Lecture Notes in Computer Science   11593

Commenced Publication in 1973
Founding and Former Series Editors:
Gerhard Goos, Juris Hartmanis, and Jan van Leeuwen

More information about this series at http://www.springer.com/series/7409

Jia Zhou · Gavriel Salvendy (Eds.)

Human Aspects of IT for the Aged Population

Social Media, Games and Assistive Environments

5th International Conference, ITAP 2019
Held as Part of the 21st HCI International Conference, HCII 2019
Orlando, FL, USA, July 26–31, 2019
Proceedings, Part II

 Springer

Editors
Jia Zhou
Chongqing University
Chongqing, China

Gavriel Salvendy
University of Central Florida
Orlando, USA

ISSN 0302-9743 ISSN 1611-3349 (electronic)
Lecture Notes in Computer Science
ISBN 978-3-030-22014-3 ISBN 978-3-030-22015-0 (eBook)
https://doi.org/10.1007/978-3-030-22015-0

LNCS Sublibrary: SL3 – Information Systems and Applications, incl. Internet/Web, and HCI

This Springer imprint is published by the registered company Springer Nature Switzerland AG
The registered company address is: Gewerbestrasse 11, 6330 Cham, Switzerland

Foreword

The 21st International Conference on Human-Computer Interaction, HCI International 2019, was held in Orlando, FL, USA, during July 26–31, 2019. The event incorporated the 18 thematic areas and affiliated conferences listed on the following page.

A total of 5,029 individuals from academia, research institutes, industry, and governmental agencies from 73 countries submitted contributions, and 1,274 papers and 209 posters were included in the pre-conference proceedings. These contributions address the latest research and development efforts and highlight the human aspects of design and use of computing systems. The contributions thoroughly cover the entire field of human-computer interaction, addressing major advances in knowledge and effective use of computers in a variety of application areas. The volumes constituting the full set of the pre-conference proceedings are listed in the following pages.

This year the HCI International (HCII) conference introduced the new option of "late-breaking work." This applies both for papers and posters and the corresponding volume(s) of the proceedings will be published just after the conference. Full papers will be included in the *HCII 2019 Late-Breaking Work Papers Proceedings* volume of the proceedings to be published in the Springer LNCS series, while poster extended abstracts will be included as short papers in the HCII 2019 *Late-Breaking Work Poster Extended Abstracts* volume to be published in the Springer CCIS series.

I would like to thank the program board chairs and the members of the program boards of all thematic areas and affiliated conferences for their contribution to the highest scientific quality and the overall success of the HCI International 2019 conference.

This conference would not have been possible without the continuous and unwavering support and advice of the founder, Conference General Chair Emeritus and Conference Scientific Advisor Prof. Gavriel Salvendy. For his outstanding efforts, I would like to express my appreciation to the communications chair and editor of *HCI International News,* Dr. Abbas Moallem.

July 2019

Constantine Stephanidis

HCI International 2019 Thematic Areas and Affiliated Conferences

Thematic areas:

- HCI 2019: Human-Computer Interaction
- HIMI 2019: Human Interface and the Management of Information

Affiliated conferences:

- EPCE 2019: 16th International Conference on Engineering Psychology and Cognitive Ergonomics
- UAHCI 2019: 13th International Conference on Universal Access in Human-Computer Interaction
- VAMR 2019: 11th International Conference on Virtual, Augmented and Mixed Reality
- CCD 2019: 11th International Conference on Cross-Cultural Design
- SCSM 2019: 11th International Conference on Social Computing and Social Media
- AC 2019: 13th International Conference on Augmented Cognition
- DHM 2019: 10th International Conference on Digital Human Modeling and Applications in Health, Safety, Ergonomics and Risk Management
- DUXU 2019: 8th International Conference on Design, User Experience, and Usability
- DAPI 2019: 7th International Conference on Distributed, Ambient and Pervasive Interactions
- HCIBGO 2019: 6th International Conference on HCI in Business, Government and Organizations
- LCT 2019: 6th International Conference on Learning and Collaboration Technologies
- ITAP 2019: 5th International Conference on Human Aspects of IT for the Aged Population
- HCI-CPT 2019: First International Conference on HCI for Cybersecurity, Privacy and Trust
- HCI-Games 2019: First International Conference on HCI in Games
- MobiTAS 2019: First International Conference on HCI in Mobility, Transport, and Automotive Systems
- AIS 2019: First International Conference on Adaptive Instructional Systems

Pre-conference Proceedings Volumes Full List

1. LNCS 11566, Human-Computer Interaction: Perspectives on Design (Part I), edited by Masaaki Kurosu
2. LNCS 11567, Human-Computer Interaction: Recognition and Interaction Technologies (Part II), edited by Masaaki Kurosu
3. LNCS 11568, Human-Computer Interaction: Design Practice in Contemporary Societies (Part III), edited by Masaaki Kurosu
4. LNCS 11569, Human Interface and the Management of Information: Visual Information and Knowledge Management (Part I), edited by Sakae Yamamoto and Hirohiko Mori
5. LNCS 11570, Human Interface and the Management of Information: Information in Intelligent Systems (Part II), edited by Sakae Yamamoto and Hirohiko Mori
6. LNAI 11571, Engineering Psychology and Cognitive Ergonomics, edited by Don Harris
7. LNCS 11572, Universal Access in Human-Computer Interaction: Theory, Methods and Tools (Part I), edited by Margherita Antona and Constantine Stephanidis
8. LNCS 11573, Universal Access in Human-Computer Interaction: Multimodality and Assistive Environments (Part II), edited by Margherita Antona and Constantine Stephanidis
9. LNCS 11574, Virtual, Augmented and Mixed Reality: Multimodal Interaction (Part I), edited by Jessie Y. C. Chen and Gino Fragomeni
10. LNCS 11575, Virtual, Augmented and Mixed Reality: Applications and Case Studies (Part II), edited by Jessie Y. C. Chen and Gino Fragomeni
11. LNCS 11576, Cross-Cultural Design: Methods, Tools and User Experience (Part I), edited by P. L. Patrick Rau
12. LNCS 11577, Cross-Cultural Design: Culture and Society (Part II), edited by P. L. Patrick Rau
13. LNCS 11578, Social Computing and Social Media: Design, Human Behavior and Analytics (Part I), edited by Gabriele Meiselwitz
14. LNCS 11579, Social Computing and Social Media: Communication and Social Communities (Part II), edited by Gabriele Meiselwitz
15. LNAI 11580, Augmented Cognition, edited by Dylan D. Schmorrow and Cali M. Fidopiastis
16. LNCS 11581, Digital Human Modeling and Applications in Health, Safety, Ergonomics and Risk Management: Human Body and Motion (Part I), edited by Vincent G. Duffy

http://2019.hci.international/proceedings

5th International Conference on Human Aspects of IT for the Aged Population (ITAP 2019)

Program Board Chair(s): Jia Zhou, *P.R. China* and Gavriel Salvendy, *USA*

- Julie A. Brown, USA
- Bessam Abdulrazak, Canada
- Ning An, P.R. China
- Marc-Eric Bobillier Chaumon, France
- Jessie Chin, USA
- Francesca Comunello, Italy
- Hua Dong, UK
- Hirokazu Kato, Japan
- Shehroz Khan, Canada
- Masatomo Kobayashi, Japan
- Chaiwoo Lee, USA
- Jiunn-Woei Lian, Taiwan
- Eugene Loos, The Netherlands
- Yan Luximon, Hong Kong, SAR China
- Andraž Petrovčič, Slovenia
- Marie Sjölinder, Sweden
- Hwee-Pink Tan, Singapore
- António Teixeira, Portugal
- Wang-Chin Tsai, Taiwan
- Ana Isabel Veloso, Portugal
- Terhi-Anna Wilska, Finland
- Fan Zhang, Canada
- Yuxiang Zhao, P.R. China
- Martina Ziefle, Germany

The full list with the Program Board Chairs and the members of the Program Boards of all thematic areas and affiliated conferences is available online at:

http://www.hci.international/board-members-2019.php

HCI International 2020

The 22nd International Conference on Human-Computer Interaction, HCI International 2020, will be held jointly with the affiliated conferences in Copenhagen, Denmark, at the Bella Center Copenhagen, July 19–24, 2020. It will cover a broad spectrum of themes related to HCI, including theoretical issues, methods, tools, processes, and case studies in HCI design, as well as novel interaction techniques, interfaces, and applications. The proceedings will be published by Springer. More information will be available on the conference website: http://2020.hci.international/.

General Chair
Prof. Constantine Stephanidis
University of Crete and ICS-FORTH
Heraklion, Crete, Greece
E-mail: general_chair@hcii2020.org

http://2020.hci.international/

Contents – Part II

Games and Exergames for the Elderly

Ambient Assisted Living

Contents – Part I

Aging and the User Experience

Elderly-Specific Web Design, Aging and Social Media

Methods and Strategies for Involving Older Adults in Branding an Online Community: The miOne Case Study

Pedro Amado[1]([⊠]) [ID], Liliana Vale Costa[2] [ID],
and Ana Isabel Veloso[2] [ID]

[1] Faculty of Fine Arts, i2ADS Research Institute, University of Porto,
Porto, Portugal
pamado@fba.up.pt
[2] Communication and Art Department, Digimedia Research Center,
University of Aveiro, Aveiro, Portugal
{lilianavale,aiv}@ua.pt

Abstract. This paper presents the methods and approaches used in the process of branding an online community for older adults, by actively involving them in its development. It starts by presenting a synthesis of the literature available on the naming and branding processes, the older adults' characteristics, and relevant participatory design methods used. Then, it presents the participatory branding process, mainly supported by a focus group workshop held with 10 older adults aged 50 and over. The participation of the older adults allowed us to embed their values and identity into the generation of a more familiar brand name, positive values and clearer messaging. Although additional testing with different focus groups is required (e.g. other age range, different ICT skills, or literacy), the results imply that the brand resonates with the target audience.

Keywords: Branding · Naming · Older adults · Participatory Design

1 Introduction

Brands play an important role in the individuals' stimuli and adherence to a product or service. They can mirror the self-image (the real and ideal self) of the subjects, creating loyal customers [1, 2]. However, so far there has been little research on creating emotionally engaging brands by involving the users in the branding process through the transference of their self-concept into brand attributes [3–5].

As it is widely known, we are living in an increasingly ageing society [5, 6]. Age-related changes in the brain are likely to influence the consumer behaviors and the values that are prioritized in a brand.

The aim of this paper is to present a method that supports the process of branding an Online Community for older adults, by involving the target audience in the process, thus generating a more meaningful brand through the effect of self-brand mirroring. This paper begins by reviewing and defining the key functional criteria behind the branding and naming processes. Then, it proceeds by highlighting what makes older

© Springer Nature Switzerland AG 2019
J. Zhou and G. Salvendy (Eds.): HCII 2019, LNCS 11593, pp. 3–19, 2019.
https://doi.org/10.1007/978-3-030-22015-0_1

adults to be attracted by brands and in what consists the process of user-generated branding. It ends with the presentation of Participatory Design methods relevant to harness the user-generated input and participation in the naming and branding development process. The methodology section describes the implementation of the participatory branding process for an online community with a focus group of older adults as its end-users. Finally, the results and conclusion sections provide an evaluation of the methods used and discusses the limitations and further research needed on this topic.

2   Literature Review

2.1   Branding and Brands

Branding can be defined as the process used to build awareness, increase the visibility, and encourage the loyalty of consumers towards a product, service, or company [7], through different associations with commercial purposes [8]. More than just a name, the Brand is both a sign and a symbol [9] resulting from the Name, Symbol, Design, or the combination of any of the previous elements that communicate the intrinsic qualities of the product, or service through its image, language, or associations. Hence, brands are decisive in the subjects' choices and self-identification towards it, or to differentiate it from others [10–13].

According to a number of authors [1, 7, 11, 14], the Brand encompasses all the elements from which it is built and unifies them into a system. These elements can be: (a) Name; (b) Logotype; (c) Tag Line, True Line, Slogan or Brand Mantra; (d) Symbol, Icon or Brand; (e) Signatures or Trademarks; (f) Color; (g) Typography; (h) Iconography; (i) Sound; (j) Motion; (k) Smell or Taste; (l) Shapes or forms of interaction; or (m) any other application or touchpoints that can be registered.

Although many authors have also highlighted some guidelines for a successful branding process [15, 16], Walvis has stressed that out of these "soft rules", we have to choose which ones serve our branding purposes in the best manner. In other words, we have to define our branding strategy and the different brand elements' Functional Criteria.

In order to do so, we should first develop a specific product strategy [7, 14, 17, 18] that usually encompasses the following: (a) Brand Brief in which it should be clear the product, or the brand' purpose, mission, values and goals; (b) the Competition and the brand's Strengths, Weaknesses, Opportunities and Threats; (c) the Brand Positioning, that is also known as the combination of the Brand Equity and Brand Parity [11, 19–23]; and (d) the product or the Brand's Essence (stated by Olgivy in the 1960' as the "Big Idea", or more recently by Kotler as the USP – Unique Selling Proposition). Once these are established, one can proceed to develop the (5) Brand Mantra [11], or Brand Messaging that comprises the Brief, Name, Descriptors, True Line, Tag Line or Slogan [7, 14, 24]. Therefore, the messaging, as a final and comprehensive step of the Branding strategy is very important, if not the most important one, as it embodies all the information of the Brand's Positioning and Values. Building a strong identity through branding has to be achieved not only through the development of a great product, but also through the values being added by the elements of the Equity elements of the Branding system [10, 11, 19, 25].

2.2 Branding and Naming Functional Criteria

The reasons that guide the choices made in the development of the brand elements should be based on objective and functional criteria [11]. These criteria have different names, and spread throughout different subjects, such as business, management, architecture, arts and communication [26]. Within the scope of these subjects, we selected the Academic (A) and Professional (P) dimensions, in the multiple practice contexts such as Communication Design (CD); Naming (N); Branding (B) and Marketing (M). We have analyzed a sample of the literature available from different dimensions and multiple contexts (Table 1).

Table 1. Sample and characterization of the number or the criteria found in the literature analyzed, according to Professional (P) and Academic (A) dimensions. And to Communication Design (CD), Naming (N), Branding (B) or Marketing (M) contexts.

Authors	Dimensions[a]	Contexts[b]	Criteria
Airey [27]	P, A	CD	7
Campbell [28]	P	N, B	8
Catchword Branding [29]	P	N, B	10
Chermayeff, Geismar and Haviv [30]	P	CD	5
Green [31]	P	N, B	5
Hart [32]	P	N, B	8
Igor [33]	P	N	8
Keller and Lehman [23]	A	N, B	7
Keller [21]	A	N, B	3
Kotler and Keller [11]	A	B, M	2
Lexicon [34]	P	N	9
Mollerup [35]	P, A	CD, N	10
Neuemeier [14]	P	CD, N, B	9
Olins [36]	P, A	CD, N, B	9
Perry and Wisnom [24]	P, A	N, B	9
Petrin [37]	P	N, B, M	4
Phillips, McQuarrie and Griffin [1]	A	B, M	8
Siegel+Gale [38]	P	N, B	9
Strategic Name Dev. [39]	P	N	9
Walvis [40]	A	B, M	6
Wheeler [7]	P, A	CD, N, B	9
Olins [41]	P	CD, N, B	7
Zinzin [42]	P	N	11

This literature review allowed us to synthesize a list of all the criteria addressed by the authors into a set of 10 Functional Criteria that can be applied in the brand messaging development (e.g. the name, wordmark, or the logotype): (1) Simple, short and easy to pronounce; (2) Relevant, descriptive and profound (it must represent the values of the product or service, links to the stakeholder's mindset and be representative); (3) Embed traditions (avoid trends) and be future-oriented; (4) Distinctive (differentiating factor and the ability to draw attention); (5) Memorable; (6) Flexible (on a formal scale), modular, extensible or translatable into other contexts; (7) Focused (convey a strong idea) and minimal (graphical excellence); (8) Transmit a positive tone and image associations; (9) Easily to like and emotionally engaging; and (10) Protectable.

Due the nature of the different contexts, the authors set a different number of criteria. Nevertheless, from the analysis of the 23 sampled references, the authors present a set of criteria that ranges from a minimum of 2 to a maximum of 11, on an average of 7,5 criteria presented by each author (Table 2).

Table 2. Number of functional criteria by author and by criteria in the sampled literature.

Authors	(1)	(2)	(3)	(4)	(5)	(6)	(7)	(8)	(9)	(10)
Airey [27]	1	1	1	1	1	1	1			
Campbell [28]	2	3			1		1	1		
Catchword Branding [29]	3	2		2			1	1		1
Chermayeff, Geismar and Haviv [30]	1	1		1	1	1				
Green [31]	1	2		2			1	2		1
Hart [32]	3	1		1	1				1	1
Igor [33]		2		2			1	3		1
Keller and Lehman [23]		1	1		1	2	1			1
Keller [21]	1	1		1						
Kotler and Keller [11]		1			1	2		1	1	1
Lexicon [34]	1			1		2				1
Mollerup [35]		1		2	1	1	1	4		
Neuemeier [14]	2	2		1	1	1			1	1
Olins [36]	2	2	1		1	1	1			1
Perry and Wisnom [24]	1	2			1	1				1
Petrin [37]	1	1		1	1	2		1	1	1
Phillips, McQuarrie and Griffin [1]		2								
Siegel+Gale [38]	1	5		1		1		1	1	1
Strategic Name Dev. [39]	2	1	1		1	1		2	1	
Walvis [40]		3	1	1	1			2		
Wheeler [7]		2	1	2		1	1	1		1
Olins [41]		4		1		1	1			1
Zinzin [42]	1	2		1						
Total by criteria	**23**	**42**	**6**	**21**	**13**	**18**	**10**	**19**	**6**	**14**

As a result, we can conclude that, from a holistic point of view relative to the 5 criteria that are the most relevant for the academic and professional dimensions, these are: (1) to be simple, short and easy to pronounce; (2) to be relevant, descriptive and profound; (4) to be distinctive; (6) to be flexible; and (8) to transmit a positive tone and image associations (setting the threshold of the analysis on double the average number of criteria per author >= 15). When analyzed only through the Naming context literature, these are also the most valued criteria alongside with the (9) Protectable. Nevertheless, this last one is not only one of the naming criteria, but also a prerequisite for registering a new brand name.

2.3 The Process of Naming

For Wheeler [7], the term Naming encompasses: (a) Revising the positioning (the objectives and target audience previously defined); (b) Evaluating the leading brand names on the market and the concurrency; (c) Planning the process (define a deadline, the teamwork, identify the brainstorm techniques, the research method and its validation); (d) Defining the naming criteria (performance, position, legal issues); (e) Conducting the brainstorm sessions; (f) Selecting the names that are easy-to-pronounce, meeting the legal issues and corresponding the brand to its market position; (g) Testing the selected name in the real context and; (h) Verifying the availability for registering the brand.

In another major study, Perry and Wisnom [24] suggest to: (a) generate a long 'master' list of names and compare them with the communication values and attributes desired for the product or service; (b) generate new names, regarding the rationale for *designing* the brand; (c) generate a shorter 'master' list with the names that meet the best communication attributes; (d) Verify the availability for registering; (e) Check the linguistic and cultural significance; and (f) Test the name with the target audience.

Hart mentions that the name development process invoices a "careful refining process" [32]. Through a process of filtering the candidates through the functional, or trademark criteria, the vast initial vast list of names can be reduced to a small number of names from which the shortlist preferred by the stakeholders is taken into testing.

Although these studies suggest testing the selected name in the real context or with the target audience [7, 24], difficulties arise when attempt is made to implement this recommendation. Nevertheless, the name testing process, regardless the method employed, should be used to identify names with a positive and negative connotation, the sound symbolism [43, 44], the latent associations and to test the name level of engagement by potential users [31, 45].

2.4 Being Attracted by Brands at a Later Age (the Older Adults' Characteristics)

During the past few years, more information has become available on branding and on the older adult consumer behavior. Indeed, there seems to be a consensus among social scientists that the older adults are more driven by emotions and personal experiences [46–48]. Nevertheless, we have to take into account that the users who experience more intense negative and positive affective states in the real world, have the least positive perceptions towards online brands [49]. This is also true for older adults.

Before analyzing the literature on what motivates the older adults to be attracted by brands, it is necessary here to clarify exactly what means being an older adult. In around 75% of world countries, an older adult can be defined as an individual aged 65 or over (legal aspect) [50]. However, this chronological standard is insufficient to encompass biological, cognitive, psychological and social effects.

During the ageing process, changes in the brain structure (i.e. whereas there is a decline in memory, emotion processing is likely to remain intact) tend to affect the older adult consumer behavior. According to Drolet et al. [51], these changes can, on the one hand, reduce the individual capacity to make free associations. On the other hand, the older adults' tendency to repeat behaviors is often increased. As a result, long-term interpersonal relationships, values (such as giving and helping), friends' behaviors [47] and self-relevant information [51] may lead this target group to act.

Moreover, as the socio-emotional selectivity theory emphasizes, during the ageing process, people tend to become more selective and guided by emotional stimuli and positive information [47, 52].

In general, further research is needed to understand the older adult consumer patterns. Despite the fact that there is some criticism around the aged market [39] the older adult segment deserves our attention as the consumer behavior also changes with ageing [53, 54].

2.5 Participatory Design

Participatory Design (PD) may be broadly defined as a method for involving the end user, as a co-designer, in the activities that inform, test and lead the development of products or services [55–57]. The research team and the end users are not necessarily united in the final result, but work together to achieve a common goal.

The participatory design method is also related to the process by which technologies are designed and stakeholders are involved [58]. In addition, participatory methodologies vary accordingly with the goals and resources provided [55, 59].

In this study, the focus group workshop was chosen because it enables stakeholders to share and communicate a set of pre-determined goals. And subsequently it helps to define strategies and assess its outcomes [55]. Even if the empirical work does not seem to strictly follow the best-known workshop format—the Future Workshop [60], the main activities involved the end-users to partake as full participants, providing enough personal information and insight for the brand development [61].

3   Methodology

A qualitative approach was deployed to provide a better understanding of the values and messages that would be important to transmit with the final brand. The development of the miOne brand presents a unique situation. We have approached the whole process by dividing the empirical work into 3 phases: (a) the brand brief development; (b) the participation of the older adults; and (c) the synthesis of the brand insights and development of the final brand.

The first phase corresponded to the involvement of the development team in defining the brand brief—the brand essence, mission, values, the naming criteria and the evaluation of the final name candidates. Then, the second phase was related with the involvement of the main stakeholders—the older adults—in the self-branding process.

Regarding the fact that some studies [62–64] and countries (e.g. Africa) consider individuals aged 50 and over as being older adults, we also included members of this age in the focus group. Thus, their inclusion allowed us to have heterogeneous group and to understand the differences and resemblances in the current and the next generation of older adults.

In the third and final phase, the data was gathered from the clinical self-concept inventory scale [65] and from the contributions of the older adults in the participatory workshop. The final candidates were generated and evaluated taking into account the functional criteria as brand heuristics alongside with the self-concept and self-brand attributes known.

3.1   A Brand for an Online Social Community: The Case Study of miOne

miOne is an online social community developed with the active participation of older adults from four community-dwelling centers of a Portuguese municipality. While the online community was being developed and tested, it was necessary to assign it a name and a distinctive brand (both by social factors, such as recognition, identification, and legal issues—the online domain and trademark registration).

Prior to this study, the research team developed a code name for the online community—'digital senior'. However, during the test sessions and thorough the iterative design sprints of the online community, the end users reported that they did not identify themselves with the name adopted for the prototype. The word 'digital' was not descriptive and meaningful enough. In addition, the word 'senior' had a negative connotation—it reminded the users of the negative aspects that occur during the ageing process.

As a consequence of this attempt to create a meaningful brand, the research team decided to involve the end-users in the process, regarding the fact that all services offered by the online social community were already a result of this design partnering.

3.2   Brand and Naming Brief

A fundamental component of the visual identity of a brand is the Brand Brief [7]. In the miOne Brand Brief (Fig. 1), the brand's vision, mission, attributes, competitive advantages, value proposition, key competitors and main stakeholders were described.

The community aims to be an open, accessible and easy to use platform for everyone, by focusing first on the older adult's needs as its interaction reference and progressively enhancing them for everyone. Users can create and strengthen their personal connections or affective bonds, since it has been also developed in a Participatory Design (PD) approach [55, 59, 66] with older adults, with a low literacy level.

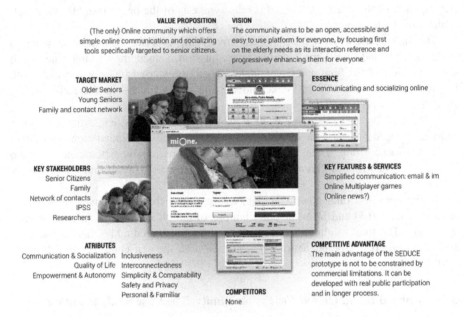

Fig. 1. Visual Brand Brief of the online social community miOne.

The brand brief (Fig. 1) defined by the research team was important in order to know the values that the internal stakeholders wanted to transmit and, then, to compare them with the results obtained from the involvement of a sample of the target market.

3.3   Defining Naming Criteria

For the purpose of identifying the most relevant criteria for choosing and evaluating brand names, the research team analyzed the literature from the theory and practice of the branding process and reviewed the desirable criteria previously defined for a brand name. From the set of the five most important ones we've highlighted the: (1) to be simple, short and easy to pronounce; (4) to be distinctive; and (8) to transmit a positive tone and image associations as the most important criteria to include in the name development process. This was mainly due to the fact that this target audience does not relate to digital technologies. So, the (2) relevant, descriptive and profound criteria would be a very difficult goal to achieve. The positive image was to be achieved not only by the name, but also mainly through the combined messaging elements (e.g. the brand with the tagline). And the last criteria, the (6) flexibility was to be achieved in combination with the (9) protectable criteria. In other words, the brand developed would have to adapt itself not only to the several areas of the community (internal flexibility) as to other languages or international settings (external flexibility). These naming criteria were the basis to formulate the questions of the focus group with main target audience (the older adults).

3.4   Creating the Panel List of Names

After having the brand brief document and the naming criteria, the process of brain writing followed. This process was iterative and continued until every member contributed as many ideas as possible in three sessions. In the end, a total of 809 names were generated. Only twenty candidates that matched the selected functional criteria were selected to proceed to the evaluation phase.

3.5   Older Adults' Participation: Sample Selection and Characterization

For the purpose of this study, a convenience sample comprised of ten participants were recruited from a day-care center and from a course of Introduction to Multimedia aimed at older adults, lectured by the authors, at the University. 60% of the sample was women and 36% were men aged between 52 and 87 ($M = 72$, $SD = 10.6$).

In addition, the criteria for selecting the subjects were: (a) being over 50; and (b) having interest in information and communication technologies (ICT). Furthermore, all participants were assured that their participation was voluntary. An overview of participants' characteristics is summarized in Table 3.

Table 3. The main characteristics of the sample

User	Age	Gender	Interests	ICT use
U1	69	F	Travelling, reading, movies, theatre and gardening	Information Search and Communication
U2	77	M	Being with family, reading and travelling	Communication and Information search
U3	62	F	Dancing, cooking, singing, reading and travelling	Social networking and Communication
U4	53	M	Fan of arts, music and poetry	Edit sound and images
U5	64	F	Painting and reading	
U6	82	F	Needlecraft, crochet	Communication and Writing
U7	87	M	Play cards and dominoes	Communication, writing and play videogames
U8	79	M	Play dominoes	Communication
U9	80	F	Play cards and dominoes, needlecraft	Communication and Play video games
U10	67	F	Travelling, reading, movies, theatre and gardening	Communication and Play video games

Although the demographic indicators are in line with our sample [50], caution must be applied, as the subjects are not representative of all older adults, and the number of subjects and the surplus of women compromises representativeness. Nevertheless, previous studies that evaluate self-brand congruity [67, 68] demonstrate that these user-generated brands are likely to positively communicate with the audience.

In our sample, we have integrated five older adults who were autonomous in using information and communication technologies (ICT) and other five older adults who used ICT, only if accompanied with somebody else (either by a caregiver, researcher, relatives or friends). Those two different profiles of the sample are important to possess the necessary characteristics about the population (older adults who feel at ease with ICT and the ones who are having the first contact with technological devices and need to be accompanied in using them).

3.6   The Involvement of the Older Adults: The Procedure

Before proceeding to the field study, the participants' consent was obtained. The empirical research began with the administration of the Clinical Self-Concept Inventory [65] and a semi-structured interview ("Describe here your personal characteristics. Please begin with the sentence 'I am...'") in order to assess participants' self-concept analysis. Closed and open-ended questions were used, as many older adults tend to manifest difficulty in self-expression. We later employed seven coders in order to analyze their answers: (A1) Sympathy/Friendliness/Positiveness/Familiarity; (A2) Communication (skills); (A3) Persistence; (A4) Tolerance; (A5) Practical; (A6) Competency/Professional (profile); (A7) Energy/Velocity/Immediacy. Nearly fifteen minutes were spent to complete the survey on paper and describe themselves.

The participants were then given a set of post-it notes in which the color corresponded to the brands' functional criteria in a self-brand exercise. They were presented with a list of 20 selected names from the master list (in no particular order) in the form of post-it boards (i.e. Raízes – Roots, Penta, Poli, Farol – Lighthouse, Atlas, Liga Digital – Digital League, Convívio – Mingle, Terra – Land, Elo – Bond, Pátio – Courtyard, Terreiro – Yard, Digital, Centro – Centre, Social, Sénior – Senior, Entre amigos – Among friends, Entre Nós – Among us, Comunique – Communicate, Sénior digital – Digital Senior and Vida – Life). The goal was for them to code each one with different color-codes, matching different characteristics they valued in the brand name, namely (B1) Familiarity, (B2) Security, (B3) Distinctiveness, (B4) Relevancy, (B5) Memorability, (B6) Extendibility and (B7) Energy. Afterwards they chose which ones corresponded better to the main branding functional criteria. For a clear understanding and richer interaction with the participants, the following questions were posed:

- Which of these names are you more familiar with?
- Which of these names inspire more confidence?
- Which are the names that stand out?
- Which are the names that suggest the concept of relationships?
- Which are the names that stay longer in memory?
- Which are the names most suitable for an online community?
- Which are the names that can be used for other things?
- Which are the names that transmit energy?

The first and last functional criteria (simple and protectable) were deprecated in this end-user evaluation. Overall, the entire procedure took 90 min to complete.

We later designed a grid to evaluate the focus group self-evaluation and name coding results in order to better understand the importance of distinct brand values for the older adults as end-users. The candidates were evaluated accordingly with the Positive, Negative and Interesting (PNI) aspects method [69]. Then, we generated a new name list by applying the SCAMPER method on the most valued ones, in order to obtain a short list of viable final name candidates.

4 Results

4.1 Self-concept Analysis

From the results of the Clinical Self-Concept Inventory and the semi-structured interview, we analyzed the answers of each participant relatively to their self-concept.

From the data obtained, we could verify that trust, a sense of connectedness, being competent and being responsible are the characteristics more valued and cited by the respondents (Table 4). Furthermore, as a group, the Older Adults of our sample are not afraid to reach out for help. Hence, these values have been added to the functional criteria in order to evaluate the final name candidates suggested for the online community.

Table 4. Sample participants' self-concepts summary

User	Age	Self-concept
U1	69	U1 considers herself a problem-solver and a pleasant person. She values connectedness between people and their honesty. For U1 a long-term and true relationship is what encourages her loyalty to a brand
U2	77	U2 considers himself talkative and rapid when completing tasks. Although he highlights that he solves his own problems, U2 usually recognizes that he needs help from others when having difficulties or troubles. He likes to be good at mastering new challenges
U3	62	U3 considers herself likeable and well accepted by others. She tends to be honest to express her opinions and assume her responsibilities until the end, even if it brings negative consequences. For her trust is everything
U4	53	U4 considers himself sincere by stating that he always tells the truth. U4 assumes his own responsibilities regardless its consequences and he tend to face his own problems
U5	64	U5 also considers herself honest when expressing her own opinions. For her velocity, energy and competency in completing tasks are very important. U5 faces her own problems and tend to assume the responsibilities for her actions
U6	82	U6 considers herself talkative and in a conversation with someone new, she would take the initiative and lead the talk. When U6 has problems, she counts on her family support. For her, succeeding well on tasks is very important
U7	87	U7 considers himself a pleasant person, with good memory and vision. For him, independency and helping other people are very important characteristics. U7 is a good listener but not very talkative
U8	79	U8 considers himself talkative, a good observer and obedient. He tends to give up from his tasks and asks for help when he has some difficulties
U9	80	U9 considers herself pleasant, stubborn, shy and hard worker. She tends to be sincere in her answers and tolerant with others. U9 is practical, persistent and energetic
U10	67	U10 considers herself extrovert, social and with initiative capacity. She actively searches for information and to be in contact with friends. She is persistent and stubborn. When she needs help, she asks for it

4.2 Self-brand Exercise

The concepts Convívio (Mingle), Centro (Centre), Social (Social), Entre Amigos (Between friends), Comunique (Communication) and Vida (Life) were the most cited in the brand name's values evaluation. These were considered important because they translated values that were defined by the development team needed in the brand. As U5 stated: "I think the concepts of Convívio (Mingle) and Digital suggest social bonds – a new generation, who gets together". U3 pointed out: "The concept of Vida (Life) suggests youth and memory. In addition, getting social is a way of being in life - a philosophy of life, a choice […]. It suggests participation, living with intensity". Meanwhile, U2 reminded us to: "Regardless the name or the concept, it should encourage trust and union".

4.3 The Online Community Brand Insights

Briefly, everybody agreed with the fact that "Life, relationships, and being digital are important concepts that the online community should transmit as values." Hence, the sense of connectedness, union, social bonds and trust will be on focus of this brand. As a result, the name miOne was developed. We opted for a coined word to enhance the distinctive and unique aspect of the community in favor of the memorability achieved with a familiar word [32]. Familiarity with the digital nature of an online community is a very difficult connection to achieve with these users. This type of name also allows for the brand to extend to additional international contexts. We have also opted for a 5-letter short word, composed by a combination of stop and fricative consonants ("m" and "n"), and stressing the lower-frequency vowel "O", in order to convey a symbolism of "largeness" [44], and to relate to the sense of union and connectedness reported by the users (Table 4). The tagline 'Life in online community. For me. For you. For everyone!' emerged in order to reinforce the memorability, description and relevance of the brand messaging. Moreover, having the members' photo embedded on the O of the logo reinforces the individuality of the online social community ('mi' – 'I am' embedded in 'One' community).

4.4 The Online Community User Interface Visual System as a Holistic Brand Experience

Throughout the brand development process, the Online Community prototype was developed and tested with a larger set of participants. As such, the miOne brand was being experienced not only through the brand messaging, but also through the online digital touch points—namely the community visual interface (Fig. 2). As described by Goodwin and Wheeler [7, 61], the careful development of the different aspects of the interface—the Visual System—extend to the Identity, Name, Logotype, Color, Typography, Content, Iconography and User Controls, Layout Grids, Application Behavior and Interaction. These are crucial touch points to support the branding process throughout the whole user experience. Hence, the Visual System was developed as an integrated documentation [70].

Fig. 2. The branded online community visual interface.

We have opted for a moderate color palette, mainly based on a low saturated blue as its primary color. Additional colors were used to provide the necessary functionality [61, 71]. In respect to the typography selection, we have opted for the font Arial—its parameters, such as body size, line height and column width were tweaked in order to achieve the best compromise between the connection performance, technical quality, and reading comfort for these users [72]. Nowadays, recent developments in Variable and Web Fonts technologies offer more options in this regard. Content was also carefully planned and, due to the public's low literacy skills, the messages were designed to be the most clear, directive and non-ambiguous as possible. Therefore, we have employed short and descriptive sentences with simple and direct-action verbs. This provides for an enhanced sense of trust within the community. For the Iconography and User Controls, we have opted for simple and familiar patterns and whenever needed, we have developed new and more simple solutions to address the lack of familiarity with the expected interface actions—such as the big and explicit scrollbar buttons. We have also highlighted the most obvious and expected actions through enlarged size and color-coded call-to-actions. Finally, the Layout Grid tries to accommodate as much white space as possible in order to improve its legibility and meet the 'openness' attribute.

5   Conclusion

This paper has addressed the process of involving the older adults in generating meaningful brands. The study was designed to develop an online community brand name, taking into account the self-concept and self-brand associations established by this target group.

In general, it seems that the process of developing a brand with the participation of the end users encompasses three phases. The first phase corresponds to the involvement of the development team in (a) discussing the brand brief, (b) brand writing, (c) defining the name criteria and (d) creating a panel list of names. The second phase is devoted to the involvement of the target audience in the process of their self-concept evaluation and transference of self-attributes into the brand being developed. Then, the third phase ended with the evaluation of final name candidates and the generation of a new name, using the PNI and SCAMPER methods. The process was guided mainly through a set of brand heuristics derived from the current list of the identified functional criteria in academic and professional literature.

Applying this process with adults aged 50 and over allowed us to experience that, as proposed by the literature review, this target group was motivated by emotions and tended to value brand names, which transmitted a sense of connectedness, trust and union. Moreover, while conducting the empirical study, we verified the importance of using both open and close-ended questions with the older adults, as these subjects experience a decline in the capacity of self-expression.

In this paper, we have proposed and described a framework for participatory branding of digital products, such as the Online Community, specifically involving older adults. It incorporates a set of 10 branding Functional Criteria that serve as heuristics for developing and evaluating the whole brand creation process.

Finally, a number of important limitations need to be considered. Firstly, we must proceed with caution, as the findings might not be transferable to other contexts, given a small sized convenience sample. Secondly, we involved a group of adults aged 50 and over in the focus group workshop and, although they formed a small heterogeneous group, their inclusion was beneficial to understand the differences and resemblances in the current and the next generation of older adults.

To sum up, further work needs to be done to achieve the generalizability of the results. Moreover, this study provides a starting point for studying older adults' brand behaviors and techniques for involving them in the user-generated branding process.

Acknowledgements. We'd like to thank and to acknowledge the contributions of four community-dwelling centers of a Portuguese municipality—PNSFV, CPSB, CESDA & CSSJP—for the availability in nurturing this project. We would also like express a special thank you to all the participants of the Introduction to Multimedia course without whom such a rich workshop and brand insights were not possible. This research is part of an ongoing project being funded by the program COMPETE, FEDER, FCT Lisbon. This work was supported by Fundação para a Ciência e Tecnologia and ESF under Community Support Framework III – the project SEDUCE 2.0 nr. POCI-01-0145-FEDER-031696.

References

1. Phillips, B.J., McQuarrie, E.F., Griffin, W.G.: How visual brand identity shapes consumer response. Psychol Mark. **31**, 225–236 (2014). https://doi.org/10.1002/mar.20689
2. Parker, B.T.: A comparison of brand personality and brand user-imagery congruence. J. Consum. Mark. **26**, 175–184 (2009)
3. Arnhold, U.: User Generated Branding: State of the Art of Research. LIT Verlag, Münster (2008)
4. Chaplin, L.N., Roedder John, D.: The development of self-brand connections in children and adolescents. J. Consum. Res. **32**, 119–129 (2005)
5. Moore, D.J., Homer, P.M.: Self-brand connections: the role of attitude strength and autobiographical memory primes. J. Bus. Res. **61**, 707–714 (2008)
6. European Commission. The 2009 Ageing Report: economic and budgetary projections for the EU-27 Member States (2008–2060) (2009)
7. Wheeler, A.: Designing Brand Identity: An Essential Guide for the Whole Branding Team. Wiley, New Jersey (2009)
8. Olins, W.: On Brand. Thames & Hudson, New York (2003)
9. Bastos, W., Levy, S.J.: A history of the concept of branding: practice and theory. J. Hist. Res. Mark. **4**, 347–368 (2012). https://doi.org/10.1108/17557501211252934
10. Doyle, P., Stern, P.: Marketing Management and Strategy. Pearson Education, New York (2006)
11. Kotler, P., Keller, K.: Marketing Management, 14th edn. Prentice Hall, New Jersey (2012)
12. Lencastre, P.: O Livro da Marca. Publicações Dom Quixote, Lisboa (2007)
13. Jevons, C.: Names, brands, branding: beyond the signs, symbols, products and services. J. Prod. Brand Manag. **14**, 117–118 (2005). https://doi.org/10.1108/10610420510592590
14. Neumeier, M.: The Brand Gap: How to Bridge the Distance Between Business Strategy and Design. New Riders, Berkeley (2006)
15. Alsop, R.J.: The 18 Immutable Laws of Corporate Reputation: Creating, Protecting and Repairing Your Most Valuable Asset. Kogan Page Publishers, London (2006)
16. Ries, A., Ries, L.: The 22 Immutable Laws of Branding. Harper Collins, New York (1998)
17. Neumeier, M.: Zag: The Number One Strategy of High-performance Brands. New Riders (2006)
18. Neumeier, M.: Brand Messaging Hierarchy. In: Liq. Agency Steal This Idea (2009)
19. Aaker, D.A.: Managing Brand Equity. Simon and Schuster, New York (1991)
20. Aaker, D.A.: Measuring brand equity across products and markets. Calif. Manag. Rev. **38**, 103 (1996)
21. Keller, K.L.: Conceptualizing, measuring, managing customer-based brand equity. J. Mark. **57**, 1–22 (1993)
22. Kay, M.J.: Strong brands and corporate brands. Eur. J. Mark. **40**, 742–760 (2006). https://doi.org/10.1108/03090560610669973
23. Keller, K.L., Lehmann, D.R.: Brands and branding: research findings and future priorities. Mark. Sci. **25**, 740–759 (2006)
24. Perry, A., Wisnom, D.: Before the Brand: Creating the Unique DNA of an Enduring Brand Identity. McGraw-Hill Publishing Co., New York (2003)
25. Aaker, D.: Building Strong Brands. Simon and Schuster, New York (1996)
26. Fetscherin, M., Usunier, J.-C.: Corporate branding: an interdisciplinary literature review. Eur. J. Mark. **46**, 733–753 (2012). https://doi.org/10.1108/03090561211212494
27. Airey, D.: Logo Design Love: A Guide to Creating Iconic Brand Identities. New Riders, Berkeley (2010)

28. Campbell, K.: Researching Brands. In: Hart, S., Murphy, J. (eds.) Brands: The New Wealth Creators. Palgrave, New York (1998)
29. Catchword Branding. Just name it. a brand name development guide (2012). http://catchwordbranding.com/static/uploads/2012/03/Naming-Guide-Final-Version-1.2.pdf. Accessed 11 Apr 2014
30. Chermayeff, I., Geismar, T., Haviv, S.: Identify: Basic Principles of Identity Design in the Iconic Trademarks of Chermayeff & Geismar. Print, New York (2011)
31. Green, D.: Improve on Naming Guidelines (2013)
32. Hart, S.: Developing new brand names. In: Hart, S., Murphy, J. (eds.) Brands: The New Wealth Creators. Palgrave, New York (1998)
33. Igor. Building th Perfect Beast: The Igor Naming Guide (2011)
34. Lexicon. Our brand naming process (2014). http://www.lexiconbranding.com/process/our-brand-naming-process.html. Accessed 28 May 2014
35. Mollerup, P.: Marks of Excellence: The History and Taxonomy of Trademarks. Phaidon, New York (2007)
36. Olins, W.: The New Guide to Identity: Corporate Identity, Retail Identity, Brand Identity, Organisational Identity, the Corporate Brand ... How to Create and Sustain Change through Managing Identity. Gower Publishing Ltd. (1996)
37. Petrin, K.: Brand. In: Millward Brown A/R/M/I-Marketing (2004). http://test.armi-marketing.com/library/Brand.pdf. Accessed 11 Apr 2014
38. Siegel+Gale. What's in a Name? (2012). http://www.slideshare.net/siegelgalebranding/whats-in-a-name-13224909. Accessed 29 May 2014
39. Strategic Name Development. Brand name research (2012). http://www.namedevelopment.com/brand-name-research.html. Accessed 29 May 2014
40. Walvis, T.H.: Three laws of branding: neuroscientific foundations of effective brand building. J. Brand Manag. **16**, 176–194 (2007). https://doi.org/10.1057/palgrave.bm.2550139
41. Olins, W.: A naming handbook (2014)
42. Zinzin. Name evaluation (2012). http://www.zinzin.com/process/name-evaluation/. Accessed 30 Jan 2019
43. Klink, R.R., Athaide, G.A.: Creating brand personality with brand names. Mark. Lett. **23**, 109–117 (2011). https://doi.org/10.1007/s11002-011-9140-7
44. Athaide, G.A., Klink, R.R.: Creating global brand names: the use of sound symbolism. J. Glob. Mark. **25**, 202–212 (2012). https://doi.org/10.1080/08911762.2012.744123
45. Green, D.: 7 steps to creating a great brand, service or product name (2014). http://www.slideshare.net/Improveon/7-steps-to-creating-a-great-brand-name. Accessed 29 May 2014
46. Regulation of emotion in the second half of life. Motiv. Emot. **27**, 103–123. https://doi.org/10.1023/A:1024569803230
47. Cole, C., Laurent, G., Drolet, A., et al.: Decision making and brand choice by older consumers. Mark. Lett. **19**, 355–365 (2008). https://doi.org/10.1007/s11002-008-9058-x
48. Williams, P., Drolet, A.: Age-related differences in responses to emotional advertisements. J. Consum. Res. **32**, 343–354 (2005). https://doi.org/10.1086/497545
49. Christodoulides, G., Michaelidou, N., Theofania Siamagka, N.: A typology of internet users based on comparative affective states: evidence from eight countries. Eur. J. Mark. **47**, 153–173 (2013). https://doi.org/10.1108/03090561311285493
50. United Nations. Population aged 60 years or over (2003)
51. Drolet, A., Bodapati, A.V., Suppes, P., et al.: Habits and free associations: free your mind but mind your habits. J. Assoc. Consum. Res. **2**, 293–305 (2017). https://doi.org/10.1086/695422

52. Fung, H.H., Carstensen, L.L.: Sending memorable messages to the old: age differences in preferences and memory for advertisements. J. Pers. Soc. Psychol. **85**, 163 (2003)
53. Gunter, B.: Understanding the Older Consumer: The Grey Market. Routledge, London (2012)
54. Goldstein, S.: The aged segment of the market, 1950 and 1960. J. Mark. **32**, 62 (1968). https://doi.org/10.2307/1248930
55. Muller, M.J.: Participatory design: the third space in HCI. In: Jacko, J.A., Sears, A. (eds.) Human-Computer Interaction Handbook, pp. 1051–1068. L. Erlbaum Associates Inc., Hillsdale (2003). Fundam Evol Technol Emerg Appl
56. Abras, C., Maloney-Krichmar, D., Preece, J.: User-centered design. In: Bainbridge, W. (ed.) Encyclopedia of Human-Computer Interaction. Sage Publications, Thousand Oaks (2004)
57. Schuler, D., Namioka, A.: Participatory Design: Principles and Practices. Lawrence Erlbaum Associates, Hillsdale (1993)
58. Agre, P., Agre, P.E.: Computation and Human Experience. Cambridge University Press, Cambridge (1997)
59. Muller, M.J., Haslwanter, J.H., Dayton, T.: Participatory practices in the software lifecycle. In: Helander, M., Landauer, T., Prabhu, P. (eds.) Handbook of Human-Computer Interaction. Elsevier Science B.V, Amsterdam (1997)
60. Kensing, F., Madsen, K.H.: Generating Visions: Future Workshops and Metaphorical Design, pp. 155–168. L. Erlbaum Associates Inc., Hillsdale (1992)
61. Goodwin, K.: Designing for the Digital Age. Wiley, Indianapolis (2009)
62. World Health Organization. Definition of an older or elderly person: proposed working definition of an older person in Africa for the MDS Project (2000)
63. Locker, D., Liddell, A., Burman, D.: Dental fear and anxiety in an older adult population. Commun. Dent. Oral Epidemiol. **19**, 120–124 (1991). https://doi.org/10.1111/j.1600-0528.1991.tb00125.x
64. Smith, A.D., Winograd, E.: Adult age differences in remembering faces. Dev. Psychol. **14**, 443–444 (1978). https://doi.org/10.1037/0012-1649.14.4.443
65. Vaz-Serra, A.: O "Inventário Clínico de Auto-Conceito" (1986)
66. Muller, M.J., Kuhn, S.: Participatory design. Commun. ACM **36**, 24–28 (1993). https://doi.org/10.1145/153571.255960
67. Sung, Y., Choi, S.M.: The influence of self-construal on self-brand congruity in the United States and Korea. J. Cross Cult. Psychol. **43**, 151–166 (2010). https://doi.org/10.1177/0022022110383318
68. Oh, H., Pizam, A.: Handbook of Hospitality Marketing Management. Elsevier, Amsterdam (2008)
69. Michalko, M.: Thinkertoys: A Handbook of Creative-Thinking Techniques, 2nd edn. Ten Speed Press, Berkeley (2006)
70. Amado, P., Fonseca, I.: Sistema visual: a identidade e a interação na comunidade miOne. In: Veloso, A., (ed.) SEDUCE: Utilização da comunicação e da informação em ecologias web pelo cidadão sénior, 1st edn. Edições Afrontamento, CETAC. Media, Porto (2014)
71. Boulton, M.: A Practical Guide to Designing for the Web. Five Simple Steps, Penarth (2009)
72. Fonseca, I., Amado, P., Costa, L.: Desenho de interfaces para seniores: desafios e oportunidades no projeto SEDUCE. Rev. Prism (2014)

(In)visibilities of Men and Aging in the Media: Discourses from Germany and Portugal

Inês Amaral[1,2(✉)], Sofia José Santos[3], Fernanda Daniel[4,5], and Filipa Filipe[6]

[1] Faculdade de Letras da Universidade de Coimbra, Coimbra, Portugal
ines.amaral@uc.pt
[2] Centro de Estudos de Comunicação e Sociedade da Universidade do Minho, Braga, Portugal
[3] Centro de Estudos Sociais da Universidade de Coimbra, Coimbra, Portugal
sjs@ces.uc.pt
[4] Instituto Superior Miguel Torga, Coimbra, Portugal
fernanda-daniel@ismt.pt
[5] Centro de Estudos e Investigação em Saúde, Universidade de Coimbra, Coimbra, Portugal
[6] Munich, Germany

Abstract. Social representations stem from wider processes of socialization within which the media perform a simultaneously reflective and co-constitutive role. Embedded in society, mainstream media discourses tend to legitimize and convey social representations in line with hegemonic ideologies. By doing so, mainstream media shed light on what are considered to be valid representations and roles and render invisible those which are not hegemonic and, hence, dismissed as less important or actively invisibilized. As European democratic societies are becoming increasingly older and gender equal, it would be expected for mainstream media to go in line with these trends, giving increasing visibility to seniors and to both women and non-hegemonic representations of what it means to be a man. This paper intends to explore whether media representations go on par with this course. To put it forward, this paper will identify how media are representing men and aging in Germany and Portugal through a quantitative content analysis of four national weekly news magazines.

Keywords: Social representations · Media representations · Masculinities · Ageism · Older men

1 Introduction

Representations used by the media are a fundamental fabric of the ideas one creates and holds about oneself, others and reality at large [1–3]. Gender and age identities are no exception to this logic. Despite entailing biological considerations, masculinities [4]

F. Filipe—Independent Scholar.

and aging [5] are socially constructed, representing models that are culturally imagined and whose evolution develops according to the different contextual settings.

Several studies show the enormous power media hold in shaping the way society percepts and understand the older people [6, 7], as well as gender norms, roles, behaviors and aspirations [8–11]. Media narratives co-constitute the construction of gender identities [12] as well as for generational identities [13, 14]. Concerning age, media promotes common societal stereotypes [15] associating old age with negative attributes including loneliness, illness and dependence [16]. In fact, "age is often used as a background variable in the construction of different audience segments and pro-files" [17]. The media depiction of older people perpetuates ageism underrepresentation and negative characterization [7]. Gender-wise, both in the North and in the Global South [18], mainstream media traditionally conveys representations of masculinities that associate "being a real man" with characteristics and attitudes of dominance, power, leadership, rationality, heterosexuality, and dominating sexual performances, among others [8–11, 19–22].

However, as media simultaneously inform and reflect society [1, 2, 23] and as European societies are becoming increasingly older [24] and progressively (even at a slow pace) gender equal [25], media representations are expected to go in line with these larger societal changes. Stemming from this presupposition, this paper intends to understand how media are representing men and aging in democratic liberal societies, exploring to which representations they shed light on, which ones they dismiss or neglect as less important, and which ones are rendered invisible. In Portugal and Germany studies on media discourses and older people have not taken a gendered approach. In the rare cases where a gendered approach is used, studies are mostly focused on women [53]. It is therefore necessary to identify the media representations of older men in both countries. In societies where hegemonic masculinities are evident in media representations, this study focuses on older men with the aim of understanding whether aging is a variable that molds media depictions of men over the age of 65. As such, this paper departs from the following research question: How are older men represented in the media? To put it forward, this study analyzed four weekly news magazines in Germany and Portugal through a quantitative content analysis. In terms of aging, and according to PORDATA data [24], in 2016 19.3% of the population of the European Union was 65 years or older. Germany is the third country with the oldest population (21.1%) and the fourth country is Portugal (20.9%). First is Italy (22.2%), followed by Greece (21.4%). In terms of overall progress toward gender equality, Germany and Portugal are on par with many other European Union countries [25].

1.1 Media and Representations

Discourses and systems of representation construct the places from which individuals can position themselves and from which they find their "place of speech" in society [12]. Assuming the changing and transformative nature of society, the enunciation in media discourses has a social nature: meaning is a product of cultures and subcultures, conveyed from shared social construction [26]. The representations that are socially shared contribute to the perception of a common reality within a particular group. Therefore, the discourses, when socially legitimated, are assumed to be a regime of truth [27].

Social representations derive from the process of socialization and are directly associated with collective identity [16], which, by definition, tends to be hegemonic. The social facts correspond to ways of acting and to representations that are external to the individual. According to Durkheim [28], society and collective consciousness are moral entities. Therefore, what people feel, think, or do is independent of their individual will and translates behavior established by society. In this perspective, social facts exercise a coercive power. It is something that exists and that remains beyond the individual. It follows that the construction of symbolic representations shared by members of social systems inhabits a universe of specific sociability [29]. This is exactly the process of forming media representations.

The media construct identities and are instruments of social legitimation [30]. Discourse emerges as a resource for power, as a way of limiting the freedom of action of the other through persuasion. Language presents itself not as a reflection of reality, but as an entity that constructs it [31]. It follows that language has the constitutive power of reality. Fairclough [32] claims that power in the media discourse refers to the idea of social construction of reality.

Discourse is the social process of making and reproducing meaning [33]. Discourses are not, in themselves, textual, but relations of power. The news does not reflect reality, but helps to constitute it as a shared social phenomenon [34]. In this perspective, the news defines, redefines, constitutes and reconstitutes permanently the social phenomena [34]. It is not in the enunciation that journalists produce discourses. It is within the discursive process itself, through multiple operations articulated by the processes of language itself, that the audience is constituted in advance [26].

1.2   Media Discourses on Men

Masculinities are socially [4] and semiotically [35] constructed, representing culturally imagined ideals. Being multiple and sometimes even contradictory, masculinities can be defined as standards of practices through which both men and women assume a position within the gender hierarchy [4]. In this context, hegemonic masculinity represents a culturally imagined ideal of what it means to be and behave as a "real man", being associated with notions of rationality, toughness, dominance, strength, power, and leadership. As Connell and Messerschmidt [4] point out, the hegemonic masculinity is normative and not necessarily statistical: it is an ideal, which creates a reference from which all men should identify themselves in a relative logic.

Traditionally, mainstream media portray men as holding personalities and behaviors in line with hegemonic understandings of what it means to be and behave as a man [8–11, 19, 21, 22]. As Silveirinha [36] summarizes, the representations on men shared by the media are social constructions embedded in the hegemonic ideology, which, in turn, perpetuates the traditional gender roles and norms. These representations are not only expressed in hyper masculinized characters like Rambo or James Bond, for example. There are other more subtle formulas which, assuming themselves as counter-hegemonic - because conceived almost in opposition to the ideal of hegemonic masculinity - also do reproduce sexist and misogynist models. The "nerd" character in several TV series is a clear example of this[1]. On the other hand, traditional gender norms are also becoming present in mediascapes. Challenging characters in popular shows on TV, such as the Joel in Parenthood or Mitch and Cam in Modern Family, are starting to emerge in the mainstream media. Nevertheless, these choices are still exceptions to the general way media have been representing men.

In terms of effects, several studies [8–10, 18, 22] show that hegemonic representations of masculinities ends up encouraging beliefs and sexist behaviors, including blaming women when victims of sexual violence perpetrated by men [37], naturalizing violence, particularly within the context of relationships [37], tolerating sexual harassment, policing what fits into the idea of "being a man" [38]. As such, these representations contribute to the perpetuation of unequal power relations between genders [19], affecting in a harmful way girls and women, but also men and boys [39, 40].

1.3   Media Discourses on Age

Around the phenomenon of aging of the population has emerged a diversity of terminologies inducing changes in social representations and public policies on the phenomenon [41]. Consequently, in European contemporary societies, representations about aging derive from discursive (re)qualifications seeking positive terminologies [42, 43]. Nevertheless, the media continue to perpetuate images with the conceptions of gender that determine the traditional roles; also the generations are usually represented statically. The population over 65 is often represented as a homogeneous group.

In the "age of mediated visibility" [44], the multiplicity of discourses conveyed by the media create and recreate social and group identities through the proliferation of social representations that assume the hegemonic ideology [16, 42]. Historical and cultural societal matrix factors represent older people and the aging of differentiated and hieratic ways [45]. Therefore, "discourses of gender and ageing have a political character: they define relations between different groups of people, establish a power structure and play a determining role in assigning certain societal spaces to individuals" [46].

According to Ylänne [5], "representations, words and images guide our thinking of ageing. They produce metaphorical images of what ageing is like". Gerbner et al. [6] identified an underrepresentation of older people on television. As the older population tends to be invisible in societies, the media perpetuate this assumption as a normalization [47]. Colombo and Fortunati [48] considered that the mediatic experience occurs within the cultural environments of the people, an idea that is associated with the belonging of a group. In this regard, Corsten [14] coined the term "We-sense", which means that historical and social experiences, whether individual or collective, within the public or private sphere, allow identification with groups. Hence, the various generations experience social and technological changes in a perspective of coexistence. The media experiences can shape the social construction of a "generational

---

[1] See "The Adorkable Misogyny of The Big Bang Theory", Pop Culture Detective Agency. Available at: https://www.youtube.com/watch?v=X3-hOigoxHs.

identity" that derives from the media representations. The representations on the feminine and the masculine shared by the media are social constructions shared by a hegemonic ideology, which perpetuates the traditional roles [36].

2   Method

This paper aims to analyze media representations of older men in Germany and Portugal, seeking to detect visibilities and invisibilities. In order to answer the research question ("How have older men been represented in the media?"), was conducted a case study through the method of content analysis [49]. The descriptive study had a quantitative approach and was focused on four news magazines: two Portuguese ("Visão" and "Sábado") and two Germans ("Der Spiegel" and "Focus"). Assuming "news magazines are important agents in the formation of public opinion" [50], the choice of the four news magazines was derived from three factors: to be a general weekly news magazine, not to be published as newspaper supplements, and to have the highest circulation within its category ("Der Spiegel" = 840,000/week, "Focus" = 441,805/week, "Visão" = 97.306/week, "Sábado" = 54,914/week). The decision to compare magazines from Germany and Portugal focused on being the third and fourth oldest country in the European Union [24].

The corpus analysis was collected from all issues published in October 2018 (four issues per magazine). For a comparative analysis between the four news magazines, thematic sections were standardized as follows: Society, Politics, National, International, Economy, Culture, Sport, Health, Entertainment, Opinion and Obituary. The quantitative content analysis assumes the following categories of analysis: the classification of the sections, the categorization of journalistic genres and formats elaborated by Melo and Assis [51] as shown in Table 1, the headlines, and the gender of the protagonists.

Table 1. Journalist genres and format

Journalist genre	Example
Informative	Note
	News
	Report
	Interview
Opinionative	Editorial
	Comment
	Article
	Review
	Column
	Caricature
	Letter
	Chronicle

(*continued*)

Table 1. (*continued*)

Journalist genre	Example
Interpretative	Analysis
	Profile
	Survey
	Chronology
	Dossier
Diversional	Human interest history
	Color history
Utility	Indicator
	Quotation
	Script
	Service

A media genre can be considered a "content category" [52] with the following characteristics: "(a) a 'collective identity', capable of being recognized by both producers and consumers; (b) the interrelation of this identity with its explicit function (information, entertainment or related), aligning form and content; (c) the permanence of that identity through the ages, attaining to the agreed parameters, aimed at preserving cultural patterns; (d) a narrative structure or a predictable sequential order, molded by stereotypes, but incorporating a 'repertoire of variants of the basic issues'" [51]. Therefore, the analysis is focused on the media genres and their formats, the sections and the gender of the protagonist of the journalistic pieces.

Due to the specificity of the news magazines, the genres "Utility" and "Diversional" were not considered. The inclusion criteria in the analysis were journalistic texts (Informative, Opinionative and Interpretative genres) whose protagonists were older people. The total of journalistic texts of the 16 analyzed numbers is 1231 ("Visão" $n = 306$, "Sábado" $n = 241$, "Der Spiegel" $n = 349$, "Focus" $n = 335$). After analyzing all the texts, 1107 articles were excluded from the sample of analyzed issues for not meeting the inclusion criteria. The final sample consisted of 124 journalistic texts (10,1%) – 38 from the Portuguese magazines ("Visão" $n = 26$, 21% and "Sábado" $n = 12$, 9.7%) and 86 from the Germans magazines ("Der Spiegel" $n = 45$, 36.3% and "Focus" $n = 41$, 33%).

3 Results and Discussion

As shown in Table 2, there are differences in the journalistic genres used in the magazines of the two countries. The interpretative genre is the most common in Portugal ($n = 20$, 52,6%), whereas in Germany the informative genre predominates ($n = 50$, 58,1%). In the total sample, the informative gender predominates ($n = 59$, 47,6%).

Table 2. Journalistic genre by country

Journalistic genre	Country		Total
	Germany (n, %)	Portugal (n, %)	
Informative	**50 (58,1%)**	9 (23,7%)	**59 (47,6%)**
Interpretative	25 (29,1)	**20 (52,6)**	45 (36,3%)
Opinionative	11 (12,8%)	9 (23,7%)	20 (16,1%)
Total	86 (100%)	38 (100%)	124 (100%)

In Table 3 it is possible to verify that the analyzed texts fall into 10 different formats, and we can observe the format used by country. The "profile" format is modal in both Germany (n = 25, 29,1%) and Portugal (n = 17, 44,7%). The "analysis" and "chronicle" formats are only used in Portugal, as well as "caricature" and "reporting" are exclusive to the German magazines in our sample.

In both Germany and Portugal magazines, the journalistic pieces of the sample are not predominantly prominent (n = 81, 92,2% vs. n = 38, 100%, respectively), as show Table 4. Therefore, it is verified that invisibility in the headlines of the journalistic pieces in which protagonists are older people. The analysis showed that stories that are not highlighted also have less visibility in the pages of the news magazines, contributing to the thesis of the invisibility of the elderly in media discourses [53].

Table 3. Journalistic format by country

Journalistic format	Country		Total
	Germany (n, %)	Portugal (n, %)	
Analysis	0 (0,0%)	3 (7,9%)	3 (2,4%)
Article	4 (4,7%)	1 (2,6%)	5 (4%)
Caricature	3 (3,5%)	0 (0,0%)	3 (2,4%)
Chronicle	0 (0,0%)	6 (15,8%)	6 (4,8%)
Column	4 (4,7%)	2 (5,3%)	6 (4,8%)
Interview	12 (14%)	5 (13,2%)	17 (13,7%)
News	14 (16,3%)	3 (7,9%)	17 (13,7%)
Note	23 (26,7%)	1 (2,6%)	24 (19,4%)
Profile	**25 (29,1%)**	**17 (44,7%)**	**42 (33,9%)**
Report	1 (1,2%)	0 (0,0%)	1 (0,8%)
Total	86 (100%)	38 (100%)	124 (100%)

It is also important to note that in the headlines of the German magazines ("Der Spiegel" $n = 3$, "Focus" $n = 2$) the protagonists are men and the news pieces fit in the sections "National" ($n = 2$) and "Politics" ($n = 3$).

Table 4. Headlines by country

Headline	Country		Total
	Germany (n, %)	Portugal (n, %)	
No	**81 (94,2%)**	**38 (100%)**	**119 (96%)**
Yes	5 (5,8)	0 (0,0%)	5 (4%)
Total	86 (100%)	38 (100%)	124 (100%)

In the gender of the protagonists, there is a predominance of male in Germany and Portugal ($n = 71$, 79,1% vs. $n = 31$, 81,6% respectively), as shown in Table 5. As empirical evidence shows media representations reproduce hegemonic cultural discourses and tend, thus, to render women invisible in the media, particularly when compared to men, as several authors have demonstrated [34, 36, 54–57].

Table 5. Gender by country

Headline	Country		Total
	Germany (n, %)	Portugal (n, %)	
Female	15 (17,4%)	7 (18,4%)	22 (17,7%)
Male	**71 (82,6%)**	**31 (81,6%)**	**102 (82,3%)**
Total	86 (100%)	38 (100%)	124 (100%)

Table 6 presents the analysis between section and gender of the protagonists. The results demonstrate that crosscutting the different sections there is a numerical expression of the male protagonists constituting a clear majority in the four analyzed news magazines, with particular emphasis on "Politics", "International" and "Culture". Also, in the "Obituary" section, although there is a female presence, men predominate. Regarding the "Opinion" section, it is important to highlight the balance in the German magazines (female $n = 2$, male $n = 3$), in contrast to a greater presence of men in the Portuguese ones (female $n = 0$, male $n = 6$).

Table 6. Section and Gender of the Protagonists by country

Section	Country					
	Germany			Portugal		
	Female	Male	Total	Female	Male	Total
Culture	5 (5,8%)	15 (17,4%)	20 (23,2%)	1 (2,6%)	4 (10,5%)	5 (13,2%)
Economics	1 (1,2%)	4 (4,7%)	5 (5,8%)	0 (0,0%)	0 (0,0%)	0 (0,0%)
Entertainment	0 (0,0%)	0 (0,0%)	0 (0,0%)	0 (0,0%)	0 (0,0%)	0 (0,0%)
Health	0 (0,0%)	0 (0,0%)	0 (0,0%)	0 (0,0%)	0 (0,0%)	0 (0,0%)
International	0 (0,0%)	**10 (11,6%)**	10 (11,6%)	0 (0,0%)	**3 (7,9%)**	3 (7,9%)
National	2 (2,3%)	9 (10,5%)	11 (12,8%)	0 (0,0%)	0 (0,0%)	0 (0,0%)
Obituary	5 (5,8%)	**19 (22,1%)**	24 (28%)	6 (15,8%)	**9 (23,7)**	15 (39,5%)
Opinion	2 (2,3%)	3 (3,5%)	5 (5,8%)	0 (0,0%)	6 (15,8%)	6 (15,8%)
Politics	0 (0,0%)	**11 (12,8%)**	11 (12,8%)	1 (2,6%)	**5 (13,2%)**	6 (15,8%)
Society	0 (0,0%)	0 (0,0%)	0 (0,0%)	0 (0,0%)	2 (5,3%)	2 (5,3%)
Sports	0 (0,0%)	0 (0,0%)	0 (0,0%)	0 (0,0%)	1 (2,6%)	1 (2,6%)
Total	15 (17,4%)	71 (82,6%)	86 (100%)	8 (21,1%)	30 (79,9%)	38 (100%)

These results are intertwined with Table 5, showing that the numerical expression quadruples between men and women (Germany: female $n = 15$, male $n = 71$; Portugal: female $n = 7$, male $n = 31$). The dominance of discourses in line with the hegemonic ideology, particularly concerning issues of Politics (national and international) and Culture, are one of the results with greater prominence of this table. In the case of the German magazines, men also dominate the "National" section. In Portugal there were no journalistic pieces of "National" that had seniors as protagonists.

This study argues that media representations, even in aging democratic liberal societies, tend to underrepresent older men and, when including them on media contents, representations go in accordance with hegemonic understandings of what the older man should be and how he should behave, dismissing other - complex, multiple and overlapping - forms of being, expressing and behaving as older men.

4   Conclusion and Limitations

This paper aimed to identify visibilities and invisibilities of older men in news magazines of Germany and Portugal in order to answer the research question: "How are older men represented in the media?".

In the "age of mediated visibility" [44], the results show a invisibility of women and older adults, being older men represented in line with traditional roles assigned to "real men", such as leadership. Older people are protagonists of only 10.1% of news stories from a total of 1231 articles, which leads to the conclusion that aging and older people are not socially represented in the discourses of the analyzed news magazines. Specifically focusing on older men, these are represented in different "places of speech" [12] according to their social position, but only with significant prominence in the "Politics", "International" and "Culture" sections in both countries. As far as political and cultural life is concerned, older men are an integral part of the hegemonic ideology. The same happens with the opinion texts and, for that very reason, with their presence itself in the media. Furthermore, it was verified that the aging of the population - which is a reality of both countries - was also rendered invisible.

The analysis also shows that the dominant journalistic genres differ in the two countries (Germany: informative genre 58,1%, Portugal: interpretative genre 52,6%). However, the journalistic format that prevails in both countries is identical and corresponds to the "Profile", which is often used in the section "Obituary".

Between visibilities and invisibilities actively produced through political and public discourses [57], the idiosyncrasy of male dominance in the two countries was verified. The results also show the invisibility of older people in the news magazines with the exception of the "Obituary" section where they have a higher presence.

Analyzed media discourses tend to reproduce the hegemonic ideology concerning age and gender. Older people are underrepresented and older men, when given the opportunity to be represented, are portrayed in line with traditional conceptions of manhood. The analyzed journalistic pieces give evidence of a mediated social construction of reality filled with stereotypes that promote the near non-existence [58] of women, non-hegemonic masculinities, or older people in the four news magazines. The power of producing absences [58] that the media holds, makes the older population almost non-existent to society. It is also important to highlight that media tend to misleadingly (re)create the image of senior people as a homogeneous group, regardless of clear differences in terms of activity, profile, health, among others. Recreating the image of the senior people as if time were of a static nature, the media continue to perpetuate the male protagonist in this almost non-existence of the older population.

The main limitations of this study are related to the quantitative approach and the analysis period. In the future we will try to analyze the same news magazines in a longitudinal study through the analysis of qualitative content, focusing on text and image.

Acknowledgments. This article was financed by national Portuguese funds through FCT (Fundação para a Ciência e a Tecnologia) in the framework of the project "(De)Coding Masculinities: Towards an enhanced understanding of media's role in shaping perceptions of masculinities in Portugal" (Reference PTDC/COM-CSS/31740/2017).

References

1. McCombs, M.E., Shaw, D.L.: The agenda-setting function of mass media. Publ. Opin. Q. **36**(2), 176–187 (1972)
2. Shoemaker, P., Eichholz, M., Kim, E., Wrigley, B.: Individual and routine forces in gatekeeping. J. Mass Commun. Q. **78**, 233–246 (2001)
3. Couldry, N., Livingstone, S., Markham, T.: Media Consumption and Public Engagement: Beyond the Presumption of Attention. Palgrave Macmillan, London (2016)
4. Connell, R.W., Messerschmidt, J.W.: Hegemonic masculinity: rethinking the concept? Gend. Soc. **19**(6), 829–859 (2005)
5. Ylänne, D.V.: Representing Ageing. Palgrave Macmillan, London (2012)

6. Gerbner, G., Gross, L., Signorielli, N., Morgan, M.: Aging with television: images on television drama and conceptions of social reality. J. Commun. **30**, 37–47 (1980)
7. Vernon, J.A., Williams, J.A., Phillips, T., Wilson, J.: Media stereotyping: a comparison of the way elderly women and men are portrayed on prime-time television. J. Women Aging **2**(4), 55–68 (1991)
8. Craig, S.: Men, Masculinity, and the Media. Sage, London (1999)
9. Katz, J., Earp, J.: Tough Guise: Violence, Media & the Crisis in Masculinity. Media Education Foundation (1999)
10. Femiano, S., Nickerson, M.: How do media images of men affect our lives. Re-Imagining the American Dream. J. Media Values (2000)
11. Katz, J.: Advertising the construction of violent white masculinity: from BMW's to Bud Light. In: Gender, Race, and Class in Media: A Critical Reader, pp. 261–269 (2011)
12. Woodward, K.: Identidade e diferença: uma introdução teórica e conceitual. In: Silva, T.T. (ed.) Identidade e diferença: a perspectiva dos estudos culturais, pp. 7–71. Petrópolis, Vozes (2000)
13. Mannheim, K.: The problem of generation. In: Mannheim, K. (ed.) Essays on the Sociology of Knowledge, pp. 276–320. Routledge & Kegan Paul, London, United Kingdom (1952)
14. Corsten, M.: The time of generations. Time & Society **8**(2–3), 249–272 (1999)
15. Vasil, L., Wass, H.: Portrayal of the elderly in the media: a literature review and implications for educational gerontologists. Educ. Gerontol. Int. Q. **19**(1), 71–85 (1993)
16. Daniel, F., Antunes, A., Amaral, I.: Representações sociais da velhice. Análise. Psicológica **33**(3), 291–301 (2015)
17. Bolin, G., Skogerbø, E.: Age, generation and the media. Northern Lights **11**, 3–14 (2013)
18. Kareithi, P.J.: Hegemonic masculinity in media contents. In: International Association For Media And Communication Research. Media and Gender: A Scholarly Agenda for the Global Alliance on Media and Gender. UNESCO, Paris (2014)
19. Todd, J.T.: Gendered Lives: Communication, Gender, and Culture. Thomson/Wadsworth, Belmont (2003)
20. Baker, K., Raney, A.A.: Equally super?: Gender-role stereotyping of superheroes in children's animated programs. Mass Commun. Soc. **10**(1), 25–41 (2007)
21. Sutherland, G., et al.: Media Representations of Violence Against Women and Their Children: Final Report. ANROWS, Sydney (2016)
22. Ward, L.M., Aubrey, J.S.: Watching gender: how stereotypes in movies and on TV impact kids' development, Common Sense, São Francisco (2017)
23. Goffman, E.: Frame Analysis: An Essay on the Organization of Experience. Harper and Row, London (1974)
24. PORDATA. https://www.pordata.pt/Europa/População+residente+total+e+por+grandes +grupos+etários+(percentagem)-1865-202233. Accessed 8 Dec 2018
25. EIGE - European Institute for Gender Equality: Gender Equality Index 2017 - Measuring gender equality in the European Union 2005–2015 (2017). https://eige.europa.eu/rdc/eige-publications/gender-equality-index-2017-measuring-gender-equality-european-union-2005-2015-report. Accessed 8 Dec 2018
26. Vizeu, A.: A produção de sentidos no jornalismo: da teoria da enunciação a enunciação jornalística. Revista Famecos **10**(22), 107–116 (2002)
27. Foucault, M.: Discipline and Punish: the Birth of a Prison. Penguin, London (1991)
28. Durkheim, É.: The Rules of Sociological Method. The Free Press of Glenco, New York (1964)
29. Amaral, I., Daniel, F.: Ageism and IT: social representations, exclusion and citizenship in the digital age. In: Zhou, J., Salvendy, G. (eds.) ITAP 2016. LNCS, vol. 9755, pp. 159–166. Springer, Cham (2016). https://doi.org/10.1007/978-3-319-39949-2_15

30. Wolton, D.: Elogio do grande público: uma teoria crítica da televisão. Ática (1996)
31. van Dijk, T.: Las estruturas de la noticia. La produccion de la noticia. In van Dijk, T. (ed.) La noticia como discurso. Comprensión, Estrutura y Producción de la Información, pp. 41–181. Ed. Paidós, Barcelona (1990)
32. Fairclough, N.: Media Discourse. Edward Arnold, London (1995)
33. Hartley, J.: Comunicação, Estudos Culturais e Media. Conceitos-chave. Quimera Editores, Lisboa (2002)
34. Tuchman, G.: Making News: A Study in the Construction of Reality. The Free Press, New York (1978)
35. Santos, M.L.: Gênero e comunicação: O masculino e o feminino em programas populares de rádio. Anna Blume, São Paulo (2004)
36. Silveirinha, M.J.: De como tanto mudou e como tanto ficou na mesma. Media Jornalismo 15, 7–11 (2009)
37. Driesmans, K., Vandenbosch, L., Eggermont, S.: Playing a videogame with a sexualized female character increases adolescents' rape myth acceptance and tolerance toward sexual harassment. Games Health J. 4(2), 91–94 (2015)
38. Hassink, A.: Men on Screen: Over-Represented, Badly Portrayed. New America (2015). https://context.newamerica.org/men-on-screen-over-representedbadly-portrayed-404a0b804c79. Accessed 5 Dec 2018
39. Fleming, P.J., et al.: Risk factors for men's lifetime perpetration of physical violence against intimate partners: results from the international men and gender equality survey (IMAGES) in eight countries. PLoS ONE 10(3) (2015)
40. Giaccardi, S., Ward, L., Seabrook, R., Manago, A., Lippman, J.: Media and modern manhood: testing associations between media consumption and young men's acceptance of traditional gender ideologies. Sex Roles 75(3–4), 151–163 (2016)
41. Daniel, F., Caetano, E., Monteiro, R., Amaral, I.: Representações sociais do envelhecimen-to ativo num olhar genderizado. Análise Psicológica 34(4), 353–364 (2016)
42. Amaral, I., Daniel, F.: The use of social media among senior citizens in Portugal: active ageing through an intergeneration approach. In: Zhou, J., Salvendy, G. (eds.) ITAP 2018. LNCS, vol. 10926, pp. 422–434. Springer, Cham (2018). https://doi.org/10.1007/978-3-319-92034-4_32
43. Loos, E., Ivan, L.: Visual ageism in the media. In: Ayalon, L., Tesch-Römer, C. (eds.) Contemporary Perspectives on Ageism. IPA, vol. 19, pp. 163–176. Springer, Cham (2018). https://doi.org/10.1007/978-3-319-73820-8_11
44. Thompson, J.B.: The Media and Modernity: A Social Theory of the Media. Stanford University Press (1995)
45. Monteiro, R.: O que dizem as mães. Quarteto, Coimbra (2005)
46. Wilińska, M.: Because women will always be women and men are just getting older: intersecting discourses of ageing and gender. Current Soc. 58(6), 879–896 (2010)
47. Ribeiro, R.: A representação dos idosos na publicidade televisiva dos canais generalistas portugueses: verdades, estereótipos e ideologias (Master dissertation). University of Minho, Braga (2012)
48. Colombo, F., Fortunati, L. (eds.): Broadband Society and Generational Changes, vol. 5. Peter Lang, Frankfurt (2011)
49. Bardin, L.: Análise de Conteúdo. Edições 70, Lisboa (1977)
50. Santos, A., Cerqueira, C., Cabecinhas, R.: Between the norm and the exception: gender asymmetries in portuguese newsmagazines. Comunicação e Sociedade 27, 457–474 (2015)
51. Melo, J.M.D., Assis, F.D.: Journalistic genres and formats: a classification model. Intercom: Revista Brasileira de Ciências da Comunicação 39(1), 39–56 (2016)
52. McQuail, D.: McQuail's Mass Communication Theory. Sage Publications (2010)

53. Raycheva, L., Tomov, M., Amaral, I., Petrović, I., Vukelić, M., Čizmić, S.: Ageing women in the media mirror maze. In: Angova, S., et al. (ed.) Media Environment, Public and Strategic Communication, pp. 39–47. Izdatelski kompleks – UNSS, Sofia (2018)
54. Pinto-Coelho, Z., Mota-Ribeiro, S.: Gender, sex and sexuality in two open access communication journals published in Portugal: a critical overview of current discursive practices. In: Cerqueira, C., Cabecinhas, R., Magalhães, S. (eds.) Gender in Focus: (New) Trends in Media, pp. 49–66. CECS, Braga (2016)
55. Byerly, C.M., Ross, K.: Women and Media: A Critical Introduction. NewMalden, Blackwell (2006)
56. Cerqueira, C.: A Imprensa e a Perspectiva de Género. Quando elas são notícia no Dia Internacional da Mulher. Observatorio (OBS*) 2(2), 139–164 (2008)
57. Amaral, I., Daniel, F., Abreu, S.G.: Policies for gender equality in Portugal: contributions to a framework for older women. Revista Prisma Social 22, 346–363 (2018)
58. Santos, B.D.S.: Para uma sociologia das ausências e uma sociologia das emergências. Revista Crítica de Ciências Sociais 63, 237–280 (2002)

Older People Are the Future of Consumption: Great Expectations and Small Starts for Brands and New Media

The French Example

Karine Berthelot-Guiet[✉]

CELSA Sorbonne Université, Paris, France
karine.berthelot-guiet@sorbonne-universite.fr

Abstract. It is now commonsense in the professional marketing sphere to say that *senior* population is the next biggest market to come. Not only regarding retirement or nursing homes which are quite common due to a longer span of life but also because, in occidental countries, of the baby boomers reaching seniorhood and, in other countries of specific demography that implies an aging population like in Japan.

This paper intends to question what we could call a paradox, especially flagrant in France, regarding what the French government promotes as the *silver economy*. In Fact, even if the marketing and communications professionals are aware of the kind of treasure these older generations represent regarding their consumption habits, they act slowly or undercover when it comes to addressing older people.

Through a semio-communicational analysis of papers coming from the professional marketing press (on and offline), we will see how this side of the question is quite talkative about older people, their mastering of consumption and their everyday use of new media in this respect. At the same time, the same kind of analysis of dedicated websites, Social media brand pages or social media senior influencer, mostly women will demonstrate how slowly senior seen as consumers are rising on the French web. We will question how this can be linked to brand communications addressing the main population in order to reach baby boomers senior.

Keywords: Brand · Advertising · Marketing professional · Social media · Elderly · Consumption

1 France: A Life-Size Laboratory About Elderly, Consumption and New Media?

It is now international commonsense among people working in the extended marketing professional field to state that more and more countries, especially the richest, are entering a new area of mass consumption that will be deeply linked and, in some respect, ruled or a least driven by older people purchases. This is especially the case in most European countries.

© Springer Nature Switzerland AG 2019
J. Zhou and G. Salvendy (Eds.): HCII 2019, LNCS 11593, pp. 33–45, 2019.
https://doi.org/10.1007/978-3-030-22015-0_3

The aging of populations is one of the great stakes of the decades to come. Its impact will be huge in society and more especially on an economic point of view. As given by the United Nations: "Globally, population aged 60 or over is growing faster than all younger age groups", this phenomenon is defined and named *population ageing*. In 2017, Japan (33%) and Israël (29%) are the countries with the most significant populations over 60, then comes Europe as a whole (from 25 to 29%), Canada and China (23%) and the USA (22%) [1]. These numbers are remarkable since, regarding the entire planet, people over 60 are only 13% and 2% over 80. However, this situation will be considerably different around 2050, when 25% of global the population will be over 60, except for Africa. In Europe, at that time, 35% of the population will be concerned.

One of the critical findings given by the United Nations concerns people over 80 whose number will triple by 2050. Their specificity in 2018 is that 27% of them live in Europe. This will decrease with time, down to 17% in 2050, and the population of other regions of the world will take the lead.

For the years to come, it gives Europe the specificity of being a kind of laboratory regarding what happens in society and economy, hence in consumption and media habits, when old people are such an essential part of the population. In 2015, Europe hosted almost 27 million people 80 and over, that are currently called in the European Union (EU) publications "elderly people." This is partly due to the increase in life expectancy which was in 2016, at the age of 80, of 9,5 years as an average. People aged 80 in EU have the longest life expectancy in France (11 years) [2]. This makes France a specific field of experience within the European case.

Focusing on European and French elderly, especially people of 65 and over, the EU statistics released in September 2017 [3] show that French elderly are massively less economically active (5%) from 65 to 74 than the other European (9,5%) which is due to the French state mandatory retirement pension system. In France, working people subscribe to the state pension, compulsory supplementary pensions and voluntary private pensions. This explains the low rate of working people after 65 and the fact that their income is quite good. Even if French elderly are not economically active, that is to say they don't have a job, they, however, have enough money and are in good shape and health.

The other specificity of France, regarding the elderly, is the public system of health insurance which gives a universal coverage. People add private health insurance, provided by employment-based mutual associations, which covers balance billing and vision and dental care. In 2010, The French health care system was ranked amongst the best by the World Health Organization for its overall efficiency [4]. Even if this ranking can be criticized [5], the French public investment in the health care system, for decades, benefits now to the older part of the population. This is not without social or geographical inequalities: some people cannot afford some specific cares that need extra-billing, and the country meets the problem of "so-called medical deserts" [6]. At the same time, the system has to take care of more and more elderly and must find a way to provide "long-term care to preserve the autonomy of elderly individuals and facilitate ageing at home while reducing the financial and care burden for the families" [6].

The same EU statistics web tool untitled "a look at the lives of the elderly in the EU today" updated in September 2017 [3] also gives elements about European elderly life habits that can be linked to consuming and media habits. In this respect, French elderly tend to live more alone (37,5%) than in the rest of UE (31,2%), and that implies that they already need or will need home care services and home adaptations in order to stay safely alone at home. They also tend to travel more than the average European elderly (EU average is 48,8%, and French average is 64%) that means a specific field of consumption and a big market regarding leisure and travel. Eventually, the statistics release focuses on Internet use in the slide "use of internet once a week." It shows that 55% of French elderly go on the web once a week at least when the average for Europe is 45%. The countries with the highest percentages are Nordic countries and UK that also happen to be countries with high percentages of economically active elderly between 65 and 74. We can induce that a longer professional life implies the use of the Internet at work. In the French case, this use cannot be linked to a working need. This is why the elderly French consumption also appears as a life-size test regarding consumption and new media.

This paper intends to question what we could call a paradox, especially flagrant in France, regarding what the French government promotes as the *silver economy*. In Fact, even if the marketing and communication professionals are aware of the kind of treasure these older generations represent regarding their consumption habits, they act slowly or undercover when it comes to addressing older people.

Focusing on the example of France, we will explore this paradox through a semio-communicational analysis of papers coming from the professional marketing press (on and offline), that will enable us to see how this professional literature is quite talkative about older people as a vast market, stressing the fact that senior and elderly are supposed to master consumption thanks to their extended training that started during the golden years of mass consumption currently called in France "Trente glorieuses" [7]. It means literally the "three glorious decades" and names the period, starting with the post Second World War, of reconstruction immediately followed by a period of prosperity, full employment, social change and constant economic growth. This era, linked to economic globalization, stopped in 1974 with economic crisis due to the first oil price shock. It is known to be the starting point and a great developing period of mass consumption in France. People who were young adults in 1945 and their children were the first to benefit from all kind of every day and technological new products from fridges to cars, television sets to chocolate spread. They were and still are very able to integrate into their daily life new products, new technologies, and new media.

Eventually, we will balance this professional marketing discourses with the rare supply dedicated to senior and elderly that appears slowly on the French market, and the analysis of dedicated websites, social media brand pages or social media senior influencers, mostly women, demonstrate how slowly senior seen as consumers are rising on the French web. We will question how this can be linked to brand communications addressing the main population to overcome the difficulty to reach baby boomers.

2 French Information and Communication Sciences as a Scientific Frame

2.1 French Communication Sciences

The analysis we intend to develop here is based on French Information and Communication Sciences contemporary approaches [8]. We choose this analytical basis firstly because we belong to it and secondly because we believe that these scientific approaches deserve to be better known outside the francophone area. We will more specifically mobilize, in French Communication Sciences, researchers focused on the conceptualization, description or analysis of social discourses as well as media and market discourses [9]. Their purpose is to comprehend how these discursive pieces, in their broadest sense including speech, images and all kind of media products, circulate between different social and media spaces thus building their media and public exposure. In this respect, media, commercial, advertising and brand speeches are considered as social discourses carrying out market mediation processes.

This specific point of view is neither psychological, sociological nor semiotic; the French information and communication sciences enable to build intermediate positions, which rely on previous analysis as the problematization developed by Barthes and Baudrillard about consumption as a social and symbolic system, basically a system of signification, linked to a sociological system of distinction, although determined by economic aspects [10–13].

In this respect, our methodology is specifically designed to deal with signs and meanings linked to consumption items and speeches in a specific sociological, economic, cultural and communication background.

The present paper is based on researches conducted in the long run that give equal weight to the communication process, the communication products (commercials, brand movies, museums, websites, social networks, and so on) and what professional people (advertising, communication and media people) publicly write or say about them. This implies to work on openly commented uses to reach practices and thus find a way towards uses, representations, and users creative appropriations. This is different from reception studies as developed in media studies because it does not stick to media uses even if some of the receiver perspectives are taken in charge. We choose a socio-semiotic based approach dealing both with the negotiation of meaning in the process of interpretation, the ongoing related infinite semiosis, and creative appropriation, or "poaching" as described by De Certeau [14].

2.2 A Sociosemiotic-Based Method: Socio-Semio-Communication Analysis

This way of doing things takes in charge what people think, say, do, especially advertising and marketing professionals, and compares it with what is happening in fact. This point of view implies what we call "creative methodology" in research. We have to find each time the proper set of methods to question it, theoretically, in a proper way. Using already existing methods is usually the mainstream, but some research topics and objects need dedicated crafted methods resulting from a thorough theoretical analysis. Then, it is a major stake to choose the best set and architecture of qualitative methods, not based on statistics or not able to give quantitative results, to question a research topic, in a proper theoretical way.

In this respect, microscale approaches are our choice especially and paradoxically to reach macro analysis. Many very detailed analysis on small elements, which in the end lead to deal with the different big corpus of small things, result in precious and unexpected results we would not have reached through direct macro analysis. Our theoretical position regarding methodology is one of a socio-semio-communication approach.

3 Senior, *Silver, etc.*: An Excellent Target for the Marketing Field

3.1 Marketing and Publishing: How to Advertise a Service

For some years now, the professional marketing sphere, either French or willing to reach French market, states globally that elderly is the next biggest market to come, especially in France. This is important, since the advertising and marketing people, especially consultants or heads of agencies, usually have a significant publishing activity in books, professional press or blogs, and other social media. This is a regular professional process that ensures the visibility of the author in his or her professional field and, at the same times, acts as a large advertising booklet for his or her practice or company. We can quote, as a good example, the case of Jean-Marie Dru, Chairman of TBWA Worldwide, who coined the word *disruption* to name his advertising method that is described as "a catalyst for creative thinking and ideas that changes the marketplace, creating business building for brands, companies and industries by upturning and challenging the conventions of that business and finding room to grow in the market" [15]. As a matter of fact, this can describe any work in any marketing or advertising agency, but the publishing work of Dru transformed the definition of *disruption* in a proprietary procedure through 6 books between 1998 and 2016 [16].

Hence, when a theme appears regularly in papers and books written by marketing professionals, one can think that it is both because some agencies try to grasp the lead and because the theme has, in some respect, a true consistency.

3.2 Senior in French Marketing Discourses: A Twenty Years Story

For more than twenty years now, the topic has been a consistent theme in French publications specialized in marketing. On this matter, one of the best sellers, published for the first time in 1994 and four-time reissued, is "Le senior marketing" [17]. The author was and still is an advertising consultant. He created in the late 90's an agency dedicated to "senior marketing" called *Senioragency*. This book started a kind of interest among French marketing people, and some other books came after, dealing more specifically with women senior, generations, etc. This publications prove a real stability of the interest for the older generation even if results remained quite elusive as the years go by.

Later, the French government, willing to boost this market created and started to promote the "Silver économie" sector [13, 18]. In 2013, the French Ministry of Economy and Finance created, as a promising niche, and defined the "Silver Economy" on an acknowledgement of the fact that for a great number of economic sectors and industries, as "gerotontechnologies", healthcare products, home equipment and leisure, the ageing of the French population is a growth opportunity. The French government defines "Silver économie" as a group of economic and industrial activities that benefit to senior and enhance their quality of life, even their life expectancy. A set of 49 priority actions was decided in 2013–2015, but the system had difficulty to work, and only half of these actions started, mainly driven by state institutions. In 2016, a new launch occurred. These different steps show at the same time a real will and some difficulties in its implementation. The field covered by the idea of silver economy goes beyond only marketing and reaches all the topics of senior citizenship and wellness. The French administration has developed practical handbook entitled "My life in Silver" and an official AFNOR standard (the French National Standards Association) named "tested and approved by senior" (Fig. 1).

Fig. 1. Silver official standard and Silver Economy handbook on www.silvereco.fr

The same kind of gap exists between the uncontested assertion of one market and even more than one, and the slow development of a true products and services offering, not only regarding retirement or nursing homes which are quite common due to a longer span of life. This is particularly flagrant analyzing in a quite extensive way different corpus of marketing professional writings about senior and elderly markets. We gathered different types of corpuses: one corpus gathered data from *Europress* database taking into account two full years of three French professional marketing magazines, amongst the most read: *Stratégies* (mostly about advertising and commu-nication agencies), *Marketing Magazine, LSA* (mostly about retail), one corpus gath-ered data from the web archives of *CB News,* the second most read magazine in the advertising field, and one corpus gathered French and international web documents about French elderly and senior as emerging or growing markets.

3.3   Aging in Marketing Discourses: A New Consumption Target

For marketing people, senior and elderly clearly appear as very promising groups of the population. Therefore, it is necessary to evaluate the potential of this coming and growing source of business and to understand their specific needs, their self-image or self-images and their new media habits [19, 20]. In France, for the first time, two, and sometimes three, generations in the same family can be referred as "senior", with young senior being 50, their parents 70 or over and their elderly grandparents being 80 to 90 or over. The middle ones (70 or over) being, most of the time, caregivers for their parents or older relatives. Even if, as seen before, the French government and marketing people are aware of the importance as a market of this part of the population they only start to look at people 50 and over as different populations of consumers, especially when it comes to new media habits.

Even if it is common sense to know that people aged 50, 60, 70, 80 or 90 must have different needs, tastes, daily activities and be dramatically different regarding autonomy, these differences almost disappear in marketing discourses. In these analysis, these different ages of life are still often categorized as one, as a whole, especially when it comes to new ways of consumption, new media, and IT products consumption [19, 21, 22]. However, marketing, media, and advertising people mostly concentrate on groups of the population known for their purchasing power and their proven activity in consumption [19, 22, 23]. It used to be marketing common sense to qualify the elderly as small buyers, especially in home equipment and fashion, and, regarding food and everyday supply, set in their ways. In this point of view, the interest to build new market offers was seen as poor. This tends to evolve in general and particularly for marketing professionals [21, 24, 25]. Senior and elderly now appear as possible marketing targets for a whole range of products, services, and media.

3.4   Senior and French Marketing: Statements More Than Achievements

Most of the papers and web publications we gathered shows that marketing professionals are globally aware of the fact that senior people are now a target since they represent, in France, an important part of social, economic, political power. The economic aspect is particularly important in this process as shown in papers as "De l'or, mon senior" (*my senior is* rich - Marketing), "Les seniors futur relais de croissance pour la grande consommation" (*senior as a coming source of growth for mass consumption* - LSA), "Fiers d'être jeunior" (*Proud to be young senior* – Stratégies), "Les "jeunes vieux" au pouvoir" (*Power to young old people*– Stratégies). The senior and elderly consumption practices and habits are also explored as new possible markets or communication tools. In this respect CB-News particularly focuses on digital aspects with papers about "on-line senior", "silver surfers", "how elderly are quick to pass along fake news". Senior shopping habits are also analyzed: what they buy, how they spend time and money in malls, how women senior are particularly active in consumption on and off-line. Some papers also concentrate on the presentation of new products, media or services dedicated to senior or/and elderly. Two launches are particularly present in the professional discourses gathered:

1. The opening of a new kind of shop called "Bien chez moi" (*I feel good at home*) opened by the big French retail group *Les Mousquetaires* also the owner or the *Intermarché* super and hypermarket brand ranked as the third French retail group,
2. The launch of a women's magazine dedicated to senior untitled "Femme Actuelle Senior." The launch has been both on and offline, with social media accounts and a newsletter.

4   Small Starts: New Retail, New Media

Hopefully, these two launches are not the first one in France, but we can say that they seem to be the first ones openly launched as designed for young senior and advertising themselves as such.

4.1   "Bien Chez Moi" (*I Feel Good at Home*): A Sustainable Model?

As already seen, "Bien chez moi" is the first store of its kind launched by a major French retail group. The store opened October 3rd, 2018 in Flers, a small town in Normandie region. The store is located in a shopping center built around an Intermarché hypermarket, which is also a brand part of Les Mousquetaires group. According to the brand manager, Flers has been chosen because of its location, in a regular French town outside Paris and its region, with the idea to promote local stores "concerned with the welfare of elderly" [26]. It has been presented as a test store implying that the group may think about a national cover or specific elderly dedicated section in its supermarket and hypermarket chain Intermarché.

Indeed, this store is the result of an ongoing and significant concern for senior consumers shown by the retail group. We can even say that Les Mousquetaires has worked on the subject with small steps before reaching the possibility to open a dedicated store. In the past years, Intermarché stores have progressively sold and put forward in their weekly promotion advertising catalogs, assisted living products in between basic daily products, these small products linked to assisted living were completely mingled with all kind of promotions. This enabled us to assume that it was part of a global strategy to standardize and normalize products related to aging and/or assisted living since they appear as mass consumption products: "In this respect, the fact that an object or service becomes a good, its *commodification,* acts as a sign of its normalization since there is no need to go in a specialized or dedicated to professionals store" [13]. Whenever you start to find senior dedicated products in your supermarket, it delivers you the message that these products are standard and that it is normal to need and buy them (Fig. 2).

The "Bien Chez moi" store has a website and a Facebook page gathering very few followers in January 2019, three months after the opening. The website has a simple, flat design with a black background and a jigsaw puzzle like the presentation of four sections dedicated to wellness, being connected (tablets, computers, and smartphones), home equipment and how to open your mind. In each section, a set of subsections are proposed with specific products. Globally, the products mingle regular products such as

Fig. 2. Intermarché hypermarket advertising catalog

Dead Sea Mud enriched cosmetics, and soaps or aromatherapy, Pilates and yoga books and accessories and senior dedicated products like posture correcting undergarment designed like sports outfit, devices and security solutions for the bathroom. The connected life section is dedicated to connected home appliances for safety, easy to use phones and tablets and devices to monitor health. Photographs show a store where the exhibition areas seem to be a mix of an organic store or Nature House shope, an Ikea staging and a small bookshop. The place appears to be vast and not so crowded with merchandise. The scarcity of the supply is not, in fact, a choice from the retail group since they issued last month an official appeal [27] to find new products and French industries to develop and produce senior dedicated products (Fig. 3).

Fig. 3. Intermarché Bien Chez Moi website

4.2   "Femme Actuelle Senior": New Media, New Discourses?

Femme Actuelle Senior (*Senior Contemporary Woman*) has been launched in April 2018, both offline and online. The magazine existed previously, since 2015, under the named *Serengo*. This previous version did not reach success, and Prisma Press Group decided to take advantage of the success of Femme Actuelle (*Contemporary Woman*), its flagship, which is the most widely read women French magazine.

At first sight, Femme Actuelle Senior, seems quite similar to other magazines, off and online, dedicated in France to senior as Pleine Vie (*Living Fully*) and Notre Temps (*Nowadays*). Pleine Vie and Notre temps give a great place to consumption topic, linking senior fulfillment with consumption. They advise about the best ways to consume, so does Femme Actuelle Senior. The section on Femme Actuelle Senior website dedicated to consumption is named "smart consumption" and announces: "we have only one obsession: save you some cash." The idea is not only about having a nice life thanks to consumption, it is to be happy because you master consumption and you don't spend more than needed. This section gathers a mix, without apparent ranking, of papers about regular topics (taxes, sales period, how to get rid of humidity at home, home to save power and money with your washing machine,…) and senior topics (retirement pension, survivor's pension, a donation between spouses). The huge discrepancy in the mix makes it difficult to follow.

The section named Smart web is dedicated to: "Finding for you the good ideas on the web and give you tips to surf the web better". This implies that the readers already use IT and are even used to it since they can improve their uses. The papers in this section are mostly small instructions manual, explaining how to use bluetooth, what are challenges on social media, how to recover the deleted content of a computer trash box, finding some specific websites, how to avoid credit card scam, etc. Only one paper is dedicated to the presentation of a tablet "simplified for seniors" which happens to be the prize to be won in a contest organized by the magazine.

The magazine both online and offline makes the difference with Notre Temps and Pleine Vie when it comes to sex life issues since it appears, in Femme Actuelle Senior as a regular topic in many papers, both on the website and in the magazine. It appears as a mandatory theme to write about as it is usually in women magazine. However, all the taboos are not overcome, and globally women and men represented in Femme Actuelle Senior fit the stereotype of the young senior that tends to appear in media in commercials. Advertising is particularly efficient in its work of stereotypy, choosing carefully nice looking even beautiful young senior people, very dynamic, beautifully tanned, hair magnificent gray or white, doing easily physically and intellectually demanding activities [12, 21, 25, 28]. Being senior is less about aging that about staying young. In this respect, the similarity between representations in advertising and Femme Actuelle Senior is flagrant (Figs. 4 and 5).

Fig. 4. Femme Actuelle Senior website

Fig. 5. Young senior stereotypy in mass advertising

5 Conclusion: Senior and Dedicated Products and Media, True Needs and Circumventing Discourses

The example of the French market experience regarding senior and elderly dedicated offer shows that a longtime interest and acknowledgment of the strength of a part of the population as a marketing target is not enough, even sustained by state action, to start a massive move in industries and companies offer as well as in older people purchases. The problem encountered by Les Mousquetaires group in order to find genuinely adapted, both technically and symbolically, items to sell in Bien chez moi, their first store dedicated to senior, is typical.

Even when the supply does exist, "young" senior or baby boomers are particularly difficult to reach with "old person" stamped products. They are the golden generation, even if the French state promotes "silver," regarding consumption. In France, they have grown up and evolved in adulthood with mass consumption and constant technological changes. They are skilled enough with IT devices. Even if they are well aware of aging issues, since many of them are caregivers for their elderly parents or relatives, they want adaptation without old persons dedicated obvious design and commercial discourses.

In this respect, the failure of attempts to launch specifically dedicated offers such as Serengo (now Femme Actuelle Senior) or the website "Vivre l'accessibilité en toute liberté" (To live accessibility in complete freedom) by Lapeyre (home improvement stores) is emblematic of the phenomenon. Once linked to the regular best seller Femme Actuelle, Femme Actuelle Senior is a media success. At the same time, the repositioning of Lapeyre senior dedicated products and personalized advice in the regular, general public, offer, presented on its website and consumer magazines has been the solution.

In this respect, taking senior as one group is not possible any more especially in the IT and new media consumption. When elderly need help, adapted and simplified devices, discovery and training workshop, baby boomers are already fluent with computers, tables, and smartphone, they master mail and well enough blogs and social media. They need tips to keep up with evolutions especially the ones linked to their grandchildren. Baby boomers want to be taken as regular consumers.

References

1. United Nations, Department of Economic and Social Affairs, Population Division. World Population Prospect: The 2017 Revision, Key Findings and Advance Tables. Working Paper No. ESA/P/WP/248 (2017)
2. Eurostat, Nearly 27 million people, aged 80 or over in the European Union, 29 September 2016. https://ec.europa.eu/eurostat
3. Eurostat, A look at the lives of the elderly in the EU today, web tool released by Eurostat, the statistical office of the European Union, 27 November 2015. Data updated in September 2017. https://ec.europa.eu/eurostat
4. World Health Organization. The world health report 2000 — Health systems: improving performance. World Health Organization, Geneva (2000)
5. Tandon, A., Murray, C., Lauer, J.A., Evans, D.B.: Measuring Overall Health Care System Performance for 191 Countries, GPE Discussion Paper Series: No. 30, EIP/GPE/EQC World Health Organization
6. Chevreul, K., Berg Brigham, K., Durand-Zaleski, I., Hernandez-Quevedo, C.: Health System Review, Health Systems in Transition, European Observatory on Health Systems and Policies partnership hosted by WHO, France, vol. 17, no. 3 (2015)
7. Fourastié, J.: Les Trente Glorieuses ou la Révolution Invisible de 1946 à 1975. Fayard, Paris (1979)
8. Jeanneret, Y., Ollivier, O.: Les Sciences de l'Information et de la Communication. Hermes, 38, Paris, CNRS Editions (2004)

9. Berthelot-Guiet, K.: La marque médiation marchande ou mythologie adolescente. In: Lachance, J., Saint-Germain, P., Mathiot, L. (eds.) Marques Cultes et Culte des Marques chez les Jeunes: Penser l'Adolescence avec la Consommation, pp. 23–38. Presses Universitaires de Laval, Laval (2016)
10. Barthes, R.: Mythologies. The Noonday Press, New York (1991)
11. Baudrillard, K.: The System of Objects. Verso, London (1996)
12. Berthelot-Guiet, K.: Paroles de Pub. La Vie Triviale de la Publicité. Éditions Non Standard, Le Havre (2013)
13. Berthelot-Guiet, K.: New media, new commodification, new consumption for older people. In: Zhou, J., Salvendy, G. (eds.) ITAP 2018, Part I. LNCS, vol. 10926, pp. 435–445. Springer, Cham (2018). https://doi.org/10.1007/978-3-319-92034-4_33
14. de Certeau, M.: The Practice of Everyday Life. University of California Press, Berkeley (1984)
15. https://tbwa.com/pirates/jean-marie-dru
16. Dru, J.-M.: Le Saut créatif, Paris, Jean-Claude Lattès (1984). Disruption, Paris, Le Village mondial (1997). Disruption Live Paris, Le Village mondial (2002). La Publicité autrement, Gallimard (2007). Jet Lag, Paris, Grasset (2011). New, Paris, Le Village Mondial (2016)
17. Treguer, J.-P.: Le senior marketing. Vendre et communiquer aux générations de plus de 50 ans, Paris, Dunod, 1994, 2007
18. La filière Silver Economie. www.entreprises.gouv.fr/politique-et-enjeux/la-silver-economy. Consulté le 11 janvier 2019
19. Colombo, F.: Ageing, media and communication. Paper Proceedings, ICA, Puerto Rico, 21–25 May, pp. 1–13 (2015)
20. Beard, J., et al.: Global Population Ageing: Peril or Promise? PGDA Working Paper, 89 (2012). http://www.hsph.harvard.edu/pgda/working.htm
21. Berthelot-Guiet, K.: Elderly and IT: brand discourses on the go. In: Zhou, J., Salvendy, G. (eds.) ITAP 2016, Part II. LNCS, vol. 9755, pp. 186–193. Springer, Cham (2016). https://doi.org/10.1007/978-3-319-39949-2_18
22. Colombo, F., Aroldi, P., Carlo, S.: New elders, old divides: ICTs, inequalities and well being amongst young elderly Italians. Comunicar Media Educ. Res. J. **XXVIII**(45), 47–55 (2015)
23. Colombo, F.: The long wave of generations. In: Colombo, F., Fortunati, L. (eds.) Broadband Society and Generational Changes, pp. 19–36. Peter Lang, Francfurt (2011)
24. Defrance, A.: Penser, classer, communiquer. Publicité et catégories sociales, Hermès **38**, 155–162 (2004)
25. Loos, E., Ivan, L.: Visual ageism in the media. In: Ayalon, L., Tesch-Römer, C. (eds.) Contemporary Perspectives on Ageism. IPA, vol. 19, pp. 163–176. Springer, Cham (2018). https://doi.org/10.1007/978-3-319-73820-8_11
26. Commerce. Intermarché pense à une enseigne pour les seniors, Alexandre Da Silva 23 mai 2018. https://www.ouest-france.fr/normandie/flers-61100/flers-un-commerce-pour-les-seniors-pense-par-les-seniors-5775046
27. BFM TV France 19, 12. https://bfmbusiness.bfmtv.com/mediaplayer/video/focus-retail-intermache-recherche-des-fabricants-pour-developper-son-activite-en-direction-des-seniors-1912-1126549.html
28. Berthelot-Guiet, K.: Analyser les discours publicitaires. Armand Colin, Paris (2015)

Methodological Strategies to Understand Smartphone Practices for Social Connectedness in Later Life

Mireia Fernández-Ardèvol[1(✉)], Andrea Rosales[1], Eugène Loos[2],
Alexander Peine[3], Roser Beneito-Montagut[1,4,5], Daniel Blanche[1],
Björn Fischer[6], Stephen Katz[7], and Britt Östlund[6]

[1] Internet Interdisciplinary Institute (IN3),
Universitat Oberta de Catalunya/Open University of Catalonia, Barcelona,
Catalonia, Spain
{mfernandezar, arosalescl, rbeneito, dblanchet}@uoc.edu
[2] Utrecht University School of Governance, Utrecht University, Utrecht
The Netherlands
e.f.loos@uu.nl
[3] Copernicus Institute of Sustainable Development, Utrecht University,
Utrecht, The Netherlands
a.peine@uu.nl
[4] Computer Science Department,
Universitat Oberta de Catalunya/Open University of Catalonia, Barcelona,
Catalonia, Spain
[5] School of Social Sciences, Cardiff University, Cardiff, UK
[6] Department for Biomedical Engineering and Health Systems,
Royal Institute of Technology, KTH, Stockholm, Sweden
{bjorfisc, brittost}@kth.se
[7] Sociology Department, Trent University, Peterborough, ON, Canada
skatz@trentu.ca

Abstract. Digital practices in later life are not yet well understood. Therefore, this paper discusses the framework for a research design project that aims at tracing differences and similarities in how older adults use their smartphones in circumstances in and outside their homes in Spain, the Netherlands, Sweden, and Canada. The research questions of this international research project focus on the extent to which digital mobile practices relate to perceived social connectedness among older adults aged 55–79 years old. While studies have shown that the subjective experience of 'being connected' supports continued well-being in later life, there remains an insufficient understanding of the processes through which digital mediated social interaction is effective for social connectedness. The analytical framework of the project prioritizes the co-constituency of (digital) technology and ageing, and takes digital practices in everyday life as its entry point. The main data collection tool will be the tracking of smartphone activity of 600 older adults (150 per country) during four weeks. An online survey and qualitative interviews will gather data about the meanings of the quantified digital practices, and how they shape (if they do) the participants' connection to the world. This approach will allow us not only to get insight into what older adults say how they used their smartphone but also to

© Springer Nature Switzerland AG 2019
J. Zhou and G. Salvendy (Eds.): HCII 2019, LNCS 11593, pp. 46–64, 2019.
https://doi.org/10.1007/978-3-030-22015-0_4

gain insight into their real-life daily use. The assessment of the challenges, strengths, and weaknesses of the methods contributes towards an accurate and appropriate interpretation of empirical results and their implications.

Keywords: Tracking · Log data · Survey data · Interviews · Mixed methods · Research design · Older adults · Later life · Smartphones · Digital practices

1 Introduction

In gerontechnological research, technologies are often regarded as mere solutions to age-related needs and problems by offering compensatory aids and supports [1, 2]. However, we contest this positioning of technological advancements as it has been associated with a deficit model of ageing and promote, instead, a critical model of socio-gerontechnology (S-G) as an alternative. This model combines traditional gerontechnology with insights from Social Studies of Science & Technology (STS) [3–6], and views ageing, technology and the social context as inextricably linked and mutually emergent (rather than separate entities [7]). Further, S-G emphasizes how technologies are contextualized and made meaningful within the lived realities of later life and the interplay between users, technology and social change [8]. Technologies only gain their characteristics over time as they are domesticated and embedded in society [9]. Hence, rather than remaining in the background, in our perspective on S-G, older persons and their immediate environments are central to the development of meaningful technologies for later life.

First launched in the 1940s, mobile phones started to be commercialized more prominently in the 1980s [10]. Since their massive consumer uptake in the late 1990s [11], they have become essential, everyday devices in most countries [12]. We consider this technological movement as part of a domestication process. Haddon [13] states that: "The earliest public and most cited reference to the concept of domestication was Silverstone, Hirsch and Morley [14], which appeared in a collection of some of the first empirical studies of ICTs. The metaphor of 'domestication' came from the taming of wild animals, but was here applied to describing the processes involved in 'domesticating ICTs' when bringing them into the home." (p. 17) [15–18]. Hartmann [19] also argues that domestication approaches, actually developed before mobile media were popular, vary amongst researchers, such that "some have tried to develop the domestication concept further, others have asked critical questions about its applicability to the mobile context, while yet others have simply applied the approach to a new set of – mobile – media." (p. 42).

Hartmann introduced the notion of 'mediated mobilism' [19] to connect mobility to social domestication through 'concurrency' and 'momentum' "as the combination of possibility and actuality in both the social and the technological. The latter in particular underlines how mediated mobilism relates to the concept of domestication: all of the above are affordances and possibilities, but they need to be enacted and interpreted by users in order to develop fully" (p. 47). Some of these affordances are related to the fact that the mobile phone is a personal device that usually moves with the individual [20]. It allows perpetual contact [21] and creates a 'lifeline' with the user's personal support network [12, 22]. In the case of older individuals, digital communication devices are not necessarily assistive technologies [23]. They are part of the communicative ecology, defined by Foth [24] as "the context in which communication processes occur" (p. 9), which refers to the whole structure of (digital) communication tools in individual's everyday life. In this sense, mobile phones are not used in isolation and often operate as an extra layer of (mediated) communication [25], if used.

Older individuals, rather than being passive users of (digital) technology, play an active role by domesticating reconfiguring, modifying or rejecting it in their everyday life. They also create meaning and incorporate technological domestication interactively within their lifestyles [26–28]. Research has demonstrated that older individuals have and often do execute their capacity to contribute to technological development and shape their technological environment [29, 30] by actively adapting the technology to their specific circumstances [31–33]. They choose to reject or not participate in the development of (digital) technologies, even while commercial messages portray older adults quite differently from how they might see themselves [34–37]. Further, from STS studies we have learned that where older adults are accused of technological 'wrong' or 'non-use,' that in reality there are reasonable and deliberate acts to defy the embedded meanings in the technology [38, 39]. Thus, not using a given technology is one way that older individuals articulate their expertise about their own lives, in the same way that attribute new meaning to those technologies they decide to use. Therefore, older individuals express their agency and autonomy through their use and non-use of technology and such expression are key to our perspective.

Our research in theorizing about the co-constitution of ageing and technology [40], steers away from the interventionist logic that characterizes mainstream approaches that reduce the lives of older people to being inputs and outputs of gero-design technologies and conceptualizing later life according to instrumental pre-defined tasks [41–43]. In contrast, co-constitution of ageing and technology highlights that ageing and technology are already intimately linked and mutually shaped (for a recent overview of empirical studies, see [44]).

Within this framework, our international research project aims to discover the uses of the smartphone within the everyday lives of 600 older adult individuals (150 × 4) 55–79 years old in four countries: Spain, the Netherlands, Sweden, and Canada. While our interest is on the third age [89], part of the participants in this research does not belong to this category as they are younger. However, by considering younger ages, it is possible to understand the differences between cohorts to have a more focused perspective on the intersection of digitization and ageing [90].

A tracking of smartphone logs over the period of four weeks in 2019 will be complemented by self-reported information [45] collected via an online survey and through qualitative interviews. This paper will present a framework for a research design project that aims at tracing differences and similarities in how older adults use their smartphones in various cultural contexts and to achieve a theoretically informed, realistic perspective on the impact of such devices in the lives of older adults, while taking into account that users create meaningful spaces for new devices in already existing digital and social arrangements [13, 18, 37, 46, 47].

We will analyze the everyday practices and motivations of (mobile) device usage by older adults, an area of knowledge currently underdeveloped in our view [48]. By looking at digital usages –and non-usages– that may be innovative, we will question widespread stereotypes of older users as passive recipients of existing technologies and designs [49]. Of particular interest is whether mobile digital communication fosters or hampers meaningful social connections; that is, the subjective experience of being connected, as meaningful social connections are essential ingredients for wellbeing (in later life). In this vein, the main research question asks to what extent digital mobile practices relate to the reported social connectedness among older adults aged 55–79 years old in the four selected countries.

Section 2 of the paper discusses a key analytical issue: social connectedness potentially afforded by digital communication technologies. Section 3 focuses on the challenges of using smartphone logs as the main data source. Section 4 discusses the research design and the characteristics of the population under study. Section 5 finishes with the conclusion.

2 Social Connectedness and Digital Technologies

At this point, much research has been devoted to the potential of digital technologies to connect older people to the world around them. However, there is still a gap in the evidence to demonstrate the impact of such technologies on problems of social isolation and loneliness. Although some gerontological literature on social relationships has shed some light on the effects of the internet on social isolation, there is not enough understanding of the processes and mechanisms through which mediated social interaction is effective for social connectedness [50]. We know that older adults differ in their inherent need for social connection and their singular ability to manage feelings of exclusion. We also know that an ecological framework is needed to assess and determine the risk factors at different levels: individual, relationships, community and societal [51]. These aspects can then affect how older adults interact with others and what they expect of these social interactions at different levels, which in turn can lead to compounding a feeling of loneliness or isolation. It is a multifaceted phenomenon and studying its intersections with current digital technologies adds a layer of complexity.

Based on the ecological framework drawn out here, we conceptualize connectivity (or connectedness) as being a fundamentally social –rather than cognitive– phenomenon. Thus, instead of only considering the lack of social connection or social isolation as an individual problem (loneliness), our suggestion is to treat meaningful social connections as essential supports of health and wellbeing in later life. Such an approach informs our methods and instruments as well as the development and testing of a new tool for data collection about the nature of social connectedness.

Our approach relies on research from social gerontology that offers new understandings into the multiple and diverse ways older people experience social connectedness, isolation and loneliness [44, 52–54]; as well as on research about technological innovations in later life [7, 40, 47]. We suggest looking at four interrelated dimensions that depict the experience of social connection in later life from an ecological perspective: (i) individual traits, (ii) personal relationships or networks, (iii) community connections, and (iv) societal engagements (Fig. 1).

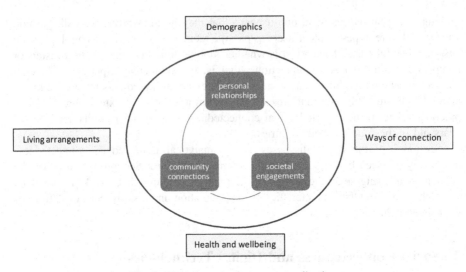

Fig. 1. Social connection conceptualization

The **individual traits** that shape social connectedness emerge from factors of age, gender, health and wellbeing, living arrangements, and life course events or transitions. We focus on the demographic characteristics, health and wellbeing, living arrangements and, given the interest of the project in digital technologies, we include the 'ways of being connected' as a relevant dimension to explore. **Personal relationships or networks** refer to both the quality and quantity of an individual's personal relationships. Having various direct and constant personal relationships increases the opportunities of getting support, while having frequent contact with others supports health and wellbeing [55]. Personal relationships or networks are comprised of several overlapping activities including frequency of contact with close friends, family or neighbors.

Community connections are the activities that happen outside the home and connect individuals across associations, neighborhoods and various communities. These community connections are usually interrelated with personal networks, but involve a stronger commitment and can enhance social connectedness in ways different from personal relationships; for example, through collective feelings of group belong. We consider the last dimension, **societal engagements**, to be one of connectedness to the broader society or the world around us. The role of media and digital technologies is crucial in this respect because of where it engages older people to feel part of the social body as a whole in ways that are relevant for connectivity. Of course media and digital technologies can also serve to alienate and marginalize older people.

A person may experience discrepancies between their actual connections and the subjective experience of being connected to varying degrees and intensity at any of the dimensions described in (ii), (iii) or (iv). Yet, there are a range of individual factors (i), such as socio-demographics, living arrangements, health, and wellbeing, as well as the means of connection that might have an effect on the experience of discrepancies in the aforementioned dimensions. Consequently, enrichment in one or more dimensions could potentially affect the social connection of older people.

The individual circumstances and the three types of connectivity (personal relations, community connections, and societal engagement) have been broadly studied in gerontology. However, the research on the study of the interrelation of these with the ways of being connected, including digital technologies. is more scarce and the research project we describe here aims to contribute in this area.

3 Smartphone Logs: Practicalities of Data Collection

Our international research project will analyze smartphone logs collected employing a tracking tool. The social sciences acknowledge the relevance of smartphones for conducting research [56] and logs are byproduct data commonly available as part of the big data revolution [57, 58]. Research relying on smartphone logs ranges from the particular analysis of the smartphone use [59] to more general digital mediated practices [60], sometimes focusing on specific age groups, such as teenagers [61] or older adults [48, 62, 63]. There is research interest in the mitigation of information overload for users while interacting with the smartphone [64] and on how the context of use affects the usage of mobile-based communication services [65]. Mobile logs can help to identify problematic usage [66] and overuse [67], and inform the analysis of the influence of socioeconomic status on smartphone usage [68]. However, logs face some limitations that must be taken into account for an appropriate interpretation of tracked use. In what follows, we discuss selected issues relevant to our research project, which we group under two categories: data interpretation and data biases.

3.1 Data Interpretation

Data interpretation is a central feature of big data analyses because logs are byproduct data that are not designed in response to particular research goals [69]. Digital logs are the raw data of apparently non-intrusive methods for data collection [70, 71]. They appear to be objective records for measuring digital usage that overcome the limitations of traditional data collection methods that are only able to gather reported use [72], but their interpretation faces some important limitations. One weakness is where smartphone logs are treated as solely human behaviour [62, 73], although in most occasions they are a mixture of human and automated or programmed activities – as we argue elsewhere [62]. Smartphone logs collect information on when and for how long the screen has displayed an app [59, 64, 67, 74, 75], but this does not necessarily mean that the user was interacting with the device. The timeout feature can keep the screen on even when the user stops interacting with the device. Logs duration, in this case, depends on the screen timeout – a feature the user can define as a general device setting.

Other features and settings would shape the information which logs provide, including the ambient display, interactive notifications, priority notifications and the unlocking system(s) the user defines. In particular, the ambient display turns the screen on and opens the app whenever there is an incoming notification. Tracking systems interpret this feature as an activity of the smartphone, but it would be inaccurate to infer it corresponds to actual users' activities in all instances.

In a similar strand, analyses usually assume that logs report data from a single user. However, in richer Western societies, some users regularly share their smartphone with relatives, as in the case of parents of young children who do not have their own device and couples with one member having limited interest in smartphones. Shared use is difficult to grasp, and it becomes more relevant when logs are used for psychometric predictions, e.g. [76–78], as they refer to a single user. Therefore, similarly to the questioning of self-reported use not being 'objective data,' tracked use also faces interpretive challenges as it is a proxy of usage not fully representing actual human use.

3.2 Data Biases

Data biases respond to technical issues, as tracking systems are not universal. First, available research does not analyze all the operating systems (OS) equally, as they impose different working conditions, in general and for tracking systems in particular. Despite some exceptions that involve the two most popular smartphone operation systems, Android and iOS [e.g., 61], or do not provide information about the operating systems included in their sample [e.g., 76, 79] most studies tend to focus on a single operating system. In this second case, most focus on Android [48, 59, 60, 64, 66, 67, 78, 80], while fewer papers track iOS [68] devices. Minority OS, like Symbian, are seldom analyzed [65]. While we have not found a discussion on such selection, our previous experience [62, 81] made it clear that different operating systems allow the collection of different information. In general terms, Android is more likely than iOS to allow tracking software(s) to function on their devices fully. This common practice of focusing only on one operating system seems to come with a bias, as the socio-demographic characteristics of diverse smartphone OS are different [e.g., 11]. One research study of personality traits found few differences between Android and iOS users that might have been due to socio-demographic differences [82]. Another issue is that tracking systems do not grant compatibility with all OS versions. The oldest and newest OS versions might be beyond the scope of particular tracking softwares. Most studies do not provide information on the particular versions of the OS compatible with the tracking system, which prevents researchers from evaluating the biases created by this technical issue – an exception is [73].

Other biases in data appear beyond technicalities. In this sense, recruitment systems usually apply snowball sampling procedures [59, 73, 83] without a reflection on the analytical consequences of generalizing results based on them. Of relevance is that demographics tend to be left out of the discussion. Beyond some exceptions [48, 62], most studies do not collect demographic data and while some papers do not discuss this lack of information [60, 61, 76], others justify it in their design. Some authors choose not to collect demographic data, like gender or age data, to grant privacy and personal security [59]. Others, instead, argue that the extra steps necessary to collect personal data, such as the provision of informed consent, would reduce the willingness of individuals to participate in the research [73]. Thus, following a big data approach, they prefer to have large amounts of data at the expense of quality and representativeness of diverse kinds of users.

4 Research Design

The first and second author defined the international research project discussed here, which benefits from the experience of previous studies [62, 84–86]. This research is part of a larger project, Being Connected at Home - Making use of digital devices in later life (BConnect@Home) (https://www.researchgate.net/project/BCONNECTHOME-Making-use-of-digital-devices-in-later-life), coordinated by the third and fourth author. As one of its parts, the results of this study will inform the other parts of BConnect@Home. At least one member of the four partner institutions participated in the discussions that fine-tuned the survey questionnaire and interview outline. This process, led by the first author, aimed at facilitating the appropriation of the tools by the international research team and, therefore, to foster future analyses and results relevant for the different participants in their respective areas of interest.

4.1 Universe Under Study

The aimed universe of study corresponds to online older adults aged 55 to 79 year old living in Canada, the Netherlands, Spain, and Sweden. Regarding **age**, this research analyzes cohorts that were born between 1939 and 1963, a group that spans a period of 25 years. In general, a cohort is a social group that shares critical experiences within the same period, with the year of birth being the variant most used by gerontologists and social scientists. Cohort scholars argue that members of the same (birth) cohort share common experiences due to their shared historical and biographical locations, which imprints certain characteristics onto its members that distinguishes them from other cohorts [87]. These cohort differences have been associated with social change, whether as a cause, a consequence, or both [88]. While in general terms, the BConnect@Home project is interested in the third age [89], part of the older adults in this research do not belong to this category as they are younger. However, by considering younger ages, it is possible to understand the differences between cohorts to have a more focused perspective on the intersection of digitization and ageing [90]. The definition of an upper threshold on age (in this case 79 years old) responds to technical limitations, as the companies that manage online panels do not expect to be able to reach older old individuals, whose levels of internet (mobile) access tend to be comparatively lower (see Table 1).

The number of older adult citizens online is on the rise, as is the use of smartphones. Available data worldwide show that although older population have lower internet uptake rates compared to younger age groups, their adoption rates are increasing at a fast pace; and growth rates are particularly faster among younger older adults [11, 91–93]; and mobile phones follow a similar path of growth [11, 92, 93]. However, the age digital divide remains comparatively higher in countries where the internet is less spread out [11].

The **geographical scope** in this project is selected to provide ample diversity regarding internet and smartphone use in later life and, thus, to enrich the analysis. As Table 1 shows, Sweden and the Netherlands are the two countries with higher internet use and higher mobile internet use at all ages for which information is reported. Canada ranks high in internet use at every age, both slightly below the Nordic countries and

Table 1. Internet and smartphone (internet) diffusion in the studied countries. Total population and selected age groups. Descendent order of internet use.

Unit: %	Total	55–64	65–74	75+
Sweden[1]				
(a) Internet users	97	97	86	..
(b) Mobile internet users	84	82	52	..
(b)/(a)	0,866	0,845	0,605	..
The Netherlands[1]				
(a) Internet users	96	96	86	..
(b) Mobile internet users	84	76	53	..
(b)/(a)	0,875	0,792	0,616	..
Canada[2]				
(a) Internet users	91	91	81	50
(b) Smartphone owners	76	69	..	18
(b)/(a)	0,835	0,758	..	0,360
EU[1]				
(a) Internet users	85	75	54	..
(b) Mobile internet users	63	42	24	..
(b)/(a)	0,741	0,560	0,444	..
Spain[1]				
(a) Internet users	85	75	45	14
(b) Mobile internet users	76	60	30	8
(b)/(a)	0,894	0,800	0,667	0,571

.. Not available.

[1] Year 2017. Individuals who accessed the internet in the last 12 months [92]. Individuals who used a mobile phone or a smartphone to access the internet [94]. EU, as for its current composition (28 members). Total refers to population aged 16 to 74.

[2] Year 2016. Individuals who used the internet last month [95]. Individuals who own a smartphone [93]. Total refers to population aged 15 and older.

clearly above the EU average and Spain. Regarding smartphones, Canadian data are on ownership instead of mobile internet usage, which is usually higher than mobile internet access [e.g., 11]. Despite this difference and the fact that direct comparison is not possible, smartphone ownership in Canada is lower than mobile internet use in Sweden and Canada. Finally, Spain is the country with lower levels of internet adoption, which are below the EU average. Mobile internet use, however, is above the EU average. Also, the ratio between mobile internet and internet, which measures the comparative popularity between the two forms of access, is higher in Spain than in the rest of the countries considered, except in the 55–64 age group, where Sweden ranks the first. Of interest are the lowest values of this ratio for Canada, mainly justified by the higher mobile telecommunication price structure [96]. In this case, the mobile digital divide increases comparatively more in Canada and narrows more in Spain. Older adults in Spain would be more likely to go online with their smartphone, while older adults in Canada would be more likely to rely on other devices for online connection.

4.2 Instruments for Data Collection

Planned for early 2019, we will proceed with data collection and follow a sequential mixed-methodology [97]. It will begin with the collection of the smartphone logs during four weeks of a sample of 150 individuals in each country (600 in total). The samples will resemble the distribution of the online population aged 55 to 79 (broken down by age and gender). The research then will follow with an online survey addressed to the whole sample, and finishes with the qualitative, semi-structured interviews with 15 individuals per country (60 in total, 10% of the total sample). With the survey and the interviews we will gather reported use, opinions and perceptions, which constitute essential information for an appropriate interpretation of the smartphone tracked use and their meanings for participants. The data collection process relies on a marketing research company with access to an online panel of consumers in each country. Those panels, managed entirely online, reward participants for their time. They allow usual sampling processes for online fieldwork and comparability at an international level. In some countries, the marketing company gains access to the panel via a (third) local partner. However, all the data collection tools are the same in every country, with adaptations in language, contextual information, and ethical requirements and procedures.

Participants' **recruitment** follows the usual strategies used in online-based research, as in the panel managed by the marketing company (or its local partners), participants receive an invitation to participate in the research project. Gender and age quotas, not reproduced here, guide the sampling process, which are established based on available data published by official statistical offices in 2018 –Eurostat for the three EU countries and Statistics Canada for Canada.

The **tracking** tool will collect smartphone logs of apps and websites running in the smartphone and displayed in the screen while the screen is on, together with the time and length of these activities during the four week period. This information is often used to calculate an indicator of use of the smartphone [48, 59, 64]. Participants have to install software on their smartphone that tracks their digital activities during the period. There is an explicit consent form which they have to approve before installing the software, and they can turn the tracking tool off whenever they consider.

The tracking will be conducted on Android smartphones, although the marketing research company originally planned the inclusion of both Android and iOS smartphones. The company based their decision on the restrictions and special certification Apple asks of providers, which complicates the process of installation of the tracking technology. In particular, including iOS devices would create extra problems for participants, who would need to give permission and (re)configure every network with which they are usually connected. The main consequence would be a bias in the data collected on iOS phones, as there is no certainty about "what networks did they manage to configure and if it covers all the navigation (…, which) will mean having partial information in a way that we cannot control" (internal communication with the company).

The **online survey** has an estimated length of 10 min. Participants will be invited by e-mail by the company once the tracking period is finished. The questionnaire gathers information on the following areas: social connectedness; digital mobile practices, including time of use and place of use; perceived essentiality of the smartphone; ecology of media; and socio-economic background and household typology. Also, an instrumental block of questions looks into the smartphone characteristics and settings for a more nuanced interpretation of tracked data.

The semi-structured **qualitative interview** is designed to last 30 min approximately. The research will discuss with participants their media with a particular interest in the role of the smartphone in creating/maintaining social connectedness at home and elsewhere, a dimension linked to the different processes of domestication. The interview will include information based on the tracked usage (for example, figures on the number of accesses to the smartphone per day and hour, and a list of the 10 most used apps during the tracking period), all in order to better understand the meanings of the data for participants. Interviewers will be members of the research team, who will contact participants who volunteer for the interview. A video call (Skype or similar) will allow accessing a more diverse group of participants possible and conversations will be recorded. Transcriptions, once translated into English, will be available for all the researchers on the team. For an easy sharing of any supporting visual material, the interviewer will share their screen with the participant.

Four individuals helped in the **validation of the questionnaire and the qualitative interview** in Spanish (two women-aged 59 and 68-, and two men-73 and 78). Their feedback helped to reword or delete questions. Final validation of the length of the questionnaire included, in addition to the initial feedback of the four volunteers, the experience of team members, colleagues, and relatives of different ages. The qualitative survey did not need extra length validation. After agreeing to the structure and the specific contents of the questionnaire and the interview outline, each local team adapted or translated it into English (Canada), Dutch (the Netherlands), Spanish (Spain), and Swedish (Sweden).

4.3 Ethics, a (G)Local Issue

Big data approaches come with questions regarding privacy and ethical protocols [98, 99], and our project had to face the concerns of the respective ethical boards in each partner institution. The deployment of the project was subject to the necessary ethical approval in the four partner institutions that lead the data collection. Ethical committees belonged to the universities in Spain and Canada, in Sweden the board is a country-wide institution, while in the Netherlands the research institution's director approved the research proposal. Reflecting differences in legislation and prevailing social values, each country had different dynamics and rules, and the research project had to adjust to them. Two main issues illustrate such differences.

On the one hand, in the Canadian context there is a particular concern about the use, storage and privacy of data where private companies are hired by publically funded research. Hence, ethical approval was of the highest importance so that equal access to participants was available under similar circumstances and with comparable data collection methods. On the other hand, the European Union is now highly concerned with the management of private, personal data while, at the same time, fosters the values of open science and open data in funded projects. As a consequence, a balance between these areas was needed in all participant countries.

5 Conclusion

The paper discusses the research design and the practicalities of an international research project about the digital practices of older adults. The research questions focus on the extent to which digital mobile practices relate to perceived social connectedness among older adults aged 55–79 years old. We conceptualize connectivity (or connectedness) as being a fundamentally social –rather than cognitive– phenomenon. Therefore, social connectedness articulates around four interrelated dimensions: individual traits, personal relationships or networks, community connections, and societal engagements.

The four selected countries, Spain, the Netherlands, Sweden, and Canada, have different systems of internet diffusion and smartphone use that shape differently the digitization of later life. The project will theorize digitization of later life in relation to social connectedness by analyzing smartphone logs of a total sample of 600 individuals aged 55–79 years old during one month. Tracked use will be complemented with quantitative and qualitative self-reported information. The analysis allows combining reported use and tracked use. Beyond actual use, self-reported use indicates what people say they do in their everyday life, which could be different from what they actually do. In contrast, tracked use reports the smartphone activities, that can combine a mixture of human and programmed activities. The analysis will triangulate the results to counterbalance these effects and, beyond the raw data, will conduct a comparative analysis of how different groups use smartphones differently to theorize digitization in later life, which particular interest of the role of digital communication in the perception of social connectedness.

Two issues are specific to this study on tracked digital practices in later life. The first one is the age scope of the empirical study. Due to the methodology of data collection and based on online tools deployed by a marketing research company for accessing participants, the age range was defined between 55 and 79 years old. In Spain, internet use and mobile internet use at the age of 75 stays at 14% and 8% respectively in 2017 (see Table 1, above). Such proportions, which are the lowest ones in the selected countries, suggest not including individuals in the older old age group in the study. They would be comparatively less accessible through digital mediated environments. For this reason, establishing an upper boundary on age appeared to be a reasonable option to grant appropriate conditions for statistical instruments.

The second issue relates to the tracking system, which finally limits its scope of participants to those using Android devices. Different industrial sources report a recent increase in popularity of iOS devices [100]. In Canada and Sweden, one in three smartphones are Android; in The Netherlands, it is one out of two; while in Spain

Android smartphones are seven out of ten [101, 102]. As discussed in Sect. 4.2, these differences introduce a bias because only Android devices are being used because, again, the tracking iOS devices faces more challenges that make collected data less consistent. Also, given that tracked use is enriched with data from the survey, we will be able to compare the socio-demographic characteristics of the samples against the online population in each country to determine the existing biases.

By describing the practicalities and the challenges of this international comparative research project, we aim at helping (young) scholars to grasp better the number of relevant decisions that shape the deployment of any (international) research project. To our understanding, transparency in research design is essential. The assessment and discussion of the challenges and limits of data collection methods include overcoming limitations, providing accurate and appropriate interpretations of empirical results and, most importantly, of the analytical implications based on them.

Acknowledgments. The research project BConnect@Home (https://www.researchgate.net/project/BCONNECTHOME-Making-use-of-digital-devices-in-later-life) is funded by the JTP 2017 - JPI More Years, Better Lives (Grant Agreement 363850). The Netherlands: ZONMW (Project 9003037411); Spain: MINECO (ref. PCI-2017-080), FORTE (ref. 2017-02301); and Canada: Canadian Institutes of Health Research (201704MYB-386097). It also received partial funding from the Ageing + Communication + Technology project http://actproject.ca/ (ref. 895-2013-1018, Social Sciences and Humanities Research Council of Canada), and the Spanish Ministry of Science, Innovation, and Universities (ref: FJCI-2015-24120).

References

1. Graafmans, J.A.M., Taipale, V., Charness, N. (eds.): Gerontechnology: A Sustainable Investment in the Future. IOS Press, Amsterdam (1998)
2. Bouma, H., Graafmans, J.A.M.: Gerontechnology. IOS Press, Amsterdam (1992)
3. Pinch, T.J., Bijker, W.E.: The social construction of facts and artefacts: or how the sociology of science and the sociology of technology might benefit each other. Soc. Stud. Sci. **14**, 399–441 (1984). https://doi.org/10.1177/030631284014003004
4. Latour, B.: Technology is society made durable. In: Law, J. (ed.) A Sociology of Monsters: Essays on Power, Technology, and Domination, pp. 103–131. MIT Press, Cambridge (1991)
5. Latour, B.: Reassembling the Social: An Introduction to Actor-Network-Theory. Oxford University Press, Oxford (2005)
6. Bijker, W.E.: Social construction of technology. In: Olsen, J.K.B., Pedersen, S.A., Hendricks, V.F. (eds.) A Companion to the Philosophy of Technology, pp. 88–94. Wiley-Blackwell, Oxford (2009)
7. Peine, A., Faulkner, A., Jæger, B., Moors, E.: Science, technology and the "grand challenge" of ageing: understanding the socio-material constitution of later life. Technol. Forecast. Soc. Change. **93**, 1–9 (2015). https://doi.org/10.1016/j.techfore.2014.11.010
8. Östlund, B., Olander, E., Jonsson, O., Frennert, S.: STS-inspired design to meet the challenges of modern aging: welfare technology as a tool to promote user driven innovations or another way to keep older users hostage? Technol. Forecast. Soc. Change. **93**, 82–90 (2015). https://doi.org/10.1016/j.techfore.2014.04.012

9. Silverstone, R., Hirsch, E.: Consuming Technologies: Media and Information in Domestic Spaces. Routledge, London (1992)
10. Agar, J.: Constant Touch: A Global History of the Mobile Phone. Icon, Cambridge (2003)
11. International Telecommunication Union: World Telecommunication/ICT Indicators Database. ITU, Geneva (2017)
12. Castells, M., Fernández-Ardèvol, M., Linchuan Qiu, J., Sey, A.: Mobile Communication and Society: A Global Perspective. MIT Press, Cambridge (2006)
13. Haddon, L.: Information and Communication Technologies in Everyday Life: A Concise Introduction and Research Guide. Berg, Oxford (2004)
14. Silverstone, R., Hirsch, E., Morley, D.: Information and communication technologies and the moral economy of the household. In: Silverstone, R., Hirsch, E. (eds.) Consuming Technologies: Media and Information in Domestic Spaces, pp. 15–31. Routledge, London (1992)
15. Loos, E., Haddon, L., Mante-Meijer, E. (eds.): Generational Use of New Media. Routledge, London (2012)
16. Haddon, L.: Domestication and mobile telephony. In: Katz, J.E. (ed.) Machines that Become Us: The Social Context of Personal Communication Technology, pp. 43–56. Transaction, New Brunswick (2003)
17. Haddon, L.: Research questions for the evolving communications landscape. In: Ling, R.S., Pedersen, P. (eds.) Mobile Communications: Renegotiation of the Social Sphere, pp. 7–22. Springer, London (2005). https://doi.org/10.1007/1-84628-248-9_2
18. Haddon, L.: Domestication analysis, objects of study, and the centrality of technologies in everyday life. Can. J. Commun. **36**, 311–323 (2011). https://doi.org/10.22230/cjc.2011 v36n2a2322
19. Hartmann, M.: From domestication to mediated mobilism. Mob. Media Commun. **1**, 42–49 (2013). https://doi.org/10.1177/2050157912464487
20. Ito, M., Matsuda, M., Okabe, D. (eds.): Personal, Portable, Pedestrian: Mobile Phones in Japanese Life. The MIT Press, Cambridge (2005)
21. Katz, J.E., Aakhus, M.: Perpetual Contact: Mobile Communication, Private Talk. Public Performance. Cambridge University Press, Cambridge (2002)
22. Wajcman, J., Bittman, M., Brown, J.E.: Families without borders: mobile phones, connectedness and work-home divisions. Sociology **42**, 635–652 (2008). https://doi.org/10.1177/0038038508091620
23. Wherton, J., Sugarhood, P., Procter, R., Greenhalgh, T.: Designing technologies for social connection with older people. In: Prendergast, D., Garattini, C. (eds.) Aging and the Digital Life Course, pp. 107–124. Berghahn Books, New York (2015)
24. Foth, M., Hearn, G.: Networked individualism of urban residents: discovering the communicative ecology in inner-city apartment buildings. Inf. Commun. Soc. **10**, 749–772 (2007). https://doi.org/10.1080/13691180701658095
25. Petrovčič, A., Fortunati, L., Vehovar, V., Kavčič, M., Dolničar, V.: Mobile phone communication in social support networks of older adults in Slovenia. Telemat. Informatics. **32**, 642–655 (2015). https://doi.org/10.1016/j.tele.2015.02.005
26. Joyce, K., Mamo, L.: Graying the cyborg: new directions in feminist analyses of aging, science, and technology. In: Calasanti, T.M., Slevin, K.F. (eds.) Age Matters: Realigning Feminist Thinking. Routledge, New York (2006)
27. Gilleard, C., Higgs, P.: Consumption and aging. In: Settersten, R.A., Angel, J.L. (eds.) Handbook of Sociology of Aging, pp. 361–375. Springer, New York (2011). https://doi.org/10.1007/978-1-4419-7374-0_23
28. Loe, M.: Comfort and medical ambivalence in old age. Technol. Forecast. Soc. Change. **93**, 141–146 (2015). https://doi.org/10.1016/j.techfore.2014.04.013

29. Essén, A., Östlund, B.: Laggards as innovators? Old users as designers of new services & service systems. Int. J. Des. **5**, 89–98 (2011)

30. Peine, A., Rollwagen, I., Neven, L.: The rise of the "innosumer": rethinking older technology users. Technol. Forecast. Soc. Change. **82**, 199–214 (2014). https://doi.org/10.1016/j.techfore.2013.06.013

31. Östlund, B.: Gammal är Äldst: En Studie av Teknikens Betydelse i Äldre Människors Liv [Older People are the Most Experienced: A Study of the Meaning of Technology in Older People's Everyday Life] (1995). https://lup.lub.lu.se/search/publication/4386c568-3b99-48b5-83a7-703093bc383a

32. Joyce, K., Loe, M.: Theorising technogenarians: a sociological approach to ageing, technology and health. In: Joyce, K., Loe, M. (eds.) Technogenarians: Studying Health and Illness Through an Ageing, Science, and Technology Lens, pp. 1–9. Wiley-Blackwell, Oxford (2010)

33. Bailey, C., Foran, T.G., Ni Scanaill, C., Dromey, B.: Older adults, falls and technologies for independent living: a life space approach. Ageing Soc. **31**, 829–848 (2011). https://doi.org/10.1017/S0144686X10001170

34. Neven, L.: "But obviously not for me": robots, laboratories and the defiant identity of elder test users. Sociol. Health Illn. **32**, 335–347 (2010). https://doi.org/10.1111/j.1467-9566.2009.01218.x

35. Mort, M., Roberts, C., Callén, B.: Ageing with telecare: care or coercion in austerity? Sociol. Health Illn. **35**, 799–812 (2013). https://doi.org/10.1111/j.1467-9566.2012.01530.x

36. Waycott, J., Vetere, F., Pedell, S., Morgans, A., Ozanne, E., Kulik, L.: Not for me: older adults choosing not to participate in a social isolation intervention. In: Proceedings of the 2016 CHI Conference on Human Factors in Computing Systems, CHI 2016, pp. 745–757. ACM Press, New York (2016)

37. Greenhalgh, T., Wherton, J., Sugarhood, P., Hinder, S., Procter, R., Stones, R.: What matters to older people with assisted living needs? A phenomenological analysis of the use and non-use of telehealth and telecare. Soc. Sci. Med. **93**, 86–94 (2013). https://doi.org/10.1016/j.socscimed.2013.05.036

38. Oudshoorn, N., Pinch, T.: How Users Matter: The Co-Construction of Users and Technologies. MIT Press, Cambridge (2003)

39. Selwyn, N.: Apart from technology: understanding people's non-use of information and communication technologies in everyday life. Technol. Soc. **25**, 99–116 (2003). https://doi.org/10.1016/S0160-791X(02)00062-3

40. Peine, A., Neven, L.: From intervention to co-constitution: new directions in theorizing about aging and technology. Gerontologist. gny050 (2018). https://doi.org/10.1093/geront/gny050

41. Schulz, R., Wahl, H.-W., Matthews, J.T., De Vito Dabbs, A., Beach, S.R., Czaja, S.J.: Advancing the aging and technology agenda in gerontology. Gerontologist **55**, 724–734 (2015). https://doi.org/10.1093/geront/gnu071

42. Peek, S.T.M., et al.: Older adults' reasons for using technology while aging in place. Gerontology **62**, 226–237 (2016). https://doi.org/10.1159/000430949

43. Mitzner, T.L., et al.: Technology adoption by older adults: findings from the PRISM trial. Gerontologist. gny113 (2018). https://doi.org/10.1093/geront/gny113

44. Joyce, K., Peine, A., Neven, L., Kohlbacher, F.: Aging: the socio-material constitution of later life. In: Felt, U., Fouché, R., Miller, C.A., Smith-Doerr, L. (eds.) The Handbook of Science and Technology Studies, pp. 915–942. MIT Press, Cambridge (2017)

45. Kvale, S.: InterViews: An Introduction to Qualitative Research Interviewing. Sage, Thousand Oaks (1996)

46. Loos, E., Haddon, L., Mante-Meijer, E. (eds.): The Social Dynamics of Information and Communication Technology. Ashgate, Aldershot (2008)
47. López Gómez, D.: Little arrangements that matter: rethinking autonomy-enabling innovations for later life. Technol. Forecast. Soc. Change. **93**, 91–101 (2015). https://doi.org/10.1016/j.techfore.2014.02.015
48. Rosales, A., Fernández-Ardèvol, M.: Smartphones, apps and older people's interests: from a generational perspective. In: Proceedings of the 18th International Conference on Human-Computer Interaction with Mobile Devices and Services, MobileHCI 2016, pp. 491–503. ACM, New York (2016)
49. Marshall, B.L., Katz, S.: How old am I? Digital culture and quantified ageing. Digit. Cult. Soc. **2**, 145–152 (2016). https://doi.org/10.14361/dcs-2016-0110
50. Beneito-Montagut, R., Cassián-Yde, N., Begueria, A.: What do we know about the relationship between internet-mediated interaction and social isolation and loneliness in later life? Qual. Ageing Older Adults. **19**, 14–30 (2018). https://doi.org/10.1108/QAOA-03-2017-0008
51. Cotterell, N., Buffel, T., Phillipson, C.: Preventing social isolation in older people. Maturitas **113**, 80–84 (2018). https://doi.org/10.1016/j.maturitas.2018.04.014
52. Cornwell, B., Laumann, E.O., Schumm, L.P.: The social connectedness of older adults: a national profile. Am. Sociol. Rev. **73**, 185–203 (2008). https://doi.org/10.1177/000312240807300201
53. Holt-Lunstad, J., Smith, T.B., Layton, J.B.: Social relationships and mortality risk: a meta-analytic review. PLoS Med. **7**, e1000316 (2010). https://doi.org/10.1371/journal.pmed.1000316
54. Waycott, J., Vetere, F., Ozanne, E.: Building social connections: a framework for enriching older adults' social connectedness through emerging information and communication technologies. In: Barbosa Neves, B., Vetere, F. (eds.) Ageing and Digital Technology: Designing and Evaluating Emerging Technologies for Older Adults, pp. 58–74. Springer, Heidelberg (2019)
55. van Tilburg, T., van Groenou, M.B.: Network and health changes among older Dutch adults. J. Soc. Issues. **58**, 697–713 (2002). https://doi.org/10.1111/1540-4560.00041
56. Raento, M., Oulasvirta, A., Eagle, N.: Smartphones: an emerging tool for social scientists. Sociol. Methods Res. **37**, 426–454 (2009). https://doi.org/10.1177/0049124108330005
57. Kitchin, R.: The Data Revolution: Big Data, Open Data, Data Infrastructures & Their Consequences. Sage, London (2014)
58. Schäfer, M.T., van Es, K. (eds.): The Datafied Society: Studying Culture Through Data. Amsterdam University Press, Amsterdam (2017)
59. Böhmer, M., Hecht, B., Schöning, J., Krüger, A., Bauer, G.: Falling asleep with Angry Birds, Facebook and Kindle: a large scale study on mobile application usage. In: Bylund, M. (ed.) Proceedings of the 13th International Conference on Human Computer Interaction with Mobile Devices and Services, MobileHCI 2011, pp. 47–56. ACM Press, New York (2011)
60. Wagner, D.T., Rice, A., Beresford, A.R.: Device analyzer: understanding smartphone usage. In: Stojmenovic, I., Cheng, Z., Guo, S. (eds.) Mobile and Ubiquitous Systems: Computing, Networking, and Services 10th International Conference: MOBIQUITOUS 2013, pp. 195–208. Springer, Cham (2014). https://doi.org/10.1007/978-3-319-11569-6_16
61. Bentley, F., Church, K., Harrison, B., Lyons, K., Rafalow, M.: Three hours a day: understanding current teen practices of smartphone application use (2015)
62. Rosales, A., Fernández-Ardèvol, M.: Beyond WhatsApp: older people and smartphones. Rom. J. Commun. Public Relations. **18**, 27 (2016). https://doi.org/10.21018/rjcpr.2016.1.200

63. Rosales, A., Fernández-Ardèvol, M.: Smartphone usage diversity among older people. In: Sayago, S. (ed.) Perspectives on Human-Computer Interaction Research with Older People. HIS, pp. 51–66. Springer, Cham (2019). https://doi.org/10.1007/978-3-030-06076-3_4

64. Ferreira, D., Goncalves, J., Kostakos, V., Barkhuus, L., Dey, A.K.: Contextual experience sampling of mobile application micro-usage. In: Proceedings of the 16th International Conference on Human-Computer Interaction with Mobile Devices & Services, MobileHCI 2014, pp. 91–100. ACM Press, New York (2014)

65. Karikoski, J., Soikkeli, T.: Contextual usage patterns in smartphone communication services. Pers. Ubiquitous Comput. **17**, 491–502 (2013). https://doi.org/10.1007/s00779-011-0503-0

66. Shin, C., Dey, A.K.: Automatically detecting problematic use of smartphones. In: Proceedings of the 2013 ACM International Joint Conference on Pervasive and Ubiquitous Computing, UbiComp 2013, pp. 335–344. ACM Press, New York (2013)

67. Lee, U., et al.: Hooked on smartphones. In: Proceedings of the 32nd Annual ACM Conference on Human Factors in Computing Systems, CHI 2014, pp. 2327–2336. ACM Press, New York (2014)

68. Rahmati, A., Tossell, C., Shepard, C., Kortum, P., Zhong, L.: Exploring iPhone usage. In: Proceedings of the 14th International Conference on Human-Computer Interaction with Mobile Devices and Services, MobileHCI 2012, pp. 11–20. ACM Press, New York (2012)

69. Boyd, D., Crawford, K.: Critical questions for big data. Inf. Commun. Soc. **15**, 662–679 (2012). https://doi.org/10.1080/1369118x.2012.678878

70. Kiukkonen, N., Blom, J., Dousse, O., Gatica-Perez, D., Laurila, J.: Towards rich mobile phone datasets: Lausanne data collection campaign. In: Proceedings of the 7th ACM International Conference on Pervasive Services, ICPS 2010. ACM Press, New York (2010)

71. Xu, R., Frey, R.M., Fleisch, E., Ilic, A.: Understanding the impact of personality traits on mobile app adoption - insights from a large-scale field study. Comput. Hum. Behav. **62**, 244–256 (2016). https://doi.org/10.1016/j.chb.2016.04.011

72. Böhmer, M., Krüger, A.: A study on icon arrangement by smartphone users. In: Proceedings of the SIGCHI Conference on Human Factors in Computing Systems, CHI 2013, pp. 2137–2146. ACM Press, New York (2013)

73. Jones, S.L., Ferreira, D., Hosio, S., Goncalves, J., Kostakos, V.: Revisitation analysis of smartphone app use. In: Proceedings of the 2015 ACM International Joint Conference on Pervasive and Ubiquitous Computing, UbiComp 2015, pp. 1197–1208. ACM Press, New York (2015)

74. Carrascal, J.P., Church, K.: An in-situ study of mobile app & mobile search interactions. In: Proceedings of the 33rd Annual ACM Conference on Human Factors in Computing Systems, CHI 2015, pp. 2739–2748. ACM Press, New York (2015)

75. Holz, C., Bentley, F., Church, K., Patel, M.: "I'm just on my phone and they're watching TV": quantifying mobile device use while watching television. In: Proceedings of the ACM International Conference on Interactive Experiences for TV and Online Video, TVX 2015, pp. 93–102. ACM Press, New York (2015)

76. Ferdous, R., Osmani, V., Mayora, O.: Smartphone app usage as a predictor of perceived stress levels at workplace. In: Proceedings of the 9th International Conference on Pervasive Computing Technologies for Healthcare, PervasiveHealth, pp. 225–228. ICST, Gent (2015)

77. Alvarez-Lozano, J., et al.: Tell me your apps and I will tell you your mood. In: Proceedings of the 7th International Conference on PErvasive Technologies Related to Assistive Environments, PETRA 2014, pp. 1–7. ACM Press, New York (2014)

78. de Montjoye, Y.-A., Quoidbach, J., Robic, F., Pentland, A.: Predicting personality using novel mobile phone-based metrics. In: Greenberg, A.M., Kennedy, W.G., Bos, N.D. (eds.) SBP 2013. LNCS, vol. 7812, pp. 48–55. Springer, Heidelberg (2013). https://doi.org/10.1007/978-3-642-37210-0_6

79. Ikebe, Y., Katagiri, M., Takemura, H.: Friendship prediction using semi-supervised learning of latent features in smartphone usage data. In: Proceedings of the International Conference on Knowledge Discovery and Information Retrieval, KDIR, vol. 1, pp. 199–205. SciTePress (2012)

80. Singh, V.K., Freeman, L., Lepri, B., Pentland, A.S.: Predicting spending behavior using socio-mobile features. In: International Conference on Social Computing (SocialCom), Washington, D.C., USA, 8–14 September 2013, pp. 174–179. IEEE, Piscataway (2013)

81. Rosales, A., Fernández-Ardèvol, M.: Generational comparison of simultaneous internet activities using smartphones and computers. In: Zhou, J., Salvendy, G. (eds.) ITAP 2016. LNCS, vol. 9754, pp. 478–489. Springer, Cham (2016). https://doi.org/10.1007/978-3-319-39943-0_46

82. Götz, F.M., Stieger, S., Reips, U.-D.: Users of the main smartphone operating systems (iOS, Android) differ only little in personality. PLoS ONE 12, e0176921 (2017). https://doi.org/10.1371/journal.pone.0176921

83. Ferreira, D., Dey, A.K., Kostakos, V.: Understanding human-smartphone concerns: a study of battery life. In: Lyons, K., Hightower, J., Huang, E.M. (eds.) Pervasive 2011. LNCS, vol. 6696, pp. 19–33. Springer, Heidelberg (2011). https://doi.org/10.1007/978-3-642-21726-5_2

84. Fernández-Ardèvol, M., Rosales, A.: My interests, my activities: learning from an intergenerational comparison of smartwatch use. In: Zhou, J., Salvendy, G. (eds.) ITAP 2017. LNCS, vol. 10298, pp. 114–129. Springer, Cham (2017). https://doi.org/10.1007/978-3-319-58536-9_10

85. Rosales, A., Fernández-Ardèvol, M., Ferran-Ferrer, N.: Long-term appropriation of smartwatches among a group of older people. In: Zhou, J., Salvendy, G. (eds.) ITAP 2018. LNCS, vol. 10926, pp. 135–148. Springer, Cham (2018). https://doi.org/10.1007/978-3-319-92034-4_11

86. Rosales, A., Fernández-Ardèvol, M., Comunello, F., Mulargia, S., Ferran-Ferrer, N.: Older people and smartwatches, initial experiences. El Prof. la Inf. 26, 457 (2017). https://doi.org/10.3145/epi.2017.may.12

87. Alwin, D.F., McCammon, R.J.: Generations, cohorts, and social change. In: Mortimer, J.T., Shanahan, M.J. (eds.) Handbook of the Life Course, pp. 23–50. Kluwer Academic Publishers, New York (2003)

88. Bristow, J.: The Sociology of Generations: New Directions and Challenges. Palgrave Macmillan, London (2016)

89. Moen, P., Spencer, D.: Converging divergences in age, gender, health, and well-being. In: Binstock, R.H., George, L.K., Cutler, S.J., Hendricks, J., Schulz, J.H. (eds.) Handbook of Aging and the Social Sciences, pp. 127–144. Elsevier, Amsterdam (2006)

90. Gilleard, C., Higgs, P., Hyde, M., Wiggins, R., Blane, D.: Class, cohort, and consumption: the British experience of the third age. J. Gerontol. Ser. B. 60, S305–S310 (2005). https://doi.org/10.1093/geronb/60.6.S305

91. Anderson, M., Perrin, A.: Tech adoption climbs among older adults. http://www.pewinternet.org/2017/05/17/tech-adoption-climbs-among-older-adults/

92. Eurostat: Individuals who accessed the internet in the last 12 months (isoc_ci_ifp_iu). http://appsso.eurostat.ec.europa.eu/nui/show.do?dataset=isoc_ci_ifp_iu&lang=en

93. Statistics Canada: Life in the fast lane: how are Canadians managing? (2016). https://www150.statcan.gc.ca/n1/daily-quotidien/171114/dq171114a-eng.htm

94. Eurostat: Individuals who used a mobile phone (or smart phone) to access the internet (isoc_ci_im_i). http://appsso.eurostat.ec.europa.eu/nui/show.do?dataset=isoc_ci_im_i&lang=en
95. Statistics Canada: Use of technology by age group and sex, Canada, provinces and regions (table 22-10-0110-01). https://www150.statcan.gc.ca/t1/tbl1/en/tv.action?pid=2210011001
96. Lagerquist, J.: Internet usage growing fastest among older Canadians: StatsCan. https://www.ctvnews.ca/sci-tech/internet-usage-growing-fastest-among-older-canadians-statscan-1.3676986, (2017)
97. Creswell, J.W.: Research Design: Qualitative, Quantitative, and Mixed Methods Approaches. Sage, Los Angeles (2014)
98. Jensen, M.: Challenges of privacy protection in big data analytics. In: BigData 2013, pp. 235–238 (2013). https://doi.org/10.1109/bigdata.congress.2013.39
99. Smith, M., Szongott, C., Henne, B., Von Voigt, G.: Big data privacy issues in public social media. In: 2012 6th IEEE International Conference on Digital Ecosystems and Technologies (DEST), pp. 1–6. IEEE (2012). https://doi.org/10.1109/dest.2012.6227909
100. Rody-Mantha, B.: Canada's prolific smartphone market skews to iOS: study (2018). http://mediaincanada.com/2018/01/23/canadas-prolific-smartphone-market-skews-to-ios-study/
101. DeviceAtlas: Android v iOS market share 2019. https://deviceatlas.com/blog/android-v-ios-market-share
102. Statcounter: Mobile operating system market share worldwide: December 2017–December 2018. http://gs.statcounter.com/os-market-share/mobile/worldwide

Exploring the Blocking Behavior Between Young Adults and Parents on WeChat Moments

Wenting Han[1], Yuxiang (Chris) Zhao[2(✉)], and Qinghua Zhu[1(✉)]

[1] Nanjing University, Nanjing 210023, Jiangsu, China
njuhanwt@smail.nju.edu.cn, qhzhu@nju.edu.cn
[2] Nanjing University of Science and Technology, Nanjing 210094,
Jiangsu, China
yxzhao@vip.163.com

Abstract. With the technology affordance of "blocking" function provided by the WeChat platform, users can have some autonomy to choose which updates can be seen by others. In everyday life information practices of social media, young adults often block their parents on WeChat Moments due to various reasons. However, the blocking behavior hinders intergenerational communication between parents and children, and may cause more misunderstandings and alienation. In this paper, semi-structured interviews are conducted with thirteen young adults between 20 to 30 years of age, exploring factors that impact blocking behaviors in young adults. According to the findings, three kinds of blocking behaviors by young people on WeChat moments are identified, and four reasons that cause blocking behaviors are also presented.

Keywords: Blocking behavior · Parent-child interaction ·
Intergenerational communication · WeChat moments ·
Semi-structured interview

1 Introduction

With the popularity of smartphones and wireless internet, there has been an increasing proportion of mobile netizens in China. The official report from CNNIC reported that the number of Chinese mobile netizens had reached 817 million by the end of 2018, increasing by 64 million and 330 thousand compared with 2017. Besides, netizens aged 20 to 29 have the highest proportion which account for 26.8% of the total Chinese netizens [1]. It is also reported that the proportion of using Instant Messaging (IM) applications (WeChat, QQ, etc.) went up to 95.6%, and the proportion of WeChat moments users reached 85.8% of the total Chinese netizens in 2016 [2]. It is not surprising to find that, Chinese netizens are accustomed to communicating with others instantly and share their daily activities through all kinds of social media, especially through WeChat application—the most representative social media application in China.

WeChat provides mixed functions with technology and social affordances. For example, users can adopt WeChat as a mobile instant messenger as well as a social

J. Zhou and G. Salvendy (Eds.): HCII 2019, LNCS 11593, pp. 65–76, 2019.
https://doi.org/10.1007/978-3-030-22015-0_5

network tool. For the self-recording and social purpose, many users employ the WeChat moment as an important information space to record their daily lives, track their trajectory changes, and share their updates with friends. However, it is important to note that, different from Facebook, Twitter and Weibo, WeChat is designed for the interaction with acquaintances. It is reported that more than 95% of users claim that their WeChat friends are filled with relatives, colleagues, and schoolmates from the real life [2]. Simonpietri [3] found that many parents were increasingly using social media to communicate with their children, while children said that they would want more face-to-face communication than connecting with social media. Some young adults even felt that communicating with parents through social media would hurt their parent-child communication. Cao et al. [4] found that the undergraduates would avoid posting moments that they were unwilling to show because of the acquaintances in their WeChat friends. In order to deal with these obstacles, WeChat has provided a series of functions with sharing affordance. For example, WeChat users can selectively make their sharing visible to some friends by identifying some tags or labels, and those who are outside the clustering tags cannot see the updates sharing. In this regard, it is of great interest for researchers and practitioners to understand user's blocking behavior in mobile social media.

Recently, many young adults reported that they often use blocking functions for their parents. Tencent News claimed that there are almost 52% of young adults who choose to block their parents [5]. Previous studies also found that there are limited interactions between young and old generations in social media because of the generation gap [6, 7]. On WeChat platform, the Chinese older people prefer to share didactic passages or articles with exaggerated titles, such as 'no share no Chinese', on their WeChat Moments, while young adults strongly resist these moments. What's more, because of the generation gap, the updates shared by young adults' WeChat Moments, are usually not understood by their parents. The differences on cognitive and values may enlarge the gap between generations, which will further lead to the blocking behavior of the young adults. In such cases, it's common for young adults to block their parents on WeChat Moments.

We believe that these blocking behaviors above are considered as obstacles for the intergenerational communication and interaction. Thus, it is of great necessity to investigate the blocking behaviors and the related antecedents and outcomes in intergenerational communication. However, prior literature on WeChat sharing behavior can offer limited insight to explain blocking behaviors on WeChat moments [8, 9]. This study aims to address the research gap by conducting an exploratory semi-structured interview to explain why and how blocking behaviors between generations on WeChat moments occur.

2   Literature Review

2.1   Selective Self-presentation on Social Media

As mentioned above, social media is an increasingly ubiquitous part of Chinese daily lives. Meanwhile, several problems have been raised regarding privacy and self-presentation on social media. The concept of self-presentation is firstly proposed by Goffman in 1959 [10], focusing on the interactions between individuals and their audiences. Individuals consciously decide to present themselves in certain manners to general or specific groups of audiences at a given circumstances.

Because of the features of computer-mediated communication (CMC), users could carefully edit and organize their self-presentation on social media [11]. Among them, public communication channels (i.e., status updates) are regarded as the most visible form of self-presentation, and users' disclosure is visible to their entire social network [12]. Consequently, a number of questions, such as invisible audience, context collapse, blurring of public & private etc., would raise some concerns for self-presentation and lead to selective self-presentation on social media [13]. Previous research has found that the concerns towards privacy exposure would reduce the profile-based disclosures on SNSs [14]. Individuals with strong concern of protecting privacy tend to adopt the 'lowest common denominator strategy' on social media, which means that users would be reluctant to post the information if they perceived that the content is not appropriate to be visible to everyone [15].

As noted above, WeChat is designed for the interaction with acquaintances. Researchers have found that users' self-presentation strategies vary from audience to audience [12]. Therefore, it is of interest to explore why users may choose to block their friends on WeChat platform.

2.2 Intergenerational Communication on Social Media

Based on the official report of CNNIC, there are increasingly social media users aged 40 and above [2]. Li and Feng reported that increasingly Chinese parents began to use social media to communicate with their young adults [8]. Based on the survey of Chinese undergraduates, Zhuang found that the dominant role of parent-child relationship was replaced by other new social relationship through social media platforms [9]. Previous study suggested that the health and well-being of the elderly is more dependent on emotionally close relatives, family and good friends [16]. Therefore, the reduction of intergenerational communication on social media will negatively affect the emotional support and social inclusion of the elderly.

According to reports, 52% of the Chinese young adults blocked their parents on WeChat moments [5]. The frequent use of blocking function will affect the intergenerational communication and mutual understanding to some extent [8]. Some studies have begun to discuss the impact of relationship building in social media context (i.e. Facebook) [17, 18]. However, there are still few studies on the blocking behavior on the WeChat platform, especially the inter-generational blocking behavior via WeChat platform [8, 9]. Therefore, this paper focuses on the blocking behavior between young adults and parents on WeChat Moments.

3 Methodology

3.1 Research Method

Since the absence of solid theoretical basis in terms of blocking behavior in social media context, we adopted a semi-structured interview as a research method in our study, which could provide deep insights on the blocking behavior between generations on WeChat platform. The semi-structured interview method is widely used in qualitative research as an explorative approach.

3.2 Procedure and Participants

Previous studies found that more and more Chinese parents aged 50 and above were willing to use social media to interact with young adults, while young adults chose to block their sharing to their parents [8]. Therefore, in order to understand the blocking behavior between young and old generations, our study selected young adults aged 20 to 30 who used WeChat for at least 3 years. We recruited 13 participants in February 2018. All of the participants were familiar with the various blocking functions provided by WeChat. The interview duration was 40 to 60 min, focusing on the interview questions listed in Sect. 3.3. Participants were allowed to talk freely with every questions and interviewee could ask relevant questions on the result of their responses. All of the interviews were recorded and transcribed for analysis. Each participants could receive a present valued 30 RMB after interview. The demographic information of participants is shown in Table 1.

Table 1. Summary of participants' demographic information.

No.	Age	Gender	Education	Occupation	Experience of using WeChat (Years)
1	24	Female	Master	Student	5
2	25	Female	Master	Student	4
3	23	Female	Master	Student	6
4	24	Female	Master	Student	5
5	25	Female	Bachelor	Employer	4
6	22	Female	Bachelor	Student	3
7	23	Male	Bachelor	Employer	4
8	24	Male	Master	Student	5
9	25	Male	Master	Student	5
10	25	Female	Bachelor	Employer	6
11	22	Female	Bachelor	Employer	4
12	29	Male	Doctor	Student	7
13	25	Female	Master	Student	5

3.3   Interview Questions

In the qualitative interview research, researchers need to extract the intricate details of phenomena such as feelings, thoughts, and emotions [19]. Our study explored how young adults thought about, felt, and experienced when they selected to block their WeChat Moments from someone else. The interview questions included the moments they chose to block, the reason for blocking and the most impressive experience about blocking behavior. The relevant questions are as follows:

(1)   What kinds of WeChat Moments would you most likely choose to block? (*What kind of moments you would like to block from your parents? What kind of your parents' moments you would like to block from yourself?*)
(2)   What are the main reasons for you to use blocking functions? (*Like blocking your own moments from parents/blocking parents' moments from yourself/setting up groups for your parents/displaying moments only shared within 3 days/6 months?*)
(3)   Please tell me the most impressive experience that you block your moments from your parents. (*What is the moment's content? Why do you choose to block it from your parents? Did your parents know that you had blocked your moments from them? How do you feel about that?*)

4   Results

4.1   Moments Blocked by Young Adults

The interviews showed that all of the participants had blocking experiences and the blocked moments could be divided into three aspects: moments blocked by young adults from their parents, moments shared by parents' that they choose to block from themselves and moments displayed only for parents.

Moments Blocked by Young Adults from Their Parents

Firstly, almost all of the participants reported that they would like to keep their privacy from their parents, especially the moments about the love affairs. Some participants said that they wanted to record and share their affection publicly on WeChat Moment, but they were unwilling to talk about their boyfriend/girlfriend with parents. So they chose to block moments from their parents.

When I was in love, I'd like to share something on my WeChat Moment. But I don't want my parents to know, because this is a relationship only between me and my boyfriend. And I don't want our parents to interfere us. You know, they certainly would ask many things about my boyfriend if they know that I am in love. So I choose to block my parents.

I don't want my parents to know that I'm in love because I think this relationship has not been determined yet, and there is no need to let my parents know.

It was understandable that young adults would not like to show their privacy to their parents. However, some participants reported a kind of moment that they shared with their parents at the beginning. And they found that their parents always misunderstood the meanings. It was really difficult to explain to them because of the generation gap. Hence, they chose to block these moments from parents afterwards.

When I travel or dating with my friends, I always like to post some beautiful photos on my WeChat moments. But if I posted these moments, my parents would mistakenly believe that I have taken too much time on the entertainment, leading to less time spent on studying or working. Then my parents would take long-winded communication to persuade me to study or work hard. That annoys me too much.

There are many things that we have different views, especially in some sensitive topics. I cannot understand my parents and my parents always think that I was too naive. These debates make me too tired, so I choose to block this kind of moments from them to avoid conflict.

I will use Internet buzzwords when I post some moments, which my parents can't understand. Then they will ask me about these Internet buzzwords, and the key point is that it's really hard to let them understand the buzzwords clearly. So, I choose to block them.

The last kind of moments that blocked by young adults is the moments that could lead to worry from their parents or make their parents unhappy. Some participants reported that they would block moments about unhealthy lifestyle (staying up, drinking excessively, staying outside late, etc.) from their parents. Besides, a few participants explained that moments that their grumble about parents would be blocked from their parents.

I will block the moments shared in midnight from my parents, you know, they will be worried because they believe that staying up late is unhealthy.

I must come back home before 10 pm before I go to college. Because my parents believe that it is not safe for a girl to come home too late. But after I attend college, sometimes I need to stay outside late because of the campus activities. So I blocked these activities from my parents.

Once my parents bought me a pink earmuff which is really unsuitable for me, so I shared a moment to ridicule them. But I knew that they would be unhappy if they browsed this moment, so I blocked them.

Moments Shared by Parents That They Choose to Block from Themselves

Some participants reported that they chose to block their parents' moments from themselves sometimes. They admitted that they have different content preferences and attitudes with their parents because of the generation gap. The moments shared by parents which were blocked most frequently by young adults were as follows: (1) moments consist of didactic articles, (2) articles with exaggerated title like 'no share no Chinese', (3) articles about health rumors, and (4) articles named 'you will get good luck if you share this article' or 'you will get misfortune if you don't share this article'.

My parents always share health rumors on their moments, like 'it has been scientifically prove that eating genetically modified food could cause cancer' or 'doctors of traditional Chinese medicine said that people must go to bed before 11 pm'. I think it is obvious that these articles have no scientific proof. So I choose to block these moments from myself.

The moments that I cannot stand mostly are the articles with exaggerated title like 'no share no Chinese'. In my opinion, these articles force audiences to repost them by abusing people's patriotism. But my parents always repost these kind of articles and my relatives will repost it too. I think that I have no choice but to block them from myself.

Moments Displayed Only for Parents

A few participants mentioned that they had shared moments that displayed only for their parents. Although there are some privacy young adults would not like to share with parents, there still some privacy that they could not share with friends or strangers but parents. Interestingly, one participants said that the moments displayed only for parents were hints which could only be understood by themselves.

When I have a hard time, the moments shared in my moments are really dark, which I don't want to display to others. But I don't mind displaying these to my parents, and my parents would always comfort me.

I always post the pictures about my family party, and these moments will be visible for my family only.

When I am short of money, I will choose to post a moment like 'I want to buy something' or 'I want to eat something', to hint my parents to give me some money.

In brief, we summarize the three types of moments that young adults may choose to block as illustrated in Fig. 1.

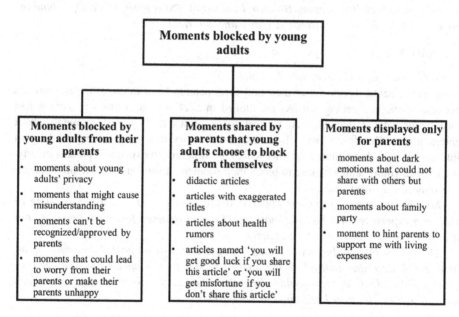

Fig. 1. Three types of moments that young adults choose to block

4.2   Factors that Impact Young Adults' Blocking Behavior

According to interviews, we summarized four factors that might lead to young adults' blocking behavior.

Psychological Factors

Independence
Many participants reported that they were more independent after going to college. On the one hand, they could be free from parents' control. On the other hand, they had to deal with many things without parents' help. Due to geographical distance and psychological independence, many young adults believe that they do not need to report the details of their lives to their parents.

My parents always don't believe in me but actually I could deal with many things by myself. So I begin to block them.

I will show the moments that are suitable for parents, and block moments that I don't want them to browse. And I think that what I have done is common.

Privacy Protection
As mentioned in Sect. 4.1, the moments that most participants chose to block from their parents was about their privacy. In such case, the reason of their blocking behavior is to protect their privacy. In the interviews, we found that some parents treated young adults' privacy as materials for chatting, which cannot be stood by young adults.

When I fall in love, the moments about my love relationship must be blocked from my parents, especially my mom. Because I am sure that my mom would talk about my private affairs with others, which is really uncomfortable for me.

Cognitive Factors

Avoid Conflicts and Unnecessary Troubles
Some participants reported that they and their parents have many different opinions because of the generation gap. As mentioned in Sect. 4.1, sometimes parents would mistakenly believe that children neglect their studies if they post moments about entertainment. Besides, it may also cause unnecessary troubles if young adults post Internet buzzwords on their moments which are different to explain to parents clearly. As a result, young adults choose to block their moments from parents to avoid conflicts and unnecessary troubles.

My parents keep nagging me about studying harder after I post my traveling or shopping experiences on WeChat moments. I have explained for many times but our discussion always end up with a quarrel.

There is an Internet buzzword called 'being drunk', when I post 'I am drunk' in my moments, it describes that I lose the interest to scold or complain anything. But my parents didn't think so, they would believe that I had drunk too much. And it's difficult to explain these Internet buzzwords to my parents.

Peer Pressure
We also found that peer pressure was one of the reasons for young adults' blocking behavior. Young adults are often keep a same tune with their friends [20]. A few participants mentioned that they began to using blocking functions because their friends had also used it.

I hardly post moments in WeChat, so there is no necessary for me to block others. But I would like to try some blocking functions after my friends told me that they had experienced it.

Emotional Factors

Don't Want Parents to Worry

As mentioned above, participants reported that the moments revealing their unhealthy lifestyle and the moments about grumble were often blocked from parents. Because they would not like to let their parents worry or make them unhappy.

My parents believe that it is not safe for a girl to come home too late. So I blocked my moments posted when I stay outside too late.

Sometimes I would post moments to grumble at my parents. But I knew that they would be unhappy if they browsed this moment, so I blocked my moments from them.

Momentary Pique

According to our interviews, young adults' blocking behavior for momentary pique would not last long. Some participants mentioned that they would block their moments from parents after they have argument with parents, and would end this blocking behavior when they reconciled with their parents.

I always block my parents after I quarrel with them, but this situation will not stay unchanged so long, I mean, the blocking will end soon after I reconcile with my parents.

Maintain a Good Impression

A few participants mentioned that they wanted to maintain an obedient impression in parents' mind. Thus, they only displayed the 'right' moments to parents.

'I don't want my father to know that I was in love, because my father always thinks that I am his good little girl, and I want to keep this impression.' Another participant said that: *'I blocked my parents when I was in love because I don't want them to browse these nauseating moments.'*

Technology Affordance

Affordance is "what the environment offers the individual, either for good or ill. It means the complementarity of individual and environment" [21]. In the interviews, some participants mentioned that they began to block others because they would like to try this new identified function on the WeChat. Other participants explained that they had deleted the skeletons from their past before the appearance of blocking functions. In this view, it is the technological factors that provided the feasibility for young adults to block others.

There is no necessary for me to block my moments to anyone, but I choose to display my moments only for 6 months. Because I would like to experience the functions that displaying moments only for 3 days/6 months. There are limited moments on my WeChat so I choose to display moments for 6 months.

In summary, we concluded psychological factors, cognitive factors, emotional factors and technology factors that impact young adults' blocking behavior, as shown in Fig. 2.

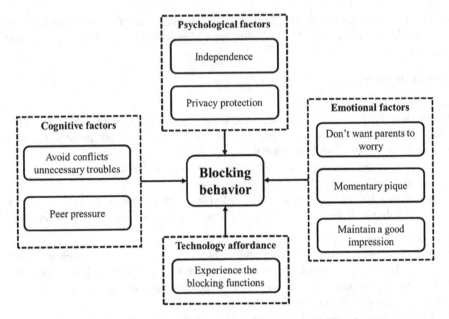

Fig. 2. Factors that impact young adults' blocking behavior.

5 Discussion and Conclusion

The study explores the blocking behavior of young adults on WeChat Moments through semi-structured interviews. Our results suggest that most young adults claim that they have the blocking experience toward their parents on WeChat moments. The moments they blocked mostly from parents were about their privacy. Besides, the moments which might cause misunderstanding because of the generation gap were also blocked by young adults from their parents. In addition, there were moments shared by parents that were blocked by young adults from themselves, such as moments consist of didactic articles, moments with exaggerated title, moments about health rumors, etc. Interestingly, some young adults would post moments that were displayed only for parents, such as the privacy issue that could not be shared with others but only with their parents. We further explore the factors that impacted young adults' blocking behaviors. Four reasons are identified, namely psychological factors (independence, protect privacy), cognitive factors (avoiding conflicts and unnecessary troubles, peer pressure), emotional factors (don't want to worry parents, momentary pique, maintain a good impression), and technology affordance (experience the blocking functions provided by WeChat).

Our study has some implications for both theory and practice. Regarding theoretical contribution, this study is among the first to identify three kinds of moments blocked by young adults. Besides, we further explore the psychological, cognitive, emotional, and technology affordance factors which impact blocking behavior of young generation. For practice, there are some suggestions for improving intergenerational communication on social media. For example, Chinese parents should be aware of protecting children's privacy, and young adults should actively communicate with their parents to reduce misunderstanding caused by the generation gap.

As an exploratory research, our study has several limitations which could be further improved. Firstly, because of the convenient sampling strategy, the sample size in our study is small that could not be general for all young adult groups. In the future research, it is necessary to conduct the empirical research with more participants. What's more, considering the blocking behavior mainly occurs in young generation, our study focuses on young adults and do not include old generation. The future study needs to recruit both young and old generation to further explore the intergenerational blocking behavior.

References

1. The 43rd China Statistical Report on Internet Development. http://www.cnnic.cn/hlwfzyj/hlwxzbg/hlwtjbg/201902/P020190228510533388308.pdf. Accessed 16 Feb 2019
2. Research report on user behavior on social application in China (2016). http://www.cnnic.cn/hlwfzyj/hlwxzbg/sqbg/201712/P020180103485975797840.pdf. Accessed 16 Feb 2019
3. Simonpietri, S.: Social media: current trends among children and their parents and implications regarding interpersonal communication. Retrieved from the University of Minnesota Digital Conservancy (2011). http://hdl.handle.net/11299/109501
4. Cao, C., Guo, S., Zhao, Y.: Exploring the characteristics and reasons of WeChat moment usage. China Youth Study **04**, 69–73 (2015)
5. White paper of family affection on WeChat Moments. http://news.qq.com/cross/20180122/3O1P30kB.html. Accessed 2 Feb 2018
6. Turnbull, C.F.: Mom just facebooked me and dad knows how to text: the influences of computer-mediated communication on interpersonal communication and differences through generations. Elon J. Undergrad. Res. Commun. **1**(1), 5–16 (2010)
7. Tang, K., Tang, J.: Analysis of interpersonal interaction on WeChat moment—discussion on the rise and governance of micro-lifestyle. J. Jiangsu Adm. Inst. **01**, 79–87 (2016)
8. Li, W., Feng, R.: Analysis of the phenomenon of blocking WeChat moment from parents by Chinese undergraduates. Today's Massmedia **11**, 34–38 (2016)
9. Zhuang, J.: Parent-child relationship in the environment of new media. Master, Nanjing University, Jiangsu China (2015)
10. Goffman, E.: The Presentation of Self in Everyday Life. Anchor, New York (1959)
11. Walther, J.B.: Computer-mediated communication: impersonal, interpersonal, and hyperpersonal interaction. Commun. Res. **23**, 3–43 (1996)
12. Vitak, J.: The impact of context collapse and privacy on social network site disclosures. J. Broadcast. Electron. Media **56**(4), 451–470 (2012)
13. Boyd, D.: Taken out of context: American teen sociality in networked publics. Doctoral dissertation, University of California, Berkeley (2008)
14. Stutzman, F., Capra, R., Thompson, J.: Factors mediating disclosure in social network sites. Comput. Hum. Behav. **27**, 590–598 (2011)
15. Hogan, B.: The presentation of self in the age of social media: distinguishing performances and exhibitions online. Bull. Sci. Technol. Soc. **30**, 377–386 (2010)
16. Gilbert, E., Karahalios, K.: Predicting tie strength with social media. In: Proceedings of the SIGCHI Conference on Human Factors in Computing Systems, pp. 211–220. ACM (2009)

17. Zhao, S., Grasmuck, S., Martin, J.: Identity construction on Facebook: digital empowerment in anchored relationships. Comput. Hum. Behav. **24**, 1816–1836 (2008)
18. Binder, H., Howes, A., Sutcliffe, A.: The problem of conflicting social spheres: effects of network structure on experienced tension in social network sites. In: Proceedings of ACM CHI 2009, pp. 965–974. ACM, New York (2009)
19. Strauss, A., Corbin, J.: Basics of Qualitative Research: Techniques, Procedures for Developing Grounded Theory. Sage, Thousand Oaks (1998)
20. Durkin, K.: Peer pressure. In: Manstead, A.S.R., Hewstone, M., Fiske, S.T., Hogg, M.A., Reis, H.T., Semin, G.R. (eds.) The Blackwell Encyclopedia of Social Psychology. Blackwell Reference/Blackwell, Cambridge (1995)
21. Gibson, J.J.: The Ecological Approach to Visual Perception, p. 127. Houghton Mifflin Harcourtm (HMH), Boston (1979)

Research on Interaction of Shopping Websites for Elderly People Based on User Experience

Mingyi Wang[✉] and Delai Men[✉]

South China University of Technology, Guangzhou 510641, GD, China
wangmy0228@qq.com, mendelai@scut.edu.cn

Abstract. The convenience of online shopping has an important impact on the change of shopping ways for the elderly. This study is based on the decline of cognitive ability of the elderly and the neglect of their shopping experience needs of the elderly in the interactive design of shopping websites. The aim of the study is to improve the experience of the elderly, and the speed of discovery browsing speed and reduce fatigue for them. In this study, 10 volunteers aged 60–65 were selected as the subjects to conduct visual flow analysis on the home pages of three shopping websites under the condition of undifferentiated testing. Participants were interviewed in depth and accessible data were collected for further analysis. The result is to discover the visual commonness of the old people's observation website, summarize the inconvenience of the interaction of shopping website, and put forward the application normative suggestions for three levels (information architecture, interaction framework and visualization framework). The contribution of the results will be helpful to the design of shopping websites for the elderly in the future, starting from the user experience and adapting to the psychological and physiological features of the elderly.

Keywords: Shopping websites · Elderly people · User experience · Interaction

1 The Background of the Elderly's Online Shopping

1.1 Ageing in China

According to the records of the first BRICS Conference on Ageing in 2017, the elderly population aged 60 years and over in BRICS countries accounted for 42% of the world's elderly population in 2016, reaching 400 million. According to experts, the elderly population will grow to 630 million by 2030 and 940 million by 2050, or 45% of the world's elderly population. From the analysis of the current situation, China is one of the most serious challenges of the aging problem. By the end of 2016, 230 million people in China had reached the age of 60 and above, accounting for 16.7% of the total population, and the aged population aged 65 and over accounted for 10.8% of the total population, exceeding 150 million. It is estimated that by 2050, 480 million people in China will reach the level of aging as showed in Fig. 1 [1].

© Springer Nature Switzerland AG 2019
J. Zhou and G. Salvendy (Eds.): HCII 2019, LNCS 11593, pp. 77–86, 2019.
https://doi.org/10.1007/978-3-030-22015-0_6

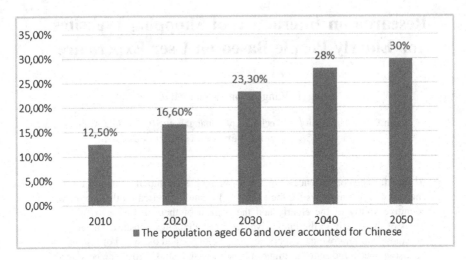

Fig. 1. Trend map of the proportion of population aged 60 and over in China

1.2 Background of Online Shopping Experience for the Chinese Elderly

The Popularity of Online Shopping. According to the survey report of China Internet Network Information Center (CNNIC), as of June 2016, the scale of Chinese netizens reached 710 million, and the penetration rate of Internet reached 51.7%, with a steady growth. According to the report of China's consumer vane, the elderly are becoming a new generation of online shopping. Whether the amount of transactions or the number of purchases, the annual ring ratio is growing at a high speed of more than 200% [2].

In the domestic shopping website market, there is almost no website interaction design for the elderly. The vast majority of older people are no different from young people in interactive design when shopping.

Physiological and Psychological Features of the Elderly. There is no significant difference in cognition and behavior pattern between the aged 60–65 and the young, but there are still some changes. However, in terms of users' visual experience on web pages, visual experience will involved in two aspects what user subjective preferences and stimulus objective presentation [3]. After sorting out the relevant knowledge, the changes of the elderly in this age group began to appear in three aspects related to online shopping.

Visual Acuity. The lens of human eyes will gradually harden with age, and the elasticity of ciliary muscles will gradually decrease. These conditions cause the decline of the visual ability of the elderly. Some small objects cannot be seen clearly. It is necessary to wear presbyopic glasses when reading newspapers and magazines to see clearly the text, and the perception of color in life will also be reduced. In addition, compared with the general population, the decline of the vision of the elderly will also lead to blurred vision movement of the elderly, which will lead to the narrowing of the field of vision of the elderly [4]. When gazing at a certain point, the ability to perceive and grasp the surrounding things decreases. For example, the sensitivity to distance and stereo sense decreases, which will also lead to the elderly's relatively blurred perception of the boundary of different things in the field of vision.

Memory and Attention. Memory refers to the reproduction of the scenes and things experienced in people's mind, which is the basis of human understanding of the world. Everyone is born with about 1 billion brain neurons, and memory function depends on them. However, with the growth of individual age and the aging of human body, brain neurons will continue to decrease, which will inevitably lead to the decline of human memory [5]. In this age group, memory deterioration and inattention are common in the elderly. They are more likely to be attracted to other non-shopping objects in other interfaces. For instance, due to the non-touchability and complex links of online shopping, they often misselect or omit payment links in the shopping links.

Psychological Changes. The elderly in this age group are often in retirement or near retirement in China. The reasons for their psychological problems are often the change of social and family roles. Because of the change of living environment and the relative alienation of interpersonal relationship, they may face the special needs of online shopping. In shopping demand, they often show two levels of differentiation. Some of them will get a sense of achievement through shopping in the relatively low-cost products of online shopping after the change of their living environment, which is manifested by indulgence in online shopping. Others, because of their own education and other background problems, show resistance and distrust to online shopping, such as turning to their children in online shopping or never doing online shopping to prevent cheating.

2 Research Objectives and Methods

2.1 Aim and Objectives

The research aim is to improve the efficiency of online shopping for the elderly and reduce the inconvenience of design based on the feature of the changes of the elderly both in psychological and physiological functions. The objectives are to explore various inconveniences of the elderly in the online shopping platform, to analyze the underlying reasons, to provide sufficient theoretical support for the follow-up interactive design principles of shop-ping websites for the elderly, and to put forward the interactive design principles of shopping websites for the elderly.

2.2 Research Methods

This study recruited 10 elderly volunteers aged 60 to 65. Based on the research questions and referring to the previous relevant literature, observation and questioning method and semi-structured interview method were used to collect data.

Flow System in Human-Computer Interaction: This is a system consisting of a user's machine environment. For users, the main interaction channels are visual input channel and touch output channel. In this interactive process involving vision and touch control, there is a flow system, including visual flow, operation flow, visual focus-to-contact guiding flow, and contact-to-visual focus feedback flow.

User Interviews: Interview is a survey method to understand the psychology of the interviewees through face-to-face communication between the researchers and the respondents. Its advantage is that it can accurately, deeply and effectively collect information about the attitudes and opinions of the respondents. It helps to provide a true and clear understanding of the online shopping situation of the elderly, the use of shopping websites and the operation experience of the shopping website interface.

3   Primary Study

3.1   Participants Survey

This study recruited 10 elderly people aged 60 to 65 who had online shopping experience and had at least one online shopping experience in the past three months. They participate in research as volunteers. Their basic information is shown in Table 1.

Table 1. The list of basic information about the subjects surveyed

Number	Gender	Age	Common consumption websites
1	Male	60	JD
2	Female	65	Taobao
3	Female	64	Taobao
4	Male	64	Taobao
5	Female	62	Taobao
6	Female	63	JD
7	Male	65	Tmall
8	Male	61	JD
9	Male	62	JD
10	Female	65	Taobao

3.2   Data Collection

Observation and Questioning on the Home Page of Shopping Website. Before the beginning of the research, it is necessary to explain the research process in detail to the participants, and explain the important concepts and related knowledge involved in the research. The participants were told that the main content of the test section today is the eye movement track of the home pages of three major shopping websites (Taobao, JD and Tmall). During the test, each participant had 30 s to browse the home page of the shopping website and they were required requests to follow the simple description of the blocks in the observation process from the most attractive area to the general attraction area. In the process of testing, besides the necessary guidance, researchers try to minimize language interference and prevent the impact of research results.

Before the research, we divide the home page of shopping website into blocks by visual rules (the proportion of pictures and words, spacing, color), and the number of plates is not fixed. The classification is as follows: Figs. 2, 3 and 4.

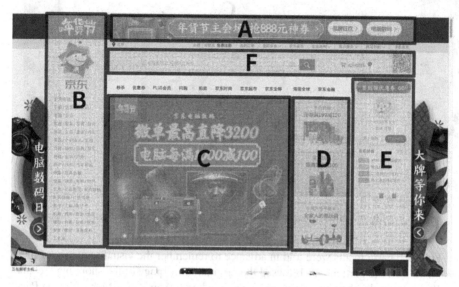

Fig. 2. Block map of home page of JD shopping website

Fig. 3. Block map of home page of tmall shopping website

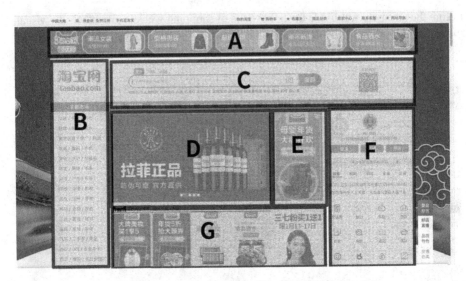

Fig. 4. Block map of home page of Taobao shopping website

First, the participants were told in advance to remember the visual sequence of their first visit, then the participants browsed the original home page of the shopping website for 30 s, and finally the participants were provided with their Block Map of Home Page of Shopping Website. Participants were asked to retell their visual order. Researchers keep records. This process is repeated three times to complete the test of three shopping website homepages.

In-depth Interview. The basic process of online shopping can be divided into seven steps: landing, entering product mall, selecting goods, putting in shopping cart, filling in information, selecting payment method, entering payment platform and confirming.

Because the research participants have the experience of online shopping, it is known that the basic operation of seven steps and ten research participants can be completed smoothly.

In the in-depth interview section, taking into account the psychological and thinking features of the 10 elderly people in the survey, the observation and interview process try to create a relaxed and pleasant atmosphere to alleviate the ideological pressure and nervousness of the elderly subjects. In the in-depth interviews with the elderly, the questions are mainly related to the problems encountered in the seven shopping sessions of the elderly (Table 2).

Table 2. Questions on in-depth interviews with the elderly

(1) Which websites do you often shop on? What are your main purchases?
(1) Do you have any difficulties or confusion in using shopping websites?
(2) What do you think are better and what are not enough about the usability of the interface design of these shopping websites?
(3) Do you have any suggestions on the color, font size, layout of the shopping website interface?

3.3   Analysis and Discussion

Observation and Questioning on the Home Page of Shopping Website.

A Brief Analysis of the Visual Elements of Shopping Websites.
Color part: Due to the youthfulness of the current shopping website, the saturation is relatively high. The JD page uses red and purple as the main color, and Taobao and Tmall use red and orange as the main colors. Color matching is also relatively bright, less dark.

Page layout: Tmall pages are relatively simple, horizontally divided into two parts: shopping guide bar and advertising page. Both JD and Taobao adopt three parts, which are divided into shopping guide bar/advertising page/user login. Vertically, the Taobao and JD interfaces have an ad bar at the top relative to Tmall.

Visual Flow Track of Home Pages of Three Mainstream Shopping Websites in China.
By sorting out the descriptions of the research participants, this part combs out the visual flow trajectories of the home pages of the three major mainstream shopping websites in China. It can be concluded that the analysis is as follows:

The visual order of observing JD website: 10 people are in the order of CBADEF. Three people are in the order of CBAEDF, and the other two people are in the order of CDBEAF and CBDAEF.

The visual order of observing Tmall website: The order of ten people is: CBA

The visual order of observing Taobao website is confusing: the most attractive part is D, the least attractive part is ACF (regardless of order). The rest of the BGE sequence is difficult to sort for participants.

Analysis and Conclusion.
Some simple conclusions can be drawn by sorting out the visual order:

Pictures in the middle of the page are usually the most attractive. The top part of the layout is often noticed at last, unless it is attracted by bright colors. Picture information often attracts more attention than text information.

Search boxes and login pages of websites are often overlooked because of text or lines.

The simpler the layout partition is, the larger the proportion between the plates is, and the clearer the visual flow is. Conversely, similar proportions between plates can cause visual confusion.

In-depth Interview. Among the online shopping platforms, Taobao has been the most selected. Ten research subjects all have visited Taobao because of its high quality, low price and complete variety of goods. As a branch of Taobao, Tmall has high reliability and a platform to ensure the quality of service. The most trusted one is JD Mall. Because of its fast and convenient logistics and high reliability, the research participants often buy relatively valuable or badly needed goods in JD. The reliability of shopping platform is the most important factor in the selection of 10 participants. Other shopping websites, such as Dangdang, Suning and Gome, are also occasionally selected.

In the process of using shopping websites, the difficulties of describing the participants of investigation are mainly manifested in several aspects: In the initial stage of use, it is difficult to find the required function entry. In the process of use, the color matching of the product is difficult to identify or the font is too small to be distinguished, resulting in long use time and fatigue. On the one hand, in the checkout part, due to the distrust of security, on the other hand, due to the complicated operation, some of the payment sessions will be handed over to the children to pay.

In the last two questions, 7 participants clearly expressed their desire to simplify the information of shopping interface, eager for interactive design with clear logic, easy to find goods. Other requirements include simple operation, timely response, clear rules of graphics and text information, reasonable size of text and pictures, and balanced color distribution. The other three participants said they could adapt to the current interactive style of shopping websites, but for the elderly, they also looked forward to more suitable interactive operation of shopping websites for the elderly.

4 Results and Findings

According to the psychophysiological features of the elderly and the results of the investigation, the interactive design optimization scheme of shopping websites for the elderly is proposed from three aspects.

4.1 Information Framework

For the interactive information framework of shopping websites for the elderly. First of all, we should fully understand the needs of users, combine the physiological and psychological needs of the elderly, simplify the interface function and strengthen the system collation. In the process of investigation, the elderly shopping is often searched by two ways: Through the search box or through the guide bar into the classification area, and then choose. In combing the information framework, we should strengthen the proportion of information sorting, classification and search convenience.

For the elderly, the depth and width of each interface cannot be too much. Depth refers to the selection times made by the elderly before they want to achieve the functions they use, while width refers to the information of the options contained in a single page. Depth and breadth are contradictory to some extent. Too much breadth and depth ratio will increase the user's use burden and reduce the operation speed. Therefore, balancing the depth and breadth of information framework is a key point for designers. It is acceptable to display 4–8 items/menus and 3–4 levels in the same system. Width is more important than depth, but it does not mean that the design of depth can be ignored. For the common functions of the elderly, we can consider to advance their depth level, such as shopping cart settings, or logistics progress location, and give priority to their level.

In the current elderly shopping website, there is always a situation: By default, all functions could be understood and be used by all users. It is undeniable that online shopping is a product of the Internet era which simulates real shopping. In the process of learning and communicating with the Internet, many young people have learnt the way of network interaction, but for the elderly, websites should always have a zero-based mentality for them. In building the platform of shopping website for the elderly, it is necessary to add the function of explaining the process and the function of timely emergency response.

4.2 Interaction Framework

Character and Pattern Selection. Language information categories (including icons and characters) should adopt the expression methods familiar to the elderly, and try to use direct and accurate product descriptions.

Principle of Repetition. In the interface structure with similar function or same category, the interface form should be consistent or similar, and the content with the same meaning should use repetitive frame structure.

Feedback System. When the user operates, the interface needs to give the user information status feedback, such as confirmation message when deleting. In addition, when the user operates incorrectly, the interface must give the feedback information of the user's current status, so as to avoid confusion and confusion for the elderly.

Location Operation. In the interactive framework, the elderly users should be given information constantly to help them determine the operation steps. For shopping, the seven steps are often not completed smoothly at one time, often repeated several of them, and ultimately completed. At the top of the shopping website, you can add a progress bar to facilitate the positioning of the elderly, such as the design of Taobao payment part (see Fig. 5).

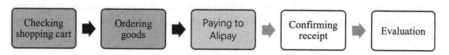

Fig. 5. Payment process of taobao shopping website (Source from: https://buy.tmall.com/order/confirm_order.htm?spm=a1z0d.6639537.0.0.undefined, 2018)

4.3 Visual Framework

Text. When using shopping websites, the text size of the webpage is generally 12px. In some cases, due to the size of the product image compression, many text sizes may be less than 12px. For the elderly, using 16px as the text reading number is more suitable for the elderly to read.

The choice of fonts should also be more square, too artistic fonts will affect the reading effect of the elderly.

Color. In the process of designing web pages for the elderly, the rational use of colors allows users to complete operations more smoothly. For example, the elderly could be dazzled by too bright colors, while the old man has a poor ability to distinguish the cool colors of blue, so we can use cool colors as the background color, and some bright warm colors can be used as the navigation information or the color of the function buttons. And the color of the home page should change with the logic level, which can prevent the elderly from feeling uncomfortable in the process of using.

Pictures. For shopping sites, images are a significant part. The appeal of displaying products is often greater than the textual description. For the elderly, in the selection and layout of pictures, do not create too many visual centers on the same layout. We can use the real shot of the product to enhance the consumer's sense of consumer safety and fully understand the product selling point. The choice of picture color should conform to the visual features of the elderly, and the color of the text and the picture must be distinguished.

5 Conclusion

This paper investigates the current situation of online shopping for the elderly by analyzing the flow system and research method in human-computer interaction, and obtains the behavior features of the elderly in online shopping, and sorts out some problems for the elderly in using the shopping website by using stream system method and user interview method. Combined with the features of intuitiveness, easy operation and easy to understand, this paper proposes a scheme that can be referenced by the interface of the elderly shopping website to make it more close to the humanized design. The results of this study complement the gap in the user experience of the elderly on shopping websites, also provides reference for the design of shopping websites for the elderly and other design criteria for the elderly.

Acknowledgment. This work was supported by a grant from the professional degree graduate education reform and construction project, South China University of Technology (zysk2016001).

References

1. Guosheng, H., Rumei, L.: An analysis of population aging, public pension expenditure and reform strategies in BRICS. Econ. Syst. Reform **5**, 56–61 (2016)
2. Jingjing, R.: A brief analysis of the development trend of "Outdoor Media + " in the mobile internet era. Art Technol. (8), 29 (2016)
3. Men, D., Hu, X., Nivala, W.C.Y., Chen, R.C.C.: A study of cognitive behavior in relation to the elderly visual experiences. In: Stephanidis, C., Antona, M. (eds.) Universal Access in Human-Computer Interaction. User and Context Diversity, UAHCI 2013. Lecture Notes in Computer Science, vol. 8010. Springer, Heidelberg (2013)
4. Lin, N., Zhe, L., Jinsong, Z.: Applying contrast sensitivity analyzer to evaluate the visual quality of cataract patients. Biomed. Eng. Clin. **13**(5), 425–430 (2009)
5. Bin, G.: Talking about the role of "memory" in vocal music teaching and learning. Art Educ. **1**, 147–148 (2009)

What Do Your Eyes Say about Your Conformity? An Observation on the Number of Sales during Online Shopping

Weibin Wang, Jia Zhou[✉], and Guangji Liao

Department of Industrial Engineering, Chongqing University, Chongqing, China
wbww1203@gmail.com, zhoujia07@gmail.com,
lgj199210@gmail.com

Abstract. This study aimed to explore the relationship between users' visual behavior and their conformity during online shopping. An experiment was conducted in which 30 young adults were asked to browse commodities differing in the number of sales and to make a purchase decision. Participants' fixation time on the commodity and the number of sales were recorded, and their conformity was measured through questionnaires. The results showed that the higher the sales, the longer the participants' fixation time on the commodity. Furthermore, the longer the fixation time, the stronger the conformity of the participants. That is, the conformity effect was observed when limited information was provided during online shopping.

Keywords: Conformity · Online shopping · Eye tracking · The number of sales

1 Introduction

In the Internet era, people spend more time online viewing news, visiting shops and blogs, and undertaking other everyday tasks. However, there is a considerable amount of false and fabricated information that might affect the users' thoughts and behavior on the Internet. On 11 March 2011, in Japan, an earthquake registering 9.0 on the Richter scale caused a tsunami, resulting in leakage of nuclear material. Shortly afterwards, rumors began to circulate that "the salt extracted from seawater that has been contaminated by nuclear radiation is not edible" and that "salt is in short supply and will soon go up in price". Many people blindly believed these rumors, causing the panic buying of salt to sweep across China's many provinces and cities. In addition, people in the United States rushed to buy potassium iodide and gas masks, and Russia and Sweden experienced panic buying of iodine. This phenomenon is called the conformity effect, which refers to individuals' thinking and behavior being consistent with the tendency of groups, and it has received substantial attention from the scientific community [1, 2]. Blindly believing in fake information eventually causes various adverse effects.

With the rapid development of the Internet, many scholars have explored the conformity effect on the Internet, but there is still no consensus on whether it exists [3, 4]. According to research reports from Marketing Land, 90% of consumers in the

© Springer Nature Switzerland AG 2019
J. Zhou and G. Salvendy (Eds.): HCII 2019, LNCS 11593, pp. 87–96, 2019.
https://doi.org/10.1007/978-3-030-22015-0_7

US and UK said they were affected by online reviews when making purchasing decisions. These data highlight the impact of online reviews on consumers. During a shopping trip, consumers will make decisions based on online reviews of commodities, which can have a considerable impact on an individual's behavior [5]. On the existing shopping websites, the number of sales is of reference value for people's purchase decision. The higher the number of commodities sold, the more popular the commodities are. Therefore, the purpose of this study was to investigate whether there is a conformity effect when people see the number of sales during online shopping.

2 Literature Review

American psychologist Sherif's "autokinetic effect" experiment was the first scientific research on the phenomenon of conformity. In the 1950s, Asch conducted a classical conformity experiment that became the start of conformity research. Conformity behavior can also be called herding behavior. In the field of psychology, scholars believe that conformity behavior is "the change of the individual's own thoughts or behaviors caused by group pressures that exist because of reality or imagination". That is, under the pressure of the group, individuals give up their original attitude or idea to maintain the same behavior as the majority.

With the rapid development of the Internet, many scholars have begun to explore whether there is a conformity effect in the online environment. For example, researchers have followed the procedure of the Asch experiment (a line judgement task) as closely as possible but in a computer-mediated communication (CMC) context. The results have shown that conformity occurred on average in only 0.17% of the selections [4]. Based on Asch's experiment, the researchers developed an online quiz that had two forms: in one form, the participant could only see other participants through one screen, and the other form was live video. It turned out that, regardless of the form of social existence, the line judgement task is not conformist [6]. The methods of the various forms of Asch's experiment can be used in the offline environment to measure conformity but cannot be combined with the context of use in the online environment. Therefore, some studies have focused on various forms of conformity on the Internet outside Asch's paradigm. For example, Lee explored conformity in the CMC context through experimental methods. Each participant made a decision about social predicaments after seeing two other (nominal) participants' conformable opinions. The result showed that visual representation of others' opinion can reduce conformity to the group in CMC [7].

Regarding the measurement of conformity, Rosander and Eriksson [8] designed a web-based survey in which the subjects were divided into a conformity group and a control group. A chart was provided for each of the conformity groups, which claimed to show the other participants' answers from their own community or network forum. The results showed that conformity increased with an increase in task difficulty, while men had higher conformity to difficulties and logical problems [8]. The scale of consumer susceptibility to interpersonal influence has been used to measure conformity in booking intentions [9].

The conceptual model of this study is shown in Fig. 1. The hypothesis is that when consumers buy commodities, their fixation time on the commodity is influenced by the sales of the commodities. The higher the sales volume, the longer the consumer's fixation time on the commodity and the higher the conformity for the consumer.

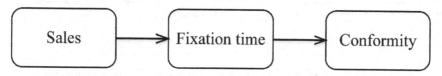

Fig. 1. The conceptual model of this study

3 Methodology

3.1 Equipment and Materials

The equipment used in the experiment was a SMI RED500 desktop eye-tracking instrument. It included an iView PC test machine, a Stimulus PC image display computer and two groups of infrared light sources. The main technical parameters were as follows: sampling rate: 50/60 Hz; tracking resolution, pupil/CR: 0.1° (typ.); gaze position accuracy: 0.5–1° (typ.); operating distance subject–camera: 0.4–1.0 m; and head tracking area 40 × 40 cm at 80 cm distance. The RED eye tracker has the function of automatic detection of participants' eyes and head. It allows participants to leave the test area of the camera for a short time during the test. When they return, the camera can continue to track the eye movements automatically. The RED eye tracker uses no restraint on the participants' head and does not cause much discomfort in long-term measurement.

In this study, we designed four e-commerce web pages, which imitated Taobao to make the laboratory simulation environment closer to the real environment, through Axure RP 8.0. Each e-commerce web page contained only one type of commodity. In this experiment, there were four types of commodities: washing machine, TV, CET-6 test paper and SPSS textbook. There were 25 similar products on each web page, and the sales volume of each commodity was different. In addition, the commodity brands, shop reputation and other interface factors were controlled on these four web pages. The sales figures were amplified to enable the participants to notice their changes more easily. To reduce the impact of the sequencing, the sequencing of commodities was processed. On half of the web pages, the commodities were arranged randomly, and, on the other half of the web pages, the commodities were arranged by sales from high to low. Figure 2 shows one of the web pages in the experiment.

Two questionnaires were used in the experiment. One of the questionnaires was a standard scale, consumer susceptibility to interpersonal relationships, which can be used to measure participants' conformity in the shopping environment [1, 9]. Another questionnaire was designed by the researcher based on the previous research results [8] to verify the accuracy of the previous questionnaire. The structure of these two questionnaires is shown in Table 1. The reliability and validity of the self-designed questionnaire were checked by the test (Cronbach's alpha = 0.837).

Fig. 2. A web page for washing machines (arranged by sales from high to low)

Table 1. The structure of the questionnaire used in the experiment

Questionnaire	Number of questions	Reference
Standard scale – consumer susceptibility to interpersonal relationships	12	Bearden et al. (1989); Tsao et al. (2015)
Self-designed questionnaire	16	Rosander and Eriksson (2012)

3.2 Participants and Tasks

A total of 30 undergraduate and master's students from Chongqing University participated in the experiment. The participants were recruited randomly. Designers issued the recruiting documents to the participants, distributed them across various QQ groups and friends, and paid attention to balancing the proportion of men and women in the process of recruiting. The participants ranged in age from 21 to 26 years, with an average age of 23.6 years (standard deviation = 1.38). There were 15 males and 15 females, all of whom had at least 1 year's experience in online shopping or Internet use. All the participants volunteered to take part in the experiment and were given a certain amount of compensation after the experiment.

In this experiment, four shopping web pages were presented to the participants, each of which corresponded to a shopping scenario. The participants needed to complete the selection of target commodities in the corresponding scenario. The specific shopping scenarios are as follows:

Scenario 1 (for a TV): Since your TV has been in use for a long time, your parents have discussed the idea of replacing it with a new one. However, your parents are busy during this period. They don't have time to go to the physical store to buy one, so they let you buy one online. You just have time today. You're going to buy it on Tmall.

Scenario 2 (for a washing machine): You and your roommates spend a lot of money on laundry every month, and you find it inconvenient, so you and your roommates have discussed buying a washing machine in partnership. You have searched for a series of washing machines in Tmall, and now you need to select one carefully that you like.

Scenario 3 (for an SPSS textbook): Recently, one of your friends needed to learn SPSS, but he has no friends who are proficient in SPSS knowledge to guide him, so you want to buy a relevant textbook online to guide his learning.

Scenario 4 (for a CET-6 text paper): Many times, you have not passed the CET-6, and once again you have indefatigably registered for it. This time you are determined to pass, so you plan to start preparing early. Today, you want to buy a test paper for CET-6 on Tmall.

The participants needed to complete three tasks in every shopping scenario: first, browse the commodity information on the web page; second, select the commodity that they want to buy from all the commodities; and, third, participate in a short interview. At the end of the experiment, the participants needed to complete two questionnaires on conformity measurement.

3.3   Variables

The independent variable is the sales volume, and the study followed a within-subject design. In this study, each shopping web page contained 25 goods, and the sales volume of each commodity was different, which means that the sales volume of each shopping web page had 25 levels.

The dependent variables were the fixation time and the participants' conformity. The fixation time was the time that the participants' eyes stayed in the area of interest. Each web page was divided into many areas of interest, which contained all the information (sketch, sales, price, etc.) on a commodity (as shown in Fig. 3). Further, to highlight the impact of the sales, the area of interest was narrowed to include only the sales (as shown in Fig. 4). The participants' conformity was measured through two questionnaires.

Fig. 3. The areas of interest

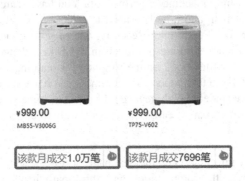

Fig. 4. The areas of interest (after being reduced)

3.4   Procedure

It took each participant approximately 45 min to complete the formal experiment. Each participant needed to browse all the web pages and complete the corresponding task. To reduce the impact of the learning effect, the order of the web pages was presented randomly. The experiment was conducted in the Human–Computer Interaction Laboratory of Chongqing University. First, the experimenter briefly introduced the experiment procedure and each participant signed a consent form. Next, the participants sat in the designated position and adjusted their sitting posture so that their eyeball could be captured by the infrared ray and the eyeball position was stably presented in the middle of the display screen.

Second, the participants' eye tracking was calibrated. The participants completed the calibration procedure according to the guidance of the eye tracker. When the calibration accuracy of the X and Y directions was less than 1.0° (preferably less than 0.5°), the experiment could start. If the error of direction of X or Y was greater than 1.0°, it needed to be calibrated again.

Third, the participants browsed the web pages and completed the corresponding tasks. For every web page, the participates were asked to browse the web page and make a shopping decision in the corresponding shopping scenario. After making their purchase decision, the participants were asked to participate in an short interview. At the end of the experiment, the participants were asked to complete two conformity questionnaires.

4   Results and Discussion

This study was conducted to validate the conformity effect on sales in online shopping. Subjects needed to browse many similar products with different sales volumes on a shopping web page and make purchase decisions. The subjects' fixation time on each commodity area was recorded, and conformity was measured through two questionnaires. The study analyzed the conformity effect on sales in online shopping in two steps.

4.1 Sales and Fixation Time

To explore the relationship between sales and fixation time, a repeated measures ANOVA was conducted. Because the sales of each web page differed, we performed a dimensionless analysis. The absolute numbers of the sales volume were divided into three levels (low, medium, and high) through quantiles on every web page. We used the subjects' average fixation time for all the commodities on each web page under the same level of sales as the final fixation time of this sales level. Because gender affects the subjects' conformity [8], the subjects' gender and Internet experience were used as covariates (as shown in Table 2). The results showed that the higher the sales, the longer the subjects' fixation time on the commodity (as shown in Fig. 5). In addition, the more Internet experience the participants had, the longer their fixation time on the commodities. According to the experimental data of the interviews, 23 subjects bought the commodity because of the high sales. The areas of interest were adjusted, and the effect of sales on the fixation time was explored further. The results of the analysis were the same as before (as shown in Table 3 and Fig. 6). However, Internet experience did not affect the participants' fixation time.

Table 2. The effect of sales, gender, and Internet experience on the fixation time

Source	df	MS	F
Sales	1.20	3.73E7	21.65**
Gender	1	2.02E7	0.55
Internet experience	1	1.90E8	5.21**
Gender*sales	1.20	968314.287	0.34
Internet experience*sales	1.20	4124510.33	1.44

** Significant at the 0.05 level

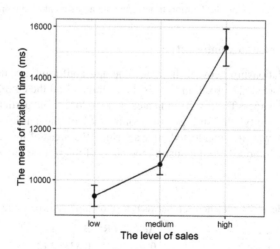

Fig. 5. The effect of sales on fixation time

Table 3. The effect of sales, gender, and Internet experience on the fixation time (after the adjustment of the areas of interest)

Source	df	MS	F
Sales	1.71	511975.99	12.22**
Gender	1	21900.33	0.07
Internet experience	1	1170716.52	3.45
Gender*sales	1.71	139568.78	3.34
Internet experience*sales	1.71	37966.35	0.91

** Significant at the 0.05 level

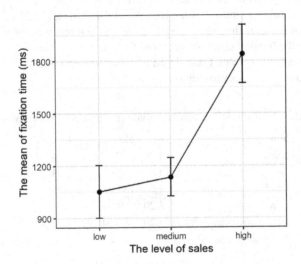

Fig. 6. The effect of sales on the fixation time (after the adjustment of the areas of interest)

4.2 Fixation Time and Conformity

To explore the relationship between fixation time and conformity, a linear regression analysis was conducted. The fixation time is the average of all the commodities on the four shopping web pages. The results indicated that the longer the participants' fixation time on the commodity, the stronger the conformity of the participants. A linear regression analysis was also conducted after adjusting the areas of interest. The results were consistent with those before adjusting the areas of interest (as shown in Table 4).

Table 4. The relationship between fixation time and conformity

Independent variable	Adjusted R^2	B	T	F
Fixation time	0.109	0.373	2.130	4.537**
Fixation time (after adjustment)	0.105	0.369	2.100	4.412**

** Significant at the 0.05 level

5 Discussion

In the results of the ANOVA, it seems that the level of sales affected the participants' fixation time on the commodities. This is consistent with the previous findings that the views of others can have a powerful influence on an individual's attitudes and attitude expression [10]. In online shopping, the sales volume is a kind of others' views and can influence the thinking of the participants as a reference for opinions. Participants generate their purchase intention according to the sales, which is the result of their own attitude communicating with other people's opinions, although the opinions of others here are a static number. In real life, those around us can influence our views through persuasion and the exchange of attitudes [10].

According to the results of the linear regression, the correlation between fixation time and conformity is significant. In summary, people with stronger conformity will have a longer fixation time on the commodity with better sales. This is consistent with the previous finding that the users' conformity will affect their behavior [11, 12]. Furthermore, according to the short interview mentioned in the task, 23 subjects chose the commodity because of the high sales. Therefore, we proved that there is a conformity effect in online shopping.

This finding can explain the click farming that is common on e-commerce platforms. On the one hand, after the sales volume has increased, the position of the commodity on the search page can be arranged to appear at the top. On the other hand, when the same commodities from different sellers are presented simultaneously to the user, the commodity with the highest sales volume receives more attention. In addition, due to the existence of the conformity phenomenon, users are more likely to purchase commodities with a high sales volume. Therefore, this may be the reason for many online sellers' willingness to pay someone for click farming, which considerably promotes sellers' profitability.

6 Conclusion

This study explored whether there is a conformity effect on sales when limited information is provided during online shopping. The relationship between sales, fixation time, and conformity was investigated, and two findings were derived.

First, the participants had a longer fixation time on the commodities with higher sales. Second, the fixation time on the commodities is influenced by conformity. Participants with higher conformity will have a longer fixation time on the commodities. Therefore, there is a conformity effect when limited information is presented in online shopping.

The limitations of this study should be noted. First, the prototypes in the experiment did not include online reviews and detailed product descriptions. Second, the participants' purchase behavior, which might be different from their visual behavior, was not considered.

Acknowledgement. This work was supported by funding from Chongqing Municipal Natural Science Foundation (cstc2016jcyjA0406) and the National Natural Science Foundation of China (Grants no. 71661167006).

References

1. Bearden, W.O., Netemeyer, R.G., Teel, J.E.: Measurement of consumer susceptibility to interpersonal influence. J. Consum. Res. **15**(4), 473–481 (1989)
2. van Leeuwen, E.J.C., Kendal, R.L., Tennie, C., Haun, D.B.M.: Conformity and its look-a-likes. Anim. Behav. **110**, e1–e4 (2015)
3. Cinnirella, M., Green, B.: Does 'cyber-conformity' vary cross-culturally? Exploring the effect of culture and communication medium on social conformity. Comput. Hum. Behav. **23**(4), 2011–2025 (2007)
4. Smilowitz, M., Chad Compton, D., Flint, L.: The effects of computer mediated communication on an individual's judgment: a study based on the methods of Asch's social influence experiment. Comput. Hum. Behav. **4**(4), 311–321 (1988)
5. Kwon, B.C., Kim, S.-H., Duket, T., Catalán, A., Yi, J.S.: Do people really experience information overload while reading online reviews? Int. J. Hum. Comput. Interact. **31**(12), 959–973 (2015)
6. Laporte, L., van Nimwegen, C., Uyttendaele, A.J.: Do people say what they think: social conformity behavior in varying degrees of online social presence. In: Proceedings of the 6th Nordic Conference on Human-Computer Interaction Extending Boundaries - NordiCHI 2010, Reykjavik, Iceland, p. 305 (2010)
7. Lee, E.-J.: Effects of visual representation on social influence in computer-mediated communication: experimental tests of the social identity model of deindividuation effects. Hum. Commun. Res. **30**(2), 234–259 (2004)
8. Rosander, M., Eriksson, O.: Conformity on the internet – the role of task difficulty and gender differences. Comput. Hum. Behav. **28**(5), 1587–1595 (2012)
9. Tsao, W.-C., Hsieh, M.-T., Shih, L.-W., Lin, T.M.Y.: Compliance with eWOM: the influence of hotel reviews on booking intention from the perspective of consumer conformity. Int. J. Hosp. Manag. **46**, 99–111 (2015)
10. Levitan, L.C., Verhulst, B.: Conformity in groups: the effects of others' views on expressed attitudes and attitude change. Polit. Behav. **38**(2), 277–315 (2016)
11. Kundu, P., Cummins, D.D.: Morality and conformity: the Asch paradigm applied to moral decisions. Soc. Influ. **8**(4), 268–279 (2013)
12. Pascual, A., Felonneau, M.L., Guéguen, N., Lafaille, E.: Conformity, obedience to authority, and compliance without pressure to control cigarette butt pollution. Soc. Influ. **9**(2), 83–98 (2014)

Health Information Literacy of the Older Adults and Their Intention to Share Health Rumors: An Analysis from the Perspective of Socioemotional Selectivity Theory

Mengqing Yang[✉]

Nanjing University, Nanjing 210023, Jiangsu, China
mqyang@nju.edu.cn

Abstract. Health rumor promises to resolve uncertainty or provide new insight into important health-related phenomena. Older adults who are more concerned about health issues are plagued by the health rumors more seriously. Why do older people prefer to share health rumors and how to protect the elderly from online health rumors are becoming a new public health concern. This study attempts to understand the health information behavior of the elderly from the perspective of socioemotional selectivity theory (SST), and to find out the possible relationship between health information literacy and health rumor sharing intention of the older adults. The results showed that health information literacy and knowledge acquisition goal were negatively related to the intention to share health rumors while emotion regulation goal had a positive influence on it. Interaction effects were also significant between the independent variables and the dependent variable. In the process of aging, the competition between knowledge acquisition goal and emotion regulation goal will play an important role in the information behaviors of individuals. Health information literacy not only helps the older adults to identify health rumors to avoid spreading them but also guides the elderly to avoid deception of false information and make incorrect health decisions.

Keywords: Health information literacy · Health rumor · Socioemotional selectivity theory (SST) · Older adult

1 Introduction

Advances in the online social network and mobile computing devices have revolutionized the way people access to and share information in daily life. People are also inclined to seek information and help from the Internet when facing health decision-making [22, 25, 34, 39]. Health rumors may be included in their search results that have a potential threat to the information seekers because they usually can't distinguish fake health information [24]. Health rumors are unverified information that lacks a secure standard of evidence. They widely spread among groups of people because this information promises to resolve uncertainty or provide new insight into important health-related phenomena [40]. Older adults who are more concerned about health

© Springer Nature Switzerland AG 2019
J. Zhou and G. Salvendy (Eds.): HCII 2019, LNCS 11593, pp. 97–108, 2019.
https://doi.org/10.1007/978-3-030-22015-0_8

issues are plagued by the health rumors more seriously. Guess et al. [18] founded that people who were over 65 had the highest rate of fake news sharing than other age groups. Why do older people prefer to share health rumors and how to protect the elderly from online health rumors are becoming a new public health concern.

Lack of competencies related to seeking, understanding and evaluating health information may impair the ability to make correct health-related decisions. Therefore, health information literacy has become a focus for understanding and exploring health behaviors. Previous research assessed people's health information literacy about perceived ability to identify a health information need, confidence in being able to find and use health information, preferences for health information sources, and determining information quality [16, 17, 28]. Individuals' ability to evaluate the quality of health information and identify health rumors is closely related to their health information literacy. It is reasonable to analyze why older adults share health rumors from the perspective of health information literacy.

In addition, the psychological factors of the elderly, which are different from those of other age groups, have to be taken into account. Socioemotional selectivity theory (SST) tells us individuals at different ages have different perceptions of future time. These differences will make people make different goal choices [7]. Generally speaking, young people perceive that the future time is relatively abundant, and they prefer to acquire knowledge as their goals, whereas older people prefer to choose emotional regulation as their goals, which is particularly evident in the process of aging [10]. This theory gives us a different perspective to explore the health information behavior of the elderly. Therefore, this study attempts to understand the health information behavior of the elderly from the perspective of SST, and to find out the possible relationship between health information literacy and health rumor sharing intention of the older adults.

2 Theory and Hypotheses

2.1 Health Rumor

Rumors are a particular form of misinformation – an acceptance of information that is factually unsubstantiated – characterized by two features. Firstly, rumors are statements that lack specific standards of evidence [3]. Secondly, rumors are more than fringe beliefs. They acquire their power through widespread social transmission [6]. Sunstein [37] defined the term to be the 'claims of fact – about people, groups, events and institutions – that have not been shown to be true, but that move from one person to another and hence have credibility not because direct evidence is known to support them, but because other people seem to believe them'. With the advent of the Internet age, the cost of information creating and dissemination has dropped sharply, and the number of rumors has also risen sharply. When health-related rumors are spread, they not only create confusion but also stir up unnecessary anxiety [11]. Depending on their ability to create anxiety, rumors are commonly classified as either dread or wish [12]. The former type of rumors usually cause panic about health threats while the latter, however, leads to a belief in false health benefits.

Attention to health rumors has led scholars to conduct relevant research. Zhang et al. [40] explored the associations between the authenticity of health rumors and some indicators of the rumors themselves. Chua et al. [11] investigated how epistemic belief affected Internet users' decision to share online health rumors. They also examined the effects of characteristics of rumors on user's decision-making. Lee and Choi [27] discussed about false rumors related to the spread of MERS virus and its influence on people's accuracy-oriented information seeking. Faced with health rumors in social networks, Sicilia et al. [35] developed a novel health-related rumor detection system on Twitter to detect if a post was either a rumor or not. It can be seen that previous rumor studies can be mainly divided into two categories: spreading mechanism studies and motivation studies [41]. However, there is still a lack of research on health rumor sharing behavior among the elderly. In the current network environment, more often than not, the elderly are not sure whether the health information they are exposed to is a rumor or not. And elderly people share health rumors without malice, just to convey information to others to improve or maintain health level. This makes it more difficult to protect the elderly from health rumors.

2.2   Health Information Literacy

The concept of health information literacy brings together the concepts of health literacy and information literacy [20, 21, 38]. American Medical Association (AMA) has defined health literacy as 'the skill set including the ability of basic reading and of performing required digital tasks for functions within the scope of health services' [1]. WTO defined it as 'the cognitive and social skills which determine the motivation and ability of individuals to gain access to, understand, and use information in ways which promote and maintain good health' [30]. As can be seen from these definitions, health literacy focuses on the abilities to apply literacy skills to health related materials. Comparatively speaking, the concept of information literacy appeared earlier, that is "a set of abilities requiring individuals to recognize when information is needed and to have the ability to locate, evaluate, and use effectively the needed information" [2]. It emphasizes the ability to process and utilize information. Under the combination of the two, the concept of health information literacy focuses on the higher level cognitive and social skills needed to cope in the complex health information environment [21]. We believe that the concept of health information literacy is 'the set of abilities needed to recognize a health information need, identify likely information sources and use them to retrieve relevant information, assess the quality of the information and its applicability to a specific situation, and analyze, understand, and use the information to make good health decisions' [4].

Exploring health information behavior from the perspective of health information literacy has become the focus of many scholars' research. Suka et al. [36] examined the relationship between health literacy, health information access, health behavior, and health status in Japanese adults aged 20–64 years. They founded that those with higher health literacy were significantly more likely to get sufficient health information from multiple sources. The study of Aydın et al. [5] proposed that the person who was health literate should have the knowledge and ability to adapt him/herself to health life style and to make healthy choices. Quinn et al. [31] pointed out that the ability to locate, evaluate and use online health information may be influenced by an individual's level of health literacy and eHealth literacy. Hirvonen et al. [21] pointed out that health information literacy is positively associated with various health-promoting behaviors. It can be seen that scholars generally believe that health information literacy can make a positive impact on individuals' health information behavior.

In the age of information explosion, many times the information we come across is not credible enough. Especially for the elderly, health concerns make them more likely to be disturbed by uncertain health information. Rather than sharing health rumors, older people share unconfirmed health information without sufficient judgment. Health information literacy represents individuals' ability to identify health information sources and assess the quality of health information. Usually we think that people with lower health information literacy have lower ability to judge the quality of health information [14]. That is to say, higher health information literacy can help individuals to judge whether health information is true or false, thereby reducing the possibility of sharing health rumors. Therefore, we propose the following research hypothesis:

H1 Health information literacy has a negative association with the intention to share health rumors.

2.3   Socioemotional Selectivity Theory (SST)

Socioemotional selectivity theory maintains that time horizons influence goals [8]. When time is perceived as open-ended, goals are most likely to be preparatory, for example, gathering information, experiencing novelty and expanding breadth of knowledge. When constraints on time are perceived, goals focus more on objectives that can be realized in their very pursuit. Under these conditions, goals emphasize feeling states, particularly regulating emotional states to optimize well-being [29]. According to this theory, there are two kinds of social goals that affect an individual's behavior. The first is acquisition of knowledge which is future-oriented, and the second is regulation of emotions which is present-oriented [9, 10]. Motivation to acquire knowledge and regulate emotions constitutes a dynamic system to stimulate social behavioral goals in the course of life. In specific situations, knowledge-related goals and emotional regulation goals compete with each other. Individuals can make choices only after weighing the importance of the two kinds of goals, and then produce corresponding behavioral responses. So we infer that knowledge-related goals will promote individuals' rational evaluation of information quality from a cognitive perspective while emotional regulation goals will pay more attention to the emotional perspective and neglect the evaluation of information quality. Thus we propose the following research hypothesis:

H2 Knowledge acquisition goal has a negative association with the intention to share health rumors.

H3 Emotion regulation goal has a positive association with the intention to share health rumors.

SST believes that older adults are more aware of the limitation of time; they tend to dissolve negative emotional experience in life, and pay more attention to the positive side, that is, to show "positive effect (the preference of the elderly for positive information)" in the process of aging [32]. It can be seen from the studies of Carstensen et al. that the main assertion of socioemotional selectivity theory is that when boundaries on time are perceived, present-oriented goals related to emotional meaning are prioritized over future-oriented goals aimed at acquiring information and expanding horizons [26]. While there are times when other goals are more highly prioritized such as when aged people reviewing decisions about health [15]. As mentioned above, health information literacy is an individual's ability to acquire information to maintain their own health. It has a negative association with individual's intention to share health rumors. Since individuals' behaviors are influenced by goals, we have reason to believe that social goals including knowledge acquisition and emotion regulation play a moderating role between health information literacy and health rumor sharing intention. Health rumor promises to resolve uncertainty or provide new insight into important health-related phenomena. This is undoubtedly a positive message for older people who are more concerned about their health. According to the SST, "positive effect" of the elderly leads to their preference for positive information and weakens their goals of information acquisition. Therefore, we hypothesize that when the goal of knowledge acquisition is high, the intention of elderly people to share health rumors will be weakened; on the contrary, when the goal of emotional regulation is higher, the elderly's intention to share health rumors will be enhanced. Thus we propose the following research hypothesis:

H4 Knowledge acquisition goal will enhance the association between health information literacy and intention to share health rumors.

H5 Emotion regulation goal will weaken the association between health information literacy and intention to share health rumors.

Figure 1 shows the theoretical framework of this study.

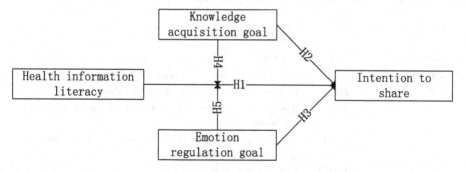

Fig. 1. Theoretical framework

3 Methods

3.1 Samples and Measures

We obtained empirical data through an online survey. Survey data were collected online through 'Tieba of the Aged' subordinate to Baidu Tieba, the largest Chinese online community. The eligible participants came from a nationwide sample of online community users who were over the age of fifty. The measures of the health information literacy construct were adopted from Jordan et al. [23] and Hirvonen et al. [21] to develop our questionnaire. Measures of the two social goals come from our self-built scale. Finally, 410 valid questionnaires were collected in this study. We investigated participants' gender and age. The demographic characteristics of the sample are shown in the Table 1.

Table 1. Demographic characteristics of the sample

Demographic characteristics		n	%
Gender	Male	201	49.0%
	Female	209	51.0%
Age	50–55	56	13.7%
	56–60	112	27.3%
	61–65	117	28.5%
	66–70	125	30.5%

Among the participants in this survey, 49.0% were men and 51.0% were women. People who are between 50 and 55 are the least and the distribution of people in other age groups was balanced, with the proportion ranging from 27.3% to 30.5%.

Table 2 shows the contents of the scale and we used a 5-point Likert scale, ranging from 'strongly disagree' (1) to 'strongly agree' (5).

Table 2. Survey scale

Construct	Item	Content
Health information literacy	HIL1	I need information about health issues
	HIL2	I know how to find the health information I need
	HIL3	It is easy to assess the reliability of health information on the Internet
	HIL4	I apply health related information to my own life and/or that of people close to me
Knowledge acquisition goal	KAG1	I like learning new knowledge
	KAG2	I have a goal of learning new knowledge
	KAG3	I am willing to constantly enrich my knowledge base

(continued)

Table 2. (*continued*)

Construct	Item	Content
Emotion regulation goal	ERG1	I think it's important to keep myself happy
	ERG2	I like to keep myself in a positive mood
	ERG3	I am more concerned about my current situation
Intention to share health rumors	INT1	I like to share health-related information, even though I don't know where it comes from
	INT2	As for health-related information, I think it's better to trust it than not
	INT3	Even if it's not clear whether health-related information is credible, I like to share it with people around me

3.2 Confirmatory Factor Analysis

We assessed the measurement model by examining the convergent validity and discriminant validity. In confirmatory factor analysis, convergent validity is measured by standardized regression weights, composite reliability (CR) and average variance extracted (AVE) [33]. As shown in the Table 3, all of the item loadings are above the recommended 0.7 and significant, and the composite reliability (CR) exceeds the recommended level of 0.7, and the average variance extracted (AVE) values are above the recommended level of 0.5 [19].

Table 3. Convergent validity of the constructs and items

Construct	Item	Loading	CR	AVE
Health information literacy	HIL1	0.723	0.895	0.681
	HIL2	0.793		
	HIL3	0.896		
	HIL4	0.878		
Knowledge acquisition goal	KAG1	0.765	0.868	0.689
	KAG2	0.933		
	KAG3	0.781		
Emotion regulation goal	ERG1	0.777	0.816	0.597
	ERG2	0.723		
	ERG3	0.815		
Intention	INT1	0.797	0.853	0.659
	INT2	0.856		
	INT3	0.780		

Then we compared the square roots of the AVEs with the latent variable correlations and the results show good discriminant validity [19] as shown in Table 4.

Table 4. Latent variable correlations & square roots of AVE

Constructs	Mean	SD	HIL	KAG	ERG	INT
HIL	2.184	0.784	**0.825**			
KAG	2.055	0.775	0.555	**0.830**		
ERG	3.532	0.802	−0.577	−0.568	**0.773**	
INT	4.038	0.781	−0.634	−0.528	0.607	**0.812**

3.3 Hypothesis Test

The results of the hierarchical multiple regression are presented in Table 5. Within the regression testing, latent variables were created as summated indexes. We standardized all variables to reduce the potential effects of multicollinearity and the values of variance inflation factor (VIF) were inspected to check for potential multicollinearity. In the process of regression, control variables entered as a block in step 1 (gender and age), followed by the main effects in step 2 (health information literacy, knowledge acquisition goal and emotion regulation goal), and the interactions were in step 3. The highest VIF value was 1.815, confirming that multicollinearity was not a problem.

Table 5. Results of the hierarchical multiple regression analyses

	Intention to share health rumors (β)		
	Model 1	Model 2	Model 3
Age	0.011	0.021	0.017
Gender	0.062	0.059	0.063
HIL		−0.368***	−0.330***
KAG		−0.166**	−0.200***
ERG		0.233***	0.211***
HIL×KAG			0.132**
HIL×ERG			0.172***
R^2	0.004	0.406	0.423
Adjusted R^2	−0.001	0.399	0.413
R^2 change	0.004	0.402	0.017

Note: HIL: Health information literacy, KAG: Knowledge acquisition goal, ERG: Emotion regulation goal, ***$p < 0.001$, **$p < 0.01$, *$p < 0.05$.

4   Results

All statistical inferences were drawn based on Model 3. Table 5 shows that age ($\beta = 0.017$, $p > 0.05$) and gender ($\beta = 0.063$, $p > 0.05$) have no significant associations with the intention to share health rumors. It proved that age and gender did not affect the intention to share health rumors among the elderly.

All the hypotheses about the main effects are supported by the data analysis results. Health information literacy was negatively related to the intention to share health rumors ($\beta = -0.330$, $p < 0.001$) and H1 was supported. The greater the health information literacy of an older adult, the lower was the intention to share health rumors. Knowledge acquisition goal was negatively related to the intention to share health rumors ($\beta = -0.200$, $p < 0.001$) and H2 was supported. The greater the knowledge acquisition goal of an older adult, the lower was the intention to share health rumors. Emotion regulation goal was positively related to the intention to share health rumors ($\beta = 0.211$, $p < 0.001$) and H3 was supported. The greater the emotion regulation goal of an older adult, the higher was the intention to share health rumors.

In the analysis of interaction effects, knowledge acquisition goal moderated the association between health information literacy and the intention to share health rumors ($\beta = 0.132$, $p < 0.01$). Though the effect was significant, the result showed that knowledge acquisition goal could weaken the association between health information literacy and the sharing intention. This result was contrary to the hypothesis so H4 was not supported. Emotion regulation goal will weaken the association between health information literacy and intention to share health rumors ($\beta = 0.172$, $p < 0.001$). The effect was significant and H5 was supported.

5   Discussion

As can be seen from the data in Table 4, the older adults as the sample of this study had a low level of health information literacy and knowledge acquisition goal. This phenomenon not only reflects the low level of health information literacy of the elderly in China, but also confirms the view of SST that future-oriented goals are less important to the elderly. In this case, it's not hard to understand why the average of health rumors sharing intentions and emotional regulation goal is relatively higher.

Health information literacy has the highest negative effect on the intention to share health rumors ($\beta = -0.330$, $p < 0.001$) following by the knowledge acquisition goal ($\beta = -0.200$, $p < 0.001$). While emotion regulation goal has a positive effect on the intention to share health rumors ($\beta = 0.211$, $p < 0.001$). Comparing the absolute values of the regression coefficients of the two social goals, the effect of emotion regulation goal is greater than that of knowledge acquisition goal. It is inevitable that individual behavior is influenced by social goals. In the process of aging, the competition between knowledge acquisition goal and emotion regulation goal will play an important role in the information behaviors of individuals and this role is to some extent uncontrollable. Although efforts cannot be made to help the elderly identify health rumors from the perspective of social goals, it is feasible to improve the health information literacy of the elderly. Improving health information literacy means improving the ability of older people to identify health information needs, evaluate health information quality and use health information to maintain their health. Health information literacy not only helps the older adults to identify health rumors to avoid spreading them but also guides the elderly to avoid deception of false information and make incorrect health decisions.

Emotion regulation goal moderated the association between health information literacy and the intention to share health rumors ($\beta = 0.172$, $p < 0.001$). According to Cohen et al. [13], if one predictor weakens the effect of the other predictor, the interactive effect is the buffering interaction. In this case, the coefficient of health information literacy on intention to share health rumors is -0.330 while the interaction of HIL$\times$ERG is 0.172. It means the negative effect of health information literacy on the intention to share health rumors will gradually weaken as the emotion regulation goal increases. For the study of health information behavior of the elderly, we should not ignore the psychological factors that the elderly are different from the young. Under the positive effect, the health information literacy of the elderly will be weakened. And preferences that favor positive and ignore negative information are either because potential warning signs are ignored or because messages about too-good-to-be-true prospects are especially salient [32]. This suggests that we should be patient enough to face this problem. When the improvement of health information literacy of the elderly is disturbed by their own psychological factors, the external intervention mechanism should play a sufficient role in helping and guiding them.

In addition, one other interesting finding emerged. Though the moderating effect was significant, the result showed that knowledge acquisition goal could weaken the association between health information literacy and the sharing intention ($\beta = 0.132$, $p < 0.01$). Although the data analysis result is inconsistent with the research hypothesis, we still think that this result is meaningful. Cohen et al. [13] believed that there was another interaction pattern named interference or antagonistic interaction. It means both predictors work on the criterion in the same direction, and the interaction is of opposite sign. How to explain this result scientifically is still lack of further validation. However, we may assume that because the health information literacy and knowledge acquisition goals of the samples in this study are at a low level, the importance of exceptional ability may be lessened by exceptional motivation, and vice versa [13].

6 Conclusion

In conclusion, this paper has found that the health information literacy, knowledge acquisition goal and emotion regulation goal have significant association with the intention of the older adults to share health rumors. It also verifies the interaction effects of the two social goals on the association between health information literacy and health rumor sharing intention. In our research, socioemotional selectivity theory was introduced into the study of health information behavior that provides a new perspective for research in related fields. And we emphasize that the study of information behavior of the elderly should not ignore the unique psychological factors of the elderly. On the other hand, the findings of this study partly explain why older people are more likely to share health rumors. We also suggest that we should start with health information literacy to improve the ability of the elderly to identify health rumors and evaluate the quality of health information. Only in this way can the elderly be fundamentally protected from health rumors. Since there is still an unsupported hypothesis in this study, future research can start with the goal of knowledge acquisition and explore its role in health information behavior of the elderly.

Acknowledgement. This research was supported by the China Postdoctoral Science Foundation (2018M642217).

References

1. American Medical Association: Health literacy: report of the council on scientific affairs. JAMA **281**(8), 552–557 (1999)
2. American Library Association: Presidential committee on information literacy: Final report. Washington, D.C. (1989). http://www.ala.org/acrl/publications/whitepapers/presidential. Accessed 28 Feb 2019
3. Allport, G.W., Postman, L.: The Psychology of Rumor. Holt Rinehart and Winston, New York (1947)
4. Medical Library Association: Health information literacy task force final report (2003)
5. Aydın, G.Ö., Kaya, N., Turan, N.: The role of health literacy in access to online health information. Procedia - Soc. Behav. Sci. **195**, 1683–1687 (2015)
6. Berinsky, A.J.: Rumors and health care reform: experiments in political misinformation. Br. J. Polit. Sci. **47**(02), 241–262 (2015)
7. Carstensen, L.L.: Age-Related Changes in Social Activity. Pergamon Press, Elmsford (1987)
8. Carstensen, L.L.: The influence of a sense of time on human development. Science **312**(5782), 1913–1915 (2006)
9. Carstensen, L.L., Fung, H.H., Charles, S.T.: Socioemotional selectivity theory and the regulation of emotion in the second half of life. Motiv. Emot. **27**(2), 103–123 (2003)
10. Carstensen, L.L., Isaacowitz, D.M., Charles, S.T.: Taking time seriously. a theory of socioemotional selectivity. Am. Psychol. **54**(3), 165 (1999)
11. Chua, A.Y.K., Banerjee, S.: To share or not to share: the role of epistemic belief in online health rumors. Int. J. Med. Inform. **108**, 36–41 (2017)
12. Chua, A.Y.K., Banerjee, S.: Intentions to trust and share online health rumors: an experiment with medical professionals. Comput. Hum. Behav. **87**, 1–9 (2018)
13. Cohen, J., Cohen, P., West, S.G., Aiken, L.S.: Applied Multiple Regression/Correlation Analysis for the Behavioral Sciences, 3rd edn. Lawrence Erlbaum, Mahwah (2003)
14. Diviani, N., van den Putte, B., Meppelink, C.S., van Weert, J.C.M.: Exploring the role of health literacy in the evaluation of online health information: insights from a mixed-methods study. Patient Educ. Couns. **99**(6), 1017–1025 (2016)
15. English, T., Carstensen, L.L.: Does positivity operate when the stakes are high? health status and decision making among older adults. Psychol. Aging **30**(2), 348–355 (2015)
16. Eriksson-Backa, K.: Elderly people, health information, and libraries: a small-scale study on seniors in a language minority. Libri **60**, 181–194 (2010)
17. Eriksson-Backa, K., Ek, S., Niemelä, R., Huotari, M.L.: Health information literacy in everyday life: a study of Finns aged 65–79 years. Health Inform. J. **18**, 83–94 (2012)
18. Guess, A., Nagler, J., Tucker, J.: Less than you think: prevalence and predictors of fake news dissemination on Facebook. Sci. Adv. **5**(1), eaau4586 (2019)
19. Hair, J.F., Black, W.C., Babin, B.J., Anderson, R.E.: Multivariate Data Analysis, 7th edn. Prentice Hall, Englewood Cliffs (2009)
20. Haruna, H., Hu, X.: International trends in designing electronic health information literacy for health sciences students: a systematic review of the literature. J. Acad. Libr. **44**(2), 300–312 (2018)

21. Hirvonen, N., et al.: Everyday health information literacy in relation to health behavior and physical fitness: a population-based study among young men. Libr. Inf. Sci. Res. **38**(4), 308–318 (2016)
22. Jin, J., Yan, X., Li, Y., Li, Y.: How users adopt healthcare information: an empirical study of an online Q&A community. Int. J. Med. Inform. **86**, 91–103 (2016)
23. Jordan, J.E., et al.: The health literacy management scale (HeLMS): a measure of an individual's capacity to seek, understand and use health information within the healthcare setting. Patient Educ. Couns. **91**(2), 228–235 (2013)
24. Kim, H., Park, S.Y., Bozeman, I.: Online health information search and evaluation: observations and semi-structured interviews with college students and maternal health experts. Health Inf. Libr. J. **28**(3), 188–199 (2011)
25. Kim, H., Xie, B.: Health literacy in the eHealth era: a systematic review of the literature. Patient Educ. Couns. **100**(6), 1073–1082 (2017)
26. Löckenhoff, C.E., Carstensen, L.L.: Socioemotional selectivity theory, aging, and health: the increasingly delicate balance between regulating emotions and making tough choices. J. Pers. **72**(6), 1395–1424 (2004)
27. Lee, J., Choi, Y.: Informed public against false rumor in the social media era: focusing on social media dependency. Telemat. Inform. **35**(5), 1071–1081 (2018)
28. Marshall, L.A., Williams, D.: Health information: does quality count for the consumer? J. Libr. Inf. Sci. **38**, 141–156 (2006)
29. Mather, M., Carstensen, L.L.: Aging and motivated cognition: the positivity effect in attention and memory. Trends Cogn. Sci. **9**(10), 496–502 (2005)
30. World Health Organization: The WHO health promotion glossary (WHO/HPR/HEP/98.1) (1998). http://www.who.int/healthpromotion/about/HPG
31. Quinn, S., Bond, R., Nugent, C.: Quantifying health literacy and eHealth literacy using existing instruments and browser-based software for tracking online health information seeking behavior. Comput. Hum. Behav. **69**, 256–267 (2017)
32. Reed, A.E., Carstensen, L.L.: The theory behind the age-related positivity effect. Front. Psychol. **3**, 339 (2012)
33. Segars, A.H.: Assessing the unidimensionality of measurement. A paradigm and illustration within the context of information systems research. Omega **25**(1), 107–121 (1997)
34. Shin, D.-H., Lee, S., Hwang, Y.: How do credibility and utility play in the user experience of health informatics services? Comput. Hum. Behav. **67**, 292–302 (2017)
35. Sicilia, R., Lo Giudice, S., Pei, Y., Pechenizkiy, M., Soda, P.: Twitter rumour detection in the health domain. Expert Syst. Appl. **110**, 33–40 (2018)
36. Suka, M.: Relationship between health literacy, health information access, health behavior, and health status in Japanese people. Patient Educ. Couns. **98**(5), 660–668 (2015)
37. Sunstein, C.R.: On Rumors: How Falsehoods Spread, Why We Believe Them, What Can Be Done. Princeton University Press, Princeton (2009)
38. Yates, C.: Exploring variation in the ways of experiencing health information literacy: a phenomenographic study. Libr. Inf. Sci. Res. **37**(3), 220–227 (2015)
39. Zhang, Y., Sun, Y., Kim, Y.: The influence of individual differences on consumer's selection of online sources for health information. Comput. Hum. Behav. **67**, 303–312 (2017)
40. Zhang, Z., Zhang, Z., Li, H.: Predictors of the authenticity of internet health rumours. Health Inf. Libr. J. **32**(3), 195–205 (2015)
41. Zhao, L., Yin, J., Song, Y.: An exploration of rumor combating behavior on social media in the context of social crises. Comput. Hum. Behav. **58**, 25–36 (2016)

A Qualitative Investigation on Miscommunication of Everyday Health Information Between Older Parents and Adult Children

Xinlin Yao[1], Xiaolun Wang[1(✉)], Jie Gu[2], and Yuxiang (Chris) Zhao[1]

[1] Nanjing University of Science and Technology, Nanjing, China
wxl@njust.edu.cn
[2] Shanghai Academy of Social Sciences, Shanghai, People's Republic of China

Abstract. With the advancement of ICTs, older adults are more actively participating in their healthcare decisions and accessing online health information. However, older adults demonstrated low levels of health literacy which calls for various interventions to improve. Given the limited accessibility and mixed results of public intervention programs, intergenerational communication/learning has been proposed as a cost-effective solution. While intergenerational communication/learning often became problematic even within family. Therefore, it is far from conclusive to employ intergenerational communication/learning to improve older adults' health literacy. To address these concerns, this study adopted semi-structured interviews to explore older adults' perceptions on their online health information seeking and sharing behaviors and on their adult children's responses. We found that older adults preferred the WeChat to seek and share everyday health information. Compared to older adults' actively involvement, adult children provided inactive or even negative responses to the sharing behaviors. Our results revealed that two miscommunications occurred in the intergenerational communication contributed to forming the problematic communication and incomplete comprehension. Implications for both theory and practice were discussed as well.

Keywords: Miscommunication · Intergenerational communication ·
Older parents · Adult children · Everyday health information · Health literacy

1 Introduction

The world is getting aging. It was predicted that the global 60-year or over ages population would be around 2 billion by 2050, and 20% of those older adults aged 80 years or above [1]. With the largest aging population in the world, China started facing salient issues resulted from the aging population. It was reported that the number of Chinese citizens aged 60 or above reached 241 million by the end of 2017, accounting for 17.3% of the total Chinese population [2]. As a part of aging process, older adults typically have a great need for health information and services [3]. With the advancement of information communication technologies (ICTs), older adults are more

© Springer Nature Switzerland AG 2019
J. Zhou and G. Salvendy (Eds.): HCII 2019, LNCS 11593, pp. 109–121, 2019.
https://doi.org/10.1007/978-3-030-22015-0_9

actively participating in their healthcare decisions, taking care of their own health, and accessing online health information [4, 5]. A recent statistic report showed that the number of internet user who aged 50 or above had been over 80 million by the end of 2017, and most of them were using smartphones [6]. However, the developing ICTs not only facilitate information accessing and sharing, but also could be hotbeds of inaccurate and misleading information. Lack of abilities on obtaining, processing, and evaluating the health-related information indicated low levels of health literacy, which might increase the likelihood of misunderstanding and misuse and impair individual's healthcare decisions [7]. Previous studies have found that older adults demonstrated low levels of healthy literacy (e.g., [8]). Therefore, it has attracted considerable attentions in both academia and policy-makers to improve health literacy among the aging population.

Previous studies have examined the public health literacy interventions and showed mixed outcomes after the interventions. Furthermore, scholars suggested that those public programs had limited accessibility and interventions targeting younger people were unlikely to reach similar results in the older population [9, 10]. Therefore, the intervention through intergenerational communication/learning was proposed as an alternative and cost-effective solution to improve older adults' health literacy [11, 12]. Nevertheless, intergenerational communication often became problematic and brought negative outcomes for both parties, even occurred within family. For instance, it has been widely discussed that adult children were troubled in failing to persuade their older parents not trusting and sharing online health-related rumors [13]. Taken together, it is far from conclusive to understand how to improve older adults' health literacy through intergenerational communication/learning and in which the miscommunication occurs.

To address these concerns, this study adopted semi-structured interviews to explore the miscommunication of health-related information between older parents and adult children. We revealed the potential vicious cycle in this intergenerational communication due to the misunderstanding between older parents and adult children, which contributed to literature in intergenerational communication and older adults' health literacy.

2   Literature Review

2.1   Health Information Needs and Sources of Older Adults

Older adults typically have greater needs to access health information than younger adults since they often have one or more chronic diseases. The paradigm shift in the patient–provider relationships to the shared decision-making model also encouraged patients to stay informed and to participate in decision making [14, 15]. For instance, Lee et al. [16] found that adults between the age of 50 to 60 used the Internet for health care purpose because they wanted to actively participate in their health care decision-making. Some scholars have identified four types of health information wants of older adults: basic, advanced, complementary, and provider-related, which included health information that would be used in decision-making but not necessarily be directly related to diagnosis or treatments [17, 18]. Furthermore, it is worth to note that the health information needs changed along with older adults' ages and health conditions [19–21].

Traditionally, older adults primarily obtained health information from healthcare providers, their social networks (e.g., family members and friends), and mass media (e.g., newspapers, broadcasts, and television) [22–25]. With the advancement and spread of information communication technologies, the Internet has become an important source of health information for the elderly [23]. Besides the effects of cognitive abilities and information quality [26, 27], considerable studies have examined the older adults' motivations, perceptions and attitudes, information needs, and query strategies of online health information seeking behaviors [5, 28–31]. However, along with an increasing number of Chinese older adults using the Internet as an easy and important source to address their health concerns [32], studies on Chinese older adults' online health information behaviors were still scant, especially regarding the misinformation and information sharing behaviors.

2.2 Online Health Literacy of the Older Adults

Health literacy refers to individuals' ability to obtain, process, evaluate, and use health information to maintain and promote health condition or make health-related decisions [33]. Online health literacy (or eHealth literacy) emphasized this ability in the online context [34]. Health literacy played an important role in health information seeking and health-related decision-making behaviors (see a literature review in [33] for more details). Recently, eHealth literacy has been conceptualized as a multi-dimensional construct including six forms of literacy: traditional, information, media, health, scientific, and computer [35], which suggested a more comprehensive perspective to understand older adults' online health information behaviors.

Previous studies have developed several measurements for evaluating online health literacy and examined the online health literacy of older adults, suggesting low levels of health literacy among older adults [8]. The poor health literacy of older adults might be attributed to the decreased cognitive skills [36], lower levels of education, poor health status [37], and limited access to the Internet (i.e., digital divide) [38]. As the core of health literacy is various social and cognitive skills, governments and communities have launched several public programs to improve older adults' health literacy (see a systematic review in [9] for more details). However, the effectiveness of these intervention programs was far from conclusive because of the reported mixed results. For instance, Xie [10] showed a significant improvement of older adults' e-health literacy through a four-week training intervention with the collaborative learning strategy. On the contrary, Campbell et al. [39] failed to find the before-after effects for most of the measured outcomes in a 5-week training course that was designed to teach older adults to use the Internet to obtain health information, which was held in public libraries and senior community centers. Given the limited programs and studies on improving older adults' health literacy, it is necessary to provide more insights on specific health literacy promotion strategies for the aging population.

2.3   Intergenerational Communication, Learning, and Miscommunication

Although governments launched several intervention programs for improving older adults' health literacy, it was obviously insufficient to meet the needs of the aging population because of the limited accessibility of this type of programs [40, 41]. Some scholars thought that one cost-effective solution to this challenge might be training older adults through intergenerational communication within or beyond the family [11, 12]. Gilbert and Karahalios [42] found that as people got old, their health and well-being were more dependent of emotionally close relationships, family members and good friends because they provided bonding social relationships and enabled specific reciprocity, emotional support and companionship. Henner [43] showed a positive effect on improving older adults' knowledge, abilities, and confidence in the Internet usage for health resources through a one-year intergenerational training program with student volunteers from universities. Furthermore, within families, intergenerational learning was regarded as the informal vehicle for systematically transferring knowledge, skills, abilities, norms and values between generations in both traditional and modern contexts. For instance, Friemel [44] found that encouragement by family was a strong predictor for Internet use, and private learning settings were preferred over professional courses among older adults.

However, intergenerational communication often became miscommunication and was characterized as dissatisfactory and problematic [45, 46]. Miscommunication refers to the misunderstanding or incomplete understanding between the intent of the speaker and the interpretation of the audience, such as misunderstanding, problematic talk, and unsuccessful interactions [47, 48]. This communicative predicament might be attributed to the salient negative assumptions about the older people, which may cause inappropriate communication (e.g., patronizing speech based on a stereotype of elder cognitive impairment), and that inappropriate communication leads to negative outcomes for both parties [45, 46, 49]. Although previous studies have examined general intergenerational communications, there was no studies concerned the intergenerational communications of every health information between older parents and their adult children to our knowledge. Therefore, it is necessary and important to address this gap because the intergenerational communication and learning within family would be a feasible and cost-effective solution to improving older adults' literacy on health information in the digital context.

3   Methodology

3.1   Method

We employed a semi-structured interview method in this study, which was well suited for understanding the phenomenon in the context and providing deeper insights on the link between older adults' perceptions and behaviors [50, 51]. The semi-structured interview approach is one of the most widely used method in qualitative research and in IS research, which helped participants recall the memory through multiple themes and topics and encouraged participants to disclosure and clarify their attitudes, opinions, and perceptions in details [50].

3.2   Procedure and Participants

A convenient sampling strategy was employed to recruit older adults who were willing to participate in this study, which included recruitment flyers in a local community in Nanjing as well as snowball sampling through word of mouth among participants. Inclusion criteria were: (1) older adults with the age of 55+ years, (2) using the Internet (including mobile Internet) for health-related information in the last month, and (3) sharing the health-related information at least one time in the last month.

Recruitment for this study was completed in November 2018. Fourteen participants were recruited and two of them were randomly invited to participate the pilot study for finalizing major interview questions. The rest of twelve formal interviews were scheduled and conducted from 40 to 60 min at the activity space of the community. Interviews were focused three main questions listed in Sect. 3.3 and relevant questions were interviewed according to participants' responses. All interviews were voice recorded and transcribed for coding and analysis. Each participant received a 30 RMB (around 5 US dollars) gift card of a local grocery store after the interview. The background information of participants was reported in Table 1.

Table 1. Summary of participants' background information

No.	Gender	Age	Education level	Experience of the internet (year)	Usage of smartphone for online information
1	F	57	College	3	Multiple times in a day
2	M	63	Middle school	1.5	Once in a day
3	M	71	Primary school	1	Once in 2 or 3 days
4	F	59	Middle school	4	Once in a week
5	M	62	Primary school	2	Once in a day
6	F	55	Middle school	6	Multiple times in a day
7	M	62	High school	2	Once in a week
8	F	58	High school	7	Multiple times in a day
9	F	67	Primary school	5.5	Once in 2 or 3 days
10	M	56	High school	4	Once in 2 or 3 days
11	F	64	Primary school	1	Once in a day
12	F	55	High school	4	Once in a day
13	M	58	College	8	Multiple times in a day
14	F	60	Middle school	3.5	Multiple times in a day

3.3   Interview Questions

The interview questions mainly focused on the following three aspects. Exemplar questions were presented in parentheses:

(1) Online health information seeking and sharing behaviors (*Have you searched or shared health-related information online in the last month? What kind of health-related information do you read most? Which source do you often use for online health information? Who do you often share the health information and why?*);

(2) Adult children's responses and feedbacks after receiving the shared health-related information (*What is your children's response when receiving your sharing health-related information? How do your children think about the shared information?*);

(3) Perceptions on the adult children's responses and feedbacks (*How do you think your behavior of sharing the health-related information? Do you think your children know or read the information that you shared? What are your thoughts and feelings about your children's responses to your information-sharing?*).

4   Results

4.1   Older Adults' Online Health Information Seeking and Sharing Behavior

The qualitative results showed that everyday health information was older adults' most interested online health-related information. Actually, participants reported that they almost never seek the health information about disease diagnosis, special treatments or medicines through the Internet. While they were interested in seeking everyday health-related information such as how to keep healthy lifestyles, how to select healthy foods, or life tips for maintaining personal health conditions.

> *"Now, I often browse health-related information since my daughter taught me how to use the smart phone to access to the Internet. It has become a part of my daily life. My favorite posts were teaching us what healthy and unhealthy lifestyles are. For instance, it is important to not stay up late and have more green vegetables in daily foods." (No. 13)*
> *"I usually search online for some life tips for keep the family healthy. Those tips are useful and practical in daily life and I often use during my cooking. If I got sick or felt uncomfortable, I prefer to ask my daughter or see a doctor rather than searching online." (No. 10)*

In terms of the source to access to the Internet, participants in this study showed obvious preferences on WeChat (i.e., one of the most popular social media in China), which might be attributed to the widely spread of smartphones and the mobile internet. WeChat not only was used as an instant messaging tool, but also supported information searching and sharing through WeChat Moments. Therefore, the health-related information could be accessed through searching or forwarding by other friends. Compared to accessing the Internet on computers, participants thought that it was easier and more convenient to use smartphones.

"Now I read the posts in my WeChat Moments most in my daily life. Furthermore, I have some chatting groups with my friends, and they often share posts about healthy cooking and healthy lifestyle. I think the posts are easier to access and very helpful." (No. 1)

However, the usage of smartphones and WeChat differed among older adults and was related to their ages and education level. For instance, older participants seemed to use smartphone less than their younger counterparts, which was consistent with previous studies that suggested the lower cognitive and sensory skills due to aging.

"My son has taught me to use the smartphone and WeChat. I can use the basic functions such as dial and pick up the phone, check the time, check the messages and so on. But I think the smartphone is too complex for me in general." (No. 3)

Given WeChat was characterized with keeping close social connections, our participants often shared health-related information to their adult children and close friends in WeChat. Therefore, the intergenerational communication from older parents to their adult children was salient in the context of everyday healthcare.

"Since I learned to use WeChat to communicate with my daughter, I also keep in touch with my old classmates through WeChat. We often share articles about important news and healthcare tips. I think those articles are useful and I will send to my daughter to remind her keep healthy. I always concern my daughter because her work is quite busy and laborious." (No. 2)

4.2   Adult Children's Responses to Old Parents' Everyday Health Information Sharing

The interviews showed that after older parents sharing the everyday health information, the major responses from their adult children were ignoring or short confirmations (e.g., OK, All right, I see), suggesting their adult children tended to avoid to actively involve in the topic. The results were different from the previous findings that showed overaccommodation (e.g., elderspeak, patronizing talk) usually occurred in intergenerational communications [49] and indicating an underaccommodation trend that inadequate communicative behaviors implementation for appropriate talk [45].

"My daughter does not response to my sharing frequently, but she does say that she knows after receiving several messages or a few days later. You can see this (the participant shows a recent chatting record on her phone) ... I understand that her work is busy and has little time to check the message." (No. 12)

"When I send my daughter the articles about maintain healthy conditions or healthy tips, she will reply me 'OK' or 'Thanks, Dad' if she is not busy." (No. 2)

In addition, two participants reported that their children gave negative responses to the everyday information sharing, which would evoke older adults' negative emotions but may not prevent their sharing behaviors.

"My son does not like to listen to me since he was a child. Now he is too busy in his work to take care his health. I send him many articles about foods, practices, and lifestyle tips through WeChat to remind him. But he said that those articles were fake and rumors, which makes me feel sad and disappointed." (No. 1)

"My daughter said that she regretted teaching me to use WeChat (laugh) because I always send her posts about healthy tips. She told me that my shared articles were unbelievable. At first, I

feel angry. But now I believe I am right because I know much more on the topic of everyday healthy habits than my daughter. I think I will keep sharing to remind my daughter." (No. 13)

It was worth to note that older parents' information-sharing behaviors seemed persistent even they received inactive and negative responses from adult children. We further explore older adults' perceptions on their information-sharing behaviors and adult children responses in the next section to attempt to reveal the underlying rationale.

4.3   Older Adults' Perceptions on Information Sharing and Adult Children's Responses

The interviews revealed that older adults' everyday heath information-sharing behaviors were shaped by their perceptions of the online heath information, their own social needs, and responses from adult children. However, the miscommunication occurred when certain party did not fully comprehend the intertwined nature of the communicative behaviors. We identified two aspects in older adults' perceptions in this study: the informative aspect and the social aspect.

The informative aspect revealed older adults' perceptions on the source (i.e., WeChat) and quality of the everyday health information, which indicated older adults' online health literacy. Although we didn't accurately measure participants' online health literacy, we found that participants' two tendency that may indicate a relatively low level of online health literacy: (1) Overconfident in online health information. Most participants showed positive attitudes towards the health-related information in the WeChat Moments. Although some participants reported that they knew there were fake articles and rumors online, they believed that they could distinguish.

"I think articles in the WeChat Moments are quite helpful and trustworthy because my old friends who was a doctor often share posts as well. Fake articles are showed in the website [searching through the search engine] and usually advertisements. But I only read posts that teaches me knowledge and experience in WeChat." (No. 2)
"I don't worry about the quality of posts in WeChat because I know WeChat is a large company. What's more, those articles are helpful and good for our health more or less. It is harmless to read more and learn more." (No. 13)

(2) Subjective mindset. Participants showed that they usually evaluated the quality and value of the online health-related information based on their experience rather than facts, which may indicate inadequate skills for information filtering.

"I trust and share posts that are consistent with my experience. You young people often despise wisdom from older generation and traditional culture. And I share those posts to remind you to attention." (No. 1)

The social aspect revealed that older adults' everyday health information-sharing behaviors not only aimed to share the health-related information, but also to satisfy their social needs and decrease social isolation. However, the social aspect may not be successfully comprehended by their adult children, resulting in the first miscommunication in this intergenerational communication. Two major reasons for participants' information-sharing behaviors were: (1) seeking social support/connections, and (2) expressing concern for adult children.

"I feel bored sometimes when I am at home alone. Reading articles can help me kill time. I often share useful articles to my son and he will reply me. It is convenient to use WeChat to communicate with him and not too disturbing compared with making a phone call." (No. 9)
"My daughter often has business trips. And I worry her sleeping conditions and daily meals. I find posts in the Moments are useful and valuable, so I often share to my daughter to remind her having deals on time and sleep early" (No. 8)

Given the inactive or even negative responses from adult children, we assume that adult children comprehended older adults' information-sharing behaviors only from informative aspect, indicating older adults' low levels of online healthy literacy. However, our interviews revealed that miscommunication occurred again among older adults because they perceived the negative responses merely from the social dimension. The qualitative results were consistent with previous studies on problematic inter-generational communications that indicating older adults felt loss of control, decreased self-esteem, lowered self-efficacy when facing the negative responses [49].

"I always think that my shared articles are beneficial and helpful. But I feel very frustrated when my daughter told me not to trust those articles. She should have confidence on me that I am capable to use the smartphone. I don't think I am too old to catch up the times." (No. 13)

In conclusion, we found a vicious cycle in the context of everyday health infor-mation communication between older adults and their adults children because of the miscommunication. We illustrated the cycle in Fig. 1, which may explain why adult children's negative responses does not prevent older parents' information-sharing behaviors.

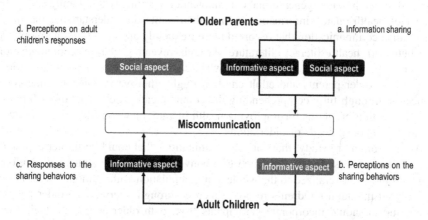

Fig. 1. The intergenerational miscommunication of everyday health information

As we mentioned in Sect. 4.1, older adults' information-sharing behaviors of everyday health information incorporated both informative aspect and social aspect, revealing their perceptions on online health information and own social needs. How-ever, adult children may only comprehend the information-sharing behavior from informative aspect because of the poor quality of the shared information. Thus, the miscommunication occurred due to the incomplete understanding the older adults' intent. Therefore, adult children offered relatively negative responses to the information-sharing behaviors to avoid reinforcing older adults' relatively poor health literacy. However, as we discussed in Sect. 4.3, older adults perceived the negative responses from the social aspect that evoked negative emotions, in where miscommunication occurred again.

5   Conclusion and Discussion

This study explored the miscommunication of everyday health information between older parents and their adult children through semi-structured interviews. Our results revealed that everyday health information was the most interesting topics for older adults. Given the widely spread and convenient supports for close communication, WeChat was the major tool and source that older adults used for seeking and sharing health-related information. Compared with older adults' actively involvement, their adult children showed inactive (e.g., ignoring or short confirmation) and even negative responses to everyday health information sharing. However, those negative cannot fully prevent older adults' from sharing health-related information. We further revealed the underlying vicious cycle through identifying two aspects of older adults' perceptions on their sharing behaviors and responses from adult children: informative aspect and social aspect. Two miscommunications occurred in the intergenerational communications contributed to forming the problematic communication and incomplete comprehension.

Our findings have several contributions for both research and practice. We extended research in intergenerational communication/learning within family and in the context of health-related information, which shed lights on understanding the intergenerational communication that occurred more frequently and easily. Furthermore, we contributed to health literacy literature through revealing the miscommunication between older parents and adult children when sharing everyday health information. For practice, older parents and adult children might improve intergenerational communication through fully comprehending the communicative behaviors of each party. And intervention programs for improving health literacy may consider the intertwined cognitive and social needs of older adults.

As an exploratory study, there are some limitations that could be further explored. The sample size was small and limited to a convenient sampling strategy. Therefore, results should be generalized to the whole aging population with caution. Furthermore, we explored the adult children's response merely through interviewing older people. Future studies should incorporate participants from both older adults and their adult children to provide a whole picture. Finally, our future study may attempt to confirm the relations in the intergenerational communication cycle with more rigorous empirical analysis.

Acknowledgements. We thank the financial support that provided by National Science Foundation of China (#71802108; #71702103), Research Funds for Young Scholars in School of Economics & Management of NJUST (#JGQN1802), Fundamental Research Funds for the Central Universities (30918013104).

References

1. United Nations. World Population Ageing: 2009. United Nations, New York (2010)
2. China's elderly population continues to rise, with 241 million now 60 or over. https:// gbtimes.com/chinas-elderly-population-continues-to-rise. Accessed 01 Feb 2019
3. Kutner, M., Greenburg, E., Jin, Y., Paulsen, C.: The health literacy of america's adults: results from the 2003 national assessment of adult literacy. NCES 2006-483. National Center for Education Statistics (2006). https://files.eric.ed.gov/fulltext/ED493284.pdf
4. Hirvonen, N., et al.: Everyday health information literacy in relation to health behavior and physical fitness: a population-based study among young men. Libr. Inf. Sci. Res. 4(38), 308–318 (2016)
5. Wu, D., Li, Y.: Online health information seeking behaviors among Chinese elderly. Libr. Inf. Sci. Res. 38(3), 272–279 (2016)
6. China's aging and senior community are finding comfort, entertainment and even fame from their smart devices. http://www.globaltimes.cn/content/1094961.shtml. Accessed 01 Feb 2019
7. Koch-Weser, S., Bradshaw, Y.S., Gualtieri, L., Gallagher, S.S.: The Internet as a health information source: findings from the 2007 health information national trends survey and implications for health communication. J. Health Commun. 15(sup3), 279–293 (2010)
8. Manafò, E., Wong, S.: Assessing the eHealth literacy skills of older adults: a preliminary study. J. Consum. Health Internet 16(4), 369–381 (2012)
9. Manafo, E., Wong, S.: Health literacy programs for older adults: a systematic literature review. Health Educ. Res. 27(6), 947–960 (2012)
10. Xie, B.: Older adults, e-health literacy, and collaborative learning: an experimental study. J. Am. Soc. Inf. Sci. Technol. 62(5), 933–946 (2011)
11. Newman, S., Hatton-Yeo, A.: Intergenerational learning and the contributions of older people. Ageing Horiz. 8(10), 31–39 (2008)
12. Magsamen-Conrad, K., Hanasono, L.K., Billotte Verhoff, C.: Health communication in the context of aging: the development of an intergenerational communication intervention to reduce biases and discrimination. In: Applications in Health Communication: Emerging Trends, pp. 101–125. Kendall Hunt, Dubuque (2013)
13. What can we do to save our parents from the rumors? http://news.cyol.com/content/2017-04/27/content_15997484.htm. Accessed 01 Feb 2019
14. Ballard-Reisch, D.S.: A model of participative decision making for physician-patient interaction. Health Commun. 2(2), 91–104 (1990)
15. McNutt, R.A.: Shared medical decision making: problems, process, progress. JAMA 292(20), 2516–2518 (2004)
16. Lee, K., Hoti, K., Hughes, J.D., Emmerton, L.: Dr Google and the consumer: a qualitative study exploring the navigational needs and online health information-seeking behaviors of consumers with chronic health conditions. J. Med. Internet Res. 16(12), e262 (2014)
17. Xie, B.: Older adults' health information wants in the Internet age: implications for patient-provider relationships. J. Health Commun. 14(6), 510–524 (2009)
18. Xie, B., Wang, M., Feldman, R., Zhou, L.: Exploring older and younger adults' preferences for health information and participation in decision making using the Health Information Wants Questionnaire (HIWQ). Health Expect. 17(6), 795–808 (2014)
19. Torp, S., Hanson, E., Hauge, S., Ulstein, I., Magnusson, L.: A pilot study of how information and communication technology may contribute to health promotion among elderly spousal carers in Norway. Health Soc. Care Commun. 16(1), 75–85 (2008)

20. Washington, K.T., Meadows, S.E., Elliott, S.G., Koopman, R.J.: Information needs of informal caregivers of older adults with chronic health conditions. Patient Educ. Counsel. **83**(1), 37–44 (2011)

21. Xie, B., Wang, M., Feldman, R., Zhou, L.: Health information and decision-making preferences in the Internet age: a pilot study using the Health Information Wants (HIW) questionnaire. In: Proceedings of the 1st ACM International Health Informatics Symposium, pp. 610–619. ACM (2010)

22. Palsdottir, A.: Elderly peoples' information behaviour: accepting support from relatives. Libri **62**(2), 135–144 (2012)

23. Wicks, D.A.: Older adults and their information seeking. Behav. Soc. Sci. Libr. **22**(2), 1–26 (2004)

24. Hirakawa, Y., Kuzuya, M., Enoki, H., Uemura, K.: Information needs and sources of family caregivers of home elderly patients. Arch. Gerontol. Geriatr. **52**(2), 202–205 (2011)

25. Niemelä, R., Huotari, M.L., Kortelainen, T.: Enactment and use of information and the media among older adults. Libr. Inf. Sci. Res. **34**(3), 212–219 (2012)

26. Anker, A.E., Reinhart, A.M., Feeley, T.H.: Health information seeking: a review of measures and methods. Patient Educ. Counsel. **82**(3), 346–354 (2011)

27. Zamarian, L., Benke, T., Buchler, M., Wenter, J., Delazer, M.: Information about medications may cause misunderstanding in older adults with cognitive impairment. J. Neurol. Sci. **298**(1–2), 46–51 (2010)

28. Flynn, K.E., Smith, M.A., Freese, J.: When do older adults turn to the Internet for health information? Findings from the Wisconsin Longitudinal Study. J. Gen. Intern. Med. **21**(12), 1295–1301 (2006)

29. Harrod, M.: "I have to keep going": why some older adults are using the Internet for health information. Ageing Int. **36**(2), 283–294 (2011)

30. Huang, M., Hansen, D., Xie, B.: Older adults' online health information seeking behavior. In: Proceedings of the 2012 iConference, pp. 338–345. ACM (2012)

31. Zulman, D.M., Kirch, M., Zheng, K., An, L.C.: Trust in the Internet as a health resource among older adults: analysis of data from a nationally representative survey. J. Med. Internet Res. **13**(1), e19 (2011)

32. Wong, C.K., Yeung, D.Y., Ho, H.C., Tse, K.P., Lam, C.Y.: Chinese older adults' Internet use for health information. J. Appl. Gerontol. **33**(3), 316–335 (2014)

33. Diviani, N., van den Putte, B., Giani, S., van Weert, J.C.: Low health literacy and evaluation of online health information: a systematic review of the literature. J. Med. Internet Res. **17**(5), e112 (2015)

34. Norman, C.D., Skinner, H.A.: eHealth literacy: essential skills for consumer health in a networked world. J. Med. Internet Res. **8**(2), e9 (2006)

35. Tennant, B., et al.: eHealth literacy and Web 2.0 health information seeking behaviors among baby boomers and older adults. J. Med. Internet Res. **17**(3), e70 (2015)

36. Federman, A.D., Sano, M., Wolf, M.S., Siu, A.L., Halm, E.A.: Health literacy and cognitive performance in older adults. J. Am. Geriatr. Soc. **57**(8), 1475–1480 (2009)

37. Eriksson-Backa, K., Ek, S., Niemelä, R., Huotari, M.L.: Health information literacy in everyday life: a study of Finns aged 65–79 years. Health Inform. J. **18**(2), 83–94 (2012)

38. Levy, H., Janke, A.T., Langa, K.M.: Health literacy and the digital divide among older Americans. J. Gen. Intern. Med. **30**(3), 284–289 (2015)

39. Campbell, R.J., Nolfi, D.A.: Teaching elderly adults to use the Internet to access health care information: before-after study. J. Med. Internet Res. **7**(2), e19 (2005)

40. Kreps, G.L., Sparks, L.: Meeting the health literacy needs of immigrant populations. Patient Educ. Couns. **71**(3), 328–332 (2008)

41. Mo, P.K., Malik, S.H., Coulson, N.S.: Gender differences in computer-mediated communication: a systematic literature review of online health-related support groups. Patient Educ. Couns. **75**(1), 16–24 (2009)
42. Gilbert, E., Karahalios, K.: Predicting tie strength with social media. In: Proceedings of the SIGCHI Conference on Human Factors in Computing Systems, pp. 211–220. ACM (2009)
43. Henner, T.: An intergenerational approach to Internet training: student-led outreach to promote seniors' use of Internet health resources. J. Consum. Health Internet **13**(4), 334–346 (2009)
44. Friemel, T.N.: The digital divide has grown old: determinants of a digital divide among seniors. New Media Soc. **18**(2), 313–331 (2016)
45. Giles, H., Gasiorek, J.: Intergenerational communication practices. In: Handbook of the Psychology of Aging (Seventh Edition), pp. 233–247 (2011)
46. Ryan, E.B., Giles, H., Bartolucci, G., Henwood, K.: Psycholinguistic and social psychological components of communication by and with the elderly. Lang. Commun. **6**(1–2), 1–24 (1986)
47. Bethea, L., Balazs, A.: Improving intergenerational health care communication. J. Health Commun. **2**(2), 129–137 (1997)
48. Coupland, N., Giles, H., Wiemann, J.M.: Miscommunication and problematic talk, vol. 11. Sage Publications, Inc., Newbury Park (1991)
49. Barker, V., Giles, H.: Integrating the communicative predicament and enhancement of aging models: the case of older Native Americans. Health Commun. **15**(3), 255–275 (2003)
50. Bradley, E.H., Curry, L.A., Devers, K.J.: Qualitative data analysis for health services research: developing taxonomy, themes, and theory. Health Serv. Res. **42**(4), 1758–1772 (2007)
51. Myers, M.D., Newman, M.: The qualitative interview in IS research: examining the craft. Inf. Organ. **17**(1), 2–26 (2007)

Games and Exergames for the Elderly

Older Adults' Perceptions of Video Game Training in the *Intervention Comparative Effectiveness for Adult Cognitive Training* (ICE-ACT) Clinical Trial: An Exploratory Analysis

Ronald Andringa, Erin R. Harell, Michael Dieciuc,
and Walter R. Boot[✉]

Department of Psychology, Florida State University, Tallahassee, USA
{andringa, harrell, dieciuc, boot}@psy.fsu.edu

Abstract. Video game-based interventions have been increasingly explored as a means to prevent or reverse age-related declines in attention, executive control, memory, and processing speed. Further, the gamification of interventions aimed at improving mental and physical health, and encouraging healthy behaviors, holds promise with respect to promoting intervention engagement and adherence. Successful implementation of game-based and gamified interventions depends on the ability to design games that older adults are willing and able to play, which ultimately depends on understanding the game preferences of older adults, and the challenges and barriers to video gameplay. To explore these issues, this paper presents data collected from U.S. participants as part of the *Intervention Comparative Effectiveness for Adult Cognitive Training* (ICE-ACT) clinical trial. This trial aimed to understand the impact of various interventions on cognition and everyday task performance. Three intervention arms involved video game play: BrainHQ training (gamified cognitive training), Rise of Nations training (commercial complex real-time strategy game), and a control group that played Sudoku, crossword, and word search computer programs. After each game session, participants rated their game experience and provided comments in a game diary. This paper presents analyses of these diary data. The largest differences observed were between attitudes toward the control games and Rise of Nations. Control games were strongly preferred and were perceived as more motivating compared to Rise of Nations, and there was a trend for Rise of Nations to be perceived as more frustrating than BrainHQ. The observed preference for puzzle games, and an aversion for the violent and complex content of Rise Nations, is consistent with previous survey and focus group data of older adults' game preferences. Results have implications for designing game-based and gamified interventions for older adults that will encourage enjoyment, engagement, and adherence.

Keywords: Older adults · Video games · Cognitive intervention · Gamification · Adherence · Engagement

© Springer Nature Switzerland AG 2019
J. Zhou and G. Salvendy (Eds.): HCII 2019, LNCS 11593, pp. 125–134, 2019.
https://doi.org/10.1007/978-3-030-22015-0_10

1 Introduction

Some researchers have proposed that video game play may serve as an effective intervention to combat age-related perceptual and cognitive decline [1, 2; but see also 3]. Others have proposed that gamification, the addition of game and video game-like elements to non-game activities, holds promise with respect to encouraging engagement with, and adherence to, health interventions and healthy behaviors [4]. This includes recent trends in the use of "exergames" to encourage physical activity and exercise [5]. Common gamification elements include the introduction of points systems, achievement badges, leaderboards, stories, themes, feedback, rewards, progress tracking, and challenges. However, a lack of experience with, and enthusiasm for, video game play by older adults has potentially important implications for the effectiveness of these interventions and techniques across the lifespan. Specifically, the age-related "digital divide" must be considered before applying these approaches to improving the cognition, wellbeing, and health of older adults.

In general, older adults are less likely to adopt many newer technologies, including the internet, smartphones, tablet computers, and smart home devices [e.g., 6, 7]. This gap in technology adoption extends to digital gaming and the devices that support video game play. In the United States, only 24% of older adults (ages 65+) report playing video games, compared to 60% of younger adults (ages 18–29), and 43% of adults in general [8]. With respect to device ownership, only 8% of older adults own a video game console, compared to 40% of adults in general [9]. Although video gameplay is a common activity for many younger adults, it is a relatively infrequent activity for many older adults.

Why are older adults reluctant to adopt video game technology? Many older adults have not adopted the prerequisite technologies necessary to engage in video game play, including the internet, smartphones, and gaming consoles. Lack of technology adoption, and as a result, technology skill, represents a substantial barrier to engaging in video gameplay. Attitudinal barriers also exist. Some older adults believe that video games are too challenging, a waste of time, or too childish [10–12]. Older adults also report an aversion to the violent content of many video games [13–16], and in the United States, erroneously attribute frequent mass-shootings to the influence of violent video games [17]. Finally, video game design that does not account for age-related ability changes (psychomotor, perceptual, and cognitive), and the relative inexperience of older adults with gaming, is an important barrier to gameplay [18, 19]. Video games are often designed by younger adults without consideration for the abilities and preferences of older adults.

This paper seeks to gain insight into older adults' perceptions of video game-based interventions to better understand barriers to cognitive intervention adoption and adherence, and the effective use of intervention gamification. Data were collected as part of the *Intervention Comparative Effectiveness for Adult Cognitive Training* (ICE-ACT) clinical trial (https://clinicaltrials.gov/ct2/show/NCT03141281). ICE-ACT aimed to test the impact of various interventions on cognition and everyday task performance [20]. Three intervention arms involved video gameplay. One group was asked to engage in BrainHQ training, which consisted of gamified neuropsychological tasks.

Another group was asked to engage in Rise of Nations training, a commercial complex real-time strategy game. Initial research has suggested that this game may improve cognition in older adults [21]. A control group played Sudoku, crossword, and word search computer programs. As part of this trial, a non-game training group completed online tutorials on driver safety and financial fraud avoidance (Instrumental Activities of Daily Living (IADL) training). As this intervention was not game-based, it is not a focus of the current paper. After each game interaction, participants rated the game experience and provided comments in a game diary. Of primary interest for the current paper, these data were analyzed to uncover older adults' experiences and challenges with this diverse set of video game and gamified interventions. Specifically, our first research question aimed to understand older adults' perceptions of the game or games they were assigned (perceptions of enjoyment, challenge, frustration, and motivation to perform well). A second research question aimed to better understand specific barriers (attitudinal and game mechanics-related) to gameplay for each game using open-ended diary responses.

2 Method and Results

A baseline paper for the ICE-ACT trial fully describes all research protocols, measures, and participant characteristics [20]. A brief summary is provided here.

2.1 Participants

In total, 230 participants were recruited from the Tallahassee, FL region, and randomized to different arms of the trial (M_{age} = 71.4, SD = 5.3). The sample was 58% female, largely White (82%), and fairly well-educated (91% with at least some college education). Random assignment resulted in 57 participants in the BrainHQ condition, 59 in the Rise of Nations (RON) condition, and 58 participants in the control condition (which played word and puzzle games). Another 56 participants were randomly assigned to the IADL training.

2.2 Game Experience

BrainHQ. Participants in the BrainHQ condition completed a subset of tasks within the BrainHQ cognitive training software suite. These tasks were: Double Decision, Freeze Frame, and Target Tracker. Double Decision is a gamified version of the Useful Field of View task, Freeze Frame is a gamified stop reaction time task, and Target Tracker is a gamified multiple object tracking task. Briefly, Double Decision presented short duration images containing road signs and vehicles and participants had to identify the vehicle and locate a peripheral road sign. Freeze Frame presented an image for participants to memorize, and then, they were shown a series of pictures. They were asked to make a response quickly if the image they saw was *not* the image they were asked to memorize, and withhold a response if it was. Target Tracker involved participants being asked to keep track of certain objects that moved randomly (e.g., fish swimming in an ocean) among identical looking distractors. Tasks were gamified in the sense that they featured appealing graphics, performance feedback, and performance tracking.

Rise of Nations. Participants in the Rise of Nations condition played a real-time strategy game. In the game, players are positioned on a map with a small civilization and few resources. The task of the player is to collect resources from the map, build structures to expand their territory and advance their civilization, and develop and maintain a military force for offense and defense. Computer-controlled players are also on the map trying to accomplish the same goals. Players win when they control 70% of the map, capture their opponent's capital city, or lead in points by constructing world wonders for a sufficiently advanced civilization.

Control Condition. In the control condition, participants played a series of three puzzle games. The crossword game emulated a traditional set of crossword puzzles. Sudoku was a computerized version of the traditional number puzzle game. Finally, word search presented participants with a matrix of letters and participants had to locate a set of target words.

2.3 Equipment and Training

All participants were provided with a laptop with their assigned game or games on it to take home. They were also provided with a mouse. In the laboratory, participants were trained by study personnel on the use of the laptop, mouse, and their assigned game or games. Participants were also given written manuals related to equipment and game use.

Home-based training consisted of a recommended 20 h of game play. This was in the form of one hour of game play on five different days each week, over the span of four weeks. To minimize fatigue, participants were asked to complete two separate thirty-minute sessions in a day.

After each session, participants were asked to complete an online diary to provide input on their experience. Participants rated four statements on a Likert-scale (1 = strongly disagree; 7 = strongly agree). These four questions were: (1) I found today's session to be enjoyable; (2) I found today's session to be challenging; (3) I found today's session to be frustrating; (4) I was motivated to perform well on today's session. Then, participants were allowed to provide any additional comments in an open-ended response box. These questions are the main focus of this paper to provide insight into older adults' game preferences and game barriers and challenges.

2.4 Results

All available diary data were entered into the reported analyses below. Participants were asked to rate their enjoyment, challenge, frustration, and motivation after each game session (Fig. 1). Note that 4 represents the neutral point of the scale (Neither agree nor disagree). For enjoyment ratings, scores were close to this neutral point, suggesting a general lack of enthusiasm for the interventions. Participants, on average, did find the games challenging and motivating, but also slightly frustrating.

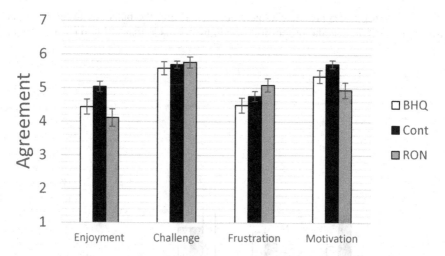

Fig. 1. Average agreement after game sessions to the four questions: (1) I found today's session to be enjoyable; (2) I found today's session to be challenging; (3) I found today's session to be frustrating; (4) I was motivated to perform well on today's session. 1 = strongly disagree; 7 = strongly agree. Error bars = ±1SEM.

The first set of analyses explored differences in game experience. Analysis of Variance (ANOVA) explored whether ratings differed between groups, and post-hoc tests with Tukey correction explored the nature of those differences. First, with respect to enjoyment, there was a significant main effect of condition ($F(2, 117) = 5.249$, $p < .01$). The control group, that played puzzle games, reported the highest enjoyment, and enjoyment was significantly higher in the control group compared to the Rise of Nations group ($p < .01$). There was no significant difference in game challenge between groups ($F(2, 117) = 0.319$, $p = .728$). There was a trend for frustration to differ between conditions ($F(2, 117) = 2.439$, $p = .092$), with this trend being associated with greater frustration being reported by the Rise of Nations group compared to the BrainHQ group ($p = .076$). Finally, there was a significant difference in reported motivation ($F(2, 117) = 4.801$, $p < .05$), driven by greater reported motivation to perform well during sessions by the control group compared to the Rise of Nations group ($p < .01$).

Next, we present data related to the open-ended question at the end of the diary entry. A rater was given categories in which they could rate participant diary comments, and was informed that comments may contain multiple ideas and clauses, and was instructed to rate each clause independently. The enjoyment category related to thoughts on positive experiences with the intervention (e.g., "The game is addictive!"; "fun"; "I'm liking the bubbles more!"). The frustration category related to negative experiences (e.g., "Not fun and frustrating"; "A little frustrating"; "glad it is over"). The challenge category contained thoughts on game difficulties and challenges to overcome (e.g., "Still trying to learn what I'm doing in this game!"; "Always find the crosswords challenging"; "The cars are VERY close in shape"). The boredom category contained expressions of poor motivation and lack of interest (e.g., "this is so boring";

"the crossword puzzles are lame"; "gets boring tracking the balls etc. in the last exercise"). Figure 2 depicts the proportion of comments made that fell into each category.

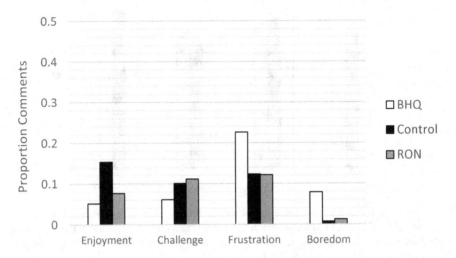

Fig. 2. Proportion of all diary entry clauses that related intervention enjoyment, challenge, frustration, and boredom.

Similar to the quantitative results, the control condition had the most comments that were positive. However, unlike the quantitative data, there were many more comments relating to frustration in the BrainHQ condition, and this condition also inspired the most comments related to boredom. More comments related to frustration may be due to the fact that this intervention was the most adaptive, and increased in difficulty as participants increased in their skill level. Other tasks, by not being as adaptive, may have allowed participants a greater sense of mastery. In a sense, the Brain HQ may have offered the least variability in game play (the same three basic exercises), which may explain the comments related to boredom. It is important to note, though, that this intervention limited their experience to three out of many BrainHQ tasks. Compared to other groups, the BrainHQ group was more likely to mention eyestrain ("The Double Decision game causes a great deal of eyestrain"; My eyes got tired doing 1 h together"; "as task continued my eyes started to fatigue"; "eyes got very tired").

The quantitative data from the Rise of Nations group suggested a trend toward greater frustration, and a lack of game motivation. The qualitative data were explored to gain insight into these patterns. In the Rise of Nations group, some participants reported being averse to the violent and war-related content of the game ("I STILL sense that the game's program tilts toward having to look for a military win. This goes against my utopian grain!!!'"; "I'm not into this level of aggression"; "Men groaning… blood splatting…shooting civilians…women screaming…Seriously? Folks play this for entertainment?"). Many negative comments related to confusion related to the complexity of the game (e.g., "So much to learn to perform well in this game"; "it was trial and error…there is so much to remember and understand") and lack of gaming experience (e.g., "Overload of information for someone not familiar with "Gaming Conventions"!"; "Don't normally play games and didn't feel comfortable doing it!"). Although the intervention provided in-lab training, and support materials for home-based training, the complexity of the game and its many rules appeared to present a learning challenge. It should be noted that although participants reported less enjoyment on average with the Rise of Nations game, some participants enjoyed the game and noted very positive comments ("Having fun building and making money"; "enjoyed game"; "Am surprised to be enjoying the game more now that I'm finally getting the hang of it!").

3   Conclusions, Limitations, and Implications for Future Research

This paper presented data related to older adults' video game experiences in the ICE-ACT randomized clinical trial. As many cognitive interventions now take the form of gamified neuropsychological tests, or commercial and custom video games, understanding older adults' game motivations, preferences, and barriers to game play is important, as these likely impact adoption and adherence to these interventions. More broadly, the introduction of game elements is being considered to improve adherence to a wide variety of interventions aimed at improving health and encouraging healthy behaviors (i.e., gamification).

Our first research question related to older adults' perceptions of the game or games they were assigned (perceptions of enjoyment, challenge, frustration, and motivation to perform well). Traditionally, there has been a digital divide between younger and older adults, including large differences in the adoption of video games as a form of leisure activity [8, 18]. This divide likely impacted participants' game experiences in the trial. For the most part, participants did not rate their game enjoyment as high, though ratings were higher for puzzle games that were part of the control condition. Overall, participants tended to rate their game experiences as challenging, and slightly frustrating. Game preferences were generally consistent with a number of prior studies [13–16]. Enjoyment was higher for puzzle games, and lower for the most violent game (Rise of Nations, which often involved combat).

Our second research question related to specific barriers to gameplay. For Rise of Nations, the most complex game, participants reported difficulty remembering the many rules and procedures of the game. However, many novice gamers with little previous experience with real-time strategy games may encounter similar difficulties. Rather than relating to age per se, these challenges may instead simply reflect a lack of experience. It should be noted that the games older adults enjoyed the most in the study (word and number puzzle games) were likely the most familiar, as they have non-digital analogues.

Although older adults in the ICE-ACT study received training on their assigned game or games within the laboratory, and help manuals and instructions for home-based training, many still reported frustration and challenges, which highlights the relationship between learnability and usability. More training may have been beneficial, especially for Rise of Nations, in order to minimize difficulty in learning how to master the game. Given that older people often rely more on help systems and error messages, it may be necessary to provide additional support aids and tutorials for older adults. Better game design and context-aware help within the game itself may be especially beneficial for older novice gamers. Adaptive support might include the option to turn this support off once it is no longer necessary. One general recommendation is that designers decrease the number of steps needed to complete a task and recognize that mistakes in any part of a serially organized sequence or process can affect the overall success or mastery of the game [22]. Just like all systems, video games and associated gaming technologies need to consider the needs, preferences, and attitudes of older adults in their design [18, 19]. This will help maximize engagement with, and adherence to, potentially beneficial game-based interventions.

Game design, however, presents a unique challenge compared to the design of other types of systems in that video games are *intended* to be challenging and slightly frustrating. That is, if a game is not challenging enough, the player will be bored and will likely disengage. However, if the demands of the game exceed the abilities of the player substantially, they will have a frustrating game experience, also resulting in disengagement. Good game design challenges players, but not too much or too little, resulting in a pleasant state known as "flow [23]." However, as a result of normative age-related changes in perceptual, cognitive, and psychomotor abilities, games that produce a flow state in younger adults might be too challenging for older adults (or novice gamers), and games that produce a flow state for older adults might not be challenging enough for younger adults. This suggests a benefit to carefully considering the range of difficulty options available to players, and having the ability to adjust game difficulty with more precision compared to typical options (easy, medium, hard) [24].

Some limitations need to be considered with respect to the data and analyses reported here. First, diary data are not available for participants who did not adhere to, or who quit, the study. Thus, data presented here may represent an underestimate of the difficulties some older adults experienced, and an overestimate of their enjoyment. Data are not available for participants who may have been so frustrated with their game, or who so disliked their game, that they dropped out of the study entirely. Second, diary questions asked participants to report their experiences with the training session. Some challenge and frustration may have come not from the game, but from their interactions with the provided technology and technical issues. For example, one participant in their diary noted a broken "U" key on their keyboard. These technical problems, unrelated to their assigned game, may have negatively influenced their ratings. Practical limitations relate to the presented analyses being based on the exploration of data from a completed study with a different purpose (to assess cognitive benefit). Much more can likely be learned in the future from studies designed specifically to understand older adults' long-term experiences with video games, including their perceptions of games and game training after extended game play, and human factors issues related to game play, using a more diverse set of video games.

Acknowledgements. We gratefully acknowledge support from the National Institute on Aging, Projects CREATE III and IV – Center for Research and Education on Aging and Technology Enhancement (www.create-center.org, NIA P01 AG017211). We are grateful to Nelson A. Roque for his assistance developing the online diary system used for this study.

References

1. Green, C.S., Bavelier, D.: Exercising your brain: a review of human brain plasticity and training-induced learning. Psychol. Aging **23**(4), 692–701 (2008)
2. Toril, P., Reales, J.M., Ballesteros, S.: Video game training enhances cognition of older adults: a meta-analytic study. Psychol. Aging **29**(3), 706–716 (2014)
3. Simons, D.J., et al.: Do "brain-training" programs work? Psychol. Sci. Publ. Interest **17**(3), 103–186 (2016)
4. Hamari, J., Koivisto, J., Sarsa, H.: Does gamification work? A literature review of empirical studies on gamification. In: 2014 47th Hawaii International Conference on System Sciences (HICSS), pp. 3025–3034. IEEE, January 2014
5. Loos, E.: Exergaming: meaningful play for older adults? In: Zhou, J., Salvendy, G. (eds.) ITAP 2017. LNCS, vol. 10298, pp. 254–265. Springer, Cham (2017). https://doi.org/10.1007/978-3-319-58536-9_21
6. Charness, N., Boot, W.R.: Aging and information technology use: potential and barriers. Curr. Dir. Psychol. Sci. **18**(5), 253–258 (2009)
7. Pew Fact Sheets. Fact sheets (2017). http://www.pewinternet.org/fact-sheet/
8. Brown, A.: Younger men play video games, but so do a diverse group of other Americans (2017). http://www.pewresearch.org/fact-tank/2017/09/11/younger-men-play-video-games-but-so-do-a-diverse-group-of-other-americans/
9. Anderson, M.: Technology device ownership: 2015 (2015). http://www.pewinternet.org/2015/10/29/technology-device-ownership-2015/
10. Brown, J.A.: Digital gaming perceptions among older adult non-gamers. In: Zhou, J., Salvendy, G. (eds.) ITAP 2017. LNCS, vol. 10298, pp. 217–227. Springer, Cham (2017). https://doi.org/10.1007/978-3-319-58536-9_18
11. De Schutter, B., Abeele, V.: Designing meaningful play within the psycho-social context of older adults. In: Proceedings of the 3rd International Conference on Fun and Games, pp. 84–93, September 2010
12. Quandt, T., Grueninger, H., Wimmer, J.: The gray haired gaming generation: findings from an explorative interview study on older computer gamers. Games Cult. **4**, 27–46 (2009)
13. Blocker, K.A., Wright, T.J., Boot, W.R.: Gaming preferences of aging generations. Gerontechnol. Int. J. Fundam. Aspects Technol. Serve Ageing Soc. **12**, 174–184 (2014)
14. De Schutter, B.: Never too old to play: the appeal of digital games to an older audience. Games Cult. **6**, 155–170 (2011)
15. Nap, H.H., de Kort, Y., IJsselsteijn, W.A.: Senior gamers: preferences, motivations and needs. Gerontechnology **8**, 247–262 (2009)
16. McKay, S.M., Maki, B.E.: Attitudes of older adults toward shooter video games: an initial study to select an acceptable game for training visual processing. Gerontechnol. Int. J. Fundam. Aspects Technol. Serve Ageing Soc. **9**, 5–17 (2010)
17. Pew Research Center. America's complex relationship with guns (2017). http://www.pewsocialtrends.org/wp-content/uploads/sites/3/2017/06/Guns-Report-FOR-WEBSITE-PDF-6-21.pdf
18. Czaja, S.J., Boot, W.R., Charness, N., Rogers, W.A.: Designing for Older Adults: Principles and Creative Human Factors Approaches, 3rd edn. CRC Press, Boca Raton (2019)
19. McLaughlin, A., Gandy, M., Allaire, J., Whitlock, L.: Putting fun into video games for older adults. Ergon. Des. **20**, 13–22 (2012)
20. Yoon, J.-S., et al.: Intervention comparative effectiveness for adult cognitive training (ICE-ACT) trial: rationale, design, and baseline characteristics. Contemp. Clin. Trials. **78**, 76 (2019)

21. Basak, C., Boot, W.R., Voss, M.W., Kramer, A.F.: Can training in a real-time strategy video game attenuate cognitive decline in older adults? Psychol. Aging **23**, 765–777 (2008)
22. Gamberini, L., Raya, M.A., Barresi, G., Fabregat, M., Ibanez, F., Prontu, L.: Cognition, technology and games for the elderly: an introduction to ELDERGAMES Project. Psychnology J. **4**(3), 285–308 (2006)
23. Belchior, P., Marsiske, M., Leite, W.L., Yam, A., Thomas, K., Mann, W.: Older adults' engagement during an intervention involving off-the-shelf videogame. Games Health J. **5**(3), 151–156 (2016)
24. de la Hera, T., Loos, E., Simons, M., Blom, J.: Benefits and factors influencing the design of intergenerational digital games: a systematic literature review. Societies **7**(3), 18 (2017)

THe Innovative Reminder in Senior-Focused Technology (THIRST)—Evaluation of Serious Games and Gadgets for Alzheimer Patients

Christian Eichhorn[1]($\boxtimes$), David A. Plecher[1], Martin Lurz[2], Nadja Leipold[2], Markus Böhm[2], Helmut Krcmar[2], Angela Ott[3], Dorothee Volkert[3], Atsushi Hiyama[4], and Gudrun Klinker[1]

[1] Chair for Computer Aided Medical Procedures and Augmented Reality, The Technical University of Munich, Munich, Germany
christian.eichhorn@tum.de,
{plecher,klinker}@in.tum.de
[2] Chair for Information Systems, The Technical University of Munich, Munich, Germany
{Martin.Lurz,Nadja.Leipold,Markus.Boehm,Krcmar}@in.tum.de
[3] Institute for Biomedicine of Aging, Friedrich-Alexander-Universität Erlangen-Nürnberg, Nürnberg, Germany
{Angela.Ott,Dorothee.Volkert}@fau.de
[4] INAMI.HIYAMA Laboratory, The University of Tokyo, Tokyo, Japan
Hiyama@star.rcast.u-tokyo.ac.jp

Abstract. We investigate the combination of a drinking gadget with *Serious Games*, designed to entice elderly/dementia patients to drink more water - with potential benefit for both, the elderlies and their caregivers. We present several strategies that are essential towards developing a *Combined Evaluation Process* needed to determine user acceptance. We report on a pilot study conducted in a retirement home with dementia patients. The goal was to gain first insights regarding the acceptance of such a technology from the viewpoint of the elderly and their caregivers.

Keywords: Dementia · Alzheimer patients · Serious Games · Gadgets for elderly · Drinking detection · Dehydration · Caregivers · Retirement home

1 Introduction

Low fluid intake is an important issue in the aging population. There are many reasons why elderly people do not drink enough – for instance because the sensation of thirst decreases with age [27]. Diseases such as dementia can increase the risk. Frequently, the result is a threatening and often overlooked state of dehydration, which is one of the most common reasons for elderly people to get

© Springer Nature Switzerland AG 2019
J. Zhou and G. Salvendy (Eds.): HCII 2019, LNCS 11593, pp. 135–154, 2019.
https://doi.org/10.1007/978-3-030-22015-0_11

hospitalized [21]. Reduced body functionality and impaired cognitive skills are some of the typical symptoms. The loss of over 15% of the water in the human body can lead to death.

In retirement homes, caregivers are responsible for many elderly people at once. They have to maintain detailed protocols of everyone's drinking habits. A system which tracks peoples' fluid intake automatically and which reminds them to drink would be of great benefit since it would reduce the administrative workload of the caregivers.

As part of the *enable* project [2], we have developed a drinking platform in the form of an inconspicuous beermat [22] for elderly people. The smart drinking gadget is wirelessly connected to an application on a mobile device which records how much a person has drunk. To stimulate a healthy amount of liquid intake, the application includes three *Serious Games* which generate drinking reminders in specified intervals. We have evaluated the system in a retirement home with dementia patients and their caregivers. To this end, we have developed a *Combined Evaluation Process* consisting of a combination of several essential evaluation strategies (short-term and long-term), as well as communication guidelines, structured into four levels. The focus lay on evaluating the gadget and application for both major user groups, the elderly/dementia patients and the caregivers. We also discuss the results of the pilot study based on the drinking data protocols and on the caregivers' opinions.

2   User-Centered Design (UCD) Approach

Applications are only useful and have a chance to be accepted when software validation aspects and design guidelines have been balanced and validated. In this respect, *usefulness* means that there is a benefit for the user towards achieving a particular goal. It should not be mistaken for good *usability*, which stands for an easy and pleasant user experience [15]. To achieve both, Holzinger and Errath [15] and researchers such as Queirós et al. [23] and Albaina et al. [7] recommend a *User-Centred Design (UCD)* approach, which focuses heavily on the end user. In the context of mobile app development, this approach consists of three phases [15]:

1. **Investigation and observation of the end-user:** To gain insights into the real-life workflows with the goal to detect benefiting elements when using applications.
2. **Paper mock-ups:** Going into detail for the workflow and parts of the application.
3. **Evaluations:** Testing the developed solution with cost-effective prototypes and iterative approaches to optimize the result [18]. In the process, user interactions with the application can be constantly improved [23].

3   Evaluation Strategies in the Context of Elderly and Dementia Patients

To evaluate a gadget and *Serious Games* for elderly people, we researched various directions of related literature to gain a better understanding of the user groups.

3.1   The Questionnaire—Evaluation Method of Choice

Stöber et al. [24] are describing guidelines for the development of questionnaires in the field of elderly people. It is important to incorporate the scientific quality criteria *objectivity*, *reliability* and *validity*. The questionnaire should start with a small instruction. On top of that, simple questions targeting previous experiences with the device should be incorporated. When formulating questions, two types of items are recommended: asking questions to discover issues (e.g. "How often are you using mobile devices?") or assertions to see the reactions (e.g. "The usage of the app is fun."). While an assertion ends with a fixed set of answers (e.g. applies, doesn't apply), normal questions can be either open-ended or closed. Stöber et al. [24] recommend closed questions when targeting the elderly to avoid receiving potentially unfinished or too short answers. A question should only contain one topic and generalizations e.g. all, always etc. and causal subordinate clauses should be avoided. Andersen et al. [8] point out that, in contrast to interviews, questionnaires can avoid the introduction of irrelevant topics. They used a two-step approach, where they first let the person rate their extent of emotion for a given topic and then investigated with other questions, why the person rated like that. On top of that, interviews and group questionnaires for the two-step approach were used.

Several standardized questionnaires have been developed for the clinical environment. The *Short Form Survey* [6] specifically focuses on the measurement of the life quality of patients. The SF-36 version is designed for being used e.g. in small-scale treatment evaluations. It takes only 5–10 min to be completed and can be used to determine each individual improvement of the life quality of a person.

3.2   Evaluation and Communication Guidelines when Communicating with Dementia Patients

When Alzheimer's disease (the most common form of dementia) progresses, communication deteriorates. Tappen et al. [25] have researched communication techniques with Alzheimer patients.

One of the most important ways of talking to patients is to use open-ended questions (asking about experiences, opinions or descriptions). This enables the Alzheimer patient to build up a relationship with the asking person and to tell more about themselves, which of course benefits the understanding of the patient's experiences and opinions. Tappen et al. [25] could clearly identify longer answers when using open-ended or mixed questions in the form of an open-ended question followed up by a closed one (only yes or no answers). The answers were richer with important content and insights [4].

When a foundation (e.g. familiar environment) for the conversation is established, more specific questions can be asked. In general, the five *Ws* (Who, Where, What, When, Why) are a good start. They are easy to understand since the direction of the question mentioned at the beginning of the sentence.

Furthermore, eye contact is important to indicate interest [1]. It is difficult to ask personal relevant questions, e.g. about the patients' illness, life in the nursing home or family members. There are a lot of traps even asking simple questions like "How are you today?" because this can lead into depressed answers about being not well or missing family members. When confusion or frustration takes over, arguing should be avoided, instead the subject should be changed to keep the person interested [4,5].

There are multiple approaches to improve communication and to talk about feelings [25]:

- **Broad openings:** Open-ended questions which encourage response. This approach counters anger, which can be experienced when asking detailed questions.
- **Speaking as equals:** Being open to learn from the person with the development of a partnership in mind where both are equally valued without a hierarchy.
- **Establishing commonalities:** Discussing and sharing of interests and perceptions to find commonalities.
- **Sharing of self:** Talking about own feelings or relating to what the patient had contributed to the conversation.
- **Maintaining the conversation:** Finding a striking topic at the beginning to start a conversation and then connecting consecutive thoughts (avoiding topic changes by the Alzheimer person).

Another helping approach could be the usage of gestures or visual cues, e.g. pointing at the toilet instead of asking [5]. These cues can also work as a memory aid. Bringing memories back, e.g. the day of the proposal or marriage, can help to start a conversation. Alzheimer patients still remember small details and *come back alive* [3,4].

Overall the recommendations suggest avoiding closed questions, when trying to establish a relationship. Showing emotions is useful, but the emotions should not dictate the conversation. They are needed to let the Alzheimer person understand the feelings and possible concerns of the talking person to gain acceptance [1]. Support can be established by encouragement in verbal and nonverbal ways, reflection or summarization. But there are limitations in the research in the direction of communication with late stage Alzheimer people [1,25].

4   Evaluation Process for Caregivers

Gaining insights from care staff can be a challenge. A lot of important details are hidden in small daily activities. For that reason, it is useful to utilize specific strategies with a focus on real-world situations and problem statements.

4.1   Naturalistic Enactment

Castro et al. [9] detected the problem with human interface evaluation for widely used techniques such as *Controlled Experiments* and *Heuristic Evaluation*. For them these approaches and their artificial environments missed the "[...] contextual conditions in which applications are used" [9, p. 371]. This problem is even more severe for mobile platforms/gadgets, which in contrast to the PC, will be used in different locations and under different conditions. There is no way around using a real-life scenario with "exposure" to technology and app content, to detect potential difficulties not only with the application, but also the devices and platforms used [9,15].

For that reason, Castro et al. [9] used the auxiliary technique called *Naturalistic Enactment* to evaluate an assistive mobile application for nurses. Their approach contains two parts, first the *Naturalistic Enactment*. This includes an *in-situ evaluation* with a combination of a controlled setting and a high *ecological validity*, which contains the integration of real users and scenarios in their environment. Secondly, a *posterior data collection* and *investigation*. While a controlled experiment focuses on speed, efficiency and effectiveness, the *Naturalistic Enactment* focuses on situations occurring when the application is used in a real scenario. Castro et al. [9] had the goal to bring structure in the interaction and diagnosis between nurses and patients. To start early with an end-user focus, Eysenbach [13] conducted a survey of different features for a mobile application and the importance of these features rated by *eHealth* experts. This strengthened the development process and the subsequent evaluation process with a pronounced focus on real life scenarios.

4.2   Focus Interviews

Focus Interviews are another important way to gain knowledge from caregivers. Hopf [16] describes focus interviews as one of the best ways to get expert knowledge. They are much more suited for gaining insights into activity alternatives or self-interpretations than e.g. questionnaires. In questionnaires people tend to rate elements only in the middle of the rating spectrum, leading to bias and often unusable results. Also losing focus can be better avoided with an interview than with a questionnaire [8].

Hopf [16] described several different types of interviews, such as the *Structure Interview* which is mostly predefined by the creator of the interview or the *Clinical Interview* which focuses on the diagnoses and condition of a disease. Yet, the two main methods of choice are *Focus interviews* and *Narrative Interviews*. While a narrative interview gives the interviewee a lot of freedom to guide the conversation in certain directions, phases of life and memories by only asking one initial question, it is not suited to ask specific questions about a gadget or application. Focus interviews are much more useful in such a scenario. They have a predefined conversation topic with the goal to collect reactions and interpretations from the expert to a certain topic and to maximize the spread of topics in the given area of the interview to gain more insights from the interviewee.

Four criteria need to be considered:

1. **Range:** The interviewee must be able to react and to introduce new aspects.
2. **Specificity:** The interview needs to cover concrete focus points.
3. **Depth:** The interviewees should be able to set own focus points with their individual opinions and interests.
4. **Personal context:** It is important to understand from which context the interviewee answers the questions.

For Hopf [16] it is important to select qualified personnel with deep understanding of the topic of the interview.

5   A Combined Evaluation Process

We have created an evaluation process for application scenarios involving a combination of hardware (gadget) and software (*Serious Games*) for two major user groups, the elderly/dementia patients and the caregivers in a retirement home. It is illustrated in Fig. 1.

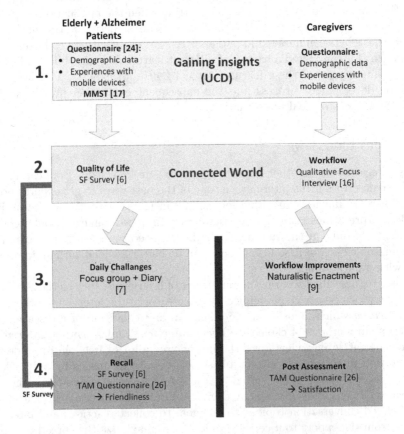

Fig. 1. The four levels of the *Combined Evaluation Process*

5.1   First Level – Gaining Insights

The goal of the first level is to obtain knowledge about the patients by using a basic questionnaire [24] with the focus on demographic data, previous experiences with mobile devices and the openness in general for modern technology (open-ended questions with closed ones as follow-ups [25]). If the questioned target group faces a common disease, it is important to measure the state of the disease with e.g. the *Mini Mental Status Test* (*MMST*) [14] to gain early insights regarding possible candidates for the study.

A second questionnaire covers demographic data of the caregivers. Additionally, previous experiences with mobile devices, with respect to their work, can be included such that an introduction can be prepared for those who are not used to the technology. The main goal is to get a basic understanding of the people and their daily challenges, especially when working with e.g. dementia patients and to establish some early relationships with them. This level is inspired by the *UCD* approach, where the early investigation and observation of the end-user is important [15].

5.2   Second Level – A Connected World

To obtain a deeper understanding of the daily routines and challenges faced by the different target groups, it is important to see the situations as a *connected flow*, rather than as independent user groups and their issues. This is essential for a gadget/application that tries to connect the elderly, dementia patients and caregivers and wants to feature advantages for all the users. To measure quality of life improvements, specific questionnaires, such as the *Short Form Survey* [6] have been created. They are typically based on a *Measurement* at the beginning and a *Recall* at the end of the evaluation.

To replace pencil and paper for recording the drinking intake, it is important to understand opportunities and limitations of the drinking gadget and the games. We use the guidelines of Hopf [16] for a qualitative focus interviews with the caregivers. The goal of the interviews is to get early feedback (reactions and interpretations) about the gadget/application to further plan the next steps and counter potential design flaws.

5.3   Third Level – Long-Term Evaluation Strategies

After establishing the first contacts and gaining insights into the connected workflow of the user groups, we test the gadget/application in a more long-term oriented evaluation. While the *First* and *Second Level* are more a combined approach for the elderly and caregivers together (see "connected" world), the *Third Level* focuses heavily on the individual user groups with the help of specialized, long-term evaluation methods.

For the caregivers, we use the *Naturalistic Enactment* approach by Castro et al. [9]. We create use cases to better understand the influence of our app (combination of hardware and software) in a specific situations in a natural environment. This gives insights into exceptional situations, which would otherwise not occur frequently. Of course, in a long-term evaluation not all use cases have to arranged, most of the situations occur naturally, enhancing the evaluation quality. Nevertheless, with a limited time frame, it is useful to intentionally play through some situations by simulating the behavior of elderly people with experienced caregivers.

For the elderly target group, a combination of multiple group sessions and a documentation of events allows to obtain a wide range of insights:

- **Focus Group:** The usage of *Focus Groups* is helpful because of the living arrangements of retirement homes, where elderly people come together in small groups and e.g. watch television or participate in small games.
- **Diary:** Another approach is to see how the elderly react to the app on a daily basis and document their behavior and thoughts in a diary such as suggested by Albaina et al. [7]. In their post-intervention step after the intensive testing and usage of the app, they used the persuasive *Technology Acceptance Model* questionnaire designed for detecting the usefulness, ease-of-use and acceptance of an app.

5.4 Fourth Level – Post Assessment After the Intervention

After the intervention period, the elderly fill out the *Short Form Survey* (long-term strategy) again as recall. Then the score is compared to their initial one to analyze improvements for the individual sections of life quality.

The conclusive perceived user friendliness of the app (perceived ease of use *PEOU*) by the elderly and caregivers' satisfaction (perceived usefulness *(PU)*) is evaluated by using the *Technology Acceptance Model* questionnaire [26].

6   Hardware

We have developed a succession of drinking gadgets for the elderly [22]. This included different design strategies, such as extending an existing cup with technology or to add features to existing smart cups. The design process went hand in hand with experimenting with different sensor strategies to measure the liquid volume in a glass or cup, such as using movable objects in the liquid, distance measurement, utilizing liquid features and weight measurement. In the process we collected important feedback and finally choose a weight measurement approach.

The final gadget imitates a traditional beermat. It fulfills three major requirements (see Fig. 2):

- **Hygiene:** A drinking glass that is used on a daily basis needs to be dishwasher safe. From previous project results and experiences of e.g. Kreutzer et al. [19], we consider it important that the sensor has no contact with the cleansing liquid. Sensors inside the liquid, such as electrodes, are a risk factor for mold and deposits. Furthermore, designing a cup with integrated sensors to be dishwater safe is difficult [20].

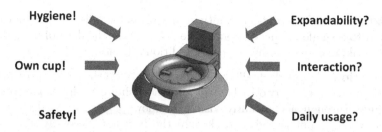

Fig. 2. Requirements for the drinking platform and additional challenges

- **Own cup:** In most cases elderly people prefer their own, existing drinking cups over prescribed ones. A common reason for such preference is stigmatization, e.g. when using a plastic cup over a regular one. Therefore, we selected a design which incorporates existing drink glasses/cups for a natural solution.
- **Safety:** Movable-objects in the liquid (e.g. a swimmer) are not suitable because parts could accidentally be swallowed. Furthermore, the solution should add no additional risk of dropping the glass, e.g. due to a slippery grip around the glass.

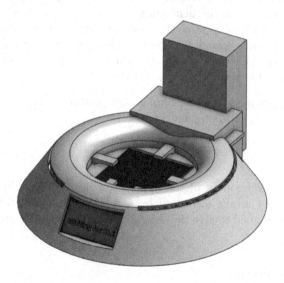

Fig. 3. CAD model with components

Our chosen solution was to take a weight measuring approach with a Force Sensing Resistor (FSR) in the form of a station which looks like an inconspicuous beermat (see Fig. 3). One platform is assigned to each patient, collecting data about their liquid intake over the day. As long as the glass stays the same, the weight loss or gain corresponds to the amount of liquid drunk by the person without the need of calibration. Multiple platforms for different people can be connected to a single mobile computing device to store the data of all gadgets.

The drinking gadget addresses three additional topics:

- **Interaction:** The gadget allows an interactive experience in two respects. Firstly, we integrated two LED stripes to show simplistic light patterns. For example, through a constantly visible rainbow pattern the elderly person is reminded to put the glass back onto the beermat. Secondly, the gadget incorporates a novel kind of interaction with the *Serious Games*, controlled by the elderly person. Drinking notifications appear, reminding the person to drink some water. The gadget then acts as control element, causing the notification to disappear when something has been drunk. The interrupted *Game Flow* [10] caused by the drink notifications acts as an incentive for the elderly.
- **Expandability:** Based on the Arduino platform with the open nature of its Bluetooth implementation, it is possible to integrate the gadget flexibly into various serious games, i.e., it is possible to expand the functionality to novel games and apps beyond the predefined one. This issue of flexibility and changeability is often overlooked in commercially available smart cups, rendering them unadaptable to novel application ideas.
- **Daily usage:** Based on previously acquired knowledge regarding the routines of the caregivers in a retirement home [11], we chose to integrate a display into the gadget which can show the caregivers status information. It can also act such that a clear association between gadgets and elderlies exists. This alleviates the need for work procedures, such as having to replace all drinking glasses on the table regularly.

In the next step we developed an application platform which builds upon the specific features of the drinking gadget.

7   Software

The management component of the application incorporates the functionality to record the liquid intake measured by a drinking gadget. Furthermore, the application was designed to give the elderly person the opportunity to play three games [11].

7.1   Serious Games

We have developed three games for dementia patients, utilizing game concepts and mechanics which focus on cognitive training:

- **Balloon game:** A simplistic game focusing on reaction time. It teaches elderly persons how to interact with the touchscreen. The player is encouraged to touch balloons of various colours and sizes, causing them to explode. Aside from familiarizing the person with the touchscreen, this concept has the goal to train the reaction speed (see Fig. 4a).

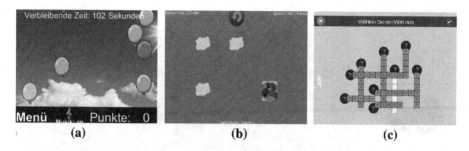

Fig. 4. (a) Balloon game (b) Pairwise matching game (c) Crossword game

- **Pairwise matching game:** A game focusing on memory training. The player has to find similar pairs of items (see Fig. 4b). Three levels of difficulty have been integrated: (a) matching pictures, (b) matching textual object descriptions and (c) matching a mixture of both. The combination of text and picture types helps elderly people to train and associate different areas in the brain.
- **Crossword quiz:** The player has to find answers to various questions based on a topic (see Fig. 4c). A game focusing on cognitive thinking and knowledge. Answers can be typed in with a senior-friendly keyboard [11]. This is the most complex game. If typing the answer is too difficult for the person, it may be played with support by a caregiver hired for mental training. It is also very suitable for group settings when several elderly people are sitting in the common room. The entire group can then be included in the game, increasing the collaborative experience.

Drinking reminders are incorporated in all three games, with the goal to motivate liquid intake. The app interacts with the smart drinking gadget via Bluetooth to transmit and receive information. The total consumed drinking volume can be calculated from the decreasing weight measurements and sent to the database for further evaluation. For this purpose, the caregivers have to create a profile for each person such that the individual drinking volume can be profiled over time.

7.2   Architecture

The system architecture is composed of three different components: the gadget, the application and the database (see Fig. 5). The database is stored at the mobile computing device. It includes information about the user in one table. A second table protocols the measured drinking volumes.

The elderly people are able to drink anytime, independently of the drink reminders which appear every 5 min when playing one of the serious games. If the person has recently drunk from the cup/glass, the notification is shown only shortly. If this is not the case, the notification will block the user from playing until something has been drunk (detected by a weight difference). If the current weight increases above a certain threshold, the application concludes that somebody has refilled the drinking glass.

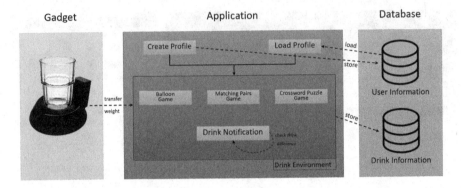

Fig. 5. System architecture: interaction between all components.

8   System Evaluation Method

8.1   Experiment Design and Recruitment Strategy

We conducted a small intervention study at an elderly home in Munich, Germany. For this first pilot study we selected residents (women and men) identified to have a potential danger of dehydration. Additionally, each of the subjects was required to be responsive, not acutely ill, not in the terminal phase of life (definition according to the clinical frailty scale), able to see, able to drink independently and able to provide consent by herself/himself in order to be included in the study. As the overall usefulness and usability in elderly homes was part of the research aim, experience in the use of tablet computers was no inclusion criteria.

To gain additional insights from the caregivers' perspective, we selected a group of caregivers. It consisted of women and men who worked at the ward of the included residents. They had to provide consent and work during the time of the study intervention.

During the entire intervention, at least one researcher was present, ensuring correct execution of the study and offering support in case of technical difficulties.

8.2   Assessment

The first visit served as an information event for the participants. We provided detailed information regarding the study procedures and each participant signed written consent. We conducted the baseline assessment for the residents. It included demographic data (age and gender), the German translation [17] of the *Mini Mental Status Test* (*MMST*) [14], as well as a short questionnaire concerning each elderlie's self-appreciation of their drinking habit as well as their self-perceived computer anxiety *(CANX)* (see Table 1). This part of the pilot study represents the *First Level* of the *Combined Evaluation Process* (see Fig. 1).

For the *Second* and *Third Level*, we visited the elderly home regularly during our evaluation period (depending on flexibility in the elderly home). When time of the caregivers was available, we conducted several spontaneous qualitative *Focus Interviews*. The drinking application and games were being used in the common room with the elderly people of the test group and their caregivers. The chosen group of participants can be seen as a small *Focus Group* and we wrote down notes as diary (*Third Level*).

At the post assessment after the intervention period (*Fourth Level*), the caregivers' satisfaction and the impression on the user friendliness of the application were evaluated using the *Technology Acceptance Model* (*TAM*) [26]. This assessment focused on perceived usefulness *s(PU)*, perceived ease of use *(PEOU)*, computer self-efficacy *(CSE)*, computer anxiety *(CANX)*, perception of external control *(PEC)*, job relevance *(REL)* and behavioral intention *(BI)*, each of which were measured on a five-point Likert scale.

Table 1. Assessment instruments, target group and measurement times. 1: Conducted during the baseline assessment; 2: Conducted during the post assessment

Assessment	Instrument	Residents	Carers
Demographics data		X^1	X^2
Mini mental status test	MMST	X^1	-
Drinking habits		X^1	-
Computer anxiety	CANX	X^1	X^2
Perceived usefulness	PU	-	X^2
Perceived ease of use	PEOU	-	X^2
Computer self-efficacy	CSE	-	X^2
Computer anxiety	CANX	-	X^2
Perception of external control	PEC	-	X^2
Job relevance	REL	-	X^2
Behavioural intention	BI	-	X^2

9   Results

9.1   Sample Description

At the beginning of the pilot study (*First Level* of the *Combined Evaluation Process*), we collected basic demographic and person specific data to gain a good understanding of our target group. A total of 5 residents (R1–R5) and 5 caregivers (C1–C5) were included. The residents' age ranged from 82 to 95 years. Two individuals were males and three were females. All residents lived in the dementia ward of the retirement home and suffered from moderate (14–18 points) dementia (majority had Alzheimer's disease) with only one participant scoring over 19 points (R2, mild cognitive impairment) while the lowest result was 14 points (R3). Participants had most difficulties with the questions of Part A (Orientation), Part D (Memory) and the drawing part in section D (Language). Three of the five participants (R1, R3, R5) stated, that they thought they drank enough every day and estimated the required amount to be 0.5 to 1 liter. Furthermore, two of the inhabitants stated during the *CANX* questions, that they were afraid of working with computers (R3, R4).

The age of the caregivers (four females, one male) ranged from 25 to 56 years. Two of them were responsible for the supervision of the residents and the preparation of the entertainment program (C1, C3), two of them were trained caregivers (C2, C5) and one of them was a caregiver in training (C4) (Table 2).

Table 2. Description of participants.

Variable	Residents	Carers
Age	88 (8.5)	43.6 (12.4)
MMST	17.2 (2.6)	-
CANX	2.6 (2.2)	-

9.2   Descriptive Analysis

Due to the small number of participants and the lack of a control group, we did not conduct a statistical analysis. Instead, we conducted a descriptive analysis to explore the results of the pilot study.

Acceptance of the Intervention by the Residents: As the residents suffered from moderate dementia, they were mostly not able to play the provided games by themselves, as they were not able to remember how to navigate through the application's menu or how to play the different games. Nevertheless, they were often open and motivated to play the games as long as a supervisor was sitting next to them to help during difficult phases. During the final assessment all participants stated that they enjoyed the game and that they would like to play them again.

Performance on Drinking Behaviour: We used the difference between single measurements of fluid intake to determine a reliable value of the fluid intake of the participants.

As the residents required constant supervision for the gameplay and since only one to two supervisors were in the retirement home at the same time, it was not possible to gain consistent overall values of the six intervention days from each participant. Furthermore, the residents were not motivated to the same degree every day and thus sometimes did not want to play with the system at all or only for a very limited time. In order to be able to see possible effects on the drinking behaviour of a user, we excluded all sessions which took less than 15 min from the final evaluation. As R3 never wanted to play the games for longer than 15 min at a time, no fluid intake tracking data was included from R3 in the final data evaluation. Nevertheless, we were able to analyze the reaction to the games and gain feedback from R3 during the post interviews at the end of the intervention period. Overall, we included five measuring sessions in the evaluation of the pilot study, of which two sessions were conducted by R2 as shown in Fig. 6.

The participants used the system for more than 280 min in total and consumed a good 400 milliliters per hour of use with an average of 11 drinking actions. About 37 mL were consumed each time with a standard deviation of 37,65. This shows the huge range of drinking amounts, as also visualized in Fig. 7. It ranged from less than 10 mL to over 150 mL, occurring once when R5 emptied the entire glass.

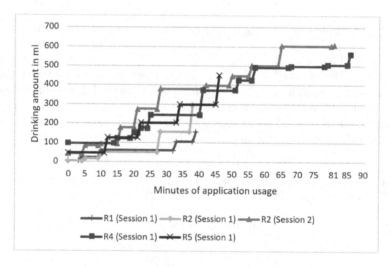

Fig. 6. Drinking amount over time for each resident (R).

Perception of the System by the Caregivers: After the intervention period, the participating caregivers were asked to fill out the *TAM* [26] questionnaire (*Fourth Level* with focus only on the caregiver side). The scores of *PU* indicate that the caregivers had a positive perception of the usefulness of the app, as shown in Table 3. None rated the usefulness with a score lower than 4. The usefulness was rated even higher with only two ratings lower than five (C3, C5 - 40%) and 4.5 being the lowest value. The values for *CSE* were a bit lower, due to the rating of CS4 who gained an end result for *CSE* of 2.0, while the rest of the caretakers rated their *CSE* as at least 4.25. Nevertheless, none of the participants perceived any general negative feelings towards digital devices, as shown through the low *CANX* value. As *CANX* measures the amount of anxiety towards computers and similar systems, low ratings (i.e., low levels of anxiety) are perceived as positive

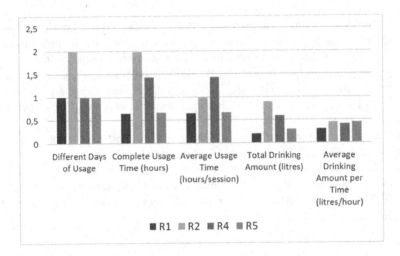

Fig. 7. Collected data during the intervention session in the elderly home

in this study. *PEC* is rated on the lower positive side at 3.5 to 4.25 with half of the rating being lower than 4. Although *REL* was perceived quite well, C5 rated it lower than 4. Nevertheless, all caregivers would like to use the system again as shown by the very good *BI* ratings with 4.3 being the lowest rating and by 3 caregivers (60%) 5.0 being the maximum.

Table 3. Mean and standard deviation of the TAM variables, assessed from the caregivers. 1: Not filled by C4 and C5; 2: Not filled by C2

Instrument	Visit 2
	M (SD)
PU	4.4 (0.5)[1]
PEOU	4.9 (0.2)
CSE	3.85 (1.0)
CANX	1.0 (0.0)
PEC	3.9 (0.3)[2]
REL	4.1 (0.6)
BI	4.8 (0.3)

10   Discussion

Through the pilot study we could collect some important insights:

- The dementia patients needed constant supervision and did not take the initiative to play by themselves. It is uncertain, if the behavior would change, if they are left alone with the option to play the games for a more prolonged time period. Nevertheless, if given the opportunity to play with the supervisors and caregivers, the interest of them in the serious games was quite high and they enjoyed themselves in most cases.
- As measured through the gadget, a healthy amount of around 400 milliliters per hour, equals 2 standard drinking glasses, has been drunk when playing. As trigger the drinking notifications were quite successful and the elderly responded to them reliably. No participant declined to drink when the application asked for it.
- The gadget was accepted by the elderly and we didn't observe any form of resentment or fear towards it. Some of them were quite interested in the blinking new technology on the table. While others simply accepted it's existence as a type of beermat (as intended by us) to put their drinking glass on.
- The feedback by the caregivers was positive and interest for the technology quite high. The low *REL* rating of C5 can be maybe pointing towards the missing digital drinking protocol. Therefore, giving us the feedback to extend the offered features for the caregivers in the future to provide advantages for both major user groups.

Overall we were pleased with our observations during the short intervention time.

11   Limitations

The pilot study included a small user group, where each individual was accompanied for around 1.5 hours per day by a supervisor. This is a typical example of a short-term evaluation. In relation to the *Combined Evaluation Process*, we limited the scope mainly to the first two levels. Therefore, excluding the *SF Survey*) and long-term oriented strategies for the caregivers from the *Third Level*, e.g. *Naturalistic Enactment*. Instead we included the post assessment (based on the *Fourth Level*) with the *TAM* questionnaire [26] to collect the caregivers' opinions.

12   Future Work

With a successful pilot study at hand, we want to start planning for future focus points of the project. This involves further gadget and application development, as well as refining our evaluation process:

- **Gadget improvements:** We plan to create a refined version of the described drinking gadget, which we will use for an extended evaluation with our project partners at FAU [22]. We will work on some design details of the overall appearance and daily usability of the gadget.

- **Drinking notification strategies:** One important result of the pilot study, was the missing initiative of the elderly to interact with the application. To solve this issue, we will have to find approaches to integrate the drinking notifications in the daily life of the elderly, which doesn't require constant supervision. We are currently working on a microcontroller gadget with an application to include notifications in the TV program of the elderly. Furthermore, a reminder application has been developed for the iPad with a specific design language for the elderly and Alzheimer patients [12].
- **Long-term evaluation with the Elderly/Alzheimer patients:** This is necessary to see what aspects are changing when the elderly are not supervised. For example, how many drinking notifications will be accepted over a longer time period by using various strategies, e.g. TV, reminder app. Another aspect would be to assess the life quality of the elderly when using the gadget and application with the *SF Survey*. This could give insights on the benefit of the *Serious Games*, as well as actual health improvements on the basis of the additional water intake.
- **Caregiver features:** To be able to include the caregivers as a major target group in future studies, we will consider aspects found in this evaluation, which suggest a need for a deeper focus on workflow improvements. For that reason, a digital drinking protocol to monitor the liquid intake with an informative user interface, including e.g. charts for visualization, will be implemented.
- **Long-term evaluation with the caregivers:** To develop benefitting features for the caregivers, a *UCD* approach by constantly gathering feedback is necessary. This includes *Focus Interviews* and the *Naturalistic Enactment* strategy, which is suited to evaluate the application with the help of scenarios and use cases.

13   Conclusion

After developing a smart drinking gadget for the elderly and dementia patients [22], we focused on a mobile device application with *Serious Games*. Our goal is to motivate the usage of modern technology through fun engagements and to stimulate a healthy liquid intake. With a working system architecture consisting out of the gadget, drinking notifications (included in the *Serious Game* application) and a working online database to store the liquid intake data, we shifted our attention towards a *Combined Evaluation Process*. It contains best practices from the literature to evaluate both major user groups, the elderly/dementia patients and their caregivers in a retirement home. The resulting process combines typical short-term assessment approaches and long-term oriented evaluation strategies for both groups. In our pilot study we had to act opportunistic to gain first results with the limited available time and mood changes of the dementia patients. Therefore, we could only identify some basic trends. But most importantly, we could show the feasibility of combining a drinking gadget with *Serious Games* with a healthy amount of liquid intake per hour during the intervention time, the acceptance of the gadget and drinking notifications. This opens the way for a future extension of the gadget and application to replace handwritten drinking protocols with a smart, automated and digital solution for the caregivers.

Acknowledgments. The preparation of this paper was supported by the enable cluster and is catalogued by the enable steering committee as enable 36 (http://enable-cluster.de). This work was funded by a grant of the German Ministry for Education and Research (BMBF) FK 01EA1409H.

The 3D shape has been designed in Onshape (https://www.onshape.com) with an Education license. Thank you to the support team for the permission to publish it. Thank you to the developer team of PDF3D (https://www.pdf3d.com) who made the interactive experience with the 3D model possible.

References

1. Alzheimer Society (2011). https://bit.ly/2NlN1XX. Accessed 26 Nov 2018
2. Enable Cluster. http://www.enable-cluster.de/. Accessed 26 Nov 2018
3. Fisher Center (2016). https://bit.ly/2Sa7tvn. Accessed 26 Nov 2018
4. Home instead (2016). https://bit.ly/2tsfpOD. Accessed 26 Nov 2018
5. Mayo Clinic (2016). https://mayocl.in/2GR1WI5. Accessed 26 Nov 2018
6. Short Form Questionnaire. https://www.rand.org/health-care/surveys_tools/mos/36-item-short-form.html. Accessed 26 Nov 2018
7. Albaina, I.M., Visser, T., Van Der Mast, C.A., Vastenburg, M.H.: Flowie: a persuasive virtual coach to motivate elderly individuals to walk. In: 2009 3rd International Conference on Pervasive Computing Technologies for Healthcare, pp. 1–7. IEEE (2009)
8. Andersen, C.L., Gudmundsson, H.P., Achiche, S., Boelskifte, P.: Challenges and limitations of applying an emotion-driven design approach on elderly users. In: ICED 11–18th International Conference on Engineering Design - Impacting Society Through Engineering Design (2011)
9. Castro, L.A., Favela, J., García-Peña, C.: Naturalistic enactment to stimulate user experience for the evaluation of a mobile elderly care application (2011)
10. Csikszentmihalyi, M.: Finding Flow: The Psychology of Engagement with Everyday Life. Basic Books, New York (1997)
11. Eichhorn, C., et al.: Innovative game concepts for Alzheimer patients. In: Zhou, J., Salvendy, G. (eds.) ITAP 2018. LNCS, vol. 10927, pp. 526–545. Springer, Cham (2018). https://doi.org/10.1007/978-3-319-92037-5_37
12. Eichhorn, C., et al.: Motivation and design guidelines focusing on mobile app development for elderly and Alzheimer patients in the area of healthcare management. ACM Trans. Accessible Comput. (TACCESS) (2019, in submission)
13. Eysenbach, G., CONSORT-EHEALTH Group: CONSORT-EHEALTH: improving and standardizing evaluation reports of web-based and mobile health interventions. J. Med. Internet Res. 13, e126 (2011)
14. Folstein, M.: A practical method for grading the cognitive state of patients for the children. J. Psychiatr. Res. **12**, 189–198 (1975)
15. Holzinger, A., Errath, M.: Mobile computer web-application design in medicine: some research based guidelines (2007)

16. Hopf, C.: Qualitative interviews: an overview. In: A Companion to QUALITATIVE RESEARCH (2004)
17. Kessler, J., Markowitsch, H., Denzler, P.: Mini-mental-status-test (MMST). Beltz Test GMBH 24, Göttingen (2000)
18. Kobayashi, M., Hiyama, A., Miura, T., Asakawa, C., Hirose, M., Ifukube, T.: Elderly user evaluation of mobile touchscreen interactions. In: Campos, P., Graham, N., Jorge, J., Nunes, N., Palanque, P., Winckler, M. (eds.) INTERACT 2011. LNCS, vol. 6946, pp. 83–99. Springer, Heidelberg (2011). https://doi.org/10.1007/978-3-642-23774-4_9
19. Kreutzer, J.F., Flaschberger, J., Hein, C.M., Lueth, T.C.: Capacitive detection of filling levels in a cup. In: 2016 IEEE 13th International Conference on Wearable and Implantable Body Sensor Networks (BSN), pp. 31–36. IEEE (2016)
20. Kreutzer, J.F., Ramesberger, S., Reimer, S.M., Entsfellner, K., Lueth, T.C.: Automatically detecting fluid intake using conductivity measurements of beverages in a cup. In: 2015 IEEE International Conference on Automation Science and Engineering (CASE), pp. 1546–1551. IEEE (2015)
21. Lehman, S., Graves, J., Mcaleer, C., Giovannetti, T., Tan, C.C.: A mobile augmented reality game to encourage hydration in the elderly. In: Yamamoto, S., Mori, H. (eds.) HIMI 2018. LNCS, vol. 10905, pp. 98–107. Springer, Cham (2018). https://doi.org/10.1007/978-3-319-92046-7_9
22. Plecher, D.A., et al.: Interactive drinking gadget for the elderly and Alzheimer patients. In: Zhou, J., Salvendy, G. (eds.) HCII 2019. LNCS, vol. 11592, Part II, pp. 444–463 (2019)
23. Queirós, A., et al.: ICF inspired personas to improve development for usability and accessibility in ambient assisted living. Procedia Comput. Sci. 27, 409 (2013)
24. Stöber, C., Williger, B., Meerkamm, H., Lang, F.: Leitfaden für die alternsgerechte produktentwicklung. Fraunhoferverlag Stuttgart (2012)
25. Tappen, R.M., Williams-Burgess, C., Edelstein, J., Touhy, T., Fishman, S.: Communicating with individuals with Alzheimer's disease: examination of recommended strategies. Arch. Psychiatr. Nurs. 11, 249 (1997)
26. Venkatesh, V., Bala, H.: Technology acceptance model 3 and a research agenda on interventions. Decis. Sci. 39(2), 273–315 (2008)
27. Volkert, D., Kreuel, K., Stehle, P.: Fluid intake of community-living, independent elderly in Germany-a nationwide, representative study. J. Nutr. Health Aging 9(5), 305–309 (2005)

Study on Baby Toy Design—From the Perspective of Audio-Visual Human Factors

Kuo-Liang Huang[1](✉), Wei Lin[2], Chia-Chen Lu[3],
and Yong-Sheng Pi[1]

[1] Department of Industrial Design, Design Academy,
Sichuan Fine Arts Institute, Chongqing, China
shashi@scfai.edu.cn, 361689378@qq.com
[2] School of Architecture, Feng Chia University, Taichung, Taiwan (R.O.C.)
wlin@fcu.edu.tw
[3] Department of Industrial Design, Tunghai University,
Taichung, Taiwan (R.O.C.)
cclu@thu.edu.tw

Abstract. Toys are partners that accompany children's growth and are indispensables that comfort children and promote their mental development. Since babies' physiology and psychology experience rapid development in babyhood (0–18 months). From the perspective of toy design and intellectual education, how to provide appropriate toys for stimulation according to perception and motor development is very important. However, it can be seen from the current toy design practice that most relevant design studies are only for school-age children; there are few studies on baby toy design. The objectives of this study are to ensure that baby toy design is based on academic and theoretical basis and make the design more rigorous to have more positive value to the physical and mental development of babies. Therefore, this study takes intelligent toy design as the viewpoint to conduct study on homologous visual and auditory human factors in babyhood and provide relevant data on human factor to achieve useful and effective design. Since the babies in this study are not yet mature in mind and body, there are a lot of limitations compared with general study objects. Therefore, this study adopts document analysis and expert interviews to study on human factors for baby toy design. The results obtained the following data on babyhood: (1) physical development process at different stages; (2) features of visual ability development at different stages; (3) features of auditory ability development at different stages; and (4) policies and suggestions for toy design for different stages.

Keywords: Educational toys · Toy design · Baby human factors

J. Zhou and G. Salvendy (Eds.): HCII 2019, LNCS 11593, pp. 155–166, 2019.
https://doi.org/10.1007/978-3-030-22015-0_12

1 Introduction

'Do not let children lose at the starting line of life' expressed most parents' expectation for their children. Therefore, they would like to grasp any opportunity that may make children grow, even 'playing'. They hope that playing 'toys' can allow their children to explore the world and develop their intelligence. 'Toys' are important partners that accompany children's growth and are indispensables that comfort children and promote their sensory and mental development. The so-called 'educational toys', which emphasize that they can enlighten intelligence, stimulate brain development and develop intelligence, have been advertised in recent years. In fact, the selection of toys is highly correlated to development stages of babies and young children. Appropriate toys selected according to the development needs at different stages can not only inspire babies' intelligence, train visual, auditory, tactile and other sensory functions and stimulate creativity, but also help physical growth and intellectual education. On the contrary, toys not in compliance with children's stages of physical and mental development are not beneficial to their development and may do harm to them.

In babyhood and childhood, the physical and psychological developments of babies and young children experience rapid changes. Although their sensation and perception systems are not mature, there is significant progress in their development every month (Shaffer and Kipp 2013). From the perspective of toy design and intellectual education, since babies develop rapidly in babyhood, it is very important to learn about their perception and motor development and provide appropriate toys for stimulation in correct development months. For example, 1-month-old babies are at an early stage of visual development when their visual angle is only 15°, they are only interested in black and white pictures, they can only slightly raise their heads, and their heads move with their eyes. Only upon learning about this can designers design effectively according to such human factors and achieve the purpose of educational toys. However, it can be seen from baby toy design practice that most relevant design studies are only for school-age children; there are few studies on human factors for baby toy design. According to the Theory of Multiple Intelligences and Physical and Psychological Development in Babyhood of Gardner (2011), a professor at Harvard University and a developmental psychologist and education scientist, the intellectual education on babies at this stage mainly focuses on visual and auditory aspects, such as spatial vision, language, body kinesthetic, natural observation and music; since babies and young children are not yet fully developed, advanced intelligence aspects, however, are relatively uncorrelated. To conclude, the objectives of this study are to ensure that visual and auditory design is based on academic and theoretical basis and make toy design more rigorous to have more positive value to the physical and mental development of babies and young children. Therefore, this study attempts to obtain the related human factors in babyhood from the perspective of intelligent toy design and that human factors can be effectively grasped during corresponding toy design, so as to achieve useful and effective design. The following questions are studied: (1) What is the process of physical development at different stages of babyhood? (2) What are the characteristics of visual development at different stages of babyhood? (3) What are the characteristics of auditory development at different stages? (4) Any suggestions for toy design based on physical and mental development at different stages?

2 Literature Review

2.1 Overview of Stages of Human Development

The course of human life begins at the moment of conception and ends with death. In this process, there are changes in quality and quantity at physical, psychological and social levels. Such changes are not temporary or incidental, but a directional and structural continued progress to maturity; and such changes are interrelated (Santrock 2006). Scholars Shaffer and Kipp (2013) further divided each stage into six stages according to developmental changes as shown in Table 1. The babyhood from birth to 18 months is a stage with the fastest rate of physical development. Babies get to know the concept of things in the world to establish schema.

Table 1. Stages of human development

Development stage	Age range
Prenatal stage	From conception to birth
Babyhood	From birth to 18 months
Toddler period (toddlerhood)	18 months - 3 years old
Preschool period	3–5 years old
School period (middle childhood)	5 - around 12 years old (before adolescence)
Adolescence	12–20 years old (the ending is defined as the time when individuals start working and can live independently)
Adulthood	20–40 years old
Middle-age period	40–65 years old
Senile period	Above 65 years old

Data source: Shaffer and Kipp (2013)

2.2 Physical, Visual and Auditory Development in Babyhood

The physical development in babyhood mainly includes two aspects: (1) physical development - development of all body parts; and (2) motor development - brought about with physical development (Shaffer and Kipp 2013; Skelton 1997; Stoppard 2007). Newborns have basic sensory functions upon birth. They can perceive surrounding visual, auditory and olfactory stimulations and can response to such stimulations. However, the relevant physical and perceptual abilities in 'babyhood' may gradually get matured with the accumulation of experiences in physical development and learning process. Perception is the meaningful sense formed from the physical and sensory information integrated by the brain. The development of perception, together with physical development, memory and experiences, is closely correlated to individuals' growth (Shaffer and Kipp 2013).

The cornea and crystalline lens in eyes are of transparent structure, thus light can be focused on the retina via the light-gathering effects of the two structures, stimulating photoreceptor cells to produce vision. Vision is the sense by which individuals distinguish the Light and shade, color, shape and other characteristics of external objects (Eysenck and Keane 2015). Babies' visual functions begin to promote visual development with visual exploration in the process of growth and mechanisms that rely on experience. Therefore, mechanisms of innate abilities and experiences will jointly promote the development of babies' visual system. The auditory sense is one of the most primitive sensory perception of humans and can be divided into three forms: language, music and noise (Shaffer and Kipp 2013). The auditory sense has developed to a certain extent in the fetal period. Especially at the end of pregnancy, the fetus is already sensitive to the sound of its mother's voice and some external sounds and even feels that the sounds heard in its mother's womb have a certain stabilizing power. Babies have some degree of auditory ability, including responding to sounds and trying to find the sound source (Shaffer and Kipp 2013). Therefore, when babies cry or are unhappy, they will gradually calm down when their mothers play some music often heard during pregnancy. See Table 2 for relevant concepts of sounds and music. Physical development and perception are necessary conditions influencing motor development. Therefore, it is important to learn about babies' perception and motor movement and providing appropriate toys for stimulation.

Table 2. List of relevant concepts of sounds and music

Perceptual element		Physical element	Description
Sounds	Volume	Amplitude size (dB)	The higher the volume, the greater the amplitude; the lower the volume, the smaller the amplitude
	Pitch	Vibration frequency (Hz)	The higher the frequency, the higher the pitch; the lower the frequency, the lower the pitch
Music	Timbre	Waveform of sound	An important feature for identifying the timbre of an instrument. The sources of different timbres can be distinguished, i.e. from different instruments or people
	Melody	A structure formed by sounds	Refers to a sequence of sounds with specific high and low and rhythm relations
	Rhythm	Frequency of sound	A fast or slow beat at a certain speed

Source: sorted in this study

2.3   Educational Toys

Such toys promote, by edutainment, players' sensory exploration and cognition of the world, including inspiring the development of language, music, logical/mathematical, visual/spatial, bodily/kinesthetic, curiosity, imagination and intellectual achievement (Frost et al. 2001; Ogata 2004). Besides, such toys also bring about joy, companionship and autonomy and improve memory, aesthetic ability and concentration (Goldstein and Goldstein 1994), thus are recognized by most educators.

3 Method

The objective of this study is to obtain the human factors for the design of educational toys for babyhood to make such design suitable for 0–18-month-old babies and ensure that the design of receive audio-visual stimuli is based on academic and theoretical basis. Since the objects in this study are not yet mature in mind and body, there are a lot of limitations compared with general study objects. Therefore, first of all, this study obtains the 'physical and psychological development progress for babies in different months' by document analysis and by widely collecting, reading and concluding from medicine, physiology, cognitive science and anthropology and other fields. Next, the deficiencies in the review results and toy design thinking are taken as the material source of 'semi-structured' interviews (expert interviews), which are carried out with four experts respectively, with interview results sorted out; finally, the 'policies and suggestions for toy design' are proposed on the basis of the 'human factors for the design of educational toys for babyhood' and toy design thinking as shown in Fig. 1 (Table 3).

Document Analysis ⟶ Semi-structured Interviews ⟶ Presented with Toy Design Thinking

• Reading and organizing • Description • Classifying • Interpretation	According to the results of the literature, the lack of literature and toy design thinking, as a source of "semi-structured" interview materials	The basis of the 'human factors for the design of educational toys for babyhood' and toy design thinking

Fig. 1. The research method used

Table 3. List of experts

No.	Background	Area of expertise
1	Doctor of Physiology	Neurophysiology and young children development, cognitive neuroscience and sensory integration
2	Doctor of Musical Arts	Music and fetal education and effects of music on young children development
3	Head of music rhythm institution for babies and young children	Music potential and rhythm, and early childhood music and rhythm
4	Doctor of Music	Music and sound therapy, sound beam assisting young children development, and regulation of young children's emotion by music

4   Results

Since relevant contents are complex, we obtained the following results and suggestions by widely collecting, reading and concluding more than 100 pieces of relevant literature from medicine, physiology, cognitive science and anthropology and by expert interviews.

4.1   Physical Development Process for Babies in 0–18 Months

This paper sorts out the Physical Development Process for Babies in 0–18 Months (Table 4) according to babies' physical and psychological development. The physical development of most babies is regular and can be used as the reference basis for babyhood toy development. However, every baby has a different constitution, thus there are still individual differences in physical development.

Table 4. Physical development process for babies in 0–18 months

Time	Motor development characteristics
Birth	Babies gradually adapt to the strange world via sleeping; crying is the only way to express their emotion; heads can rotate slightly when supported; they can move and lift their hands and feet; they can clench their palms when someone touches the palm
1 month	The head moves with eyes; babies can slightly raise their head; when they lie down, they can lift the chin; they will unconsciously suck fingers; reflex actions of the palm are reduced, but the palms are still clenched; when they are awake, they can play alone for about 30 min
2 months	2-month-old babies can keep their head straight when they are held by someone; their upper and lower limbs can stretch and kick; they will not go to sleep immediately after drinking milk and may play for about 30 min; when they lie flat on the stomach, they can briefly raise the head for 45°
3 months	Reflex actions of the palm completely disappear; babies often stare at their hands; when they lie flat on the stomach, they can raise the head for 45°; when they are held and lifted, they can kick alternately
4 months	They become interested in their hands and often suck fingers; they can control their hands and feet and can simply turn over; they can sit when assisted by supports; when they lie flat on the stomach, they can raise the head for 45–90° and like to look around; they can catch toys, suck toys with mouth and shake toys; they can babble and smile cordially at their mothers; they can see distant things, stare at people, reach for distant objects and track moving objects; they may suck fingers and make sounds to amuse themselves
5 months	Babies lick everything with their mouth to learn about the world; they can catch things without using their thumbs; their muscles are strengthened and they can fully control their neck muscles; they can lift the chest; their feet can support their weight and can turn over; they know the existence of toes and put fist into mouth, indicating that they can use eyes and hands simultaneously; they can distinguish acquaintances and strangers and begin to be afraid of strangers and clingy

(continued)

Table 4. (*continued*)

Time	Motor development characteristics
6 months	Babies can turn over by themselves; they can sit on chairs with a back; they can catch hanging objects and can pass objects from one hand to another hand; they can point the corresponding position with thumb or other fingers and can pick up things or grasp with both hands; they know that things in hands should be thrown away before getting a new thing; the muscles of both arms are strong enough to support the body; they can reach out for hugging and may put things into mouth due to the tickle of gingiva
7 months	Babies can sit by themselves for several minutes and can support with hands, knock with toys and help themselves to finger food
8 months	Babies begin to crawl and can use the thumb to grab something and pick up small things with the thumb and the index finger; they can tear paper, hold things and crawl (pull the body and feet with hands); they can move the body to get close to things they want; they may try to stand when someone holds their arms
9 months	Babies can stand with the help of something and can sit on their own for 10 min and will not fall down even they shake back and forth; they can roll, want to get up, and can push, pull, drag or hold objects
10 months	When babies are sitting, they can be free to move and rotate the body with hands and knees and can stand up by themselves and begin to walk along tables and chairs; they can control their index fingers to get things and put them down; they can eat the food in their hands and like to throw things
11 months	Babies can crawl with the help of hands and feet and may try to walk a few steps; they can give things to others and put them into containers
12 months	Babies can stand by themselves and try to walk a few steps; they can catch and put down the ball and may try to take two objects with one hand
13–18 months	Babies can climb stairs, stoop to pick something up and scratch with a pen; they like to throw things and walk independently and can run awkwardly; They can stoop and bend their knees and like to push and pull, throw balls, turn pages and scribe

Source: sorted in this study

4.2 Arguments for the Characteristics of Visual Development at Different Stages of Babyhood

Babies' visual functions begin to promote visual development with visual exploration in the process of growth and mechanisms that rely on experience. Therefore, mechanisms of innate abilities and experiences will jointly promote the development of babies' visual system. Since various visual abilities in babyhood have different development in different growing periods, in order to help to understand such development and further apply such development in the development and design of toys, we further conclude and sort out the 'visual ability processes in babyhood' in this study. See Table 5.

Table 5. Visual ability processes in babyhood

Time	Visual ability development
0 month	The optimum staring distance is 20 cm. Babies cannot clearly see too close or too far objects and can respond to 'light'. When the light is too bright and strong, babies may not adapt to this and may turn the head to the other side. Their visual acuity is 20/600 and their vision is about 0.05–0.025; they like faces and objects with clear and simple contour. Visual angle: 15° from the midline on the left and right respectively
1 month	Babies can see objects 20–30 cm from their faces. Visual angle: 30° from the midline on the left and right respectively. The fixation time can be up to 3–5 s
2 months	Color discrimination ability: babies can distinguish different colors (such as red, yellow and orange), but they prefer white and black (neutrals); the fixation time in 2–3 months can be up to 7–10 min; their eyeballs can accurately chase objects and can chase objects horizontally and vertically, but cannot chase the object beyond the midline of the body)
3 months	Red is the most attractive color for babies; they can see objects 4–7 m away, chase objects to the midline of the body and actively find visual stimuli. Since they can see a distance of a room, they begin to identify the environment
4 months	Their vision is about 0.1 and can see the difference between near and far; their stereoscopic sense also develops rapidly at this time; 4–8-month-old babies are interested in things in warm colors (red, yellow and orange) and do not like cool colors (such as blue and green) and pale colors (such as gray and brown); they may show a preference for a certain color;
5 months	Visual angle: 45° from the midline on the left and right respectively
6 months	Their vision is 0.5; they can distinguish 3D patterns and establish stereoscopic vision; visual acuity: 20/100;
9 months	They can see things as near as 2–3 cm;
12–18 months	13-month-old babies can recognize and correctly point out red, green, blue and yellow

Source: sorted in this study

Since the wave length of soft yellow-green light is long, eyes are highly sensitive to yellow-green light and are not easy to be fatigue. In terms of colors, in the first 3 months after birth, babies can only recognize white and black; 3–4-month-old babies can recognize red, green and blue. Later, with the accumulation of life experiences, babies may have different color preferences in different periods. This cannot be judged according to physiological factors. With regard to shapes, 3–4-month-old babies can only recognize the basic contour of objects. Later, they will begin to recognize details and are especially absorbed in moving objects.

4.3 Arguments for the Characteristics of Visual Development at Different Stages of Babyhood

Normal newborns have auditory sense immediately after birth (Shaffer and Kipp 2013) and can 'stare at the person who speaks' (Rheingold and Adams 1980; Rosenthal 1982); and are most focused on high frequency sound (Ecklund-Flores and Turkewitz 1996).

Thus, babies can quickly learn to recognize the words that they often hear. 4–5-month-old babies can turn their heads when someone call their names but have no response to other names (Mandel et al. 1995); when they are 7 months old, they can generalize the patterns learned from language to other sounds, such as pitch, the timbre of an instrument and the sound of an animal (Marcus et al. 2007). Therefore, from the perspective of cognitive learning, repeating simple nursery rhymes, singing sweet songs and saying loving words will be highly favorable to the development of auditory sense, emotion and movement. On the contrary, excessively loud, sharp, irritating or unpleasant sounds may scare babies. Their brain and auditory system will repel these sounds, which is extremely detrimental to brain development (Karmiloff and Karmiloff-Smith 2004; Stoppard 2007).

It can be concluded that babies' auditory sense starts in the fetal period. In the process of auditory development, babies can recognize multiple sounds in surrounding environment and master human languages. Babies' auditory susceptibility has significant individual difference. Some have higher susceptibility and that of others is lower, but such individual difference is not unchanging. In fact, babies' auditory sense keeps developing under the influence of living conditions and education. Lastly, in order to help to further understand auditory development processes and apply them in toy development and design. We further conclude and sort out auditory development processes in this study. See Table 6.

Table 6. Auditory development processes in babyhood

Time	Auditory ability development
0 month	Normal newborns have auditory sense immediately after birth and can 'stare at the person who speaks'; they can recognize their mothers' voices, for which they show obvious preference
1 month	Babies can distinguish 200 Hz and 500 Hz pure tones; when they are sleeping, if they suddenly hear some sound, they may open their eyes and cry
2 months	When babies are sleeping, if there are noises, they may open their eyes but they will not cry; they can distinguish flutes and bells
3 months	They begin to identify and distinguish sounds and can preliminarily distinguish 'pitches'; they may be uneasy when hearing a quarrel and may be happy when hearing music and like high frequency sounds
4 months	Babies can combine auditory sense and visual sense and can turn their heads towards the direction of sounds
5 months	The auditory differential threshold within 200–2000 Hz among in 5–8-month-old babies doubles that among adults; the auditory differential threshold within 4000–8000 Hz is the same as that among adults; in case of any sudden sound, babies may rush to hug the caregiver (such as mothers) and may turn their heads when hearing their names
6 months	Babies can hear external sounds below 1000 Hz and respond to mothers' voice
7 months	Babies can distinguish different sounds in a language and can extract patterns from voices
8 months	Babies may actively make some sounds and imitate others' words that they hear

(*continued*)

Table 6. (*continued*)

Time	Auditory ability development
9 months	Babies can distinguish whether sounds are meaningful, for example, someone calls their names
10 months	Babies can imitate to call father and mother
12–18 months	Babies can rapidly and directly search for sound sources and can distinguish finer sound of different phonetic symbols, such as barking and honking

Source: sorted in this study

If babies are exposed to music early, the music elements in music tunes that vary in height, speed, and strength can better inspire the development of children's sensory perception and music ability (Karmiloff and Karmiloff-Smith 2004). Babies' musical ability first is that their auditory sense hears music and generates feelings. Then such delighted feelings drive them to find 'sounds' and make 'sounds' by themselves to experience the relationship between sounds and people, things, objects, time and space. Thus, such interests increase with time, leading to the music ability cultivation and skill learning. For this point, Moog (1976a, b) pointed out on the basis of a study on babies cognitive abilities: 0–4 months: babies are sensitive and feel safe to high frequency music and noise, thus women's and children's voices can make babies calm down; after 4 months: babies like 'delighted music' and 'beautiful voices': after 6 months: strong sounds cannot make babies physically move with music, but 'delighted music' and 'beautiful voices' can; 18 months: 10% of babies can physically move with music rhythm (Moog 1976a, b). Besides, relevant studies also proved that when babies are 2 months old, they can lie still and listen to music; when they are 2–3 months old, they can preliminarily distinguish 'pitches'; when they are 3–3.5 months old, they can distinguish 'timbres'; 5–6-month fetuses have music perception; when they are 6–7 months old, they can distinguish simple 'pitches'.

Sinor (1980), an American scholar of music education proposed, according to the 'cognitive-developmental theory' of Jean Piaget, a developmental psychologist, the 'musical development of children', which shows that 0–1-year-old babies begin to develop the dynamic and timbre of perception, and listening and moving abilities of response. The musical activities before 1 year old emphasize tunes and intonation related to music, rather than linguistic speech on the rhythm of music. Babies can also distinguish different rhythms.

It can be concluded that music does soothe emotions. The frequency of music is very important in soothing music. Low frequency is for comfort. However, this does not mean always playing low frequency music to fetuses. The music should have some changes, such as the changes in tone and cadence. A cradlesong is soothing, but it should be accompanied by the hug from adults. A cradlesong should be slow with stable pitch, such as the stability of Baroque music, the rhythm of which is close to heart rate. The mind-inspiring music should be diversified, not too long, highly comparative and repetitive. Music for mental development should have design lesson plans and music with meaningful guidance. Babies' audition is very sensitive, thus the volume of toys with sound should be below 50 dB.

4.4   Suggestions for Design of Acousto-Optic Toys Based on Physical Development of Babies and Young Children

For visual sense, although light can easily attract their attention, hurts can be easily caused. Therefore, light should be carefully designed. Please use indirect light. Among lights, blue light is terrible, thus do not apply it. It is suggested not to develop the visual sense of 0–3-month-old babies. Hanging toys can be added to babies above 4 months. Toys may not be dynamic and in black, white and warm colors with high saturation, such as red, yellow and orange. For babies above 5 months, toys may be dynamic to allow babies and young children to practice eyeball tracking.

For auditory sense, the sounds of music should be from real instruments with stable melody and range, for example, there are a total of seven tones, the range of which should not be too wide. The melody should be within one range without large fluctuations. The speed of music should be one beat in one second, that is, sixty beats in one minute. Generally speaking, such speed is in line with heart rate. For voice, mothers' voices can be used (for example, when clicking the pictures of cars, "car" will be said) to enhance babies cognition. The adding to motherese to the sound feature of products can increase babies' preference. Such motherese can also be interspersed in different paragraphs by playing motherese first to lead babies stare on left and right sides to promote their visual development. Since sounds have the synesthesia of colors and visual perception, the match of sounds and colors can be used to train the synesthesia of babies and young children. Meanwhile, the match of visual features with sounds, such as the match of a dog shape with barking, should be taken into account when designing toys for babies and young children above 12 months.

Finally, we propose the following summaries and suggestions for different stages:

(1) 0–3 months: this stage emphasizes the soothing sound rather than the soothing light/visual objects.
    For 0–3-month-old babies, since their visual sense has not been fully developed, the staring distance increases from 20 cm to 7 m, and the staring can last as long as 10 min, the stimulation development for this stage should be based on sound, rather than visual ability.

(2) Above 4 months: addition of object space concept
    Babies above 4 months begin to develop synesthesia and 3D concept. At this stage, the combination of sounds and objects can be used to train babies' sense of space.

(3) 5–12 months: learning of music and training of perception
    Babies and young children above 5 months can identify timbres, pitches, tones, melodies and simple tunes in music. Therefore, it is suggested to train babies' music perception, including different timbres, rhythms and melodies.

(4) Above 12 months: emphasis of the interaction between sound and movement
    Babies and young children above 12 months begin to have body movements, thus different music or sounds can be used to guide the learning of body movements of babies and young children at this stage.

5 Conclusions and Suggestions

This study enriched the relevant human factors for baby toy design by different academic literature review and expert interviews and proposed design suggestions for different stages. The results can be applied to the development of educational toys for babies. Therefore, it can be concluded from this study that the design of the educational toys for 0–18-month-old babies should be focus on the development of sound senses. If visual lights are used, please use indirect lighting; blue light is prohibited. Mothers' voices are important for children. However, the design of few products on the market has applied mothers' voices. It is suggested to apply such voices during design.

References

Ecklund-Flores, L., Turkewitz, G.: Asymmetric headturning to speech and nonspeech in human newborns. Dev. Psychobiol. **29**(3), 205–217 (1996)

Eysenck, M.W., Keane, M.T.: Cognitive Psychology: A Student's Handbook, 7th edn. Psychology Press, London and New York (2015)

Frost, J.L., Wortham, S.C., Reifel, R.S.: Play and Child Development. Merrill, Prentice Hall, Upper Saddle River (2001)

Gardner, H.E.: Multiple Intelligences: New Horizons in Theory and Practice, 3rd edn. Basic Books, New York (2011)

Goldstein, J.H., Goldstein, R.: Toys, Play, and Child Development. Cambridge University Press, Cambridge (1994)

Karmiloff, K., Karmiloff-Smith, A.: Everything Your Baby Would Ask: If Only Babies Could Talk. Firefly Books, Buffalo (2004)

Mandel, D.R., Jusczyk, P.W., Pisoni, D.B.: Infants' recognition of the sound patterns of their own names. Psychol. Sci. **6**(5), 314–317 (1995)

Marcus, G.F., Fernandes, K.J., Johnson, S.P.: Infant rule learning facilitated by speech. Psychol. Sci. **18**(5), 387–391 (2007)

Moog, H.: The development of musical experience in children of pre-school age. Psychol. Music **4**(2), 38–45 (1976a)

Moog, H.: The Musical Experience of the Pre-school Child. Schott Music Corp., London (1976b)

Ogata, A.F.: Creative playthings: educational toys and postwar American culture. Winterthur Portf. **39**(2/3), 129–156 (2004)

Rheingold, H.L., Adams, J.L.: The significance of speech to newborns. Dev. Psychol. **16**(5), 397 (1980)

Rosenthal, M.: Vocal dialogues in the neonatal period. Dev. Psychol. **18**(1), 17 (1982)

Santrock, J.W.: Human adjustment. McGraw-Hill, New York (2006)

Shaffer, D.R., Kipp, K.: Developmental Psychology: Childhood and Adolescence. Cengage Learning, Belmont (2013)

Sinor, J.: Musical development of children and Kodály pedagogy. Kodály Envoy **6**(3), 6–10 (1980)

Skelton, K.J.: Paraprofessionals in Education. Delmar Publishers, New York (1997)

Stoppard, M.: New Baby Care: A Practical Guide to the First 3 Years. Penguin, New York (2007)

Digital Gaming by Older Adults: Can It Enhance Social Connectedness?

David Kaufman[1] and Louise Sauve[2(✉)]

[1] Faculty of Education, Simon Fraser University, Surrey, BC, Canada
dkaufman@sfu.ca
[2] Teleuniversite, Quebec, QC, Canada
louisesauve25@gmail.com

Abstract. It has been well established that social engagement is an important component of positive aging, yet little is known about whether and in what forms digital games can provide social benefits. This paper addresses this issue by discussing research we have conducted during the past four years. The research question addressed in this paper is: Can playing digital games provide social benefits to older adults? To address this question, we provide overviews of four of our research studies that have investigated the social aspects of playing digital games. These are: (1) a face-to-face survey of 463 older adults in Canada who play digital games; (2) an eight-week Wii Bowling tournament involving 73 older adults from 14 long-term care facilities; (3) a four-week Bingo 'frame game' study involving 50 older adults in long-term care facilities; and (4) an online survey of 176 older adults who play the Internet game entitled *World of Warcraft*. The findings of these four research studies are encouraging as we found social benefits in each study. Although many older adults play digital games, a minority play games with others. These findings suggest that promotion and education would be helpful to encourage and support older adults to play digital games with others to gain the social benefits.

Keywords: Older adults · Social connectedness · Social benefits ·
Digital games · Survey · Wii games · Bingo · World of Warcraft

1 Introduction

Although social isolation (lack of social relationships) and loneliness (a feeling that one's social relationships are insufficient) can be issues at any age [1], older adults are often at increased risk of both, due to causes such as smaller social networks, mobility difficulties, and the death of spouses. Both social isolation and loneliness are associated with increased health and mortality risk [2–4]. Previous studies have shown that a lack of communication and social connection to others can contribute to isolation and loneliness [5], which in turn can result in problems such as depression and cognitive decline for older adults. It is well established that social engagement is seen as an important component of positive aging [6, 7]. In addition, social engagement provides opportunities for older adults to deal with stress and receive social support and connect with friends. One unique study [8] with 30 participants yielded supportive evidence

© Springer Nature Switzerland AG 2019
J. Zhou and G. Salvendy (Eds.): HCII 2019, LNCS 11593, pp. 167–176, 2019.
https://doi.org/10.1007/978-3-030-22015-0_13

that individuals with regular social interaction over 10 days showed diminished neuroendocrine stress responses and distress of social separation. Therefore, there are numerous reasons why creating opportunities for older adults to connect socially can be valuable [9]. Such opportunities may help reduce feelings of loneliness or isolation, increase self-esteem and facilitate the process of forming new social relationships, creating community, and expanding social networks.

For these reasons, it is important to provide opportunities where older adults can build relationships with others in a positive and supportive social environment. Digital gameplay is one activity that can draw older players to engage and interact socially with other players [10, 11]. Digital games can support and encourage social interaction and socializing is an important reason that many older adults play digital games [11, 12]. In some studies, older adults have reported that playing games socially has led them to make new friends and strengthen connections with current friends and family [13–16]. Social connectedness can be conceptualized as the degree to which people have and perceive a sufficient number and diversity of relationships that allow them to give and receive information, emotional support, and material aid [17]. This creates a sense of belonging and value and fosters growth. Social connectedness is important because it provides people with the emotional support, material help, and information they need to thrive. Social connectedness—both the sum of individual relationships and a sense of belonging—is crucial to overall health and wellbeing. Social connectedness decreases feelings of loneliness [18–21]. De Schutter [11] identified connectedness with family and friends as well as the broader community as one of five categories of perceived needs motivating older adult game players. In a study by De Schutter and Brown [22], older adults valued their digital gameplay because it distracted them from feelings of loneliness and helped them to connect with younger generations. Based on observation and interviews, other researchers [23] reported that playing digital games together led older adults to experience social and emotional benefits including social interaction, increased self-esteem, positive emotions, and wellbeing.

Several other studies have shown that social interaction that takes place when playing digital games is very important to older players [12, 24, 25]. Playing digital videogames promotes positive health outcomes associated with alleviating depression, and reducing feelings of loneliness, and isolation [25]. Digital gaming also provides a venue for developing social capital that strengthens strong social ties both on- and offline [26]. Despite the potential benefits of digital game playing, little is known about whether and in what forms digital games can best and most efficiently benefit older adults. Within the limited research reported, there is more focus on the efficacy of playing digital games to improve the *cognitive* abilities that tend to decline with age. There is not much research on the *social* benefits of digital game playing for older adults [28].

2 Statement of Purpose and Research Question

This paper addresses this issue by discussing several studies conducted during the past four years within the Canadian National Centre of Excellence Project entitled *AGE-WELL* (see https://agewell-nce.ca). The research question addressed in this paper is:

Can playing digital games provide social benefits to older adults? In particular, we addressed social connectedness in the quantitative research methods and, to some extent, in the qualitative research.

To address this question, we provide overviews of four of our research studies that have investigated the social aspects of playing digital games. These are: (1) a face-to-face survey of 463 older adults in western Canada who play digital games [28]; (2) an eight-week Wii Bowling tournament involving 73 older adults from 14 long-term care facilities [13]; (3) a four-week Bingo 'frame game' study involving 50 older adults in long-term care facilities [14]; (4) an online survey of 176 older adults who play the Internet game entitled *World of Warcraft* [15]. The key results of each study are discussed below.

3 Overview of Research Studies

This section provides an overview of our research studies that addressed the research question given above.

3.1 Survey of Older Adults in Canada

This study employed a closed-ended cross-sectional survey developed by the author and his team aimed at understanding older adults' (aged 55 years and older) experiences of playing digital games and their opinions regarding these [31]. The questionnaire included questions about older adult respondents' characteristics, experiences of playing digital games, patterns of playing, and opinions about digital games. It was administered to older adults in shopping malls, local community centers, nursing homes and seniors' centers. A total of 463 questionnaires were analyzed; 27.5% of respondents reported that they play online with other players and 15.3% reported that they met new people while playing online (Table 1).

Table 1. Social Benefits of Playing Digital Games (n = 463)

Benefits	% Reporting an Increase
General Benefit	
Social interaction	25.9
Specific Social Benefits	
Dealing with loneliness	34.5
Connecting with family	32.5
Connecting with various age groups	28.1
Connecting with current friends	26.6
Developing new friendships	25.6

Note: Respondents could select more than one benefit

A total of 25.9% of respondents selected social interaction as one benefit of playing digital games. Respondents also reported that digital games increased specific social benefits of dealing with loneliness, connecting with family and various age groups, connecting with current friends and developing new friendships.

These results show that a minority of older adults actually play games online or face-to-face with others. Therefore, fewer older players reported socio-emotional benefits although those that did play digital games reported an increase.

3.2 Social Benefits for Older Adults of Playing Wii Bowling

The primary research question in this study was 'Does playing a digital game with others increase social connectedness and reduce social isolation?' The purpose of this study was to explore the social experiences of older adults (60 yrs and older) who played the digital game Wii bowling in an eight-week tournament. The 73 participants aged 60 years or older were recruited from 14 centers in Greater Vancouver including independent living centers, senior recreation centers, and assisted living centers. Those recruited to play in the tournament were organized into teams formed within each participating site. Scores were posted weekly on a website and paper copies were provided at each site as not all players used or had access to the Internet.

We used a mixed methods research approach in this study. For the quantitative data collection, players were asked to rate their agreement on a Likert scale with statements relating to loneliness and social connectedness. The questions relating to social connectedness and loneliness were adapted from two existing social scales: the UCLA Loneliness Scale and Social Connectedness Scale. The pre-and post-tests were analyzed using a paired samples t-test. The qualitative study interviewed players' about their perceptions such as friendships and social contacts they made during the tournament, their conversations with friends and family about their involvement in the tournament, and the team experience.

It is notable that 80% of our group were 70 years of age or older with half of all participants being 80 years old or older. The key results were as follows: There was a statistically significant decrease in loneliness (M = 2.214, SD = 0.528) before game playing and (M = 2.049, SD = 0.54) after game playing (t = 3.518, p = 0.001. There was also a statistically significant increase in social connectedness (M = 3.410, SD = 0.528) before and (M = 3.526, SD = 0.485) after game playing (t = −2.180, p = 0.03).

Themes relating to the category of social connectedness were:

- Interaction with others because of Wii
- Conversations about Wii with family and friends
- Better social connections
- Team experience

In this mixed methods study, both the quantitative and qualitative analyses showed socio-emotional benefits for older adults who played Wii bowling. When measured before and after the tournament, quantitative results suggest that participants experienced an increased level of social connectedness and decreased level of loneliness. The results of the qualitative study show that some participants made social connections that extended beyond their teammates to family and friends and in some cases created opportunities to meet and socialize in other contexts outside the tournament.

3.3   A Customized Digital Bingo Game

The purpose of this study was to investigate learning and social connectedness through a digital game for older players. The two primary research questions were:

1. Are there increases in older adults' knowledge, social connectedness, and attitudes toward digital games as a result of playing a multiplayer, educational digital Bingo game?
2. What is the social experience of older adult players while playing a multi-player, educational digital game?

Participants played an enhanced online "Bingo Nutrition and Health" game for four weekly sessions, after first playing for one familiarization session with a similar "Bingo Canada" game with different learning content. Quantitative data were collected using pre- and post-tests for knowledge of the game's learning content and for changes in participants' social connectedness. Qualitative data on the players' gameplay experiences and preferences were collected through semi-structured post-game interviews. For this paper, only the social connectedness results are discussed. A complete report of this study is available elsewhere [14]. We spent more than a month visiting residential seniors centres to recruit 50 participants who completed the study.

The Bingo Nutrition and Health game chosen for this study is a replica of traditional Bingo that has been digitized as a multiplayer online game. Our team developed this game following a user-centered design process and applied ergonomic principles appropriate for this target audience, i.e., older adults [31]. Due to server limitations, gameplay during this study was limited to eight players at one time. As in traditional Bingo, each player had a Bingo card or board, of five columns, with five rows of numbers, and a score panel that displayed all players' scores. The game was modified to include pop-up educational content in the form of questions. When a Bingo number was "called" by the game (e.g., "B 13"), a player checks on his or her Bingo board's column B to see if the number matches. If the number matches, the player clicks on the number on his or her board, followed by receiving a question in a pop-up frame. The number will be registered or covered if s/he answered correctly. Players needed to have a row of numbers registered or covered—horizontally, vertically, or diagonally—in order to win. Points were also awarded to the player based on question difficulty, and the player with the most points when "Bingo" was called was declared as the winner of the game.

Bingo was chosen as the game for this study because it is a common, yet, traditional game, popularly played by many older adults. Its embedded educational content and competition encourage players to learn the topics embedded in the game, and at the same time have fun playing socially with other players. Although this game could be played without a computer, the affordances provided by the digital version make it much easier for older adults to play, even without a game facilitator. The immediate feedback provided, pop-up windows, scoring system, and touch screen capability provide a comfortable and smooth game experience for older adults. The questions were in True/False and multiple choice formats with easy, medium, and difficult levels. The questions were entered into the game by the researchers and fell into the four categories of Nutrition, Physical Exercise, Socialization, and Prevention.

Each gameplay session lasted for about 30 to 45 min. Each week, each group played two game sessions at their respective centres. Players played seated around a table in a group of four to eight persons, using touch-screen laptop computers that were logged into the Bingo game server. Each player had an individual laptop for gameplay. Players were free to collaborate or socialize during the gameplay.

Both pre- and post-tests included sections on knowledge of the game's learning content, participants' social connectedness, and their attitudes toward digital games. The pre- and post-test social connectedness questionnaire used a five-point Likert scale and post-gameplay interviews were used to collect qualitative data. The open ended, semi-structured, face-to-face interviews of 10 participants asked about their perception of the gameplay experience and about learning socially with other players.

The quantitative results showed that participants' scores on social connectedness showed a statistically significant increase from before ($M = 3.54$, $SD = 0.43$), to after ($M = 3.73$, $SD = 0.48$) their gameplay ($t = 2.32$, $p = 0.02$).

The qualitative analysis resulted in two main themes and five sub-themes shown in Table 2.

Table 2. Results of qualitative analysis in Bingo study

Theme	Sub-themes	Sample quotes
Playing with others	Player Connectedness	Player 31: "I would like to continue playing the game with the same group – we became very close doing it. Good to come out of my room to socialize and do other things, be connected with others ..."
	Player Interactivity	Player 17: "I am more interested to play with others – much better than playing alone. It's better because I could communicate with others and interact with them."
	Player collaboration	Player 31: "It's a game you are playing together, working together.... It's teamwork."
	Talking to other players	Player 10: "Playing, I talk to people who play with me, and we talk about playing, about the food and something like that."
	Positive co-playing experience	Player 02: "Playing in a group, I have more fun and can hear the sounds of other players. It also improves your mood while playing..."
Making new friends		Player 21: "I can see how other elderly people are playing and get to know others I haven't met before. They can share their life stories, too"

This study adds to the evidence that certain types of digital games can be both entertaining activities and valuable resources for older adults. Participants in this study acquired new and useful knowledge; expanded their social connectedness; valued the enjoyment, learning, and socializing that took place during their digital Bingo gameplay. As a result, they finished the study with more favorable attitudes toward digital games.

3.4   Older Adults' Social Interactions in an MMORPG

The purpose of this study was to investigate older adults' social interactions in MMORPGs. An online survey was developed and posted to eight World of Warcraft (WoW) player forums to gather information about older gamers' demographic characteristics, play patterns, social interactions in WoW, and challenges facing older adults while playing WoW. This is the most played MMORPG in North America. Invitation messages including the URL to the Web questionnaire were posted on the WoW player forums. The study addressed several research questions regarding older adults' play of the MMORPG entitled World of Warcraft (WoW). One of the research question is addressed here: What are older adults' social experiences within MMORPGs? The other questions are discussed in another paper published earlier [31].

Participants were asked to complete a Web questionnaire that consists of four sections. The section relevant to this paper asks questions about older adults' social interactions within WoW, including (1) methods used to communicate with other players; (2) with whom older adults play; (3) discussing with other players; (4) depth of relationships; and (5) quality of guild play.

Playing MMORPGs is not only about mindlessly killing monsters, but also about learning and participating in the shared practices of a game community [32]. To progress quickly through the games, players need to group with others and work together to overcome challenging quests for mutual benefits. Due to these mechanisms, playing MMORPGs provides many opportunities for social interactions. Compatible with previous findings, playing MMORPGs not only offers older adults many opportunities to sustain offline relationships with family and real-life friends, but also build meaningful and supportive relationships with game friends. MMORPGs also have the potential to function as a "third place" for older adults to socialize and be entertained similar to a real-world club or coffee shop.

Data from 176 older adult participants aged 50 and over who play WoW were analyzed. The majority of older WoW players were young older adults who were in their late 50s or early 60s. A substantial majority of them still maintained a certain amount of social contact, and were well-educated. In addition, the majority of them could be defined as heavy gamers (who played video games more than 2.5 h a day) based on De Schutter's criteria [11].

The questionnaire consisted of four sections and one section is discussed here. This section asked questions about older adults' social interactions within WoW, including: (1) methods used to communicate with other players; (2) with whom older adults play; (3) discussing with other players; (4) depth of relationships; and (5) quality of guild play. The complete study has been described elsewhere [15]. The results of the social research question are summarized here.

With Whom Older Adults Play. A larger number of older adults played with their family and real-life friends.

Discussing with Other Players. The majority of older adults never or rarely shared their personal problems with game friends. Older adults were more likely to discuss game play and general information within WoW such as weapons, rules and trades.

Depth of Relationships. Almost half of participants agreed or strongly agreed that playing with family members made them feel closer, and that they developed closer relationships with their real-life friends due to playing with them.

Guild Life. Guild life is a major part of the social interactions that take place within the game. Most participants mentioned they were either satisfied or very satisfied with the organization of guild, leadership, and interaction with guild members.

4   Conclusions, Limitations and Implications

The results from these research studies are encouraging. We addressed the research question: Can playing digital games provide social benefits to older adults? In particular, we addressed social connectedness in the quantitative research methods and, to some extent, in the qualitative research. We conducted four very different digital game studies with older adults and found social benefits in each study. Social connectedness was enhanced in all studies and was a consistent theme.

The survey conducted in the first study demonstrated that a minority of older adults actually play games online or face-to-face with others. As a consequence, fewer older players reported socio-emotional benefits, although those that played social games reported an increase in social benefits that were all aspects of social connectedness. The Wii Bowling and Bingo studies demonstrated that providing older adults with the opportunity to play a digital game with others resulted in positive social benefits; once again these benefits were types of social connectedness. These findings were confirmed by both the qualitative and quantitative results. Finally, the WoW study showed that playing online in stable groups, called guilds, with family members and friends resulted in closer bonds. It also demonstrated that new friendships could be formed by playing online with others. This study also demonstrated that MMORPGs have the potential to function as a "third place" for older adults to socialize and be entertained similar to a real-world club or coffee shop.

Overall, these findings suggest that promotion and education are needed to encourage and support older adults to play digital games with others to provide them with the social benefits and social connectedness that can be gained from this enjoyable activity.

Acknowledgement. This work was funded by AGE-WELL NCE Inc., a national research network in Canada supporting research, networking, commercialization, knowledge mobilization and capacity building activities in technology and aging to improve the quality of life of Canadians and contribute to the economic impact of Canada. AGE-WELL is a member of the Networks of Centres of Excellence (NCE), a Government of Canada program that funds partnerships between universities, industry, government and not-for-profit organizations.

References

1. Dykstra, P.A.: Older adult loneliness: myths and realities. Eur. J. Aging **6**(2), 91–100 (2009)
2. Ong, A.D., Uchino, B.N., Wethington, E.: Loneliness and health in older adults: a mini-review and synthesis. Gerontology **62**, 443–449 (2016)
3. Shankar, A., Mcmunn, A., Banks, J., Steptoe, A.: Loneliness, social isolation, and behavioral and biological health indicators in older adults. Health Psychol. **30**(4), 377–385 (2011)
4. Holt-Lunstad, J., Smith, T.B., Baker, M., Harris, T., Stephenson, D.: Loneliness and social isolation as risk factors for mortality: a meta-analytic review. Perspect. Psychol. Sci. **10**(2), 227–237 (2015)
5. Cacioppo, J.T., Patrick, W.: Loneliness: Human Nature and the Need for Social Connection. W. W. Norton & Company, Inc., New York (2008)
6. von Faber, M., et al.: Successful aging in the oldest old: who can be characterized as successfully aged? Arch. Int. Med. **161**(11), 2694–2700 (2001)
7. Reichstadt, J., Depp, C.A., Palinkas, L.A., Folsom, D.P., Jeste, D.V.: Building blocks of successful aging: a focus group study of older adults' perceived contributors to successful aging. Am. J. Geriatr. Psychiatry **15**(3), 194–201 (2007)
8. Eisenberger, N.I., Taylor, S.E., Gable, S.L., Hilmert, C.J., Lieberman, M.D.: Neural pathways link social support to attenuated neuroendocrine stress responses. Neuroimage **35**, 1601–1612 (2007)
9. Adams, K.B., Leibbrandt, S., Moon, H.: A critical review of the literature on social and leisure activity and wellbeing in later life. Ageing Soc. **31**(4), 683–712 (2011)
10. Delwiche, A.A., Henderson, J.J.: The players they are A-Changin': the rise of older MMO gamers. J. Broadcast. Electron. Media **57**(2), 205–223 (2013)
11. De Schutter, B.: Never too old to play: the appeal of digital games to an older audience. Games Cult. **6**(2), 155–170 (2011)
12. De Schutter, B., Vanden Abeele, V.: Designing meaningful play within the psycho-social context of older adults. In: Vanden Abeele, V., Zaman, B., Obrist, M., IJsselsteijn, W. (eds.) Fun and Games 2010: Proceedings of the 3rd International Conference on Fun and Games, Leuven, Belgium, pp. 84–93 (2010)
13. Schell, R., Hausknecht, S., Zhang, F., Kaufman, D.: Social benefits of playing Wii Bowling for older adults. Games Cult. **11**(8), 1–103 (2016)
14. Kaufman, D., Seah, E.T.-W., Zhang, F., Ireland, A.: Play, learn, connect: Older adults' experience with a digital educational Bingo game. J. Educ. Comput. Res. **56**(5), 675–700 (2018)
15. Zhang, F., Kaufman, D.: Older adults' social interactions in MMORPGs. Games Cult. **11**(1–2), 150–169 (2016)
16. Loos, E., Kaufman, D.: Positive impact of exergaming on older adults' mental and social well-being: in search of evidence. In: Zhou, J., Salvendy, G. (eds.) ITAP 2018, Part II. LNCS, vol. 10927, pp. 101–112. Springer, Cham (2018). https://doi.org/10.1007/978-3-319-92037-5_9
17. https://fullframeinitiative.org/wp-content/uploads/2011/05/SocialConnectedness_Factsheet.pdf
18. Hausknecht, S., Schell, R., Zhang, F., Kaufman, D.: Building seniors' social connections and reducing loneliness through a digital game. In: Helfert, M., Restiva, M.T., Svacek, S., Uhomoibhi, J. (eds.) Proceedings of the 7th International Conference on Computer Supported Education, pp. 276–284. Science and Technology Publications, Lda., Setúbal (2015)

19. Ijsselsteijn, W., Nap, H.H., de Kort, Y., Poels, K.: Digital game design for elderly users. In: Kapralos, B., Katchabaw, M., Rajnovich, J. (eds.) Future Play 2007: Proceedings of the 2007 Conference on Future Play, pp. 17–22. ACM, New York (2007)
20. van Bel, D.T., Smolders, K.C., Ijsselsteijn, W., de Kort, Y.: Social connectedness: concept and measurement. In: Callaghan, V., Kameas, A., Reyes, A., Royo, D., Weber, M. (eds.) Intelligent Environments 2009: Proceedings of the 5th International Conference on Intelligent Environments, pp. 67–74. IOS Press, Amsterdam (2009)
21. De Schutter, B., Maillet, S.: The older player of digital games: a classification based on perceived need satisfaction. Communications 39(1), 67–88 (2014)
22. De Schutter, B., Brown, J.A.: Digital games as a source of enjoyment in later life. Games Cult. 11(1–2), 28–52 (2016)
23. McLaughlin, A., Gandy, M., Allaire, J., Whitlock, L.: Putting fun into video games for older adults. Ergon. Des. Q. Hum. Factors Appl. 20(2), 13–22 (2012)
24. Khoo, E., Cheok, A.: Age invaders: intergenerational mixed reality family game. The International Journal of Virtual Reality 5(2), 45–50 (2006)
25. Wollersheim, D., et al.: Physical and psychosocial effects of Wii video game use among older women. Int. J. Emerg. Technol. Soc. 8(2), 85–98 (2010)
26. Trepte, R., Juechems, K.: The social side of gaming: how playing online computer games creates online and offline social support. Comput. Hum. Behav. 28(3), 832–839 (2012)
27. Allaire, J.C., McLaughlin, A.C., Trujillo, A., Whitlock, L.A., laPorte, L., Gandy, M.: Successful aging through digital games: socioemotional differences between older adult games and non-gamers. Comput. Hum. Behav. 29, 1302–1306 (2013)
28. Kaufman, D.: Aging well: can digital games help older adults? In: Bastiaens, T., Marks, G. (eds.) Proceedings of World Conference on E-Learning in Corporate, Government, Healthcare, and Higher Education 2013, pp. 1943–1949. AACE, Chesapeake (2013)
29. Kaufman, D., Sauvé, L., Renaud, L., Sixsmith, A., Mortenson, B.: Digital gameplay by older adults: patterns, benefits, and challenges. Simul. Gaming 47(4), 475–489 (2016)
30. Sauve, L., Renaud, L., Kaufman, D., Duplaa, E.: Ergonomic criteria for creating online educational games for seniors. In: Sourina, O., Wortley, D., Kim, S. (eds.) Subconscious Learning via Games and Social Media. GMSE, pp. 115–134. Springer, Singapore (2015). https://doi.org/10.1007/978-981-287-408-5_9
31. Zhang, F., Kaufman, D.: Massively Multiplayer Online Role-Playing Games (MMORPGs) and socio-emotional wellbeing. Comput. Hum. Behav. 73(c), 451–458 (2017)
32. Ducheneaut, N., Moore, R.: The social side of gaming: a study of interaction patterns in a massively multiplayer online game. In: Proceedings of the ACM Conference on Computer-Supported Cooperative Work, Chicago, USA, pp. 360–369. ACM Press (2004)

The Gamer Types of Seniors and Gamification Strategies Toward Physical Activity

Chia-Ming Kuo[(✉)] and Hsi-Jen Chen

Department of Industrial Design, National Cheng Kung University, No. 1,
University Road, East District, Tainan 701, Taiwan
p900372012@gmail.com, hsijen_chen@mail.ncku.edu.tw

Abstract. Gamification strategies were utilized as persuasive designs for promoting physical activities in recent years. However, the "one-size-fits-all"
design approach cannot be employed effectively to convince all users to engage
in targeted behaviors. Consequently, personalized gamified interactions which
require an adaptation of gameful experiences to the user's preferences were
applied to drive users more effectively. The aim of this study was to investigate
the gamer types among the seniors, and which gamification strategies are
affected by the same gamer types, thereby engaging in more physical activities.
We conducted an online questionnaire to investigate the gamer types of seniors.
Based on the results, seniors can be divided into three categories of gamers:
Easygoing, Socializer and Achiever. For the Easygoing, they showed little
preference for gamification strategies and were more difficult to drive by specific
strategies. The Socializer tends to be driven by socially oriented gamification
strategies, but disliked punishment in games. Furthermore, the Achiever preferred to pursue personal achievements rather than interacting with others in
games. The findings of this study contribute to HCI Community with the preliminary investigations on the gamer types of seniors, arriving at a better
understanding of how persuasive technology can be designed to meet the needs
of seniors.

Keywords: Gamification strategy · Senior · Gamer type · Physical activity

1 Introduction

Previous research has revealed that aging is associated with physical and psychological
changes, including the decline in cognitive abilities [1, 2], the loss of long-term partners and social support, etc. [3]. These changes in life increase the prevalence of
depression and chronic diseases [3, 4]. Nevertheless, many preventive strategies have
been demonstrated to help seniors facing life changes. Past research suggested that the
types and amounts of physical activities relevant to slow down the aging process,
which were also associated with lower risks of cognitive decline [5–7] and chronic
diseases such as cardiovascular diseases, diabetes, hypertension, obesity, etc. [8]. In
addition, physical activities are factors that help to relax and relieve stress, promote the
quality of life and increase sense of happiness [9].

© Springer Nature Switzerland AG 2019
J. Zhou and G. Salvendy (Eds.): HCII 2019, LNCS 11593, pp. 177–188, 2019.
https://doi.org/10.1007/978-3-030-22015-0_14

On the other hand, as the advancement of technology and the popularity of mobile devices, there have been many studies on how to use technology to persuade people to engage in more physical activities in recent years. The method of using designed technologies to change attitudes or behaviors of the users are so-called "Persuasive Technology" [10]. Gamification is a persuasive technology that attempts to influence user's behaviors by activating individual motives via game-design elements [11]. However, not all game-design elements can drive users to engage in targeted behaviors. The differences in personality traits, personality, gamer type, and age between users affect their perception and preference, and in turn affect their execution motivation for targeted behaviors [12–15]. Therefore, specific gamification strategies have to be applied for users with different personality traits to persuade them to engage in targeted behaviors. However, past researches made were mostly focusing on the applications of gamification for the young communities, rarely made on the gamer types of seniors, and preferences regarding technologies that motivate them for more targeted behaviors. Thus this paper conducted a questionnaire to investigate the gamer types of seniors and classify those who could be driven via similar gamification strategies into different "gamer types", and investigate the characteristics of each gamer types.

2   Literature Review

2.1   Persuasive Technology and Gamification

Persuasive Technology. Persuasive Technology has been proposed by Fogg [10], which was defined as a technology that was designed to change attitudes or behaviors of the users through persuasion and social influence rather than coercion. Increased popularity of smartphones made technology become vital to our daily life. Smartphones storage various visual information and the data from users' everyday-life scenarios could be collected by connecting with a variety of sensors for analyses [17, 18]. We could conduct experiments and collect data that are closer to reality easily with the assistance of such technologies. Likewise technologies such as internet, wearable devices, environmental sensors, and virtual reality have also become good tools for interacting and persuading people.

Gamification. The concept of Gamification is often adopted in the field of persuasive technology to enhance the motives of the targeted groups, and which in turn achieve behavior changes. Gamification is defined based on two perspectives, (1) the use of game elements in non-gaming system contexts [19]; (2) the use of game thinking and game mechanics to encourage for further activities and problem solving [20]. Some behaviors can bring benefits and have a significant influence to people's health in everyday life, such as healthy diets, physical activities, etc. Nevertheless, people may require amount of efforts and easily get bored for these positive behaviors. Therefore, studies were focused on gamification for persuading people by more enjoyable way to drive low-motivation behaviors.

Core Drives of Gamification. Hamari et al. [21] reviewed 24 studies on gamification and compiled ten "Motivational Affordances" that can drive users to engage in targeted behavior; Sailer et al. classified 7 "Gamification Elements" by reviewing research literature on gamification mechanisms; Orji, Nacke and Di Marco [23] have co-compiled the induction of Fogg [10] and Oinas-Kukkonen et al. [24], attributing into 10 "Persuasive Strategies" that can be applied to the gamification system. Furthermore, Chou [11] indicated his point on gamification in academic works "Actionable Gami-fication", suggesting "human-oriented design" to provide users with motivation rather than the "functionalities-oriented design" during the gamification design process. Chou deemed it important to investigate how the Gamification Elements drive the users to change their behaviors thus he has concluded 8 "Gamification Core Drives" via gamified theory examples in daily life, and named as "Octalysis":

- **Epic meaning and calling:** This Core Drive is in play when a person believes he or she is doing something meaningful, or has come up with sense of adventure or competency.
- **Development and Accomplishment:** This Core Drive is to make players focus on growth, making efforts for achieving mastery, and obtain the sense of achievement during the process.
- **Empowerment of Creativity & Feedback:** It emphasizes on allowing players to exert their creativity and see the results immediately. Because the creativity of each game is different, the result of the game is different too, so that the users are deeply attracted and not bored.
- **Ownership & Possession:** The players may feel themselves running certain types of things according to their own thoughts, such as a foster type of game, or a collection of virtual currency or virtual items.
- **Social influence and relatedness:** They are originated from people's desires for social contacts. In order to be integrated into social groups, people would comply to the commonly-recognized behaviors to avoid social rejection. This core drive has been applied in games, and the what we can see frequently are cooperation, com-petition, etc.
- **Scarcity and impatience:** Scarcity is resulted when the demand of something is greater than the supply. The cherished things may make users amazed that they won't hesitate to pay money and time to obtain them.
- **Unpredictability and curiosity:** People are usually curious upon things unpre-dictable, and this core drive is to drive the players by utilizing curiosity.
- **Loss and avoidance:** This core drive is from the fear of losing some things. The players would regret much if they losing some things in the games after spending all the time and efforts, thus they would prevent such loss from happening.

In spite of the discrepancy for above-mentioned terms of "Motivational Affordance", "Gamification Element", "Persuasive Strategy" or "Core Drives", these concepts have applied gamified elements to strategically drive the targeted gamers' groups, and the definitions are also similar. We consolidated these theories and summarize them into 12 gamification design frameworks as shown in the table below:

Table 1. Gamification design strategies and descriptions

Core drives [11]	Gamification design strategies			Naming and description	
	Persuasive strategy [23]	Motivation [21]	Gamification elements [22]		
Epic meaning and calling	Simulation			Simulation	By means of simulation, let users know the meaning and benefits of engaging in the targeted behaviors
Development and accomplishment		Points, Badges, Levels	Points, Badges	Point/Level/Badge	Driving and motivating users to engage in targeted behaviors by points, badges, and levels
	Self-monitoring and Feedback	Progress	Performance Graphs	Performance Graphs	Providing information about the users' performance compared to their preceding performance during a game.
	Goal-setting and Suggestion	Clear goals, Feedback		Goal-setting	Users set their own goals and provide appropriate advice
Empowerment of creativity and feedback	Customization			Customization	Users create their own ideas in the game
Ownership and possession			Avatars	Avatar	Offering users virtual avatars on behalf of themselves
Social influence and relatedness	Competition	Leaderboard	Leaderboards	Leaderboard	Competing with others, the scores of the competition will be presented in the rankings
	Cooperation		Teammates	Cooperation	Co-working with others to get more rewards in the games
Scarcity and impatience		Reward		Scarce Reward	Using rare and precious rewards to entice users to engage in targeted behaviors
Unpredictability and curiously		Story/Theme	Meaningful stories	Narrative Story	Creating a relevant story and attracting users about the follow-up
		Reward		Unpredictable Reward	Using a variable mechanism to earn the rewards randomly
Loss and avoidance	Punishment			Punishment	Conduct punishment to take away the belongings of gamers

2.2 Gamer Types and Gamification

Most gamification designs were developed as a one-size-fits-all approach which was used to explore whether the gamification strategies can drive targeted groups to engage in targeted behaviors. The concept of this design faces criticism as not considering the idiosyncratic needs of users. Hamari et al. [21] reviewed 24 studies on gamification and found that the application of gamification strategies can indeed provide users with additional motivations. However, part of the gamers showed negative attitudes toward the respective approaches, indicating the "one-size-fits-all" design cannot drive users efficiently and accurately. It was also revealed in the study by Orji et al. [25], which argued that individual differences need to be considered, and specific strategies are required to drive specific groups to engage in targeted behaviors. Orji et al. [25] investigated how persuasive game applications can be personalized by tailoring the persuasive strategies to various personality types. Therefore, studies on gamification relevant to gamers' motivation in recent year were focused on concerning the motivation of individuals. Ferro et al. [26] proposed the design of gamification elements by investigating possible relations among player types, personality traits, and game elements, suggesting a more practical design for gamification. The study of Orji et al. [16] investigated the perception of individual gamification strategies by different users with a "Healthy Diet Apps". The results revealed that different types of gamers showed significant differences for gamification strategies. For example, gamers of the "player" type are driven by gamification strategies such as competition, cooperation, and rewards. However, gamers of the "disruptors" type are not being driven by gamification strategies such as punishment, goal setting, simulation, and self-monitoring. Furthermore, Jia et al. [15] explored the relationship between the "Big Five" traits and gamified motivation preferences. It was found that different personality traits affect the perception of gamification strategies. This research also indicated that the age growth and emotional stability were negatively correlated with their preferences for all gamification strategy, suggesting that people are less likely to be driven by these gamification strategies along with the growth of the age. She concluded that the emotional stability will get better as aging, thus not easily affected by the sensory stimuli that gamification brings to the gamers. In Taiwan, numerous of seniors play mobile games, such as "Pokémon" and "Star Mahjong ", indicating a large potential market size of the game for senior players. We conducted a better understanding of how persuasive technology can be designed to meet the needs of the seniors in this paper.

3   Method

In this article, we conducted an online questionnaire to investigate the perception of gamification among seniors. Prior researches on gamification were reviewed to have a comprehensive understanding of gamification. This study summarized the core drives of "Octalysis" proposed by Chou [11] and the gamification motivates and strategies proposed by Sailer et al. [22], Orji et al. [23], Jia et al. [15] and conclude into 12 Gamification design strategies (See Table 1). Referring to the method proposed by Jia et al. [15], we demonstrated these gamification strategies with an online video in the online questionnaire to help the participants understand how the gamification strategies works.

3.1   Participants for the Online Questionnaire

The design of gamified applications targeting elderly people aged 55 to 65. Those over the age of 65 were excluded in the research for reasons given below: (1) Aging is a gradual process. It is meaningful for seniors to continue their habits of pursuing physical activities against aging before entering aged population. (2) Older adults over the age of 65 have less experiences with digital technologies. They may not be able to understand the gamification strategies through demonstration videos and use their own mobile phones and computers to complete the questionnaire. Finally 60 valid questionnaires have been collected for analysis in this study.

3.2   Questionnaire Design

The questionnaires were divided into two parts. In the first part, participants were asked to fill in their general information, physical activity habits, and frequency of playing mobile games. The second part was an aim to know how the participants perceive gamification. Participants fill in a five-point Likert scale questionnaire about their perceptions of gamification after viewing the demonstration video (See left picture of Fig. 1). The questions were designed to ask the answerers for their understanding of the gamification, whether the game can bring fun to them and help them to carry out physical activities, whether the game can drive them to engage in more physical activities, and whether the game has used simple rules and interfaces. In addition, the question design for level of understanding was to confirm whether participants fully understand the operation mode of the gamification presented in the film. If the participants who are not able to understand gamification, the collected information will be regarded as an invalid data. Other questions are referenced from the studies by Halko et al. [27] and by Jia et al. [15]. This questionnaire took about 15 or 20 min to complete.

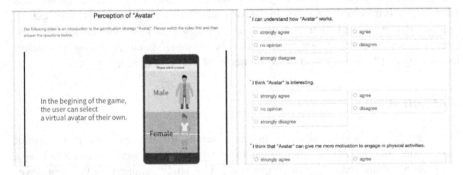

Fig. 1. Online questionnaire design

4   Results

The participant's driving scores for each question were standardized in the beginning of analysis, and the SPSS software was used for cluster analysis. The groupings were based on the driving scores according to their attribute preferences from "fun scores", "driving scores", and "helpful scores". To determine how the participants can be identified into groups, a hierarchical cluster analysis was used to examine the decision tree in the report. According to the structure of the decision tree, a relevant conclusion has been made to divide into three groups. Furthermore, K-Means Cluster Analysis has been implemented to know about the grouping status of each participant.

The results of K-means cluster analysis showed the amount of the three groups were 40, 6, and 14, respectively, but it did not indicate whether there were any significant differences between each group. Therefore, we applied one way analysis of variance (ANOVA) to examine the differences between the three groups. We served the numbers of groups as the independent variables, and the standardized values of "fun scores", "driving scores", and "helpful scores" as the dependent variables for comparing the differences between the groups. Based on the analysis results, we named the three groups as "Easygoing", "Socializer" and "Achiever", and the details were shown as follows.

4.1 Comparison of Three Groups

Table 2 showed the differences between three groups after ANOVA, and * the mark indicated the significant difference (p $\leq$ 0.05). Italic was marked on the items with low driving scores, while bold was marked on the items with high driving scores. It was found that the "Easygoing" exhibited lower driving scores in the items "Point/Level/Badge" and "Performance Graph"; higher driving scores in the items "Unpredictable Reward" and "Punishment". In spite of higher driving scores in the items "Unpredictable Reward" and "Punishment", the driving scores were close to zero, revealing that the "Easygoing" group showed no particularly preference in these 2 gamified items. The seniors in the "Socializer" group preferred the socially oriented gamification strategies, showing higher driving scores in the items "Leaderboard" and "Cooperation", and lower driving scores in the items "Unpredictable Reward". They do not prefer the gamification strategies of Unpredictable Reward that the motivation scores were significantly lower than those of the other two groups. In addition, the Socializers extremely disliked the gamification of "Punishment" with the driving scores all below −2 in all three indicators. On the contrary, those in "Achiever" have shown less preference on the socially-oriented gamification strategies, especially the item "Leaderboard". They preferred a gamification strategy for personal achievement orientation, such as Point/Level/Badge and Performance Graph.

4.2 Comparing the Driving Scores Within a Group

This study investigated the role of gamer type among seniors, and which gamification strategies were affected by the same gamer types, thereby engaging in more physical activities. The driving scores of core drives for each group of 12 gamification strategies were also discussed in this article. Table 3 lists the top three driving scores and the bottom three cores of the core drives in each group.

Seniors in the "Easygoing" group preferred the gamified items "Leaderboard", "Customization", "Narrative Story" and "Unpredictable Reward", showing less preference in the items "Punishment", "Avatar" and "Scarce Reward". All the driving scores of core drives for "Easygoing" group were close to zero, suggesting that there's no specific gamification strategies for driving them in the games. Nevertheless, this conclusion requires further verification.

The top 2 preferences of core drives for the "Socializer" were "Cooperation" and "Leaderboard". Both of the 2 items used social influence to drive gamers to engage in targeted behaviors. In addition, the driving scores in the item "Progress Graph" are similar to "Leaderboard". Those of the "Socializer" disliked and concerned about the "Punishment" mechanism. It should be verified by further experiment whether them would lose their motives as "Punishment" mechanism was applied on them.

Table 2. Differences between three groups after ANOVA

Items	Group 1 (Easygoing)	Group 2 (Socializer)	Group 3 (Achiever)
Point/Level/Badge_Fun Scores	*0.02**	0.46	0.46
Point/Level/Badge_Driving Scores	−0.03	0.17	**0.66***
Point/Level/Badge_Helpful Scores	*−0.03**	0.42	0.49
Performance Graph_Fun Scores	*−0.01**	0.13*	**0.46***
Performance Graph_Driving Scores	*0.05**	0.67	0.58
Performance Graph_Helpful Scores	*0.02**	–	**0.35***
Leaderboard_Fun Scores	0.17*	**0.79***	*−0.69**
Leaderboard_Driving Scores	0.20	0.67	*−0.49**
Leaderboard_Helpful Scores	0.20*	**0.92***	*−0.65**
Cooperation_Fun Scores	−0.11	**1.13***	-0.33
Cooperation_Driving Scores	−0.10	**1.50***	−0.42
Cooperation_Helpful Scores	−0.05	**1.08***	−0.22
Unpredictable Reward_Fun Scores	**−0.01***	−0.87	−0.4
Unpredictable Reward_Driving Scores	**0.07***	*−0.67**	*−0.35**
Unpredictable Reward_Helpful Scores	**0.17***	−0.75	−0.29
Punishment_Fun Scores	**−0.21***	*−2.37**	*−0.97**
Punishment_Driving Scores	**−0.23***	*−2.34**	−1.06*
Punishment_Helpful Scores	**−0.15***	*−2.08**	−0.94*
Simulation_Helpful Scores	0.02	−0.25	**0.42***
Customization_Fun Scores	*0.14**	–	**0.53***
Total Amount	40	6	14

Table 3. The top three high driving scores and the last three low driving scores of the gamification strategy for each tree group

Rank		Group		
		Easygoing	Socializer	Achiever
Top	1	Leaderboard (0.2) Customization (0.2)	Cooperation (1.5)	Point/Level/Badge (0.66)
	2	Narrative Story (0.12)	Leaderboard (0.67)	Performance Graph (0.58)
	3	Unpredictable Reward (0.07)	Scarce Reward (0.33)	Goal-setting (0.39)
Last	1	Punishment (−0.23)	Punishment (−2.34)	Punishment (−1.06)
	2	Avatar (−0.18)	Unpredictable Reward (−0.67)	Leaderboard (−0.49)
	3	Scarce Reward (−0.13)	Goal-setting (−0.37)	Cooperation (−0.42)

As for those of the "Achiever", they preferred the core drives of "Point/Level/Badge", "Progress Graph" and "Goal-setting" which attributed to personal-achievement-oriented items in the gamification strategies. They like single-player games and got a sense of achievements from them, but showed no preference on cooperating and competing with others in games.

Furthermore, the lowest driving scores showed in the three groups were "Punishment". It was suggested that "Punishment" was a core drive with "Black Hat Gamification Design" defined by Chou [11]. This type of gamification design make gamers feel urgent, stressful or uncomfortable that gamers tend to engage in targeted behaviors to eliminate such negative feelings. However, the cost of engaging in physical activities may be greater than the incentives provided by the games, causing the gamers to give up physical activities directly as they get punished in the games.

5 Discussion

Previous studies indicated that there are different preferences of gamification strategies between different gamer types. Thus specific gamification strategies are required to effectively drive the specific gamer groups [15, 23]. In this study, it is found that different gamer groups showed different preferences in the gamification strategies too. Based on the analysis of the questionnaire, we divided the gamer types of the seniors into three categories. The characteristics of three types of gamer were discussed as follows:

Easygoing. The "Easygoing" type of gamers predominate the overall samples, with 40 out of 60 ones belonging to this type. All the driving scores of the core drives for "Easygoing" group were close to zero, the highest driving scores were shown on the "Driving Score" and "Helpful Score" of the "Leaderboard", but just 0.2, suggesting that there's no specific preference of gamification strategies for driving them into the games. Compared to the other 2 groups of gamers, the "Easygoing" exhibited less preference for the two gamification items of "Point/Level/Badge" and "Performance Graph". In addition, the gamers in the "Easygoing" group showed less aversion for the item "Punishment" than the "Socializer" and "Achiever" even though the driving scores have shown negative values. Most of the gamification strategies can be applied for the "Easygoing" type gamers, and so can the "Black Hat" Types games.

Socializer. The "Socializer" type of gamers have accounted for the least percentage, with only 6 persons in our samples that we guess it could be attributing to the cultural difference. For the seniors in the "Socializer" group, their preferences of gamification strategy were focused on two items related to social impact: Leaderboard and Cooperation. Compared to other 2 groups, the "Socializer" scores significantly higher on the items "Leaderboard" & "Cooperation" than other groups. Furthermore, the "Socializer" gamers cannot be driven by the core drives of "Punishment" and "Unpredictable Reward". The best way to drive the "Socializer" gamer is using socially-oriented gamification strategies and avoid the "Punishment" and "Unpredictable" mechanisms.

Achiever. The "Achiever" gamers preferred achievement-oriented gamification strategies, such as "Point/Level/Badge" and "Performance Graph", which got higher "fun scores" of "Performance Graph" than the other 2 groups. To the Contrary with the "Socializer" gamers, the "Achiever" gamers showed no preference for socially-oriented gamification strategies, especially for the item of "Leaderboard". Their driving scores for "Leaderboard" were much lower than that of "Cooperation", indicating that "Achiever" gamers tend to pursue the self-breakthrough pleasure in the games, and showed no preference for having social intervention or competing with others. For the gamer type of "Achiever", the design of the games should focus on the characteristics of self-breakthrough and self-growth, and avoid the use of socially-oriented gamification strategies. The "Cooperation" way of design should be applied in case social-oriented of strategy was a must.

6 Conclusion

In this research, prior studies of gamification were collected and summarized into 12 strategies for promoting physical activities. We conducted an online questionnaire to investigate the gamer types of seniors aged 50–65 by applying these 12 gamification strategies. Based on the scores of the questionnaire items, seniors can be grouped into three categories of gamers in accordance to their preferences eventually: "Easygoing", "Socializer" and "Achiever". Seniors in the "Easygoing" group showed no particular preference for the gamified items, and they did not dislike black-hat gamification design of the item "Punishment" much either. The "Socializer" gamers interested in the socially-oriented gamification items, and extremely disgusted with the "Punishment" mechanism. As to the"Achiever" gamers, they preferred personal-achievement-oriented gamification strategies, but could not be driven by socially-oriented items for physical activities.

In conclusion, past researches have been studied mostly on the applications of gamification for the young communities. Since more and more seniors have experiences in using digital technologies thus it does worth it to persuade seniors with such technologies. The findings of the study contribute to HCI Community with the preliminary investigation on the gamer types of seniors, and future research should be further focused on practical experiments to verify the conclusions of the self-reports.

References

1. Kappen, D.L., Nacke, L.E., Gerling, K.M., Tsotsos, L.E.: Design strategies for gamified physical activity applications for older adults. In: 49th Hawaii International Conference on System Sciences (HICSS), pp. 1309–1318, IEEE (2016)
2. Ijsselsteijn, W., Nap, H.H., de Kort, Y., Poels, K.: Digital game design for elderly users. In: Proceedings of the 2007 Conference on Future Play, pp. 17–22. ACM (2007)
3. Vasconcelos, A., Silva, P.A., Caseiro, J., Nunes, F., Teixeira, L.F.: Designing tablet-based games for seniors: the example of CogniPlay, a cognitive gaming platform. In: Proceedings of the 4th International Conference on Fun and Games, pp. 1–10. ACM (2012)

4. Kaufman, D.: Aging Well: Can Digital Games Help? Overview of the Project. World Social Science Forum, Montreal (2013)
5. Yaffe, K., Barnes, D., Nevitt, M., Lui, L.Y., Covinsky, K.: A prospective study of physical activity and cognitive decline in elderly women: women who walk. Arch. Intern. Med. **161**(14), 1703–1708 (2001)
6. Clarkson-Smith, L., Hartley, A.A.: Relationships between physical exercise and cognitive abilities in older adults. Psychol. Aging **4**(2), 183 (1989)
7. Hultsch, D.F., Hammer, M., Small, B.J.: Age differences in cognitive performance in later life: relationships to self-reported health and activity life style. J. Gerontol. **48**(1), P1–P11 (1993)
8. Warburton, D.E., Nicol, C.W., Bredin, S.S.: Health benefits of physical activity: the evidence. Canad. Med. Assoc. J. **174**(6), 801–809 (2006)
9. Penedo, F.J., Dahn, J.R.: Exercise and well-being: a review of mental and physical health benefits associated with physical activity. Curr. Opin. Psychiatry **18**(2), 189–193 (2005)
10. Fogg, B.J.: Persuasive technology: using computers to change what we think and do. Ubiquity **2002**, Article no. 5 (2002)
11. Chou, Y.K.: Actionable Gamification: Beyond Points, Badges, and Leaderboards. Octalysis Group, Milipitas (2016)
12. Jia, Y., Liu, Y., Yu, X., Voida, S.: Designing leaderboards for gamification: perceived differences based on user ranking, application domain, and personality traits. In: Proceedings of the 2017 CHI Conference on Human Factors in Computing Systems, pp. 1949–1960. ACM (2017)
13. Klock, A.C., Gasparini, I., Pimenta, M.S., de Oliveira, J.P.M.: 'Everybody is playing the game but nobody's rules are the same': towards adaptation of gamification based on users' characteristics. Bull. IEEE Techn. Committee Learn. Technol. **17**(4), 22 (2015)
14. Orji, R., Vassileva, J., Mandryk, R.L.: Modeling the efficacy of persuasive strategies for different gamer types in serious games for health. User Model. User-Adapt. Interact. **24**(5), 453–498 (2014)
15. Jia, Y., Xu, B., Karanam, Y., Voida, S.: Personality-targeted gamification: a survey study on personality traits and motivational affordances. In: Proceedings of the 2016 CHI Conference on Human Factors in Computing Systems, pp. 2001–2013. ACM (2016)
16. Orji, R., Tondello, G.F., Nacke, L.E.: Personalizing persuasive strategies in gameful systems to gamification user types. In: Proceedings of the 2018 CHI Conference on Human Factors in Computing Systems, p. 435. ACM (2018)
17. Koch, S., Marschollek, M., Wolf, K., Plischke, M., Haux, R.: On health-enabling and ambient-assistive technologies. Methods Inf. Med. **48**(1), 29–37 (2009)
18. Zuckerman, O., Gal-Oz, A.: Deconstructing gamification: evaluating the effectiveness of continuous measurement, virtual rewards, and social comparison for promoting physical activity. Pers. Ubiquit. Comput. **18**(7), 1705–1719 (2014)
19. Deterding, S., Dixon, D., Khaled, R., Nacke, L.: From game design elements to gamefulness: defining gamification. In: Proceedings of the 15th International Academic MindTrek Conference: Envisioning Future Media Environments, pp. 9–15. ACM (2011)
20. Zichermann, G., Cunningham, C.: Gamification by Design: Implementing Game Mechanics in Web and Mobile Apps. O'Reilly Media, Inc., Sebastopol (2011)
21. Hamari, J., Koivisto, J., Sarsa, H.: Does gamification work? A literature review of empirical studies on gamification. In: 47th Hawaii International Conference on System Sciences (HICSS), pp. 3025–3034. IEEE (2014)
22. Sailer, M., Hense, J.U., Mayr, S.K., Mandl, H.: How gamification motivates: an experimental study of the effects of specific game design elements on psychological need satisfaction. Comput. Hum. Behav. **69**, 371–380 (2017)

23. Orji, R., Nacke, L.E., Di Marco, C.: Towards personality-driven persuasive health games and gamified systems. In: Proceedings of the 2017 CHI Conference on Human Factors in Computing Systems, pp. 1015–1027. ACM (2017)

24. Oinas-Kukkonen, H., Harjumaa, M.: A systematic framework for designing and evaluating persuasive systems. In: Oinas-Kukkonen, H., Hasle, P., Harjumaa, M., Segerståhl, K., Øhrstrøm, P. (eds.) PERSUASIVE 2008. LNCS, vol. 5033, pp. 164–176. Springer, Heidelberg (2008). https://doi.org/10.1007/978-3-540-68504-3_15

25. Orji, R., Mandryk, R.L., Vassileva, J., Gerling, K.M.: Tailoring persuasive health games to gamer type. In: Proceedings of the SIGCHI Conference on Human Factors in Computing Systems, pp. 2467–2476. ACM (2013)

26. Ferro, L.S., Walz, S.P., Greuter, S.: Towards personalised, gamified systems: an investigation into game design, personality and user typologies. In: Proceedings of the 9th Australasian Conference on Interactive Entertainment: Matters of Life and Death, p. 7. ACM (2013)

27. Halko, S., Kientz, J.A.: Personality and persuasive technology: an exploratory study on health-promoting mobile applications. In: Ploug, T., Hasle, P., Oinas-Kukkonen, H. (eds.) PERSUASIVE 2010. LNCS, vol. 6137, pp. 150–161. Springer, Heidelberg (2010). https://doi.org/10.1007/978-3-642-13226-1_16

Playing with Words: The Experience of Self-disclosure in Intergenerational Gaming

Sanela Osmanovic[⊠] and Loretta L. Pecchioni

Department of Communication Studies, Louisiana State University,
Baton Rouge, USA
{sosman3,lpecch1}@lsu.edu

Abstract. While small and large technological miracles have undoubtedly made our lives easier, they have potentially also made a significant part of our daily social routine obsolete. People live in the same space but rarely spend quality time together, interacting and bonding. One of the solutions to enhance family relationships may lie in the technology itself—video games. Previous research having shown the sociability of video games, and in this study, we examined their potential in creating closer family relationships, especially among different generations. Participants (n = 183) were asked to play video games together over a period of six weeks. Participants completed a modified version of the self-disclosure and relationship closeness inventories before and after the treatment and responded to a series of open-ended questions post-treatment. Results indicate an increase in breadth and depth of self-disclosure, and in relationship closeness in both younger and older adults. Gathering around a novel shared activity, both younger and older adults found new ways of connecting to their family members, whether through more frequent conversations, broader selection of topics, shared subjects, or pure entertainment. The findings suggest that video games can provide a platform for family communication, resulting in the rejuvenation and maintenance of intergenerational relationships.

Keywords: Family relationships · Video games · Older adults · Relationship closeness · Intergenerational gaming

1 Introduction

Decades of scientific research have placed family communication in a prominent position as the source for a child's attitudes, beliefs, and behaviors. Family members provide a foundation for the development of self, serving as primary socialization agents in the acquisition of interpersonal skills necessary for social wellbeing and relationship development [1, 2], and healthy behaviors [3] to name a few. While the emphasis in research is usually placed on parent-child relationships, the family as a unit affects the child's development and one of these influential family relationships is that between a grandparent and a grandchild. Distinct due to the usually large generational gap, positive grandparent-grandchild relationships have been shown to produce positive psychosocial outcomes for both parties, where grandchildren gain a source of

© Springer Nature Switzerland AG 2019
J. Zhou and G. Salvendy (Eds.): HCII 2019, LNCS 11593, pp. 189–203, 2019.
https://doi.org/10.1007/978-3-030-22015-0_15

family values, beliefs, and history, as well as social support, and grandparents gain a source of pride and the feeling of being young again [4]. Studies have shown that young adults have a rather negative view of older adults, holding up the stereotypes of old age—deterioration of physical and mental faculties—undervaluing their competence, their perceived intelligence or abilities [5]. On the other hand, close relationships with grandparents have been found to generate positive stereotyping of older adults [6]. Thus, it is important to provide younger and older adults with an opportunity and means to create closer family bonds, improving not only their relationships, but also potentially affecting the views of and interactions among the generations on the whole. In this study, we examine the outcome of joint video gaming on intergenerational relationship development within families, especially as it pertains to an important element of relationships—the role grandparents and grandchildren play in each other's lives.

1.1 Aging and Family Relationships

Population aging is one of the sturdiest demographic trends of the past few decades, particularly in developed countries. According to the National Institute of Aging [7], "in 2006, almost 500 million people worldwide were 65 and older. By 2030, that total is projected to increase to 1 billion—1 in every 8 of the earth's inhabitants" (p. 2). The rise in life expectancy combined with the decline in natality is making older adults an increasingly large fraction of the world's population [7], leaving a significant mark on the relationships and the structure of families. Three and even four generations are now in a position to spend significant parts of their lives together, with older adults having a much larger span of years to perform their family roles, and "intergenerational relationships...take on an added dimension as the number of grandparents and great-grandparents increase" (p. 10). Thus, it becomes increasingly important to form and maintain strong bonds among older and younger adults in families, especially since these relationships are typically involuntary and tend to be sacrificed on the altar of the all-consuming adolescence and newfound independence. As adolescents become involved in the unforgiving whirlpool of new romantic, academic, and social activities, family ties take a back seat and the frequency and intensity of relationships weakens, especially with the grandparents [8, 9]. One way to maintain important intergenerational relationships within families is through shared activities appealing to both sides of the age spectrum and, potentially, also creating closeness to further strengthen the bonds.

1.2 Video Games as a Relationship-Building Tool

The technological advancements of the past few decades have created a large gap among younger and older adults, alienating them from each other's worlds, and video games are a significant part of that process. While small and large technological miracles have undoubtedly made our lives easier, they have potentially also made a significant part of our daily social routine obsolete. Families and friends still gather, but now around television sets, or even more solitarily in the past decade, around computers, tablets and smartphones. Watching television, the activity on which families spend five hours a day on average, does not require nor necessitate much interaction [10]. Thus, those gathered around the screen may share the space but they share little else, either preoccupied by the program or otherwise immersed into social media on other devices and being only physically present. Such lack of communication and interpersonal interaction has led to weaker family ties, distant relationships, and even a breakdown of families and friendships [11]. While popular media continuously emphasize the importance of meaningful interactions among family members and friends for the strength of the relationships, resulting in calls for sharing meals without distractions, with the wide introduction of personal computers, tablets and smart-phones, the silence and distance are becoming more pervasive. A toddler with a phone in her hands, swiping surprisingly expertly with yet-to-become-nimble fingers in search of its favorite *Dora the Explorer* episode on YouTube has become a far more common sight than a toddler on a swing in the park. So, technology is also serving as a replacement for interaction with developing children while science scrambles to uncover long-term consequences of this new trend in parenting.

However, as postulated above, there may be a solution, and it may lie in the technology itself—after all, as the old idiom says, we have to fight fire with fire. The fire of recovery in this case may lie in one of the most controversial and discussed outcomes of the technological golden age—video games. As the biggest entertainment industry in the world, perpetually drawing attention of young adults especially, video games may hold the potential to make people happier and help them maintain a healthy social life within and outside their families. Indeed, research has shown that video gameplay, especially in the circle of friends and family members, can yield positive physical and mental outcomes, as well as improve relationships and promote connectedness [12–15]. Older adults are increasingly responding to their call as well— between 1999 and 2011, the number of gamers older than 50 has increased from 9 to 26% [16, 17]. Older adults, it transpires, enjoy demanding, intellectually challenging games with rich narratives, and large, involved communities in which they can take part—in short, they just want to have fun [18]. And they especially enjoy the social side of gaming [19, 20], as a means to spending time together, requesting help and attention from children and grandchildren, or something to structure the conversation with friends and family. In intergenerational family gaming, in particular, positive emotions such as happiness and enjoyment coalesced with–and stemmed from–the bonding, the conversations, the feeling of being closer to loved ones and of maintaining relationships across distances [12, 13, 21–23]. To look at how the sociability of video games affects relationship closeness, we employed the Social Penetration Theory.

1.3 Self-disclosure in Interpersonal Relationships

Social penetration theory (SPT) posits that relational closeness develops as a product of interpersonal communication advancing from superficial to more personal levels, and mainly through reciprocal self-disclosure [24]. Self-disclosure encompasses exchange of information, expressions of positive and negative emotions, as well as mutual activities [25]. In other words, behaviors considered in social penetration theory range from disclosure of low-risk personal information to the sharing of personal experiences, hopes and dreams, ambitions, and goals.

When it comes to the selectivity of self-disclosure—with whom we share information about ourselves and to what extent—Altman and Taylor drew on Thibaut and Kelley's [26] social exchange theory, viewing relationships in economic terms and self-disclosure in terms of the cost/reward ratio. As humans are rational creatures seeking rewards and avoiding punishment, we make judicious choices on disclosing information, considering not only the interests of the relationship, but also what effect given information will have on the other person. The initial, low-level self-disclosures serve to reduce uncertainty. As the relationship progresses, higher-level self-disclosures serve to promote a close relationship, and with it potentially gain help and support, satisfaction and contentment. On the other end of the spectrum, higher-level self-disclosures also carry a higher cost through greater vulnerability, potential rejection, loss of trust and the relationship. In every relationship, individuals weigh costs against the rewards, and if the perceived mutual benefits outweigh the cost of greater vulnerability, the self-disclosure and with it the social penetration will continue.

With this in mind, in social penetration theory Altman and Taylor [24] postulated that, after the initial encounter, the closeness of the relationship progresses through the linear stages as the breadth and depth—or the number of topics discussed, and the importance of the topic to the person respectively—of self-disclosure increase. Positive responses to self-disclosure have a positive effect on existing relationships; in family relationships, which are of interest for this study, it has been strongly associated with openness in family communication, cohesiveness, identity development, and satisfaction with family relationships [27]. Reciprocal self-disclosure between grandparents and grandchildren was found to be positively associated with perceptions of shared family identity [28].

These findings were also reflected in the few studies of self-disclosure in a mediated video game environment. Taylor and Taylor [29] found that game-mediated conversations were characterized by intimacy, where participants reported feeling safe disclosing personal information. In a study of 6000 messages exchanged among the players of a task-oriented game, Peña and Hancock [30] found the majority of them not to be task-related, but rather socioemotional and positively valenced. However, besides this work, few studies have looked specifically at self-disclosure and how it is used and perpetuated around gameplay to advance relationships. In this study, we sought to examine how intergenerational gameplay among family members affects the breadth and depth of the players' self-disclosure and thus relational closeness, postulating that:

H_1: Regularly playing video games together increases the breadth and depth of self-disclosure among family members of different generations.

H_2: Increase in breadth and depth of self-disclosure is positively associated with relationship closeness.

To summarize, how technology and society shape each other in a reciprocal process is the basic question of this study, since video games are both shaped by and shape the lives of those engaging in them. Digital technology has changed the fundamentals of how we interact and bond in society, taking away old and offering new infrastructure through which we can act [31]. Therefore, the aim of this study is to provide an interactional understanding of social video gaming within families. More specifically, what are the effects of social gaming on relationships, and what is its current and potential role as a social leisure activity in everyday family life? The main focus of the research presented here is the intergenerational social interaction in, around, and through video games, and how it potentially changes self-disclosure and closeness in family relationships.

1.4 Purpose of the Study

The aim of this study was to explore the effects of intergenerational video gaming on the bonds between older and younger family members. At the heart of the inquiry was the potential of the shared leisurely activity to build or maintain relationship closeness between family members, especially of different generations, through the increase in self-disclosure. To assess the effect of sharing the activity of playing video games as opposed to simply bonding over a conversation, we employed a mixed-methods longitudinal design to collect both survey data on self-disclosure and detailed personal accounts of the effects of gaming on dyadic family relationships. For comparison purposes, the same design was used to collect data on the effects of regular conversations on intergenerational family relationships, removing the shared gaming factor. The results of this investigation are presented below.

2 Method

To fully understand player interactions and relationship development in and around video gameplay, data were collected through a multi-method, longitudinal study. The participants were recruited from two classes at a large Southern USA university after receiving approval from the appropriate Institutional Review Board. Each participant was asked to select an older adult, age 55 and above, from their immediate family circle who will consent to play video games with him/her at least three hours a week, either in a mediated or co-located setting. Younger adults received partial course credit while older adults did not receive any compensation for taking part in the research. The data from the dyads was collected over a period of six weeks. The duration of six weeks was determined based on the research findings of a pilot study implemented during the summer of 2016.

Participants. The sample consisted of 182 participants: 89 older adults, 58 females and 31 males (M = 1.65, SD = .48), ages 55–77 (M = 59.43, SD = 4.57), and 93 younger adults, 51 females and 42 males (M = 1.59, SD = .50), ages 17–28 (M = 20.39, SD = 2.05). The older cohort (n = 89) comprised 75 (84.27%) grandparents, 11 (12.36%) parents, 2 (2.25%) stepparents, and 1 (1.12%) aunt. The younger cohort (n = 93) comprised 77 (82.80%) grandchildren, 13 (13.98%) children, 2 (2.15%) stepchildren, and 1 (1.08%) niece.

Data Collection. Considering the pretest-posttest nature of the study, self-completed questionnaires were used to collect standardized and thus comparable information from the participants. All questionnaires were web-based, administered using the Qualtrics survey tool. Web surveys were employed for being easily available and accessible, with the possibility to prompt for missing data or explain potentially difficult sections, which is important given the age of some of the participants and lack of funding for the study.

For the same reason and also given the potentially mediated nature of the study, thus placing participants at greater distances, the questionnaires were used to collect narrative data as well, allowing for a broader accessibility. The survey was distributed online. The questionnaire took approximately 30 min to fill out, with the narrative section approximated at 10 min.

All participants were tasked with completing a questionnaire at the beginning and the end of the study. The initial questionnaire consisted of six sections. The first section contained questions on demographic information (including gender, age, and relationship status) and the relationship between the two family members (i.e., parent-child or grandparent-grandchild) participating in the study. The second section comprised questions on previous gaming experiences (e.g. "Have you ever played video games?", "What games do you play most frequently?", "Do you play or have you played video games with older family members (age 55 and up)?"). The third section was available to those who positively responded to the query on previous gaming experience with older family members and comprised related to that experience (e.g. "With which older family member do you play video games most frequently?", "Within the past three months, how often have you played video games with this family member?"). Participants were then asked to complete the following two sections addressing self-disclosure, and relationship closeness items which were coded per their respective scales, detailed below.

Self-disclosure Rating Scale. The fourth and final survey section comprised questions on breadth and depth of self-disclosure, measured using the Revised Self-Disclosure Scale developed by Wheeless and Grotz [32]. Both breadth (8 items, e.g., "I usually talk about myself for fairly long periods at a time"; $\alpha = 0.82$) and depth (10 items, e.g., "Once I get started, my self-disclosures last a long time"; $\alpha = .84$) were measured using a 7-point Likert-type scale ranging from 1 = "strongly disagree" to 7 = "strongly agree." In hypotheses testing, both variables were treated as continuous.

Relationship Closeness. The fifth section comprised questions on relationship closeness, measured on a 7-point Likert scale using categories from the modified Friendship Qualities Scale [33], with predetermined questions for closeness (12 items; e.g. "_____ and I have a strong connection"; $\alpha = .77$). In hypotheses testing, the variable was treated as continuous.

The post-test survey, completed after six weeks of interaction, comprised five sections. The first section contained questions on demographic information and the relationship between the two family members participating in the study. The second section comprised questions on games played, gaming type (collaborative, cooperative, or other) and location (collocated, remote, or other) during the experiment. The following two sections comprised repeated self-disclosure, and relationship closeness measures.

Digital Postcards. The fifth and final section of the post-test survey was designed for narrative data collection, consisting of digital postcards asking the participants to share their experience of the six-week study in their own words. Participants were asked to reflect on their gaming/conversation rituals, the expectations, outcomes, and future plans in relation to joint gaming or conversations. Questions to aid in reflecting on the experience and writing the postcards were provided on the same page.

Data Analysis. Responses to the scaled items for both groups were examined using pretest-posttest statistical analysis, which is presented in greater detail in the Results chapters for both experimental groups. Narrative data was examined using careful, line-by-line content analysis, investigating the context, perspectives, and overall character of the responses. Emerging patterns and themes were uncovered by searching for word repetitions, then analyzing keywords and their context. Themes were grouped and assigned colors, and the narrative data was highlighted accordingly. The detailed analysis of pretest-posttest studies and the narrative data for both groups are presented in the next section.

3 Findings

Based on the responses from our participants, we answer our questions about if and in what ways intergenerational game playing may affect self-disclosure and relationship closeness between family members. Both older and younger adults largely reported positive outcomes from playing video games with family members–while enjoyment was an important aspect, maintaining connections with each other and with the home, and training cognitive and physical abilities were repeatedly emphasized. The changes in self-disclosure were also noted, as both gained more insight into each other's lives, knowledge, and thoughts.

Video Gaming Experience. The majority of the older adults who participated in the study—63 or 70.8%—reported never having previously played video games. None of the remaining 29.2% identified as active gamers or playing video games on a regular basis, but stated they had either tried video games in the past or play sporadically. Their gaming experience included a wide variety of games and platforms, from mobile apps to exergames and sports simulations, to more complex first-person shooters. Younger adults who participated in the study predominantly (82, 88.2%) reported playing or having played video games, of which 29 (31.2%) identified as active gamers who play six or more hours per week. They too reported having played or playing a variety of games on different platforms.

3.1 Self-disclosure

The first hypothesis posited that regularly playing video games together increases the breadth and depth of self-disclosure among family members of different generations. A paired t-test was employed to determine whether there was a statistically significant mean difference between breadth and depth of self-disclosure before and after the six-week gaming treatment. The results of the paired t-tests are presented in Table 1. Among younger adults, there was a statistically significant difference between pretest (M = 34.07, SD = 6.28) and posttest breadth of self-disclosure (M = 38.90,

SD = 15.00), t(92) = 2.94, p = .0042, CI.95 1.56, 8.09. Cohen's effect size (d = .42) suggests a moderate increase in the breadth of self-disclosure for this test group. Older adults also experienced an increase in the breadth of self-disclosure between pretest (M = 33.16, SD = 5.26) and posttest (M = 36.25, SD = 9.18), t(88) = 4.62 p = .0041, CI.95 1.75, 4.40. Cohen's effect size for older adults (d = 0.41) similarly suggests a moderate increase in the breadth of self-disclosure.

Table 1. Results of pretest and posttest self-disclosure dimensions for younger and older adults

Variable/Results	N	Pretest-posttest diff. of M	SD	t	p
Breadth of self-disclosure - younger adults	93	4.83	15.85	2.94	.0042
Depth of self-disclosure - younger adults	93	5.03	22.15	2.19	.0310
Breadth of self-disclosure - older adults	89	3.07	9.86	2.94	.0041
Depth of self-disclosure - older adults	89	3.98	17.49	2.15	.0347

Depth of self-disclosure also underwent a statistically significant increase for both groups. For younger adults, pretest (M = 44.15, SD = 11.64) and posttest (M = 49.18, SD = 17.11), t(92) = 2.19, p = .0310, CI.95 .47, 9.59, and Cohen's effect size value (d = 0.35) suggests a small to moderate increase in the depth of self-disclosure. Older adults also experienced a small to moderate increase in the depth of self-disclosure between pretest (M = 39.62, SD = 12.41) and posttest (M = 43.59, SD = 11.68), t(88) = 2.15, p = .0347, CI.95 .29, 7.66, and with Cohen's effect size score of d = .36. Therefore, the first hypothesis was supported for both older and younger adults, with a larger positive effect on breadth of self-disclosure than on depth.

3.2 Relationship Closeness

The second hypothesis predicted that an increase in the breadth and depth of self-disclosure results in an increase in the perception of relationship closeness. A Pearson's product-moment correlation was used to assess the relationship among the variables. Tables 2 and 3 present the results of the correlation analysis, where a statistically significant positive correlation was found between the change in the breadth of self-disclosure after the treatment, and the change in the perception of relationship closeness for both younger and older adults, with a more significant effect for the older cohort. In the same time, a statistically significant correlation was not found for the change in the depth of self-disclosure, and the change in the perception of relationship closeness for either younger and older adults. Thus, the second hypothesis was partially supported.

Table 2. Correlation matrix for relationship closeness, and breadth and depth of self-disclosure for younger adults

	N	Breadth	Depth	Closeness
Breadth	93	1.000		
Depth	93	.4461**	1.000	
Closeness	93	.3008*	.1427	1.000

Correlation is statistically significant at:
*$p < 0.05$; **$p < 0.01$*

Table 3. Correlation matrix for relationship closeness, and breadth and depth of self-disclosure for older adults

	N	Breadth	Depth	Closeness
Breadth	89	1.000		
Depth	89	.6025**	1.000	
Closeness	89	.6523**	−.0141	1.000

Correlation is statistically significant at:
*$p < 0.05$; **$p < 0.01$*

3.3   Qualitative Findings

In the final part of the closing survey, participants were asked to describe their six-week joint gaming experience—which games they played, did they compete or collaborate, what was the usual gaming ritual, what stood out to them the most, how did they feel about it at the beginning and the end of the study, will they continue playing video games together.

Games Played. Games were largely selected by the younger cohort, and comprised a variety of genres. Most of the dyads—60.7% (54)—played casual, turn-based app games such as Words with Friends and Trivia Crack. Other popular choices were Wii games (13, 14.6%), Minecraft (9, 10.1%), sports games such as Madden (6, 6.7%), first-person shooters such as Call of Duty (4, 4.5%), and simulations such as Need for Speed (3, 3.4%). An overwhelming number of older adults (80, 89.9%) reported enjoying the experience of playing games with their family members over the course of the study, citing fun, gratification of spending time together, learning something new, as well as feeling happy for being involved and able to help their child or grandchild with a school assignment. The majority of the younger cohort (77, 82.8%) also reported having enjoyed the experience of playing games with their family members over the course of the study, referencing connectedness, sharing an activity with a family member, and fun.

Self-disclosure. Both breadth and depth of self-disclosure featured prominently in the participants' comments about their shared experiences. An abundance of conversation brought along a slew of topics, both previously discussed and not. The participants reported sharing more of their lives, past and present, with their family members as they played together. A male participant, age 55, said:

I used to teach him how to play these games; and now he teaches me. This realization brought our relationship to a new level. We spoke about his station in life and his plans, relationships with others and long and short terms goals and achievements. We spoke a lot about politics and life itself.

Another male participant, age 59, had a similar experience:

Me and my stepson enjoyed playing video games together. He asked me how life was when I was growing up. We talked about how things were so different. It was a great opportunity for us to catch up. We often joked about all kinds of different things, but we also had serious conversations about how times are changing. It was really a great opportunity to connect with each other.

Younger participants also found enjoyment in the communication and conversations with their gaming partner, and learned more about them. As one male participant (19) explained:

I liked that we had the ability to communicate and actually play a game together. I feel like I learned more about how my mom thinks, I can understand better our different choices. I did not like that she was really close to beating me every time.

A female participant (21) from the younger cohort concurred:

This was the first time that I have ever played a game with any older family member. Throughout these six weeks, I learned more about myself as well as my family members than I had in all this time living an hour away from each other. Playing this game caused my grandfather and I to joke and talk more than normal, which really helped our relationship. I now know where my competitiveness [comes] from.

Older adults hope to continue gaming together. Said a male participant (57):

We plan on continuing our poker competition and adding my other son into our competition. After partaking in this experiment, I can say that I feel like we were able to grow in our relationship and become better friends. I also learned that my son is better than me at online poker.

A female participant (63) had the same idea:

I would continue to play video games with my grandchildren to connect with them and learn personal information about them. It is a good relaxed and neutral ground for both parties. It gives us a chance to slow down and listen to one another. I wish I could have used it with my own parents to learn about their history and lives before my existence.

Overall, about one-third (30, 33.1%) of older adults and younger adults (27, 29.1%) listed examples of one or both dimensions of self-disclosure as a part of their six-week gaming experience.

Relationship Closeness. Time spent together and the resulting closeness were in the center of most responses. As one female participant (57) noted:

My daughter is my oldest child so we have an extremely close bond. Now that she's older, it's hard for us to do fun things together even though we live in the same city. Even though it was a silly phone game for school, I appreciated the extra time we were able to spend together and I was surprised at the amount of time we actually spent engaged in conversation while doing this project. I think that more than anything that time actually made our relationship stronger.

Younger adults shared similar experiences, as a male participant (19) elaborated:

I found that we exchanged text messages more often during this time because my dad is a big trash talker. My dad and I already are very close but I'd say that this added an extra element to our relationship! It was great doing something together and it gave us something out of the norm to look forward to!

For some, it was about feeling physically closer to their family member, said one grandmother (63):

Watching your children become their own person is something all parents wish for. Yet, you still feel this loss of your child not being in your daily routine anymore. With these video games, as simple as it may sound, reconnects you again no matter how far. While I played, it made me think of her, and when she played, it made me feel like we were connected even thought we were not in the same city. It made me feel close to her and we enjoyed it.

A younger female participant (18) concurred:

I liked that we were playing together. It was a nice since the game put us both in position to have conversations about the game and other things in her and my life at the moment. She is about 900 miles away from me so it was a nice way to keep connected and share in each other's lives.

Others brought the family in on the gaming experience. A female participant (22) described her experience:

It made me want to expand my vocabulary. It also made me want to play more games with family members because it feels like you do get closer. You are constantly thinking about beating them when you play. Which means you are constantly thinking about them as well. Overall, I enjoyed this experience. I would not have started playing games with older relatives without this study. I will continue to do so now. The most fun was trash talk among and to family members because you shouldn't usually be doing that. When it comes to games though, it is totally acceptable to do so. I enjoyed playing games but I may switch to other games to play intergenerationally because I need spell check.

More than two-thirds of both older and younger adults (74.2% and 69.9% respectively) cited more frequent communication and spending more time together as the outcomes of the six-week joint gaming, while 24 (25.8%) younger adults and 31 (34.8%) older adults specifically cited an effect on relationship closeness. A female participant, age 74, said:

Playing games with my grandson keeps me sharp. We joke and talk and compliment each other on good moves. I love that he treats me as an equal and doesn't hold back. Playing games has brought us closer, in my opinion. Doing this with [my grandson] is now one of the joys in my life. I feel that playing games together has taught us both different things, we have learned from each other and about each other.

Participants' narratives provided a deeper understanding of their experiences, and perhaps an insight into potential moderating elements that occurred during the study. Primarily, both younger and older adults found new ways of connecting to their family members, whether through more frequent conversations, broader selection of topics, shared subjects, or pure entertainment. Gathering around the novel activity allowed participants the space to talk and listen in a relaxed environment, and they largely reported bonding and enjoyment, with older adults also placing emphasis on learning and acquiring new skills. Not all was fun and games, however, as the repetitiveness and simplicity of the selected games resulted in boredom and loss of interest for some participants of both cohorts. Several dyads who played more demanding and involving games relished the experience, but some older were left frustrated after struggling with complex controls, while their younger counterparts were annoyed with having to repeatedly provide instructions.

To summarize, after spending six weeks playing video games together, both younger and older adults experienced a moderate increase in the breadth and depth of self-disclosure. The broadening of the range of conversational topics and the increasingly personal nature of self-disclosures were positively associated with the enhancement of relationship closeness for both groups.

It is important to note that biological sex, location (collocated vs. mediated play) or type of gaming (collaborative vs. competitive) were not significantly correlated with the difference in self-disclosure and relationship closeness for either group. This shows that physical presence is not imperative in gaining benefits from intergenerational gaming, and whether players prefer collaborative or competitive games is not likely to affect the relational outcome of their joint activity.

4   Conclusion

In this study, we explored intergenerational video game playing among family members, seeking to find whether such shared activity provides a platform for building and maintaining interpersonal; relationships. Using a mixed-methods longitudinal design allowed us to collect both disclosure and closeness-specific quantitative data and detailed qualitative accounts of the effects of long-term gaming on dyadic family relationships.

Corresponding to the findings of previous studies [12, 13, 15, 19, 20, 23], the social side of gaming, the opportunity for conversation and bonding, drew in both younger and older adults. The older cohort, largely consisting of individuals who have never played video games before, found the experience entertaining, interesting, and gratifying. The younger cohort enjoyed the opportunity to display their expertise to older family members while in turn discovering more about them and receiving the benefit of an interested listener and adviser. While they played video games, in the background their relationships changed. In this study, we hypothesized that joint video gaming will increase the breadth and depth of self-disclosure between family members, as well as that said increase will result in higher perceived relationship closeness. The first hypothesis was supported as self-disclosure thrived during the shared activity—indeed, there was a moderate increase in breadth and depth of self-disclosure for both younger and older adults after the six-week gaming period. These findings resonate with the postulates of the Social Penetration Theory [24] that, as relationships progress, breadth and depth of self-disclosure increase. Breadth of self-disclosure was positively correlated with relationship closeness, more so for older than for younger adults. However, the correlation between depth of self-disclosure and relationship closeness, while positive, was not significant, thus the second hypothesis was not supported.

Again, narrative accounts may shed more light on these findings. Participants largely reported sharing more with and finding out more about their family members, connecting and understanding each other better. However, almost two-thirds of dyads played online games in a remote setting. While this platform provides for joking, small talk, and challenging each other, it is not the best channel for deeper, more intimate questions or revelations. It did still, however, provide a connection.

With each year, the aging population grows. In the same time, especially in the Western world, the use of technology has led to people living in the same space but rarely spending "quality time together," actually interacting and bonding. While popular media continuously emphasize the importance of meaningful interactions among family members and friends for the strength of the relationships, resulting in calls for sharing meals without distractions, with the wide introduction of personal computers, tablets and smartphones, the silence and distance are becoming more pervasive. In order to enhance lives across generations, the same technology can be used to counter this effect. With careful design and consideration of current and potential players, video games have the capacity to positively impact families, and social life in general, bridging the distance and drowning the silence.

5 Implications

With each year, the aging population grows [7]. In the same time, especially in the Western world, it seems that the use of technology has led to people living in the same space but rarely spending "quality time together," actually interacting and bonding. While popular media continuously emphasize the importance of meaningful interactions among family members and friends for the strength of the relationships, resulting in calls for sharing meals without distractions, with the wide introduction of personal computers, tablets and smartphones, the silence and distance are becoming more pervasive. However, as this and other recent studies show, the same technology can be used to counter this effect and enhance lives across generations. With careful design and consideration of current and potential players, video games have the capacity to positively impact families and social life in general, bridging the distance and drowning the silence [12, 13, 23].

6 Limitations

As with any research, this project has its limitations. The number of participants was relatively small, and they were all from the United States. As a consequence, we should not over-generalize our findings. In addition, for younger adults the participation was a part of the course requirement, which may have impacted their perception of the project —must vs. want—and thus the level of their participation and satisfaction. Future research should address the limitations to this study, as well as examine more specific aspects of influences, examining the effect of existing relationships, family patterns, and emotional and physical states. These additional motivations are important to gaining a more complete picture of shifts in family relationships and how video games can be used to help balance them.

References

1. Kunkel, A., Hummert, M.L., Dennis, M.R.: Social learning theory: modeling and communication in the family context. In: Braithwaite, D.O., Baxter, L.A. (eds.) Engaging Theories in Family Communication: Multiple Perspectives, pp. 260—275 (2006)
2. Koerner, A.F., Fitzpatrick, M.A.: Toward a theory of family communication. Commun. Theor. **12**, 70–91 (2002)
3. Baiocchi-Wagner, E.A.: Future directions in communication research: individual health behaviors and the influence of family communication. Health Commun. **30**(8), 810–819 (2015)
4. Lin, M., Harwood, J., Bonnesen, J.L.: Conversation topics and communication satisfaction in grandparent-grandchild relationships. J. Lang. Soc. Psychol. **21**(3), 302–323 (2002)
5. Kite, M.E., Stockdale, G.D., Whitley, B.E., Johnson, B.T.: Attitudes toward younger and older adults: an updated meta-analytic review. J. Soc. Issues **61**(2), 241–266 (2005)
6. Pecchioni, L.L., Croghan, J.M.: Young adults' stereotypes of older adults with their grandparents as the targets. J. Commun. **52**(4), 715–730 (2005)
7. National Institute of Aging: Why population aging matters. A global perspective (2015). https://www.nia.nih.gov/publication/why-population-aging-matters-global-perspective/over view-our-aging-world
8. King, V., Elder Jr., G.H.: American children view their grandparents: linked lives across three rural generations. J. Marriage Fam. **57**, 165–178 (1995)
9. Roberto, K.A., Stroes, J.: Grandchildren and grandparents: roles, influences, and relationships. Int. J. Aging Hum. Dev. **34**(3), 227–239 (1992)
10. Kirkorian, H.L., Pempek, T.A., Murphy, L.A., Schmidt, M.E., Anderson, D.R.: The impact of background television on parent–child interaction. Child Dev. **80**(5), 1350–1359 (2009)
11. Segrin, C., Flora, J.: Family Communication. Routledge, New York (2011)
12. Osmanovic, S., Pecchioni, L.: Beyond entertainment: motivations and outcomes of video game playing by older adults and their younger family members. Games Cult. Spec. Ed. Games Ageing **11**, 130–149 (2015)
13. Osmanovic, S., Pecchioni, L.: Family matters: the role of intergenerational gameplay in successful aging. In: Zhou, J., Salvendy, G. (eds.) ITAP 2016. LNCS, vol. 9755, pp. 352–363. Springer, Cham (2016). https://doi.org/10.1007/978-3-319-39949-2_34
14. Przybylski, A.K., Mishkin, A.F.: How the quantity and quality of electronic gaming relates to adolescents' academic engagement and psychosocial adjustment. Psychol. Popular Media Cult. (2015)
15. de la Hera Conde-Pumpido, T., Loos, E.F., Simons, M., Blom, J.: Benefits and factors influencing the design of intergenerational digital games: a systematic literature review. Societies **7**(18) (2017)
16. ESA: 2004 essential facts about the computer and video game industry (2004). http://www.theesa.com/facts/pdfs/ESA_EF_2004.pdf
17. ESA: 2017 Essential facts about the computer and video game industry (2017). http://www.theesa.com/wp-content/uploads/2017/04/EF2017_FinalDigital.pdf
18. Pearce, C.: The truth about baby boomer gamers: A study of over-forty computer game players. Games Cult. J. Interact. Media **3**(2), 142–174 (2008)
19. Gajadhar, B.J., Nap, H.H., de Kort, Y.A., IJsselsteijn, W.A.: Out of sight, out of mind: co-player effects on seniors' player experience. In: Proceedings of the 3rd International Conference on Fun and Games, pp. 74—83 (2010)

20. Coyne, S.M., Padilla-Walker, L.M., Stockdale, L., Day, R.D.: Game on… girls: associations between co-playing video games and adolescent behavioral and family outcomes. J. Adolesc. Health **49**(2), 160–165 (2011)

21. Costa, L., Veloso, A.: Being (grand) players: review of digital games and their potential to enhance intergenerational interactions. J. Intergenerational Relat. **14**(1), 43–59 (2016)

22. Zhang, F., Kaufman, D.: A review of intergenerational play for facilitating interactions and learning. Gerontechnology **14**, 127–138 (2016)

23. Loos, E., Zonneveld, A.: Silver gaming: serious fun for seniors? In: Zhou, J., Salvendy, G. (eds.) ITAP 2016. LNCS, vol. 9755, pp. 330–341. Springer, Cham (2016). https://doi.org/10.1007/978-3-319-39949-2_32

24. Altman, I., Taylor, D.: Social Penetration: The Development of Interpersonal Relationships. Holt, Rinehart and Winston, New York (1973)

25. Taylor, D.A.: The development of interpersonal relationships: social penetration processes. J. Soc. Psychol. **75**(1), 79–90 (1968)

26. Thibaut, J.W., Kelley, H.H.: The Social Psychology of Groups. Transaction Publishers, Piscataway (1959)

27. Papini, D.R., Farmer, F.F., Clark, S.M., Micka, J.C., Barnett, J.K.: Early adolescent age and gender differences in patterns of emotional self-disclosure to parents and friends. Adolescence **25**(100), 959–976 (1990)

28. Soliz, J., Harwood, J.: Shared family identity, age salience, and intergroup contact: investigation of the grandparent–grandchild relationship. Commun. Monogr. **73**(1), 87–107 (2006)

29. Taylor, J., Taylor, J.: A content analysis of interviews with players of massively multiplayer online role-play games (MMORPGs): motivating factors and the impact on relationships. In: Ozok, A.A., Zaphiris, P. (eds.) OCSC 2009. LNCS, vol. 5621, pp. 613–621. Springer, Heidelberg (2009). https://doi.org/10.1007/978-3-642-02774-1_66

30. Peña, J., Hancock, J.T.: An analysis of socioemotional and task communication in online multiplayer video games. Commun. Res. **33**(1), 92–109 (2006)

31. Castells, M.: The Internet Galaxy: Reflections on the Internet, Business, and Society. Oxford University Press, New York (2001)

32. Wheeless, L., Grotz, J.: Conceptualization and measurement of reported self-disclosure. Hum. Commun. Res. **2**(4), 338–346 (1976)

33. Bukowski, W.M., Hoza, B., Boivin, M.: Measuring friendship quality during pre- and early adolescence: the development and psychometric properties of 50 the friendship qualities scale. J. Soc. Pers. Relat. **11**, 471–484 (1994)

Design Elements of Pervasive Games for Elderly Players: A Social Interaction Study Case

Luciano H. O. Santos[1]([✉]), Kazuya Okamoto[1,2], Shusuke Hiragi[1,2],
Goshiro Yamamoto[2], Osamu Sugiyama[3], Tomoki Aoyama[4],
and Tomohiro Kuroda[1,2]

[1] Graduate School of Informatics, Kyoto University, Kyoto, Japan
lhsantos@kuhp.kyoto-u.ac.jp
[2] Division of Medical Information Technology and Administration Planning,
Kyoto University Hospital, Kyoto, Japan
[3] Preemptive Medicine and Lifestyle-Related Disease Research Center,
Kyoto University Hospital, Kyoto, Japan
[4] Graduate School of Medicine, Kyoto University, Kyoto, Japan

Abstract. We present the design process and evaluation of a pervasive, location-based mobile game created to act as an experiment system and allow evaluation of how different design elements can influence player behaviour, using social interaction as a study case. A feasibility study with a group of community dwelling elderly volunteers from the city of Kyoto, Japan, was performed to evaluate the system. Results showed that the choice of theme and overall design of game was adequate, and that elderly people could understand the game rules and their goals while playing. Points of improvement included reducing the complexity of game controls and changing social interaction mechanics to account for situations when there are only a few players active or players are too far apart.

Keywords: Elderly · Pervasive games · Serious games ·
Physical activity · Social interaction

1 Introduction

Populations are ageing worldwide [1] and societies face an increasing number of challenges to promote quality of life for elderly citizens. Aiming at preserving their health, many studies have employed electronic games as an approach help elderly people lead more active lifestyles, with varied levels of success [2].

In that context, a new family of games that has yet to be fully explored are the so-called *pervasive games* [3], a term that describes any game that mixes elements from the real world in their mechanics, blurring the edges of the "magic circle" – *i.e.*, the perceived boundaries where playing takes place [4]. For that reason, such games have also been called *ubiquitous* [5], *context aware* [6],

© Springer Nature Switzerland AG 2019
J. Zhou and G. Salvendy (Eds.): HCII 2019, LNCS 11593, pp. 204–215, 2019.
https://doi.org/10.1007/978-3-030-22015-0_16

mixed reality [7] or even *trans-reality* [8]. The main goal is to create higher levels of immersion and, thus, more fun experiences. Many commercial pervasive games became very popular – *e.g.*, Pokémon GO[1], Ingress[2] and Dead Rising 3[3] –, illustrating their potential to engage large groups of players.

Not only pervasive games are particularly immersive and engaging for players of all ages, they can be also especially beneficial for elderly players, since two of the most commonly explored design elements in these games are *physical location* and *social relations* among users. By inviting players to visit places in the real world, a pervasive game can promote regular physical activity; and by asking these players to interact with other people, it can help prevent social isolation. Both effects are strongly correlated with higher qualify of life among the elderly and lower incidence of age-related diseases [9–13].

One issue commonly found in previous works – not specific to pervasive games, but affecting any game in general targeting the elderly – is that, even though these studies part from the assumption that electronic games can engage people because they are fun, there's still an excessive or even exclusive focus on health benefits, with aspects such as user's motivations to play and sought experiences left to secondary roles. Nonetheless, any study using games should take these aspects into consideration – a deep and meaningful connection with activities of *play* and *fun* is an inherent aspect of human nature [14], and elderly people are no exception. By understanding which design principles can generate the most fun and engaging experiences, it is possible to further increase the results of game-based approaches to health promotion.

In this paper, we describe a pervasive game that was designed specifically to test different design elements, and how they affect player behaviour. To evaluate our system, we chose social interaction as study case and performed a feasibility study with community dwelling elderly volunteers from Kyoto city.

The remaining of this text is organized as follows. Section 2 makes a brief literature review of relevant related works. Section 3 describes the design process and the resulting system. Section 4 presents the evaluation method and the results. Finally, Sect. 5 makes final considerations and lists possible future steps.

2   Related Works

Pervasive games have emerged as research field in the last decade, with several games made [15] and there are a few works focusing particularly on design [16, 17], while games for elderly became a research topic on its own in the context of serious games for health [18,19].

Some works investigated challenges when designing for older audiences [20–22], identifying common physical and cognitive limitations that should be considered. De Schutter et al. point out that older players of electronic games do

---

[1] Niantic Labs, 2016 – https://www.pokemongo.com/.

[2] Niantic Labs, 2013 – https://www.ingress.com/.

[3] Microsoft Studios and Capcom, 2013 – https://www.microsoft.com/en-us/p/dead-rising-3/.

not form an homogeneous group, but instead, like any other demographic, show highly varied behaviours and preferences deeply influenced by culture, background and both intrinsic and extrinsic motivations [23]. They propose 5 basic profiles of older players [24] based on the Uses and Gratifications Theory [25] and the Self-Determination Theory [26]. Recent research has started to analyze elements of fun and engagement more deeply [27], following the principle that games should first be fun, and all additional benefits will come later as a natural consequence of playing [28].

A few studies tried to identify preferences of elderly people regarding content and/or genre of the games, primarily using surveys [29–31]. Recent works evaluated elderly players' experiences with different kinds of games, focusing on specific styles of game, such as casual games [32]. A commonly explored genre is the one of *exergames*, *i.e.*, games in which the player must perform specific kinds of coordinated movements to control the input, sometimes in association with other cognitive tasks [33]. Many studies used varied interfaces for such games, evaluating the user's acceptance of the technology and/or motivation to play [34,35]. There are also some examples of pervasive games targeting older adults, usually focusing on specific goals, such as cognitive training [36] and promotion of physical activity using social incentives [37].

3   Methods

While previous works using games to help the elderly focused on basically comparing *game* and *non-game* strategies [15,16], this research compares variations on the design of the *same game*. In order to do that, the first problem that must be addressed is how to appropriately test *design*.

Hebert Simon defines any design problem as a "wicked" or "ill-defined" problem [38], *i.e.*, a problem that cannot be fully understood from start, but must be continuously redefined and worked out via in an iterative process. A good strategy to perform this process is by using an *experiment system*, a system that rather than immediately *solving* a problem, focuses on *understanding* it to evaluate how specific elements can change the outcome. In the next sections, we describe the design process we followed to create such a system.

3.1   Design Principles

If the game's purpose is to act as an *experiment system*, it should not only be pervasive, but also allow for easy *contextual adaptations* in its pervasive mechanics. One way of framing this problem is by using Schell's elemental tetrad (Fig. 1), that describes a game in terms of four domains that affect each other and combine to create specific experiences to the player.

A pervasive game is one that integrates elements from the real world into one or more of these domains [17], thus, a pervasive game that is also an appropriate *experiment system* should allow for changes on these integrations that can be isolated and controlled for testing.

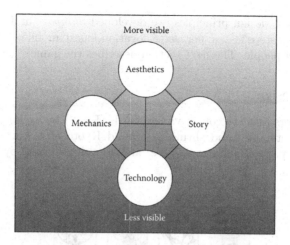

Fig. 1. Schell's elemental tetrad [39]: **aesthetics** – all parts of the game accessible to the player, such as visuals, sounds and controls; **mechanics** – all game rules, valid states and constraints; **story** – the elements of narrative; **technology** – set of physical components that allow the game to take place.

Taking on this idea as a guide, we used an iterative design process that analyzed existing (pervasive) games and took the input of specialists from varied fields and from final users, to lay out general design principles:

– the main goal is **collection of items** – this is a play element present in almost every culture and appreciated by players of varied ages, backgrounds and motivations; since the main point is the *abstraction* of collecting items, the nature of the items can be easily changed; this allows for adaptations on:
  • *aesthetics* – different representations and visual styles;
  • *story* – different meanings of the items in the game narrative;
  • *technology* – different media, such as virtual or physical items;
– items are collected by **walking to specific locations** – this serves the research goal of promoting physical activity, but also allows for flexibility, with variations on:
  • *mechanics* – varied constraints of navigation and access to places;
  • *story* – different meanings and roles of places in the game narrative;
  • *technology* – different types and arrangements of places, as well as levels of scale (*e.g.*, within a room, a building, a city);
– players should be able to **collaborate** for mutual benefit and the game should use **positive reinforcement** to promote pro-social behaviour – even though social interaction in the form of player vs player competition is enjoyed by some people, collaboration can be enjoyed by any person; this allows for variations on:
  • *mechanics, technology* – direct *vs* virtual, static *vs* casual, known people *vs* strangers, groups *vs* individuals, *etc...*;
  • *story* – different roles of people in the game narrative.

Based on these design principles, we developed *Shinpo* – in Japanese, 神歩, meaning "sacred steps" –, a pervasive location-based mobile game targeting Japanese elderly people. The next section describes the game.

3.2 Game Design

In Shinpo, players must to collect virtual cards (Fig. 2) by walking and visiting real locations – temples and shrines – around Kyoto city. Each card has an animal (from Japanese fauna or folklore) and a level, indicated by its color (1 – violet, 2 – green, 3 – blue, 4 – gold).

Fig. 2. Examples of game cards. (Color figure online)

Using the map (Fig. 3(a)), players can locate nearby hotspots and receive some card by visiting them. Cards are earned the first time within a day that the player enters a shrine and periodically depending on how much they walked and how many hotspots they visited on the previous days.

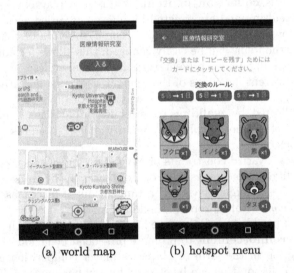

(a) world map   (b) hotspot menu

Fig. 3. Some screenshots from *Shinpo*.

Inside the hotspot, players can see their current cards (Fig. 3(b)) and trade a certain number of cards of a level for one card of the next level. Because there are 4 levels, it takes a long time to achieve the game's goal of having all the possible gold cards. By design, players with higher levels of physical activity can win the game faster.

Shinpo uses a specific theme to appeal to Japanese (elderly) people – shrines and card game references –, but, as explained in Sect. 3.1, its design principles allow for variations of these choices, while keeping the core elements.

For instance, other abstractions could be used (e.g., zodiac signs instead of animals or coins instead of cards); different rules and interaction strategies (e.g., cooperation, competition, challenges, hierarchies); different visual styles (e.g., traditional, cute, cartoonish); and different technologies (e.g., physical objects, IoT devices). These adaptations, when limited within a closed context, could also be presented to different groups of players to evaluate their specific experience. As an example, the color schemes or the illustration style could be changed and evaluated for their appeal to different audiences.

To test the adaptability of the game, we proposed a variation using including social interaction. The proposed variation includes these additional rules:

- players have customized profiles that identify them to other players within the game and also see and "like" other players' actions;
- players can, once per day, leave a card at a hotspot; other players will be notified about it and will receive a copy when they enter that hotspot; the owner is rewarded with additional random cards of same level based on the number of total copies distributed this way;
- everyday, players receive a challenge of visiting a certain number of shrines in collaboration with other players, if they join the challenge and reach their goal, all members of the group can get more cards;
- nearby players can meet in person, and receive cards by doing so.

4   Evaluation

To evaluate the game, we performed a 3-week feasibility study (Fig. 4) with volunteer community dwelling senior citizens. Participants were recruited from a group of people who attend a program run by Kyoto University Hospital, offering weekly sessions of exercise-based cognitive training at a local community center.

At the beginning of the study, participants answered a questionnaires about their previous experience with technology (if they have and use smartphones and/or personal computers, how often they use them and what kind of tasks they use them for) and with games in general and electronic games specifically (what kinds of games they play, how often, using which devices and with whom). No previous experience was required to join the experiment, volunteers received a preconfigured smartphone and were given an explanation about its basic operation.

During the first week, subjects were asked to simply carry the smartphone around with them, to register their baseline level of physical activity,

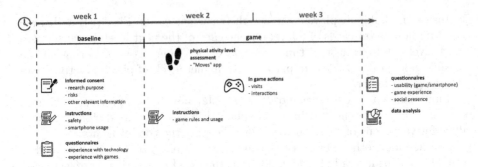

Fig. 4. Feasibility study protocol.

measured by the number of steps as calculated using the smartphone sensor data. On the following 2 weeks, they played the game, while their step count continued to be monitored.

At the end of the study, volunteers were asked to answer questionnaires to assess the usability of the game, and to report their experience during the game, including their sense of social presence. The questions were based and/or adapted from the Game Experience Questionnaire (GEQ) [40] and translated to Japanese by native speakers. All questions had a 5-level Likert scale of one of two types: agreement level (0 = strongly disagree, 4 = strongly agree) and frequency (0 = never, 4 = always).

4.1   Results

In Table 1, basic demographic data about the participants is presented. The average scores of the usability, game experience and social presence evaluation are presented in Table 2.

Results indicated that the proposed design was successful in appealing to Japanese elderly people. Users could learn the basic operation of the smartphone without problems, even if most of them had never used one before. Players were able to understand the game rules and goals and overall liked its visual style. There were mixed results about learning the game controls.

Players also enjoyed the challenge level of the game and also reported engagement and satisfaction/motivation to play and enjoyment/fulfillment. There was a general sense that the game stimulates players to explore their surroundings and discover new things, which was also corroborated by some open questions comments. There was strong approval of the game theme (Japanese shrines).

The Social Presence Questionnaire section of GEQ had overall low scores for all items. We hypothesized that this was due to the small number of participants, *i.e.*, the proposed mechanics require a large number of simultaneous players to be effective, thus a revision of such mechanics is necessary for the next steps of the research.

Table 1. Participants' demographic data and previous experience technology and games.

Demographics		Non-electronic games	
Average age (σ)	74.6 (3.3)	Doesn't play	9 (75%)
Number of participants	12	Everyday	0 (0%)
Female	9 (75%)	2+ times/week	2 (17%)
Dropouts	3 (F=2)	1- times/week	1 (8%)
Experience with PCs		**Electronic games**	
Frequency of usage		Frequency of play	
Everyday	1 (8%)	Doesn't play	9 (75%)
2+ times/week	5 (42%)	Everyday	1 (8%)
1- times/week	1 (8%)	2+ times/week	1 (8%)
Never	5 (42%)	1- times/week	1 (8%)
Skills		Partners	
Internet, email	1 (8%)	(% of those who play)	
Social networks	3 (25%)	Alone	3 (100%)
Experience with smartphones		Family (adults)	1 (33%)
Never used	5 (42%)	Family (children)	0 (0%)
Make calls	6 (50%)	Friends	0 (0%)
Internet, e-mail	6 (50%)	Strangers	0 (0%)
Social networks	3 (20%)		
Install apps	3 (20%)		

Table 2. Usability, game experience, and social presence average scores.

Category	Score
Usability	
Controls	1.50
Learn curve	1.90
Feedback	2.25
Game rules	2.06
Game experience	
Theme and visual style	2.45
Originality	2.17
Feeling of Immersion	2.02
Feeling of Enjoyment	2.40
Feeling of Engagement	2.21
Feeling of Freedom/Ability to explore	1.78
Feeling of (positive) Challenge	2.11
Social presence	0.48

Even though the sample was too small for any further analysis and the feasibility stage didn't focus on evaluating the main outcome yet, a slight positive effect in comparison to the baseline was observed (Table 3).

Table 3. Number of steps of the whole group during the study.

Week	Mean (σ)	Effect (relative to σ)
1	22567.2 (16347.8)	–
2	24272.9 (16995.3)	+1705.7 (7.6%)
3	24393.3 (14203.8)	+1826.1 (8.1%)

5   Conclusion

In this paper, we presented the design process and implementation of an experiment system that allows for testing of variations in pervasive game design targeting elderly people and evaluate their effect on player's behaviour.

The results indicate that the choice of theme and visual style for the proposed game was adequate, and that elderly people could understand the rules and goals of the game. Participants also reported feeling challenged and engaged, but there might be difficulties when it comes to learning complex controls.

The proposed social interaction mechanics weren't very effective. We believe this happened because the proposed mechanics require a large number of simultaneous players to be effective, thus a revision of such mechanics taking these findings into account is necessary for future iterations.

A deeper understanding of how pervasive mechanics affect older audiences can be a powerful asset for researchers and designers aiming at using pervasive games to promote the well-being of elderly people. In our future steps, we will improve our design to address the issues identified in our study, and investigate other variations on design, aiming at further expanding our understanding of how design choices can affect player experience and behaviour.

References

1. UN: World Population Ageing. Technical report, United Nations, Department of Economic and Social Affairs, Population Division (2017)
2. Bleakley, C.M., Charles, D., Porter-Armstrong, A., McNeill, M.D.J., McDonough, S.M., McCormack, B.: Gaming for health: a systematic review of the physical and cognitive effects of interactive computer games in older adults. J. Appl. Gerontol. **34**(3) (2013) https://doi.org/10.1177/0733464812470747
3. Kasapakis, V., Gavalas, D.: Pervasive gaming: status, trends and design principles. J. Netw. Comput. Appl. **55**, 213–236 (2015)
4. Montola, M.: Exploring the edge of the magic circle: Defining pervasive games. In: Proceedings of DAC, vol. 1966, pp. 16–19 (2005)

5. Björk, S., et al.: Designing ubiquitous computing games: a report from a workshop exploring ubiquitous computing entertainment. Personal Ubiquitous Comput. **6**(5–6), 443–458 (2002)
6. Koskinen, K., Suomela, R.: Rapid prototyping of context-aware games. In: 2nd IET International Conference on Intelligent Environments (IE 06), vol. 2006, pp. v1-135-v1-142. IEEE (2006)
7. Bonsignore, E.M., Hansen, D.L., Toups, Z.O., Nacke, L.E., Salter, A., Lutters, W.: Mixed reality games. In: Proceedings of the ACM 2012 Conference on Computer Supported Cooperative Work Companion - CSCW 2012, p. 7. ACM Press, New York (2012)
8. Gutierrez, L., Stroulia, E., Nikolaidis, I.: fAARS: a platform for location-aware trans-reality games. In: Herrlich, M., Malaka, R., Masuch, M. (eds.) ICEC 2012. LNCS, vol. 7522, pp. 185–192. Springer, Heidelberg (2012). https://doi.org/10.1007/978-3-642-33542-6_16
9. Colcombe, S., Kramer, A.F.: Fitness effects on the cognitive function of older adults. Psychol. Sci. **14**(2), 125–130 (2003)
10. Larsen, L.H., Schou, L., Lund, H.H., Langberg, H.: The physical effect of exergames in healthy elderly-a systematic review. Games Health J. **2**(4), 205–212 (2013)
11. Vagetti, G.C., Barbosa Filho, V.C., Moreira, N.B., de Oliveira, V., Mazzardo, O., de Campos, W.: Association between physical activity and quality of life in the elderly: a systematic review, 2000–2012. Revista Brasileira de Psiquiatria **36**(1), 76–88 (2014)
12. Tomaka, J., Thompson, S., Palacios, R.: The Relation of social isolation, loneliness, and social support to disease outcomes among the elderly. J. Aging Health **18**(3), 359–384 (2006)
13. Lee, G.R., Ishii-Kuntz, M.: Social interaction, loneliness, and emotional well-being among the elderly. Res. Aging **9**(4), 459–482 (1987)
14. Huizinga, J.: Homo Ludens: A Study of Play-Element in Culture. Routledge, London (1949)
15. Buzeto, F.N.F., Castillo, A.H.O.R., Castanho, C.D., Jacobi, R.P.: What is going on with ubicomp games. In: XI Brazilian Symposium on Games and Digital Entertainment, Brasília, DF, Brazil, Universidade de Brasília, SBC, pp. 1–7 (2012)
16. Kasapakis, V., Gavalas, D., Bubaris, N.: Pervasive games research: a design aspects-based state of the art report. In: Proceedings of the 17th Panhellenic Conference on Informatics - PCI 2013, p. 152. ACM Press, New York (2013)
17. Buzeto, F.N., e Silva, T.B.P., Castanho, C.D., Jacobi, R.P.: Reconfigurable games: games that change with the environment. In: 2014 Brazilian Symposium on Computer Games and Digital Entertainment, pp. 61–70. IEEE, November 2014
18. Smith, S.T., Talaei-Khoei, A., Ray, M., Ray, P.: Electronic games for aged care and rehabilitation. In: 2009 11th International Conference on e-Health Networking, Applications and Services (Healthcom), pp. 42–47. IEEE, December 2009
19. Garcia Marin, J., Felix Navarro, K., Lawrence, E.: Serious games to improve the physical health of the elderly: a categorization scheme. In: International Conference on Advances in Human-Oriented and Personalized Mechanisms, Technologies, and Services, CENTERIC 2011 (c), pp. 64–71 (2011)
20. Ijsselsteijn, W., Nap, H.H., de Kort, Y., Poels, K.: Digital game design for elderly users. In: Proceedings of the 2007 Conference on Future Play - Future Play 2007, p. 17. ACM Press, New York (2007)

21. Ogomori, K., Nagamachi, M., Ishihara, K., Ishihara, S., Kohchi, M.: Requirements for a cognitive training game for elderly or disabled people. In: 2011 International Conference on Biometrics and Kansei Engineering, pp. 150–154. IEEE, September 2011

22. Barnard, Y., Bradley, M.D., Hodgson, F., Lloyd, A.D.: Learning to use new technologies by older adults: perceived difficulties, experimentation behaviour and usability. Comput. Hum. Behav. **29**(4), 1715–1724 (2013)

23. De Schutter, B., Brown, J.A., Vanden Abeele, V.: The domestication of digital games in the lives of older adults. New Media Soc. **17**(7), 1170–1186 (2015)

24. De Schutter, B., Malliet, S.: The older player of digital games: a classification based on perceived need satisfaction. Communications **39**(1), 67–88 (2014)

25. Katz, E., Blumler, J., Gurevitch, M.: The Uses of Mass Communication: Current Perspectives on Gratifications Research. Sage Publications, Beverly Hills (1974)

26. Ryan, R., Deci, E.: Self-determination theory and the facilitation of intrinsic motivation. Am. Psychol. **55**(1), 68–78 (2000)

27. Gerling, K., De Schutter, B., Brown, J., Allaire, J.: Ageing playfully: advancing research on games for older adults beyond accessibility and health benefits. In: Proceedings of the 2015 Annual Symposium on Computer-Human Interaction in Play, CHI PLAY 2015, pp. 817–820. ACM, New York (2015)

28. De Schutter, B., Vanden Abeele, V.: Towards a gerontoludic manifesto. Anthropol. Aging **36**(2), 112–120 (2015)

29. Carvalho, R.N.S.D., Ishitani, L., Nogueira Sales De Carvalho, R., Ishitani, L.: Motivational factors for mobile serious games for elderly users. In: XI Brazilian Symposium on Games and Digital Entertainment, Brasília, DF, Brazil, Universidade de Brasília, SBC, pp. 19–28 (2012)

30. Cota, T.T., Ishitani, L., Vieira, N.: Mobile game design for the elderly: a study with focus on the motivation to play. Comput. Hum. Behav. **51**, 96–105 (2015)

31. Kaufman, D., Sauve, L., Renaud, L., Sixsmith, A., Mortenson, B.: Older adults digital gameplay: patterns, benefits, and challenges. Simul. Gaming **47**(4), 465–489 (2016)

32. Chesham, A., Wyss, P., Müri, M.R., Mosimann, P.U., Nef, T.: What older people like to play: genre preferences and acceptance of casual games. JMIR Serious Games **5**(2), e8 (2017)

33. Kayama, H., Okamoto, K., Nishiguchi, S., Yamada, M., Kuroda, T., Aoyama, T.: Effect of a kinect-based exercise game on improving executive cognitive performance in community-dwelling elderly. J. Med. Internet Res. **16**(2), e61 (2014)

34. Brox, E., Konstantinidis, T.S., Evertsen, G.: User-centered design of serious games for older adults following 3 years of experience with exergames for seniors: a study design. JMIR Serious Games **5**(1), e2 (2017)

35. Meekes, W., Stanmore, K.E.: Motivational determinants of exergame participation for older people in assisted living facilities: mixed-methods study. J. Med. Internet Res. **19**(7), e238 (2017)

36. Gamberini, L., et al.: Eldergames project: an innovative mixed reality table-top solution to preserve cognitive functions in elderly people. In: 2009 2nd Conference on Human System Interactions, pp. 164–169. IEEE, May 2009

37. Brox, E., Fernandez-Luque, L., Evertsen, G., González-Hernández, J.: Exergames for elderly: social exergames to persuade seniors to increase physical activity. In: Proceedings of the 5th International ICST Conference on Pervasive Computing Technologies for Healthcare, pp. 546–549. IEEE (2011)

38. Simon, H.A.: The Sciences of the Artificial, 1st edn. MIT Press, Cambridge (1969)

39. Schell, J.: The Art of Game Design: A Book of Lenses. Morgan Kaufmann Publishers Inc., San Francisco (2008)
40. Poels, K., de Kort, Y.A.W., Ijsselsteijn, W.A.: D3.3: game experience questionnaire. Technical report, Technische Universiteit Eindhoven, Eindhoven (2007)

Are We Ready to Dance at Home?: A Review and Reflection of Available Technologies

Paula Alexandra Silva[(⊠)]

DigiMedia Research Centre – Universidade de Aveiro, Aveiro, Portugal
palexa@gmail.com

Abstract. It is well acknowledged that engaging in physical exercise is important to live a longer healthier life. In this context, dance is an especially interesting activity that may hold much potential in an ageing society. Dance combines the essence for successful ageing in a panoply of benefits that range from the physical to the cognitive and psychosocial. To be able to engage in dancing activities from home can then be a valuable add on to people's health, wellbeing and quality of life; this paves the way for technology-mediated dance activities at home. This paper reviews the research in this area, to develop an understanding of currently available technologies and to provide researchers and practitioners alike with an overview of how the technologies reviewed can address the specific characteristics of dance.

Keywords: Older adults · Physical activity · Dance · Entertainment ·
Active Ageing · Fitness · Games · Technology

1 Introduction

Between the year 2000 and the year of 2016, the global average life expectancy saw its largest increase since 1960, of 5.5 years, with people born in 2016 being estimated to live until they are ~72 years old [1]. As our society ages and continues to conquer longevity, a growing concern is how to sustain more active, happier, and healthier lives.

Pushed by the challenges of demographic change, European and International governments and organizations have developed strategic plans to adequately address demographic change, namely though policies and partnerships for Healthy and Active Ageing [2–8]. An important mark among those actions is the World Health Organization's policy framework on Active Ageing developed in 2002 [2]. Currently, and more precisely, between 2015–2030, the focus of WHO's work on ageing is Healthy Ageing [4, 8]. Those actions emphasize, for example, the importance of sustaining health and well-being, of promoting participation and an active contribution to society, and of remaining physically, socially, and mentally active across the life course.

Another important idea that has been gaining momentum in the context of ageing successfully is the one of ageing in place, also referred to as ageing at home [8, 9]. Ageing in place expresses and gives voice to older people's preference to remain home, as they grow older. "New technologies provide opportunities to achieve ageing in place, to enhance the quality of older people's environments and to increase life

J. Zhou and G. Salvendy (Eds.): HCII 2019, LNCS 11593, pp. 216–231, 2019.
https://doi.org/10.1007/978-3-030-22015-0_17

fulfillment and quality of life" [10]. The rising interest and acknowledgment of the importance of ageing at home underlines the need for research in the home context.

The research presented in this paper concerns the use of technology as a facilitator of ageing in place with a view to promoting a healthy and active lifestyle at home. In particular, this paper discusses the relevance, potential, and adequacy of existing technologies in supporting dance – here defined as "a physical, cognitive, and psychosocial activity, either done alone or in a group, which encompasses a sequence of movements usually performed to the sound of music or some sort of rhythm" [11] – at home.

Two research questions guide this research: i. What types of technology have been used to support the context of technology-mediated dance targeted at older adults? and ii. To what extent do those types of technology address the specific characteristics of dance? In addressing these questions, this paper engages in a review of research reporting on the use of technology-mediated dance interventions targeted at older adults. A purposive sampling selection of articles is applied to the studies retrieved from an extensive literature search, to then elicit the different types of technology in use and to develop a preliminary discussion around those technologies and to what extent they address the characteristics of dance. This review contributes to developing an overview and gaining a better understanding of the area.

2 Physical Activity, Health and Well-Being

2.1 Benefits of Engaging in Physical Activity

Physical activity is a key lifestyle factor contributing to living a longer healthy life [12]. Showing a panoply of benefits, physical exercise decreases risk of falling, reduces physical disability, improves sleep, and enhances mood and well being [13]. With physical activity prompting positive results that range from reducing pain to fostering functional mobility [14], to remain physically active offers an effective way to counterbalance the risk factors and functional decline associated with age [12].

Aware of the advantages of physical activity, the World Health Organization (WHO) has created a set of physical activity guidelines [15] that member states of the Europe Union (EU) are advised to implement [16]. In short, these guidelines recommend that older adults engage in: i. 150 min of moderate-intensity *aerobic physical activity* per week, or in at least 75 min of vigorous-intensity aerobic physical activity; ii. *muscle-strengthening activities*, involving major muscle groups, two or more days a week, and iii. *balance training activities* three or more days per week.

In addition to the evidence demonstrating that physical activity is effective in preventing or delaying chronic diseases [17], evidence also shows positive compelling results in addressing specific neurodegenerative conditions, such as Parkinson's disease (PD), where physical activity not only lowers the risk of developing PD, but also improves the symptoms associated with it [18].

2.2 Previous Uses of Technology in Promoting Physical Activity

With a growing body of literature showing that to stay physically active is a precursor of good health and well-being, leading to successful ageing [19], it is important to both motivate older adults to exercise and to create opportunities for them to exercise. A possibility of doing so is to leverage on the potential of technology to make solutions available to older adults at the convenience of their home.

Several research projects have focused on developing solutions that promote the uptake of physical exercise (for a review see [20]). Regardless of the different approaches followed, a popular strategy used by those projects, resorts to exergames and serious games to motivate older adults to take up physical activity [20].

There is also a wealth of research reporting on the use of commercial game consoles (e.g.: [21, 22]) and of custom made solutions (e.g.: [23–26]) for exercise purposes among older adults.

While a number of studies shows positive results in physical function, cognition and quality of life, socialization and motivation to exercise [13], research on exergames still shows conflicting results in terms of health benefits [27], namely in psychosocial well-being [28, 29] with some interventions holding only short-term effects [30]; this underlines the need for further research in the area.

2.3 Dance as a Unique Form of Physical Activity

While intuitively one may think of dance mostly as a form of physical exercise, possibly also as a social activity, dance is a much more complete activity, that equally involves cognitive elements – triggered, for example, while one tries to memorize or recall a sequence of steps – and psychological elements – such as those that convey a sense of satisfaction with life.

Looking at dance from a diversity of perspectives, research has investigated the health benefits of dancing and found positive health effects in older adults across domains, being those physical (e.g. [31]), cognitive (e.g. [32, 33], or psychosocial (e.g. [34]). A systematic review on the effectiveness of dance interventions in improving health among older adults has concluded that, irrespective of the style, dance improves older adults' functional fitness, in terms of muscular strength, endurance, and balance [31]. The health benefits of dance also extend to neuro-cognitive function [33] and dual-task performance [32]. Moreover, from a psychosocial viewpoint, studies have shown decrease in pain levels [14], improvements in psychological well-being related to general health and the decrease of bodily pain [34] as well as in social activity and community involvement [35]. Furthermore, dance has shown the highest levels of efficacy in terms of gait and quality of life with regards to specific neurodegenerative conditions, such as PD [18], both in the form of Argentine tango [36] and Irish step dancing [37], with some boldly stating that dance may hold the potential to demedicalize PD [38].

When compared to other types of exercise, dance shows increased physical and cognitive benefits, namely in terms of balance and brain structure, delaying cognitive deterioration [12] as well as brain plasticity [39]. Furthermore, a recent systematic review and meta-analysis on the effectiveness of dance interventions in comparison with other types of interventions on physical health outcomes shows that structured dance of at least four weeks' duration can significantly improve physical health outcomes [40]. Research results like these, make dance a promising candidate in counteracting the age-related decline in physical and mental abilities [12], considered by Dhami et al. [41] as *the* framework for rehabilitation, where dance is not only effective, but also enjoyable.

2.4 Motivation to Exercise Among Older Adults

Regardless of the benefits that engaging in physical activity entails, older adults are not regular exercisers [42]. This problem of adherence is one of the pitfalls of interventions with exergames, which use has shown to decrease over time [27]. This is not unique to technology–mediated interventions, as 50% of the older adults tend to drop involvement in regular exercise programs within the first six months into the program [13], with the decrease in motivation to exercise starting 16 weeks into it [13, 43].

Although willing to exercise, older adults fear injury and would rather exercise in a cost-effective way and at their convenience in the safety of their homes [44]. Considering the home scenario as a hypothetical alternative, previous studies [40] have found that a home-based program was as effective in increasing health benefits and exercise participation as the face-to-face interventions. These results indicate that home-based programs are not only desirable but also feasible and effective, which is encouraging if a home-based scenario is to be considered.

Socializing or the possibility for increased social interaction is seen as a motivating factor to exercise [44, 45]. While older adults may find typical forms of exercise monotonous and boring [22], dance is seen as an enjoyable activity among older adults [34, 37] that makes them feel happy [34]. Psychological benefits have been observed in previous studies involving dance, where improvements could be attributed to the social network and friendship developed while dancing [34].

In addition, having fun is one of the reasons older adults adhere to physical activity programs [43, 45]. The idea of fun is intrinsic to games, which then may mean that games hold the potential of making exercise more fun and, in this way, of increasing adherence [22]. Previous researchers have argued that physical and occupational therapy activities delivered through games, or 'therapytainment' systems (i.e.: systems that simultaneously engage older adults in learning, working, and play [46]), do transform physical therapy from a chore into a fun activity, while older adults are still doing hard work [46].

In the specific case of dance, the appealing recreational nature of interactive dance exercise may further help promote adherence to physical activity [42]. In line with this, other forms of technology-mediated dance have reportedly received a very positive and emotional response in the context of dance for PD [47].

The aspects discussed in this section put technology-mediated dance interventions in an advantageous position to promote physical activity among older adults at home. Dance is an attractive form of exercise, that has shown to hold positive physical, cognitive, and psychosocial health benefits among older adults [48]. Furthermore, the possibility of offering it in a home scenario is likely to further strengthen its potential, not only because these type of interventions have shown feasibility and effectiveness

[49], but also because engaging in exercise programs at home increases chances of adherence to physical activity in the long term [50].

3 Research Methodology

The goal of this study is to develop a greater understanding of what characterizes the technologies available in the context of technology-mediated dance for older adults. With that goal in mind, two research questions guided this research: i. What types of technology have been used to support the context of technology-mediated dance targeted at older adults? and ii. To what extent do those types of technology address the specific characteristics of dance?

In addressing the research questions above, this study engaged in an exhaustive literature search across a number of databases (PubMed, ACM Digital Library, Academic Search Complete, IEEE, Scopus, and Web of Science Core Collection) to locate research on technology-mediated dance targeted at older adults (for the full details on the search string please refer to Appendix A). All study designs and all types of dance were considered, for research published between the year 2000 and 2018.

During a second phase, studies were selected based on a purposive sampling technique (also known as judgment, selective, or subjective sampling), a method inspired in anthropology research, that involves a deliberate choice, in which the researcher decides what needs to be known and sets out to find it [51]. With the aim of getting a good overview of the spectrum of technology-mediated solutions for dance targeted at older adults, an heterogeneous sampling [52] was used with the purpose of eliciting as many unique solutions as possible, both in terms of designs and technology components.

Once the papers that fitted within the topic of this research were retrieved, they were further analyzed regarding the properties and features of the solutions.

4 Technology to Support Dance at Home

Following an extensive and comprehensive searching phase, the records retrieved were reviewed to identify eligible studies. Relevant studies reported on the use of technology-mediated dance systems designed and/or assessed with older adults. As previously mentioned, this research considered dance as "a physical, cognitive, and psychosocial activity, either done alone or in a group, which encompasses a sequence of movements usually performed to the sound of music or some sort of rhythm" [11].

In order to correctly interpret the results presented in this section, it is important to note that not all eligible studies were necessarily included in the review. This was the case, because this research aimed at identifying solutions, which were different enough from one another. So, if there were a number of different manuscripts, all reporting on the use of identical versions of the a given system, for example, StepMania and a dance mat with panels (e.g.: [53, 54]), only one, maximum a couple of studies, were explicitly mentioned in the analysis, in representation of the remaining identical ones. Conversely, if there were a system, which contained similar components but at least one that would make the overall solution different enough, a different instance would be considered. An example of this would be the use of the above system – StepMania and a dance mat with panels –, but in which ropes to which participants could hold on too while using the system were added (see for example [55]).

The following two sections briefly describe and analyze the included studies. Findings are organized by the underlying purposes of the study in which systems were involved and by type of solution.

4.1 Studies' Purposes

The studies included in this review investigated technology-mediated dance interventions with a number of purposes. Looking at specific health conditions or frequent issues among older adults, fall risk and fall prevention have been repeatedly a target of investigation [23, 53, 56]. Other conditions which have been a focus of research include multiple sclerosis [54], Parkinson's [57, 58], and Huntington's disease [59].

A number of studies included in this review have focused on assessing foundational aspects of these systems, such as feasibility [55, 60]; feasibility and safety [61]; feasibility, acceptance, and usability [62]; and adherence, perceptions of the game, and safety [59]. Studies were also performed with the goal of tweaking the systems [63] and of understanding older adults' perceived advantages and disadvantages of such approaches [42]. With encouraging results on these dimensions, studies set out also to evaluate the systems' effectiveness in improving specific dimensions of health and wellbeing in older adults.

Into what concerns physical health outcomes, studies again assessed a number of different aspects, including spatiotemporal gait measures [59]; balance [57, 64]; exercise capacity [65]; balance and gait [58]; and stepping performance [61].

Aware of the multidimensional nature of dance, studies further evaluated walking dual task performance [55, 66] and balance, stepping, cognition and functional performance [54]. Turning more into the assessment of cognitive outcomes, studies investigated, for example, cognitive performance [66] and cognitive control and attention [67].

Although less frequent, studies also looked into psychosocial health outcomes. Among this type of studies, there are articles focusing on the development of social connections [68], quality of life [59, 65], and the effect of interventions on activities of daily living and depressive disorder [57]. Finally, there are studies specifically investigating motivation [69] and the effects of interventions on other specific health outcomes such as blood lipid and blood pressure [70, 71].

With more or less significant results obtained, the range of studies above shows the perceived potential that technology-mediated dance interventions entail. It also shows that this area has been gathering the attention of several researchers in a number of different domains.

4.2   Main Types of Technology-Mediated Dance Systems

To report on the different types of solutions found, this research developed a classification, which captures the main types of technology-mediated dance systems in a structured way. Figure 1 shows a classification divided into four groups, organized according to the ways in which technology is used and the level of adaptation of the system to cater for older adults' characteristics.

While the first two groups are mostly illustrative containing only a couple of examples each, the second two groups are more complete. This is the case not only because records fitting into the first two groups are very scarce, but also because the second two groups refer to solutions which have been adapted and specifically tailored to be inclusive of the needs of older adults and thus are, considering the scope of this study, the most interesting and relevant.

The top group *'Dance therapies delivered through technology'* includes conventional dance therapies, which are delivered exactly as they would be delivered in a normal face-to-face scenario, yet they are mediated by technology. Two examples were found that fitted this category: in one case, the therapy is delivered by a regular therapist via Skype [60]; in the other, the dance exercise is displayed from a video disk that the participants follow, while a facilitator supervises them *in locu* (se for example, [65, 70]. In this category, technology plays a merely instrumental role – that of a means of communication –, which purpose is simply to transcend geographic constraints.

The second group *'Commercial dance games'* contains references to mainstream commercial games, which have been used and assessed in interventions with older adults. Two types of examples were found, two instances using Dance Dance Revolution [59, 67] and another using K-Pop Dance Festival for the Wii game console [57].

The following group *'Adapted commercial dance games'* consists of adapted versions of commercial dance games. Aware of the issues imposed by commercial games, designed for mainstream users, likely to include jumps and fast-paced music [64, 72], commercial games were modified to accommodate older adults needs and characteristics. This is the group for which the largest number of instances were retrieved, with the majority of the research making use of StepMania, an open source version of Dance Dance Revolution (DDR) (for specific studies, see, for example, [22, 69, 73] but also [11]). Similarly to the original DDR, to play this game participants would follow the instructions on a screen while at the same stepping on a dance mat with panels. Variations of this system followed the initial attempts developed on MatLab [63], and included, for example, a version that included a set of ropes to which the participants could hold on to while performing the moves [55]. Another variation of DDR used an accelerometer, a gyroscope, and a mobile phone [74]. Another adaptation was found of Dancetown, in a version that played songs from the 50's and presented simplified graphics and dance step sequences that progressed slower in difficulty [42].

Finally, the last group, *'Custom made solutions'*, includes solutions that have been specifically designed to cater for older adults and their specific needs. Examples in this category are extremely diverse, resorting to a smartphone-based game [23, 56] to a robot [58], or the Google Glass [38, 47].

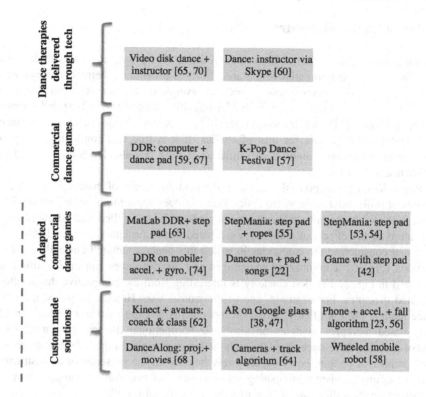

Fig. 1. Classification of studies according to type of technology-mediated dance system.

The example using the smartphone leverages on the potential of its embedded sensors and of a fall algorithm, to offer the user an experience that consists of mimicking the movements of a virtual coach [23, 56]. A similar approach uses a dance video game coupled with a low cost camera tracking [64]. Another example uses 'Movioke', allowing players to dance along with scenes from popular movies [68]. In this example, in addition to the song selection in the DanceAlong interface, the system uses three projectors, two showing the steps and another displaying the video of the movie. The Google Glass is used for rehabilitation with people with PD and is a sort of augmented reality class, where the specific dance therapy moves are displayed in the goggles and the person executes the movements accordingly [38, 47]. Another solution leverages on Kinect to create a virtual reality group dance class, where the dance participants see their avatars and those of the coach and other participants on the television screen and hear each other via headsets [62]. The last example uses a wheeled robot for partner dancing [58].

The specific strengths and drawbacks of each category are discussed in the next section.

5   Discussion and Future Work

Several purposes have been at the center of the studies presented in this review that show the interest and potential of the area. Still, as previous systematic reviews conclude [11, 75], the effectiveness of such interventions has not yet been definitely demonstrated. This is the case, namely, for cognitive–motor effects [75] and for psychosocial factors [11], where both systematic reviews report on the weak evidence, low-quality, and high risk for bias of studies. If it is true that conflicting and poor evidence have also been reported in similar areas [76], this also indicates the need for further research in the area.

Regardless of the possible learning demand in terms of basic technical and movement skills, interactive video dance exercise, does appear to be an appealing form of exercise for older adults [42] and several randomized controlled trials show positive indications of the effects of technology-mediated dance systems [53, 54, 61, 66].

When considering the categories in which this paper structured currently existing solutions (Fig. 1), a number of advantages and disadvantages can be identified, as displayed in Fig. 2. The first category is interesting from the perspective that it offers validated therapies. For example, one of the studies uses Healthy Steps, which is "a dance therapy program that is based on movements that are used in allopathic, medically based therapies, such as physical and occupational therapy programs" [60]. Approaches like these once shred through the Internet or placed on a player can reach a large number of people, however, they rely heavily on the presence of an instructor, who, for example, when participating remotely may not even have a complete view of the person on the other side, which may be a significant pitfall.

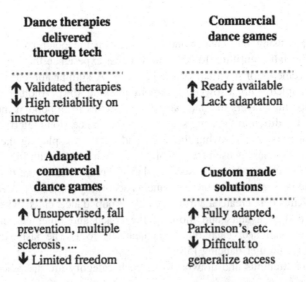

Fig. 2. Main advantages and pitfalls of each type of technology-mediated dance system.

Regarding the second category, if it is true that commercial games are of widespread access, they are generally not suitable for older adults, given their fast-paced music, frequent jumping, and overload of information on the screen [64, 72]. Still, these games have been assessed in improving the conditions of specific diseases, such as Huntington's [59].

As mentioned before, the third group *'Adapted commercial dance games'* is the one for which we found the most instances, with most of the studies resorting to StepMania and a dance pad with panels to step on. In spite if this approach showing positive results, namely in addressing specific health conditions (see for e.g. [54, 66]), the fact that the game requires players to step on specific panels and focuses very much on precision may remove the fun, and freedom of movement and expression that usually characterize the nature of dance.

The most diversity is found in the last category of systems, which includes technology-mediated dance systems that have been adapted or specifically designed to suit older adult's characteristics. The solutions found in this group cater for the necessary freedom of movement that a holistic dance experience entails. While some solutions focus on providing users with an experience that includes other dance class participants [62], or an actual dance partner [58], other approaches favor wearable, yet non-intrusive or limiting technologies [23, 56]. There are also solutions that leverage on the potential of depth cameras to offer a seamless technological solution [64, 68]. One of the seminal works in this area [68], additionally builds upon the reminiscence potential of old movies to offer a more rewarding user experience. This last category includes promising, compelling, and more recent technologies where researchers are experimenting with a robot [58] and augmented reality glasses [38, 47], much like a science fiction movie would anticipate. To some extent uncharted territory, these solutions therefore hold undiscovered potential in enabling an experience that is more natural and closer to what a dance experience would involve. However, these technologies are not easily accessible nor in their final commercial phase. They also have not been conveniently validated that they can be made available for health prescription.

It is therefore necessary to continue investigating, on the one hand, what constitutes a system that is both designed to be inclusive of the older adult population and to allow for a complete positive dance experience, and, on the other hand, the effectiveness of such systems.

To design for the rich context of dance and movement, constitutes a significant technological challenge. Fast-paced music, negative feedback, among others are problematic and may be intimidating [64, 72]. Having to use a dance pad may be limitative in terms of movement as well as dangerous [72], so other approaches have tried, using. for example, a mobile version integrating an accelerometer and gyroscope [74] or the Kinect [45]. There are also other sensors entering the market, such as Real sense (https://realsense.intel.com/), that may hold the necessary features that a complete dance experience requires, namely freedom of movement and partnered or group dancing, but also music, a sequence of steps, etc.

Dance is a positive health activity that nurtures body and mind. The research reported in this paper compiled and structured existent solutions for dance and older adults to then develop an understanding of the characteristics of those solutions and gauge to what extent they fitted and addressed the properties of a dance context.

Despite a thorough search of the existing literature, it is possible that other relevant studies may have been left out. Moreover, for a complete understanding of the existing types of systems that can be used to support dance, a more exhaustive study would be needed describing all solutions and deconstructing them into their different components. This offers a relevant opportunity for further research, as it is important to assess, for example, how to appropriately design for freedom of movement, customization of therapy, provisions health feedback, and group or partnered dancing.

6 Conclusions and Limitations

Regardless of the hypothetical potential of technology-mediated dance, to our knowledge, no studies have yet reviewed the types of technologies, which have been used in this context, nor have given careful consideration to how those technologies attend to the specific characteristics of dance and the experience it affords. This research aimed at shedding light into this area and to develop an awareness of the strengths and limitations of existing technologies in addressing the specific characteristics of dance.

An extensive search of databases was done that served as the basis for selecting relevant research. Based on a set of eligible papers, this research elicited distinct groups of technology to contribute with a classification that systematizes and organizes the technologies reported in the studies reviewed according to its main features and characteristics. This addresses RQ1: What types of technology have been used to support the context of technology-mediated dance targeted at older adults? where this research found that there are four main types of solutions: i. Dance therapies delivered through technology, ii. Commercial dance games, iii. Adapted commercial dance games, and iv. Custom made solutions.

Additionally, and in addressing RQ2: To what extent do those types of technology address the specific characteristics of dance?, this research sparks a discussion on the extent to which the types of solutions found address the specific characteristics of dance and enable a positive and complete dance experience at home. While the first two types of solutions present considerable limitations, the last two types hold significant potential, especially the last type, which includes technologies that have been specifically designed to cater for dancing and older adults. Still, findings point to the need of future research in the area.

Other research could additionally inform the relevance, potential, and adequacy of existing technologies in supporting dance that have not been considered in this study. These are, for example, studies on the general area of exergames for older adults that could help understand what works and what does not, as well as research involving other populations, that while less conservative, can point into alternative technological directions that could lend more freedom and completeness to the dance experience.

Health promotion actions and alternatives that can be offered to older adults in the home context have the potential to extend seniors' years of active and healthy living, while promoting their independence and continued engagement with society at large. Alternatives with the potential to improve physical, cognitive and psychosocial health may be particularly relevant for those living with temporary disability or in regional or remote areas, yet technology-mediated dance offers great value, holding the prospect of a joyful active future to us all.

Acknowledgments. This research was developed with the support of the Research Program "CeNTER - Community-led Territorial Innovation" (CENTRO-01-0145-FEDER- 000002), funded by Programa Operacional Regional do Centro (CENTRO 2020), PT2020.

Appendix A

The following filters were applied in PubMed: Publication date from 2000; Humans; English; middle aged + aged: 45+ years; Middle aged: 45–64 years; aged: 65+ years; 80 and over: 80+ years.

Two search strategies were used in PubMed. The first used Mesh Terms "dance therapy" "dancing" combined with the terms "technology," "software," "apps," "playware," "edutainment," "exergaming," "robot," "game," or "haptics" as search terms in all fields.

A keyword search was also run, using a combination of keywords: "technology," "software" "apps" "playware" "edutainment," "exergaming," "AI games", "robot," "game," "haptics," all of which were combined with "dance," "dancing," "dance therapy" and also with the terms "older," "elderly," "frail elderly" "older-adults," "Old-Old," "geriatric" and "senior."

References

1. WHO: Life expectancy. http://www.who.int/gho/mortality_burden_disease/life_tables/situation_trends_text/en/
2. WHO: Active ageing: a policy framework. http://www.who.int/ageing/publications/active_ageing/en/
3. Active ageing - Employment, Social Affairs & Inclusion - European Commission. https://ec.europa.eu/social/main.jsp?catId=1062&langId=en
4. WHO: What is Healthy Ageing? http://www.who.int/ageing/healthy-ageing/en/
5. Healthy Ageing. http://www.healthyageing.eu/
6. European Innovation Partnership. https://ec.europa.eu/eip/ageing/home_en
7. World Health Organization: Policies and priority interventions for healthy ageing. http://www.euro.who.int/__data/assets/pdf_file/0006/161637/WHD-Policies-and-Priority-Interventions-for-Healthy-Ageing.pdf?ua=1
8. WHO (World Health Organization): The Global strategy and action plan on ageing and health, Geneva, Switzerland (2017)
9. Aging in Place: Growing Old at Home. https://www.nia.nih.gov/health/aging-place-growing-old-home
10. Bond, J., Peace, S., Dittmann-Kohli, F., Westerhof, G.: Ageing in Society: European Perspectives on Gerontology. SAGE Publications Ltd., London (2007)
11. Silva, P.A., Cochrane, A., Farrell, H.: The effectiveness of technology-mediated dance interventions and their impact on psychosocial factors in older adults: a systematic review and meta-analysis. Games Health J. (2018). https://doi.org/10.1089/g4h.2017.0197

12. Rehfeld, K., et al.: Dancing or fitness sport? The effects of two training programs on hippocampal plasticity and balance abilities in healthy seniors. Front. Hum. Neurosci. **11** (2017). https://doi.org/10.3389/fnhum.2017.00305

13. Resnick, B.: Prescribing an exercise program and motivating older adults to comply. Educ. Gerontol. **27**, 209–226 (2001). https://doi.org/10.1080/036012701750194950

14. Tse, M.M., Wan, V.T., Ho, S.S.: Physical exercise: does it help in relieving pain and increasing mobility among older adults with chronic pain? J. Clin. Nurs. **20**, 635–644 (2011). https://doi.org/10.1111/j.1365-2702.2010.03548.x

15. WHO: Physical Activity and Older Adults. http://www.who.int/dietphysicalactivity/factsheet_olderadults/en/

16. EU Working Group "Sport and Health": EU Physical Activity Guidelines: Recommended Policy Actions in Support of Health-Enhancing Physical Activity (2008). https://eacea.ec.europa.eu/sites/eacea-site/files/eu-physical-activity-guidelines-2008.pdf

17. Booth, F.W., Roberts, C.K., Laye, M.J.: Lack of exercise is a major cause of chronic diseases. Compr. Physiol. **2**, 1143–1211 (2012)

18. Grazina, R., Massano, J.: Physical exercise and Parkinson's disease: influence on symptoms, disease course and prevention. Rev. Neurosci. **24**, 139–152 (2013). https://doi.org/10.1515/revneuro-2012-0087

19. Martin, P., et al.: Defining successful aging: a tangible or elusive concept? The Gerontologist. **55**, 14–25 (2015). https://doi.org/10.1093/geront/gnu044

20. Silva, P.A.: Physical activity among older adults: a meta-review of Eu-funded research projects. In: Clua, E., Roque, L., Lugmayr, A., Tuomi, P. (eds.) ICEC 2018. LNCS, vol. 11112, pp. 374 387. Springer, Cham (2018). https://doi.org/10.1007/978-3-319-99426-0_47

21. Pisan, Y., Garcia Marin, J.A., Felix Navarro, K.M.: Improving lives: using microsoft kinect to predict the loss of balance for elderly users under cognitive load. ACM Press (2013)

22. Studenski, S., Perera, S., Hile, E., Keller, V., Spadola-Bogard, J., Garcia, J.: Interactive video dance games for healthy older adults. J. Nutr. Health Aging **14**, 850–852 (2010)

23. Silva, P.A., Nunes, F., Vasconcelos, A., Kerwin, M., Moutinho, R., Teixeira, P.: Using the smartphone accelerometer to monitor fall risk while playing a game: the design and usability evaluation of dance! Don't fall. In: Schmorrow, D.D., Fidopiastis, C.M. (eds.) AC 2013. LNCS (LNAI), vol. 8027, pp. 754–763. Springer, Heidelberg (2013). https://doi.org/10.1007/978-3-642-39454-6_81

24. Clawson, J., Patel, N., Starner, T.: Dancing in the streets: the design and evaluation of a wearable health game. In: International Symposium on Wearable Computers (ISWC 2010), pp. 1–4 (2010)

25. de Bruin, E.D., Schoene, D., Pichierri, G., Smith, S.T.: Use of virtual reality technique for the training of motor control in the elderly. Z. Für Gerontol. Geriatr. **43**, 229–234 (2010). https://doi.org/10.1007/s00391-010-0124-7

26. Bock, B.C., et al.: Exercise videogames for physical activity and fitness: design and rationale of the Wii heart fitness trial. Contemp. Clin. Trials. **42**, 204–212 (2015). https://doi.org/10.1016/j.cct.2015.04.007

27. Chen, F.X., King, A.C., Hekler, E.B.: "Healthifying" exergames: improving health outcomes through intentional priming. In: Proceedings of the SIGCHI Conference on Human Factors in Computing Systems, pp. 1855–1864. ACM, New York (2014)

28. Li, J., Theng, Y.-L., Foo, S.: Exergames for older adults with subthreshold depression: does higher playfulness lead to better improvement in depression? Games Health J. **5**, 175–182 (2016). https://doi.org/10.1089/g4h.2015.0100

29. Li, J., Xu, X., Pham, T.P., Theng, Y.-L., Katajapuu, N., Luimula, M.: Exergames designed for older adults: a pilot evaluation on psychosocial well-being. Games Health J. **6**, 371–378 (2017). https://doi.org/10.1089/g4h.2017.0072

30. Sardi, L., Idri, A., Fernández-Alemán, J.L.: A systematic review of gamification in e-Health. J. Biomed. Inform. **71**, 31–48 (2017). https://doi.org/10.1016/j.jbi.2017.05.011

31. Hwang, P.W.-N., Braun, K.L.: The effectiveness of dance interventions to improve older adults' health: a systematic literature review. Altern. Ther. Health Med. **21**, 64–70 (2015)

32. Hamacher, D., Hamacher, D., Rehfeld, K., Hökelmann, A., Schega, L.: The effect of a six-month dancing program on motor-cognitive dual-task performance in older adults. J. Aging Phys. Act. **23**, 647–652 (2015). https://doi.org/10.1123/japa.2014-0067

33. Kimura, K., Hozumi, N.: Investigating the acute effect of an aerobic dance exercise program on neuro-cognitive function in the elderly. Psychol. Sport Exerc. **13**, 623–629 (2012). https://doi.org/10.1016/j.psychsport.2012.04.001

34. Hui, E., Chui, B.T., Woo, J.: Effects of dance on physical and psychological well-being in older persons. Arch. Gerontol. Geriatr. **49**, e45–e50 (2009). https://doi.org/10.1016/j.archger.2008.08.006

35. Nadasen, K.: 'We are too busy being active and enjoying ourselves to feel the aches and pains': perceived health benefits of line dancing for older women. Qual. Ageing Older Adults **8**, 4–14 (2007). https://doi.org/10.1108/14717794200700016

36. Duncan, R.P., Earhart, G.M.: randomized controlled trial of community-based dancing to modify disease progression in Parkinson disease. Neurorehabil. Neural Repair. **26**, 132–143 (2011). https://doi.org/10.1177/1545968311421614

37. Shanahan, J., Morris, M.E., Bhriain, O.N., Volpe, D., Lynch, T., Clifford, A.M.: Dancing for Parkinson disease: a randomized trial of Irish set dancing compared with usual care. Arch. Phys. Med. Rehabil. **98**, 1744–1751 (2017). https://doi.org/10.1016/j.apmr.2017.02.017

38. Butt, C.A.: "Move Your Arm Like a Swan": Dance for PD Demedicalizes Parkinson disease. JAMA **317**, 342–343 (2017). https://doi.org/10.1001/jama.2016.21033

39. Rehfeld, K., et al.: Dance training is superior to repetitive physical exercise in inducing brain plasticity in the elderly. PLoS ONE **13**, e0196636 (2018). https://doi.org/10.1371/journal.pone.0196636

40. Fong Yan, A., et al.: The effectiveness of dance interventions on physical health outcomes compared to other forms of physical activity: a systematic review and meta-analysis. Sports Med. **48**, 933–951 (2018). https://doi.org/10.1007/s40279-017-0853-5

41. Dhami, P., Moreno, S., DeSouza, J.F.X.: New framework for rehabilitation – fusion of cognitive and physical rehabilitation: the hope for dancing. Front. Psychol. **5** (2015). https://doi.org/10.3389/fpsyg.2014.01478

42. Inzitari, M., Greenlee, A., Hess, R., Perera, S., Studenski, S.A.: Attitudes of postmenopausal women toward interactive video dance for exercise. J. Womens Health **18**, 1239–1243 (2009). https://doi.org/10.1089/jwh.2008.1176

43. Resnick, B., Spellbring, A.M.: Understanding what motivates older adults to exercise. J. Gerontol. Nurs. **26**, 34–42 (2000)

44. Dishman, R.K.: Motivating older adults to exercise. South. Med. J. **87**, S79–S82 (1994)

45. Ganesan, S., Anthony, L.: Using the kinect to encourage older adults to exercise: a prototype. In: CHI 2012 Extended Abstracts on Human Factors in Computing Systems, pp. 2297–2302. ACM, New York (2012)

46. Tabar, P.: Dance, cycle and play: techno-gaming makes rehab fun. Long-Term Living Contin. Care Prof. **62**, 18 (2013)

47. Abbasi, J.: Augmented reality takes parkinson disease dance therapy out of the classroom. JAMA **317**, 346–348 (2017). https://doi.org/10.1001/jama.2016.18122

48. Kattenstroth, J.-C., Kalisch, T., Holt, S., Tegenthoff, M., Dinse, H.R.: Six months of dance intervention enhances postural, sensorimotor, and cognitive performance in elderly without affecting cardio-respiratory functions. Front. Aging Neurosci. **5** (2013). https://doi.org/10.3389/fnagi.2013.00005

49. Miller, K.J., Adair, B.S., Pearce, A.J., Said, C.M., Ozanne, E., Morris, M.M.: Effectiveness and feasibility of virtual reality and gaming system use at home by older adults for enabling physical activity to improve health-related domains: a systematic review. Age Ageing **43**, 188–195 (2014). https://doi.org/10.1093/ageing/aft194

50. Ashworth, N.L., Chad, K.E., Harrison, E.L., Reeder, B.A., Marshall, S.C.: Home versus center based physical activity programs in older adults. Cochrane Database Syst. Rev. CD004017 (2005). https://doi.org/10.1002/14651858.cd004017.pub2

51. Bernard, H.R.: Research Methods in Anthropology: Qualitative And Quantitative Approaches. AltaMira Press, Lanham (2006)

52. Etikan, I., Musa, S.A., Alkassim, R.S.: Comparison of convenience sampling and purposive sampling. Am. J. Theor. Appl. Stat. **5**, 1 (2015). https://doi.org/10.11648/j.ajtas.20160501.11

53. Schoene, D., et al.: Interactive cognitive-motor step training improves cognitive risk factors of falling in older adults – a randomized controlled trial. PLoS ONE **10**, e0145161 (2015). https://doi.org/10.1371/journal.pone.0145161

54. Hoang, P., Schoene, D., Gandevia, S., Smith, S., Lord, S.R.: Effects of a home-based step training programme on balance, stepping, cognition and functional performance in people with multiple sclerosis – a randomized controlled trial. Mult. Scler. J. **22**, 94–103 (2016). https://doi.org/10.1177/1352458515579442

55. de Bruin, E.D., Reith, A., Dorflinger, M., Murer, K.: Feasibility of strength-balance training extended with computer game dancing in older people; does it affect dual task costs of walking? J. Nov. Physiother. (2011). https://doi.org/10.4172/2165-7025.1000104

56. Kerwin, M., Nunes, F., Silva, P.A.: Dance! Don't Fall - preventing falls and promoting exercise at home. Stud. Health Technol. Inform. **177**, 254–259 (2012). https://doi.org/10.3233/978-1-61499-069-7-254

57. Lee, N.-Y., Lee, D.-K., Song, H.-S.: Effect of virtual reality dance exercise on the balance, activities of daily living, and depressive disorder status of Parkinson's disease patients. J. Phys. Ther. Sci. **27**, 145–147 (2015). https://doi.org/10.1589/jpts.27.145

58. Chen, T.L., et al.: Evaluation by expert dancers of a robot that performs partnered stepping via haptic interaction. PLoS ONE **10**, e0125179 (2015). https://doi.org/10.1371/journal.pone.0125179

59. Kloos, A.D., Fritz, N.E., Kostyk, S.K., Young, G.S., Kegelmeyer, D.A.: Video game play (Dance Dance Revolution) as a potential exercise therapy in Huntington's disease: a controlled clinical trial. Clin. Rehabil. **27**, 972–982 (2013). https://doi.org/10.1177/0269215513487235

60. Krampe, J., Musterman, K.: Shall we skype dance? Connecting nursing students with older adults via skype for dance-based therapy. Comput. Inform. Nurs. CIN **31**, 151–154 (2013). https://doi.org/10.1097/NXN.0b013e31828e2faf

61. Schoene, D., Lord, S.R., Delbaere, K., Severino, C., Davies, T.A., Smith, S.T.: A randomized controlled pilot study of home-based step training in older people using videogame technology. PLoS ONE **8** (2013). https://doi.org/10.1371/journal.pone.0057734

62. Cyarto, E.V., Batchelor, F., Baker, S., Dow, B.: Active ageing with avatars: a virtual exercise class for older adults. In: Proceedings of the 28th Australian Conference on Computer-Human Interaction, pp. 302–309. ACM, New York (2016)

63. Smith, S.T., Talaei-Khoei, A., Ray, M., Ray, P.: Electronic games for aged care and rehabilitation. In: 2009 11th International Conference on e-Health Networking, Applications and Services (Healthcom), pp. 42–47 (2009)

64. Lange, B., et al.: 'Skip': development of an interactive stepping game to reduce falls in older adults. Int. J. Disabil. Hum. Dev. **10**, 331–335 (2011). https://doi.org/10.1515/IJDHD.2011.056

65. Maruf, F.A., Akinpelu, A.O., Salako, B.L.: Self-reported quality of life before and after aerobic exercise training in individuals with hypertension: a randomised-controlled trial. Appl. Psychol. Health Well-Being **5**, 209–224 (2013). https://doi.org/10.1111/aphw.12005

66. Eggenberger, P., Theill, N., Holenstein, S., Schumacher, V., de Bruin, E.D.: Multicomponent physical exercise with simultaneous cognitive training to enhance dual-task walking of older adults: a secondary analysis of a 6-month randomized controlled trial with 1-year follow-up. https://www.dovepress.com/multicomponent-physical-exercise-with-simultaneous-cognitive-training–peer-reviewed-article-CIA

67. Chuang, L.-Y., Hung, H.-Y., Huang, C.-J., Chang, Y.-K., Hung, T.-M.: A 3-month intervention of Dance Dance Revolution improves interference control in elderly females: a preliminary investigation. Exp. Brain Res. **233**, 1181–1188 (2015). https://doi.org/10.1007/s00221-015-4196-x

68. Keyani, P., Hsieh, G., Mutlu, B., Easterday, M., Forlizzi, J.: DanceAlong: supporting positive social exchange and exercise for the elderly through dance. In: CHI 2005 Extended Abstracts on Human Factors in Computing Systems, Portland, OR, USA, pp. 1541–1544. ACM (2005)

69. Rogan, S., Radlinger, L., Baur, H., Schmidtbleicher, D., de Bie, R.A., de Bruin, E.D.: Sensory-motor training targeting motor dysfunction and muscle weakness in long-term care elderly combined with motivational strategies: a single blind randomized controlled study. Eur. Rev. Aging Phys. Act. **13** (2016). https://doi.org/10.1186/s11556-016-0164-0

70. Maruf, F., Akinpelu, A., Salako, B.: Effects of aerobic exercise and drug therapy on blood pressure and antihypertensive drugs: a randomized controlled trial. Afr. Health Sci. **13**, 1–9 (2013). https://doi.org/10.4314/ahs.v13i1.1

71. Maruf, F.A., Akinpelu, A.O., Salako, B.L.: A randomized controlled trial of the effects of aerobic dance training on blood lipids among individuals with hypertension on a thiazide. High Blood Press. Cardiovasc. Prev. **21**, 275–283 (2014). https://doi.org/10.1007/s40292-014-0063-2

72. Theng, Y.-L., Dahlan, A.B., Akmal, M.L., Myint, T.Z.: An exploratory study on senior citizens' perceptions of the nintendo WII: the case of Singapore. In: Proceedings of the 3rd International Convention on Rehabilitation Engineering & Assistive Technology, pp. 10:1–10:5. ACM, New York (2009)

73. Smith, S.T., Davies, T.A., Lennox, J.: Step training system: an ICT solution to measure and reduce fall risk in older adults. In: 2013 35th Annual International Conference of the IEEE Engineering in Medicine and Biology Society (EMBC), pp. 7033–7035 (2013)

74. Kailas, A.: Basic human motion tracking using a pair of gyro + accelerometer MEMS devices. In: 2012 IEEE 14th International Conference on e-Health Networking, Applications and Services (Healthcom), pp. 298–302 (2012)

75. Schoene, D., Valenzuela, T., Lord, S.R., de Bruin, E.D.: The effect of interactive cognitive-motor training in reducing fall risk in older people: a systematic review. BMC Geriatr. **14**, 107 (2014). https://doi.org/10.1186/1471-2318-14-107

76. Larsen, L.H., Schou, L., Lund, H.H., Langberg, H.: The physical effect of exergames in healthy elderly—a systematic review. Games Health J. **2**, 205–212 (2013). https://doi.org/10.1089/g4h.2013.0036

Exergames in Augmented Reality for Older Adults with Hypertension: A Qualitative Study Exploring User Requirements

Oskar Stamm$^{(\boxtimes)}$, Susan Vorwerg, and Ursula Müller-Werdan

Geriatrics Research Group, Charité – Universitätsmedizin Berlin,
Reinickendorfer Strasse 61, 13347 Berlin, Germany
{oskar.stamm,susan.vorwerg,ursula.mueller-werdan}@charite.de

Abstract. The development of Augmented Reality head-mounted displays for the commercial market offers new application possibilities in combination with exercise therapy. Patients who are medically advised to exercise regularly, such as hypertensive patients, could increase adherence through gamification elements combined with immersive projections in their real-world environment. Furthermore, different vital data could be displayed during their training. In order to determine the needs and preferences for an exergame for elderly hypertensive patients we conducted a requirements analysis through semi-structured interviews in older adults (n = 11) over 65 years with diagnosed essential hypertension. The data collected was analyzed through a summarizing content analysis. The requirements analysis revealed mandatory requirements in the areas of: overall system, hardware, software, gamification and monitoring. The results indicate that these potential users of an AR exergame, who are vulnerable target group, must be considered separately from others in terms of additional factors such as comorbidities, danger of falling or acceptance of technology.

Keywords: Augmented Reality · Rehabilitation · Hypertension · Requirements analysis · Seniors

1 Introduction

Arterial hypertension is highly prevalent among older adults and is a risk factor for developing e.g. coronary artery disease, stroke, myocardial infarction and kidney insufficiency. Studies have shown that every third adult in Germany suffers from hypertension, which affects approximately 25 million adults in total [1]. In the highest age group of 70–79 year-olds, even three out of four adults have hypertension in Germany. Along with other lifestyle modifications, physical activity is a commonly recommended non-pharmacological treatment for hypertensive patients. Guidelines of the European Society of Hypertension and the European

© Springer Nature Switzerland AG 2019
J. Zhou and G. Salvendy (Eds.): HCII 2019, LNCS 11593, pp. 232–244, 2019.
https://doi.org/10.1007/978-3-030-22015-0_18

Society of Cardiology suggest performing moderate–intensity dynamic aerobic exercise 5–7 days per week to reduce blood pressure [2]. In the longer term, only regularly performed workouts seem to be effective for hypertensive patients. However, the continuity of practice can be an obstacle for many older adults. Since it is hard to motivate oneself for daily exercises, exergames developed specially for the target group could increase the motivation of elderly users. By utilizing gamification elements, it might be possible to promote long-term usage of the system and thus a higher training frequency.

Previous studies have shown that Augmented Reality (AR) exergames are motivating during therapy and suitable for in-home rehabilitation, what has already been shown in existing studies with a Microsoft Kinect System [3,4]. The study by Hino et al. [5] did find out that the number of step in their sample of middle-aged and elderly players was higher than in non-players until 7 months after the release of PokémonGo. With the development of Augmented Reality (AR) head-mounted displays (HMD) for the commercial market, such as the Microsoft HoloLens or the Magic Leap One, the use of AR in combination with exercise therapy offers new opportunities. In addition to increasing adherence of the patients through gamification techniques combined with immersive projections in their real-world environment, it is also possible to display assistive health parameters during exercises in AR exergames. Hypertension patients could benefit from this new technology, which is interactive, adaptable to individual needs and applicable at home.

Our study was carried out as part of the BewARe project, which aims to develop technically assisted movement training for seniors with hypertension, based on an intelligent augmented reality system consisting of an augmented reality application and various sensors. The BewARe project is a joint project financed by the German Federal Ministry of Education and Research (BMBF). The project lasts three years and began in August 2018.

2   Methods

The purpose of this qualitative study was to determine the requirements for a sensor-assisted exergame in an AR system for elderly hypertensive patients. A requirements analysis was carried out to ascertain the requirements. In the course of identifying the requirements, we conducted semi-structured interviews with seniors over 65 years. The interviews were held in German; the quotations used in this paper were translated.

2.1   Procedure

In a telephone call, interested seniors were first informed about the study and if they agreed were subsequently interviewed about the inclusion and exclusion criteria in a screening. Before the interviews, the corresponding screening assessments were carried out on site. The fall risk was tested by the Tinetti Test [6] and cognitive impairments was measured using the Mini Mental State Examination

(MMSE) [7]. The semi-structured interviews included 11 subjects and consisted of three parts: a first part for personal/non-technical requirements, a second in which the subjects tested a user experience demo in a VR and AR environment, and a third part concerning individual requirements for an AR system. The interview guideline created by the Geriatrics Research Group included the following main content categories: dealing with hypertension, forms of exercise in the past and today, technology usage, monitoring of health data, general requirements for an AR movement training, hardware and software requirements, requirements for motivational elements and requirements for safety aspects. The ethics committee of the Charité – Universitätsmedizin Berlin approved the study (no.: EA2/212/18).

2.2 Participants

Semi-structured interviews were conducted with 11 elderly adults diagnosed with essential hypertension (Stage 1). The sample consisted of 6 women and 5 men with an age range from 65 to 91 (mean 73.09, SD 7.53). The subjects included had no increased danger of falling (Tinetti Test: 27.91, SD 0.302), had no cognitive impairments (MMSE: 28.91, SD 1.221) and their hypertension was drug-adjusted. The results of the MMSE between 24 and 30 were interpreted as no cognitive impairment. A score in the Tinetti Test in the range of 19–24 points indicates a risk of fall. All of the examined subjects had low risk of falling ($\geq$24 = low risk of fall).

2.3 Materials

Exergame Prototypes. Exergame prototypes were used to create a common understanding for AR and VR among older adults. Due to the lack of prior experience in the living environment of older people, it cannot be assumed that every senior knows how the VR and AR environments differ. For this reason three different user experience prototypes were used, two in VR and one in AR.

The first exercise variation was in a standing position and involves a squat in the VR environment. During the task the user can see an animation model similar to a mannequin that replicates his or her movements. When the users hands are stretched forward with the controllers, a large dumbbell appears. The user has to perform the squats in the defined execution area. The control of the exercise execution is graphically represented by a transparent cylinder. If the exercise is carried out correctly, the dumbbell turns green. The instructions were presented as text in the game.

The second exercise variation was conducted in a sitting position and involved a seated trunk rotation, also in the VR environment. In this prototype a transparent bar appears in front of the user. The user moves the controllers through this preset path. If the exercise is performed correctly, the displayed grips will turn green. The user sees, as in the first exercise, a figure who simultaneously turns with his or her movements. The instructions in this prototype were presented by a speaker.

The third exercise variation was similar to the first, although an AR environment was used instead of a VR environment. The users are in a standing position and see their real environment and a virtual figure that appears in the space in front of them. The instructions were presented as text in the game. The user is asked to perform squats. While performing, the user sees a simultaneous movement of the figure and of a green dot.

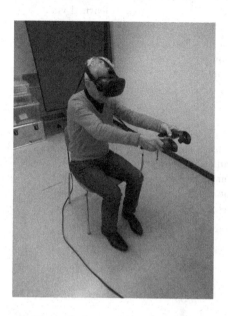

Fig. 1. Task-based part in VR.   **Fig. 2.** Task-based part in AR.

HMDs for the Prototypes Used. In the task-based part two different HMDs were used in order to show the differences between a VR and AR experience (see Figs. 1 and 2). As VR headset we used a HTC Vive [8] with two stationary reference units, which were tracking the users headset and controllers in space. As AR headset the HoloLens [9] was used, which has its own native tracking system built into the HMD.

2.4   Data Analysis

All interviews were recorded and transcribed using the transcription software f4. A summarizing content analysis by Mayring [10] was carried out with the data analysis program ATLAS.ti 8. The aim of the content analysis is to reduce the material and to create an overview through abstractions. The analysis contains among other things paraphrasing, generalization to abstraction level and reduction of data units. The example given in Table 1 shows the process of clustering in the analysis using the example of category: education of the system.

Table 1. Procedure example of the summarizing content analysis within a category.

Case	Quote	Paraphrase	Generalization	Reduction
4	"You can read it through beforehand, but it's like any other instruction manual, you don't understand it anyway"	Read beforehand, like any other manual - you don't understand it	Manuals not understand-able for the peer group	**Education of the system:** The system should not be learned via a manual
5	"So the best thing is, if you have it while you have the glasses on, then you get it explained somewhere here in the program"	Explanation in the program while wearing glasses	Tutorial	The system should be learned by a tutorial in the game
9	"I don't think I'd like to read a manual so much, so the best thing is if you get it explained somewhere in the program while you're wearing the glasses, or if someone explains it to you but then not with the glasses on. Reading a manual before or something like that, I wouldn't find that very helpful"	Reading a manual is not very helpful, explanation in the program or by someone	~~No manual, tutorial,~~ personal assistance	The system should be learned by personal assistance

The first step was to determine that parts of a single sentence, entire sentences and entire paragraphs could be used as analysis units. Subsequently (step 2) we paraphrased the 803 content-bearing passages. In the third step we determined the envisaged level of abstraction and a generalization of the paraphrases was conducted. In step 4 a first reduction was done through the selection of semantically identical paraphrases. The paraphrases with the same meaning were deleted. The second reduction (step 5) merged paraphrases to the envisaged level of abstraction. In the sixth step we compiled the new statements as a category system. Finally we compared the statements to the source documents. Table 1 shows an exemplary process that was carried out within the framework of the study.

All relevant data units (quotations) were assigned manually to specially drafted coding rules. Two scientists independently analyzed the 11 documents using the four-eyes principle. The coded quotations were grouped into semantic domains and an inter-rater reliability according to Krippendorff was calculated with Atlas.ti 8 for each domain along with the overall concordance degree among the raters.

3   Results

The following paragraphs describe the main results for individual technical requirements (e.g. hardware, software) and non-technical requirements (e.g. motivational concepts, application possibilities) for an exergame in AR. The results presented in the next subsections are organized into the following semantic domains: overall system, hardware, software, gamification and monitoring.

3.1   Overall System

The requirements of the overall system gathered during the interviews are presented here. The interviews with hypertensive seniors revealed concerns about the application of a VR systems. The non-existent perception of the real environment is seen as a factor that increases the risk of falls. *"The other thing about stumbling is of course interesting, so you would have to, let's say, I would use such a device [VR] in the apartment, i.e. I would have to somehow think about it first, that there is nothing I could trip over and that I also have to think about that I can't bump into anything." (Subject03, female, 70 years old).* The recognition of the dangers in the room makes the application of the AR system in comparison to a VR system for elderly users more universally adaptable in different locations e.g. in their domestic environment. Since the domestic environment was the most frequently indicated setting of use, elderly users should be able to recognize the dangers in the room and thus the AR system enables the users a more secure usage.

In addition to the question of the setting, an important decision for the development of an exergame was the type of game. Many of the hypertensive seniors have already been active in sport clubs for years or are active in cardiac rehab groups. For the seniors these groups play an important role in their social participation and offer social support from which friendships emerge. *"So with this swim group, they're steady girlfriends, you can see that clearly." (S11, female, 78y).* Some interviewees worried that if the subjects were to use an AR exergame they would miss the interaction with others. Therefore, some subjects require that the system should include a multiplayer mode.

Another important aspect is the operation of the system. Especially with the task-based part it became clear that controlling the demo with gesture control was more difficult for the subjects than with a controller. For some, gesture control caused frustration. *"I'm always under so much pressure when I think I didn't get it right away." (S03, female, 70y).* The operation with a controller felt more natural to many. Other test persons said that the correct gesture execution is very practice-dependent and not directly understandable the first time. *"So, once I really understand it, it's easy too. But the other one [controller] is of course even easier." (S11, female, 78y).*

In order to test the homogeneity of the coders in this semantic domain about the overall system, an inter-coder reliability was computed with Krippendorff cu α, which was 0.968.

3.2   Hardware

The hardware requirements of the interviewed subjects are described below. Many of their responses regarding the hardware focused on the effects on their safety. Almost all seniors considered a cable to be an unnecessary tripping risk. *"I do not know, I personally always find the easier it is, the better and [...] whenever there is so much there and there, I find it easier without a cable"* (S02, female, 71y). The transparent display of the HoloLens allowed the seniors to perceive their surroundings, which was seen as very important. *"That's the way it is, if you turn back and forth a few times or walk [in VR], you lose a bit of the overview. That's normal, I think." (S04, male, 71y).* The subjects also expressed the desire that the headset should be easy to put on and take off. In addition the headset should be lighter than the headsets demonstrated.

The Krippendorff's cu α was calculated for the semantic domain at 0.981.

3.3   Software

This subsection describes the main requirements for the software of the exergame in detail. The interviews identified two groups of potential users of the software: Users with low intrinsic motivation and users with high intrinsic motivation. The statements of these two groups on the environments they could imagine being displayed in AR were related to their self-determination. The users with a high intrinsic motivation did not want an illusory environment; instead they preferred the real environment with additional vital data or the explanation of the execution of the exercise. *"The pure practicality, that would be more to me" (S04, male, 71y).* The users with a low intrinsic motivation or the users who needed an extrinsic motivation wanted environments that are illusory and allow the user to experience and get motivated by a different place through immersion. *"So I could go for a walk in the mountains, even though I'm walking around on the carpet at home." (S03, female, 70y).* In terms of the exergame environment, these users mentioned natural environments in the game such as forests, mountains and meadows. Figure 3 shows a sample network of two desired environments and the relations to the motivation of the subjects. Some subjects who wanted to perform ADLs in the illusory environment expressed an additional requirement for the environment: *"I know, light gardening, [...] raking or something like that" (S06, female, 66y).*

Subjects could learn the system in a variety of ways. Many of the subjects do not want to learn the system through a manual. The seniors preferred a video sequence, a tutorial or personal operating instructions instead. *"If that were possible, yes. That one then says:'Now you have to do faster' [...] or adjust your field of view more precisely and therefore a voice control in the background that draws attention to the errors. Yes. Or which reads out the manual and then errors can be corrected immediately by the respondent or me then, in that case." (S09, male, 71y).*

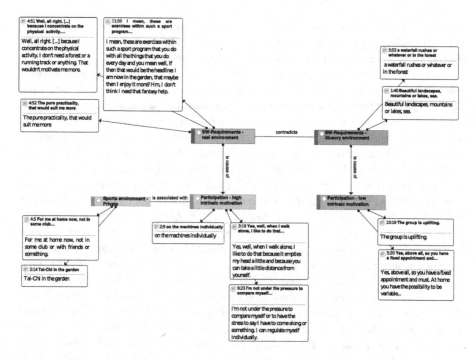

Fig. 3. Atlas.ti network view of the desired game environments.

The inter-coder reliability, computed with the Krippendorff cu α was on this semantic domain 0.970.

3.4 Gamification

The following subsection describes the main requirements of the game mechanics for a potential augmented reality exergame based on the conducted interviews. Many of the seniors wanted as progression feedback a comparison with their own previous data rather than a comparison against other players. This allows the user to compete with his or her own performance, which increases motivation and allows the subjects to monitor their own progress. This type of data monitoring makes it possible to detect progress e.g. through a decreasing heart rate or blood pressure during training. *"So I would consider a comparison to past times or periods of data in relation to the data, which are then detected. Now, as I said, I write this down and then I watch how it has developed. I could also imagine that it could be implemented graphically."(S09, male, 71y).* However, the subjects indicated that the data should only be available afterwards, not while they conduct in-game activities, because that would distract them. Furthermore, the target of the exercises in an exergame should be individually adaptable and individual training load benchmarks should be considered. *"Yes, yes! Maybe it's a target setting, it's not 3 squats, but 10 and at some point it has to be 15 and maybe 20 and then at some point it's over again. Well, I don't want to go to the*

Olympics. I want to be 100 years old, but I don't have to go to the Olympics."
(S01, male, 81y). For an individual adjustment of the goals, the current fitness
status of the users should be essential in an AR exergame.

The story telling in the game was also perceived as an important element.
Since video game experience could not be assumed in the sample, movies were
used to classify the game genre and the story line. The seniors interviewed mentioned historical movies ten times as movie preferences, crime films five times,
political television content four times, nature movies twice and action movies
once. As a narrative story in the game, most could also imagine historical actions,
as they indicated in their movie preferences. "Something historical, for example
on the basis of a uh yes of a fate basically, so that one says yes that interests you,
how does that go on, how has he or she mastered that in his or her life. Basically
it is, of course, a primitive crime thriller." (S11, female, 78y). It was interesting that many subjects experienced the Second World War or its consequences,
for this reason a war scenario would be unthinkable for the target group. "For
example, I don't want to be involved in any theatres of war here. I also don't
want to drive a tank and as many games today, as I said I have no game, but
what you get or what you see, as I said I dont want to be involved." (S10, male,
69y). Moreover, the Bartle Test of Gamer Psychology [11] was applied in order
to find out possible player types of the target group based on Bartles taxonomy.
The Bartle Test of Gamer Psychology showed that 8 seniors can be classified as
explorers and 3 as socializers in a gaming scenario. Figure 4 shows a radar chart
of the average scoring of the subjects in the four categories, each of which can be
rated up to 100%. Both player types, socializers and explorers, are interested in
interacting. For socializers the interaction with other players is the focus of the
game. For explorers the interaction with the virtual world plays a decisive role.
While the explorers enjoy discovering new worlds and details of game mechanics,
the socializers are interested in connecting with other players and want to get
involved in the community. The results met our expectations from the interviews,
as many stated that they greatly appreciated the group dynamics.

The Krippendorff cu α for the semantic domain was 0.989.

3.5   Monitoring

This subsection shows the main monitoring requirements of the seniors. The
subjects indicated that they consider it important to control their blood pressure
and heart rate. "Oh no I mean my blood pressure, pulse and so on, if it is not
somehow such a giant apparatus, but some small device I could quite well imagine
that." (S01, male, 81y). The wish was expressed for a kind of training history
with various health determinants to be displayed in order to achieve progress.
However, the data should not be displayed during the game. "And during the
exercise you would get distracted and feel disturbed [by vital data]." (S05, female,
71y). It would be most pleasant for the test persons if the heart rate could be
recorded via a wristband, e.g. via a smartwatch. This wearable should also be
usable in their everyday life beyond the training.

The Krippendorff cu α for the semantic domain was 0.968.

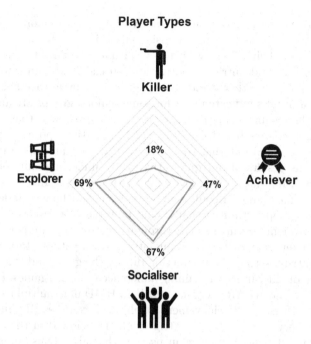

Fig. 4. Radar chart of the rounded average scoring of the subjects for the four player types according to Bartle's taxonomy. Each category can be rated up to 100%. The responses represent a total of 200% distributed across the four categories.

4   Discussion

The aim of the study was to determine the user requirements for a sensor-assisted exergame in an AR system in elderly hypertensive patients. We performed a requirements analysis through a qualitative analysis of semi-structured interviews with hypertensive seniors in order to gather mandatory requirements.

The results indicated that many seniors would prefer an AR system to a VR system because of the lower risk of falling, which is based on the visibility of the environment and the wireless nature of the AR HMD. However, the AR system should not be controlled through gestures and or if so, it must be practiced personally beforehand with the older users, whereby the technical socialization of the generation and of the individual in his or her personal history must be taken into account. Optionally, the Hololens clickers, which interact with holograms, could be used and further explored. The subjects also stated that the headset should be easy to put on and take off and be lighter than the headsets used in our study, which were 579 g.

The results presented under software requirements show that involving seniors in the development of an AR exergame is advisable to increase the successful adherence of this user group. The requirements analysis offered insights about the game type to be developed. The findings demonstrated that the desirable game type is connected with the motivation of the seniors. Hypertensive seniors who already have a strong intrinsic motivation need more of an assistive AR exergame that helps them with the vital data documentation. Hypertensive seniors with a weak intrinsic motivation, on the other hand, would like to immerse themselves in other worlds and play an exergame together with other seniors. The interviews indicated that for some seniors, groups are an important facilitator in their habit formation. Previous research showed that a portion of the elderly prefer home-based exercises [12,13]. In their position paper Brox et al. [14] have pointed out that social interactions are an important factor in exergaming. The results of our qualitative study underline and connect these opinions by showing that seniors have a strong desire to interact socially even in the exergame, which however could still be performed at home. Modern technology opens up new opportunities that should be further researched; e.g. through online multiplayer modes in the AR, through meetings of interest groups for a collective AR exergame, or through simulated groups with avatars, it might be possible to contribute to social interaction during the game and thus increase of the motivation of older users for training adherence with exergames. First studies have shown that playing AR exergames with an HMD in a multiplayer mode can be combined with the goal achievement of physical exercises [15] and enjoyable for people of every age group [16]. Attig et al. [17] showed in their study that there is a strong dependency effect in users with high extrinsic motivation for tracker usage during physical activity, which should be also considered in developing an AR exergame. Thus, even if the exergame promotes social interaction, it should also intrinsically motivate the users.

Furthermore, our paper highlighted the main requirements for the game mechanics. During the exergame the target group don't want to see their vital data continuously, as it would distract them. This implies that the vital parameters should only appear as a result in retrospect or as a warning during the game and need to be recorded in the background. Heart rate, blood pressure and exercise time were perceived as the most important parameters. The target of the exercises should be individually adaptable and individual training load benchmarks should be taken into account. For this reason, machine learning for exercise data evaluation was integrated in the BewARe-Project. The individual adaptability plays a decisive role for the group of hypertensive patients, as some individual comorbidities lead to movement limitations or various medications reduce the load intensity of the patients, i.e. if these limitations are not respected, the AR exergame users will be exposed to a potential danger. For this reason, it is worth considering having the input parameters entered by a doctor or medical staff. The Bartle Test of Gamer Psychology used here showed that the two most frequent player types in the sample were explorers and socializers. This supports the results of the interviews, in which social interaction with other seniors in exercise was the main concern. Important conclusions can be drawn from the player types of the target group about the goals and motivations to play the future exergame.

The 130 mandatory requirements collected from the interviews will be prioritized within the consortium in the BewARe-Project according to the MoSCoW-Method. The requirements serve in the ongoing project for the conception and the use-case ideation of the exergame to be developed.

5 Conclusion

The use of modern AR HMDs during home exercises could greatly benefit elderly hypertensive patients by increasing their adherence. This target group of older adults must be considered separately from others in terms of additional factors such as comorbidities, danger of falling or acceptance of technology. The results obtained will be used to define use cases for the BewARe-Project to generate a concept for exergames.

References

1. Neuhauser, H., Thamm, M., Ellert, U.: Blutdruck in Deutschland 2008–2011. Bundesgesundheitsblatt - Gesundheitsforschung - Gesundheitsschutz **56**(5), 795–801 (2013). https://doi.org/10.1007/s00103-013-1669-6
2. Williams, B., Mancia, G., Spiering, W., Agabiti Rosei, E., et al.: 2018 ESC/ESH guidelines for the management of arterial hypertension. Eur. Heart J. **39**(33), 3021–3104 (2018). https://doi.org/10.1093/eurheartj/ehy339. https://academic.oup.com/eurheartj/article/39/33/3021/5079119
3. Desai, K., Bahirat, K., Ramalingam, S., Prabhakaran, B., Annaswamy, T., Makris, U.E.: Augmented Reality-based exergames for rehabilitation. In: Proceedings of the 7th International Conference on Multimedia Systems, Klagenfurt, Austria, pp. 22:1–22:10 (2016). https://doi.org/10.1145/2910017.2910612
4. Tannous, H., Grbonval, C., Istrate, D., Perrochon, A., Dao, T.T.: Cognitive and functional rehabilitation using serious games and a system of systems approach. In: 2018 13th Annual Conference on System of Systems Engineering (SoSE), pp. 189–194, June 2018. https://doi.org/10.1109/SYSOSE.2018.8428731
5. Hino, K., Asami, Y., Lee, J.S.: Step counts of middle-aged and elderly adults for 10 months before and after the release of Pokémon GO in Yokohama, Japan. J. Med. Internet Res. **21**(2), e10724 (2019). https://doi.org/10.2196/jmir.10724. https://www.jmir.org/2019/2/e10724/
6. Tinetti, M.E., Williams, T.F., Mayewski, R.: Fall risk index for elderly patients based on number of chronic disabilities. Am. J. Med. **80**(3), 429–434 (1986)
7. Folstein, M.F., Folstein, S.E., McHugh, P.R.: "Mini-mental state". A practical method for grading the cognitive state of patients for the clinician. J. Psychiatr. Res. **12**(3), 189–198 (1975)
8. HTC: VIVE — (2016). https://www.vive.com
9. Microsoft: Microsoft HoloLens (2016). https://www.microsoft.com/hololens
10. Mayring, P.: Qualitative Inhaltsanalyse: Grundlagen und Techniken. Beltz, Weinheim Basel, neuausgabe, 12, aktualisierte edn., February 2015
11. Bartle, R.: Hearts, clubs, diamonds, spades: players who suit MUDs. J. MUD Res. **1**, 28 (1996)
12. Yardley, L., et al.: Older people's views of falls-prevention interventions in six European countries. Gerontologist **46**(5), 650–660 (2006)

13. Brawley, L.R., Rejeski, W.J., King, A.C.: Promoting physical activity for older adults: the challenges for changing behavior. Am. J. Prev. Med. **25**(3 Suppl 2), 172–183 (2003)

14. Brox, E., Fernandez-Luque, L., Evertsen, G., Gonzlez-Hernndez, J.: Exergames for elderly: social exergames to persuade seniors to increase physical activity. In: Proceedings of the 5th International ICST Conference on Pervasive Computing Technologies for Healthcare. IEEE, Dublin (2011). https://doi.org/10.4108/icst.pervasivehealth.2011.246049, http://eudl.eu/doi/10. 4108/icst.pervasivehealth.2011.246049

15. Kegeleers, M., et al.: STAR: superhuman training in augmented reality. In: Proceedings of the First Superhuman Sports Design Challenge: First International Symposium on Amplifying Capabilities and Competing in Mixed Realities, Delft, Netherlands, pp. 7:1–7:6 (2018). https://doi.org/10.1145/3210299.3210306, http://doi.acm.org/10.1145/3210299.3210306

16. Buckers, T., Gong, B., Eisemann, E., Lukosch, S.: VRabl: stimulating physical activities through a multiplayer augmented reality sports game. In: Proceedings of the First Superhuman Sports Design Challenge on First International Symposium on Amplifying Capabilities and Competing in Mixed Realities - SHS 2018, pp. 1–5 (2018). https://doi.org/10.1145/3210299.3210300, http://dl.acm.org/citation. cfm?doid=3210299.3210300

17. Attig, C., Franke, T.: I track, therefore I walk exploring the motivational costs of wearing activity trackers in actual users. Int. J. Hum.-Comput. Stud. (2018). https://doi.org/10.1016/j.ijhcs.2018.04.007, http://www. sciencedirect.com/science/article/pii/S1071581918301915

Age Stereotyping in the Game Context: Introducing the Game-Ageism and Age-Gameism Phenomena

Liliana Vale Costa[1]([⊠]), Ana Isabel Veloso[1], and Eugène Loos[2]

[1] DigiMedia Research Centre, Department of Communication and Art,
University of Aveiro, Campus Universitário de Santiago,
3810-193 Aveiro, Portugal
{lilianavale,aiv}@ua.pt
[2] Utrecht University School of Governance, Utrecht, The Netherlands
e.f.loos@uu.nl

Abstract. Digital games are frequently described as media that can be crucial in strengthening relationships, enhancing cognitive skills and providing social support. Although considerable empirical research on the use of digital games in youth and stereotypes on gender or ethnicity has been widely covered, there have been few studies on age stereotyping in the game context. In addition, this type of stereotype – game-ageism is likely to negatively affect age identity and intergroup communication amongst players, which could hinder to bridge the gap between different generations. Drawn on a literature review, this position paper introduces the concept of game-ageism as an age stereotype that is still set in our game culture. It also seeks to remedy this problem by suggesting an opposite ideological movement – age-gameism that refers to widening the audience of the game industry to all ages. In general, this paper offers a contribution in the field of media and society by highlighting the need for developing games for all ages, encouraging a positive age identity, enhancing intergroup communication and a heterogeneous game culture.

Keywords: Information and Communication Society ·
Ageism · Intergenerational communication · Digital games ·
Stereotypes · Game-ageism · Age-gameism

1 Introduction

One of the most significant current issues in Information and Communication Sciences is the increasing complexity of global networks and their impact on today's societal crisis. In fact, Information and Communication Technologies (ICT) play an important role in the maintenance and creation of post-industrial [1] network structures. Castells [2] points out that these networks are built according to our individual and societal choices, changing the way individuals communicate and interact. A "new technological divide" [2] can result from unequal access to digital platforms, insufficient ICT skills or a geographic or demographic digital divide [3].

© Springer Nature Switzerland AG 2019
J. Zhou and G. Salvendy (Eds.): HCII 2019, LNCS 11593, pp. 245–255, 2019.
https://doi.org/10.1007/978-3-030-22015-0_19

Considering the population ageing, the older target group is likely to become the next generation of consumers in the entertainment sector [4, 5]. However, the research to date is still too much focused on the use of ICT, especially digital entertainment, by children or young people rather than by (older) adults [6–8]. For example, the game's market tends to overlook some proper effects of the ageing process (e.g. reaction time), consequently leading to gaps in the balance between the players' skills and the challenges provided [9–14].

This paper, therefore, debates on age stereotyping in the game context by introducing the terms of game-ageism and age-gameism. The findings are drawn from theory-driven perspectives in the domain of Information, Communication and Society [2]; Communication, media and playfulness [15]; Ageing Studies [16]; and Game Studies – e.g. [17–20].

Throughout the paper, the term 'game-ageism' will be introduced and used to refer to the stereotype against individuals based on their age, in the context of games. This term stems from the concepts of 'ageism' [21] and 'techno-ageism' [22], presented in the section: Ageism, techno-ageism and game-ageism.

2 Games as an Ageless Experience

Over the past few years, a large body of literature – e.g. [18, 23] has investigated the game experience and the network relationships that are established in virtual environments. These studies have revealed that an effective game experience should be context-sensitive and centered on the player's mindset (their feelings, stimuli, motivations, and the depth of the relationship between the player and the ludic artefact).

Game experience is a commonly used notion in game studies and yet it is a difficult concept to define precisely. For Ermi and Mayra [18, p. 37], game experience 'emerges in a unique interaction process between the game and the player' and embodies the concepts of immersion, presence, fun, engagement and flow.

Whereas the term of 'presence' refers to a sense of being in a mediated space (either spatial, physical, social or of self-presence), players' immersion, fun, engagement and flow are related with an intense pleasure, lack of awareness of the outside world, a pleasant activity and a sense of novelty. This latter concept of flow is also associated to an optimal experience that results in a balance between the players' skills and challenges [24]. One question that needs to be asked, however, is whether these experiences are democratic and accessible to a multigenerational context.

In our ageing society, we acquire and loose different skills. Although games might have some benefits to the player such as training and improving specific skills as memory, attention and problem-solving [25–28], physical skills or social skills through the use of exergames [29–32], the game interfaces must be easy-to-use and adaptive to the player [10, 33–36].

One example of these adaptive interfaces can be found in the game Guitar Hero 3, in which the challenge is adapted to the player's performance. As these may have the potential to encourage the sense of mentoring and a peer culture in which experiences are in line with the players' goals [24], games and players are likely to be reinvented in a "casual revolution" overstated by Juul [20]. Indeed, the strategy of Nintendo for widening the audience of digital games has been crucial to leap games into a more natural experience and the game remotes have been evolving from buttons to simple gestures. Despite the fact that these interfaces have become mimetic (the player interacts with the system through mimesis. The character on the screen imitates and reproduces the real gestures that come from the player) and socially embeddable (the appropriateness of the interfaces to the user by being natural and ubiquitous within the social context) [20], further developments have to be done in order to straighten the value of inclusive game communities and player-centered environments.

There are a number of similarities between age stereotypes and others (e.g. racial, cultural), which often derive from social emotions. They are mostly activated when detecting differences between oneself in relation to other individuals or groups [37, 38] and if in our primates, these differences were a sign of potential aggression or danger, there is no reason to perpetuate these in today's society. Furthermore, our minds, artefacts and society tend to be enriched by a cultural pluralism. One way to dissipate the reflection of these stereotypes on the game culture is to provide the players with *remappable keys* (providing the option to reconfigure keys) context-aware and personalized environments without affecting the quality of the graphics, the type of the game and the equilibrium between the game challenges and the players' skills. A player versus environment conflict is also likely to be preferred in order to not creating 'unfair' game scenarios and meet the game challenges to the skills of gamers from different generations.

In terms of the older adult player, a positive game experience is very important as his/her brain tends to release *dopamine* (a neurotransmitter that when released, it vis thought to give a sense of pleasure and reward) and this chemical is likely to stimulate the *amygdalae* (brain region that takes part of the limbic system and it is suggested that this region is important to the memory and emotions processing as well as in decision-making), which is responsible for the transmission of emotions, social behaviours and social interactions [39]. In addition, games can overcome some physical [30, 31], cognitive [25, 26] and social effects [40] of the ageing process.

Relative to the reported motivations for playing videogames by older adult gamers, these are: spending free time [6, 7], maintaining an active mind and escaping from reality [8]. Gajadhar, Nap, De Kort and Ijsselsteijn [41] point out that this target group also enjoy teaching and helping other players. These results corroborate the Meaningful Elderly Play (MEP) model proposed by De Schutter and Vero Vanden [40], which suggests the following keys to create a meaningful play environment and attract an older audience to play: fostering connectedness; cultivating oneself; and contributing to society.

Finally, the bases for creating an ageless gameplay experience lie in combining the aforementioned age-related adaptive interfaces and meeting the older adult motivations with the elements that are proposed by Csikszentmihalyi [24] to generate an optimal experience: (a) a challenge; (b) a task; (c) the ability to concentrate on the task; (d) a sense of control over actions and of worry about losing control; (e) a loss of self-consciousness; and (f) transformation of time. These elements can be designed and stimulated by creating a game environment that enables players to exchange their experiences and bring daily moments of their lives, knowledge, feelings, thoughts and desires into games.

Having discussed the potential of a positive game experience to all ages, the following section reports on the concepts of ageism, techno-ageism and game-ageism.

3   Ageism, Techno-Ageism and Game-Ageism

Age identity and stereotypes tend to strongly influence communication and social relationships. Indeed, Tajfel and Turner [42] state that the popularity, likeability or discrimination of a group is dependent on the sense of belonging felt by their members. Furthermore, the individual's identity can be affected by [16, 42]: (a) social mobility (moving from one social group to another); (b) social change (changes in the relationships); (c) social creativity (individuals tend to concentrate on positive distinctiveness) and (d) social competition (competition between groups).

In 2007, Harwood [16] examined the Tajfel and Turner's theory in the context of older adults by suggesting that they can: (a) act as youngsters; (b) emphasize the positive aspects of being an older adult (positive stereotypes), successively comparing themselves to others who are older or impaired; and (c) compete with younger generations.

Regardless of the attitude of individuals towards groups, the sense of membership and shared fellowship shape the age identity, which is determinant to the communication process (e.g. second- versus third- person in speech, authority) and the sense of self.

Meanwhile, it is worth noting that there are slight differences between the concepts of stereotype, prejudice and discrimination. Whereas stereotypes are cognitive schemas, prejudices are affective and discrimination is behavioural [16]. In this paper, one type of stereotype is covered – ageism, which can be applied to different contexts (e.g. both in the use of technology and digital games).

3.1   Ageism

Ageism may be broadly defined as an age-related stereotype [43], prejudice and discrimination against people because of their age [44, 45]. This type of stereotype is mostly applied to older adults and it often relates to the denial or violation of Human Rights in older adults [43]. See [46] for more information about the origins of this notion.

Ageism is a blend of the words "Age" and "-ism". In specific, age corresponds mainly to biological, psychological and social changes [47, 48] that occur during a certain period of time, in which a person has lived. Regarding the suffix "-ism", a multitude of meanings may be subsumed – e.g.: a distinctive practice; a system; a political ideology; an artistic movement or the basics for prejudice or discrimination.

A number of studies [49, 50] have attempted to explain the reason this stereotype occurred in society, given that each generation age from the moment they start to live. Martens, Greenberg, Schimel and Landau [49] claim that the stereotype may be due to the fear of mortality and thus, being in contact with older adults reminds us of this Human condition and the limitations of time.

Cuddy, Norton and Fiske [50] found that younger generations had contradictory views relative to older adults. In their study, younger generations have seen older adults as incompetents (low status) but at the same time warm (passive). On the one hand, negative stereotypes related with the ageing process are often associated with an increase in loneliness [51], boredom [52] and disabilities [53]. On the other hand, positive stereotypes are likely to be related with wisdom [54], caring [55] and politeness [56].

Older men seem to benefit from positive stereotypes rather than women and this may owe to the women's longer life expectancy and the negative perceptions of their physical appearance as society tends to value beauty, women fertility and youth [16, 57].

In brief, understanding ageism is very important in order to know its impact on social networks, intergenerational friendships and attitudes towards the ageing process.

3.2   Techno-Ageism

One of the most significant current concerns of the Preparatory Committee for the Second World on Assembly on Ageing [43] and of the International Strategy for Action on Ageing 2002 [58] is the abuse and ageism towards older adults. Indeed, these recent developments in the study of the older adult's discrimination have led to the definition of their rights in different forms of abuse: (a) physical; (b) emotional; (c) financial; and (d) neglect.

Although advances in the Human's Rights related with the freedom of opinion and the use of media (Art.19) have been made [59], there is still insufficient data for such network vulnerabilities that can occur in the Information and Communication Society – e.g. techno-ageism and game-ageism.

Pires [22] was apparently the first to use the term techno-ageism. For Pires [22], techno-ageism refers to a set of stereotypes and prejudices regarding the older adults' capabilities to use Information and Communication Technologies. Furthermore, this concept is also used to describe the digital divide between younger and older generations and their own attitudes towards the Internet.

The term techno-ageism is also associated to the incapability to adapt to new learning contexts – e.g. the proverb "You can't teach an old dog a new trick" and a positive stereotype would be related with a sense of independence and extra cognitive activity. Another form of techno-ageism refers to the design of digital artefacts that are neither accessible nor suitable for older adults, despite the fact that it is, thus, worth to remember that the Web is designed to serve everyone, despite their inabilities, languages and software or hardware used [60].

3.3   Game-Ageism

The use of new media introduces new terms and changes in everyday speech [61]. In fact, having defined what is meant by Ageism and Techno-ageism, the term Game-ageism is proposed in this paper to refer to:

The belief that all members of an age group possess certain game characteristics, skills or attitudes that distinguishes them as inferior or superior to other gamers.

This term also encompasses the following meaning:

Stereotype, prejudice or discrimination against gamers, based on their age and the assumption that being youngster is the gamers' standard.

Game-Ageism is a blend of the words "Game" and "Ageism". Like Techno-Ageism (technologies + ageism), the word game has been added before in order to give its context and although the game concept embodies different definitions, it is intertwined with the concept of playing.

According to Huizinga [19], play is a free and unserious activity, almost situated outside of everyday life and Caillois [62, p. 63] adds that "play is a parallel, independent activity, opposed to the acts and decisions of ordinary life by special characteristics appropriate to play." These mentioned characteristics are: (a) being free and voluntary; (b) independent from every day's life; (c) uncertain; (d) unproductive; (e) reigned by rules; and to (f) create an imaginary world.

In the digital game context, Salen and Zimmerman [63, p. 80] describe games as "a system in which players engage in an artificial conflict, defined by rules, that results in quantifiable outcome." Juul [20] also highlights the characteristics of "rule-based" and "quantifiable outcome."

In this paper, we use, therefore, the term "game" with the meaning of a voluntary activity defined by a set of rules and outcome-oriented goals as overstated by previous studies [19, 20, 62, 63].

Game-ageism may affect intergroup communication, forming exclusive "digital tribes" or "virtual clans" [64], using age criteria. In fact, a survey conducted by Costa [65] has revealed that individuals who tend to be in favor of playing in later age base their opinion on reasons for playing, whereas those who are against are likely to support on game experiences.

The inverse phenomenon of Age-Gameism can also occur. It is proposed in this paper to refer to:

Gaining pleasure from playing games and, thus, overcoming age-related psychological and social constraints.

This term also encompasses the following meanings:

Action of playing games vigorously on a certain age, aimed at bringing a social change;

The willingness to play games and develop gamer skills, regardless age;

Age-related benefits brought through the ritual of playing games;

Be proud of maintaining a 'gamer soul' (be avid in games) throughout the ageing process;

The belief that games are for all ages.

In this particular case, gameism (game+ism) refers to the activity, a state/quality and ideological movement of playing games on a certain age. The term 'age' moved to the beginning of the sentence (expressing the context) instead of the word 'game.' It functions as the opposite of game-ageism.

On the one hand, in recent years, grandchildren have been disseminating videos on Youtube showing grandparents playing games, especially digital games, as if it was a "coolest grandma or grandpa" contest. This trend is an example of a social movement for the use of games and digital games regardless of the players' age. In addition, many online communities addressed to older gamers (e.g. The older gamers, 2old2play,

Greezer Gamers) have been created. On the other hand the analysis of the Dutch short film Pony Place shows how grandparents trying to play a digital game are stereotypically represented as digital immigrants [66], which could be labeled as a form of visual ageism [67].

Overall, these initiatives help to reduce the sense of Game-Ageism and some of them even spread the doctrine of Age-Gameism.

4 Discussion

This paper debated on age stereotyping in the game context, introducing the terms of Game-ageism and Age-gameism. In fact, discussing the presence of age identity and intergroup communication in the context of digital games is relevant, considering that game experiences need to be democratic and accessible to a multigenerational context, inviting to a "casual revolution" [20].

Another aspect is that owing to the rise of a global network society, as posited by Castells [2], changes in the complexity of social and family structures are likely to be perceived. The idea of a social divide does not fit with the flexibility and adaptability model of these networks and conflicts between generations are likely to occur because of the lack of an age identity and a set of learning, communication and authority gaps.

The Ageism phenomenon spills over to another context, such as the use of Information and Communication Technologies and Digital Games. That said, the movement of Age-gameism should be encouraged over Game-ageism.

This study pleads for the potential of digital games in reshaping our stereotypes related with the ageing process and stimulating solidarity and collaboration between different generations.

A limitation of this study is that it is theory-driven and there is a general lack of field work in the area. The comparison between different generations about their perceived attitude towards the ageing process before and after gameplay was also not covered in this paper. Further research would be necessary to understand in which way this type of stereotype is covered in different media and formats (e.g. news, animations, movies, visual novels, games) and assess the potential of intergenerational gameplay to demystify this ageing bias – game-ageism and foster age-gameism by comparing the end-users' perceived attitude towards ageing before and after gameplay, in comparison with other intergenerational mediated activity.

Acknowledgements. This work was supported by Fundação para a Ciência e Tecnologia and ESF under Community Support Framework III – the project SEDUCE 2.0 nr. POCI-01-0145-FEDER-031696.

References

1. Toffler, A.: The Third Wave. Bantam Books, New York (1984)
2. Castells, M.: The Internet Galaxy: Reflections on the Internet, Business, and Society. Oxford University Press, Oxford (2004)

3. Friemel, T.: The digital divide has grown old: determinants of a digital divide among seniors. New Media Soc. **18**, 313–331 (2014). https://doi.org/10.1177/1461444814538648
4. Lenhart, A., Jones, S., Macgill, A.: Pew Internet Project Data Memo Adults and video games. Pew Internet & American Life Project, USA (2008). http://www.pewinternet.org/wp-content/uploads/sites/9/media/Files/Reports/2008/PIP_Adult_gaming_memo.pdf.pdf. Access 13 Jan 2019
5. Brown, J.A., Marston, H.R.: Gen X and digital games: looking back to look forward. In: Zhou, J., Salvendy, G. (eds.) ITAP 2018, Part II. LNCS, vol. 10927, pp. 485–500. Springer, Cham (2018). https://doi.org/10.1007/978-3-319-92037-5_34
6. Costa, L., Veloso, A.: Factors influencing the adoption of video games in late adulthood. Int. J. Technol. Hum. Interact. **12**, 35–50 (2016). https://doi.org/10.4018/ijthi.2016010103
7. Marston, H.: Design recommendations for digital game design within an ageing society. Educ. Gerontol. **39**, 103–118 (2013). https://doi.org/10.1080/03601277.2012.689936
8. Pearce, C.: The truth about baby boomer gamers. Games Cult. **3**, 142–174 (2008). https://doi.org/10.1177/1555412008314132
9. Costa, L., Veloso, A.: Being (Grand) players: review of digital games and their potential to enhance intergenerational interactions. J. Intergener. Relatsh. **14**, 43–59 (2016). https://doi.org/10.1080/15350770.2016.1138273
10. Loos, E.: Designing meaningful intergenerational digital games. In: International Conference on Communication, Media, Technology and Design, pp. 46–51 (2014)
11. Khoo, E., Merritt, T., Cheok, A.: Designing a mixed reality intergenerational entertainment system. In: Dubois, E., Gray, P., Nigay, L. (eds.) The Engineering of Mixed Reality Systems. Human-Computer Interaction Series, pp. 121–141. Springer, London (2010). https://doi.org/10.1007/978-1-84882-733-2_7
12. Davis, H., Vetere, F., Gibbs, M., Francis, P.: Come play with me: designing technologies for intergenerational play. Univ. Access Inf. Soc. **11**, 17–29 (2011). https://doi.org/10.1007/s10209-011-0230-3
13. Khoo, E., Cheok, A., Nguyen, T., Pan, Z.: Age invaders: social and physical intergenerational mixed reality family entertainment. Virtual Real. **12**, 3–16 (2008). https://doi.org/10.1007/s10055-008-0083-0
14. Mahmud, A., Mubin, O., Shahid, S., Martens, J.: Designing social games for children and older adults: two related case studies. Entertain. Comput. **1**, 147–156 (2010). https://doi.org/10.1016/j.entcom.2010.09.001
15. Jenkins, H.: Convergence Culture: Where Old and New Media Collide. NYU Press, New York (2006)
16. Harwood: Understanding Communication and Aging: Developing Knowledge and Awareness. SAGE Publications, University of Arizon, USA (2007)
17. Crawford, C.: Chris Crawford on Game Design. New Riders Publishers, Indianapolis (2003)
18. Ermi, L., Mäyrä, F.: Fundamental components of the gameplay experience: analysing immersion. In: DIGRA 2005 – Proceedings of the 2005 DIGRA International Conference: Changing Views, Worlds in Play, vol. 3, pp. 15–27 (2005)
19. Huizinga, J.: Homo Ludens: A Study of the Play-Element in Culture. Routledge & Kegan Paul Limited, London (1949)
20. Juul, J.: A Casual Revolution: Reinventing Video Games and Their Players. The MIT Press, Cambridge (2012)
21. Butler, R.: Ageism: looking back over my shoulder. Generations **29**, 84–86 (2005)
22. Pires, A.: Efeitos dos videojogos nas funções cognitivas da pessoa idosa [Master's Thesis], Faculdade de Medicina da Universidade do Porto (2011)

23. De Kort, Y., Ijsselsteijn, W.: People, places, and play: player experience in a socio-spatial context. In: Computers in Entertainment (CIE) - Theoretical and Practical Computer Applications in Entertainment. ACM, New York (2008). https://doi.org/10.1145/1371216. 1371221

24. Csikzentmihalyi, M.: Flow: The Psychology of Optimal Experience. Harper Perennial Modern Classics, New York (2008)

25. Gamberini, L., Barresi, G., Majer, A., Scarpetta, F.: A game a day keeps the doctor away: a short review of computer games in mental healthcare. J. CyberTherapy Rehabil. 1, 127–145 (2008)

26. Whitlock, L., McLaughlin, A., Allaire, J.: Individual differences in response to cognitive training: using a multi-modal, attentionally demanding game-based intervention for older adults. Comput. Hum. Behav. 28, 1091–1096 (2012). https://doi.org/10.1016/j.chb.2012.01. 012

27. Nouchi, R., et al.: Brain training game improves executive functions and processing speed in the elderly: a randomized controlled trial. PLoS ONE 7, e29676 (2012). https://doi.org/10. 1371/journal.pone.0029676

28. Belchior, P., et al.: Video game training to improve selective visual attention in older adults. Comput. Hum. Behav. 29, 1318–1324 (2013). https://doi.org/10.1016/j.chb.2013.01.034

29. Leinonen, M., Koivisto, A., Sirkka, A., Kristian, K.: Designing games for well-being; exergames for elderly people. In: European Conference on Games Based Learning (ECGBL 2012), pp. 635–639. Academic Publishing International Limited, Reading (2012)

30. Brox, E., Luque, L., Evertsen, G., Hernandez, J.: Exergames for elderly: social exergames to persuade seniors to increase physical activity. In: 5th International Conference on Pervasive Computing Technologies for Healthcare, PervasiveHealth 2011, pp. 635–639. IEEE (2011). https://doi.org/10.4108/icst.pervasivehealth.2011.246049

31. Loos, E., Kaufman, D.: Positive impact of exergaming on older adults' mental and social well-being: in search of evidence. In: Zhou, J., Salvendy, G. (eds.) ITAP 2018, Part II. LNCS, vol. 10927, pp. 101–112. Springer, Cham (2018). https://doi.org/10.1007/978-3-319-92037-5_9

32. Schell, R., Kaufman, D.: Cognitive benefits of digital games for older adults. In: Proceedings of the International Conference on Computer Supported Education, CSEDU 2016, pp. 137–141 (2016). https://doi.org/10.5220/0005878501370141

33. Anguera, J., et al.: Video game training enhances cognitive control in older adults. Nature 501, 97–101 (2013). https://doi.org/10.1038/nature12486

34. Basak, C., Boot, W., Voss, M., Kramer, A.: Can training in a real-time strategy video game attenuate cognitive decline in older adults? Psychol. Aging 23, 765–777 (2008). https://doi. org/10.1037/a0013494

35. Fisk, A., Czaja, S., Rogers, W., Charness, N., Czaja, S., Sharit, J.: Designing for Older Adults: Principles and Creative Human Factors Approaches. CRC Press, Boca Raton (2009)

36. Costa, L., Veloso, A.: The Gamer's Soul never dies: review of digital games for an active ageing. In: 2015 10th Iberian Conference on Information Systems and Technologies (CISTI), pp. 1–6. IEEE (2015). https://doi.org/10.1109/cisti.2015.7170614

37. Damásio, A.: Looking for Spinoza: Joy, Sorrow and the Feeling Brain. Houghton Mifflin Harcourt Publishing Company, New York (2003)

38. United Nations: The Universal Declaration of Human Rights. United Nations, Paris (1948). http://www.un.org/en/documents/udhr. Access 13 Jan 2019

39. Adolphs, R.: Social cognition and the human brain. Trend Cogn. Sci. 3, 469–479 (1999)

40. DeSchutter, B., Vero Vanden, A.: Designing meaningful play within the psycho-social context of older adults. In: Proceedings of the 3rd International Conference on Fun and Games, pp. 46–51. ACM, New York (2010). https://doi.org/10.1145/1823818.1823827

41. Gajadhar, B., Nap, H., De Kort, Y., Ijsselsteijn, W.: Out of sight, out of mind: co-player effects on seniors' player experience. In: Proceeding Fun and Games 2010 Proceedings of the 3rd International Conference on Fun and Games, pp. 74–83. ACM, New York (2010). https://doi.org/10.1145/1823818.1823826

42. Tajfel, H., Turner, J., Austin, W., Worchel, S.: An integrative theory of intergroup conflict. In: Hatch, M., Schultz, M. (eds.) Organizational Identity: A Reader, pp. 56–65. Oxford University Press, New York (2004)

43. United Nations Economic and Social Council: Abuse of older persons: recognizing and responding to abuse of older persons in a global context. World Assembly on Ageing, New York (2002)

44. Australian Human Rights Commission: Age Discrimination – exposing the hidden barrier for mature age workers. Australian Human Rights Commission, Sydney (2010)

45. Nelson, T.: Ageism: Stereotyping and Prejudice Against Older Persons. MIT Press, Cambridge (2004)

46. Butler, R.: Age-ism: another form of bigotry. Gerontologist 9, 243–246 (1969)

47. Going, S., Williams, D., Lohman, T.: Aging and body composition: biological changes and methodological issues. Exerc. Sport Sci. Rev. 23, 411–458 (1995). https://doi.org/10.1249/00003677-199500230-00016

48. Perlmutter, M., Hall, E.: Adult Development and Aging. Wiley, New York (1992)

49. Martens, A., Greenberg, J., Schimel, J., Landau, M.: Ageism and death: effects of mortality salience and perceived similarity to elders on reactions to elderly people. Pers. Soc. Psychol. Bull. 30, 1524–1536 (2004). https://doi.org/10.1177/0146167204271185

50. Cuddy, A., Norton, M., Fiske, S.: This old stereotype: the pervasiveness and persistence of the elderly stereotype. J. Soc. Issues 61, 267–285 (2005). https://doi.org/10.1111/j.1540-4560.2005.00405.x

51. Dykstra, P.A.: Older adult loneliness: myths and realities. Eur. J. Ageing 6, 91–100 (2009). https://doi.org/10.1007/s10433-009-0110-3

52. Palmore, E.: Ageism: Negative and Positive. Springer, New York (1999)

53. Sheets, D.: Aging with disabilities: ageism and more. Generations 29, 37–41 (2005)

54. Staudinger, U.: Older and wiser? Integrating results on the relationship between age and wisdom-related performance. Int. J. Behav. Dev. 23, 641–664 (1999)

55. Hank, K., Buber, I.: Grandparents caring for their grandchildren: findings from the 2004 survey of health, ageing, and retirement in Europe. J. Fam. Issues 30, 53–73 (2014). https://doi.org/10.1177/0192513X08322627

56. Harwood, J., McKee, J., Lin, M.: Younger and older adults' schematic representations of intergenerational communication. Commun. Monogr. 67, 20–41 (2000). https://doi.org/10.1080/03637750009376493

57. Saucier, M.: Midlife and beyond: issues for aging women. J. Couns. Dev. 82, 420–425 (2011). https://doi.org/10.1002/j.1556-6678.2004.tb00329.x

58. Sidorenko, A., Walker, A.: The Madrid International Plan of Action on Ageing: from conception to implementation. Ageing Soc. 24, 147–165 (2004)

59. Kerr, I., Bailey, J.: The implications of digital rights management for privacy and freedom of expression. J. Inf. Commun. Ethics Soc. 2, 85–95 (2004). https://doi.org/10.1108/14779960480000245

60. Accessibility - W3C. http://www.w3.org/standards/webdesign/accessibility

61. Postman, N.: Technopoly: The Surrender of Culture to Technology. Random House Digital, Inc., New York (1992)

62. Caillois, R.: Man, Play and Games. University of Illinois Press, Chicago (1992)

63. Salen, K., Zimmerman, E.: Rules of Play: Game Design Fundamentals. MIT Press, Cambridge (2003)

64. Wheeler, S.: Connected Minds, Emerging Cultures: Cybercultures in Online Learning. Information Age Publishing, Inc., Charlotte (2009)
65. Costa, L.: Networked video games for older adults [Master's thesis], Universidade de Aveiro (2013)
66. Loos, E., Kubiński, P., Romero, M.: The representation of older people playing a digital game in the short film 'Pony Place': a semiotic and narratological analysis. J. Comp. Res. Anthropol. Sociol. **8**, 43–62 (2017)
67. Loos, E., Ivan, L.: Visual ageism in the media. In: Ayalon, L., Tesch-Römer, C. (eds.) Contemporary Perspectives on Ageism. IPA, vol. 19, pp. 163–176. Springer, Cham (2018). https://doi.org/10.1007/978-3-319-73820-8_11

Attraction and Addiction Factors of Online Games on Older Adults: A Qualitative Study

Xiaolun Wang[1], Xinlin Yao[1(✉)], and Jie Gu[2]

[1] Nanjing University of Science and Technology, Nanjing, China
xinlinyao@njust.edu.cn
[2] Shanghai Academy of Social Sciences, Shanghai, China

Abstract. With the development of technology and new devices, online games have attracted more and more older adults. Exploring chances and challenges of the elder players become an important issue in the game industry. First of all, older adults have a lot of accesses to reach a new game, but it is unclear which way is the most effective one. Secondly, although adequate game playing is good for elders' mental and physical conditions, game addiction is not. It is emergent to distinguish between the attractive and addictive factors of online games on older adults, and find a balance between them. A semi-structure interview is employed in this study. We analyze the qualitative data from four themes: older adults' access to online games, factors that attract older adults to play online games, factors that lead to older adults' addiction in online games, game design features that alleviate game addiction for older adults. This research is among the first to distinguish the attractive and addictive factors on elder game players, as well as provide practical implications for game company and designers.

Keywords: Game attraction · Game addiction · Older adults · Game design

1 Introduction

Online games have increasingly become an integral part of daily life for people of all ages and genders [1]. An official report from ESA and ARRP announced that there were over 41 million elder game players, constituting 36 percent of all the population with an age above 50 [2]. From the social benefit perspective, online games have been proved to enhance the quality of elders' lives, such as improving their mental and cognitive abilities, strengthening social connectedness, as well as offering a joyful way of spending time [3, 4]. From a commercial view, elder players are a potential user base due to large numbers and lots of free time. Therefore, it is of great importance to explore the chances and challenges of the elder players in the game industry.

To open this potential market, the first problem is game publicity and promotion. Different from the younger generation, older adults are usually with low technical literacy and have almost none information seeking techniques. Therefore, our first research question is: *Where do the elders access game information? And which is the most effective one?*

© Springer Nature Switzerland AG 2019
J. Zhou and G. Salvendy (Eds.): HCII 2019, LNCS 11593, pp. 256–266, 2019.
https://doi.org/10.1007/978-3-030-22015-0_20

Even if a game successfully reaches the aged population, it does not mean the older players will be willing to click in the game. Most games have not fully taken older adults' needs and interests into consideration, which build solid healthy, social and technical barriers that keep the elders away from playing online games [5, 6]. Fortunately, A few literatures have paid attention to the problem and proposed several game design features that might be attractive for older adults, such as font size, color brightness, theme relevance, goal simplicity, and necessary social functions [7–9]. These changes significantly increase the number of elder players but unintentionally lead to a negative consequence: game addition, which caused serious bodily impairments on older adults' eyes, necks, and waists. So, it is emergent for academicians and practitioners to distinguish between the attractive and addictive factors of online games on older adults, and find a balance between them. In other words, *which factors can attract elder players to play an online game? Which factors will lead to their addiction in games? And how can we motivate older adults to play games but not be addicted to it through game designs?*

To solve the above questions, this study adopts a semi-structured interview as the research method. 12 respondents with an average age of 66.7 who have played at least one kind of online game are recruited. We analyze the qualitative data from four themes: older adults' access to online games, factors that attract older adults to play online games, factors that lead to older adults' addiction in online games, game design features that alleviate game addiction for older adults. This research is among the first to distinguish the attractive and addictive factors on elder game players, as well as provides practical implications for game company and designers.

The rest of the paper is organized as follows. We first review relevant literatures. Then we propose our research design. After that, we report on the qualitative results. Finally, we discuss the implications, limitations and future directions of this study.

2   Literature Review

2.1   Barriers that Hinder Older Adults from Playing Online Games

Older adults are a homogeneous group facing similar age-related changes and impairments, which may hinder them from playing online games [1]. According to previous literatures, we categorize these factors into healthy, social and technical barriers.

First and foremost, older adults face serious health problems including sensory decrements in vision and hearing, decaying cognitive abilities, reduced physical skills, as well as chronic illnesses [6]. Secondly, the "old" is recognized as a group irrelevant to online games under current social norms [3], few seniors do play online, and therefore, few peers in games lead to few social benefits [4]. Thirdly, current generation of older adults have not experienced the same degree of computer and Internet technology as the younger ones do [5], who have significant difficulties in handling diverse game interfaces and operations.

Overall, these healthy, social and technical problems limit older adults' possibilities of participating in most online games and lead to special requirements in the process of game design and promotion [8].

2.2 Game Design Features for Older Adults in Online Games

In fact, older adults are a group of under-investigated users in online games with particular needs and interests [1]. Till now, a few researches have begun to understand the ageing population and attempt to incorporate specific design features into online games. We summarize these features from four aspects: interface, user-computer interaction, user-user interaction, and content.

First of all, the interface has to be adjusted to meet the needs of older adults in consideration of their healthy barriers, including basic settings of size, color and voice [8]. Secondly, according to Choi and Kim [10], user-computer interaction can be facilitated by providing appropriate goals, operators and feedback. Besides, devices with technology that are easy-to-operate are the mostly preferred [7]. Thirdly, user-user interaction is important in improving social capital and support for elders [9]. Last, appropriate themes and funny game contents play a significant role in attracting older adults [7, 11]. Details are illustrated in Table 1 below.

Table 1. Game design features for older adults in online games

Game design factors	Objects	Features	References
Interface	Size	Large font size and figures	[5, 8]
	Color	Bright and soft color	
	Voice	Low-frequency voice	
User-computer interaction	Goal	Easy and large targets	[5, 10]
	Operators	Minimize the number of operators, and help elder to get full control over the game	
	Feedback	Frequent tactile or vibration feedbacks	
	Device & technology	Prefer touch screen	[7]
User-user interaction	Social interaction	Effective communication places and tools	[9]
	Social recommendation	Sharing and ranking function in popular social media platforms	
Contents	Theme	Appropriate themes for elders	[7, 11, 12]
	Entertainment	Funny and attractive	

Although previous literatures proposed specific features of online game design for older adults, they have not distinguished them into short-term and long-term factors. In other words, the ageing population may be attracted to an online game with certain features, but the reasons why they addict to an online game is different. It is important to identify and classify these features to better guide the game design for elders.

2.3 Impacts of Playing Online Games on Older Adults

Ample studies have demonstrated that online games can help older adults to improve their cognitive abilities, mental health, social networks, and technical literacy. First of all, games are proved to be efficient in improving elders' hand-eye coordination, recognition memory, attentional control, and processing speed [4]. Secondly, as an alternative to television, the initial purpose of online games is for relaxation and entertainment [5], which improves the elders' quality of life [3]. Thirdly, many older adults enjoy online game because it provides a place to communicate with others, thus improve their social capital and support social relationships [4]. Last, online games also generate positive attitudes towards technology and encourage their technological learning impetus [7].

However, every coin has two sides. A number of negative impacts of playing online games on older adults have been put forward recently. On one hand, it is widely known that playing online games too long will lead to cervical spondylosis, lumbar strain, and eye impairment, especially for older adults with a relatively bad healthy condition. On the other hand, although elders regard games as a means of escaping from daily routines [7], it will be troublesome if they put too much time on games, which eventually disturbs their daily life and offline social activities.

In this regard, playing online games adequately is good for the aged population, but the challenge is to avoid them from being too addictive to those games. Therefore, it is emergent and important to find the boundary between attractive and addictive factors, and alleviate the addiction phenomenon through specific game designs features.

3 Research Design

3.1 Research Method

This research adopts a semi-structured interview as the research method, which follows a general interview approach [13]. The reasons why I choose this method are twofold. Firstly, attractive and addictive factors are difficult to distinguish with simple survey questions when the sample group is elder people, so prior studies with quantitative data can only investigate all related factors but cannot tell the difference. Secondly, semi-structured interview can help respondents recall the memory, and report their detailed attitudes with multiple choices, which is widely recognized as an effective approach in social research.

3.2 Interviewees and Interview Process

We recruited 12 respondents with an average age of 66.7 who have played at least one kind of online game (i.e., QQ Chinese Poker, AniPop) during the year 2018. All interviews were conducted in China by the same researcher. Every interview started with an open question: What is your favorite game? Then, participants were invited to talk freely about how they know the game, why and when they begin to play the game, their attitudes towards the game, and so on. Later on, they were asked about the average time they spend in playing this game every day, and following questions are based on their answers. Two hours were regarded as the boundary between normal and addictive game players. For addictive older adults, they recalled the reason why they keep playing this game so long, as well as the perceived negative effects of their addiction. The average interview duration was 40 min. Each participant was offered a small gift valued around 30 RMB after the interview. The demographic summary is shown in Table 2.

Table 2. Demographic Summary

Age	Gender	Education	Game playing experience (Years)	Game playing time (Hours/Day)
60	F	Bachelor	4	1
66	M	Senior secondary school	6	2.5
59	M	Junior college	5.5	1
62	M	Junior secondary school	2	3
58	F	Bachelor	3	6.5
64	F	Primary school	4.5	1
81	M	Bachelor	3	4.5
73	F	Junior secondary school	3	2
80	M	Senior secondary school	10	6
60	M	Senior secondary school	1	2
72	F	Primary school	9	1
65	M	Junior secondary school	5	2.5

4   Qualitative Results

The qualitative results are demonstrated under four themes that guided the interview: (1) where do you know online game information? (2) Which factors of the game that attract you to play it? (3) Which factors of the game that make you addict to it? (4) Are there any ways to alleviate the symptom of game addiction?

4.1   Older Adults' Access to Online Games

This qualitative results reveal that there are four approaches that take older adults to online games.

The first and most effective way is from peers' recommendation. In fact, respondents were usually introduced to games by their spouse, relatives or friends, because they share common interests and trust each other. Healthy, social and technical barriers can be easily broken when your peers play the same game. Interestingly, different from the younger generation, even if suggested by their friends, the elders are not necessarily playing together, they prefer play games alone and have a competition in the system-uploaded high scores.

> "My elder sister has been playing AniPop for a couple of years, and taught me how to play the game in our family party last year. It seemed easy and I believed I could play well since she could...In most times, we don't play together, but we always check and compare our highest scores. Sometimes she won me and then I would try to surpass her as soon as possible."

The second approach is an unintentional one. A few respondents played games which were originally prepared for their grandchildren. Under this circumstance, online games unexpectedly narrow the intergenerational distance, and become a new way for older adults to spend more time and have more interactions with the younger generations.

> "My son downloaded the game 'Baby Crocodiles Love Baths' for my granddaughter. Sometimes she could not pass a barrier and asked me for help. Then I found the game interesting and began to play whenever I was free. Finally, this game became a shared activity with my granddaughter. It is incredible!"

In addition, marketing messages are delivered everywhere by the game company. Due to unfamiliarity with most devices, older adults frequently click into pop-up windows unconsciously. They are so cautious that they feel afraid of the advertisements, because they think these are possibly virus. But when the game seems well developed, older adults' worry may be dispelled and even to play it.

> "Last time, when I opened the game 'Fruit Slice', another game appeared and I accidentally clicked in. This game seemed poorly developed thus I quickly quit in case it was a virus...If the game seemed better, it was likely that I may try it."

The last way to access game information is from self-seeking. One advantage of playing online games is the improvement in older adults' technological literacy [7]. They are motivated to learn as long as they want to play more and better. Therefore, some of them have gradually acquired the ability to search for games that they are interested in.

> "I like playing AniPop and have already cleared all the stages. Then I felt bored and my daughter taught me how to search and download new games from my tablet PC. I used the key word 'elimination' and found a few similar games. That's great!"

4.2 Factors that Attract Older Adults to Play Online Games

Just as we summarized in Sect. 2.1, there are three barriers that hinder older adults from playing games. Except for social recommendation approach proposed in Sect. 4.1, game design features that are directed at breaking healthy, social and technical barriers can play a key role in attracting elders to play a new game.

First and foremost, interface design makes a first impression that directly impacts elders' willingness to try. For a game to attract older adults, the principle is a bit different because it has to consider their healthy conditions first. Due to the eye and ear impairments, older adults will only be interested in games that allow players to change the font, color and voice settings, as well as window resizing and figure zooming. With regard to their low cognitive ability, easy operation and basic instructions is necessary for older adults when they first enter the game.

> *"Once I clicked in a game, I was scared by dense words and figures. You know, I have got presbyopia for a long time, I cannot see the words clearly if the font cannot be enlarged...Some games seem difficult to play with no instructions, I will be in a loss because I don't know what I should do. I will quickly quit the game with no hesitation."*

Social barriers also keep elders away from certain games. For instance, massively multiplayer online games are mainly designed for young adults, where elders cannot find any peers in the game. Bloody, childish, and dating games are also not suitable for older adults under current social norms. Therefore, the best way to broke social barriers is to design games with relevant themes attractive to older adults. For instance, puzzle games like poker, mahjong, and chess is popular in the elders' life because it corresponds to their offline activity. Simple games such as AniPop and Fruit Slice may also attract older adults since their peers are playing it too.

> *"I am interested in Chinese chess, which I am good at since I was a child. Online games help me to find matched rivals, and I don't need to go out early to occupy a seat. This technology really improves my recreational life."*
>
> *"AniPop is so interesting, many of my friends play it. And when I conquered my friend, I might even share the score in my friend cycle."*

With a low technical literacy, older adults stated their worry about the ability to use a computer, but felt relieved after the prevalence of touch screen laptop. Besides, the mobility nature of tablet affords the possibility to play games everywhere at any time. Therefore, the development of new device breaks the longstanding technical barriers for elders. However, older adults are not followers of all new technology. WII somatic games and virtual reality games have not attracted the elders at all, because they are relatively complex even compared with PCs.

> *"It is difficult to use a PC because I have to learn how to start up, how to find the game, how to use the mouse and keyboard. I never played any online games before my son gave me an iPad. It is an amazing technology and so easy to learn and use! My son also bought a VR glass last year, I really don't like it. I keep playing my iPad since there are countless new games."*

In addition, money is also important in older adults' selection of online games. They seldom play any games that are not free because they don't know how to pay and are afraid of being cheated. The reasons seem totally different from the younger generation.

> *"I don't want to spend any money in a game. It is just a game, and what if they stole my bank account information? The Internet is unsafe."*

4.3   Factors that Lead to Older Adults' Addiction in Online Games

Game addiction is not a rare phenomenon nowadays. Among the interviewees in our study, two thirds of them spend 2 h or above in playing online games every day, who can be identified as game addiction users. Although they know this is a bad habit, it is difficult to change.

> "I originally started playing online games just because I was bored...But now I am completely fascinated by QQ Chinese chess. I almost spend all my free time on it, I have to admit that I am totally addicted to it."

In fact, older adults might be attracted to an online game with certain factors, but being addicted is another thing. Some game design factors can be experienced only when the elders play the game for a while. First of all, although easy goals and simple operations can attract older adults at first glance, these games cannot lead to user loyalty. In other words, a good game for elders should increase the level of difficulty progressively, and demands some challenges thus improves a sense of accomplishment and self-efficacy.

> "The game should be very simple at the beginning, and as we are learning and progressing, it can become harder and more complicated gradually. It allures me to play again and again to achieve a higher level...It is a perfect way for us to learn new things, we can train our brains while having fun."

Another important factor is frequent and exaggerated feedbacks for elder players. As they are lacking in technical literacy, it may take longer time for older adults to pass a new stage. If the feedback can only be achieved when players make a big progress, they will feel disappointed in most times. Therefore, respondents stated their requirements for more encouragements either with words or props, which can attract them to play longer.

> "Actually, I played better and better each time although I failed to pass the level. Every time, the game continued to tell me that "you lose", which made me angry and abandon the game though it was a good one...Different with it, AniPop always gave me game props which helped me to pass a new stage more easily, so I felt my effort was worthy."

In addition, social interaction is also proved to be important for the time that interviewees spent in online games. Most older adults regard games as an approach to build social contact with offline friends, relatives, and even grandchildren, and some of them also make new friends online with same age and common interests when playing. In other words, the social interaction functions attach more value than simple entertainment on playing games.

> "I will be bored when I play QQ Landlords alone, but I feel satisfied when playing it with my friends. Maybe it is because we can chat online and have a close teamwork."
> "I am good as Chinese chess, and cannot find a rival in real life. Fortunately, the QQ game assigned one to me according to my level, who was two years older than me and lived in a neighboring province. We had so much to talk because we shared common interest and experiences. I really treasure this friend."

Actually, the ultimate purpose of playing games is to get entertainment. Only when an older adult feels happy in a game, he or she will continue playing it, no matter the fun comes from challenging tasks, social interactions, or both.

"The only reason that I am addicted to the game is that I could get great fun from it."

4.4 Game Design Features that Alleviate Game Addiction for Older Adults

We confirm previous findings that there are two negative impacts of online games if older adults put too much time on it: serious healthy problems and disturbance of normal daily life. The following quote describes how an old man aged 81 spend so much time in online games, even to the degree that he has to face wife's criticism and physical illness as a consequence.

"Three years ago, I began to play QQ Chinese Chess online. In the beginning, I didn't have any problems with it, but my wife complained from time to time. Because this game could not stop once I begun, otherwise my marks would be deducted. I even missed the meals and she had to eat alone...Besides, it was bad for my neck and eyes after I played it for a long time. I kept sitting in my desk and stared at the screen for at least four hours every day. I think I should change my addiction but I lack self-control, and I have made an appointment with my online friend."

Therefore, it is urgent to find solutions to alleviate the above phenomenon. Fortunately, our respondents both pointed out several existing useful game design features and suggested a few potential changes of online games that might work in the future. Among them, time control function has already been adopted by a few games, while time warning and counting functions are rarely seen since the purpose of game designers is to make users play as long as possible.

"In all the games I played, only AniPop has a time control function. You have to rest for a period of time before starting a new round. Sometimes, because I did not want to wait idly, I would do some cleaning and washing instead. At first, I hated this function because it interrupted my desire to gain a higher score. But now, I thought it was good since I could not control myself without this specific function."

"Sometimes, I wanted to know how long I have been playing the game, but I could not see the clock in most game interfaces. I think it might work if the game reminds me every other hour. This function will definitely alert me."

5 Discussion and Implications

5.1 Discussion of Findings

Based on the qualitative analysis, we not only answer all our research questions, but also have a few unexpected findings. First of all, older adults have four approaches to reach online game information: peers' recommendation, unintentionally attracted by grandchildren's games, advertisements in pop-up windows, self-seeking by keywords searching. Among them, peers' recommendation is the most effective one.

Secondly, just as we summarized in Sect. 2.2, a number of game design features are useful for older adults in online games, which can be separated into attractive and addictive factors. For instance, easy operations, interface design, social recommendation, theme, technology and device can conquer healthy, social and technical barriers for elder people, which is vital in attracting them to play a new game. Besides, free price is also found to be a basic requirement to attract elder players. Differently, because game is an experience product, additive factors can only be perceived after the older adults play the game, including progressive challenging goals and operations, frequent and exaggerated feedbacks, social interaction functions, and entertainment. We find that the most obvious distinction lies in the difficulty of games. At the beginning, older adults will be attracted by easy games due to low cognitive ability, but when they play more, only challenging games allure them to play longer.

Last, we also confirmed the bad healthy and social consequences caused by online games, and provide time control, time warning, and time counting functions to alleviate game addiction phenomenon for older adults.

5.2   Implications, Limitations and Future Research

This study has profound theoretical and practical implications. Theoretically, we are among the first to distinguish the attractive and addictive factors on elder game players. We also indicate a few neglected game design features. In practice, game company should adopt social recommendation approach in promotion because it is the most effective method. Game designers should find a balance between the proposed two groups of factors, and may incorporate time control features into their design especially for elder players.

As an exploratory research, this study contains a few limits which can be further explored. Firstly, with a small sample size, maybe we have missed some important clues. A focus group research with more respondents will be conducted in the future. Secondly, the qualitative research approach has relatively low external validity. Our next step is to confirm the relationship between certain factors and corresponding attractive and addictive behaviors by quantitative methods like survey and experiment.

Acknowledgement. This work was supported by National Science Foundation of China (#71802108; #71702103), Research Funds for Young Scholars in School of Economics & Management of NJUST (#JGQN1802), Fundamental Research Funds for the Central Universities (30918013104).

References

1. Iversen, S.M.: Play and productivity: the constitution of ageing adults in research on digital games. Games Cult. 11(1–2), 7–27 (2016)
2. Sohu News. https://www.sohu.com/a/81181091_352928. Accessed 23 Jan 2018
3. De Schutter, B., Brown, J.A., Vanden Abeele, V.: The domestication of digital games in the lives of older adults. New Media Soc. 17(7), 1170–1186 (2015)

4. Duplàa, E., Kaufman, D., Sauvé, L., Renaud, L.: A questionnaire-based study on the perceptions of canadian seniors about cognitive, social, and psychological benefits of digital games. Games Health J. **6**(3), 171–178 (2017)
5. Ijsselsteijn, W., Nap, H.H., de Kort, Y., Poels, K.: Digital game design for elderly users. In: Proceedings of the 2007 Conference on Future Play, pp. 17–22. ACM, New York (2007)
6. Smeddinck, J., Gerling, K., Tiemko, S.: Visual complexity, player experience, performance and physical exertion in motion-based games for older adults. In: Proceedings of the 15th International ACM SIGACCESS Conference on Computers and Accessibility, pp. 25–32. ACM, New York (2013)
7. Diaz-Orueta, U., Facal, D., Nap, H.H., Ranga, M.M.: What is the key for older people to show interest in playing digital learning games? Initial qualitative findings from the LEAGE project on a multicultural European sample. Games Health: Res. Dev. Clin. Appl. **1**(2), 115–123 (2012)
8. Gerling, K.M., Schulte, F.P., Smeddinck, J., Masuch, M.: Game design for older adults: effects of age-related changes on structural elements of digital games. In: Herrlich, M., Malaka, R., Masuch, M. (eds.) ICEC 2012. LNCS, vol. 7522, pp. 235–242. Springer, Heidelberg (2012). https://doi.org/10.1007/978-3-642-33542-6_20
9. Zhang, F., Kaufman, D.: Older adults' social interactions in massively multiplayer online role-playing games (MMORPGs). Games Cult. **11**(1–2), 150–169 (2016)
10. Choi, D., Kim, J.: Why people continue to play online games: in search of critical design factors to increase customer loyalty to online contents. Cyber Psychol. Behav. **7**(1), 11–24 (2004)
11. Gerling, K.M., Schulte, F.P., Masuch, M.: Designing and evaluating digital games for frail elderly persons. In: Proceedings of the 8th International Conference on Advances in Computer Entertainment Technology, pp. 62–69. ACM, New York (2011)
12. De Schutter, B., Malliet, S.: The older player of digital games: a classification based on perceived need satisfaction. Communications **39**(1), 67–88 (2014)
13. Myers, M.D., Newman, M.: The qualitative interview in IS research: examining the craft. Inf. Organ. **17**(1), 2–26 (2007)

Impact of Intergenerational Play on Young People's Perceptions Towards Old Adults

Fan Zhang[✉]

Faculty of Education, Simon Fraser University, Burnaby, BC, Canada
fza26@sfu.ca

Abstract. This study explored the impact of intergenerational play on young people's perceptions towards old adults. It analyzed how intergenerational play is associated with the three factors of ageism (i.e., antilocution, discrimination, and avoidance). To address the research question, seven research hypotheses were proposed. A total of 150 young people aged between 15 and 30 completed an online survey. To test the research hypotheses and determine the amount of variance in ageism attributable to gender and education level, a series of two-stage hierarchical regression analyses were carried out. The results of regression analyses revealed that the frequency of playing with parents and grandparents and the frequency of playing either against or collaboratively with old family members is not significantly associated with ageism. However, expecting to play with old family members, the quality of intergenerational play, the sense of closeness to old family members due to gameplay, and the enjoyment of playing with old family members were positively associated with young people's perceptions towards old adults. The findings indicate that young people's perceptions towards old adults are strongly associated with the quality and enjoyment of gameplay with old family members rather than the quantity of gameplay.

Keywords: Intergenerational play · Younger people · Older adults · Ageism

1 Introduction

1.1 Ageing and Ageism

The world population is ageing. By 2050, the number of people aged 60 years and over in the world is projected to double its size in 2015 [1]. Intergenerational communication and interactions are expected to play an important role in an aging society due to the likelihood that young people would interact with and provide support to a larger proportion of old adults in near future [2]. However, society generally has a negative attitude towards old adults [3]. Ageism is widespread and extremely common [4].

Negative attitudes about age can begin to form among children as young as six years old, and these attitudes will solidify as they grow older [5]. The research report published by Australian Human Rights Commission in 2013 indicated that ageing has predominantly negative connotations. In general, Australians aged 18–24 years were the most negative about old adults. The majority of Australians (71%) believed that age discrimination in Australia is common. In addition, negative portrayal of older Australians would result in negative behaviors towards older Australians. Similar findings

© Springer Nature Switzerland AG 2019
J. Zhou and G. Salvendy (Eds.): HCII 2019, LNCS 11593, pp. 267–276, 2019.
https://doi.org/10.1007/978-3-030-22015-0_21

were reported in UK [5]. Ageism harms the public's health [5]. Stereotypes of ageing affect the physical and mental functioning, overall wellbeing and perceived quality of life of old adults [6]. Negative attitudes about age harm young people because they apply negative age stereotypes to themselves as they grow older. The self-perceptions of stigmatized groups can influence longevity [7]. People with more positive self-perceptions of ageing could live 7.5 years longer than those with less positive self-perception of ageing [7]. The negative effects of ageism indicate the need of methods to bridge intergenerational gap.

1.2   Gameplay as an Enjoyable Leisure Activity

Research has indicated the potential of joint activity to maintain relationships [8]. Flora and Segrin [9] explored the impact of activity type, social skills, relationship type and positivity on relationship maintenance. The results indicated that joint activity time is more satisfying and rewarding when people exhibited good social skills and interactions and perceived positivity in their partners. The quality of time spent together in the leisure events makes a significant impact on relationships. The authors stated

> Joint activity time may serve to maintain relationships largely because of the quality of social interaction exchanged during that time together. High quality interaction contributes to high leisure satisfaction, and the strong relationship between leisure satisfaction and relational satisfaction [9, p. 717].

Digital games are symbolic and cultural tools that promote meaningful interactions [10]. Lazzaro [11] examined why people play digital games, and concluded that "people play games not so much for the game itself as for the experience that the game creates: an exciting adrenaline rush, a vicarious adventure, a mental challenge; and the structure games provide for time, such as a moment of solitude or the company of friends" [p. 1]. The context of gameplay naturally provides situational factors for collaboration, competition, common goals and thoughts sharing which are key to satisfying interactions [2, 12]. Collaborative gameplay allows people to "make creative, playful and social use of their leisure time" [13, p 417].

1.3   Intergenerational Play and Intergenerational Perceptions

Previous research has explored the design and use of digital games for intergenerational interaction and learning [12, 14–16]. Theng et al. [17] investigated how Wii games could improve old adults' socialization. The results of this study showed that both old adults and teenaged players improved attitudes toward the other age group [17]. Zhang et al. [18] Investigated how the structures of talk-in-interaction during intergenerational play provide opportunities for situated learning between young people and old adults. Old adults learned gaming skills and made sense of collaborative gaming activities through young people's guidance. As old adults gradually became more experienced users, they were able to coordinate with their younger partners to overcome setbacks and engaged in mutual encouragement to reach a common goal. Chua et al. [2] conducted a two-group (i.e., experiment group and control group) pre-post design study to examine the impacts of intergenerational play on young people's perceptions towards old adults. In this study, digital gameplay was viewed as a form of shared leisure activities in which individuals from different age groups could engage without much resistance. The results revealed that when older adults and young people play digital games together, they could develop positive perceptions towards both their particular play partners and the members of the other age group as spill-over effects. In addition, it was found that the more participants enjoyed intergenerational play, the greater attraction and less intergroup anxiety they reported. Chua et al. concluded that the results of this study could support the potential of intergenerational play in developing positive perceptions towards other age groups as a means of shared leisure activities.

In family contexts intergenerational play could serve as a resource for family interactions and communication, especially in families with communication difficulty [19]. It creates opportunities for family members in different age groups to pursue common goals and share experiences, resulted in improving family relationships [20]. Wang, Taylor and Sun [21] investigated the effects of digital gameplay among family members on family satisfaction and closeness. It was found that the more frequently family members play digital games together, the better family satisfaction and family closeness they have [21]. Costa and Veloso [16] reviewed the benefits of intergenerational play and summarized that intergenerational game-mediated interactions between different generations, especially between grandparents and grandchildren, have the potential to break age stereotypes, develop civic engagement, and give a sense of purpose and companionship. However, few studies have collected quantitative data to examine whether intergenerational play with family members affects intergenerational perceptions, especially young people's perceptions towards old adults.

1.4   Research Purpose and Hypotheses

The author conducted an online survey to investigate the patterns, benefits and challenges of intergenerational play between young people and old family members in 2018 [22]. The results of this study revealed that although young people aged 15+ do not frequently play digital games with their old family members (i.e., parents and grandparents), intergenerational play is a fun way to bond with family members. The motivation for intergenerational play is to maintain closeness and connection with family members. There are different portrayals of the value of intergenerational play within family contexts, such as common hobby among family members, getting every member involved during big festivals or family gathering, giving them something to talk about and a way to maintain contact across geographical distance. The author concluded that "(intergenerational play) is more about the quality of gameplay and related interaction than quantity" [22, p. 591].

Building on the findings of the author's prior study, the purpose of the current study was to examine whether intergenerational play affects young people's perceptions towards old adults. The findings of previous research conducted by other researchers have indicated the potential of intergenerational play in developing family relationships and young people's perceptions towards old adults [2, 16, 20, 21]. Therefore, the author proposed that intergenerational play as an enjoyable leisure activity is negatively associated with ageism (Fig. 1).

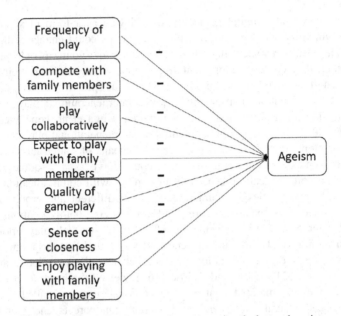

Fig. 1. Relationships between intergenerational play and ageism

This study did not use frequency of playing with family members as a gross measure of intergenerational play. Playing frequently with family members could increase the opportunities for meaningful interactions, but it did not depict the whole picture of intergenerational play. In this study intergenerational play was viewed as an enjoyable leisure activity that offers satisfying and rewarding interactions. Flora and Segrin [9] emphasized that "Without considering the quality of time spent together, joint leisure time cannot uniformly be guaranteed to enhance relationships" [9, p. 717]. Zhang [23] conceptualized older adults' social interactions in online games as communication methods, frequency of playing with other players, enjoyment of relationships and quality of gameplay, and found that enjoyment of relationships and quality of gameplay were significantly associated with older adults' social-emotional wellbeing. For young people, the motivation for playing games with family members is to maintain family closeness [22]. So, in this study the author examined seven of the factors involved in intergenerational play experiences: (1) frequency of gameplay with old family members, (2) play against with old family members, (3) play collaboratively with old family members, (4) expect to play with old family members, (5) quality of gameplay with old family members, (6) sense of closeness due to gameplay with old family members, and (7) enjoy playing with old family members. This study would test the hypotheses in Table 1.

Table 1. Summary of research hypotheses

Hypothesis 1	Higher frequency of playing with old family members is associated with lower level of ageism
Hypothesis 2	Higher frequency of competing with old family members is associated with lower level of ageism
Hypothesis 3	Higher frequency of playing collaboratively with old family members is associated with lower level of ageism
Hypothesis 4	Higher level of expecting to play with old family members is associated with lower level of ageism
Hypothesis 5	Higher quality of intergenerational play is associated with lower level of ageism
Hypothesis 6	Higher level of sense of closeness to family members is associated with lower level of ageism
Hypothesis 7	Higher level of enjoyment of playing with old family members is associated with lower level of ageism

2 Methods

2.1 Survey Design

A total of 150 young people who had played digital games with their old family members (e.g., parents and grandparents) completed an online survey. The participants were aged between 15 and 35 with an average age of 22.46. With regards to gender, roughly 55% of the participants were male and 45% were female. A significant majority of participants had a high school degree (25.2%), some college (28.5%) or a four-year degree (25.8%), while 4.6% had a Master's degree and 1.3% had a doctoral degree.

The online survey consisted of three sections. The first section asked questions related to intergenerational play experience, such as frequency of playing digital games with parents and grandparents, frequency of playing collaboratively or compete with old family members, closeness to old family members, and enjoyment and quality of gameplay. The second section asked questions measuring three factors of ageism. The third section asked demographic questions.

The Fraboni Scale of Ageism (FSA) was used to measure young people's ageism [24]. The FSA construct is derived from Butler's [25] definition of ageism which refers to a "...profound psychosocial disorder characterized by institutionalized and individual prejudice against the elderly, stereotyping, myth-making, distaste, and/or avoidance" [24, p. 14].

The FSA has a high internal reliability ($\alpha = .86$). It specifically measures three factors of ageism: (1) acceptance of others, (2) factual knowledge about elderly people, and (3) social desirability. The FSA has three subscales: Antilocution ($\alpha = .76$), Discrimination ($\alpha = .65$), and Avoidance ($\alpha = .77$). Fraboni et al. indicated that "the three primary factors are not independent, and because they represent theoretically additive constructs, division of the FSA into subscales is possibly not warranted" [24, p. 64]. In this study, we used all items of the three subscales to measure the three factors of ageism. Items in the FSA (either negative or positive in content) were in a 5-point Likert format. Responses choices were presented as "Strongly disagree", "Disagree", "Neutral", "Agree", and "Strongly agree". Responses were scored from 5 to 1 for negative statements and 1 to 5 for positive statements with unanswered items scored as 3. Higher scores revealed a higher level of ageism.

2.2 Data Analysis

In this study multiple regression was the method of data analysis. The statistical goal of multiple regression is to produce a model in the form of a linear equation that represents the relationships between a dependent variable and a number of predictors or independent variables. A multiple correlation coefficient indexes the degree of linear association of one variable with a set of other variables, and the squared multiple correlations (R^2) indicate how much variance of dependent variable is explained by the model. In general, R^2 values, .01, .06, and .14 are considered to be small, medium, and large respectively [26].

To test the seven research hypotheses and understand the amount of variance in ageism attributable to gender and education level, a series of two-stage hierarchical regression analyses were carried out. For each analysis, each of the three factors of ageism was the dependent variable; gender and education level were entered to the first block as covariates; and each of the seven factors of intergenerational play was entered to the second block as predictor. For hierarchical multiple regression, researchers should look at the change of R^2 with and without the predictor rather than an overall model R^2 [23].

3 Results of Data Analysis

The means of antilocution ($M = 2.82$), discrimination ($M = 2.27$), and avoidance ($M = 2.52$) were lower than the neutral value of 3 on the 5-item Likert-type subscales. The R^2 change of frequency of playing with old family members, frequency of playing against with family members, and frequency of playing collaboratively with family members was not statistically different from zero.

Table 2 presents the analysis results for expecting to play with old family members. Gender and education level were not significant covariates for the three types of ageism. When expecting to play was added to the block, the prediction model for avoidance was statistically significant, F_c (1, 141) = 8.480, p_c = .004, R^2_c = .057.

Table 3 describes that when quality of gameplay was added to Model 1, the second prediction models of discrimination and avoidance were significance. However, the R^2 changes for all three types of ageism were statistically different from zero. Quality of gameplay accounted for 1.3% of the variance of antilocution (F_c (1, 140) = 4.676, p_c = .032, R^2_c = .013), 14.2% of the variance of discrimination (F_c (1, 140) = 23.639, p_c < .001, R^2_c = .057), and 6.8% of the variance of avoidance (F_c (1, 140) = 10.216, p_c = .002, R^2_c = .068).

Table 2. Results for expecting to play with old family members

Outcome measures	Model 1[a]			Model 2[b]			Change		
	F	p	R^2	F	p	R^2	F_c	p_c	R^2_c
Antilocution	.911	.405	.013	1.280	.284	.027	2.005	.159	.014
Discrimination	1.331	.268	.018	1.038	.378	.022	.464	.497	.003
Avoidance	.046	.955	.001	2.859	.039	.057	8.480	.004*	.057

Note. *p < .05, [a]Includes gender and education level, [b]Model 1 with expecting to play with old family members

Table 3. Results for quality of gameplay with old family members

Outcome measures	Model 1[a]			Model 2[b]			Change		
	F	p	R^2	F	p	R^2	F_c	p_c	R^2_c
Antilocution	.901	.409	.013	2.175	.094	.045	4.676	.032*	.013
Discrimination	1.301	.276	.018	8.886	<.001*	.160	23.639	<.001*	.142
Avoidance	.124	.883	.002	3.493	.017*	.070	10.216	.002*	.068

Note. *p < .05, [a]Includes gender and education level, [b]Model 1 with quality of gameplay with old family members

As shown in Table 4, the second prediction models for discrimination and avoidance were statistically significant when closeness to family members was added to Model 1. Their R^2 changes were also statistically significant. For discrimination, closeness to family members explained 14.2% of its variance, F_c (1, 140) = 23.622, p_c = < .001, R^2_c = .142. For avoidance, closeness to family members explained 6.9% of its variance, F_c (1, 140) = 10.374, p_c = .002, R^2_c = .069.

Table 4. Results for closeness to old family members due to gameplay

Outcome measures	Model 1[a]			Model 2[b]			Change		
	F	p	R^2	F	p	R^2	F_c	p_c	R^2_c
Antilocution	.911	.405	.013	1.378	.252	.029	2.295	.132	.016
Discrimination	1.282	.281	.018	8.866	<.001*	.160	23.622	<.001*	.142
Avoidance	.068	.934	.001	3.507	.017*	.070	10.374	.002*	.069

Note. *p < .05, [a]Includes gender and education level, [b]Model 1 with closeness to family members due to gameplay

Table 5 shows that all of the second prediction models were statistically significant when enjoyment of gameplay was entered. Enjoyment of gameplay accounted for 5.1% of the variance of antilocution (F_c (1, 141) = 7.637, p_c = .006, R^2_c = .051), 10.2% of the variance of discrimination (F_c (1, 141) = 16.362, p_c < .001, R^2_c = .102), and 7.6% of the variance of avoidance (F_c (1, 141) = 11.650, p_c = .001, R^2_c = .079).

Table 5. Results for enjoyment of gameplay with old family members

Outcome measures	Model 1			Model 2			Change		
	F	p	R^2	F	p	R^2	F_c	p_c	R_c^2
Antilocution	.911	.405	.013	3.181	.026*	.063	7.637	.006*	.051
Discrimination	1.331	.268	.018	6.437	<.001*	.120	16.362	<.001*	.102
Avoidance	.046	.955	.001	3.916	.01*	.077	11.650	.001*	.076

Note. *p < .05, [a]Includes gender and education level, [b]Model 1 with enjoyment of gameplay with old family members

4 Discussion, Conclusion and Limitations

Previous study has indicated that although young people do not play digital games with their old family members frequently, intergenerational play is a fun way for them to bond with and stay close to family members [22]. In this study, intergenerational play was viewed as an enjoyable leisure activity in which people from different groups can engage in rewarding and satisfying social and emotional exchanges. The author focused on seven of the factors involved in intergenerational play experiences rather than quantity of gameplay alone, and investigated how each of those factors is associated with the three types of ageism (i.e., antilocution, discrimination and avoidance).

Consist with the findings of previous research, the positive social-emotional impacts of digital gameplay are not associated with the quantity of gameplay [26]. The findings of this study indicated that hypotheses 1–3 were not supported. The frequency of playing with old family members and the frequency of competing or playing collaboratively with old family members were not significantly related to young people's perceptions towards old adults. Instead, hypotheses 4–7 were all supported. Expecting to play with old family members explained 5.7% of the variance of avoidance. For the quality of gameplay and enjoyment of gameplay with old family members, the R2 changes for all three types of ageism were statistically different from zero. The magnitude of those R2 changes (see Tables 3 and 5) was medium to large based on the criteria of Cohen [26]. Closeness to old family members explained 14.2% of the variance of discrimination and 6.9% of the variance of avoidance. The magnitude of these two R2 changes was medium to large. Therefore, the findings of this study indicate that young people's perceptions towards old adults are strongly associated with the quality and enjoyment of gameplay with old family members rather than the quantity of gameplay. In addition, the results support the potential of intergenerational play as an enjoyable leisure activity in developing young people's perceptions towards old adults.

The author is aware of two limitations. First, the participants were aged 15 and over. So, the findings could not be applied to people younger than 15. Second, this study used a self-report questionnaire to measure young people's perceptions towards old adults. The results do not imply causal relationships. However, this study sheds light on the relationships between intergenerational play and positive perceptions towards old adults.

Acknowledgement. This work was supported by AGE-WELL NCE Inc., a national research network supporting research, networking, commercialization, knowledge mobilization and capacity building activities in technology and aging to improve the quality of life of Canadians and contribute to the economic impact of Canada. AGE-WELL is a member of the Networks of Centres of Excellence (NCE), a Government of Canada program that funds partnerships between universities, industry, government and not-for-profit organizations.

References

1. United Nations: World Population Ageing 2015 Report (2015). http://www.un.org/en/development/desa/population/publications/pdf/ageing/WPA2015_Report.pdf. Accessed 08 Mar 2017
2. Chua, P.H., Jung, Y., Lwin, M.O., Theng, Y.L.: Let's play together: effects of videogameplay on intergenerational perceptions among youth and elderly participants. Comput. Hum. Behav. **29**(6), 2303–2311 (2013)
3. Hernandez, C.R., Gonzalez, M.Z.: Effects of intergenerational interaction on aging. Educ. Gerontol. **34**(4), 292–305 (2008)
4. World Health Organization: Discrimination and negative attitudes about ageing are bad for your health (2016). https://www.who.int/news-room/detail/29-09-2016-discrimination-and-negative-attitudes-about-ageing-are-bad-for-your-health
5. Calouste Gulbenkian Foundation UK Branch: The Age Old Question: How Attitudes to Ageing Affect our Health and Wellbeing (2018). https://www.rsph.org.uk/uploads/assets/uploaded/010d3159-0d36-4707-aee54e29047c8e3a.pdf
6. Dionigi, R.A.: Stereotypes of aging: their effects on the health of older adults. J. Geriatr. **2015**, 1–9 (2015)
7. Levy, B., Slade, M.D., Kasl, S.V., Kunkel, S.R.: Longevity increased by positive self-perceptions of ageing. J. Pers. Soc. Psychol. **83**(2), 261–270 (2002)
8. Canary, D.J., Stafford, L., Hause, K.S., Wallace, L.A.: An inductive analysis of relational maintenance strategies: comparisons among lovers, relatives, friends, and others. Commun. Res. Rep. **10**, 5–14 (1993)
9. Flora, J., Segrin, C.: Joint leisure time in friend and romantic relationships: the role of activity type, social skills and positivity. J. Soc. Pers. Relat. **15**, 711–718 (1998)
10. Piirainen-Marsh, A.: Bilingual practices and the social organisation of video gaming activities. J. Pragmat. **42**(11), 3012–3030 (2010)
11. Lazzaro N.: Why we play games: four keys to more emotion without story (2004). http://twvideo01.ubm-us.net/o1/vault/gdc04/slides/why_we_play_games.pdf. Accessed 01 Jan 2019
12. Zhang, F., Kaufman, D.: Review of intergenerational play for facilitating interactions and learning. Gerontechnology **14**, 127–138 (2016)
13. Kern, D., Stringer, M., Fitzpatrick, G., Schmidt, A.: Curball. A prototype tangible game for inter-generational play. In: Proceedings of the Workshop on Enabling Technologies: Infrastructure for Collaborative Enterprises, pp. 412–417. IEEE press, Manchester (2006)
14. De la Hera, T., Loos, E.F., Simons, M., Blom, J.: Benefits and factors influencing the design of intergenerational digital games: a systematic literature review. Societies **7**, 18 (2017)
15. Loos, E.F.: Designing meaningful intergenerational digital games. In: Proceedings of the International Conference on Communication, Media, Technology and Design, Istanbul, pp. 46–51, 24–26 April 2014
16. Costa, L., Veloso, A.: Being (Grand) players: review of digital games and their potential to enhance intergenerational interactions. J. Intergenerational Relat. **14**, 43–59 (2016)

17. Theng, Y.L., Chua, P.H., Pham, T.P.: Wii as entertainment and socialisation aids for mental and social health of the elderly. In: Proceedings of the 2012 ACM Annual Conference Extended Abstracts on Human Factors in Computing Systems, Austin, Texas, USA, pp. 691–702 (2012)
18. Zhang, F., Schell, R., Kaufman, D., Salgado, G., Erik, T., Jeremic, J.: Situated learning through intergenerational play between older adults and undergraduates. Int. J. Educ. Technol. High. Educ. **14**(16), 1–16 (2017)
19. Aarsand, P.A.: Computer and video games in family life: the digital divide as a resource in intergenerational interactions. Childhood **14**(2), 235–256 (2007)
20. Voida, A., Greenberg, S.: Console gaming across generations: exploring intergenerational interactions in collocated console gaming. Univers. Access Inf. Soc. **11**(1), 45–56 (2012)
21. Wang, B., Taylor, L., Sun, Q.: Families that play together stay together: Investigating family bonding through video games. New Media Soc. **20**(11), 4074–4094 (2018)
22. Zhang, F.: Intergenerational play between young people and old family members: patterns, benefits, and challenges. In: Zhou, J., Salvendy, G. (eds.) ITAP 2018. LNCS, vol. 10926, pp. 581–593. Springer, Cham (2018). https://doi.org/10.1007/978-3-319-92034-4_44
23. Zhang, F.: Social-emotional impacts of MMORPGs on older adults. Ph.D. Dissertation, Simon Fraser University (2014)
24. Fraboni, M., Saltstone, R., Hughes, S.: The fraboni scale of ageism (FSA): an attempt at a more precise measure of ageism. Can. J. Aging **9**(1), 56–66 (1990)
25. Butler, R.N.: Thoughts on aging. Am. J. Psychiatry **135**(Suppl), 14–16 (1978)
26. Cohen, J.: Statistical Power Analysis for the Behavioral Science, 2nd edn. Lawrence Erlbaum, Hillsdale (1988)

The Effect of Familiarity on Older Adults' Engagement in Exergames

Hao Zhang[1,2], Chunyan Miao[2(✉)], Qiong Wu[2], Xuehong Tao[3], and Zhiqi Shen[2]

[1] Interdisciplinary Graduate School, Nanyang Technological University,
Singapore, Singapore
i150001@e.ntu.edu.sg
[2] Joint NTU-UBC Research Centre of Excellence in Active Living for the Elderly,
Nanyang Technological University, Singapore, Singapore
{ascymiao,wu.qiong,zqshen}@ntu.edu.sg
[3] Swinburne University of Technology, Melbourne, Australia
xtao@swin.edu.au

Abstract. With entertaining game graphics and tasks, exergames can provide benefits for older adults to effectively exercise their physical and mental capabilities. However, it is sometimes difficult for exergames to engage older adults due to maladaptation. In this work, we suggest that the feeling of familiarity can positively influence older adult's adaptation to exergames. Based on this intuition, to help exercise older adult's upper limbs, we design a Ping Pong Exergame (PPE) infused with table tennis activities, which has been shown to be one of the most popular (thus familiar) sports among Singaporean older adults. A five-week study involving 44 Singaporean older adults shows that the participants who have higher levels of familiarity to table tennis exhibit higher motivation and ability in playing PPE, which indicate that familiarity can improve older adults' adaptation to exergames.

Keywords: Familiarity · Exergame · Person-Environment fit

1 Introduction

The pace of aging is accelerating all over the world in the coming decades [26]. Older adults may encounter various health related issues as they age, such as the reduction in their motor and cognitive abilities. Rehabilitation exercise has been designed to help older adults recover from their deteriorated capabilities effectively and efficiently. Older adults are advised to frequently take those rehabilitation exercises designed based on their specific conditions. However, the adherence rate to rehabilitation exercises is often low, due to the fact that most rehabilitation exercises contain repetitive physical movements which tend to be boring for older adults [24]. As technology advances, gamified rehabilitation exercises, or exergames, has been shown to be more attractive to older adults with entertaining game graphics and interactive tasks [23]. Moreover, exergames with

© Springer Nature Switzerland AG 2019
J. Zhou and G. Salvendy (Eds.): HCII 2019, LNCS 11593, pp. 277–288, 2019.
https://doi.org/10.1007/978-3-030-22015-0_22

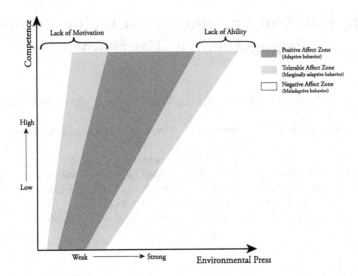

Fig. 1. P-E fit model.

motion detection devices, such as Microsoft Kinect, make it easy for older adults to interact with exergames using natural body movements. Hence, exergames have been widely studied to help older adults recover their physical and mental capabilities [6,7,29].

However, it is not easy to motivate older adults to voluntarily play exergames unless the games are attractive enough [1]. One of the key reasons that make exergames unappealing is the lack of engagement and enjoyment [18]. Moreover, some of the new technologies and devices may be over complex and difficult for older adults to use [18]. All these reasons lead to older adult's maladaptation to exergames. To understand why maladaptation occurs, we refer to the Person-Environment (P-E) fit theory originated from the gerontology research [16]. According to this theory, a person's Behavior (B) reflects how well the Person's competence (P, personal abilities) matches the Environmental press (E, environmental stimuli and barriers): $B = f(P, E, P \times E)$ [16]. As shown in Fig. 1, optimal adaptation will occur only when older adults' personal competence can appropriately fit the surrounding environment. Good adaptation will result in a feeling of comfort and enhance engagement and enjoyment [16]. However, maladaptation can occur in the following two cases: older adults with high competence in low press environments (low motivation) and older adults with low competence in high press environments (low ability).

As maladaptation occurs when personal competence does not match environmental press, we suggest that maladaptation can be mitigated by familiarity, which characterizes the relationship between a person and something (such as the environment) that the person has had considerable experience with [15]. Previous research shows that familiarity has an activating effect to arouse older adults' past feelings and emotions [14]. In familiar environment, old adults may feel more comfortable and be more willing to improve their social and functional capabilities. Moreover, familiarity can evoke the older adults' past implicit and explicit memories [15], from which to recall the approaches to interact with the familiar environment [2].

To test whether familiarity has a positive effect in improving older adult's adaptation to exergames, we designed a Ping Pong Exergame (PPE) infused with table tennis activities for exercising older adults' upper limbs. The game offers older adults an enjoyable interactive environment for physical exercise and cognitive training. Table tennis is one of the most common sports in Singapore.[1] For older adults who often play table tennis, PPE offers familiar game environments and tasks. A five-week study with PPE involving 44 able-bodied Singaporean older adults was conducted. The participants were divided into three groups based on different levels of familiarity to table tennis. The experimental results indicate that familiarity has significant positive influence on older adults' ability and motivation during exergame playing.

The rest of this paper is organized as follows. Section 2 reviews the related works on P-E fit theory and familiarity design. Section 3 presents the framework of P-E fit theory with familiarity incorporated. We show the methodology and results of our study in Sect. 4. In the end, we make a discussion and conclude this paper.

2   Related Work

Comparing with traditional rehabilitation exercises, exergames can provide attractive graphical virtual environments designed in various ways to encourage users to become more engaged, immersed, and motivated [28]. In this section, we first review the P-E fit theory and then the existing research on familiarity.

2.1   P-E Fit Theory

Lewin first proposed the heuristic formula $B = f(P, E)$ in the initial P-E fit model, which is used to characterize the behavioural effect caused by the matching between the state of a person P and his/her surrounding environment E [19]. Lawton then added another interactive term $P \times E$ into the original formula: $B = f(P, E, P \times E)$, to account for the behaviors influenced by the interaction between an individual's competence and the environmental press [16]. This theory was used to analyze older adults' physical and psychological well-being [17]. As older adults age, they need to cope with both the external environment change and the internal capability decline. Iwarsson et al. [11,13] applied the P-E fit theory to developed a tool for evaluating interaction design of the surrounding environment for older adults. They stated that in order to help older adults age well, it is important to understand the relationship between the person and the

---

[1] https://www.channelnewsasia.com/news/singapore/table-tennis-gains-popularity-in-singapore-8127732.

environment [12]. However, research on new technology design for older adults seldom consider P-E fit. Our research aims to improve P-E fit between older adults and exergames.

2.2   Familiarity

Familiarity is thought to be an unconscious, automatic process that demands minimal attention [27]. Prior research on memory indicates that aging leads to a decrease in recollection, but does not influence familiarity [22]. Being familiar with a system means we are ready to operate it in an appropriate way based on our prior experiences [8]. On the one hand, familiarity plays an important role in any products use; if a user can implicitly recognize a thing, then he or she is more likely to understand its purpose and how to use it [21]. Son et al. [25] stated that familiarity can enhance older adults' functional ability (physical, psychological, and emotional abilities). Boger et al. [4] also found that familiarity can enhance faucet usability for older adults. On the other hand, familiarity can bring about emotional meaning and increase safety, usability, and attractiveness of the environment. Brittain et al. [5] found that familiar surroundings can provide the older adults with the confidence to get outdoors. Barry [3] also encouraged the incorporation of familiarity into the home design to bring positive changes for older adults.

In addition, familiarity has also been applied in new technology design for older adults. Leonardi et al. [18] designed WIMP (Window, Icons, Menus and Pointing) interfaces with familiar interaction modalities to enhance user experience for older adults. Hollinworth and Hwang [10] designed an e-mail application for older adults with familiar visual objects and operations. All the senior participants found the familiar interface easy to understand and they can quickly master how to use it. Prior research showed the effectiveness of familiarity in helping older adults to understand and interact with new technology, which encourages us to employ familiarity in exergame design to improve older adults' adaptation.

3   Modeling Familiarity in P-E Fit Theory

As shown in Fig. 1, Lewin defined three zones, i.e., positive affect zone, tolerable affect zone and negative affect zone, where adaptive, marginally adaptive and maladaptive behaviors can be produced, respectively. Familiarity characterizes a positive relationship between a person and the past experienced environment, which can improve the fit between older adults and the environment. Figure 2 illustrates how familiarity can impact Lewin's P-E fit model. We argue that familiarity can potentially enlarge the positive affect zone by improving both ability and motivation, referred to as zone A and zone M respectively. On the one hand, a sense of familiarity can evoke a person's implicit and explicit memories, so as to enhance their functional abilities [25]. On the other hand, familiarity can

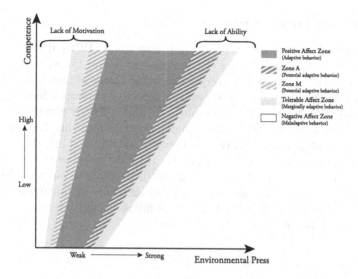

Fig. 2. Improved P-E fit model.

arouse a person's past positive emotions, so as to enhance their motivation [9,14]. Based on the original P-E fit formula, we extend it as:

$$B = f(P, E, P \times E \mid F), \tag{1}$$

where F represents familiarity that can induce positive adaptation changes.

4   The Study

To investigate whether familiarity can improve the P-E fit between older adults and exergames, we conducted a field study involving 44 Singaporean older adults. After the experiment, each participant received compensation in the form of shopping vouchers worth 20 Singapore dollars. IRB approval was obtained ahead of the experiment.

Fig. 3. Ping Pong Exergame.

4.1 The Ping Pong Exergame

In this experiment, we use a Ping Pong Exergame (PPE) designed by the Joint NTU-UBC Research Centre of Excellence in Active Living for the Elderly (LILY). PPE is an upper limb exercise game in the theme of table tennis (Fig. 3). Some fundamental cognitive tasks such as selective attention have also been infused into PPE for cognitive training. To play PPE, a participant simply stands in front of a Microsoft Kinect and naturally wave his/her chosen arm as if holding a table tennis bat. He/she needs to identify and hits the Ping Pong ball with designated color and ignore others (to practise selective attention). In this way, PPE offers both physical and cognitive training to older adults. Table tennis is one of the most common sports for older adults in Singapore. For older adult who frequently play table tennis, the interface and interaction mode of PPE tend to be familiar for them.

4.2 Participants

44 able-bodied Singaporean senior citizens (10 males and 34 females) volunteered to participate in this study. The study was conducted at a community center in Singapore. Participants were aged between 58 to 90 ($M = 71.7, SD = 7.88$). They were divided into three groups (never play, played a few time, often play) according to their prior experiences to table tennis, which are summarized in Table 1. Considering the fact that a person's age can have a significant impact on his/her game performance, we conducted ANOVA and pairwise T-test to investigate whether there are significant age differences among the three groups. From the statistical results (as shown in Table 2), it can be observed that all the computed $p > 0.05$, which indicates that there is no significant age difference

Table 1. Participants categorization based on their prior experiences to table tennis.

	Never play	Played a few times	Often play
Group	A	B	C
No.	7	10	27
Mean age	75	74	70
SD	3.28	2.23	1.26

Table 2. Pairwise T test and ANOVA results for group age difference.

Pairwise T test	t	p
Group A&B	0.16	0.877
Group A&C	1.53	0.135
Group B&C	1.62	0.114

ANOVA: $F = 2.01, p = 0.15$

among different groups. Based on this results, we can exclude the effect of age to some extent on players' performance in different groups.

4.3 Experiment Design

A five-week longitudinal study is conducted to collect participants' long-term performance change and their adherence rate to PPE. A questionnaire with five-level Likert scale was designed to collect participants' subjective opinions. The questionnaire includes rated scores for enjoyment, satisfaction and perceived difficulty while playing PPE. Meanwhile, participants' game performance was automatically tracked by the game system. These results allow us to compare the motivation and ability of the participants in different groups, so as to find the impact of familiarity on users' P-E fit. The following four hypotheses were tested in this study:

H1: *Familiarity positively impacts older adults' performance in exergames.*
H2: *Familiarity reduces older adults' perceived difficulty of exergames.*
H3: *Familiarity improves older adults' enjoyment while playing exergames.*
H4: *Familiarity improves older adults' satisfaction for exergames.*

Hypothesis 1 and Hypothesis 2 are related to participants' ability while Hypothesis 3 and Hypothesis 4 concerns their motivation while playing PPE.

4.4 Procedure

Participants are required to play PPE once a week in the community center for five consecutive weeks (Fig. 4). Upon the first arrival at the experiment venue, all participants filled in a consent form and a short demographic survey before the experiment start. Each participant was allocated a QR code to track their long-term performance. During the experiment, participants were required to play PPE for about 20 min each time. Throughout the whole experiment, one researcher accompanied each elderly participant in case they encounter any problem during the experiment. After completing all five game sessions, the participants filled the questionnaire to collect their opinions about PPE. Although we

Fig. 4. Participants are playing PPE.

divided the participants into three groups based on their prior experiences of table tennis, they were not aware of the grouping during the whole experiment.

4.5   Results

38 out of 44 participants completed all the five sessions of the experiment. The other six participants each completed four sessions due to their unavailability in one of the five weeks. All participants joined the first and last game sessions.

H1: Does familiarity improve participants' performance? Participants' performance can be reflected by the in-game scores they received after each game session. We recorded their game scores for all the game sessions and calculated the average scores as their final game performance. We first conducted ANCOVA test to check the interactive effect between familiarity and age on participants' performance. The ANCOVA results show that the interactive effect between familiarity and age on participants' performance is not significant ($F = 1.33$, $p = 0.321$). Then, one-way ANOVA was conducted to compare the performance between different familiarity groups. Table 3 shows the ANOVA results. The results indicate that there is significant performance difference among three groups. In addition, the group with higher levels of familiarity received higher scores. These results support Hypothesis 1 that familiarity can positively impact older adults' performance in exergames.

Table 3. Game performance ANOVA results.

	Mean score	SD
Group A	2658	375.2
Group B	2905	225.3
Group C	3076	417.5
ANOVA: $F = 3.61, p = 0.036$		

H2: Does familiarity decrease participants' perceived difficulty? To evaluate the participants' perceived difficulty, we collected their self-rated understanding of the game rules through a five-level Likert scale in the questionnaire. Higher scores represent that the participants perceive less difficulty and they are more confident to complete the game tasks. As Hypothesis 2 is also related to the participants' ability to play the exergame, we first conducted ANCOVA to see the interactive effect between familiarity and age. The ANCOVA result indicates that this interactive effect is not significant ($F = 0.81, p = 0.611$) and the influence of age on participants' rated scores is not significant ($F = 0.93, p = 0.578$). Then, Kruskal-Wallis test was conducted to compare rated scores among different familiarity groups and the results are shown in Table 4. The results indicate a significant difference of rated scores in different familiarity groups. However, the mean score of Group B is smaller than Group A, which is in contrary to the hypothesis. To test whether the difference between Group B and Group A is significant, we then conducted a pairwise analysis through Mann-Whitney test. The Mann-Whitney test result indicates that there is no significant difference between the two groups ($z = 0.745, p = 0.456$). In summary, the data provides partial support for Hypothesis 2. In particular, the group with the highest level of familiarity to table tennis would perceive significantly less difficulty when playing PPE than other groups.

Table 4. Perceived difficulty Kruskal-Wallis test results.

	Mean score	SD
Group A	4.0	0.22
Group B	3.7	0.26
Group C	4.4	0.14
Kruskal-Wallis: $H = 7.61, p = 0.022$		

H3: Does familiarity improve participants' enjoyment? Participants' enjoyment was also collected through a five-level Likert scale in the questionnaire. We conducted Kruskal Wallis test to compare the rated enjoyment among different familiarity groups. Table 5 shows the Kruskal Wallis test results, which indicate that the influence of familiarity on participants' enjoyment is not significant ($p > 0.05$). Hypothesis 3 is not supported from this results. However, the mean values of the rated enjoyment increase with higher levels of familiarity, which indicates some effect of familiarity on improving participants' enjoyment during the exergame.

Table 5. Enjoyment Kruskal-Wallis test results.

	Mean score	SD
Group A	3.57	0.37
Group B	3.60	0.27
Group C	4.19	0.16
Kruskal-Wallis: $H = 4.91, p = 0.086$		

H4: Does familiarity improve participants' satisfaction? In the questionnaire, we asked participants to rate their overall satisfaction to PPE with a five-level Likert scale. The Kruskal-Wallis test results of rated satisfaction in different groups are shown in Table 6. The results indicate that familiarity has significant influence on participants' overall satisfaction to PPE. From the mean scores we can find that groups with a higher level of familiarity rated higher satisfaction scores. Therefore, Hypothesis 4 is strongly supported by our data.

Table 6. Overall satisfaction Kruskal-Wallis test results.

	Mean score	SD
Group A	3	0.22
Group B	3.1	0.18
Group C	3.7	0.13
Kruskal-Wallis: $H = 8.93, p = 0.012$		

4.6 Discussion

In this section we discuss the experimental results and summarize the contribution of our work. We explored the effect of familiarity on the P-E fit between older adults and exergames. Hypothesis 1 and Hypothesis 2 concerns older adults' ability during the exergame play. The results indicate that participants' prior experience to table tennis significantly influence their game performance and their perceived game difficulty. During the study, we found some participants who are familiar with table tennis showed professional posture and mastered the rhythm of hitting quickly. They quickly understand the rules of PPE and received high scores after the game sessions. In terms of perceived difficulty, we found only Group C rated higher scores for their understanding the game rules. This suggests that the participants who often play table tennis are really confident to play PPE. Although participants in Group B did not rate higher score for their understanding of game rules than those in Group A, the in-game performance of Group B is actually significantly higher than Group A. Therefore, although the participants only play table tennis a few times in their daily life and they are not confident enough of their table tennis skills, they still perform better than participants with no experience of table tennis at all.

Hypothesis 3 and Hypothesis 4 focus on participants' motivation while playing PPE. However, Hypothesis 3 is not supported by the statistical results, which means that participants' enjoyment is not significantly improved with familiarity. Yet some effect of familiarity can be found because the mean enjoyment scores is growing with increased level of familiarity. Moreover, participants' enjoyment is influenced by many factors. For example, five weeks of the same exergame playing may decrease their enjoyment. Hypothesis 4 is supported by the collected data. Higher satisfaction represents higher motivation of the participants to play PPE, which can improve the P-E fit between older adults and the exergames. In addition, we found no significant difference of rated scores for enjoyment and satisfaction between Group A and Group B. However, a significant increase of those scores is observed in Group C. This indicates that the influence of familiarity on improving older adults' motivation is more effective when the exergames are highly familiar for them.

5   Conclusion

In this work, we suggest that older adults' feeling of familiarity can improve their adaptation to exergames. We incorporate familiarity into the initial P-E fit model and show that familiarity can improve P-E fit by enhancing older adults' motivation and ability. A study involving 44 Singaporean older adults was conducted to evaluate the impact of familiarity. The experimental results show that familiarity can positively influence participants' ability and motivation in the exergame. Thus, we suggest that familiarity design can increase older adults' engagement in exergames. Although the feeling of familiarity is related to people's past experiences and varies from person to person, we can always find some shared experiences and stories for the older adults from the same region, culture or with the same hobbies.

Acknowledgements. This research is supported, in part, by the National Research Foundation, Prime Ministers Office, Singapore under its IDM Futures Funding Initiative and the Singapore Ministry of Health under its National Innovation Challenge on Active and Confident Ageing (NIC Project No. MOH/NIC/COG04/2017).

References

1. Balaam, M., et al. Motivating mobility: designing for lived motivation in stroke rehabilitation. In: Proceedings of the SIGCHI Conference on Human Factors in Computing Systems, pp. 3073–3082. ACM (2011)
2. Barba, G.D.: Recognition memory and recollective experience in Alzheimer's disease. Memory **5**(6), 657–672 (1997)
3. Barry, J.E.: Everyday habits and routines: Design strategies to individualize home modifications for older people. Ph.D. dissertation, Washington State University (2008)
4. Boger, J., Craig, T., Mihailidis, A.: Examining the impact of familiarity on faucet usability for older adults with dementia. BMC Geriatr. **13**(1), 63 (2013)
5. Brittain, K., et al.: Ageing in place and technologies of place: the lived experience of people with dementia in changing social, physical and technological environments. Sociol. Health Illn. **32**(2), 272–287 (2010)
6. Brox, E., et al.: Experiences from long-term exergaming with elderly. In: Proceedings of the 18th International Academic MindTrek Conference: Media Business, Management, Content & Services, pp. 216–220. ACM (2014)
7. De Boissieu, P., et al.: Exergames and elderly: a non-systematic review of the literature. Eur. Geriatr. Med. **8**(2), 111–116 (2017)
8. Herstad, J., Holone, H.: Making sense of co-creative tangibles through the concept of familiarity. In: Proceedings of the 7th Nordic Conference on Human-Computer Interaction: Making Sense Through Design, pp. 89–98. ACM (2012)
9. Holland, A.C., Kensinger, E.A.: Emotion and autobiographical memory. Phys. Life Rev. **7**(1), 88–131 (2010)
10. Hollinworth, N., Hwang, F.: Investigating familiar interactions to help older adults learn computer applications more easily. In: Proceedings of the 25th BCS Conference on Human-Computer Interaction, pp. 473–478. British Computer Society (2011)

11. Iwarsson, S., Isacsson, Å.: Development of a novel instrument for occupational therapy of assessment of the physical environment in the home–a methodologic study on the enabler. Occup. Ther. J. Res. **16**(4), 227–244 (1996)
12. Iwarsson, S., Slaug, B.: Housing enabler—a method for rating/screening and analysing accessibility problems in housing. Manual for the complete instrument and screening tool (2010)
13. Iwarsson, S., et al.: Importance of the home environment for healthy aging: conceptual and methodological background of the European ENABLE-AGE Project. Gerontol. **47**(1), 78–84 (2007)
14. Küller, R.: Environmental activation of old persons suffering from senile dementia. In: 10th International Conference of the IAPS, vol. 2, pp. 133–139. Delft University Press (1988)
15. Kaplan, S., Kaplan, R.: Cognitive and Environment: Functioning in an Uncertain World. Ulrichs Books, Ann Arbor (1982)
16. Lawton, M.P., Nahemow, L.: Ecology and the aging process (1973)
17. Lawton, M.P.: Competence, environmental press, and the adaptations of older people. In: Lawton, M.P., Windley, P.G., Byerts, T.O. (eds.) Aging and the Environment: Theoretical Approaches, pp. 97–120. Springer, New York (1982)
18. Leonardi, C., et al.: Designing a familiar technology for elderly people. Gerontechnology **7**(2), 151 (2008)
19. Lewin, K.: Behavior and development as a function of the total situation (1946)
20. Moreland, R.L., Zajonc, R.B.: Exposure effects in person perception: familiarity, similarity, and attraction. J. Exp. Soc. Psychol. **18**(5), 395–415 (1982)
21. Norman, D.: The Design of Everyday Things: Revised and Expanded Edition, expanded edn. Basic Books, New York (2013)
22. Perfect, T.J., Williams, R.B., Anderton-Brown, C.: Age differences in reported recollective experience are due to encoding effects, not response bias. Memory **3**(2), 169–186 (1995)
23. Rizzo, A.S., Kim, G.J.: A SWOT analysis of the field of virtual reality rehabilitation and therapy. Presence: Teleoperators Virtual Environ. **14**(2), 119–146 (2005)
24. Shaughnessy, M., Resnick, B.M., Macko, R.F.: Testing a model of post-stroke exercise behavior. Rehabil. Nurs. **31**(1), 15–21 (2006)
25. Son, G.R., Therrien, B., Whall, A.: Implicit memory and familiarity among elders with dementia. J. Nurs. Sch. **34**(3), 263–267 (2002)
26. United Nations World population ageing 2017 Department of economic and social affairs (2017)
27. Wagner, A.D., Gabrieli, D.E., Verfaellie, M.: Dissociations between familiarity processes in explicit recognition and implicit perceptual memory. J. Exp. Psychol. Learn. Mem. Cogn. **23**(2), 305 (1997)
28. Witmer, B.G., Singer, M.J.: Measuring presence in virtual environments: a presence questionnaire. Presence: Teleoperators Virtual Environ. **73**, 225–240 (1998)
29. Zhang, H., Miao, C., Yu, H.: Fuzzy logic based assessment on the adaptive level of rehabilitation exergames for the elderly. In: 2017 IEEE Global Conference on Signal and Information Processing (GlobalSIP), pp. 423–427 (2017)

Ambient Assisted Living

Combining Mixed Reality and Internet of Things: An Interaction Design Research on Developing Assistive Technologies for Elderly People

Ryan Anthony J. de Belen[1(✉)], Dennis Del Favero[1],
and Tomasz Bednarz[1,2]

[1] Faculty of Art & Design, University of New South Wales,
Paddington, NSW 2021, Australia
r.debelen@student.unsw.edu.au,
{d.delfavero,t.bednarz}@unsw.edu.au
[2] CSIRO Data61, Australian Technology Park, Eveleigh, NSW 2015, Australia

Abstract. Ambient Assistive Living (AAL) technologies have the capacity to provide a safe environment for elderly people and to monitor and analyse gathered data which have been proven to be valuable in detecting activities that underpin health decline. Although there is a growing interest for these technologies, older people face some difficulties interacting with the technology. In an AAL environment, the interaction problem due to changes in perceptual and motor skill capabilities that often accompany the aging process in elderly people is further complicated as the immense quantity of sensors, with varying user interface and user interaction, makes full interoperability difficult. As elderly people navigate through this environment, they should be able to discover, configure, and directly interact with a myriad smart objects and digital information delivered to them. To increase the uptake of these technologies, there is a need for an intuitive interaction technique that considers elderly people's personal profile and presents contextual information when needed. In this paper, we present an interaction design research which aims to explore opportunities and challenges inherent to the development of an Assistive Technology (AT) for elderly people. The proposed AT, which is a combination of Mixed Reality (MR) and Internet of Things (IoT) technologies, aims to improve the Quality of Life (QoL) and to maintain the self-independence of people aged 65 or above. The intended users are elderly people, their family, their closest friends, and their healthcare network. The main contribution of this project is to provide a set of interaction design principles for combining MR and IoT as an AT. This is achieved by a carefully planned participatory design approach. The benefits and drawbacks of each phase are discussed transparently to inform current practices which are still mostly technology driven.

Keywords: Accommodations for aging-in-place ·
Aging and technology acceptance · Aging and ubiquitous computing ·
Interaction design · Assistive technologies · Mixed Reality ·
Internet of Things · Quality of Life

© Springer Nature Switzerland AG 2019
J. Zhou and G. Salvendy (Eds.): HCII 2019, LNCS 11593, pp. 291–304, 2019.
https://doi.org/10.1007/978-3-030-22015-0_23

1   Background

Australia's ageing population is associated with a growth in demand for health services and with an increase in residential care costs, creating a public health challenge. It is projected that by 2056, 22% of Australians will be 65 or over [1]. A similar trend is observed globally [2]. As this demographic continues to grow, discussions will need to focus on how elderly people can safely live at home longer, while improving their Quality of Life (QoL) and maintaining their self-independence. This challenge can be met with technologies that not only meet the needs and expectations of elderly people, but also are reliable, usable, and are suitable for everyday use. Over the past decade, there is an increasing number of technological developments and research projects (i.e. the main ICT-Agenda of the European Union: Horizon 2020) dedicated to the healthcare sector. In this regard, we argue that although the developments are promising, most are mostly technology-driven with little focus on the intended users.

2   Introduction

In general, Internet of Things (IoT) is a paradigm which consists of internet tech-nologies where everyday objects are inherently connected allowing them to commu-nicate and interact often bi-directionally with other networked objects [3]. Recently, various IoT solutions are being explored to sense, measure, and control indoor and outdoor smart connected objects [4], which aim to analyse and monitor the wellbeing of elderly people and to support their independent living. Although there is a growing interest for these technologies, older people are unfamiliar or they face some difficulties interacting with the technology [5–7]. In addition, older people are faced with per-ceived challenges and barriers (e.g. privacy and ethical concerns) [8, 9]. This is partly due to the fact that recent developments in these areas are mostly technology-driven [10–12], with only a few guidelines and principles on how to design and develop these technologies [13–16]. However, it is imperative that assistive technologies are relevant, easy to use, usable, appealing, and beneficial to the everyday lives of elderly people. We use a participatory design approach to address the social and ethical concerns of developing assistive technologies and ensure an optimised user experience meeting the needs and expectations of elderly people.

Participatory design plays an important role in influencing the technology adoption rates. This method actively involves different stakeholders – elderly people, family members, closest friends, and healthcare providers – in conceptualising design ideas and evaluating new technologies. With proper design and careful consideration, the quality of user interaction and user experience might improve adoption rates, especially of elderly people [17]. The long-term aim of this research is to present interaction design principles for combining Mixed Reality (MR) and Internet of Things (IoT) technologies as an Assistive Technology (AT). We hope that it can lead to more successful technical and social outcomes. In this research, MR is envisaged as a tool for elderly people to improve interactions with IoT technology, to enhance remote com-munication with their family, their closest friends, and their healthcare networks, to properly aid and assist them in their daily activities, and to address loneliness and social isolation which are often key components of depression among elderly people.

This paper is organized as follows: Sect. 3 discusses the applied research design. Section 4 outlines interaction design principles for developing ATs for elderly people. Finally, Sect. 5 presents a discussion of the implications of our study and suggests directions for future work.

3   Methodology

In this section, the applied research design is discussed. The first phase is conducted as a participatory design workshop that brought elderly people aged 65 or over, their family, their closest friends, and their healthcare network together for contextual inquiry. The second phase consists of an iterative development cycle that draws feedbacks from the previous phase to inform the development. The final phase is carried out as an evaluation workshop through quantitative and qualitative analysis. We outline a set of interaction design principles for developing Assistive Technologies (AT) for elderly people. In addition, we provide a series of future direction and recommendations for similar works in this research area. Finally, we constructively discuss the benefits and drawbacks of each phase to inform current practices which are still mostly technology driven.

3.1   Participatory Design Workshop

To provide the elderly people with a platform to have their voices heard and generate collaborative discussions with the other stakeholders, a participatory design workshop was conducted. The aim of the participatory design workshop was to explore the opportunities and challenges inherent to the development of an Assistive Technology (AT) to improve the Quality of Life (QoL) and to maintain the self-independence of elderly people. Overall, the participatory design approach is premised on the assumption that different stakeholders, including the elderly, families, closest friends, and healthcare providers, play an important role in the system development [18]. Besides technological developments, focusing on user experience and acceptance is important for a successful adoption. The ideal coordination and communication with the target group enables us to imagine how the AT can be adjusted based on the needs and wishes of the intended users. The system development should be driven completely and without exception by the needs of the target group at stake. However, there should be an optimal balance between users' desires and technical feasibility.

Participant Profiles. To ensure high utility and usability, different stakeholders were included throughout the design process. Participants were recruited from a local healthcare facility (refer to Table 1). They were selected for their expression of interest in participating in the study. All of them signed a consent form and agreed to voluntarily participate without compensation in the study. Afterwards, they answered a questionnaire which addressed demographic aspects, such as age, gender, and sex.

Elderly People. Most developed world countries have accepted the chronological age of 65 years as a definition of 'elderly' or older person [19]. Although a number is not a good predictor of functional status in biological, psychological and social processes [20], it should be sufficient to identify people who are starting to experience the ageing process. As such, we considered people aged 65 or above as potential participants in this study. We did not exclude those with physical disabilities or cognitive decline.

Family Members. Elderly people usually live or lived with family members who know their usual habits. Involving family members in the participatory design workshop brings valuable insights and different perspectives in the design of innovative technologies for elderly people [21]. We considered people who live with a family member aged 65 or above as potential participants to this study.

Healthcare Provider. Using healthcare providers as proxies for elderly in the development of assistive technologies showed promising and positive results [22]. Since they are to a great extent familiar with the needs and demands of elderly people, their inclusion is immensely important as they support and complete the understanding of how and where assistive technologies could be beneficial to the intended users. Thus, their contribution to the development is perceived as more meaningful, both to elderly and healthcare providers. In this regard, we recruited elderly healthcare providers to participate in this study.

Table 1. Participant profiles

Characteristics	Description	N	%
Stakeholder	Elderly people	10	71
	Family member	2	14
	Healthcare provider	2	14
Age	65–74 years old	3	21
	75–84 years old	5	36
	85 or above	3	21
	Other or no answer	3	21
Gender	Male	2	14
	Female	12	86
	Other or no answer	0	0

Workshop Setting. The participants were recruited through a local community centre ('Holdsworth Community') in Sydney, who had expressed an interest after being introduced to the research project. Holdsworth Community also provided the setting for the workshop. The community centre describes itself as *"a community that supports older people who may be frail, ill, lacking mobility, experiencing social isolation or living with dementia"* throughout Sydney, Australia. They also aim to *"build a community where all people have the support and services that they need in order to build their personal capacity; have a voice and make choices; and make the meaningful connections they need to live an active and happy life in the community."*

The Holdsworth Community carries out discussion group sessions which run weekly on Mondays and Tuesdays, where older people are invited to attend to socialise.

Ethics Approval. Ethics approval to conduct this research was granted by the University of New South Wales Human Research Ethics Committee Executive (HREC) with HC No: HC180805. This ensures that the research meets the requirements of the National Statement of Ethical Conduct in Human Research (2007), updated 2018 [23]. Particular attention was paid to configuring informed consent for elderly people within this study. A different version of consent forms to support the provision of consent by an elderly person's family member or healthcare provider was also prepared. Participation in any of the activities was voluntary. Mixed Reality (MR) activities were ensured to be safe and easy to use for the study participants. Participant information sheet and consent forms were handed over to the participants prior to any of the activities. These documents informed the participants about the possibility of feeling nauseous after using the system and the risk of falls and injury since they will be moving around while wearing the headset. To mitigate the risks, potential participants, who have previously experienced motion sickness, were asked to confirm if they still want to proceed with the activities. In addition, proper precaution was taken to ensure that the environment was free of loose objects to minimize the risk of falls and injury. As an introduction to the activities, details about what participants could expect by wearing the headset were provided. If a participant expressed doubt or hesitation to take part in any of the activities, they will not be forced to continue. Furthermore, they have the option to withdraw their participation anytime.

Mixed Reality Activities. As it is expected that the participants will have little to no knowledge about the current technologies, a background introduction was administered at the start of the workshops. This included the process of introducing the Internet of Things (IoT) technologies, showing participants photos and videos of people trying out Mixed Reality (MR) devices, asking them to try out MR devices, and then discussing current approaches on how technologies are being used to improve the Quality of Life (QoL) of elderly people.

During the activities, participants frequently interacted with a Microsoft HoloLens device. At the beginning of each activity, each participant did a calibration setup using an application that is pre-installed on the Microsoft HoloLens. The application calibrates the HoloLens display according to the users' individual inter-pupillary distance. By going through the calibration setup, all participants were introduced to the basic controls of the HoloLens. Afterwards, each participant finished a tutorial session which made them familiar and comfortable with the device.

User Study – Object Selection. The first activity is an object selection task (shown in Fig. 1). During this activity, elderly people are surrounded by coloured boxes and asked to select boxes with a colour that was randomly chosen by the system. The goal is to select the correct coloured boxes with the least amount of time possible. It consisted of different session with each session only allowing them to select a box using only one of the following selection techniques:

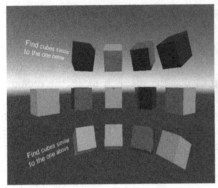

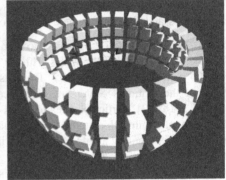

Fig. 1. User study – object selection   **Fig. 2.** User study – navigation

- By pressing a button on a remote control
- By performing a specific hand gesture
- By looking at the coloured box for at least 3 s
- By saying the word, "Select"

User Study – Navigation. The second activity is a navigation task (refer to Fig. 2). The goal of this activity is to determine the most effective way to provide directions in a mixed reality environment. In each session, audio, visual, and haptic cues were used to provide directions and to help participants locate virtual objects. Arrows were used as a visual cue to show direction and location of the target objects. The goal is to find and select virtual objects with the least amount of time possible.

User Study – Assistance. The third activity is an assistance task. The goal of this activity is to determine how mixed reality (MR) can enhance the communication between elderly people, their family members, and their closest friends, as well as how it can provide remote consultation between elderly people and healthcare providers.

Each activity, as well as the measurement of completion times and error, will begin as soon as the participants perform any of the selection technique discussed above.

Three activities were constructed with an overall aim of gathering enough information about the most suitable and preferred interaction techniques of AT for elderly people. This will be done through quantitative analysis of the participants' performance and qualitative analysis of participants' feedbacks.

Quantitative Evaluation - Questionnaire Design. After completing each activity, participants will be asked to complete a questionnaire. The questionnaire consisted of several parts which aims to determine the efficiency and effectiveness, along with user acceptability and user satisfaction. The perceived ease of use of the developed system was measured using the System Usability Scale (SUS). SUS aims to cover different aspects of the system:

- Effectiveness (how well users successfully achieve their objectives)
- Efficiency (how much effort and resources are necessary to achieve their objectives)
- Satisfaction (how much the users' expectations are met when they achieve their objectives)

Qualitative Evaluation - Interview Design. Semi-structured interviews were conducted during the initial workshop. The focus of questions to participants was to learn what the participants think of emerging technologies, how they see these technologies to be useful to their daily lives, what is the impact such technologies might bring, whether they can see themselves using such technologies, what are the barriers for technology adoption, and what they would want such technologies to have. In addition, the interview was complemented with observations about their current life situation and experiences, the social relationship they currently have, specific issues they encounter daily, and the types and uses of technology in their daily lives. This was done to capture how current technologies address the needs of elderly people, and how emerging technologies can improve aspects that are not currently being focused. Gathered data were analysed by creating affinity diagrams.

A scenario was designed in order to ensure that all participants refer to the same vision – a smart personal home environment where everyday objects are 'smart' with diverse functions: full automation, remote control functionality, indoor monitoring of daily activity, etc. The other stakeholders (e.g. family members, closest friends, and healthcare providers) were asked to put themselves in an elderly person's position, to identify everyday objects that might need to be smart, and to imagine how he will interact with these smart objects. Subsequent to the scenario, the participants were asked to assess the perceived benefits, barriers, and the acceptance of as well as intention to use the described smart personal home environment.

3.2   Iterative Development Cycle

During this stage, an initial prototype using Mixed Reality (MR) and Internet of Things (IoT) technologies is developed. The system requirements were obtained through affinity diagrams constructed based from participants' performance and feedback during the participatory design workshop.

3.3   Evaluation Workshop

In this workshop, the prototype is presented to the participants and evaluated through quantitative and qualitative measures.

4   Results

An initial workshop with 12 elderly people was conducted to introduce the emerging technologies (such as Internet of Things, Smart Home, Mixed Reality Technology) and the different perspectives of the elderly people are presented below. In this section, we summarise the lessons that we have learned and draw observations from the initial workshop. In addition, we constructively discuss the benefits and drawbacks of each phase to inform current practices which are still mostly technology driven.

4.1   Participatory Design Workshop

The initial workshop was carried out as part of Holdsworth Community's afternoon discussion group sessions on Tuesdays. It lasted for lasted approximately two hours. Our primary aim was to explore the initial reactions to Mixed Reality (MR) environments for elderly people. In the initial workshop, where participants were seated around a table, an introduction about the research was conducted. This included the process of introducing the Internet of Things (IoT) technologies, explaining how IoT devices are being incorporated in a house to make it smart, showing participants photos and videos of people trying out Mixed Reality (MR) devices, asking them to try out MR devices, and then discussing current approaches on how technologies are being used to improve the Quality of Life (QoL) of elderly people.

Data Collection and Analysis. Data from the initial workshop was collected through video and audio recording of the session. The workshop questions were semi-structured. The interviews were transcribed and interpreted through thematic analysis. This allowed us to investigate recurring themes and requirements. Affinity diagrams were constructed to organize ideas, issues, insights into a collection showing common themes and structures [24]. The affinity diagram revealed the scope of the user problem (i.e. issues, worries, etc.) and defined the key system requirements (i.e. reliability, performance, etc.) to generate design ideas. The themes emerged from the interviews through a process of induction [25]. The analysis focused on answering the questions, "what are the opportunities and challenges present when designing and developing an assistive technology for elderly people?"

Establishing Effective Communication. Effective communication between researchers and participants is one of the most important elements during the initial workshop. Age-related changes in hearing, vision, cognitive, and physical abilities can make face-to-face communication even more demanding [26]. Before the interview, it is useful to gather preliminary data on user background which can help assess the level of sensory impairments of the older person. Following the advice of the Holdsworth Community, proper care was taken to make sure that the researchers conducted the interview in a room with a low background noise, the workshop instructor had a moderate speech rate, audible voice, and clear articulation, and the workshop slides contain texts which are readable from a distance.

Mixed Reality Device Introduction. Older participants are generally unfamiliar with the Microsoft HoloLens device due to its relative newness and less accessibility of the consumer market owing to its high cost. When introducing the device to the participants, it was necessary to play videos of people trying the device and to show a live demonstration where they learned the basic interactions with the device. In addition, the live demonstration was supplemented with a live-stream first view of the scene. This allowed the workshop instructor to share the experience with the participants by allowing them to see the holograms as he sees them. During the workshop, the HoloLens was connected to the community centre's wireless internet connection (over WiFi) and the Mixed Reality Capture feature was accessed through the Windows Device Portal.

Genuine Interest. During the initial workshop, the participants expressed great interest in integrating emerging technologies into their daily lives. After listening to the workshop introduction, the participants immediately wished to try the HoloLens. The initial workshop showed that elderly people are interested and able to take part in participatory design workshop on combining Internet of Things (IoT) and Mixed Reality (MR) technologies as an Assistive Technology (AT).

Basic HoloLens Interactions. Because of the time constraints during the initial workshop, only half of the participants were able to try the HoloLens. They were amazed on how the workshop instructor can interact with virtual objects around him. One participant even said: *"You can click the air"*. Although the participants worried that they might not be able to perform the gestures correctly, they showed particular interest in learning how to use it. After trying the different gestures, one participant said, *"Once you are used to doing that [referring to the gestures], you can do anything!"*

Initial Reactions. After learning the basic HoloLens interactions, the participants were asked to try the 3D Viewer which is a pre-installed and standalone application on HoloLens. It allowed them to easy place, scale, and rotate 3D models and view animations in real-time. The participants were immediately impressed - *"This is amazing!" "Absolutely incredible."*

Entertainment. The participants thought that Mixed Reality devices can be used to revisit memorable places but could not visit anymore or explore unfamiliar places that are hard for them to visit. Someone argued that instead of spending money to travel overseas, one can just buy the device, put it on, and stay in the comfort of your own home. She said, *"You could go on holidays but sit on your own armchair."* and added, *"You could also go underwater and see, you could go swimming."* Most participants affirmed by saying, *"I can imagine."* Although it is convenient to visit places without physically being there, the older participants think that would make them feel isolated. One argued, *"Don't you think that's really sad?"* In line with this, discussions about how the HoloLens can be used to improve social communication between elderly people, their family, their closest friends, and their healthcare providers were talked about. The older participants were likely to perceive the usefulness of this technology for staying in touch with people over long distances. It is important to consider how elderly people can share entertaining experiences and meaningful experiences with their loved ones when using Mixed Reality devices.

Assistive Technology. Interesting suggestions on the feasibility of the HoloLens device as an assistive technology for older people were drawn from the initial workshop. Participants were convinced that the device can be used as a navigational aid to help in wayfinding in indoor and outdoor environments, especially when they get lost. In addition, they suggested that the device can be useful in locating important objects around their houses. Finally, they argued that the device can be used to connect with smart objects around the house and to talk to them if they forgot to turn off something.

Perceived Usefulness Outweighs Device Cost. One participant expressed curiosity about how expensive it is to use the technology. She asked, *"Is it too expensive to use each time you get on it?"* When told about the unit price of one Microsoft HoloLens device, some participants expressed their shock: *"So, we're not talking about little bits and pieces. It is a serious money."* Although the device itself is expensive, participants discussed about the perceived usefulness of the device. They think that the potential benefits outweigh the device cost. *"Well, you have to need it. If you need it, then it's cheap. It's fabulous!"* A participant asked the group and said *"Would you like to use it and what for? Forget about the cost."* The group noted that they are currently unaware on how it could be useful for them. However, they think that if developers are able to make applications that are useful to them, they definitely would buy and use the device. We also believe that based on early prototypes, we can provide scalable and cheap solutions by utilizing commonly available mobile devices or tablets such as iPad.

Social Acceptance. Older participants expressed great concern on how social inter-actions will be like in the future. While the workshop instructor was performing ges-tures on the HoloLens, a participant said, *"So, if you think that kids are unresponsive now, imagine how will the world interact with each other. We will be different people then."* Older participants also express their concerns about the potential of stigma from others who think that wearing HoloLens makes them look foolish. One participant said, *"Can you imagine yourself going to Woolies? [a supermarket]"* Everyone laughed with her. When queried about this, participants indicated that they found the large form factor of the HoloLens a bit intimidating. For this reason, participants talked about the need to have an aesthetically-pleasing device. It is clear that developing an assistive technology for elderly people should be done in such a way that they are evaluated as socially acceptable and even desirable.

Perceived Drawbacks. The participants argue that the automation brought by the Internet of Things (IoT) technologies may promote sedentary living conditions making elderly people more immobile. When asked if the participants are willing to use the device to operate smart objects in the house, one argued, *"We were told that we got to be moving all the time and exercise. Why would we be doing that? Say, turn the lights on. [then proceeds with an air tap gesture]"* However, one participant suggests that elderly people who are physically infirmed will greatly benefit from this kind of technology because of the convenience it offers. When designing for an assistive technology for elderly people, it is important to offer convenience without sacrificing the need for them to physically move.

Device Comfort/Ease of Use. Most of the participants found the HoloLens device problematic due to its weight. While putting on the device, one participant was shocked: *"Oh my God! It is so heavy!"* During the initial workshop, older participants found it hard to carry the device for an extended period of time. A smaller and lighter device form factor might deal with this issue. In addition, one participant noticed that using the device can be quite disorienting. When asked to explain further, she added *"You'd have to have a really good balance. Because it is so disorienting. It's quite freaky that you are looking at something that is not reality."* Another participant affirmed by saying, *"You lose association with reality."* When asked about the experience, she said, *"It is like as if I was sitting in a cinema."* Another one explained:

"It'd be like trying new glasses" However, they pointed out that it just needs getting used to – *"There's a lot of learning to go with it."*

Benefits and Drawbacks. While it can be difficult for participants to talk about how emerging technologies can help elderly people in their daily lives, showing videos of people trying the devices and explaining how these devices are being used in different application areas elicit views and provide opportunities for specific design ideas to be critiqued.

5 Discussion

In this study, we considered and compared diverse stakeholder perspectives (elderly people, family members, closest friends, and healthcare networks) in order to explore the opportunities and challenges inherent to the development of an Assistive Technology (AT) to improve the Quality of Life (QoL) and to maintain the self-independence of elderly people. The results provide valuable interaction design principles in developing ATs for elderly people.

5.1 Interaction Design Principles

Understanding the increasing needs of elderly people is critical and crucial to the design and development of ATs. There is a common perception that there is a digital divide where the current old generation is comparatively inexperienced with technology than the younger generation [27]. However, this is a huge misconception since the current share of the population that is over 65 has been through a number of technological innovations during their lifetime [28]. The real and pressing problem when designing and developing ATs for elderly people lies on how to overcome the gradual changes in perceptual and motor skill capabilities that often accompany the aging process in elderly people. In this section, interaction design principles for developing Assistive Technology (AT) for elderly people are outlined. Given the relative newness of this area of research, this can be used as a foundation principle to ensure that ATs are designed in a sensitive way and optimized for elderly people, to provide high-quality positive experiences, and to maximise user satisfaction.

Effective communication between researchers and participants is one of the most important elements during the initial workshop. During the initial workshop, it was evident that the older participants have a limited knowledge about the emerging technologies, such as Mixed Reality (MR) and Internet of Things (IoT). While it can be difficult for participants to talk about how emerging technologies can help elderly people in their daily lives, showing videos of people trying the devices and explaining how these devices are being used in different application areas elicit views and provide opportunities for specific design ideas to be critiqued. A positive interest towards how these technologies can be integrated in elderly people's daily lives were observed during the initial workshop. The initial workshop captured the elderly participants' initial reactions on what they think of emerging technologies, how they see these technologies to be useful in their daily lives, what is the impact such technologies might bring, whether they can see themselves using such technologies, what are the barriers for technology adoption, and what they would want such technologies to have.

5.2 Limitations and Further Research

When interpreting the results, the reader should be aware of certain limitations. First, the low number of participants during the initial workshop limited the statistical analyses that could be completed by the study. Instead, we present observations from the initial workshop with 12 elderly people. Arrangements with the Holdsworth Community were already made to recruit more participants and to perform statistical analyses and make generalisations in the future. Second, an ideal scenario where elderly people wearing a Mixed Reality (MR) headset and interacting with smart objects in a smart home was presented to the participants. A working prototype is currently being developed to validate the presented observations. Thirdly, the time constraints during the first visit to the community centre limited the user study that the researchers were able to perform. Although the three activities (selection, navigation, and assistance) for the user study were already fully implemented in a standalone application, only an initial workshop was conducted during the first visit. This is considered as the first phase of the project which informs the succeeding workshops and refines the final Assistive Technology (AT) for elderly people.

6 Conclusion

In this paper, we present an interaction design research which aims to explore opportunities and challenges inherent to the development of an Assistive Technology (AT) for elderly people. The proposed AT, which is a combination of Mixed Reality (MR) and Internet of Things (IoT) technologies, aims to improve the Quality of Life (QOL) and to maintain the self-independence of people aged 65 or above. The intended users are elderly people, their family, their closest friends, and their healthcare network. The main contribution of this project is to provide a set of interaction design principles for combining MR and IoT as an AT. This is achieved by a carefully planned participatory design approach. The benefits and drawbacks of each phase are discussed transparently to inform current practices which are still mostly technology driven. In addition, interesting observations captured during the initial workshop with elderly people, family members, closest friends, and healthcare networks were presented. This included their initial reactions, perceived benefits, impact of technology on their daily lives, barriers to technology adoption, and their suggestions on how these technologies can be integrated in their daily lives.

Acknowledgements. We would like to thank all participating clients of Holdsworth Community, as well as to staff of the community centre for their time and interest, especially to Shaun Zingel. This research is supported by an Australian Government Research Training Program (RTP) Scholarship and Expanded Perception and Interaction Centre (EPICentre) located at the UNSW Art & Design in Paddington, Australia.

References

1. Australian Institute of Health and Welfare. Older Australia at a glance, September 2018
2. United Nations Department of Economic and Social Affairs PD, World Population Ageing (2015)
3. Giusto, D., Iera, A., Morabito, G., Atzori, L.: The Internet of Things: 20th Tyrrhenian Workshop on Digital Communications, 1st edn. Springer, New York (2010). https://doi.org/10.1007/978-1-4419-1674-7
4. Jang, J., Bednarz, T.: HoloSensor for smart home, health, entertainment, p. 2. ACM (2018)
5. Tomita, M.R., Mann, W.C., Stanton, K., et al.: Use of currently available smart home technology by frail elders: process and outcomes. Top. Geriatr. Rehabil. **23**, 24–34 (2007)
6. Hill, R., Beynon-Davies, P., Williams, M.D.: Older people and internet engagement: acknowledging social moderators of internet adoption, access and use. Inf. Technol. People **21**, 244–266 (2008)
7. Rogers, W.A., Stronge, A.J., Fisk, A.D.: Technology and Aging. Rev. Hum. Factors Ergon. **1**, 130–171 (2005)
8. van Heek, J., Himmel, S., Ziefle, M.: Privacy, data security, and the acceptance of AAL-systems – a user-specific perspective. In: Zhou, J., Salvendy, G. (eds.) ITAP 2017. LNCS, vol. 10297, pp. 38–56. Springer, Cham (2017). https://doi.org/10.1007/978-3-319-58530-7_4
9. Kolkowska, E., Avatare Nöu, A., Sjölinder, M., Scandurra, I.: To capture the diverse needs of welfare technology stakeholders – evaluation of a value matrix. In: Zhou, J., Salvendy, G. (eds.) ITAP 2017. LNCS, vol. 10298, pp. 404–419. Springer, Cham (2017). https://doi.org/10.1007/978-3-319-58536-9_32
10. Eason, K., Waterson, P., Davda, P.: The sociotechnical challenge of integrating telehealth and telecare into health and social care for the elderly. In: Healthcare Administration: Concepts, Methodologies, Tools, and Applications, pp. 1177–1189. IGI Global (2015)
11. Oishi, M.M.K., Mitchell, I.M., Van der Loos, H.M.: Design and Use of Assistive Technology: Social, Technical, Ethical, and Economic Challenges. Springer, New York (2010). https://doi.org/10.1007/978-1-4419-7031-2
12. Baxter, G., Sommerville, I.: Socio-technical systems: from design methods to systems engineering. Interact. Comput. **23**, 4–17 (2011)
13. Kourouthanassis, P.E., Boletsis, C., Lekakos, G.: Demystifying the design of mobile augmented reality applications. Multimed. Tools Appl. **74**, 1045–1066 (2015)
14. Gruenerbl, A., Bahle, G., Weppner, J., et al.: Ubiquitous context aware monitoring systems in psychiatric and mental care: challenges and issues of real life deployments, pp. 105–109. ICST (Institute for Computer Sciences, Social-Informatics and Telecommunications Engineering) (2014)
15. Vichitvanichphong, S., Talaei-Khoei, A., Kerr, D., et al.: Adoption of assistive technologies for aged care: a realist review of recent studies, pp. 2706–2715. IEEE (2014)
16. Peek, S.T., Wouters, E.J., van Hoof, J., et al.: Factors influencing acceptance of technology for aging in place: a systematic review. Int. J. Med. Inform. **83**, 235–248 (2014)
17. Östlund, B.: The benefits of involving older people in the design process. In: Zhou, J., Salvendy, G. (eds.) ITAP 2015. LNCS, vol. 9193, pp. 3–14. Springer, Cham (2015). https://doi.org/10.1007/978-3-319-20892-3_1
18. Sjölinder, M., Scandurra, I., Avatare Nöu, A., Kolkowska, E.: To meet the needs of aging users and the prerequisites of innovators in the design process. In: Zhou, J., Salvendy, G. (eds.) ITAP 2016. LNCS, vol. 9754, pp. 92–104. Springer, Cham (2016). https://doi.org/10.1007/978-3-319-39943-0_10
19. World report on ageing and health: World Health Organization (2015)

20. Markson, E.W., Jordan, K.S.: Social Gerontology Today: An Introduction. Roxbury Publishing Company, Los Angeles (2003)
21. Lawrence, V., Fossey, J., Ballard, C., et al.: Improving quality of life for people with dementia in care homes: making psychosocial interventions work. Br. J. Psychiatry **201**, 344–351 (2012)
22. Sjölinder, M., Scandurra, I., Avatare Nou, A., Kolkowska, E.: Using care professionals as proxies in the design process of welfare technology – perspectives from municipality care. In: Zhou, J., Salvendy, G. (eds.) ITAP 2017. LNCS, vol. 10297, pp. 184–198. Springer, Cham (2017). https://doi.org/10.1007/978-3-319-58530-7_13
23. National statement on ethical conduct in human research. National Health and Medical Research Council (2007)
24. Holtzblatt, K., Wendell, J.B., Wood, S.: Rapid Contextual Design: A How-to Guide to Key Techniques for User-Centered Design. Elsevier, San Francisco (2004)
25. Fowler, T.: The Elements of Inductive Logic. Clarendon Press, Oxford (1883)
26. Jiang, Y., Dong, H., Yuan, S.: Developing a framework for effective communication with older people. In: Zhou, J., Salvendy, G. (eds.) ITAP 2015. LNCS, vol. 9193, pp. 61–72. Springer, Cham (2015). https://doi.org/10.1007/978-3-319-20892-3_7
27. Selwyn, N.: Defining the 'digital divide': developing a theoretical understanding of inequalities in the information age. School of Social Sciences, Cardiff University (2002)
28. Eriksson, Y.: Technologically mature but with limited capabilities. In: Zhou, J., Salvendy, G. (eds.) ITAP 2016. LNCS, vol. 9754, pp. 3–12. Springer, Cham (2016). https://doi.org/10.1007/978-3-319-39943-0_1

Smarter Homes for Older Adults: Building a Framework Around Types and Levels of Autonomy

Maryam FakhrHosseini[(✉)], Chaiwoo Lee[(✉)],
and Joseph F. Coughlin[(✉)]

Massachusetts Institute of Technology, 77 Massachusetts Avenue,
Cambridge, MA 02139, USA
{shabnaml,chaiwoo,coughlin}@mit.com

Abstract. The types and levels of autonomy have been deeply discussed and, in some cases, standardized in the areas of human robot interaction, autonomous vehicles, and spaceflight vehicles. However, there is not an established framework for in-home technologies, which is a growing area of technological development. Home technologies have had significant effects on how people live, especially improving the ways in which older adults and their caregivers navigate various daily tasks. Having a framework to define the types and levels of automation in home technologies is necessary to better understand the state of the art, identify current and future directions for development, and facilitate communication between stakeholders. This paper reviews existing studies on smart home technologies and previous efforts around building taxonomies of automation in different domains. Literature around technology adoption among older adults and related design considerations are also discussed to further describe home automation as it applies to improving independence among older adults.

Keywords: Smart home · Home technologies · Older adults · Automation

"The last place we think will need us is our own home. We need it more than it should need us which is what makes it so relaxing. It doesn't need anything from us when we leave it and it is always there for us to come back to."

Alexandra Deschamps-Sonsino.

1 Introduction

Life expectancy has increased from 61.7 years in 1980 to 71.8 years in 2015 [1], and this trend has been observed more in higher income countries [2] and higher income populations [3]. A comprehensive study on cause-specific and all-cause mortality factors predicted an increasing trend of life expectancy by 2040 in 116 of 195 countries [4]. According to a report released by [5], the global population aged 60 years or over numbered 962 million in 2017 which was more than twice as large as in 1980 when

© Springer Nature Switzerland AG 2019
J. Zhou and G. Salvendy (Eds.): HCII 2019, LNCS 11593, pp. 305–313, 2019.
https://doi.org/10.1007/978-3-030-22015-0_24

there were 382 million older adults worldwide. In this report, it has been estimated that the proportion of older adults aged 60 years and older, compared to the total population, is expected to double between 2007 and 2050 and will reach to 2 billion by 2050 [5].

Aging in place has been recognized as one of preferred models of aging due to the growth of the older adult population [6]. Most of older adults prefer to continue living in their own homes [7]. Feeling attachment to their homes and independence, sustaining self-identity, memories of the past, quality of neighborhood, and sense of freedom are all underlying factors associated with this preference [7, 8]. According to [9], more than 20% of adults aged 65 to 84 and around 40% of adults 85 and older live alone in their households. However, while many older adults can easily continue to live independently, aging in place may be problematic for older adults at the higher end of the age spectrum (i.e., those 80 years of age or older) [7]. Also, people are likely to experience physical and mental changes as they age, which also pose difficulties in doing daily tasks independently [10]. A further complication for aging in place stems from having to manage chronic conditions or disabilities, which is prevalent among older populations. According to a recent report from the United States Census, about 39% of Americans aged 65 or older reported having at least one disability; and among those 85 and older, 73% had at least one disability, and 42% have three or more types of disabilities [11].

While aging in place alone can be difficult since many older adults suffer from chronic diseases, physical, visual, and hearing limitations [12, 13], a wide variety of technological advancements have been made to support the wellness and independence of older adults (e.g. [14–18]). Few studies have investigated the potential values that these technologies may being to the older population. For example, in order to find if there is any correlation between the use of home-based technology (HBT) devices and the quality of life among older people, [19] interviewed 160 older people 75 and older. Using regression analysis, results showed that the use of multiple HBT devices is associated with better quality of life of among the residents. A review study of 48 papers investigated the clinical outcomes of smart homes and home health-monitoring technologies between 2010 and 2014. Results from this review showed that home health-monitoring technologies reduced the symptoms of depression and frequency of visits to the emergency department in older adults with chronic illness and facilitated sharing data with clinicians. However, it did not help with the conditions of disease, disability prediction, health-related quality of life, and fall prevention [14].

Many home technologies are posed to help older adults to live independently and age in place, as well as to make daily tasks easier and more convenient for the general population. Enabled by recent technological advancements, there is now a greater variety of home technologies, varying in their degrees of automation, available to users across generations. However, unlike other domains such as aviation and surface transportation, where the concept of automation has been established with widely accepted taxonomies, there is no clear description of automation and its applications among home technologies. This study aims to address the gap by reviewing existing definitions and models of home automation and smart home technologies. With a survey of previously suggested concepts, this study seeks to identify key directions to work toward with the objective of creating and establishing a universal definition and taxonomy of home automation and smart home technologies.

2 Smart Home Technologies

The term "smart home" was first used in 1984 in a consortium hold by the National Association of Home Builders [20]. The terms, "Domotics" and "home automation" were used to describe in-home technologies of the upper class in the 80s and 90s. [21] defined the term "smart home" as "a residence equipped with technology that facilitates monitoring of residents and/or promotes independence and increases residents' quality of life" [21]. Smart home technologies passively collect multiple types of data (e.g. physiological and location data) from the resident, and, depending on the goals, share it with the residents, family members, and/or care providers [22].

The purpose of smart homes is to enhance resident security, safety, health and quality of life by non-obtrusive monitoring of activities. Characteristics of case models of smart houses such as Gator Tech Smart House, Matilda Smart House, the Aware Home, Duke University Smart House, Drexel Smart House, and MIT Smart House were reviewed by [23]. They discusses that the interrelations between the residents, spaces, technologies, social behavior, and the communications are important and there is not a harmony between the users' daily routines and the design of the house. A systematic review on smart home technologies showed that physical and functional health are the top 2 priorities [21] and less attention has been paid to the issues of social interactions.

While users across the age spectrum, researchers, developers and designers, and service providers alike are moving toward making the smart home a reality, there is not yet a comprehensive framework to describe the various forms of in-home technologies. Home technologies vary greatly in the level of automation and the areas of application. In order to facilitate a streamlined discussion among stakeholders, as well as to ensure a successful deployment of potential solutions, it is necessary to better understand the current state of in-home technologies and to work toward developing a framework defining various application types and levels of automation.

3 Technology Adoption

The older population has been traditionally regarded and stereotyped as late adopters or rejects of technological innovations. Recent studies, however, have found evidence to argue that older adults, especially Baby Boomers, are interested in new technologies, willing to learn about them, and in fact using a variety of them [24–26]. While older adults have been slower than younger generations to adopt new technologies, they are increasingly embracing new technologies and related applications. For example, Pew Research Center reported that smartphone adoption among older adults 65 and older has almost quadrupled between 2011 and 2016, and that the vast majority of the segment is using the internet [27].

The desire of older adults to age in place leads them accept in-home technologies [28]. However, due to the physical and cognitive constraints, older adults accept new technologies under the influence of specific factors [29]. Older adults' willingness to adopt smart home technologies within continuing care retirement community living environment was explored through individual interviews and focus groups. Results of the qualitative analysis showed that perceived need was a critical factor in older adults' willingness to adopt smart home technologies [22]. In 2010, Coleman et al. found the same thing: older adults accept a technology if they find a direct benefit of it. Older adults want technologies that are useful, trustable, help them to age in place, and improve their quality of life [14].

[14] in their review paper concluded that the level of technology readiness for smart homes and home health monitoring technologies is still low. Previous studies showed ten factors as the key determinants for older adults' technology adoption: value [28], usability [30], affordability, accessibility, technical support, social support, emotion, independence (Hawley-Hague, Boulton, Hall, Pfeiffer, & Todd, 2014; 30], experience, and confidence (Lee and Coughlin, 2015). In addition to these factors, [28] found that older adults express concerns of stigmatization when the technology is too noticeable or obtrusive within their homes. They concluded that stigmatization and privacy are the two factors that do not persist over time. Finally, they concluded that the role of family and friends on older adults' perception of needing a technology in technology adoption process should not be ignored [28].

When it comes to in-home technologies, privacy is one of the biggest user concerns. Older adults prefer to have a system that tells them when cameras are activated, with a very clear indicator which assures the users that their privacy is not being compromised (Hawley-Hague, Boulton, Hall, Pfeiffer, & Todd, 2014; 28, 30]. Older adults usually refuse video cameras at home but have not fear of being recorded by microphone [30]. However, [22] said that privacy concerns rarely impacted users' adoption choices and they are willing to trade privacy with the potential benefits of smart home technologies.

Smart homes, also called "automated homes," aim to automate the tasks for the residents [31]. We call a technology "smart" if that technology possess an awareness of its situation and is capable of reacting to it [32]. If smart home technologies are supposed to accomplish tasks autonomously, then what tasks should be automated and to what extent? A taxonomy of smart houses was developed by [33] (Fig. 1). In this taxonomy, smart houses are divided into three categories: controllable houses, programmable houses, and intelligent houses. Classes in this taxonomy, from the top to the bottom, imply the evolution of houses and the complexity of the systems. Although the taxonomy provides a good source of information and a discussion platform on the complexity of smart houses, it mainly focuses on the input data and lacks the detailed information on the role of users and possible human factors outcomes.

Although one of the fundamental aims of automation and autonomous systems is to eliminate burden [34], older adults are concerned with being dependent on smart home technologies. They believe that smart homes would decrease their independence rather than improving it [30]. For example, older adults fear that smart home technologies are tools that substitute for personal forms of care and communication [21]. To alleviate these concerns researchers need to know how autonomous smart home technologies

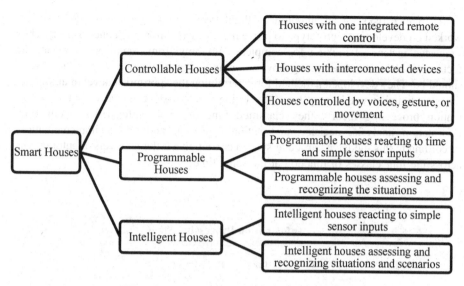

Fig. 1. A taxonomy of smart houses by [33]

should be designed for the target users. A framework that conceptualizes autonomy and identifies human automation interaction variables is necessary to answer these questions. Moreover, any changes in the level of autonomy of a system, influences the role of the users. To understand what roles should be given to users based on the environmental conditions and user characteristics, researchers need a framework to communicate the design decisions and predict the human-automation interaction outcomes.

4   Level of Autonomy

Autonomy has been conceptualized in different domains. [35] defined automation as "full or partial replacement of a function previously carried out by the human operator." They suggested a continuum of levels for automation that starts from the lowest level of fully manual performance to the highest level of full automation. Similar approaches have been applied to the levels of driving automation for on-road vehicles and medical robots [36] that describe the allocation of responsibility on the user versus the technology.

In the area of human robot interaction (HRI), [37] provided a cohesive framework on robot autonomy. This framework allows designers and researchers to identify a robot's autonomy level on a 10-point scale. In their definition of autonomy, they distinguished the psychological and artificial aspects of the term and defined robot autonomy as "the extent to which a robot can sense its environment, plan based on that environment, and act upon that environment with the intent of reaching some task-specific goal (either given to or created by the robot) without external control." Sensing, planning, and acting have been considered as the important aspects of function allocation between a robot and a human in this framework.

To reduce risks for an autonomous flight management system, NASA engineers worked on developing a prototype to prove the utility of autonomy concepts [38]. They suggested instead of looking for complete autonomy from human intervention, the focus should be on determining how autonomous each function within the system should be. They developed a method for determining the appropriate level of autonomy for each function within a system [38]. Using the four-stage model of human information processing theory, they classified functions into: information acquisition, information analysis, decision and action selection, and action implementation. According to this model, a particular system can involve different levels of automations across the four classes of function at the same time.

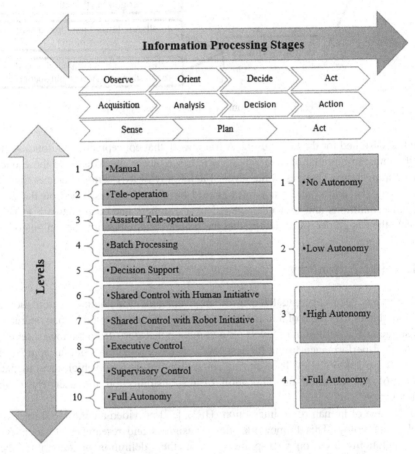

Fig. 2. A summary of existing frameworks on the level of autonomy.

Most existing frameworks use the stages from information processing theory as a measurable concept to assess functions within human automation interaction [35, 38] which raises a few questions: what if the underlying mechanisms for processing automation related information is different from non-automated information? Is there any other mechanisms above the information processing stages for analyzing automation related information?

Another aspect in the level of autonomy frameworks is a continuum from fully manual to fully automated. For example, there are 10 levels in LORA by [37], 8 levels in the level of autonomy assessment scale by [38], and 4 levels in adjustable autonomy in intelligent environment by [34]. Figure 2 summarizes some of the existing frameworks. Since any changes in the level of autonomy requires the user to adopt new demands, these continuums are efforts to understand user reactions to autonomy and facilitate the interaction between the user and the systems.

As previously mentioned, there are a lot of common perspectives in the existing frameworks on the level of automation. However, most of them do not explain causal relationships between variables and outcomes [37]. To understand the ability of the frameworks on predicting the outcomes, experimental evidences as evaluative criteria need to be provided, specifically in the domain of home automation in order to alleviate concerns of safety, security, and user trust.

5 Discussion

Homes play a key role in the health and lifestyle of older adults. It has been estimated that older people spend 80 to 90% of their time in their homes [19], and one out of five adults aged 65 to 74 and two out of five adults aged 85 and older live alone [9]. While living alone and aging in place might be a challenge for older adults, home-based technologies and automation have been the focus of research to identify needs and enhance their safety and security.

Researchers have been using technology adoption models to uncover factors that influence technology acceptance and usage. However, little is known about users' acceptance and performance in interaction with automated systems in homes. For example, although home-based technologies are being automated to eliminate burden and help older adults accomplish the tasks faster and easier, some of the older adults avoid depending on automated systems for the fear of skill degradation in the long term [35].

Having a framework in the area of automated home technologies and level of autonomy can help researchers to understand users' roles and predicting their performance. In this paper, we reviewed some of the existing taxonomies and frameworks on the level of autonomy. Most of the frameworks have used the information processing stages as one aspect of to show who, system or human, is responsible at each of the different functional stages. In addition, a continuum of fully manual to fully automate was another aspect in defining the level of autonomy. Although the origin of many of these perspectives are similar, there are differences in their taxonomies and definitions. To build a framework that researchers and stakeholders agree on, further research is required to understand the role of autonomy within smart home technologies and models for predicting human and system performance to support design.

References

1. Wang, H., et al.: Global, regional, and national life expectancy, all-cause mortality, and cause-specific mortality for 249 causes of death, 1980–2015: a systematic analysis for the global burden of disease study 2015. Lancet **388**(10053), 1459–1544 (2016)
2. Kontis, V., Bennett, J.E., Mathers, C.D., Li, G., Foreman, K., Ezzati, M.: Future life expectancy in 35 industrialised countries: projections with a Bayesian model ensemble. Lancet **389**(10076), 1323–1335 (2017)
3. Chetty, R., et al.: The association between income and life expectancy in the United States, 2001–2014. JAMA **315**(16), 1750–1766 (2016)
4. Foreman, K.J., et al.: Forecasting life expectancy, years of life lost, and all-cause and cause-specific mortality for 250 causes of death: reference and alternative scenarios for 2016–40 for 195 countries and territories. Lancet **392**(10159), 2052–2090 (2018)
5. United Nations Department of Economic & Social Affairs. 2017 Annual Report on World Population Ageing (2017)
6. Marek, K.D., Rantz, M.J.: Aging in place: a new model for long-term care. Nurs. Admin. Q. **24**(3), 1–11 (2000)
7. Stones, D., Gullifer, J.: 'At home it's just so much easier to be yourself': older adults' perceptions of ageing in place. Ageing Soc. **36**(3), 449–481 (2016)
8. Iecovich, E.: Aging in place: from theory to practice. Anthropol. Notebooks **20**(1), 21–33 (2014)
9. Roberts, A., Ogunwole, S., Blakeslee, L., Rabe, M.: The Population 65 Years and Older in the United States: 2016. American Community Survey Report (2018)
10. Blaschke, C.M., Freddolino, P.P., Mullen, E.E.: Ageing and technology: a review of the research literature. Br. J. Soc. Work **39**(4), 641–656 (2009)
11. He, W., Larson, L.J.: Older Americans With a Disability: 2008–2012. American 39 Community Survey Reports, ACS-29. U.S. Census Bureau (2014)
12. Hung, W.W., Ross, J.S., Boockvar, K.S., Siu, A.L.: Recent trends in chronic disease, impairment and disability among older adults in the United States. BMC Geriatr. **11**(1), 47 (2011)
13. Salkeld, G., et al.: Quality of life related to fear of falling and hip fracture in older women: a time trade off study commentary: older people's perspectives on life after hip fractures. BMJ **320**(7231), 341–346 (2000)
14. Liu, L., Stroulia, E., Nikolaidis, I., Miguel-Cruz, A., Rincon, A.R.: Smart homes and home health monitoring technologies for older adults: a systematic review. Int. J. Med. Inform. **91**, 44–59 (2016)
15. Pearce, A.J., et al.: Robotics to enable older adults to remain living at home. J. Aging Res. **2012**, 10 (2012)
16. Portugal, D., Alvito, P., Christodoulou, E., Samaras, G., Dias, J.: A study on the deployment of a service robot in an elderly care center. Int. J. Soc. Robot. **11**, 1–25 (2018)
17. Rashidi, P., Mihailidis, A.: A survey on ambient-assisted living tools for older adults. IEEE J. Biomed. Health Inform. **17**(3), 579–590 (2013)
18. Smarr, C.A., Fausset, C.B., Rogers, W.A.: Understanding the potential for robot assistance for older adults in the home environment. Georgia Institute of Technology (2011)
19. Matlabi, H., Parker, S.G., McKee, K.: The contribution of home-based technology to older people's quality of life in extra care housing. BMC Geriatr. **11**(1), 68 (2011)
20. Deschamps-Sonsino, A.: Smarter Homes: How Technology Will Change Your Home Life. Apress, New York (2018)

21. Demiris, G., Hensel, B.K.: Technologies for an aging society: a systematic review of "smart home" applications. Yearb. Med. Inform. **17**(01), 33–40 (2008)
22. Courtney, K.L., Demeris, G., Rantz, M., Skubic, M.: Needing smart home technologies: the perspectives of older adults in continuing care retirement communities (2008)
23. GhaffarianHoseini, A., Dahlan, N.D., Berardi, U., GhaffarianHoseini, A., Makaremi, N.: The essence of future smart houses: from embedding ICT to adapting to sustainability principles. Renew. Sustain. Energy Rev. **24**, 593–607 (2013)
24. Anderson, G.O.: Getting Connected: Older Americans Embrace Technology to Enhance Their Live. American Association of Retired Persons, Washington, DC (2018)
25. Niemelä-Nyrhinen, J.: Baby boom consumers and technology: shooting down stereotypes. J. Consum. Mark. **24**(5), 305–312 (2007)
26. Rogers, W.A., Fisk, A.D.: Toward a psychological science of advanced technology design for older adults. J. Gerontol. Psychol. Sci. **65B**(6), 645–653 (2010). https://doi.org/10.1093/geronb/gbq065. Accessed 10 Sept 2010
27. Anderson, M., Perrin, A.: Technology Use Among Seniors. Pew Research Center for Internet & Technology, Washington, DC (2017)
28. Peek, S.T., Wouters, E.J., van Hoof, J., Luijkx, K.G., Boeije, H.R., Vrijhoef, H.J.: Factors influencing acceptance of technology for aging in place: a systematic review. Int. J. Med. Inform. **83**(4), 235–248 (2014)
29. Lee, C., Coughlin, J.F.: PERSPECTIVE: older adults' adoption of technology: an integrated approach to identifying determinants and barriers. J. Prod. Innov. Manage **32**(5), 747–759 (2015)
30. Portet, F., Vacher, M., Golanski, C., Roux, C., Meillon, B.: Design and evaluation of a smart home voice interface for the elderly: acceptability and objection aspects. Pers. Ubiquit. Comput. **17**(1), 127–144 (2013)
31. Madakam, S., Ramaswamy, R.: Smart homes (conceptual views). In: 2014 2nd International Symposium on Computational and Business Intelligence (ISCBI), pp. 63–66. IEEE, December 2014
32. Worden, K., Bullough, W.A., Haywood, J.: Smart Technologies. World Scientific, Singapore (2003)
33. Pilich, B.: Engineering Smart Houses, Lyngby, Informatics and Mathematical Modelling. Technical University of Denmark (2004)
34. Ball, M., Callaghan, V.: Explorations of autonomy: an investigation of adjustable autonomy in intelligent environments. In: 2012 8th International Conference on Intelligent Environments (IE), pp. 114–121. IEEE, June 2012
35. Parasuraman, R., Sheridan, T.B., Wickens, C.D.: A model for types and levels of human interaction with automation. IEEE Trans. Syst. Man Cybern. Part A Syst. Hum. **30**(3), 286–297 (2000)
36. Yang, G.Z., et al.: Medical robotics—regulatory, ethical, and legal considerations for increasing levels of autonomy. Sci. Robot. **2**(4), 8638 (2017)
37. Beer, J.M., Fisk, A.D., Rogers, W.A.: Toward a framework for levels of robot autonomy in human-robot interaction. J. Hum.-Robot Interact. **3**(2), 74–99 (2014)
38. Proud, R.W., Hart, J.J., Mrozinski, R.B.: Methods for determining the level of autonomy to design into a human spaceflight vehicle: a function specific approach. National Aeronautics and Space Administration, Lyndon B Johnson Space Center, Houston TX (2003)

Visualizing Organizational Culture in Old People's Homes and Hospitals in Japan: Human Interaction in the IoT Era

Koji Hara[1,2], Takayo Nakabe[1], Toshiya Naka[2,3], Masayuki Tanaka[1], and Yuichi Imanaka[1(✉)]

[1] Department of Healthcare Economics and Quality Management, Graduate School of Medicine, Kyoto University, Kyoto, Japan
{hara-k, tanaka-msyk, imanaka-y}@umin.net,
nakabe.takayo.74v@st.kyoto-u.ac.jp
[2] Advanced Research Department, Panasonic, Kyoto University, Kyoto, Japan
naka.tosiya@jp.panasonic.com
[3] Panasonic Corporation, Osaka, Japan

Abstract. In Japan, which has the highest aging rate in the world, demand for long-term care (LTC) is rapidly increasing. However, the labor force is decreasing nationwide, and in particular the shortage of staff for LTC services is a serious problem. Japanese government aims to reduce the burden on staff at old people's homes and improve the quality of LTC services by introducing ICT/IoT. The organizational culture in old people's homes is the basis of the quality of LTC services; hence, we aimed to visualize it. For the purposes of this research, organizational culture is divided into the following eight domains: "teamwork," "information sharing," "morale," "professional growth," "common values," "resource allocation prioritization," "responsibility and authority," and "improvement orientation." A questionnaire survey on organizational culture was administered to 366 staffs in 23 old people's homes and 4053 staffs in 4 hospitals. The response rates were 71.9% and 82.0%, respectively. The results revealed that old people's homes have higher scores compared to hospitals on teamwork, information sharing, and organizational values, and that old people's homes have problems in securing and fostering middle managers. It was suggested that effectively introducing ICT/IoT could enhance the organizational culture and increase the job satisfaction.

Keywords: Old people's home · Long-term care · Hospitals · Organizational culture

1 Introduction

Japan currently has the highest proportion of people aged 65 years or older in the world, and has become one of the first "super-aged" societies. Following the increase in demand for long-term care (LTC) services, the number of old people's homes has greatly increased in Japan [1]. On the other hand, the number of staffs engaged in LTC services is not sufficient. According to the Ministry of Economy, Trade and Industry in

© Springer Nature Switzerland AG 2019
J. Zhou and G. Salvendy (Eds.): HCII 2019, LNCS 11593, pp. 314–325, 2019.
https://doi.org/10.1007/978-3-030-22015-0_25

Japan, with the increase in the demand of LTC services due to the aging of the population, there will be a shortage of 790,000 care workers [2]. Due to the declining birthrate, human resources are lacking in all industries, particularly in the service industry. However, it is said that physical and mental burden and low salaries are responsible for human resource shortage in old people's homes [3].

Under these circumstances, Japanese government is actively promoting the introduction of ICT/IoT/robots in LTC services to resolve the problem of staff shortage. These measures are not intended to merely reduce the physical burden of staff. Rather, by introducing ICT/IoT/robots, it is expected that the quality of LTC services can be improved by increasing the duration of contact with the user, and it will facilitate quick detection of the change in the user's state. If these initiatives can help improve the satisfaction level of staff, it may contribute to securing staff.

The organizational culture of the staff can be considered as the basis of the quality of LTC services. Organizational culture is defined as the pattern of shared basic assumptions, invented, discovered, or developed by a given group, as it learns to cope with its external and internal problems [4]. In particular, in medical care and LTC services, human-human interaction is very frequent. Previous studies have shown that the organizational culture of hospital staff is related to the quality of medical care provided at a given hospital [5]. It is assumed that a similar relationship is found in LTC services. However, organizational culture in LTC services has hardly been investigated and elucidated so far. Kobuse et al. (2014) developed the questionnaire for organizational culture in hospitals and confirmed statistical validity [6]. Based on the questionnaire, we developed a revised questionnaire for LTC services, and its statistical reliability and validity was confirmed [7].

As shown in Fig. 1, organizational culture is related to the interaction between staff, the interaction between staff and users, and the interaction between staff and system (including ICT/IoT). Thus, through the visualization of organizational culture, it is also possible to verify the effect of introducing ICT/IoT. Therefore, we aimed to visualize the organizational culture in LTC services, which is the basis of the quality of LTC services, and describe its characteristics. To clarify the characteristics of organizational culture in old people's homes, we compared it with that of hospitals. In the future, these findings can become the basis for verifying the impact of introducing IoT/ICT on organizational culture.

In this study, we compared the organizational culture in hospitals and old people's homes, and across professions and management/non-management positions in old people's homes. In addition, we investigated factors related to job satisfaction. Finally, we will provide examples of initiatives that utilize ICT and IoT at old people's homes.

2   Methods

2.1   Organizational Culture

As shown in Table 1, organizational culture is composed of the following eight domains: "collaboration," "information sharing," "professional growth," "morale," "common values," "resource allocation prioritization," "responsibility and authority,"

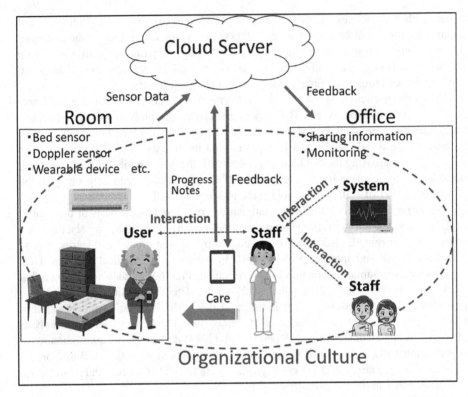

Fig. 1. The concept of organizational culture and user, staff, system in old people's home

and "improvement orientation." In addition to organizational culture, domains related to work/workplace environments such as "job satisfaction" and "workload and burden" are also measured. There are 2 to 7 questions for each domain, and the total number of questions is 58. We used the established scoring method where a higher score is better.

2.2   Questionnaire Survey and Statistical Analysis

We administered the questionnaire survey to 366 staffs in 23 old people's homes of 3 corporations. In addition, 4,053 hospital staffs in 4 hospitals were surveyed as comparison subjects. These included doctors, nurses, allied health personnel, administrative staff, and others. These surveys in both LTC and hospitals settings were conducted from October 2017 to August 2018. The participants were informed that there was no obligation to participate in the study, but that submitting a questionnaire would imply consent to participation. The answered questionnaires were sealed and collected by the researchers. Confidentiality and anonymity were protected during the entire study procedure. This study was approved by the Ethics Committee, Kyoto University Graduate School and Faculty of Medicine.

For the comparison, t test and one-way analysis of variance were used. To clarify factors related to job satisfaction, we performed multiple regression analysis. Our

Table 1. Domains and items of organizational culture

Domains	Example of items
Teamwork	• Free discussion and reporting of problems at workplace • Mutual help to prevent errors
Information sharing	• Prompt distribution of information to relevant units • Appropriate sharing of information to prevent errors
Morale	• Active commitment to care at the individual level • High level of commitment to care by colleagues • Enthusiastic commitment to improvement of care at the organization level
Professional growth	• Professional skill-building opportunities • Professional inspiration from peers • Sufficient opportunity for training and development
Common Value	• Concrete goals set at workplace • Good understanding of organizational policy • Non-punitive and system-focused approaches
Resource allocation prioritization	• Sufficient number and quality of staff • Sufficient time for delivering quality care and services • Sufficient facilities, equipment, and safety devices
Responsibility and authority	• Clearly defined chain of command • Adequate authorization to fulfill responsibilities
Improvement orientation	• Promotion of safety practices, thoroughness in implementation and follow up of improvement measures • Collection of information within the facility as well as outside

model used job satisfaction as the objective variable. Explanatory variables included the eight domain scores, as well as the respondents' profession, position, and dummy variable of each corporation. Analyses were performed using R 3.5.1.

2.3   Interview

Among old people's homes cooperated in our questionnaire survey, we conducted an interview with the administrator of an advanced old people's home (Home A) that had effectively adopted ICT/IoT. We asked what aspects of ICT/IoT were introduced, what impact they had on the work of staff. In addition, the organizational culture survey was also conducted at that home (its data are included in the above analysis).

3   Results

Of the 366 staffs surveyed in old people's home, 263 responded (overall response rate: 71.9%). Of the 4053 staffs surveyed in hospitals, 3323 responded (overall response rate: 82.0%).

As shown in Fig. 2, when comparing the results for the hospitals and the old people's homes, it was found that the old people's homes had a significantly higher score in "team work," "information sharing," and "organization values" (p < 0.05). On the other hand, "growth as a professional" and "improvement orientation" were higher in the hospitals, but the difference was not significant. With regard to work/workplace environment, the old people's homes had higher "job satisfaction" than the hospitals (p < 0.05) (Table 2).

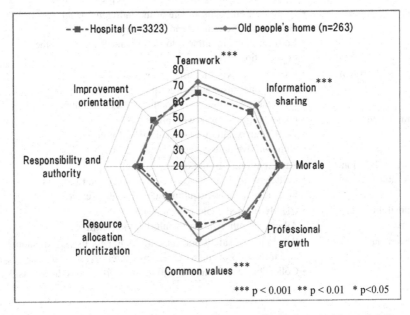

Fig. 2. Comparison of organizational culture scores of hospitals and old people's homes

In addition, when comparing staffs across positions in old people's homes, executives had a high overall score compared to other positions (see Fig. 3). Note that the scores of the middle managers were lower than those of the non-managers in all domains except "responsibility and authority." In the case of hospitals, the score of middle managers was higher than that of non-managers. There may be a problem in the middle management positions in old people's homes.

Multiple regression analysis showed that "Teamwork," "Professional growth," "resource allocation prioritization," "responsibility and authority," middle manager, and non-manager were significantly associated with job satisfaction.

We conducted interviews at Home A, an old people's home actively using ICT/IoT. The characteristic of this home is the three monitors in the office (see Fig. 4). The monitor on the left shows activity status and sleeping state of each resident sent from the air conditioner equipped with monitoring system. This system reduces the number of staff visits to the residents' rooms, which leads to the reduction of burden on staff. The right side of it is the picture of the surveillance camera installed in the corridor, cafeteria, and building surroundings. It is possible for the camera to capture falls, wandering residents, and other troubles among residents. By looking at these two

Table 2. Associations of job satisfaction with organizational culture domains

	B	SE	β		VIF
Organizational culture domains					
Teamwork	0.12	0.05	0.13	*	2.39
Information sharing	−0.06	0.05	−0.07		2.68
Morale	0.06	0.06	0.07		2.83
Professional growth	0.12	0.05	0.17	*	2.67
Common values	−0.01	0.06	0.00		2.18
Resource allocation prioritization	0.19	0.04	0.25	***	2.08
Responsibility and authority	0.23	0.04	0.31	***	2.24
Improvement orientation	0.02	0.05	0.03		2.86
Corporations (ref: Corp. A)					
Corp. B	0.05	0.08	0.03		1.05
Corp. C	0.22	0.08	0.07		1.20
Positions (ref: Executive)					
Middle manger	−0.47	0.15	−0.17	**	1.74
Non-manager	−0.24	0.11	−0.16	*	3.19
Part-time worker	−0.01	0.11	−0.01		3.48
Explanatory power					
Adjusted R-squared	0.57				

*Significant at α = 0.05 level, **Significant at α = 0.01 level, ***Significant at α = 0.001 level.
β, standardized coefficient; B, unstandardized coefficient; ref, referent category;
SE, standard error; VIF, variance inflation factor.

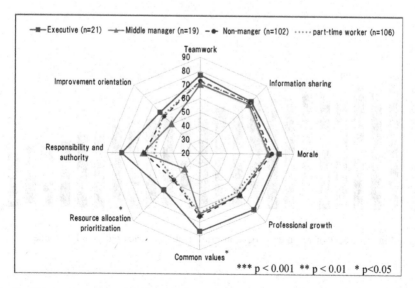

Fig. 3. Comparison of organizational culture scores across positions in old people's homes

monitors, the staff instantaneously grasps the situation of the residents and prioritize their tasks. The monitor in the middle has a different function; it is interlocked with a car navigation system of a shuttle car, and provides business support by using AI in pickup scheduling, route guidance, safe driving, etc. This system can reduce business hours.

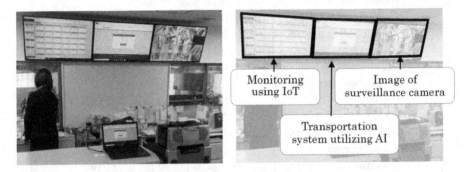

Fig. 4. Photo showing the use of ICT/IoT in the office of Home A

In fact, home A had higher scores in "resources" and "responsibility and authority" than in other homes (see Figs. 5 and 6). In addition, "employee satisfaction level," "workload and burden," "work improvement," "facility effort" also gave higher scores than other homes.

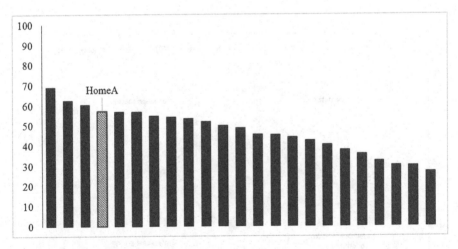

Fig. 5. Score of resource allocation prioritization at each old people's home

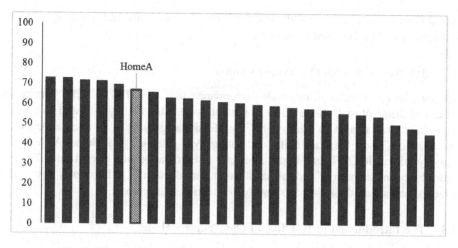

Fig. 6. Score of responsibility and authority at each old people's home

4 Discussion

4.1 Characteristics of Organizational Culture in Old People's Home

Old people's homes had higher scores than hospitals in "team work," "information sharing," "common values." This difference may be due to the fact that old people's homes are smaller in size than hospitals (number of staffs, number of patients/users, buildings, etc.). In fact, the average number of staffs at the surveyed hospital was 1013.3 people, whereas at the old people's home there were 15.9 people. Some old people's homes that were surveyed have conferences in which all staff members participate. In addition, differences in the length of stay of patients/users may also influence information sharing. The average length of stay in hospitals is about 16.3 days [8], but many users of old people's homes stay in them for several years. In old people's homes, staff frequently share information on users.

On the other hand, in the "professional growth" and "improvement orientation" domains, although not statistically significant, the hospital's score was slightly higher than that of the old people's home. It is important to provide opportunities for education and training to employees in medical care and LTC services as professionals. However, since old people's homes generally have limited financial capability and a small number of staffs, many homes are unable to provide such opportunities. In order to raise the quality of nursing staff, Japanese government offers common national training and national qualifications, and is supporting the improvement of their career path [9]. Some homes utilize educational opportunities through e-learning. In addition, it is reported that when staffs for care provided an educational program using printed educational materials on dementia, the stress of staffs reduced [10].

Comparing the organizational culture scores for different positions in old people's homes, the scores for middle managers tended to be generally lower than non-managers. When interviewing the executives of the surveyed old people's home, the staff tended not to want to become managers, which was seen as an increase in burden and difficulties in managing staff. For LTC services, securing and fostering middle managers can be mentioned as an issue.

4.2 Job Satisfaction in Old People's Home

Job satisfaction is an important Key Performance Indicator (KPI) in LTC services, where securing of staff is the most important issue. Our findings showed that job satisfaction was related to "teamwork," "professional growth," "resource allocation prioritization," and "responsibility and authority." Interestingly, Home A, which actively utilizes ICT/IoT, had high scores on "resource allocation prioritization," "responsibility and authority," and job satisfaction. Introduction of ICT/IoT may have the effect of enhancing these domains and help retention management.

4.3 The Introduction of ICT/IoT in Old People's Home

There are several reasons why the introduction of ICT/IoT does not progress in old people's homes. In LTC services industry, handwritten documents are used in most workplaces, and many nursing staffs are accustomed to writing in Japan as well as US [11]. Therefore, it is necessary to change workplace practices and educate and skill staff for the introduction of ICT/IoT. Further, as many staffs in LTC services are relatively older compared to those in other industries [12], their IT literacy is insufficient, which is a challenge while introducing ICT/IoT. In addition, it is difficult to introduce new technologies in old people's homes because they have limited funds and human resources. Finally, there are few easy-to-use products and services. For example, products that take time to set up or cause discomfort to users cannot be used in old people's homes, even when they can lower the physical burden of staff. In the future, further collaboration between staff in LTC services and engineers is desirable. We will continue research to support the development of products/services that can resolve these problems.

4.4 Limitations

There are several limitations in the study. First, the number of survey participants at the facility utilizing IoT was small, and the effect of IoT could not be verified sufficiently. In the future, we will increase the number of participants. Second, we could not administer a questionnaire survey to users. Improvement of user satisfaction and quality of life is an important outcome in nursing care services, and its relation to IoT introduction is also very interesting. We are currently working on questionnaires for users.

5 Future Work

Through our research, we have clarified the characteristics of organizational culture in old people's homes. In the future, we will verify the effect before and after introducing IoT concretely through organizational culture survey and user survey.

We have started building monitoring services using IoT in collaboration with Panasonic, with the aim of "reducing the burden on old people's homes and improving the QoL of users."

The overall structure of this system is as follows (see Fig. 7).

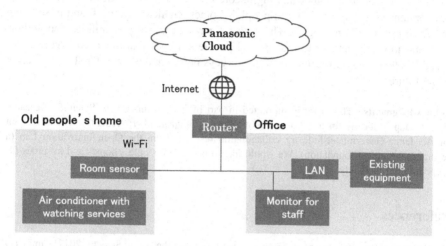

Fig. 7. System diagram of watching security system

System configuration

- High sensitivity room sensor (Doppler sensor, Pressure sensor, etc.):
  - Detects incidents such as heat stroke and dehydration symptoms in users, monitors safety at night
- IP-Camera system:
  - Extensively captures the activities and condition of the residents in old people's homes.
- Tablet terminal · Mobile phone
  - Automatic record of staff behavior, such as the behavior of a caregiver. Reflect on progress notes, etc.
- Cloud server
  - Aggregate the big data of user's activities and visualize them
    Health rehabilitation. Creation of LTC services program
- AI prediction technology
  - Forecasting and prediction with AI-based data analysis using all the aspects/elements of health and LTC services data.

In the future, we will evaluate and visualize the quality of LTC services before and after introduction of the IoT watching service, using the organizational culture and user satisfaction survey. Moreover, we would like to analyze the causal relation between comparisons and differences among homes.

6 Conclusion

Through the visualization of the organizational culture, which is the basis of the quality of LTC services, we clarified the characteristics of old people's home. Compared to hospitals, old people's homes had high score on "team work," "information sharing," and "organizational values." In old people's homes, challenges were found in securing and fostering middle managers. The scores for resources, responsibilities and authorities, and job satisfaction are high in old people's homes that have effectively introduced ICT/IoT. We will further conduct surveys before and after ICT/IoT introduction in the future.

Acknowledgments. This work is supported in part by a Grant-in-Aid for Scientific Research from the Japan Society for the Promotion of Science (Grant number: A16H02634) and a Grant for Academia-Government-Industry collaboration research from the Open Innovation Lab (a general incorporated foundation). We would like to thank old people's homes and hospitals for cooperating in the study.

References

1. Cabinet office, Government of Japan, Annual Report on the Aging Society: 2017 (summary) (2017)
2. Ministry of Economy, Trade, and Industry, the Report by the Study Group on the Provision of Nursing Care Services in Response to Future Nursing Care Demand (2016). (in Japanese)
3. Ministry of Health, Labour and Welfare: Securing care workers (2014). (in Japanese) https://www.mhlw.go.jp/file/05-Shingikai-12201000-Shakaiengokyokushougaihokenfukushibu-Kikakuka/0000047617.pdf
4. Schein, E.: Organizational Culture and Leadership. Jossey-Bass, San Francisco (1985)
5. Ukawa, N., Tanaka, M., Morishima, T., Imanaka, Y.: Organizational culture affecting quality of care: guideline adherence in perioperative antibiotic use. Int. J. Qual. Health Care **27**, 37–45 (2015)
6. Kobuse, H., et al.: Visualizing variations in organizational safety culture across an inter-hospital multifaceted workforce. J. Eval. Clin. Pract. **20**, 273–280 (2014)
7. Hara, K., Nakabe, T., Imanaka, Y.: Visualized organizational culture by type of old people's home/occupation type and consideration factors related to desire to continue working. In: The 56th Conference of the Japan Society for Healthcare Administration, The Japan Society for Healthcare Administration, Fukushima (2018)
8. OECD: Health at a Glance 2017 - OECD Indicators. OECD Publishing, Paris (2017)
9. Ministry of Health, Labour and Welfare: Comprehensive and systematic promotion of securing care workers (2015). (in Japanese) https://www.mhlw.go.jp/file/05-Shingikai-12201000-Shakaiengokyokushougaihokenfukushibu-Kikakuka/document2-1.pdf
10. Fukuda, K., et al.: Effectiveness of educational program using printed educational material on care burden distress among staff of residential aged care facilities without medical specialists and/or registered nurses: cluster quasi-randomization study. Geriatr. Gerontol. Int. **18**, 487–494 (2018)

11. Bjarnadottir, R.I., Herzig, C.T.A., Travers, J.L., Castle, N.G., Stone, P.W.: Implementation of electronic health records in US nursing homes. Comput. Inform. Nurs. **35**, 417–424 (2017)
12. Ministry of Health, Labour and Welfare: The current state of LTC service labor (2017). (in Japanese) https://www.mhlw.go.jp/file/05-Shingikai-12602000-Seisakutoukatsukan-Sanjikan shitsu_Roudouseisakutantou/0000071241.pdf

A Fingerprinting Trilateration Method FTM for Indoor Positioning and Its Performance

Makio Ishihara[✉] and Ryo Kawashima

Fukuoka Institute of Technology, 3-30-1 Wajiro-higashi, Higashi-ku,
Fukuoka 811-0295, Japan
m-ishihara@fit.ac.jp
http://www.fit.ac.jp/~m-ishihara/Lab/

Abstract. This manuscript discusses a new indoor positioning method called a fingerprinting trilateration method or FTM using BLE beacons. The strength of BLE signals, referred to as received signal strength indicators or RSSI, decrease as they travel through space. FTM employs a list of fingerprints of RSSIs and performs trilateration between the three closest fingerprints to locate a receiver's current position. An experiment in positioning performance is conducted in comparison with a traditional method of fingerprinting and the result shows that FTM could locate the current position with a positioning error of 0.615 m while it is 1.162 m for fingerprinting using a Between-points condition.

Keywords: Trilateration · Centroid · Fingerprinting · Indoor positioning

1 Introduction

Nowadays the population of elderly people in Japan is increasing and the percentage of those who live alone at home is arising as well. Figure 1 shows the increase in population of elderly people aged 65 or older in Japan and it is believed to reach 35 million in 2020. Figure 2 shows the number of households where elderly people live alone in Japan and it will reach 7,000 in 2020. In this circumstance, one of the ongoing and urgent problems is that no one is aware if their lives ever are in danger. Figure 3 shows the number of cases in which elderly people have died alone and it has been increasing constantly over the past 16 years. To keep elderly people safe while preventing their privacy from being invaded, an indirect and ambiguous way to protect them would be preferred. For example, a way of using cameras to visually capture them and recognize their activity accurately would obviously not be preferred. On the other hand, a way of using sounds like footsteps to ambiguously recognize their activity and learn they are not in danger would definitely be more preferred. This manuscript discusses an indirect way of locating elderly people in a room to make sure they are not in danger, utilizing a technique of fingerprinting.

© Springer Nature Switzerland AG 2019
J. Zhou and G. Salvendy (Eds.): HCII 2019, LNCS 11593, pp. 326–335, 2019.
https://doi.org/10.1007/978-3-030-22015-0_26

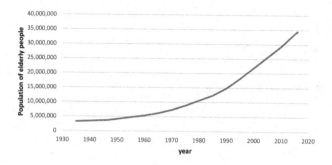

Fig. 1. Population of elderly people aged greater than or equal to 65 years old in Japan.

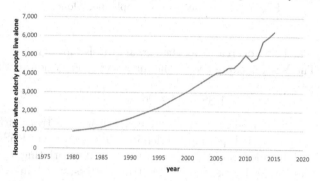

Fig. 2. Households where elderly people live alone in Japan.

Section 2 introduces traditional indoor positioning methods and Sect. 3 describes the related work to differentiate our approach. Section 4 explains our approach of a fingerprinting trilateration method or FTM. Section 5 conducts an experiment in positioning performance of FTM for a traditional method of fingerprinting and Sect. 6 gives a brief report of the results. Section 7 gives the concluding remarks.

2 Traditional Methods

Indoor positioning systems mainly rely on radio signals from multiple transmitters whose positions are already known. Centroid and fingerprinting [7] are common traditional methods.

Centroid is a way of locating a receiver's current position by averaging all the positions of transmitters whose signals can be observed by the receiver. The process of positioning is simple and the accuracy is comparatively high but it is affected easily by interference between multiple signals that bounce off the walls, ceilings and floor, especially in the case that transmitters are placed in a small space.

To deal with this problem, fingerprinting is introduced. It works with the strength of radio signals, called a received signal strength indicator (RSSI).

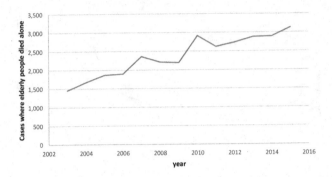

Fig. 3. Cases that elderly people died alone.

Theoretically, an RSSI decreases as the signal travels through space from the transmitter. The RSSI is expressed as the following propagation model of radio signals:

$$\text{RSSI} = A - 20\log(r) \tag{1}$$

where r denotes the physical distance in meter from the transmitter and A denotes RSSI when $r = 1$. Equation (1) denotes that decrease of RSSI indicates a longer physical distance from the transmitter. For fingerprinting, a fingerprint is defined as an array of RSSIs from all the transmitters, which are observed at a given reference point. A fingerprint works as a signature of the reference point and multiple fingerprints are stored in a DB. The receiver's current position is located by calculating Euclidean distance between the measured fingerprint at the current position and the stored fingerprint in the DB. Once the closest fingerprint to the measured one is found, its reference point is returned as the current position.

Based on centroid and fingerprinting, various indoor positioning methods and the related topics have been studied so far. Nakajima et al. [6] proposed a directional fingerprint that consists of multiple child-fingerprints. A child-fingerprint is an array of the RSSIs measured by a receiver facing in a given direction at the same reference point with the parent one. The child-fingerprint can express angular changes of radio waves due to interference between signals, obstructions by people, nearby obstacles, diffraction and other communication signals. Fu et al. [3] proposed a method of updating fingerprints automatically by numerous users because building a bunch of fingerprints is a time-consuming task. In their method, accelerometer and gyroscope built in a smartphone are used to track the user's position and the fingerprint at the position is updated by measuring the RSSIs there. Subhan et al. [9] and Bose et al. [1] investigated a gap between RSSIs and the propagation model RSSI expressed by Equation (1), and proposed a method to absorb the gap. The gap is caused by indoor environments such as interference between signals, obstruction by people, nearby objects and diffraction, especially in the case that the transmitters are placed in a small space. Fan et al. [2] utilized change of the magnetic field as fingerprints. Their method does not rely on infrastructure of the building. Tung et al. [10] employed acoustic signature to locate the current position. A receiver emits a sound actively and records its reflection, and analyzes features of the spectrum. Their method does not rely on infrastructure of the building as well.

3   Related Work

This manuscript discusses a weighted 3-nearest neighbor (W3-NN) fingerprinting method using Bluetooth (Bluetooth low energy or BLE) signals for indoor positioning. A BLE beacon is a one-way transmitter running on 2.4 GHz, which sends signals or messages to nearby receivers such as smartphones and tablets.

A k-nearest neighbor (k-NN) fingerprinting method is an extended version of fingerprinting. It locates a receiver's current position by averaging reference points of the nearest k fingerprints. Furthermore, a weighted k-NN (Wk-NN) fingerprinting method is an extended version of k-NN fingerprinting. It locates the current position by weighting the reference points of the nearest k fingerprints and averaging them. The weight should carefully be designed to reflect the physical distance between the reference point and the current position.

Gao et al. [4] built a system that employs a k-NN fingerprinting for radio signals of Wi-Fi that has commonly been installed throughout a building. Our method relies on BLE because it is a low-cost low-power lightweight transmitter and it is capable of working by solar power. In the long term, it has the advantage of low running-cost as compared to Wi-Fi devices.

Subedi et al. [8] built a hybrid system of a weighted centroid method and a Wk-NN fingerprinting method for radio signals of BLE to reduce the number of transmitters. Here a weighted centroid method (WCM) locates a receiver's current position by weighting positions of the transmitters whose signals can be observed by the receiver and averaging them. A provisional current position is obtained by WCM and its position is used to perform Wk-NN fingerprinting for refining it. Our method is based on only a Wk-NN fingerprinting method by turning the weight carefully to the physical distance between the reference point and the current position.

Previously, the authors [5] proposed an indoor positioning method called a fingerprinting trilateration method or FTM, which is classified into a W3-NN fingerprinting, and conducted a pilot experiment on positioning performance of FTM. The result showed that their method is feasible. The objective of this manuscript is to conduct a further experiment for obtaining more data and report the latest result on positioning performance of FTM in comparison with a traditional indoor positioning method of fingerprinting.

4   Fingerprinting Trilateration Method [5]

An array of m BLE beacons is regularly attached on the ceiling and an array of n reference points are defined. A list of n fingerprints at the reference points is

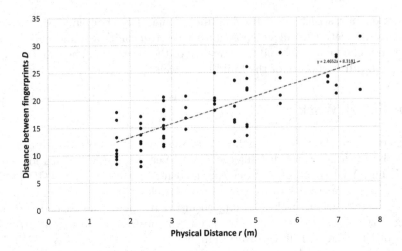

Fig. 4. Relation of distance between fingerprints with physical distance.

obtained. Each fingerprint comes from a different reference point it consists of m RSSIs obtained from all the m BLE beacons.

Locating the current position P_{crt} is performed as the following steps. Here let a symbol f_i be a i-th fingerprint, $RP(f_i)$ be the corresponding reference point, and D_{f_i,f_j} be the distance between fingerprints f_i and f_j.

Step 1. Measure the fingerprint f_{crt} at the current position P_{crt}.
Step 2. Calculate every distance between fingerprints $D_{f_{crt},f_i}, i \in \{1,2,\ldots,n\}$.
Step 3. Find the top three closest fingerprints $f_i, i \in \{top3\}$.
Step 4. Convert the distance $D_{f_{crt},f_i}, i \in \{top3\}$ in physical distance. They are represented as $toPhy(D_{f_{crt},f_i}), i \in \{top3\}$.
Step 5. Determine the current position P_{crt} by performing trilateration among the three physical distances $toPhy(D_{f_{crt},f_i}), i \in \{top3\}$ and the reference points $RP(f_i), i \in \{top3\}$.

The distance between fingerprints D_{f_i,f_j} is defined as Euclidean distance as follows:

$$D_{f_i,f_j} = \sqrt{\sum_a (f_i[a] - f_j[a])^2}, \tag{2}$$

where $f_i[a]$ denotes the RSSI of the fingerprint f_i, which is observed from the a-th BLE beacon. The distance between fingerprints D_{f_i,f_j} is converted into the physical distance r by the following equation which is obtained experimentally in the previous work [5].

$$r = toPhy(D) = \frac{D - 8.32}{2.47} \tag{3}$$

Figure 4 shows a relation of the distance between fingerprints defined in Equation (2) with the physical distance between the corresponding reference points.

Fig. 5. A photo of our laboratory.

Regression Analysis confirms that the relation is significant [$t(65) = 14.969$ at $p < .01$]. The regression line is given in Eq. (3). When the physical distance r increases 1 m, it adds more 2.47 to the distance between fingerprints D.

5 Experiment on Positioning Performance

5.1 Settings and Preparation

Figure 5 shows a photo of our laboratory where an experiment is conducted in comparison with a traditional indoor positioning method of fingerprinting. There are a number of desktop computers and a television, a WiFi router etc. which create interference in radio signals of 2.4 GHz band.

In our experiment setting, a 3 by 4 array of 12 BLE beacons ($m = 12$) is attached on the ceiling of the laboratory whose dimension is 5 m wide by 9 m long as shown in Fig. 6. The grey boxes denote desks and the desktop computers and the dark gray boxes denote the television and the Wi-Fi router. An array of small circles denotes the array of 12 BLE beacons numbered from 1 to 12.

The reference points used in our experiment are placed at positions just under the 12 BLE beacons shown in Fig. 6, resulting in the 12 reference points ($n = 12$), and a list of 12 fingerprints at the corresponding reference points is obtained. While receiving each RSSI to build a fingerprint at each reference point, the receiver is held 1.7 m under the ceiling (1.0 m from the ground) and a temporal sequence of RSSIs for 4 min at 5-s intervals is stored and averaged for the fingerprint. Figure 7 shows all the 12 fingerprints. A value in a fingerprint shows the RSSI observed from the corresponding BLE beacon. For example, the RSSI of −63.52 in the top left corner in the fingerprint 1 comes from the BLE beacon 1 which is placed in the top left corner in Fig. 6.

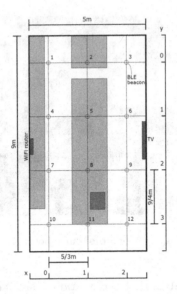

Fig. 6. Floor plan of our laboratory.

5.2 Procedure

An experiment on positioning performance of FTM in comparison with a traditional method of fingerprinting was conducted.

The experiment takes two layouts of evaluation positions into consideration, where indoor positioning methods are performed for evaluation. One is called a condition of Between-points and the other is a condition of On-points. For Between-points condition, evaluation positions are placed between neighboring four reference points. For example, the first evaluation position is in the center between reference points 1, 2, 4 and 5. There are six evaluation positions at all. For On-points condition, they are right under reference points. There are 12 evaluation positions at all. For each of those evaluation positions, fingerprinting and FTM are performed. The receiver is held 1.7 m under the ceiling (1.0 m from the ground) and a temporal fingerprint f_{crt} is obtained and the current position P_{crt} is calculated by the given method for 4 min at 5-s intervals, resulting in 49 pieces of positioning data P_{crt} at every single evaluation position:

$$49 \text{ pieces of positioning data}$$
$$\times \ (6 + 12) \text{ evaluation positions} = 882 \text{ in total} \tag{4}$$

The receiver used in this experiment is Nexus7 for both the preparation and evaluation.

6   Results

Figure 8 shows the positioning result performed by FTM and fingerprinting under Between-points condition and Fig. 9 is for On-points condition. The hori-

1	x		
	0	1	2
y 0	-63.52	-68.67	-81.09
1	-67.02	-66.96	-72.79
2	-66.79	-66.88	-72.90
3	-72.94	-82.76	-74.18

2	x		
	0	1	2
y 0	-63.76	-66.48	-76.70
1	-67.57	-64.75	-67.29
2	-68.80	-71.25	-69.98
3	-72.36	-82.27	-72.25

3	x		
	0	1	2
y 0	-65.47	-64.15	-74.81
1	-71.78	-66.95	-63.67
2	-71.96	-70.49	-71.21
3	-74.36	-84.01	-74.19

4	x		
	0	1	2
y 0	-64.30	-69.46	-82.47
1	-60.32	-66.26	-69.42
2	-65.07	-68.78	-71.61
3	-70.26	-81.23	-74.18

5	x		
	0	1	2
y 0	-64.17	-65.02	-79.04
1	-65.93	-65.64	-68.41
2	-65.42	-60.70	-66.48
3	-72.62	-79.76	-70.74

6	x		
	0	1	2
y 0	-67.98	-71.23	-76.17
1	-71.91	-64.86	-60.37
2	-72.48	-69.64	-65.98
3	-71.16	-80.90	-66.05

7	x		
	0	1	2
y 0	-67.20	-68.04	-83.17
1	-66.08	-66.13	-72.67
2	-65.75	-67.21	-73.84
3	-65.53	-76.57	-67.87

8	x		
	0	1	2
y 0	-65.36	-68.76	-82.61
1	-66.52	-68.02	-72.27
2	-63.19	-64.05	-66.12
3	-66.24	-77.21	-68.49

9	x		
	0	1	2
y 0	-68.59	-69.18	-80.48
1	-71.45	-68.33	-62.89
2	-72.53	-66.20	-63.30
3	-70.88	-79.95	-64.84

10	x		
	0	1	2
y 0	-74.08	-76.59	-90.32
1	-70.36	-72.57	-76.36
2	-67.13	-65.22	-70.83
3	-62.76	-72.84	-70.92

11	x		
	0	1	2
y 0	-74.56	-76.22	-85.04
1	-70.07	-73.75	-75.63
2	-65.89	-67.51	-69.57
3	-65.13	-77.81	-64.82

12	x		
	0	1	2
y 0	-75.52	-74.71	-82.27
1	-73.61	-74.17	-71.60
2	-70.26	-67.14	-65.97
3	-71.88	-76.53	-64.63

Fig. 7. The 12 fingerprints used in our experiment.

zontal and vertical axes correspond to those with the floor plan of Fig. 6. Each arrow represents accuracy of positioning at the corresponding evaluation position. The start point of the arrow denotes each evaluation position and the end does the predicted current position, and the length of the arrow denotes positioning error.

As shown in the positioning result under Between-points condition, FTM has a better positioning performance than fingerprinting. The average of positioning error for FTM is 0.615 in meter and it is 1.162 for fingerprinting, and the standard deviation is 0.375 and 0.305 for FTM and fingerprinting, respectively. Statistically, the unpaired t test confirmed that there is a significant impact over positioning error between FTM and fingerprinting [$t(10) = -2.772$ at $p < .05$].

For the positioning result under On-points condition, FTM has a worse positioning performance than fingerprinting. The average of positioning error for FTM is 1.246 in meter and it is 0.050 for fingerprinting, and the standard deviation is 0.574 and 0.087 for FTM and fingerprinting, respectively. Statistically, the unpaired t test confirmed that there is a significant impact over positioning error between FTM and fingerprinting [$t(12) = 7.128$ at $p < .01$ with Welch's correction]. The positioning error of FTM is 20 times or more worse than finger-

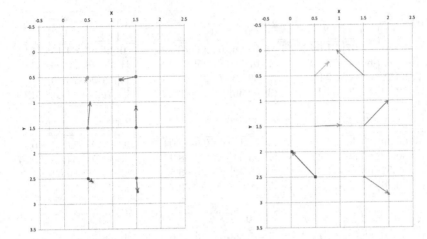

Fig. 8. Positioning performance performed by FTM (Left) and fingerprinting (Right) under Between-points condition.

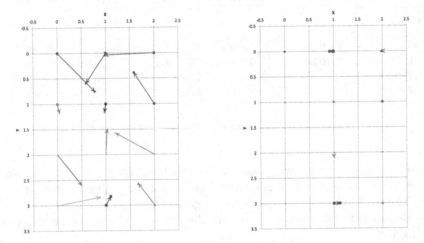

Fig. 9. Positioning performance performed by FTM (Left) and fingerprinting (Right) under On-points condition.

printing. This result could stem from difference of layouts of evaluation positions and lack of fidelity of Eq. (3) for conversion into physical distance from finger-prints distance, especially around physical distance of 0–2.

7   Conclusions

This manuscript proposed an indoor positioning method called a fingerprinting trilateration method or FTM using BLE beacons. FTM employs a list of fin-gerprints of RSSIs and performs trilateration between three closest fingerprints to locate a receiver's current position. The experiment result showed that FTM could locate the current position with positioning error of 0.615 m while it was 1.162 m for fingerprinting under Between-points condition.

References

1. Bose, A., Foh, C.H.: A practical path loss model for indoor WiFi positioning enhancement. In: 6th International Conference on Information, Communications Signal Processing, pp. 1–5, December 2007
2. Fan, X., Wu, J., Long, C., Zhu, Y.: Accurate and low-cost mobile indoor localization with 2-D magnetic fingerprints. In: Proceedings of the First ACM Workshop on Mobile Crowdsensing Systems and Applications, CrowdSenSys 2017, pp. 13–18. ACM, New York (2017). http://doi.acm.org/10.1145/3139243.3139244
3. Fu, N., Zhang, J., Yu, W., Wang, C.: Crowdsourcing-based WiFi fingerprint update for indoor localization. In: Proceedings of the ACM Turing 50th Celebration Conference, TUR-C 2017, China, pp. 34:1–34:9. ACM, New York (2017). http://doi.acm.org/10.1145/3063955.3063989
4. Gao, S., Prasad, S.: Employing spatial analysis in indoor positioning and tracking using Wi-Fi access points. In: Proceedings of the Eighth ACM SIGSPATIAL International Workshop on Indoor Spatial Awareness, ISA 2016, pp. 27–34. ACM, New York (2016). http://doi.acm.org/10.1145/3005422.3005425
5. Ishihara, M., Kawashima, R.: A fingerprinting trilateration method FTM for indoor positioning. In: Proceedings of the 33rd International Technical Conference on Circuits/Systems, Computers and Communications, pp. 422–425 (2018)
6. Nakajima, N., Tang, S., Ogishi, T., Obana, S.: Improving precision of BLE-based indoor positioning by using multiple wearable devices. In: Adjunct Proceedings of the 13th International Conference on Mobile and Ubiquitous Systems: Computing Networking and Services, MOBIQUITOUS 2016, pp. 118–123. ACM, New York (2016). http://doi.acm.org/10.1145/3004010.3004041
7. Shahra, E.Q., Sheltami, T.R., Shakshuki, E.M.: Comparative study of fingerprint and centroid localization protocol using Cooja. Procedia Comput. Sci. **98**, 16–23 (2016). http://www.sciencedirect.com/science/article/pii/S1877050916321275. The 7th International Conference on Emerging Ubiquitous Systems and Pervasive Networks (EUSPN 2016)/The 6th International Conference on Current and Future Trends of Information and Communication Technologies in Healthcare (ICTH-2016)/Affiliated Workshops
8. Subedi, S., Pyun, J.Y.: Practical fingerprinting localization for indoor positioning system by using beacons. J. Sens. 1–16 (2017). https://doi.org/10.1155/2017/9742170
9. Subhan, F., Hasbullah, H., Rozyyev, A., Bakhsh, S.T.: Indoor positioning in Bluetooth networks using fingerprinting and lateration approach. In: International Conference on Information Science and Applications, pp. 1–9, April 2011
10. Tung, Y.C., Shin, K.G.: EchoTag: accurate infrastructure-free indoor location tagging with smartphones. In: Proceedings of the 21st Annual International Conference on Mobile Computing and Networking, MobiCom 2015, pp. 525–536. ACM, New York (2015). http://doi.acm.org/10.1145/2789168.2790102
lastpage

Gifts and Parasites

Paro the Healthcare Robot and the Logics of Care

Joni Jaakola[✉] and Jukka Vuorinen

Department of Social Research, University of Turku, Turku, Finland
{joni.jaakola, jukka.vuorinen}@utu.fi

Abstract. This social theory and philosophy-oriented paper offers a framework to analyze changes in the logics of care, and their connections to robots in healthcare. If care can be historically understood as a gift given to one another and given back in return, in many post-industrial societies care has been separated from the sphere of family to an independent area of care labor, obscuring the idea of reciprocity commonly linked to care-as-gift. Correspondingly, the robots utilized in healthcare defy the idea of reciprocity yet more extremely. In care robotics social relations go only one way, adhering to the logic of the parasite. Starting with a discussion of the theories of care-as-gift, the paper argues that the logic of the parasite has (partially) replaced the logic of gift in the organization of care. Furthermore, the human-computer interaction implied in the design of the social robot Paro are analyzed in more detail, elucidating the logic of the parasite in action.

Keywords: Care · Gift · Logic · Parasite · Social theory

1 Introduction

Care robots are designed to help care workers in their daily tasks, like bathing and lifting, or to replace the care-giver by answering the needs of the care-receiver directly (van Wynsberghe 2013, p. 408). In the recent social scientific discussion, robots have been offered as a solution to many problems occurring in healthcare markets that are struggling to face the needs of ageing societies (see for example Rantanen et al. 2018). This article develops a theoretical and conceptual framework to analyze the changes in the logic of care in postindustrial societies and the implementation of robotics in healthcare. In other words, we argue that the introduction of robots in healthcare also requires a certain way of thinking in regard to healthcare; with the robots comes a particular *logic of care*.

In this paper, we explore the ways in which the logics of care can be analyzed through the theories of giving and taking–the gift and the parasite–and how these logics of gift and parasite are connected to the rationale of care robots. While there are many theories of care and how it is organized in society (see England 2005), we focus on analyzing the ways in which care has been, and could be, conceptualized as a form of gift in informal and formal care through existing theoretical and empirical literature mainly drawn from the fields of sociology, anthropology and philosophy. How does a

© Springer Nature Switzerland AG 2019
J. Zhou and G. Salvendy (Eds.): HCII 2019, LNCS 11593, pp. 336–352, 2019.
https://doi.org/10.1007/978-3-030-22015-0_27

robot mediate care? What kind of giving, taking, and reciprocity is included in the process of caring in terms of robots?

We concentrate on the relation of care-giving and - receiving and ask: How do robotics change the logics of care? Moreover, how can care alter when robots are involved in social care interaction? Our main argument is that the gift–which has been a central concept in explaining care–is in itself insufficient when theorizing the logic of care in familial and professional settings. We further argue that there is a certain kind of logic of care that is connected to the introduction of healthcare robotics. We elaborate this argument further with a brief and illustrative analysis of the care-giving robot Paro and the human-robot interaction it entails. Our aim is to typify and propose concepts to analyze how robots change the social dynamics in care relations. However, we do not claim that all care robots function with the same logics.

It is worth noting that we use the term "logic" in a slightly unconventional manner as we connect logics to ways of thinking. However, in our way of using it we are quite aligned with a number of researchers. In her book *The Logic of Care* (2008), Dutch philosopher Annemarie Mol distinguishes two different and often contradicting ways to deal with diseases: the logic of choice and the logic of care. The logic of choice, most prominently found in different neoliberal healthcare policies, highlights the individual customer's freedom to choose, whereas the logic of care refers to the complex and multiple collective ways of prolonging a patient's life. Like Mol (ibid., p. 9), we utilize the concept of logic not in the conventional and philosophical sense, but more as a discursive tool: "logic" is a certain kind of historically and culturally situated way, *a rationale*, of organizing care in different times and places.

For us, "logic" is a system of thinking and functioning through which care can be assessed and understood. With the concept of logic, it is also possible to ask which are the coherent and appropriate ways of acting when dealing with care practices (ibid., p. 10). In this sense, logic is also fundamentally about ethics and normativity–what care practices are considered as legitimate: "For not only does each logic define its own version of the good, each also has its own take on how to 'do' it." (ibid., p. 85). The difference between us and Mol is that we are not interested in the different logics of tackling diseases; Mol speaks of only one kind of logic of care, but we are keen to inspect the inner logics of care itself. Our aim is not to *explain* the socio-technical change but to describe logics that come with the robots, and importantly provide theoretical tools to be utilized in further research on healthcare and its different logics.

Giving and receiving care is fundamentally a social interaction and an interdependence between people (Fisher and Tronto 1990; Tronto 1993, pp. 105–108, 127, 162). Care is a relation that joins humans (and non-humans) together[1]. Even though the care-giver and - receiver are conceptually separated from one another, this does not

---

[1] The relation-oriented literature on the gift has also been criticized: gift-relations are always formed around material objects–the given–as well as people. These "quasi-objects", in the Serresian sense, collect people together and keep them together (from time to time), and make the intersubjective relationships possible in the first place. (Pyyhtinen 2014). However, in care relations, objects are multiple and ever-changing; care is an open-ended and continuing process, not a transaction but an interaction (Mol 2008, pp. 20–23). This is why we take a more relation-oriented look on the logic of gift and care.

imply that the former is an active and the latter a passive actor. Instead, care is a mutual co-construction, where every participant in the care relation is an active force (Browne 2010). However, the question of power is evident in care. Caring in principle puts the care-receiver into a position of vulnerability; care relations are unequal and asymmetrical–they question the autonomy of individuals (Tronto 1993, p. 103). Even though we take a relation-oriented view of care, care need not be a dyadic relation between two individuals. Care between giver and receiver is the third in the combination (see Latour 2005; Serres 2007); the health issue that is taken care of is the fourth. The setting in which care is given is the fifth. Diagnosis is the sixth. The list is long. In other words, care actualizes through a number of actors including the patient and healthcare giver but also including knowledge.

In sociological and anthropological literature, care has been conceptualized through the theory of the gift and often as an opposite to care-as-discipline (Bolton 2000; Browne 2010; Claassen 2011; Fox 1995; Lewinter 2003; MacBride-Stewart 2014; Russ 2005; Torres et al. 2015). In his famous essay *The Gift* (1990), the French sociologist Marcel Mauss's theoretical outcome is that all of the social networks in the "archaic" cultures he has studied are based on gifts: giving, receiving and returning gifts. These three dimensions of the gift are (moral) obligations (ibid., p. 41). Once received, the gift has to be returned to its sender. In this way the logic of the gift is based on the social expectation of reciprocity: the gift should be returned. If the chain of giving, receiving and returning gifts gets broken, the breaker "loses face" and is a moral outcast in the eyes of the community. As paraphrased by anthropologist Douglas (1990, p. x: "A gift that does nothing to enhance solidarity is a contradiction"; gifts and the relations they gather keep society together.

It can be argued that in familial relations care has been organized mostly around intergenerational ties and duties, the moral obligations of giving and receiving care gifts, and the idea of reciprocity: parents take care of their children, and in return receive care from them when they grow old and frail. Present day care markets are said to be organized at least partly on the logic of the gift as well (see for example Lewinter 2003; MacBride-Stewart 2014; Russ 2005; Torres et al. 2015). However, the gift-oriented approach forgets, simplifies, and blurs the societal changes that have made possible and modified different kinds of logics of care, most importantly the commodification of care and the formation of care markets–this is the setting in which the robots enter. Even though care given inside the family is still an important aspect of organizing care (see for example Wolf 2004, p. 111), it too is subject to societal changes. The theory of the gift does not fully grasp the logic of informal care. Furthermore, socio–technical changes in healthcare, like the introduction of care robots, complicate the logics of care even further. We argue that in terms of reciprocity, care robots can cut down or simplify the part of giving back that is crucial to all care relations.

Thinking in terms of the parasite clarifies the logic of care-giving in human-robot interaction and the disappearance of giving back in care relations. We argue that the concept of the parasite hailing from the theory of French philosopher Serres (2007) captures the contradictions and multiplicities in human-computer care settings. The parasite does not promote reciprocity but opposes it. So, the logic of the parasite is a stark contrast when compared to the logic of the gift; "the parasite is a reverse of the gift" (Pyyhtinen 2014, pp. 11, 94). Certainly, the concept of the parasite has many negative connotations in everyday thinking. However, our aim is not to romanticize the past nor is it to judge the present or the future. Following Serres, we see parasitic relations as an important facet and common feature of all societal (or, in his terms, collective) life: "man is the universal parasite" (Serres 2007, p. 24). Taking and giving, being host and guest (parasite that is), are the basic foundations of a relationship. Through these essential elements, the relation that care brings about can be grasped.

First, we examine care as a gift and the logic this entails, and engage in discussion with Mauss and other scholars of the gift. We also make the distinction between gifts and true gifts. Second, we analyze care as a commodity. Third, we introduce the idea of care as a parasitic relation, and as a reverse of the gift, as a presupposition in the design of care robotics. Through these sections, we show how the logics of gift, commodity and parasite relate to and differ from one another: what kinds of reciprocity, economy or form of exchange, hierarchy and power relations, interaction, and obligations are promoted? Additionally, as the concept of logic also implies the forms of action which are seen as proper and desirable, we discuss the ethical questions raised by care robotics. We end the paper with a conclusion and proposals for future research in the field of healthcare robotics and care labor.

2 Care and the Logic of the Gift

The gift has been a popular concept in the field of social sciences because it actualizes and (re)establishes a social relationship. Importantly, care as a relation has also been conceptualized as a gift. However, the gift is not a simple concept and it is used in different and contradictory ways. Thus, we propose that a distinction between gifts and true gifts needs to be made. In the literature, "gift" and "exchange" are constantly mixed together. Mauss provides the most famous example of this. Although he separates market exchange from the exchange of gifts, he takes the gift as a pre-economic form of exchange: his argument is based on the discourse of "exchangism" (Elder-Vass 2015, pp. 452–453). Current care research re-establishes a similar mix of gift and exchange. Russ (2005, p. 29), when studying hospice practices, uses the term "the economy of 'pure gift'", which is organized around charity, in contrast to an economy, which is characterized "by standards of efficiency and discipline, cost containment, [and] profit making". Following Elder-Vass (2015, p. 455), we want to highlight that care work is one mode of giving that doesn't fit indisputably the "exchangist" model of the gift.

The logic of the true gift is ruled by moral duty and personal emotions: "the world of the gift moves through a continual affirmation of bonds, based on responsibility, trust, and gratitude and premised on a capacity for emotional attachment" (Hochschild 2011, p. 23). Moreover, true gifts are motivated by love, generosity, trust and delight (Fox 1995, p. 108). In more detail, the logic of the true gift is composed of voluntariness, unconditionality, and spontaneity; gifts are not given solely on the basis of exchange (like money) (Pyyhtinen 2014, p. 15). In addition, sacrifice and loss are key components of the true gift as well. "The gift is a sacrifice offered to the other and for the other" (ibid., p. 26) and, Pyyhtinen argues, "sacrifice is a precondition of the gift" (ibid., p. 29). These factors–moral duty and responsibility, personal emotions and attachment, trust, generosity, gratitude, spontaneity, unconditionality, voluntariness, and sacrifice–form the basis of care as a true gift.

Sacrifices are an important facet of true care gifts: parents sacrifice most of their time when taking care of their children, they leave their jobs with the aid of paternity or maternity leaves, for example; "it is only when [...] one gives one's life for the other that the gift may be possible" (Pyyhtinen 2014, p. 151). In the same sense, a family care-giver sacrifices much of his/her time when answering the needs of a frail family member. The voluntariness of gift-giving emphasizes the importance of sacrifices: nothing assures that care gifts given ever get returned. Caring for the other in the logic of a true gift is truly "a leap of faith" in the Kierkegaardian (2009) sense.

Just as Mauss suggests, reciprocity is at the core of the logic of the gift. Even though gifts do not have a price–it would be inappropriate to leave a price tag on a Christmas present–the gift-receiver is obliged to give something in return, a return-gift, a "compensation for their effort and the sacrifices they've made" (Pyyhtinen 2014, pp. 15–16). For our purposes, Mauss's conception of reciprocity as a law and basis for solidarity doesn't quite get to the core of care as a true gift. Additionally, there are different kinds of reciprocity taking place in gift relations. We argue that the reciprocity that true gifts entail differs from the reciprocity of gift exchange in general. Gift relations cannot form solely around the idea of exchange because the logic of the gift and exchange contradict one another. "Giving may be distinguished from market exchange because, unlike market exchange, it is a *voluntary* transfer of goods or services that *does not entail an immediate return of agreed benefits of equivalent value*" (Elder-Vass 2015, pp. 456, emphasis added).

The element of exchange is a crucial part of the logic of the gift, but it is not an important aspect of true gifts: when one *has to* return the gift to its sender, the gift becomes only a form of exchange, and the logic of gift becomes correlative to that of an economic system (Derrida 1992, p. 23; Pyyhtinen 2014). True gifts must remain uneconomic (Derrida 1992, p. 7). Reciprocity as a fundamental rule would make gift-giving only a form of economic exchange; true gifts are given without the expectation of reciprocity (Fox 1995, p. 118). It would be quite hard to form an economy around true gifts, like donating blood and sharing material on the Internet (Elder-Vass 2015), because they do not entice the flow of exchange but stagnate it. Whereas a pre-economy can be formed around exchanging gifts, true gifts do not easily create an economy.

Even though there is always exchange going on in care relations–giving and receiving food, clothing, and shelter, for example–there is an important difference between the moral sense of responsibility and the official contracts of exchange: when one buys groceries, they are obliged to give a monetary compensation for the goods directly and usually in the moment. When the contract is broken, one refuses to pay and instead steals, to put it bluntly, there are juridical and legal consequences. However, care as a true gift on the other hand only implies reciprocity which may never actualize in the future. In fact, a return-gift of care, the compensation for a care received in the past, nulls care as a gift. When returned, the idea of the true gift disappears and is replaced by economic exchange, debt and paying back the loan (Derrida 1992, pp. 7,

24; Pyyhtinen 2014, pp. 21–25). Moral obligations, rather than legal contracts, are the basis of the logic of true gift.

What kind of reciprocity, then, is known in true gift relations? Familial and other personally and emotionally attached care relations are not solely based on contracts, so the gifts received are not usually returned right away but on a later, undecided, and ambiguous date (Browne 2010, p. 582). This kind of reciprocity is best described by the concepts of generalized reciprocity and positional giving.

In generalized reciprocity, relations are formed by "assistance given and [...] assistance returned" (Sahlins 1972, pp. 193–194). Sahlins (ibid., p. 194, emphasis added) elaborates the altruistic dimensions of general reciprocity further.

> The material side of the transaction is repressed by the social: reckoning of debts outstanding cannot be overt and is typically left out of account. This is not to say that handing over things in such form, even to "loved ones," generates no counter-obligation. But [...] *the expectation of reciprocity is indefinite*. It usually works out that the time and worth of reciprocation are not alone conditional on what was given by the donor, but also upon what he will need and when, and likewise what the recipient can afford and when. [...] The requital thus may be very soon, but then again it may be never.

In generalized reciprocity the moral standards of gift-giving and - receiving are highlighted, as opposed to the question of when, if ever, the exchange is made and the transaction complete. In this sense, the logic of the true gift is foggy. It is possible that gifts never get returned; there are no imperative obligations, no real market-based contracts. Sahlins (ibid., p. 194) goes on to say that in generalized reciprocity the flow of gifts does not stop if the receiver fails in giving a return-gift. This makes sense: who would stop caring for an aged parent if s/he fails at recognizing the care-gifts received, if s/he momentarily forgets the name of a loved family member due to a memory loss, for example?

Just as care as a true gift can be seen through generalized reciprocity, it can be grasped with the idea of positional giving as well. In positional giving, giving is based on a normative expectation that people who occupy certain positions, a parent for example, will give gifts to certain other people, let's say children. A return-gift is not expected at once, and here we can concur with Sahlins: instead, if and when found in the same position, one is expected to make similar gifts. (Elder-Vass 2015, pp. 457, 460.) This applies when children compensate the care received in the past to their aged parents, for example. Positional giving also highlights the hierarchical relations in gift giving: the one who gives is empowered, s/he becomes the subject. In contrast s/he who receives must return the favor on an undecided date in the future.

Care as a form of labor cannot be organized solely around the idea of true gifts. Care as a formal profession by no means entails any given and returned *gifts*, in the sense of the true uneconomic gift. Formal care is usually compensated. These care relations are not based on reciprocal true gifts, but on the conceptions of exchange and the rationale of the market: care as a commodity. Furthermore, the logic of care implied by certain care robots like Paro differs from the logic of the gift significantly.

3 Care as a Commodity

How can care–closely connected to reciprocal networks, deep emotions and feelings, familial ties, even blood relations; to obligations which, when bypassed, can make one a moral outcast in community–transform into a commodity that is constantly reproduced, sold and consumed in healthcare markets? According to Browne (2010) care markets are born because gift-based care relations are, in general, insufficient to offer a stable and predictable guarantee of adequate care. This implies that care markets are formed in accordance with a different logic than care-as-gift. We call this rationale the logic of commodification.

According to the sociologist Hochschild (2011) care is mutated into a consumable product through commodification (see also Claassen 2011). In terms of healthcare markets, care-gifts are not merely given and received but as they are given they are compensated in return, ideally through monetary transactions. Correspondingly, the one getting care–the care-receiver–is not expected to give anything in return other than the monetary transaction. This way care becomes a commodity. In present day post-industrial societies, care has partly been withdrawn from the sphere of family and familial relations to a form of care production and an area of care labor.

When people, be it sociologists, politicians or care-receivers and - givers, are urged to "find ways to make room for the spirit of the gift [in a market-oriented world]" (Hochschild 2011, p. 32), it is troublingly forgotten that the gift is not the primary logic for the organization of care in professionalized care labor. In care labor nothing is given as a gift–at least this is not the logic that dominates, or is desired, in healthcare markets. Reciprocity, in the sense of "balanced reciprocity", where one gets a direct and equivalent compensation for the things given (Sahlins 1972, pp. 194–195), and the economic system of exchanges that follow, are the basis for the logic of care-as-commodity to work.

There are many transactions going on in care labor: the exchange of money for food, housing and other basic needs. The law of the gift no longer applies, as care-commodities are produced because there is a market-based demand for them, a demand of balanced reciprocity. In the logic of commodification, care becomes a form of exchange. The exchange is incommensurable: the care received is no longer returned with care-gifts, but primarily with money. "When the language of the market is mobilized, patients are referred to as 'customers'. They buy their care in exchange for money. This implies that patients do not need to feel gratitude for the care they receive, which they might feel obliged to *if care were a gift*" (Mol 2008, p. 16, emphasis added). In addition to the possible lack of gratitude, the care economy renders it possible that family members do not need to feel guilty when passing their care-obligations on to care professionals and organizations, nor does their moral status necessarily decline in the eyes of the community. In addition to moral obligations, like the need to obey ethical rules, care as a commodity is also ruled by clearer contractual and legal obligations than care-as-gift.

In the relations of commodified care work the care-receiver (a resident in a nursing home, for example), or his/her relatives, pays a compensation for the care given, with or without the aid of state provision. There are no other obligations for the care-receiver. Mutually, the care-giver expects monetary compensation for his or her services; it would be intuitively absurd to expect any true return-gift of care in the future (or care received in the past). In fact, it is even common to formally *forbid* the care-receiver to give any sort of return-gifts besides that of money.

The hierarchy and asymmetry in commodified care relations, like those in hospice practices and home care, are strong. There are stable roles that should be executed: the care worker is the constant host, the one who gives, and the care-receiver an everlasting parasite, the one who takes. Nevertheless, these roles are not as immutable as it might seem. The social expectation of reciprocity is present in formal care relations as well. In Danish home care, for example, it is still common to defy the prohibition to return the favor: care-receivers often want to offer a cup of coffee for the services they receive (Lewinter 2003, p. 370). Gifts are given in formal care work as well. As Douglas (1990, p. ix) puts it, when talking about charity: "the recipient does not like the giver".

3.1 Care-Gifts in Care Markets

The gift received should be returned in some way. The gifts given in commodified care labor are not true gifts, but neither are they mere particles of economic exchange. The gifts given in commodified care work are an important tool to enforce the subjectivity of the care-receiver.

When a Danish care-receiver offers the care-giver a cup of coffee, the beverage is not only a hot "cup of joe". The coffee signifies "a sign of welcome and hospitality; it put[s] the care-receiver in the role of *host/hostess* and not just help recipient" (Lewinter 2003, p. 371, emphasis added). The coffee, as a way to reciprocate the services received, is a way of showing hospitality and a means to increase and enforce one's integrity and independence (Gibson 1985; Lewinter 2003, p. 371). It makes one an active participant, a host, rather than just a passive help-recipient a parasite; coffee is a route to empowerment; a way to strengthen the care-receiver's subjectivity and autonomy, to make the distinctively hierarchical care relation more symmetrical. Even though return-gifts like the cups of coffee render possible direct compensation for the care given, and form a brief economy of gifts in the Maussian sense inside the actual care markets, they are more a means of empowerment on the part of the care-recipient. Return-gifts like coffee make it possible to "save face" and restore the status quo of face-to-face interaction.

Correspondingly, it is also possible, if not common, that care-givers are expected to give gifts in commodified care labor. When they work overtime without pay, professional care workers are presumed to give care as a gift (see for example Kröger et al. 2018; Torres et al., 2015; Twigg 2000). In this host–parasite dichotomy the worker only gives and the employer-parasite only takes (the labor input), giving nothing (no payment) in return.

However, it is important to notice that the logic of gift-as-commodity is no longer fully compatible with the ideals of a true gift. While there can be important aspects involved in care labor that resemble the components of the gift, like mutual respect and trust, deep personal attachment and emotions, recognition, and so on, these seem not to be the *necessary* conditions of care for the actual care markets to work. For example, in a Finnish job satisfaction survey, the appreciation professional home care-givers get from their clients or employers seems to be something extra: the feeling of inadequacy is omnipresent due to increasing workloads, and there seems to be no trust between the worker and the employer (Kröger et al. 2018). So, the quality of the care given seems not to be the precondition for getting the job done. This would not be the case, if care were a true gift in professional labor, if the logic of the gift ruled care markets: to give a bad gift would be shameful. This is not to accuse the workers of being incompetent, lazy or anything else; rather, the problem is probably within the care markets and their policies. Additionally, when home care is organized efficiently around tight timetables (Browne 2010, pp. 586–587), there is no time for coffee or any other return-gifts.

The logic of the gift is also insufficient when capturing the logics of care robots. So, we develop the notion of the parasite as a grounding logic embedded in care robots in the next section.

4   Care in Parasitic Relations

In Serres's (2007) work, "parasite" has three different meanings. First, the term parasite can refer to a biological parasite. A biological parasite uses its host and gives nothing back. Secondly, the parasite can refer to a social parasite that takes "hard" things such as food and money but gives back nothing, or "soft" things such as words. Thus, in Serresian terminology a consultant would be a parasite. Thirdly, "parasite" refers to noise–static in a message for example.

For Serres, the concept of "parasite" is all about *relation*–moreover, it is a position in a relation. A parasitic relation is "a one-way arrow": the parasite takes but gives nothing in return (ibid., pp. 24, 27). A host serves a guest. In some relations we all are or have been parasites. For example, an infant is a parasite in Serres's terms. However, every parasite requires a host, which means that there must be a producer to be parasitized. Importantly, parasitizing is always connected to a particular aspect of the relation. This means that a parasite in one particular manner can serve as a host in another manner. For example, a human wearing leather shoes parasitizes an animal but can be a host in terms of social relationships. In other words, there are parasites upon parasites. Sooner or later, the parasite has to give compensation in return to another parasite and thus to work as a host. In "parasitic chains", parasites are parasitized. The roles in a parasitic relation are not necessarily stable. Everyone in the chain can be a host and a parasite in turn. (Ibid., pp. 14, 16, 19.)

What happens when a care robot enters the "parasitic chain"? We argue that the logic of the parasite is an important aspect of the functioning of certain care robots. Care robots are usually divided into three different types: the assisting, the monitoring, and the social (Sharkey and Sharkey 2012). Assisting robots can help in lifting, for example, monitoring robots can keep an eye on one's vital functions and movements like falls, and social robots offer company and responses to one's emotional needs.

We will now investigate robots as "socially functioning" care-givers. First, we take a look at what the introduction of robotics to care relations implies in terms of logic. Second, we examine the human-computer interaction formula embedded in the design of the robot Paro. In the discussion section, we take a closer look at some of the ethical dilemmas of the robotization of care work and the robot-parasite as a noise, the third type of parasite. We will focus mostly on the role of the care-receiver, and how robotics makes possible an increasingly parasite-oriented logic of care in care labor.

4.1   Care Robots, Reciprocity and Emotional Labor

A robot doesn't demand much from the care-receiver, and it makes possible the role of the parasite for the user: s/he only takes and gives nothing in return. In fact, it is quite impossible for the care-receiver to be anything but a parasite in the direct human-robot care-relations. The care-giver robot imposes the position of parasite on the care-receiver; with its impenetrable shield of autonomy and absence of needs, the robot invites the patient to become nothing but a parasite. Certainly, the robot requires maintenance at some point, but this is not done by the care-receiver. So, the logic is different from that of commodified care where the giving of gifts was still a possibility and the dynamics of giving and receiving, hosting and parasitizing, more fluid. We will investigate this with an example mentioned earlier. When a care-receiver gives coffee or other return-gifts to the care-giver, s/he not only compensates the care received but asserts his/her integrity, independence, autonomy, and subjectivity. It can be quite difficult to give return-gifts to the care robot. The robot by giving care prepares and provides an irreversible position of a parasite.

What happens when reciprocity gets annulled in care relations? As mentioned earlier, gifts of coffee are already scarce in present-day care labor; in home care there is usually no time for any return-gifts or - favors. The robot highlights the parasitic logic even further: it renders it impossible to give anything in return for the services received—not in the traditional sense of a cup of coffee at least. Any mechanical gift, an answer to the robot's needs, that the robot would "like" seems odd and unlikely. The robot provides opportunities to be heard, but does not itself require any attention. This raises an important question: why would the care-receiver want to compensate an inanimate technological object? Our target is not to seek an answer to this question, but the increasing impossibility of reciprocity, which has crucial effects on one's subjectivity, independence, empowerment, and integrity, should be addressed more thoroughly in future research. In the meantime, we examine the interconnectedness between care robots and care as "emotional labor."

In her book *The Managed Heart* (1983) Hochschild argues that in service sector jobs there is a need to produce human feelings regardless of the "real" emotions experienced by the subject-worker: "the *emotional style of offering the service is part of the service itself*" (ibid., p. 5, emphasis in original). Flight attendants need to keep a happy smile on their faces when on the job, no matter how angry or frustrated they get because of the customer's actions. This applies to other service jobs, like care labor, as well.

As much as care work is physical labor—it consists of heavy lifting, for example—it is also "emotional labor": there is a need to suppress or induce personal feeling and emotions to produce the desired emotions in the costumer (Hochschild 1983, p. 7), to produce a feeling of integrity in the care-receiver, and so on. If one fails in producing the desired feelings, if the care-receiver gets hatred instead of empathy, one has failed in the job as well. Ideally in service jobs emotions like empathy should be omnipresent, but there are situations when the worker does not feel the "needed" sensation. A patient with Alzheimer's can arouse many contradicting emotions but only the likes of empathy should be expressed. Hochschild's notions on emotional labor and the production of human feelings are highly useful when exploring the logic of the parasite and the introduction of robotics to care labor.

As Hochschild (ibid., p. 23) herself notes ironically: "every day [...] we see human beings whose show of feeling has a robot quality."[2] The commercialization of human feeling makes humans more or less robot-like in some situations in service work. To simplify, it is only logical that these robot-like workers are partly replaceable with real robots. The care robots only need to produce a feeling in the care-receiver that his/her emotions have been replied to in an appropriate manner. A robot does not need to "feel" anything; the fact that the care-receiver gets the support needed and his/her needs answered is enough. In fact, a robot having "real" human-like feelings and emotions can be considered a worst-case scenario that brings to mind the products of science fiction, where the robot, having reached the singularity, wants to avenge the slavery it has gone through.

One problem with care as emotional labor is that care is seen as coming "less *from* the self and being less directed *to* the other." (Hochschild 1983, p. 13, emphasis in original). One downside of emotional, as well as physical, labor, is that the worker can get estranged and alienated from him/herself and his/her surroundings (ibid., p. 7). When it comes to robots, this problem is not so prevailing–quite the opposite. As far as a robot cannot feel human-like emotions, like that of estrangement, the introduction of care robotics can be considered as an answer to solve the problem of alienation in care work–on the part of the care-giver at least. The alienation of the care-receiver, it is argued, the care robots can possibly increase (Sharkey and Sharkey 2012). To illustrate this and the parasitic logics of care robotics further, we will next examine the functioning of Paro, the care-giving robot seal, which can enter into relations with the care-receiver directly and (supposedly) independently.

4.2   The Paradoxes of Paro

Paro is a commercial, zoomorphic, baby seal-like social robot used primarily in eldercare as a therapeutic device (Kerruish 2016; Šabanović 2014; Šabanović and Chang 2016). It is designed to arouse experiences, memories and associations in its user. For example, the form of a seal infant with oversized eyes is supposed to evoke the nurturing instinct. Likewise, Paro weighs as much as an average human baby. Its soft, antibacterial "fur" invites petting, and the cylindrical shape makes hugging and holding easy. Since a diurnal rhythm controls the robot, it is thus the most active in the daytime, just as most human babies are. In addition, Paro can respond to the attention it has drawn, and to its surroundings, by making seal-like sounds, moving its tail or blinking its eyes. Nevertheless, Paro's animality is stripped down: it does not bite, eat or defecate. (Kerruish 2016, p. 6; Šabanović and Chang 2016, pp. 542, 544.)

---

[2] Despite the robot-like quality, the feelings produced need to seem real, not produced or fake. "Going into robot" is actually one form of resistance or defense conducted by the worker, a refusal to enact emotional labor (Hochschild 1983, pp. 129, 135).

Zoomorphic robots' animality, like Paro's, is stereotypical and human-created (Kerruish 2016, p. 13).

Although socially oriented care robots differ from industrial ones in many ways, they are designed and evaluated on the basis of autonomy: how well do they perform their duties, produce the desired effects, like the feeling of wellbeing, in their user as "independent" entities, while potentially replacing human workers (Kerruish 2016, p. 5; Šabanović and Chang 2016, p. 539). In this sense social robots like Paro become actors in emotional labor. They are emotional workers trying to stimulate the desired emotions and feelings in their users or, in the case of formal care work, customers. Paro's exaggerated big button eyes call for eye contact. Still, the feeling of connection is only an attribute (Kerruish 2016, p. 6).

If we follow Hochschild (1983, p. 219) and take emotions as one of the biological senses, as an orientation toward action and cognition, robots, being the non-biological entities they are, cannot have emotions. However, they can imitate feelings. Thus, Paro is well suited for emotional labor: it produces feelings in its user without itself experiencing them in terms of human affection and attachment. It is well compatible with care labor. Although Paro cannot feel in the sense humans feel, it can also stimulate emotions other than positive ones in its user, and decide which feelings or actions are positive and which ones negative. Normativity is embedded in its functions. We will now investigate the sociality of Paro and its dynamics.

Technically speaking, Paro has a Reinforcement Learning Framework and algorithmic software that processes the information gathered by physical sensors in its body. This framework is Paro's system of perception; its expressions are formed through the quantification of the user's responses. Stroking too roughly can lead to an expression of pain–a high-pitched voice, "crying", for example–while soft stroking can lead to a joyful and excited waggling of its body. These expressions set in motion associations of satisfaction, pain or need in the user. (Kerruish 2016, pp. 6–8.) These measurements are Paro's "feelings" and "emotions".

In contrast to both care as a gift and care as a commodity, there are no legal or moral obligations inherent in direct care-related human-robot interactions; robots are not (yet) moral or legal subjects, and only their human designers, users, and providers are legally and morally responsible actors. Nevertheless, ethics and norms are always present in the design of robots. In a way, Paro's user "takes care" of the baby seal robot and moreover is encouraged, or even ordered, to take care of it according to certain culturally approved norms and ethical codes that are programmed and embedded in Paro's design: stroke gently, don't hit. Paro is a tool of self-care, even self-formation, but only insofar as it is treated "correctly": "In establishing a circulation of normative affect through mechanical entrainment, Paro and other social robots produce not only affects and sensations but also subjectivities, bodies and selves." (Kerruish 2016, p. 12).

How does the subjectivity–the development and formation of self, how one thinks about oneself–created by the circulation of affects and their quantification in Paro, and the subjectivity gained from reciprocity in care relations differ? In comparison to human-related care, Paro's reactions are, when it is working correctly, predictable and invariable. Paro is not very sensitive. It acts before it thinks and expects certain kinds of behavior–input–to get the wanted results; a human care-giver would perhaps not mind if the gift of coffee is too cold, but Paro screams in agony when given a "bad" gift, like overly rough petting. Humans are capable of creativity and resistance, in robots these could be considered flaws in the design process. Interaction, when it is predictable, becomes noiseless and thus lifeless.

Is Paro only a device of self-care, a way to minimize care and care relations traditionally composed of giving and receiving, hosting and parasitizing, to solely receiving and parasitizing from the user's point of view? Is Paro a means to entice egocentrism even? Does it call on the user to give care rather than receive it, and, correspondingly, to get the satisfaction and feeling of wellbeing that care-giving can produce? It seems that Paro turns the roles of care-receiver and care-giver upside down. The robot's user nurtures the seal only in order to get positive feedback[3], a sensation of care given, in return. The robot uses the user.

Since Paro can never fully give care on its own merits, it renders possible the giving of true gifts–or at least associations of the true gift for the user. Likewise, Paro seems to be a preeminent parasite, always taking, never giving. Paro tries to bring to the fore the ideal of care as an act of gift-giving, "a labor of love" (Graham 1983). The paradox is that while Paro's user seems to be the ultimate host, giving gifts that cannot be returned, s/he is the obvious parasite. For true gifts or even conventional gifts to exist, there needs to be the possibility of reciprocity, giving back gifts. Paro only imitates reciprocity. Paradoxically, Paro the seal is designed around the logic of care as a gift, but functions according to the logic of a parasite. The user can hug Paro, but Paro cannot hug the user. Gifts given to and given by Paro are only quasi-gifts. The attention, the care Paro receives, is only a way to evoke the positive associations that caring and nurturing bring about.

5 Discussion

Care robots complicate the logics of care and the social expectations they include. Instrumentally and functionally, robots like Paro succeed when fulfilling the social expectations of care. They seem to operate on the basis of the logic of the gift but at the same time defy it. They seem to render possible the giving of instant true gifts, but this is only an imitation; the logic of the gift implies that the gift can be returned. In the case of care robots like Paro, giving gifts in return seems impossible. In imitating the logic of the gift but actually functioning according to the logic of the parasite, Paro simplifies the social dimensions of care. Nevertheless, it is not only the care-receivers who are parasites. In its turn the robot parasitizes too: it takes advantage of its mechanic and the power-distribution network, for example. In the parasitic chains the parts of the host and the parasite can be interchangeable and brief. The dynamics of the logic of gift and the possibilities of reciprocity in human-robot relations of care are presented in Table 1.

---

[3] This is the robot's main function in nursing homes and care work in general; of course, it can be used to other purposes and means as well.

Table 1. Care as gift and non-gift

	Care as gift	Care as non-gift
Possibility of reciprocity	Participants potentially "socially equal", enforcement of autonomy and agency	Healthcare markets, care as a commodity
No possibility of reciprocity	Parasitic relation, socially functioning healthcare robot	Care as or through an instrument, technically functioning healthcare robot

In recent discussions, many ethical problems and questions have been raised concerning care robots. Our analysis has shown that the logics of care and ethics are firmly connected to one another. This can be seen in close encounter interaction in care relations as well as in professional care labor in a broader sense. In giving feedback and evoking the pleasures of giving care, care robots can give the sensation of strengthening one's autonomy. Simultaneously, as the giving of care gifts encouraged by robots is based on imitation and associating the quantified feedback with "true" emotional attachment and feelings, the robots can delude the user and dissolve the distinction between "true" care and the imitation of care.

The fear of diminishing human contacts, and the loss of control, personal freedom and privacy, are some anxieties the robots raise (see for example Sharkey and Sharkey 2012). Many of the ethical issues, however, are the same, whether it be a robot or a human as the care-giver (Etzioni and Etzioni 2017). So, these ethical problems should not be considered as something that the robotics bring with themselves. Instead, we emphasize that when robots are introduced to the system of care labor as parasitic "noise", they bring to the fore problems and uncertainties that already exist. As the ethical discussions care robots raise concern not only technology, but the labor given by humans as well, the parasitic care relation should be considered as an enticement to tackle problems inherited in present-day care labor.

"There is no system without parasites. This constant is a law" (Serres 2007, p. 12). If one wants to erase the crackling, the noise, of a poor telephone line, one has to erase the whole line, the channel in its entirety[4]. Likewise, if you erase the parasites–be they human or non-human–in a care labor that is formed around the logic of a parasite, the whole system breaks. Accordingly, the parasite is the means of transformation and change. The ethical issues are in many ways something already inscribed in the healthcare markets and their semi-parasitic logic of care. At the same time as they raise ethical questions, like the problem of alienation in emotional labor, anew, the robots are also the key to change in the existing care systems. The noise that the parasite creates is the beginning of change (ibid., p. 184). "The parasite is always an exciter" (ibid., p. 192). Care robots excite the conversation to say the least, but, in addition, they make the ethical problems already embedded in the current care labor and organization more visible, and in this way stimulate policies surrounding the organization of care.

---

[4] This example is from Pyyhtinen (2014, p. 74).

Concurrently, one ethical dilemma of care robots is that they can be used to dodge problems in care labor in a broader sense. If tight timetables force the employee to work overtime, free of charge and as a gift, the gift of care transforms into a tool of producing surplus value for the employer (Browne 2009, 2010, p. 587). The employer (and possibly the care-receiver) becomes a parasite, the one who takes but gives nothing in return. If situations like these are rationalized only with the theory of the gift, the exploitation, deception, oppression and reification of care are left out of sight and unproblematized. With the theory of the parasite it is possible to reveal and analyze these issues and examine care as a dynamic process comprised of gifts and parasites.

6 Conclusions

In this paper we have presented how care can be conceptualized as a gift, and clarified the reciprocal gift relations connected to care with the distinction between true gifts and gifts. We argued that commodified care in present day care markets cannot be grasped fully with the logic of the gift. The logic of the parasite, we further highlighted, is the discursive precondition implied in the design and functioning of social care robots like Paro.

This theoretical framework is offered as a conceptual topology to examine the changes of care in different societal settings, mainly those in post-industrial welfare societies. Mol's notion of the logic of care does not imply, and neither do we, that there is solely a single kind of logic that occurs always in certain times and places. In practice, care is formed to a greater or lesser extent according to different overlapping rationales and logics: care is composed of different kinds of hybrids (Fine 2005, p. 249). The framework offered here should be considered as an ideal type, a topology to use to get a grasp on certain features of reality, and especially the changes in the logics of care and advancements in care technology. The parasite is always the counterpart of the gift-giving host, so the logic of the gift and the logic of the parasite actualize simultaneously in care practices. Although the industry of healthcare robots is more or less booming, the utilization of robots in healthcare is still a work in progress. Our argument and many of our examples are hypothetical in nature–they should be seen as a call for further, empirical, research on the subject at hand.

As there are many different types of healthcare robots, empirical research is needed to dissect the ways in which different logics of care are actualized in actual care practices. Furthermore, the effects of the parasitic relation to the psyche and wellbeing of the robot's user as well as the impacts of robots on care labor policies should be addressed in future research. The present paper has implications on the design of healthcare robots as well: should the logic of the gift or the idea of reciprocity be acknowledged more closely? Should the robot be able to say "thank you"? Should the logics of care inscribed and embedded in robots be solely about functioning efficiently and working as an instrument, a mediator, of care? Or should robots be seen as social actors producing the social expectations of interaction connected to care-giving and - receiving?

References

Bolton, S.C.: Who cares? Offering emotion work as a 'gift' in the nursing labour process. J. Adv. Nurs. **32**(3), 580–586 (2000)

Browne, P.L.: Conflict, competition and cooperation in the social division of healthcare. In: Denis, A., Fishman, D.K. (eds.) The ISA Handbook in Contemporary Sociology, pp. 250–264. SAGE, London (2009)

Browne, P.L.: The dialectics of health and social care: toward a conceptual framework. Theory Soc. **39**(5), 575–591 (2010). https://doi.org/10.1007/s11186-010-9120-6

Claassen, R.: The commodification of care. Hypatia **26**(1), 43–64 (2011). https://doi.org/10.1111/j.1527-2001.2010.01146.x

Derrida, J.: Given Time 1: Counterfeit Money. The University of Chicago Press, Chicago (1992). Trans. Kamuf, P.

Douglas, M.: Foreword: no free gifts. In: Mauss, M. (ed.) The Gift, pp. ix–xxiii. Routledge, London (1990)

Elder-Vass, D.: Free gifts and positional gifts: beyond exchangism. Eur. J. Soc. Theory **8**(4), 451–468 (2015). https://doi.org/10.1177/1368431014566562

England, P.: Emerging theories of care work. Ann. Rev. Sociol. **31**, 381–399 (2005). https://doi.org/10.1146/annurev.soc.31.041304.122317

Etzioni, A., Etzioni, O.: The ethics of robotic caregivers. Interact. Stud. **18**(2), 174–190 (2017). https://doi.org/10.1075/is.18.2.02etz

Fine, M.: Individualization, risk and the body: sociology and care. J. Sociol. **41**(3), 247–266 (2005). https://doi.org/10.1177/1440783305057077

Fisher, B., Tronto, J.: Toward a feminist theory of caring. In: Able, E.K., Nelson, M. (eds.) Circles of Care – Work and Identity in Women's Lives, pp. 35–62. State University of New York Press, Albany (1990)

Fox, N.: Postmodern perspectives on care: the vigil and the gift. Crit. Soc. Policy **15**(44–45), 107–125 (1995). https://doi.org/10.1177/026101839501504407

Gibson, D.M.: The dormouse syndrome-restructuring the dependency of the elderly. J. Sociol. **21**(1), 44–63 (1985). https://doi.org/10.1177/144078338502100103

Graham, H.: Caring: a labour of love. In: Finch, J., Groves, D. (eds.) A Labour of Love: Women, Work and Caring, pp. 13–30. Routledge and Kegan Paul, London (1983)

Hochschild, A.: Emotional life on the market frontier. Ann. Rev. Sociol. **37**(1), 21–33 (2011). https://doi.org/10.1146/annurev-soc-081309-150137

Hochschild, A.: The Managed Heart: Commercialization of Human Feeling. University of California Press, Berkeley, Los Angeles and London (1983)

Kerruish, E.: Perception, imagination and affect in human-robot relationships. Cult. Stud. Rev. **22**(2), 4–20 (2016). https://doi.org/10.5130/csr.v22i2.4823

Kierkegaard, S.: Concluding Unscientific Postscript to the Philosophical Crumbs. Hannay, A. (ed. and Trans.). Cambridge University Press, Cambridge (2009). https://doi.org/10.1017/CBO9780511626760

Kröger, T., van Aerschot, L., Puthenparambil, J.M.: Hoivatyö muutoksessa: Suomalainen vanhustyö pohjoismaisessa vertailussa. University of Jyväskylä, Jyväskylä (2018)

Latour, B.: Reassembling the Social: An Introduction to Actor-Network-Theory. Oxford University Press, Oxford (2005)

Lewinter, M.: Reciprocities in caregiving relationships in danish elder care. J. Aging Stud. **17**(3), 357–377 (2003). https://doi.org/10.1016/S0890-4065(03)00025-

MacBride-Stewart, S.: Motivations for the 'gift-of-care' in the context of the modernisation of medicine. Soc. Theory Health **12**(1), 84–104 (2014)

Mauss, M.: The Gift, 2nd edn. Routledge, London and New York (1990)

Mol, A.: The Logic of Care. Routledge, London (2008). https://doi.org/10.4324/9780203927076

Pyyhtinen, O.: The Gift and Its Paradoxes: Beyond Mauss. Routledge, London and New York (2014)

Rantanen, T., Lehto, P., Vuorinen, P., Coco, K.: The adoption of care robots in home care–a survey on the attitudes of finnish home care personnel. J. Clin. Nurs. **27**(9–10), 1846–1859 (2018). https://doi.org/10.1111/jocn.14355

Russ, A.J.: Love's labor paid for: gift and commodity at the threshold of death. Cult. Anthropol. **20**(1), 128–155 (2005)

Šabanović, S., Chang, W.-L.: Socializing robots: constructing robotic sociality in the design and use of the assistive robot PARO. AI Soc. **31**(4), 537–551 (2016). https://doi.org/10.1007/s00146-015-0636-1

Šabanović, S.: Inventing Japan's 'robotics culture': the repeated assembly of science, technology, and culture in social robotics. Soc. Stud. Sci. **44**(3), 342–367 (2014). https://doi.org/10.1177/0306312713509704

Sahlins, M.: Stone Age Economics. Aldine de Gruyter, New York (1972)

Serres, M.: The Parasite. University of Minnesota Press, Minneapolis (2007). Trans. Schehr, L.R.

Sharkey, A., Sharkey, N.: Granny and the robots: ethical issues in robot care for the elderly. Ethics Inf. Technol. **14**(1), 27–40 (2012). https://doi.org/10.1007/s10676-010-9234-6

Torres, J.M., Kietzman, K.G., Wallace, S.P.: Walking the line: navigating market and gift economies of care in a consumer-directed home-based care program for older adults. Milbank Q. **93**(4), 732–760 (2015). https://doi.org/10.1111/1468-0009.12163

Tronto, J.: Moral Boundaries: A Political Argument for an Ethic of Care. Routledge, New York (1993)

Twigg, J.: Bathing-The Body and Community Care. Routledge, London (2000)

Van Wynsberghe, A.: Designing robots for care. care centered value-sensitive design. Sci. Eng. Ethics **19**(2), 407–433 (2013). https://doi.org/10.1007/s11948-011-9343-6

Wolf, D.A.: Valuing informal elder care. In: Folbre, N., Bittman, M. (eds.) Family Time: The Social Organization of Care, pp. 110–129. Routledge, New York (2004)

Design and Implementation of Age-Friendly Activity for Supporting Elderly's Daily Life by IoT

Soo In Kang[1]([⊠]), Reina Yoshizaki[2], Koki Nakano[5], Taiyu Okatani[6], Akihiko Kamesawa[4], Daisuke Yoshioka[3], Jiang Wu[3], Yuriki Sakurai[3], Kenichiro Ito[7], Mahiro Fujisaki-Sueda-Sakai[7], Ikuko Sugawara[7], Misato Nihei[3], Takahiro Miura[7], Ken-ichiro Yabu[7], Taketoshi Mori[7], Tohru Ifukube[7], and Junichiro Okata[7]

[1] Graduate School of Medicine, The University of Tokyo,
7-3-1 Hongo, Bunkyo-Ku, Tokyo 113-8656, Japan
skang-tky@umin.ac.jp
[2] Graduate School of Engineering, The University of Tokyo,
7-3-1 Hongo, Bunkyo-Ku, Tokyo 113-8656, Japan
[3] Graduate School of Frontier Sciences, The University of Tokyo,
7-3-1 Hongo, Bunkyo-Ku, Tokyo 113-8656, Japan
[4] Graduate School of Arts and Sciences, The University of Tokyo,
7-3-1 Hongo, Bunkyo-Ku, Tokyo 113-8656, Japan
[5] Graduate School of Humanities and Sociology, The University of Tokyo,
7-3-1 Hongo, Bunkyo-Ku, Tokyo 113-8656, Japan
[6] Graduate School of Information Science and Technology,
The University of Tokyo, 7-3-1 Hongo, Bunkyo-Ku, Tokyo 113-8656, Japan
[7] Institute of Gerontology, The University of Tokyo, 7-3-1 Hongo,
Bunkyo-Ku, Tokyo 113-8656, Japan

Abstract. Internet of Things (IoT) is highly expected to contribute in making elderly people's quality of life better, especially by detecting early health risks and supporting livings. However, most elderly people are not friendly to IoT technologies, which is a barrier to implement IoT technologies into the elderly people' livings. In this study, we designed a card-based age-friendly workshop to help elderly people being friendly and having confidence with IoT. The cards composed of 16 "trigger cards" and 14 "feedback cards" about several IoT devices, which reflects our degraded but age-friendly explanation of IoT that IoT devices give a "feedback" when a "trigger" happens. The participants were asked to come up with ideas for use cases of IoT by combining a trigger card with a feedback card. Within three workshops, 22 people of 65 years of age or older were recruited, and 134 ideas were totally obtained. We revealed that the ideas were categorized into nine groups based on the purpose of each use case. Moreover, survey results indicated that the elderlies became friendly with IoT through coming up with ideas in the workshop. In this study, we confirmed that carefully designed cards and example ideas can help participants bring out more

© Springer Nature Switzerland AG 2019
J. Zhou and G. Salvendy (Eds.): HCII 2019, LNCS 11593, pp. 353–368, 2019.
https://doi.org/10.1007/978-3-030-22015-0_28

ideas and higher confidence in IoT. Experiencing and imaging about the use of IoT in their own personal needs will encourage elderlies to use IoT technologies.

Keywords: Aging and technology acceptance ·
Involving the elderly in HCI methodology ·
Training the elderly in the use of IT

1   Introduction

State-of-art technologies such as Internet of Things (IoT) is highly expected to contribute in making elderly's quality of life better. One of the advantages of utilizing IoT technology is that it can be customized easily according to user's preference. In IoT technology, inputs and outputs are connected via the Internet, and since they are inherently independent from each other, adjustment of their functions can be easily done. By connecting various things in the house to the internet, users can solve their own problem such as achieving the status information, receiving alert of dangers, controlling motors in furniture, classifying life patterns by accumulated data, and so on. Also, the concept of connecting everything to the internet has a high expectation of medical support for home clinical care setting which requires care and warning to patient's daily life. Thus, users can change and utilize the functions of IoT technology in a manner suited to their own lifestyle.

Elderly people have their own requirements for their own life style which might be different with imagination from assistant device developer. Age-related functional decline is a gradual loss of physical and psychological ability which occurs with changes in the human body in every moment from the 20 s until the end [1]. Changes in physical ability such as the sensorimotor system can cause risk of falls or accidents and it might bring limitation in independent lifestyle [1–3]. Not threatening, but gradual macular degenerations, loss of hearing, weakness in bones, memory problems and brain problems will also bring changes in lifestyle. At the point of specific levels of decline in ability, elderly's will stop driving, unable to read a book, less cooking recipe, quitting outdoor sports and less challenges toward new experience. These kind of various problems might not be enough to maintain their quality of life by using current assistant devices. In the other hand, IoT devices which can be easily changed and utilized for user can effectively solve the elderly's needs.

IoT technology has not prevailed much in the lives of elderly people. In Japan, where the population aging is progressing, technology is expected to support home life of elderly people. Under these circumstances, IoT technology, which is easy to customize according to individuals, can play an effective role in the lives of elderly people whose physical and psychological conditions have large differences among individuals. Therefore, elucidation of the barriers in introducing IoT technologies into the daily lives of elderly people is an important subject.

One hypothesis of the reasons why the IoT technologies do not prevail in the elderly people is that the elderly people may not be able to imagine the living scene using IoT technology by themselves. In other words, whether they can envision use case of IoT technology may be an important aspect for the friendliness of elderly people with such technology. If so, it will be indispensable for the introduction of IoT technology not only to improve the functional convenience of the technology, but also to promote elderly people's understanding of the technology.

The purpose of our study is to introduce IoT to elderly people using carefully designed age-friendly workshop and to verify that helping elderly people to imagine they use IoT in their livings, can encourage elderly people to bring out solutions for their own specific problems. In the workshop, we asked the elderly people's ideas to make better their lives by using IoT technology and measured how much they are friendly and having confidence with the IoT technology by questionnaire. By considering the result of this survey, this study explored guidelines for introducing IoT technology to the lives of elderly people.

2 Related Works

This chapter reviews previous researches related to this study. First, we review how the workshop is acceptable for IoT experience. Then, we review how the workshop is acceptable for encouragement for elderly people to generate as many ideas as possible in a short time. These studies focus on the usefulness and impact of card-based workshop to encourage elderly people to think about more convenient life by using and trying, feeling IoT possibility.

2.1 Workshop for IoT Experience

Research projects found that workshops which install card-based tools are effective to support idea generation [4]. Cards are a good tool for experiencing a difficult concept because it makes people enjoyable and let the people at the center of the process [5, 6].

It is effective not only for logical thinking, but also for facilitating creative thinking. When a participant's idea gets unproductive, using cards can lead to discussing actively and generating diverse ideas [7]. It has been introduced to the design of IoT related technology such as interfaces, influencing behaviors and design for games [8–10]. From these previous researches, the card-based workshop is acceptable for IoT experience. So, we use card-based workshop for IoT experience and led people to generate ideas in a new way for IoT.

2.2 Workshop for Encouraging Elderly to Generate Ideas by Themselves

It is difficult for not only elderly people but also young people or even children to generate new ideas in a short period. For developing new technology for elderly people, many companies or researchers tried various methods such as interview, workshop and observation of their lifestyle in order to prevent mismatches of needs between caregivers and developers, extract new ideas, find potential needs and evaluate acceptance [11–13].

When we talk with elderly people, they probably shared their life experience, memory, and events. Even though dementia, it is known that they remembered past events or special story like their childhood story. Remembering and sharing it with another person is meaningful (Ricoeur's words 1999, Jelin 2001). This meaning action does not occur only by themselves, but need groups and social networks.

The workshop that provides the place where elderly people can talk or recall their life stories and share with other people give benefit to the elderly people, because it is a good opportunity for them to experience new thing and develop social skills by discussing with the group members. During the workshop, it was found that workshop constitutes a tool of access to the subjective experience of elderly people and storytelling gives new meaning to their life trajectory. So, the workshop is a good way to encourage them to think of their lifestyle and discuss about what is their problems or worries in their life or what kind of technology will need or can be installed in order to have an enjoyable time at home.

3   Methods

3.1   Overview and Subject Attributes

In order to have the elderly people themselves discover ideas for utilizing IoT based on their own specific needs, "Workshop on Information Utilization in Life" targeting over 65 years old was held (Fig. 1). We constructed the WS based on the ideas of card-based design tools [14, 15]. We look at IoT from a "things-oriented" [16] perspective. Since the basic operation of the tablet PC is necessary in this WS, the ones who owns a tablet PC or a smartphone were elected. The workshop was held in two different places and we named each group as group A and group B. Activity for group A was held in an activity center which is called Fuseshinmachi Furusato Center in Fuseshinmachi, Kashiwa, Chiba prefecture, Japan. And activity for group B was held in University of Tokyo in Bunkyo-ku, Tokyo, Japan.

Fig. 1. Elderly people trying to use IoT devices in the designed workshop

3.2   Flow of WS

We implemented WS as shown in Fig. 2. First, we briefed about IoT and demonstrated IoT equipment for about 10 min. This explanation is not intended for the participants to acquire general knowledge about IoT, but intended to improve their confidence in understanding with helping to establish an image to IoT. The definition and explanation of IoT has been prepared with reference to ICT skills comprehensive learning materials [17] by the Japanese Ministry of Internal Affairs and Communications.

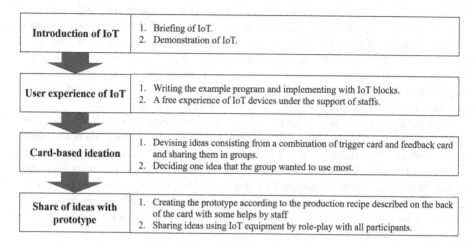

Introduction of IoT	1. Briefing of IoT. 2. Demonstration of IoT.
User experience of IoT	1. Writing the example program and implementing with IoT blocks. 2. A free experience of IoT devices under the support of staffs.
Card-based ideation	1. Devising ideas consisting from a combination of trigger card and feedback card and sharing them in groups. 2. Deciding one idea that the group wanted to use most.
Share of ideas with prototype	1. Creating the prototype according to the production recipe described on the back of the card with some helps by staff 2. Sharing ideas using IoT equipment by role-play with all participants.

Fig. 2. Flowchart of the workshop

Next, the subject experienced IoT equipment. As IoT equipment, we have prepared devices, which have functions of communication and sensing, and devices which have functions of communication and feedback. Specifically, a tablet PC (iPad, Apple), a set of IoT blocks (MESH, SONY), a smart light bulb (KL110, TP-Link) has been prepared and each function can be connected by visual programming (MESH, SONY) (Fig. 3). We used the web service for connecting APIs (IFTTT) to easily realize IoT system, but the participants never touched this web service not to be confused.

Fig. 3. Used IoT devices

The experiential program is divided into two parts, a fixed experience according to the manual and a free experience by the subjects. In the first part, they experienced the method of visual programming that connects Trigger which is expressed as a conditional clause and Feedback which is expressed as a main clause with two programming examples. Then they checked the operation of two examples by the IoT blocks and they have experienced the connection between the visual programming and the real operation. In the second part, the subjects freely experienced a combination of the sensor devices and the feedback devices under the support of staffs for about 10 min, while using prepared cards expressing functions of the sensor and feedback devices. This set of cards is the same as that used in the third program, the card-based ideation. The card set will be described in detail in the following paragraphs. In these experiences, we emphasized that the connection between visual programming and its implementation result is intuitive for the subjects, and we kept in mind that the implementation result could be confirmed by the subjects immediately.

The third part is the card-based ideation by senior subjects. As it is difficult for non-expert senior to understand the engineering functions of sensors and others and make them available in a limited time, we prepared the set of cards in two categories of Trigger and Feedback category with words and pictures abstractly showing examples of utilization of equipments prepared for this workshop (Fig. 4). Words written on the card were unified into descriptions having one or less subject and one predicate when written in Japanese and the expression of words and pictures didn't limit the place of use with the notation.

Fig. 4. Example of cards used in the workshop. Left is trigger card and right is feedback card.

The card-based ideation consisted of two parts, that was devising ideas and sharing them in groups and deciding one idea that the group wanted to use most. Devising ideas and sharing took place in about 20 min. We informed participants that the participants themselves should devise the ideas that make their lives more convenient, or more pleasant. For these objectives, they thought the idea consisting from a combination of trigger and feedback, where they wanted to use and how they wanted to use. During devising and sharing ideas, the staff made remarks to hear the detailed content of the idea. When the elderly people need help, the staffs advised for improvement of the ideas, but the idea was conceived and formed by the elderly people themselves. In order to get ideas closely related to living, the position of physical trigger and physical feedback operation is limited to within the home premises, and the non-physical trigger and feedback cards are stamped for distinction. For ideas that came out about functions not provided as cards, we recorded in post it.

As the final part of idea delivery, the participants themselves determined one idea to prototype in the group based on the degree of hope of using at home. In order to share their ideas of all groups with participants, elderly people created prototypes of the ideas that were decided according to the production recipe described on the back of the card with some helps by staff. The role-play type prototype using IoT equipment was examined for over 15 min. Then, WS activity was closed with presentations of ideas by role-play (Fig. 5).

Fig. 5. Idea delivery part in workshops

3.3 Senior-Friendly Design of the WS Cards

Cards are devised to make it easy for elderly people to understand and utilize. The cards are sized as large as 148 × 105 mm and the main letters are sized more than 8 mm (Fig. 6). The letter size is large enough for seniors under the ordinal room light [18]. Because elderly people do not memorize the contents of the all cards, we simplified the card type so that they expanded all kinds of cards on the table to look every card. The contents of Trigger card and Feedback card are summarized in Table 1. With reference to some designs [14, 15], Trigger category and Feedback category are color-coded to be discernible from each other. On the backside of the card, to help to write a program for implementation of the idea, the screenshot of the visual programming shows what sensor can be used and how to set up [15].

3.4 Evaluation Process

The WS aimed at the senior-friendly introduction of IoT and the excavation of the unconscious individual IoT needs of elderly individuals, so WS was evaluated at these two points. In order to evaluate confidence in understanding, questionnaires with a five point Likert scale are conducted before the workshop and after the workshop. In

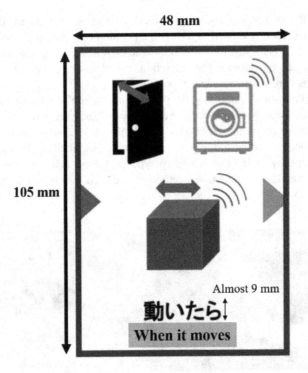

Fig. 6. Design of cards for elderly people

Table 1. Contents of trigger cards and feedback cards

Trigger card	Feedback card
When it gets warm	Turn off the small light
When it gets cold	Turn on the small light
When it gets dry	Turn on the light
When it gets humid	Turn off the light
When it gets brighter	Play sound
When it gets dark	Stop the sound
When a sound comes	Send the e-mail
When some creature passes by in front	Send the notification
When some creature has gone out	Take a photo
When a mail comes	Record on the sheet online
When it is blocked	Lock[*]
When something to block has gone out	Unlock[*]
When turning in a certain direction	Turn on the consumer electronics[*]
When it turns over	Turn off the consumer electronics[*]
When it moves	
When the button is pressed	

[*]Card that wasn't tried in this workshop, and only provided to group A

addition, in order to evaluate the acceptability for seniors of a series of systems used in the workshop, a questionnaire on SUS [18] was done after the workshop.

In order to evaluate the excavation of the unconscious individual IoT needs of elderly individuals, we compared the free answer of "Recent Trouble" by a prior questionnaire with the idea that resulted from WS. Video data and audio data were recorded for every two groups, and the contents of listening to ideas at WS were used for concrete representation of ideas that resulted from WS.

3.5   Statistical Analysis

Spearman's rank correlation coefficient was calculated for showing the relationship between the individual's number of idea and friendliness to IoT. To compare between before and after questionnaire score, Mann-Whitney U test was used. Mann-Whitney U test was also used for comparing between groups' characteristics using before survey to confirm there is no big difference between 3 different workshops. These calculations were done by statistic program R-3.5.2.

4   Result

4.1   Participant Characteristics

In the two times of the workshop, total 22 elderly people participated to experience using IoT in their real life. Participants' characteristics were obtained as Table 2 during survey time. Our research team recruited those who understand drag and drop of the touch panel. Thus, except one participant, 21 participants were using smartphone with understanding their house internet environment. And also for preventing result from reflecting gender characteristic, 10 female participants and 12 male participants were chosen. Most of the participants were living with their partner or children while only two participants lived alone.

4.2   Before Workshop

Participants also provided pilot survey of 4 different questions. Group A was asked about what kind of troubles exist in their current life. We collected these data for knowing how much participants are friendly toward IoT or new technology. Participants showed various answers to whether they are used to the word IoT (median: 3, IQR: 2-4). But most of the participants thought, internet can help their trouble in life (median 4, IQR 4-4). Also, various people came to experience about IoT, those who felt different trouble level with diverse reasons in their lifestyle (median 3, IQR 2-4). Figure 7 shows how much they are active toward experiencing new technology. In group A 29% of the participants shown the most expectation for this workshop while 64% shown interest and left 7% shown difficulty. On the other hand, group B was mostly showing their interest (75%), and some of them shown difficulty (25%) before they join this workshop. Group B was significantly younger compare to group A.

Table 2. Characteristics of the participants

Characteristics	Total (n = 22)	Group A (n = 14)	Group B (n = 8)
Age, year, mean (SD)	73 (5.11)	75 (5.02)	69 (1.80)
65–74, n (%)	13 (59)	5 (36)	8 (59)
75–84, n (%)	9 (41)	9 (64)	0 (41)
Gender			
Male, n (%)	12 (55)	8 (57)	4 (50)
Female, n (%)	10 (45)	6 (43)	4 (50)
Living state			
Living with someone, n (%)	20 (91)	14 (100)	6 (75)
Living alone, n (%)	2 (9)	0 (0)	2 (25)
Internet environment in home			
Wired network, n (%)	5 (23)	3 (21)	2 (25)
Wireless network, n (%)	21 (95)	14 (100)	7 (86)
None, n (%)	1 (5)	0 (0)	1 (0)
Internet device usage			
Smart phone, n (%)	20 (91)	12 (86)	8 (100)
Tablet PC, n (%)	13 (59)	9 (64)	4 (50)
Desktop PC, Laptop PC, n (%)	19 (86)	12 (86)	7 (86)
Smart speaker, n (%)	2 (9)	2 (14)	0 (13)
Questionnaires[*]			
Used to the word "IoT", score, median (IQR)	3 (2-4)	2.5 (2-4)	3 (2-4)
Agree with internet can be helpful, score, median (IQR)	4 (4-4)	4 (4-5)	4 (4-4)
Feel troubles in recent life, score, median (IQR)	3 (2-4)	3 (2-4)	3 (2-3)

[*]In these questionnaires, 5 scale scoring was used. Score 1 is greatly disagree while 5 is greatly agree.

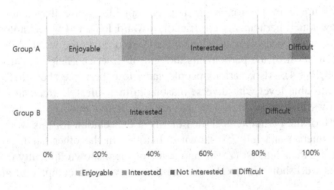

Fig. 7. Each group's activeness of the participants

4.3   Idea from Workshop

In these two workshops, 22 participants suggested 134 ideas, including 15 ideas which were the external idea from workshops' card based idea. Each group's number of ideas are shown in Table 3. Group A expressed 94 ideas which is 6.71 ideas per one person. And group B expressed 40 ideas with 5 ideas per one person.

Table 3. Number of idea from each group

Group	Card based idea	External idea	Average idea per 1 person
Group A (n = 14)	87	7	6.71
Group B (n = 8)	32	8	5.00
Total (N = 22)	119	15	6.09

After the workshop ended, participants provided their feeling toward IoT using surveys. Table 4 shows the result of after survey. The median score of questionnaire about how much they enjoyed was 5 (IQR, 4.75-5) showing that they greatly agreed. And in other questions scored 4 showing that they agreed. Only, 13 participants joined in SUS test, and the average score was 54.62 (SD, 13). Most of the participants have shown positive score for thinking and try making prototype IoT devices (Fig. 8).

Table 4. Scores of after workshop survey to confirm their friendly and acceptability

Survey contents	Total (n = 22)	Group A (n = 14)	Group B (n = 8)
Questionnaires[*]			
Enjoyed, score, median (IQR)	5 (4.75-5)	5 (5-5)	5 (3-5)
Understood, score, median (IQR)	4 (4-5)	4 (4-5)	4 (4-5)
Will use in future, score, median (IQR)[**]	4 (4-5)	4 (4-5)	
Will use in home, score, median (IQR)	4 (3-4.25)	3 (3-4)	4 (3-5)
Will introduce to friends or family, score, median (IQR)	4 (3-5)	5 (3-5)	4 (4-5)
SUS, total score, mean (SD)[***]	54 (13)		

[*]In this questionnaires 5 scale scoring was used. Score 1 is greatly disagree while 5 is greatly agree.
[**]This question was only offered to group A.
[***]Total 13 participants joined for SUS survey

Most of the participants gave high score on their understanding level. As, this question is about asking their confidence level, we compared with question about whether they are used to IoT. There was a significant difference in participant's confidence between before and after ($p < 0.05$, Fig. 9). Rather than explaining the whole system of IoT, just making them understand what is obtaining information and what can be feedback, lead elderly people to try to make or design by themselves. Degraded

Fig. 8. Elderly people thinking about what can be help for their lives

but friendly explanations could have made participants obtain more confidence in IoT devices.

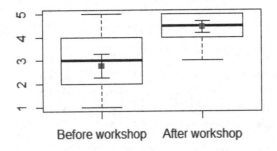

Before workshop   After workshop

Fig. 9. Confidence in using IoT

5   Discussion

Age-friendly designed workshop introduced IoT to elderly people by experiencing various IoT devices and imaging the usage in their own life. Participants expressed 119 ideas based on card combination and among those ideas 12 best ideas were selected based on elderly people's consensus. Most of the participants replied positively about IoT devices after the workshop, compared to participants shown various feelings toward experiencing new technology before the workshop. Encouraging elderly people to imagine how to solve problems from their own problems using IoT technologies, might bring them better achievement and bigger consensus with others.

In previous research, finding elderly's difficulty and solving with house monitoring technology was done, by trying to make elderly people imagine their normal life to figure out their needs [19]. This approach might discover common needs that can basically occur in various elderly people as the researcher were focusing on ideas that came out frequently, but not individual specific needs. Using and customizing IoT might help finding elderly's individual specific needs. As IoT is not easy to be used by elderly, our research group tried to introduce the IoT technology to elderly people, to build their own smart house with their own requirement, expecting elderly people to become friendly with IoT technology.

A number of ideas were considered as how well participants can imagine about where to use this new experienced technology. And friendly score was measured by asking how much they enjoyed using IoT devices. By using Spearman's rank correlation coefficient, we confirmed there is significant correlation between knowledge of where to use and friendly toward IoT (ρ = 0.44, p < 0.05, Fig. 10). Though it is hard to say there is a causal relationship, verification of importance in imagination toward usage was done in this study.

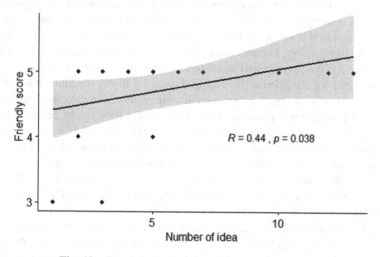

Fig. 10. Correlation with friendly and number of ideas

Many different kinds of ideas might indicate that the workshop was effective enough to support idea generation. Thus, what kind of problems does elderly people imagine before the workshop was achieved by the survey. And for the imagination of during the workshop was collected by card based ideas. In the survey, participants were asked before the workshop is started, about their troubles they can easily think about (Table 5). Four participants wanted to solve their memory problem and three participants shown difficulty in driving and multitasking. These result show that most of the troubles came from age-related functional decline which might have changed their life style [2, 3].

Table 5. Troubles that participants had before workshop

Answers	Number of similar answers (N = 14)
Forgetting problem	4
Forgetting things in fridge[*]	
Forgetting what was done[*]	
Forgetting appointment time[*]	
Difficulty in using PC	3
Difficulty in driving	2
Difficulty in multitask	1
Want to know temperature of bottle	1
No troubles	3

[*]Answers with detail story

To show what kind of imaginations came out from the workshop, our research team categorized ideas into each objective that elderly people wanted to detect by sensor and what they wanted to do with that information. Categorize was based on the purpose of used card by elderly people. For example, sensing the pushed button is basically detecting thing, but if it was for detecting interphone pressed by someone, we classified as, detecting living thing. For another example, we classified turning on the light as changing status if the purpose was to make a brighter place, and if the purpose was to notice someone, we classified as informing. Figure 11 shows the number of the categorized idea. Most of the participants were having needs about detecting environment changes. They were greatly interested at dangers that they might couldn't feel, or maintaining daily cycle as they don't have any works. Also, they wanted to get the information or send the information, rather than changing or recording automatically. It seems that elderly people prefer to get informed and solve by themselves, which is comparable with young people who wants everything done automatically. Moreover, feedback of inform was greatly important for elderly people to alert the sudden danger to neighbors and family.

Previous studies found that card-based workshop is effective for supporting idea generation [4]. Nine categorized 119 ideas from this workshop also indicate that the card based workshop was effective enough to bring out elderly people's idea generation. This study was done with elderly people who know how to use tablet PC or smartphone. The reason was we failed to explain well toward elderly people who don't even have a smartphone. And this kind of difficulty brought many additional efforts until now to develop new technologies for elderly people [11–13]. In this study, we suggest card based workshop to help elderly people to be able to solve their problem by imaging where they can use IoT devices.

Our research group expected, we could find elderly people's specific own needs by asking the thinking pathway of came out idea. However, obtaining such kind of data with consistency was greatly difficult. Also, comparing before with after wasn't clearly done as activity time was only one and a half hour. If we can have held this kind of activity in same area periodically, we might could be successful to do before and after comparison and also obtain how they are experiencing and using.

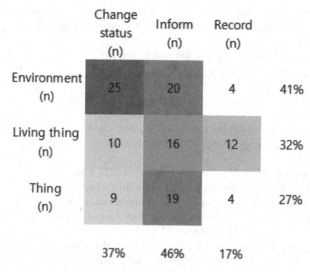

	Change status (n)	Inform (n)	Record (n)	
Environment (n)	25	20	4	41%
Living thing (n)	10	16	12	32%
Thing (n)	9	19	4	27%
	37%	46%	17%	

Fig. 11. Numbers of each categorized idea.

6 Conclusion

In this study, we verified that the knowledge of where to use with connecting to their own specific needs will bring elderly people friendly with IoT devices. Carefully designed cards and example ideas helped participants bring out more ideas and higher confidence. We are suggesting that future age-friendly IoT device can be more intuitive by using a degrading concept of IoT using card activity.

References

1. Samson, M.M., Meeuwsen, I.B., Crowe, A., Dessens, J.A., Duursma, S.A., Verhaar, H.J.: Relationships between physical performance measures, age, height and body weight in healthy adults. Age Ageing **29**(3), 235–242 (2000)
2. Wolfson, L., Whipple, R., Judge, J., Amerman, P., Derby, C., King, M.: Training balance and strength in the elderly to improve function. J. Am. Geriatr. Soc. **41**(3), 341–343 (1993). https://doi.org/10.1111/j.1532-5415.1993.tb06716.x
3. Brown, M., Sinacore, D.R., Host, H.H.: The relationship of strength to function in the older adult. J. Gerontol. A Biol. Sci. Med. Sci. **50**(Special_Issue), 55–59 (1995)
4. Vaajakallio, K., Mattelmäki, T.: Design games in codesign: as a tool, a mindset and a structure. CoDesign **10**(1), 63–77 (2014). https://doi.org/10.1080/15710882.2014.881886
5. IDEO Method Cards: 51 ways to inspire design. IDEO Homepage (2013). https://www.ideo.com/post/method-cards
6. Lucero, A., Arrasvuori, J.: PLEX Cards: a source of inspiration when designing for playfulness. In: 3rd International Conference on Fun and Games, pp. 28–37 (2010). http://doi.org/10.1145/1823818.1823821
7. Carneiro, G., Li, Z.: i|o cards: a tool to support collaborative design of interactive objects. In: Proceedings of DESIRE, pp. 357–358 (2011). http://doi.org/10.1145/2079216.2079268

8. Hornecker, E.: Creative idea exploration within the structure of a guiding framework: the card brainstorming game. In: Proceedings of TEI, pp. 101–108 (2010). http://doi.org/10.1145/1709886.1709905

9. Dan, L., David, H., Neville, A.S.: Design with Intent: 101 Patterns for Influencing Behaviour Through Design. Equifine, Windsor (2010)

10. Mueller, F., Gibbs, M.R., Vetere, F., Edge, D.: Supporting the creative game design process with exertion cards. In: Proceedings of CHI, pp. 2211–2220 (2014). http://doi.org/10.1145/2556288.2557272

11. The Japanese Ministry of Health, Labor, and Welfare: Guideline for development of welfare equipment and nursing care robot (2014). http://www.techno-aids.or.jp/research/robotebiki_mhlw_140922.pdf

12. Inoue, T.: Development of life support robot system in community based on field-based-innovation. J. Robot. Soc. Jpn. **34**(5), 304–308 (2016). https://doi.org/10.7210/jrsj.34.304

13. Otsuki, R., Okamoto, M.: Research of the communication tool for the visually impaired person using the participatory design. In: The 60th Annual Conference of JSSD, 20th June 2013. https://doi.org/10.11247/jssd.60.0_43

14. Mora, S., Gianni, F., Divitini, M.: Tiles: a card-based ideation toolkit for the internet of things. In: Proceedings of the 2017 Conference on Designing Interactive Systems, pp. 587–598 (2017). http://doi.org/10.1145/3064663.3064699

15. MESH Homepage. http://blog.meshprj.com/entry/designpatterncard

16. Atzori, L., Iera, A., Morabito, G.: The internet of things: a survey. Comput. Netw. **54**(15), 2787–2805 (2010). https://doi.org/10.1016/j.comnet.2010.05.010

17. The Japanese Ministry of Internal Affairs and Communications Homepage. http://www.soumu.go.jp/ict_skill/

18. Sagawa, K., Ujike, H., Sasaki, T.: Legibility of Japanese characters and sentences as a function of age. Proc. IEA **7**, 496–499 (2003)

19. Wu, J., et al.: Design implications and methodology based on the potential needs of seniors for home monitoring systems. In: Asian Conference on Design and Digital Engineering, Okinawa (2018)

A Cooking Support System for Seasoning with Smart Cruet

Yuta Kido[1], Teruhiro Mizumoto[2(✉)], Hirohiko Suwa[1], Yutaka Arakawa[1], and Keiichi Yasumoto[1]

[1] Graduate School of Science and Technology,
Nara Institute of Science and Technology, Ikoma, Japan
yasumoto@is.naist.jp
[2] Graduate School of Information Science and Technology,
Osaka University, Suita, Japan
teruhiro-m@is.naist.jp
http://ubi-lab.naist.jp/

Abstract. In recent years, the number of people who use online recipe services in order to cook has increased. It is difficult to match food taste to user's preference because an online recipe page shows a recipe to realize just one taste even though there are countless numbers of recipes in an online recipe service. Our preliminary experiment using convenience food to investigate the user's preference showed that the preference of almost participants differed from the taste of food cooked following the recipe printed in the package. It has also been reported that 76.5% of housewives are interested in cooking activities. However, using measuring spoon is difficult to use in order to determine the exact amount of seasonings. When we conducted a preliminary experiment to confirm the error between the input amount based on a rough estimation and the specific amount, the average error for small spoon was 46.2%, and the average error for large spoon was 31.8% even though the participants cook frequently. Especially, for an elderly person requiring low salt or low sugar, if the error becomes too big than appropriate amount, leading to endangering his life or losing the pleasures of eating. However, since there is no device currently in use that can assist in putting seasonings, a device other than measuring spoon is needed to determine the amount of seasoning for cooking. In this research, we aim to bring the taste of food with an online recipe close to the user's preferable taste without burdening the user. In this paper, we propose a cooking support system which analyzes user's preference from user's feedback according to the five grade evaluation for each meal, adjusts the amount of seasoning for a recipe depending on user's preference, and supports to add the seasoning by Smart Cruet equipped with motion sensors, LED light, and BLE communication interface. We conducted an experiment for 14 days to confirm how many days are needed to bring the adjustment of the seasonings close to the preferable taste for the user. We were able to reach the desired adjustment in 7 days. Furthermore, we found Smart Cruet could measure the adding amount of seasoning with 5.56% average error.

© Springer Nature Switzerland AG 2019
J. Zhou and G. Salvendy (Eds.): HCII 2019, LNCS 11593, pp. 369–382, 2019.
https://doi.org/10.1007/978-3-030-22015-0_29

Keywords: Cooking support system · Elderly support · IoT

1   Introduction

With the spread of smartphones, users of online recipe services such as Allrecipe and Cookpad are on the rise. For example, in Cookpad[1], the number of users has increased from 26 million in 2013 to almost 60 million by 2017 [1]. According to a survey by Cookpad, more than 60% of respondent have shown increment in the use of online recipes and almost half of the respondents have stopped purchasing cookbooks and magazines. This proves that there is a rapid increase in the interest of people towards using online recipes.

It is expected that online recipe service users and the number of online recipes will continue to increase. However, even if you cook in accordance with an online recipe, it does not necessarily match the preferable taste of the person who eats it because the preference of taste is different depending on the person. It is desirable to match dishes to the preferable taste as much as possible even though using online recipes because it is apparent that eating tasty dishes affects human satisfaction.

In recent years, the paradigm called IoT (Internet of Things) has become widespread. Not only smart devices such as smartphone and tablet but various items used in everyday life have now become equipped with sensors and Internet connectivity. Introduction of IoT into industrial, medical and other fields is progressing, but a movement to apply IoT to cooking utensils and the kitchen itself has also begun. For example, Pantelligent [2], a frying pan embedded with a temperature sensor and radio communication function, can provide the time to heat as well as to flip the ingredients by performing temperature management in cooperation with smartphone. As a result of the Panasonic survey [3], 76.5% of housewives have been devising to save the trouble of cooking. From these movements, it appears that various smart kitchen utensils with IoT will spread to homes in the future. However, there is no cooking utensil focusing on adjusting the amount of seasoning depending on the user's preference.

As a preliminary experiment, we investigated about rough estimation and preference. The result showed that even though the subject user cooked on a regular basis, the difference between rough estimation and preferable amount of seasoning was about 35%. Moreover, we served instant soups with different amount of hot water to the 24 participants, by letting them choose their favorite from the soups. As a result, 12 participants chose strong soups, 11 participants chose weak soups, and only one participant chose the soup with the appropriate amount written on the official package. From these results, we assume that it is useful to realize a method that brings the taste close to the user's preference and supports to add the precise amount of seasoning.

In this paper, we propose a cooking support system that adjusts the amount of seasoning for a recipe depending on user's preference and supports adding

---

[1] Cookpad is Japan's largest recipe-sharing service launched in March 1998 (http://info.cookpad.com/en).

seasoning by Smart Cruet. The system has three main functions: (1) to extract a user's preference by learning the assessment of individual tasty for the consumed amount of seasoning; (2) to determine the amount of seasoning depending on user's preference; (3) to measure and notify the input amount of seasoning by Smart Cruet in real time. Our system analyzes the user's preference for five basic tastes, such as saltiness, sweetness, sourness, bitterness, and umami (savoriness) [4,5], based on feedback according to the five-grade evaluation for each meal, and to adjust the amount of seasonings depending on the user's preference. In addition, the system facilitates to add the seasonings by Smart Cruet. We assume that the users of our system can improve their satisfaction with eating, which also serves as a factor to improve their QoL. We conducted two experiments to know the user's preference. At first, we served a dish cooked in accordance with the original recipe, and then, collected the feedback according to the five grades evaluation, such as very strong, strong, favorite, weak and very weak for the dish. Then, in the next step, we served a dish adjusted based on the feedback and collected the feedback for the dish again. As a result, we confirmed that approximately half of subjects who did not evaluate 'favorite' to the first dish evaluated 'favorite' for the adjusted dish. For the second experiment, we conducted an experiment for 14 days to confirm determine how many days are needed to bring the adjustment model close to the user's preferable taste. We do so because the adjustment based on one-time feedback in the first experiment was not able to reach the preference level of all the participants. As a result, we found that it took approximately seven days to bring the taste close to the user's preference.

2   Related Works

2.1   Food Recognition

Mirtchouk et al. [6] proposed a food recognition method, which uses audio sensor and accelerometers from smart watch and Google Glass to automatically detect food type and amount. This method can classify food into 40 types and estimate consumed amount by mastication sound and arm and head actions. Another device, CogKnife [7], a knife equipped with a microphone, recognizes food types from the cutting sounds. This method can classify food into six types with 96% accuracy from the cutting sounds by a classification model based on SVM (Support Vector Machine). These methods mainly recognize the food type but do not support to recognize the seasoning type and to estimate the amount of seasonings.

FoodCam [8] is a food recognition system by using camera of smartphone. This system classifies a food photo into five food types, from 100 food types with 79% accuracy by a classification model based on SVM. Bettadapura et al. [9] also proposed a food recognition system which recognizes the types of restaurant and food by location context and photo from smartphone. These systems can recognize the food type from a food photo but cannot identify the types of consumed seasonings and also cannot estimate the amount of the seasonings.

2.2   Food Recommendation

Kadowaki et al. [10] proposed a recipe recommendation system by using tweets on Twitter. The system analyzes user's preference based on the eaten food within 3 h from posting of the tweet, and recommends a suitable recipe by estimation of current context from the latest tweet. Li et al. [11] also proposed a recipe recommendation algorithm by combining content-based filtering and collaborative filtering algorithms. The system analyzes user's preference with the recipes evaluated as Light or Piquancy to recommend the suitable recipes. Furthermore, Yamamoto et al. [12] proposed a recipe recommendation system based on cooking history. Hence, there are many studies about recipe recommendation however these studies don't focus on the adjustment of seasoning, thus, users can only select from the recommended recipes, that is, users cannot eat dishes that the users want to eat based on their preferable taste.

2.3   Commercial Smart Kitchen Utensils

Pantelligent [2], a frying pan with a temperature sensor, realizes the proper doneness for each food ingredient. This utensil shows the proper time to heat the food ingredient and the proper timing to flip the food ingredient, to a smartphone by the management of the temperature on the frying pan. Another device, Grill alert [13] measures the temperature of grill and can notify the proper doneness to smartphone. However, these utensils do not support to show the proper amount of seasonings. Crock pot, a cooking pot [14] embedded with a temperature sensor and radio communication function, can detect the temperature of the cooking pot and then adjust to the proper temperature but cannot adjust the taste of food.

There has been lot of studies about food recognition, recipe recommendation, and smart kitchen utensils. However, there is no study to adjust the amount of seasonings from a recipe depending on the user's preferable taste. Therefore, we propose a cooking support system, which (1) analyzes the user's preference for the five basic tastes [4,5], such as saltiness, sourness, bitterness, sweetness, and umami (savoriness), (2) adjusts the amount of seasoning depending on the user's preference, and (3) uses a LED light embedded in the Smart Cruet to indicate the moment to stop adding the seasoning.

3   Preliminary Experiments

3.1   Investigation of Individual Differences in Taste Preference

In order to find out, whether there are individual differences in user,s preference, we conducted an experiment in which the participants eat miso soups with different amounts of hot water, and then choose the most favorite soup. In this investigation, we prepared the instant miso soups with five different amounts of hot water, such as 128 ml (−20%), 144 ml (−10%), 160 ml (correct amount on the recipe), 176 ml (+10%) and 192 ml (+20%). To avoid bias from prior knowledge, we didn't tell the participants the amount of hot water in each soup.

The participants rated each soup according to their personal taste. Table 1 shows the count of favorites for each soup. 12 participants answered that the soups with 128 ml and 144 ml, which are stronger soups than the correct soup with 160 ml, are the most favorite. On the other hand, 11 participants answered that 176 ml and 192 ml, which are weaker soups, are the most favorite. There was only one participant answered that the correct amount of soup with 160 ml is the most favorite soup. From this result, we found that there are the individual differences in user's preference even though the food is too strong/weak like the case of differing with 20% than the correct amount defined by the manufacturer.

Table 1. Individual Differences in user's preference for miso soups with different amount of hot water

Taste: reduction rate of water	# of participants
Too Strong: −20%	6
Strong: −10%	6
Correct: ±0%	1
Weak +10%	9
Too Weak +20%	2

3.2 Investigation of Error in the Input Amount by Adding Seasoning Based on Rough Estimation

Over half of Japanese housewives add seasoning based on rough estimation. Adding seasonings based on rough estimation opens the possibility that the taste of the dish differs greatly from the intended taste of the cook or of the eater's preference due to a too high or small amount of seasoning in comparison with the recipe. Therefore, we conducted an experiment to confirm the error between the input amount based on a rough estimation and the specific amounts. In this experiment, we prepared seven cups written the input amount of seasoning soy sauce such as large spoon: '1 (, 2, 3, or 4)', and 'small spoon: 1 (, 2, or 3)'. One measure of a large spoon represents 15 ml, and the measure of one small spoon represents 5 ml. We let 15 participants add soy sauce seasoning based on rough estimation to each cup. Among the 15 participants, six participants have been cooking more than three days in a week, the other nine participants usually cook less than three days in a week.

Figure 1a and b show the difference between rough estimation and preferable amount as stated in the recipe for the small and large spoon measure, for the nine participants, which did not cook very frequently. In the figures, the points represent the amount of seasoning with rough estimation and the red line represents the preferable amount of seasoning with measuring spoons. For these participants, the average error for small spoon was 71.8% and the average error

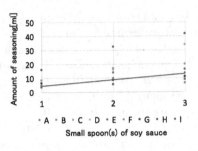
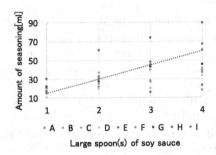

(a) Amount of seasoning for small spoon

(b) Amount of seasoning for large spoon

Fig. 1. Difference between rough estimation and preferable amount of seasoning in six participants with daily cooking habits (Points: Amount based on Rough Estimation, Led Line: Preferable Amount)

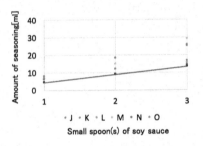
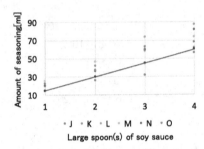

(a) Amount of seasoning for small spoon

(b) Amount of seasoning for large spoon

Fig. 2. Difference between rough estimation and preferable amount of seasoning in six participants with cooking habit (Points: Amount based on Rough Estimation, Led Line: Preferable Amount)

for large spoon was 41.4%. Both of the average errors were understandably large because these participants don't cook very frequently. On the other hand, Fig. 2a and b show the difference for the six participants, who cook frequently. For these participants, the average error for small spoon was 46.2% and the average error for large spoon was 31.8%. Even if the dish is cooked using the recipe, the dish does not always match the user's preference because of the measuring error of the seasoning which differs from the recipe.

From these results, we assume that a system is needed to be able to adjust the amount of seasoning depending on the user's preference in order to serve the dish to satisfy user's preference, and assist putting seasonings correctly.

4 Cooking Support System for Seasoning with Smart Cruet

4.1 System Architecture

The system architecture for the proposed system is shown in Fig. 3. The system consists of a smartphone application, a server and Smart Cruet. Users can check details about the dish and cooking process by using their smartphones. Users are required to evaluate the dish after eating, which is then stored in the user preference database. The server also consists of recipe database, a preference analysis mechanism, and amount adjustment mechanism. Smart Cruet is used to add salt and soy sauce adjusted according to user's preferable taste.

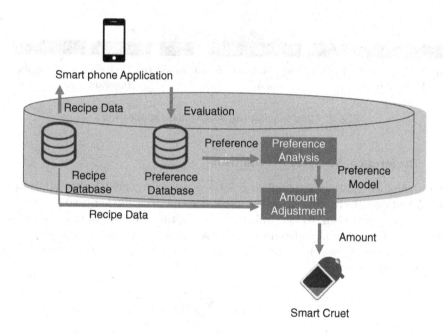

Fig. 3. System architecture

4.2 Smartphone Application

Figure 4a shows the details of the cooking process and recipes for the dish. The smartphone application is used to record feedbacks of users which are recorded as evaluation data to the server. The smartphone application also displays recipe data and user's preference. The users submit their evaluation based on the five basic tastes (Sweet, Salty, Sour, Bitter, Umami (savoriness)) after each meal as shown in Fig. 4b. Figure 4c shows a preference display function for the five basic tastes created for each user using their feedbacks.

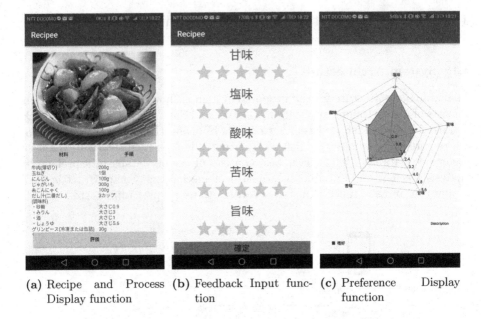

(a) Recipe and Process Display function

(b) Feedback Input function

(c) Preference Display function

Fig. 4. Main functions of smartphone application

4.3 Preference Analysis Mechanism

The preference analysis mechanism creates a preference model after analyzing the evaluation data received from the users. This model is further used in amount adjustment mechanism, to determine the appropriate amount of seasonings for each user. To create a preference model, we analyze the evaluation feedback received after each meal from the user and calculate the preference model value using the following formula:

$$M_i = \sum_{k=1}^{i-1} (M_k - F_k) \, / \, i$$
$$(M_1 = 0, \ F_1 = 0, \ -2 \leq F_k \leq 2, \ i > 1)$$

M_i and F_i represent the preference model value and feedback value for each day i, respectively.

4.4 Amount Adjustment Mechanism

The amount adjustment mechanism is used for adjusting the amount of seasoning according to the user's preference. By using the preference model developed, the appropriate amount of seasoning for each user is derived using the following formula:

$$Adjusted \, amt. = M_i \times 0.1 \times Amt. \, of \, seasoning$$

This adjusted amount is added to the current amount of seasoning used in the recipe.

4.5   Smart Cruet

Smart Cruet is developed to make it easier for users to add amount of seasonings according to their preferable taste. The Smart Cruet, as shown in Fig. 5, is composed of an acceleration sensor, a gyro sensor, a Bluetooth low energy (BLE) module, a battery, and a light emitting diode (LED). While using Smart Cruet, the embedded LED blinks to indicate that the appropriate amount of seasoning has been added and hence the user can now stop adding the seasoning to the dish.

Fig. 5. Smart cruet prototype

4.6   Recipe Dataset

Since our aim is to analyze user's preferable taste and adjust the amount of seasoning according to that taste, we required recipes that have not been affected by user's preference. Therefore, we used Bob & Angie [15] dataset provided by OGIS-RI Co., Ltd[2]. We believe that the dataset is suitable as a basic recipe dataset because it contains four thousand recipes supervised with emphasis on health and nutrition by registered dietitians.

5   Experiment

Experiments were conducted to determine if the proposed system could be used to get the amount of seasoning closer to the user's preferable taste. We also conducted experiments to check the accuracy of the Smart Cruet in real time.

---

[2] OGIS-RI Co., Ltd.: http://www.ogis-ri.co.jp/corporate_e/n-00.html.

5.1   Confirming Effect of One Feedback

Experimental Method. On the first day, we gathered feedbacks from 15 participants for Japanese Beef and Potato Stew dish, as shown in Fig. 6a. On the second day, the participants were asked to rate the dish prepared based on their feedbacks earlier on the level of saltiness from scale 1–5. Participants then tried the dish Boiling Spinach with Tube-shaped Fish Paste as shown in Fig. 6b in which soy sauce and salt were adjusted based on feedback received on the first day. This helped us to determine if we can approximate the preference level of users based on the feedbacks received after each meal.

(a) Dish before adjustment (Japanese Beef and Potato Stew)

(b) Dish after adjustment (Boiling Spinach with Tube-shaped Fish Paste)

Fig. 6. Dishes before and after adjustment

Experimental Result. Figure 7 shows the number of feedbacks received from the 10 participants before the adjustment of saltiness, while Fig. 8 depicts the number of feedbacks received after adjustment. The feedback for the amount of seasonings is depicted from scale 1 to 5, with 1 indicating the lowest amount of saltiness, 5 indicating the highest amount, and 3 indicating the optimal amount. The feedback before the adjustment showed that out of all the participants, optimal rating i.e. 3 was provided by 5, two participants rated the seasoning as 1, while the highest saltiness scale was 4 as provided by three participants. After the adjustment, four participants rated the seasoning as optimal i.e. 3. While five participants rated the seasoning in the scale of 2, only one participant provided the rating scale of 5. Table 2 shows that we were able to increase the preferable taste to the optimal amount for four participants. We were also able to improve the taste for one participant, up to the scale of 2.

Consideration. Four out of 10 participants rated the taste of the seasoning to be optimal, while six participants did not. We believe that the results from one-day experiment explained above were inconclusive. Therefore, we decided to test the efficiency of our system for a longer period of time.

Table 2. Evaluation before and after adjustment (bold columns represent the participants who could be closer to themselves preference)

Evaluation	**A**	**B**	C	D	**E**	F	G	**H**	I	**J**
Before adjustment	1	1	2	2	2	2	2	4	4	4
After adjustment	2	3	2	2	3	2	2	3	5	3

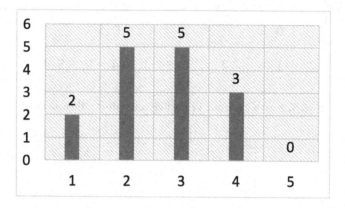

Fig. 7. Feedback from 15 participants before adjustment

5.2 Confirming Effects of Feedback After Two Weeks

Experimental Method. We conducted this experiment to investigate personal preferences over a long term period. The first day, the user cooks following a basic recipe. The user evaluates five levels of the introduced five basic tastes after the meal. Based on the feedback, the proposed system adjusts the amount of seasoning on on the second day. The users evaluate again their meal but this time with the adjusted amount of seasonings based on user's preference. This process was repeated for 14 days, each time taking the new feedback into account. We evaluate the proposed system based on how close it approaches the user's preference.

Experimental Result. Figure 9 shows the preference model for the five different tastes evaluated, which greatly changed until the seventh day except for bitter taste. However, the preference model on the final day did not vary much from the preference model that was created at the 7th day. It can be seen that a person's taste preference could be modeled and improved to some extent in seven days from the start of the experiment.

Consideration. Since the preference model estimation in two days was not able to approach the majority or more of the participants, we decided that the period was not sufficiently long. Therefore, the period was extended. After

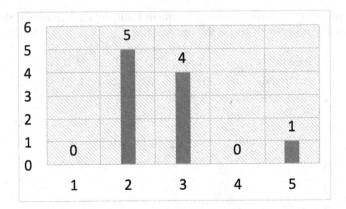

Fig. 8. Feedback from 10 participants after adjustment

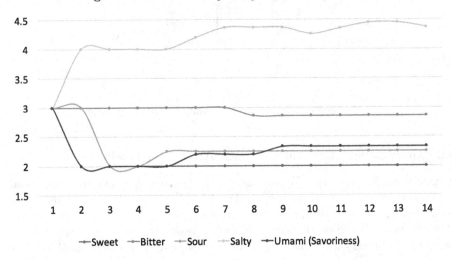

Fig. 9. Transition of feedback for five basic tastes during two weeks

conducting the additional experiments, the preference model estimation in a two week time period was able to estimate roughly the individual preference model. However, since there was only one participant in the preference model estimation experiment in the two week period, there was a possibility that it is not representative. In the future, we think that it is necessary to verify the preference analysis time period by increasing the number of participants and estimating different preference models.

5.3   Confirming Accuracy of Smart Cruet

To confirm the accuracy of adding seasoning with the Smart Cruet, we conducted an experiment. In this experiment, we added 50 ml of soy sauce 10 times using the Smart Cruet. After this we compared the amount estimated by the Smart Cruet to the actual added amount. As a result, the average of the added amount was 51.37 ml, the average of the estimated amount was 54.23 ml, thus, the average error between the actual amount and the estimated amount was 5.56%. Moreover, the error between the average estimated amount and the preferable amount (50 ml) was 8.46%.

As we showed in Sect. 3.2, even if the cooks are experienced, there is approximately 30% error between rough estimation and preferable amount. Therefore, it is assumed that a dish seasoned by the Smart Cruet is closer to user's preference than by using rough estimation. Furthermore, it is easier to use than using measuring spoons.

6 Conclusion

In this paper, we proposed a cooking support system that adjusts the amount of seasoning depending on the user's preference and support adding the correct amount of seasoning, through smartphone and Smart Cruet. The system analyzes the user's preference based on the feedback for five basic tastes evaluated by five grades after each eating a dish and adjust the amount of seasoning in the selected recipe depending on the user's preference. For the adjusted amount of seasoning, Smart Cruet, which embeds motion sensors, LED light, and BLE communication interface, indicates the moment to stop adding the seasoning. We were successful in improving the adjustment to user's preference in 7 days through a two week feedback experiment. Furthermore, Smart Cruet achieved a 5.56% average error, which is clearly lower than adding seasoning based on rough estimation. Because we used the recipes made by registered dietitians in this paper, as future work, we will mainly focus on adjusting the amount of seasoning for online recipes registered by non professional cooks. We also plan to test the efficiency of our system with higher number of participants.

References

1. Cookpad: To our corporate customers. https://info.cookpad.com/en/ads Accessed 3 Dec 2017
2. Inc., Circuitlab: Pantelligent - the easiest way to make great steaks, salmon, and much more. https://www.pantelligent.com. Accessed 26 Nov 2017
3. Panasonic: an attitude survey for cooking and kitchen (in Japanese). http://news.panasonic.com/jp/press/data/2013/04/jn130405-3/jn130405-3.pdf.   Accessed 3 Dec 2017
4. Chandrashekar, J., Hoon, M.A., Ryba, N.J.P., Zuker, C.S.: The receptors and cells for mammalian taste. Nature **444**(7117), 288–294 (2006)
5. Kobayashi, Y., Habara, M., Ikezazki, H., Chen, R., Naito, Y., Toko, K.: Advanced taste sensors based on artificial lipids with global selectivity to basic taste qualities and high correlation to sensory scores. Sensors **10**(4), 3411–3443 (2010)

6. Mirtchouk, M., Merck, C., Kleinberg, S.: Automated estimation of food type and amount consumed from body-worn audio and motion sensors. In: Proceedings of the 2016 ACM International Joint Conference on Pervasive and Ubiquitous Computing, UbiComp 2016, pp. 451–462. ACM (2016)

7. Kojima, T., Ijiri, T., White, J., Kataoka, H., Hirabayashi, A.: CogKnife: food recognition from their cutting sounds. In: 2016 IEEE International Conference on Multimedia Expo Workshops (ICMEW), pp. 1–6. ieeexplore.ieee.org, July 2016

8. Kawano, Y., Yanai, K.: FoodCam: a real-time food recognition system on a smartphone. Multimed. Tools Appl. **74**(14), 5263–5287 (2015)

9. Bettadapura, V., Thomaz, E., Parnami, A., Abowd, G., Essa, I.: Leveraging context to support automated food recognition in restaurants, pp. 580–587 (2015)

10. Kadowaki, T., Yamakata, Y., Tanaka, K.: Situation-based food recommendation for yielding good results. In: 2015 IEEE International Conference on Multimedia Expo Workshops (ICMEW), pp. 1–6 (2015)

11. Li, Z., Hu, J., Shen, J., Xu, Y.: A scalable recipe recommendation system for mobile application. In: 2016 3rd International Conference on Information Science and Control Engineering (ICISCE), pp. 91–94 (2016)

12. Yamamoto, S., Kando, N., Satoh, T.: Continuous recipe selection model based on cooking history. In: Spiro, E., Ahn, Y.-Y. (eds.) SocInfo 2016, Part I. LNCS, vol. 10046, pp. 138–151. Springer, Cham (2016). https://doi.org/10.1007/978-3-319-47880-7_9

13. Brookstone: Grill alert bluetooth connected thermometer. http://www.brookstone.com/pd/grill-alert-bluetooth-connected-thermometer/919441p.html. Accessed 3 Dec 2017

14. Crock-Pot: Crock-Pot WeMo enabled slow cooker. https://www.crock-pot.com/wemo-landing-page.html Accessed 3 Dec 2017

15. OGIS-RI Co., Ltd: Recipe SiteBob & AngieHealth recipes supervised by national registered dietitian. https://www.bob-an.com/. Accessed 3 Dec 2017

Assistive Technology for Active and Independent Aging

Blanka Klimova$^{(\boxtimes)}$

University of Hradec Kralove, Rokitanskeho 62,
500 03 Hradec Kralove 3, Czech Republic
blanka.klimova@uhk.cz

Abstract. Due to a rising number of older population groups, there is a need to prolong an active life of elderly people, who are ready and want to lead active and quality life in a sense of their inclusion, socialization and independence. Especially, the independence in their everyday activities is crucial for them. In this process, assistive technology seems to play a promising role. The purpose of this article is to discuss the role of assistive technology (AT) for active and independent aging, summarize its benefits and constraints for the elderly people, as well as describe its types. The methods include a method of literature search of available sources describing this issue in the world's databases Web of Science, Scopus, and PubMed, and a method of comparison and evaluation of the findings of the selected studies on the research topic. The findings of all the detected studies confirmed that the use of AT had a positive impact on the enhancement of active and independent living of the elderly people. Most of the trials researched the effectiveness of AT on the enhancement of physical conditions of healthy older people, followed by social assistive robots, memory aid systems, or protection AT. Nevertheless, it is important to target all AT devices at meeting both the elderly people's and their caregivers' individual needs. Therefore, developers should tailor these technological devices to the needs of the elderly people, which can be achieved through multidisciplinary cooperation of all interested stakeholders such the end-users, their caregivers, developers, and possibly, doctors.

Keywords: Assistive technology · Elderly · Quality of life · Benefits · Constraints

1 Introduction

Due to the demographic changes, the number of the elderly people is rapidly changing nowadays. In fact, aging is becoming a big social and economic issue. For instance, in 2030, the number of the elderly people aged 65+ years should reach 19%, which is 7% more in comparison with the year of 2000 [1]. In developed countries, this number of older adults forms 24% and it should rise to 33% by 2050 [2]. Thus, by 2050, the number of the elderly people should outnumber the young population in most of these countries [3]. This shift in the population groups obviously brings about a lot of problems, such as an increase in the costs on care (both institutional and non-institutional) about these elderly people [4]. Nevertheless, currently, there is a trend to

J. Zhou and G. Salvendy (Eds.): HCII 2019, LNCS 11593, pp. 383–392, 2019.
https://doi.org/10.1007/978-3-030-22015-0_30

move the institutional care to the community care [5]. According to the data from the SHARE project, 21% (in France and Switzerland) to 43% (Czech Republic) of the non-institutionalized population at the age of 65+ years receive help or support at least sometimes on an informal basis [6]. In fact, in the UK, informal care is the most important source of care for the elderly [7]. In addition, those are especially older family caregivers who take care of their infirm ones. These informal caregivers are also physically and emotionally burdened because they often experience isolation, low self-esteem, as well as depression [8]. Therefore, there is a need to prolong an active life of elderly people, who are ready and want to lead active and quality life in a sense of their inclusion, socialization and independence [9]. Especially, the independence in their everyday activities is crucial for them. In this process, assistive technology seems to play a promising role [10, 11].

The purpose of this article is to discuss the role of assistive technology for active and independent aging, summarize its benefits and constraints for the elderly people, as well as describe its types.

2 Assistive Technology

Assistive technology (AT) can be generally defined as any item, piece of equipment, or product system, whether acquired commercially, modified, or customized, that is used to increase, maintain, or improve functional capabilities of individuals with disabilities [12]. However, for the purpose of this article, a more appropriate definition is that AT is any product or service designed to enable independence of disabled and older people [13]. At present, more than one billion people need one or more assistive devices [14].

There exist different divisions of AT. According to its purpose, one can divide it into supportive technologies, which help people to complete tasks; responsive technologies, which can help to manage stress and raise alarms; and preventive technologies, which can help to prevent harm and raise alarms [15]. AT can range from a very simple device, such as crutches, walkers or calendar clocks, to a very sophisticated device, such as fall detectors that automatically send a signal via a base unit connected to a telephone line to a caregiver, community alarm or monitoring service, and which can call for assistance when necessary [15]. A more detailed division of AT is provided by Sisay [11]. Please consult Fig. 1 below.

AT for Social Interaction

Apart from living independently and safe, it is important for elderly people to stay in touch with their family, friends and peers since such a social contact has a positive impact on their cognition, mood and well-being [16]. And with the boom of mobile technologies it is quite easy. Patients can play games, get involved into computer brain training programs or just chat with their loved ones [15]. Moreover, social media play an important role in this respect because they can assist elderly people in developing social networking through which they can share and exchange information [17].

AT for Safety and Security

The safety devices can enable people to live independently, as well as, reduce worries of their loved ones about them. These technologies comprise different devices such as

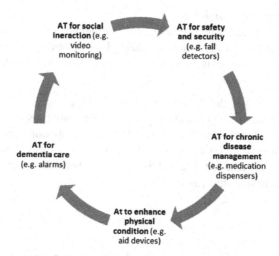

Fig. 1. Types of AT (author's own processing).

automatic lights, automated shut-off devices that can stop the gas supply if the gas has been left on, water isolation devices that control water taps and prevents flooding, or fall sensors that can register if a person has fallen. These sensors are usually small devices worn on the waist or on the upper chest. They have a button which, when activated, sends a signal to a caregiver or community alarm service [18]. Moreover, these safety devices also include tracking devices or location monitoring services, which enable to find the person if s/he gets lost and at the same time it enables the person with AD to call for help is s/he is disoriented and cannot find the way on his/her own [19].

For the above described reasons, AT is sometimes referred to as Ambient Assisted Living (AAL) since its aim is also support people to live independently. In addition, the AAL technologies can collect characteristics/data about the elderly through a non-intrusive wireless sensor system, whose data can provide valuable information about the elderly in real-time [20].

AT for Chronic Disease Management

Chronic diseases cover anything from diabetes to cancer, cardiovascular diseases and respiratory conditions. They can result in illness and hospitalization if they are not managed well. They are also among the leading causes of death. They can affect person's quality of life but they do not have to be detrimental to person's sense of independence [8]. Once again, AT can contribute to the maintenance or even improvement of their quality of life. There is, for instance, mobile app BlueStar Diabetes Manager for Type 2 diabetes. It enables patients to track their symptoms, food and medical information. It can also produce reports, which can be then shared with their caregivers and doctors [21].

AT to Enhance Physical Condition
Physical conditions of elderly people vary. Some of them do not need any mobility aids while the others are heavily dependent on them. These mobility aids include walkers, crutches, canes, prosthetic devices, scooters, wheel chairs, even mouth stick [21].

AT for Dementia Care
These technologies include the devices, which help people with AD with their memory, orientation and communication difficulties. These are mainly prospective memory aids including devices focused on time orientation, keeping appointments, or reminding people of attending social activities [22]. Furthermore, clocks calendar clocks help them to be aware of the relevant date and time, while the orientation devices such as the locaters help them to find the way or things.

3   Methods

The methods of this article comprise a method of literature review of available studies found on the research topic in the world's databases Web of Science, Scopus, and PubMed. The search keywords were *assistive technology* AND *elderly*; *assistive technology* AND *older people*; *assistive technology* AND *healthy aging*. Furthermore, a method of comparison and evaluation of the findings was used. All studies were written in English. Thus, articles written, for instance, in Chinese (cf. [23]) were excluded.

Altogether 2,127 articles were generated from all three databases. Most of the articles were found in Scopus (935). The oldest one dates to the year of 1991. The search was limited by December 2018. Nevertheless, majority of the articles did not focus on the research topic. Furthermore, most of the articles started to be published after the year of 2005. This can be illustrated on the articles identified in the Web of Science (consult Fig. 2 below). In addition, in searching the articles based on the keywords *assistive technology* AND *healthy aging*, only few studies were generated. They were mainly related to social robots, e.g. [24, 25], and devices aimed at physical abilities of older people, e.g. [26, 27]. However, the author concentrated only on clinical trials, which seemed to prove the efficacy of the use of assistive technology by elderly.

The selection inclusion criteria were as follows:

- the article had to be peer-reviewed and written in English;
- the end of the search period was December 2018, otherwise the beginning of the search was not limited by any year;
- it had to be a clinical trial;
- it had to focus on the research topic, i.e. active and independent aging, thus
- the articles which included, for example, older people who were not able to take care of themselves and required somebody else's care, were excluded [16, 19, 20, 22];
- the articles focused on caregivers and their use of AT were also excluded.

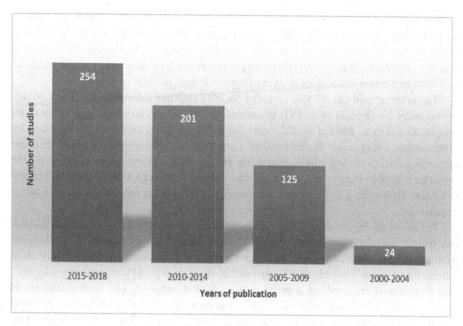

Fig. 2. An overview of the number of publications on the research topic in the Web of Science from 2000 till 2018, authors' own processing based on the data from the Web of Science [28].

Eventually, after removing duplicates and titles/abstracts unrelated to the research topic, 48 peer-reviewed, English-written studies were identified. After the full-text analysis, seven studies were included into the final analysis. Nevertheless, some of the other articles were used as a source of information for discussion.

4 Findings and Discussion

Altogether seven clinical trials were identified [29–35]. The oldest ones date back to the year of 2013 [31–34]. All studies concluded that the use of AT had a positive impact on the enhancement of active and independent living of the elderly people.

Most of the trials researched the effectiveness of AT on the enhancement of physical conditions of healthy older people [29–32]. In fact, these studies predominantly focused on the use of AT for maintaining balance in elderly [29–31]. Research shows that older people aged 65 years and above tend to increase likelihood of falling since their muscle function and strength are both relatively unstable and weak [30].

For example, Guitard et al. [31] tried to identify if artificial intelligence could raise grab bar use by seniors and to determine the efficacy of different cues (auditory, visual, and audiovisual combination) on the frequency of use of a grab bar. Their findings showed that participants had preferred the visual cue but the auditory cue had been the most powerful. Furthermore, their results revealed that artificial intelligence might be an interesting opportunity to raise grab bar use in healthy elderly people in order to decrease the risk of falls during bathing or bathtub transfers. Silveira et al. [32] maintain that the adoption of assistive technology devices for physical intervention tends to motivate and retain older people exercising for longer periods of time.

The other area of the AT use included socially assistive robots (SAR). The findings of the study by Granata et al. [33] illustrated that robot services were usable by older people. In addition, Pino et al. [25] state that SAR can help improve care delivery for older people living alone in the form of supporting the end-user's cognitive abilities, enhancing social participations, providing remote and continuous monitoring of the end-user's health status, and coaching the user in the promotion of his/her healthy behavior. However, it is important to customize SAR appearance, services, and social capabilities.

Furthermore, Bayen et al. [34] assessed the effectiveness of a memory aid system, the InBad (InBath), for bathroom-related daily care. They simulated a challenging morning routine consisting of 22 bathroom activities with a sample of 60 healthy older adults. Participants were randomly assigned to three groups: (1) 'no memory support', i.e., participants received no support at all, (2) 'list support', i.e., participants could retrieve a list of all activities, and (3) 'system support', i.e., participants received prompts for specific activities that had not yet been executed. The results revealed that both support groups executed significantly more activities compared to the 'no support' group. Thus, the findings confirmed that the use of AT had the potential to enable older adults to remain safe and independent in their own home.

Research also shows that all AT should be targeted at meeting the elderly people's individual needs and thus, developers should tailor these technological devices to the needs of the elderly people. This can be achieved through multidisciplinary cooperation of all interested stakeholders such the end-users, their caregivers, developers, and possibly doctors. Righi et al. [36] emphasize that technological devices focused on the elderly people should be designed to meet situated and dynamic needs/interests of the communities (and not only of care) to which they belong. This is quite important since as research [36–38] indicate, the elderly people are still reluctant to adopt AT. This can be improved by making the elderly people aware of the benefits of AT devices, such lowering their travel costs (i.e., they do not inevitably have to see their doctor face-to-face about the prescription they need); avoiding social isolation (i.e., AT devices can enable them easier communication with their family members or friends and in this way eliminate their loneliness); reducing pressure on both formal and informal care-givers; enhancing their independence in performing their everyday activities; or increasing their feeling of safety [39–42]. On the basis of the research studies, Fig. 3 below then summarizes the key benefits and constraints of the use of AT by the elderly.

Benefits	Constraints
• enhancement of independent and active living, aging in place; • lowering of economic burden of social system; • reduction of distress and loneliness; • increasing the feeling of safety and security; • monitoring of the elderly people's state of health; • willingness of younger generation of the elderly to adopt AT.	• inappropriate technical parameters of AT for the elderly; • a lack of awareness of the benefits which AT devices can generate; • fear of misuse of personal data; • costs barriers; • stigmatization of the use of AT; • unequal access and a lack of support; • older people's reluctance to accept and adopt AT; • a lack of political will and cooperation.

Fig. 3. Benefits and constraints of the use of AT by the elderly people (author's own processing).

5 Conclusion

The findings of all the detected studies confirmed that the use of AT had a positive impact on the enhancement of active and independent living of the elderly people. Most of the trials researched the effectiveness of AT on the enhancement of physical conditions of healthy older people, followed by social assistive robots, memory aid systems or protection AT.

Nevertheless, it is important to target all AT devices at meeting the elderly people's individual needs. Therefore, developers should tailor these technological devices to the needs of the elderly people, which can be achieved through multidisciplinary cooperation of all interested stakeholders such the end-users, their caregivers, developers, and possibly, doctors (cf. [43]). In addition, Garcon et al. [44] indicate that many countries need much greater official awareness of older adults' needs and preferences. Such attitudinal changes should then be reflected in laws and regulations to address the specificities of care for older people.

Acknowledgements. This study is supported by the SPEV project 2019, run at the Faculty of Informatics and Management, University of Hradec Kralove, Czech Republic. The author thanks Josef Toman for his help with the data collection.

References

1. Vafa, K.: Census bureau releases demographic estimates and projections for countries of the world (2016). http://blogs.census.gov/2012/06/27/census-bureau-releases-demographic-estimates-and-projections-for-countries-of-the-world/
2. World population Ageing 2013. UN, New York (2013)

3. Statista: Proportion of selected age groups of world population in 2017, by region (2017). https://www.statista.com/statistics/265759/world-population-by-age-and-region/
4. Klimova, B., Maresova, P., Kuca, K.: Non-pharmacological approaches to the prevention and treatment of Alzheimer's disease with respect to the rising treatment costs. Curr. Alzheimer Res. 13(11), 1249–1258 (2016)
5. De Vliegher, K., Aertgeerts, B., Declercq, A., Milisen, K., Sermeus, W., Moons, P.: Shifting care from hospital to home: a qualitative study. Prim. Health Care 25(9), 24–31 (2015)
6. Riedel, M., Kraus, M.: Informal care provision in Europe: Regulation and profile of providers. ENEPRI Research Report no. 96 (2011). http://aei.pitt.edu/32970/
7. Cook, E.J., et al.: Exploring factors that impact the decision to use assistive telecare: perspectives of family care-givers of older people in the United Kingdom. Ageing Soc. 38(9), 1912–1932 (2018)
8. Maresova, P., Klimova, B.: Non-pharmacological approaches in the depression treatment - strengths and weaknesses of mobile applications use. In: Oliver, N., Serino, S., Matic, A., Cipresso, P., Filipovic, N., Gavrilovska, L. (eds.) MindCare/FABULOUS/IIOT 2015-2016. LNICST, vol. 207, pp. 73–77. Springer, Cham (2018). https://doi.org/10.1007/978-3-319-74935-8_10
9. Klimova, B., Valis, M., Kuca, K.: Cognitive decline in normal aging and its prevention: A review on non-pharmacological lifestyle strategies. Clin. Interv. Aging 12, 903–910 (2017)
10. Nagode, M., Dolnicar, V.: Assistive technology for older people and its potential for intergenerational cooperation. Teorija in Praksa 47, 1278–1294 (2010)
11. Sisay, M.: The use of assistive technology to support selfcare of elderly people at home (2017). https://www.theseus.fi/bitstream/handle/10024/127841/Thesis%20Final%20version.pdf?sequence=1&isAllowed=y
12. Assistive Technology Act of 1998 (1998). https://section508.gov/assistive-technology-act-1998
13. Beech, R., Roberts, D.: SCIE Research briefing 28: Assistive technology and older people (2008). http://www.scie.org.uk/publications/briefings/briefing28/index.asp
14. Assistive technology (2018). http://www.who.int/news-room/fact-sheets/detail/assistive-technology
15. Alzheimer's Society: Assistive technology (2018). https://www.alzheimers.org.uk/info/20091/what_we_think/85/assistive_technology
16. Vahia, I.V., Kamat, R., Vang, C., Posada, C., Ross, L., Oreck, S., et al.: Use of tablet devices in the management of agitation among patients with dementia: an open-label study. Am. J. Geriatr. Psychiatry 25(8), 860–864 (2017)
17. Iqbal, S., Ahsan, K., Hussain, M.A., Nadeem, A.: Social media as assistive technology for elderly. J. Basic Appl. Sci. 12, 211–222 (2016)
18. Miskelly, F.G.: Assistive technology in elderly care. Age Ageing 30, 455–458 (2001)
19. McKinstry, B., Sheikh, A.: The use of global positioning systems in promoting safer walking for people with dementia. J. Telemed. Telecare 19(5), 288–292 (2013)
20. Stucki, R.A., Urwyler, P., Rampa, L., Müri, R., Mosimann, U.P., Nef, T.: A web-based non-intrusive ambient system to measure and classify activities of daily living. J. Med. Internet Res. 16(7), e175 (2014)
21. Chronic illness: Common assistive technologies (2018). http://guides.library.illinois.edu/c.php?g=598148&p=4140793
22. King, A.C., Dwan, C.: Electronic memory aids for people with dementia experiencing prospective memory loss: a review of empirical studies. Dementia (2017). https://doi.org/10.1177/1471301217735180
23. Chu, H.T., Chen, M.H.: Assistive technology devices for the elderly at home. Hu Li Za Zhi 53(5), 20–27 (2006)

24. Susel, G.A., Hamrioui, S., de la Torre Díez, I., Cruz, E.M., López-Coronado, M., Franco, M.: Social robots for people with aging and dementia: a systematic review of literature. Telemedicine E-health. https://doi.org/10.1089/tmj.2018.0051

25. Pino, M., Boulay, M., Jouen, F., Rigaud, A.S.: Are we ready for robots that care for us? Attitudes and opinions of older adults toward socially assistive robots. Front. Aging Neurosci. 7, 141 (2015)

26. Maclean, L.M., Brown, L.J.E., Khadra, H., Astell, A.J.: Observing prioritization effects on cognition and gait: the effect of increased cognitive load on cognitively healthy older adults' dual-task performance. Gait Posture 53, 139–144 (2017)

27. King, E.C., Novak, A.C.: Effect of bathroom aids and age on balance control during bathing transfers. Am. J. Occup. Ther. 71(6), 7106165030p1–7106165030p9 (2017)

28. Web of Science (2018). http://apps.webofknowledge.com/

29. Chiang, S.L., et al.: Measurement of bed turning and comparison with age, gender, and body mass index in a healthy population: application of a novel mobility detection system. Biomed. Res. Int. 2014, 819615 (2014)

30. Chen, T.H., Chou, L.W., Tsai, M.W., Lo, M.J., Kao, M.J.: Effectiveness of a heel cup with an arch support insole on the standing balance of the elderly. Clin. Interv. Aging 9, 351–356 (2014)

31. Guitard, P., Sveistrup, H., Fahim, A., Leonard, C.: Smart grab bars: a potential initiative to encourage bath grab bar use in community dwelling older adults. Assist. Technol. 25(3), 139–148 (2013)

32. Silveira, P., van de Langenberg, R., van Het Reve, E., Daniel, F., Casati, F., de Bruin, E.D.: Tablet-based strength-balance training to motivate and improve adherence to exercise in independently living older people: a phase II preclinical exploratory trial. J. Med. Internet Res. 15(8), e159 (2013)

33. Granata, C., Pino, M., Legouverneur, G., Vidal, J.S., Bidaud, P., Rigaud, A.S.: Robot services for elderly with cognitive impairment: testing usability of graphical user interfaces. Technol. Health Care 21(3), 217–231 (2013)

34. Bayen, U.J., Dogangün, A., Grundgeiger, T., Haese, A., Stockmanns, G., Ziegler, J.: Evaluating the effectiveness of a memory aid system. Gerontology 59(1), 77–84 (2013)

35. Ong, N.W.R., et al.: Utility of a medical alert protection system compared to telephone follow-up only for home-alone elderly presenting to the ED - a randomized controlled trial. Am. J. Emerg. Med. 36(4), 594–601 (2018)

36. Righi, V., Sayago, S., Blat, J.: When we talk about older people in HCI, who are we talking about? Towards a 'turn to community' in the design of technologies for a growing ageing population. Int. J. Hum.-Comput. Stud. 108, 15–31 (2017)

37. Chernbumroong, S., Atkins, A.S., Yu, H.: Perception of smart home technologies to assist elderly people. In: Proceedings of the 4th International Conference on Software. Knowledge, Information Management and Applications (SKIMA 2010), Bhutan, pp. 1–7 (2015)

38. Iancu, I., Iancu, B.: Elderly in the digital era. Theor. Perspect. Assist. Technol. Technol. 5(60), 1–13 (2017)

39. Beer, J.M., Takayama, L.: Mobile remote presence systems for older adults: acceptance, benefits, and concerns. In: Proceedings of the 6th ACM IEEE International Conference on Human-Robot Interactions (HKI 2011), Lausanne: ACM, pp. 19–26 (2011)

40. Mitzner, T.L., Boron, J.B., Fausset, C.B., Adams, A.E., Charness, N., Czaja, S.J.: Older adults talk technology: technology usage and attitudes. Comput. Human Behav. 26(6), 1710–1721 (2010)

41. Hola, J., Pikhart, M.: The implementation of internal communication system as a way to company efficiency. E&M 17(2), 161–169 (2010)

42. Yusif, S., Soar, J., Hafeez-Baig, A.: Older people, assistive technologies, and the barriers to adoption: a systematic review. Int. J. Med. Inform. **94**, 112–116 (2016)
43. Góngora, A.S., Hamrioui, S., de la Torre Díez, I., Motta Cruz, E., López-Coronado, M., Franco, M.: Social robots for people with aging and dementia: a systematic review of literature. Telemed. J. E Health (2018). https://doi.org/10.1089/tmj.2018.0051
44. Garçon, L., et al.: Medical and assistive health technology: meeting the needs of aging populations. Gerontologist **56**(Suppl 2), S293–S302 (2016)

Digital Home: Life Transitions and Digital Domestic Practices in Later Life

Sanna Kuoppamäki[✉]

University of Jyväskylä, Jyväskylä, Finland
sanna.kuoppamaki@jyu.fi

Abstract. As older adults become active users of digital technologies, digital activity among this age group is increasingly associated with life stage factors. This paper discusses the understanding of life stage as explanatory factors in older adults' digital engagement by exploring the association between life transitions and digital domestic practices in Finland. The study is based on an analysis of qualitative, in-person interview data from 20 participants between the ages of 50 and 78 who recently bought their own apartment in Western or Central Finland. The aims are to identify variances of life transitions in relation to domestic practices, investigate the association between life transitions and digital engagement at home, and evaluate the possibilities for incorporating digital domestic ecosystems into the daily lives of older adults. The study makes three main propositions: digital domestic practices are influenced by financial decision-making processes in households; life transitions and changes in social and personal relationships influence the emergence and creation of digital practices at home; and the appropriation of digital domestic ecosystems requires social and cultural changes regarding the desirability and accessibility of digital services. To this end, the study considers the extent to which the concept of life stages could be taken into consideration in the digital design of domestic practices among older people in Finland.

Keywords: Digital technologies · Ageing · Life transitions · Digital domestic practices · Digital home

1 Introduction

Older adults' engagement with digital technologies is influenced by various personal, socio-demographic and socio-economic factors, such as age, attitudes towards technology, cognitive abilities, personal interests, education level, as well as availability and access to technology [6, 15, 18, 19]. A key question has been whether age predicts digital activity, or whether digital engagement is shaped by life stage factors, such as life transitions and changes in social and personal relationships [8]. This paper discusses the understanding of life stage as an explanatory factor in older adults' digital engagement. It explores the association between life transitions and digital domestic practices among older adults in Finland. These issues are becoming more relevant as the number of older people is increasing and societies need to develop new solutions to

© Springer Nature Switzerland AG 2019
J. Zhou and G. Salvendy (Eds.): HCII 2019, LNCS 11593, pp. 393–404, 2019.
https://doi.org/10.1007/978-3-030-22015-0_31

support independent living among older adults, and engage them in exploiting digital technologies widely in various servicescapes [10, 18].

The study investigates the role of life transitions in digital domestic practices among older adults from three standpoints. The first is to identify the variances of life transitions among older adults in relation to domestic practices (research question RQ1). This is conducted by addressing certain life events in the life courses of older adults that contribute to creation of new alterations and inspirations for digital engagement.

Second, the study aims to investigate the association between life transitions and digital engagement by analysing the interfaces where life transitions and digital engagement overlap (RQ2). Research has suggested that certain life events, such as the departure of children from home, or retirement, may provide new drivers for older adult's digital engagement [18, 19]. Typically, the presence of children in the household may improve adults' digital skills and motivation to use digital technologies [8]. When children leave home, the family dynamics changes which may result in changes in digital engagement among adult family members.

The third objective of the study is to evaluate the emergence of digital domestic ecosystems and possibilities to appropriate these technologies in older adults' daily lives (RQ3).

The paper begins with an introduction to the concepts of digital domestic practices and life transitions. This is followed by an analysis of a qualitative data set collected in 2016 as semi-structured in-person interview data for participants ages 50 to 80. Finally, the study discusses the extent to which life transitions can be considered an explanatory factor when investigating older adults' digital engagement, and how life stage could be taken into consideration in the digital design of domestic services for older people in Finland.

2   Digital Practices in Domestic Environments

Digital domestic practices refer to the application and usage of digital technologies in domestic environments and domestic management [13]. Previous research discusses managing digital content at home in terms of 'digital housekeeping', which refers to the management of networked home, encompassing a multitude of devices and services and their interrelations in an ecology of media [23]. Digital domestic practices are constructed around specialised knowledge, skills and comprehension and specialised strategies, activities and characteristics understood as agency in decision-making [13]. Digital domestic 'expertise' thus involves social and cultural capital to media and literacies to apply in the contexts of daily home life.

The domestication of technologies in the home is a process in which all family members influence the formation and negotiation of social rules around particular technologies [11]. The household structure is connected to the practices through which digital technologies are integrated into the organisation of everyday life, involving an element of social interaction between family members in the household. The influence of household structure on digital domestic practices can be evaluated by addressing the presence of young people in the household. Young people are usually regarded as motivators or teachers in adults' technology use, as they encourage adults in the same household to use the internet and use different digital technologies in ways unfamiliar to them [8, 20, 21]. Parents, on the other hand, finance and regulate children's computer use [25]. Adults are presented as newcomers in digital environments in comparison to young children, who often limit adults' access to digital technologies by dominating the spatial environment of the household [24].

Digital domestic practices include housekeeping activities that serve to maintain the functioning and maintenance of the household, such as meal planning and preparation, shopping, cleaning, laundry, maintenance and repairs, care of adults, children and pets, management of bills and expenses and transportation [5]. Digital domestic practices also involve managing digital content in the form of identifying, accessing, storing and organising digital content in relation to household needs [23]. Media activity practices, such as selecting and downloading movies, organising TV, radio or music content are part of digital management in daily life that also include aesthetic requirements of the home environment, such as stacking hard drives neatly, hiding wires, making devices look orderly, and so on [13]. This digital household management occurs in relation to and within the interaction of family relationships and household members that affect the development of digital practices at home.

3 Digital Practices in the Lives of Older Adults

The application of digital technologies to domestic practices is influenced by age, but also by other socio-demographic and socio-economic factors that represent the life stage of older adults [6, 15, 18, 19]. Older adults, aged approximately 50 to 74, are influenced by various life transitions, including changes in family or employment status, that may influence on their abilities, skills and needs in digital technology use. Quite often, these life transitions are associated with changes in living arrangements and living environments.

At this life stage, adults typically encounter transitions related to social and personal relationships [2, 14]. These transitions are embodied in relation to changes in work life and changes in family structures [12], and they may act as a driving force behind new living solutions. For instance, changes in work life may motivate older adults to relocate to a new city or even to a new country [16]. Changes in family structures may inspire older adults to pursue their own interests, which are often related to housing and living. With ageing, social networks may narrow, but become more meaningful [2], and older adults may thus have a stronger need for maintaining ties with established social networks [1, 7]. Older adults are highly motivated to use these to keep in touch with family members in particular, and to strengthen social and personal relationships that are often transformed in later stages of life [19].

In a qualitative study of adoption of information and communication technologies, older adults' motivations and reasons for computer use in the household were investigated [21]. The interviewees, who were aged 60 and over, said they had started using computers as a consequence of some significant life event, such as a heart attack, which motivated them to keep up to date with technology that helped in maintaining independence when financial security and mobility were threatened. Technological innovations thus provide opportunities for independent, safe and secure living for older adults [3].

In the appropriation of digital technologies, encouragement from children or younger members of the household who want their parents to use technology may significantly influence decisions to acquire new technology [21]. In the incorporation of technologies, older adults use social strategies that involve families and friends as driving forces in the acquisition process of technology [17]. In all phases of making sense of technology, older adults thus rely significantly on the social relationships that encourage and support them in the acquisition of these devices [21]. Incorporation of digital technologies into daily life is thus influenced by users' networks, which affect the social understandings of these artefacts [3, 4].

4   Materials and Methods

The study analyses a qualitative data set entitled *Housing, Digitalisation and the Life Course*, which was collected between November and December 2016 as part of a research project entitled '*DIGI50 + Mature consumers, customer experience and value creation in digital and physical environments.*

The data set includes 20 in-person interviews conducted among 11 males and nine females. The participants were recruited using a database owned by YIT Group, one of the largest housing manufacturers in Finland. The recruitment of participants was conducted under two criteria: they had bought a new apartment during the last 12 months in Western or Central Finland, more specifically Jyväskylä or Tampere area, and they belonged to the over 50 age group. An invitation was sent to 157 members of the data base (107 in Tampere area and 50 in Jyväskylä area), and 20 reported as volunteers. Each of the interviews lasted approximately 60 to 75 min, and were held in the University of Jyväskylä or in the University of Tampere as in-person interviews with one or two interviewers present in each interview. Of the interviewees, nine lived in the Tampere area and 11 in the Jyväskylä area that are growing regions in Western and Central Finland.

The interviews, carried out as semi-structured in-depth interviews, covered the following research areas: the person's current housing and living situation, life transitions that resulted in changes in housing, and digitalisation of domestic environments. In the interviews, participants were asked to describe these issues in their current living, and the interviewers presented specific sub-questions to explore these issues in more depth. The interviews were guided by the presumption that housing is associated with life stages, and therefore the interviewers wanted to gain an overall view of the interviewee's life situation.

The analysis was guided by conceptual presumptions regarding life stage, life transitions and digital engagement [6, 8, 12, 15, 18]. In the first phase of the analysis, all expressions related to digital technologies in domestic environments were separated from the main text. In the second phase, expressions were thematised under three categories: financial decision-making in digital environments, life transitions and digital domestic practices, and designing the digital home in later life. In both phases of the analysis, the unit of analysis was a sentence or statement articulated by a particular interviewee. The data expressions were interpreted in order to understand and explain the association between life stage and digital engagement.

5 Research Findings

5.1 Financial Decision-Making in Digital Environments

When reflecting on their choice of housing, the participants generally felt the decision was primarily guided by financial considerations. Many shared an experience of living their young adulthood years with limited financial resources which reflected their housing conditions as young adults. The participants generally described their housing path as a desire to improve on their past housing conditions and quality of life. Now, in their fifties and sixties, the participants who represented property owners, generally had a good level of income, which enabled many to re-evaluate their housing choices and make improvements. This experience was associated with ideas regarding smart home solutions and emergence of digital technologies in domestic environments:

> Now when I have it [a higher income] I can buy it [a new digital technology] if needed. I don't want to buy new things all the time, only when something is broken. (Male, 68)

For most of the participants in the 50–60 age group, digital technologies were integrated into their daily lives to a wide extent, and they actively described their use of digital technologies for banking, communication, social media, searching for information and other daily necessities. Participants in this age group generally said they had much less difficulty in digital engagement in comparison to older participants, who did not articulate their opinions or impressions of digitalisation of domestic environments as clearly. However, many participants from all ages considered themselves to be careful and moderate users of digital domestic technologies, and rarely described their relationship with digital technologies with enthusiasm. Older adults were digitally active in those practices that were associated with utility value, whereas digital media practices with a focus on gratification or entertainment were considered less appealing or important by the participants.

> We have a very fancy [smart] television and we cannot really use it, it requires updating all the time, you can use the television for the internet, YouTube and Twitter and all that [...] but we rarely use it [...] luckily we have these online help services to help up with that. (Male, 68)

> I don't trust them [digital domestic technologies]. If I leave the house and could turn the washing machine on with an app, I wouldn't trust it. I would only do damage [*laughs*]. (Female, 50)

Decisions to acquire new technologies at home were thus carefully considered by the participants, and they did so in relation to their social and family situations. The presence of new technologies in the home was seen as something involving the whole family, and which thus influenced the lives of others in the household. Despite that many of the participants said they used digital media for communication with family members, application of digital domestic technologies was still relatively rare.

> I ask my family members which technologies I should buy, and which software is best. (Male, 52)

> If we have a home cinema or something like that at home, it's our son who always fixes it. I have delegated it to him; it [home cinema] is more for the young people. (Male, 52)

For many participants, the question of digitalisation of domestic practices involved finances and financing one's own housing decisions. Most of the participants considered digital domestic technologies and smart home solutions to be something they cannot afford, and that are too expensive for their everyday lives:

Technological developments and new apartments are quite expensive, and many people cannot afford to buy [*laughs*] unless they receive a heritage or win the lottery. It limits things a lot, how technology is developed at home. (Male, 52)

That would be nice, if you are coming home and you could turn on the sauna, I don't have that kind of possibility [*laughs*] but that would be nice, or to see what is in your refrigerator and you could order food when you come home. [...] I might pay for that. But I suppose that would be so expensive that I could not afford it [*laughs*]. (Female, 53)

Finland has a long tradition of house ownership, and many still consider ownership one of the most important factors behind housing decisions. One of the interviewees, who has in the past lived abroad for several years, could not understand the Finnish practice of spending majority of one's income on housing:

For us [the Finns], housing is given too much importance. It takes too much of your income, it restricts other things. [...] You need to buy a home and then pay the mortgage for several decades, you cannot afford to travel or have expensive hobbies. It would be much more reasonable to live in a more urban environment so that you can walk to cultural events, restaurants, movies and meet people. (Male, 78)

When understanding and interpreting older adults' needs and capabilities in relation to digital housing solutions, therefore, cultural factors regarding housing decisions as established practices of financing them may explain the extent to which older adults in Finland are willing to apply digital technologies at home. The Finnish culture of independent living and ownership of one's home encourages consumers to invest their resources in improving their quality of life through advanced housing solutions. Despite many of the participants evaluating their income level as relatively good, they still considered new digital technologies to be too expensive for their daily lives. These financial decision-making processes regarding housing decisions and digital solutions therefore reflect the characteristics of Finnish consumer culture more generally.

5.2   Life Transitions and Digital Domestic Practices

During the interviews, the participants generally described changes in their housing path in relation to changes in family status or employment situation. When sharing their experiences from their personal housing history, the participants discussed changes in their relationships such as starting a new relationship, ending a relationship, starting and ending education and establishing a work life [9]. Female interviewees in particular stated changes in their personal relationships as the main inspiration for alternative housing solutions. However, these reasons were pronounced among the male interviewees:

Could you describe what has influenced [your decisions] along with ageing?

I had a divorce process and I was looking for an apartment, I went to all kinds of awful places [*laughs*]. Then I thought, I have to move to a great place. Somewhere that feels like home. And after that, I've learned to appreciate it. (Male, 53)

For many of the participants, changes in their housing path were characterised by positive emotional changes, particularly if housing decisions were accompanied by starting of new relationships. During their life courses, many of the participants had experienced various forms of housing and living arrangements, both living alone as a single person, living together with a spouse and living together with other family members. At the later stages of life, interviewees described their living in terms of established habits and routines. Despite that, most participants orientate themselves positively towards new changes and alterations:

It is a positive change to move in with someone. Prior to that, I lived alone for nine years, before that I was married. It was a big change, after getting used to living alone, with all the personal characteristics that I have [*laughs*]. (Female, 50)

For some of the interviewees, these changes resulted to new contemplations in digital domestic practices. For particularly the female participants, moving together with someone and starting a new relationship brought along new digital routines and habits from the part of their spouses. Interviewees described these new digital practices brought along by their spouses with consideration and sometimes with judgement, and in many cases they were not willing to adopt same digital habits, particularly if these new digital practices were in contraction with their own identities and values in general:

I use a tablet computer due to work and my personal interest. It's now my world, it's more my spouse who takes care of it. It's his hobby. My work has forced me to use them, and sometimes I browse the internet at home. But I don't play with computers or like gaming at home, even though [my spouse] does that. I'm spending all my days with the computer, so at home I want to do something else. (Female, 50)

The adoption and use of digital domestic technologies occur in the household where all members influence on technological decisions [8, 11, 21], individuals and families show a lot of variance in the extent to which children and other family members influence the application of digital technologies at home. During the interviews, this heterogeneity was clearly highlighted. For some of the participants, children had a major role when teaching or motivating adults to embrace digital domestic practices, but this was not the case for all:

Did you notice that children would teach you or bring technology into your everyday life?

Well, some have. But not all. My niece, who is 20, is not very active with digital [devices]. (Female, 50)

Whether children could actually teach their parent how to use technology at home could therefore be highly dependent on other factors. According to the interviews, these factors may include, for instance, the digital skills levels of younger people at home, the frequency of communication between family members, the extent to which older adults participate in working life, and the quality and intensity of other social relationships in daily life. For some of the interviewees, it was older adults at work who had a stronger impact on the adoption and use of digital technologies in domestic environments than the presence of children in their daily life:

In your case, have your children influenced your use of technology in any way?

Yes, they have. My kids have taught me what they knew themselves. Or then [I learnt] at work. It's mostly from work where these laptops and tablet computers, smartphones come from, there I can get help. (Female, 53)

For those participants who were still actively involved in work life, it was the work environment that influenced domestication practices of technologies, particularly if the children or other young people possessed less advanced digital skills or were not involved with similar technologies as the older family members in the household. Interviewees who were approaching retirement mentioned children as the most important source of incorporating digital technologies to domestic environments:

Do your kids use technology more than you do?

Yes, they do. I have a son, and I call him when something is not working. My son fixed my computer at home. He was here in the summer. He ordered the parts from the internet. (Male, 60)

We have very close relationships in our family. There are six people in our household, we are actively involved during holidays. We just spent our holiday in Germany, for all six of us. We always try to get the whole family together (—) We will send videos and pictures, and it does help us to get the whole family together. (Male, 60)

Offline communication practices between younger and older adults in the household thus significantly influenced to what extent the children encouraged or supported older adults' with their participation in digital environments at home. Those participants with more frequent offline communication practices between family members discussed the role of their children in digital engagement more often than those who possessed less frequent contact or communication with their children. If the family members were actively involved in each other's lives outside of digital environments, it was perhaps easier for them to ask or offer support in digital domestic practices at home. The frequency of digital communication in general thus seemed to be associated with support that was provided in the usage of digital technologies in the context of home in particular. Those participants who did not actively discus or mention the role of their children in the incorporation of digital domestic practices, rather discussed about other social and personal relationships that influenced the help and support that was available to them in the usage of digital technologies. Being seen as part of the household environment, mothers and sisters were sometimes considered equally important enablers or supporters of digital technology use. Therefore, life transitions that inspired or motivated older adults to adopt new digital practices were experienced in relation to all social and personal relationships:

Was your decision [to buy a home] preceded by some kind of life changes?

Well, my children moved away from home, that is. I was laughing, now when I don't have the kids anymore, then it's my mom who moves to my house! (Female, 53)

I had a new internet connection. I had to learn it.. but then I received help from my sister so that I could have the laptop in my use. At first it wasn't working, but my sister helped me with it. (Female, 56)

5.3 Designing a Digital Home in Later Life

During the interviews, the participants were shown a prototype (a picture) of a digital ecosystem representing the emergence of digital and physical services integrated to everyday living and housing. In this ecosystem, digital and physical services regarding domestic tasks, food delivery, health applications, care services and physical exercise were provided by the housing cooperative, indicating the easy accessibility of these services through digital platforms. The participants generally considered the emergence of new digital ecosystems to be valuable, but they discussed the importance of the ability to access these services independently:

What kind of thoughts do you have about housing services, that would be connected to your home, for example the possibility to have care or help with domestic tasks?

I suppose they are important for older people. But I can stand with my own feet, I don't really need them. But perhaps later I will. (Male, 58)

Many of those [services] are important. But maybe I don't need them in my own life. I like to go to my own gym in the city. And services regarding other domestic tasks... well I like to use my favourite ones that I have used for many years. I have a close relationship with them [*laughs*]. I like to go to a certain hairdresser, food store... I don't need them at home. (Female, 50)

For the older adults, using digital services at home was thus associated with old adulthood when the individual is more dependent on the help of other people [12]. In their fifties, the participants evaluated their physical abilities as good and wanted to maintain these abilities and skills by using physical services instead. Many of the interviewees already had existing relationships with service providers, which was perceived more important than having increased accessibility to physical services through digital platforms.

The participants discussed their personal needs regarding the emergence of digital ecosystems in relation to health and wellbeing. A possibility to enjoy nature or time with pets in an urban environment was considered desirable; gardens and pets, for example, were mentioned as being important to a sense of personal wellbeing. Most participants mentioned the importance of going to the gym or other possibilities for physical exercise. The idea of creating hybrid practices in urban environments received attention, and the emergence of new ecosystems integrating physical services to natural and authentic environment was regarded as a pleasant experience for older people.

Green house, or a room with pets, for example cats and dogs. And maybe a hairdresser. To have services near you. (Male, 50)

I would like to be able to talk and chat with people. Especially when you are old, to have social connection and community. Now when I'm still working, I don't need it, but when I'm old... I'd like to have it nearby. (Male, 52)

Regarding the life stages of the participants, the life transitions represented in the form of changes in social and personal relationships and employment status were thus well represented in how they discussed their needs in relation to the emergence of new digital ecosystems. Needs and aspirations were associated with work and family status that created the framework for everyday living. When still employed and actively participating in work life and having social contacts and interaction in the workplace, participants did not see the value of having social or community living near them. Despite this, they recognised the changing needs followed by life transitions and were preparing themselves to adjust their living environment to these changing aspirations.

The emergence of digital ecosystems that increase the accessibility of physical services through digital platforms is a new phenomenon in Finland, and most of the participants lacked experience in using these kinds of services. Most of the participants has positive images of new digital domestic services, but many still appreciated the possibility to carry out domestic activities on their own. Based on the interviews, older adults expressed their concern at not being able to actively participate in cleaning, renovating and taking care of the home or garden, rather than their willingness to participate in digital ecosystems in their old age:

> We have not used or needed anybody's help [with domestic tasks]. When moving to an apartment, it felt as if there's nothing to do here. Living in a detached house of your own, you have always lots of things to do. Renovating, cleaning and such. (Female, 73)

6   Conclusions

This study has shed light the role of life transitions in older adults' engagement with digital domestic technologies from the perspective of life transitions that occur in relation to social and personal relationships. In response to RQ1, the study identified changes in personal and social relationships as well as work life and employment situation that influence the life stage among adults in their fifties and sixties. For the lives of older adults, these life changes were seen as an inspiration for creation of new living solutions and domestic practices. Some previous research has found that a person's relationship with their spouse is one of the most important factors representing developmental phases of later life [9, 12], suggesting that changes in this relationship could inspire the creation of new digital practices simultaneously. For the participants in the present study, this relationship was regarded as perhaps one of the most significant in their daily life and domestic practices, indicating that it could influence the incorporation of digital practices in the household.

In response to RQ2, the study aimed to address the associations between life transitions and digital engagement in domestic environments. Based on the findings, this association was not clearly pronounced in participants' speech, but was instead included in the way digital technologies were understood as part of the household structure and family situation in general. For the adults in their fifties and sixties, digital technologies were already integrated to daily living to a wider extent, thus the incorporation of these technologies to domestic environments was understood also as a financial decision. Many of the interviewed adults experienced digital domestic technologies as too expensive for their daily life. Life transitions, particularly those related to work and employment changes, may be associated with financial resources and therefore these changes could both weaken or strengthen engagement with digital domestic practices. Thus, when the household structure or income level changes, it provides older adults new aspirations to re-evaluate and re-create the already established domestic practices.

Regarding the role of children as motivators and teachers in older adults' digital engagement [8, 20, 21], participants expressed many variances and heterogeneities in their speech. For participants with close family relationships, the children played a major role in domesticating digital technologies at home, but for other participants it was rather other relatives or adults in the workplace who provided support in digital technology usage. This suggests that life transitions related to the departure of children from the household may create a need to establish or strengthen new social and personal relationships. For most of the participants, this life transition was not seen as a negative thing but rather as something that could bring new possibilities for personal interests and pursuits.

In response to RQ3, the paper aimed to evaluate the possibilities for older adults to incorporate digital domestic ecosystems in their daily living. The study concludes that application of digital technologies to increase the accessibility of physical and digital services is not considered an appealing choice in older adults in their fifties and sixties. In that life stage, which is typically characterised by employment and a relatively good income, older adults typically perceive themselves as capable and interested in acquiring personalised services or maintaining existing ones. Incorporation of digital ecosystems was associated with a life stage when the capabilities are limited, and possibilities are restricted in terms of individualised choices. For these reasons, cultural and social changes related to the desirability and accessibility of digital ecosystems are needed in order to support the engagement of older adults with digital technologies for domestic practices.

References

1. Ashida, S., Heaney, C.A.: Differential associations of social support and social connectedness with structural features of social networks and the health status of older adults. J. Ageing Health **20**(7), 872–893 (2008)
2. Charles, S.T., Carstensen, L.L.: Social and emotional aging. Annu. Rev. Psychol. **61**, 383–409 (2010)
3. Comunello, F., Mulargia, S., Belotti, F., Fernández-Ardèvol, M.: Older people's attitude towards mobile communication in everyday life: digital literacy and domestication processes. In: Zhou, J., Salvendy, G. (eds.) ITAP 2015. LNCS, vol. 9193, pp. 439–450. Springer, Cham (2015). https://doi.org/10.1007/978-3-319-20892-3_43
4. Comunello, F., Fernández-Ardèvol, M.F., Muargia, S., Belotti, F.: Women, youth and everything else: age-based and gendered stereotypes in relation to digital technology among elderly Italian mobile phone users. Media Cult. Soc. **39**, 1–18 (2016)
5. Cunningham, M.: Influences of women's employment on the gendered division of household labor over the life course: evidence from a 31-year panel study. J. Fam. Issues **28**, 422–444 (2007)

6. Dutton, W.H., Reisdorf, B.C.: The internet through the ages. In: Nixon, P.G., Rawal, R., Funk, A. (eds.) Digital Media Usage Across the Life Course, pp. 16–28. Routledge, London (2016)

7. English, T., Carstensen, L.: Selective narrowing of social networks across adulthood is associated with improved emotional experience in daily life. Int. J. Behav. Dev. **38**(2), 195–202 (2014)

8. Eynon, R., Helsper, E.: Family dynamics and internet use in Britain: what role do children play in adults' engagement with the internet? Inf. Commun. Soc. **18**(2), 156–171 (2015)

9. Green, L.: Understanding the Life Course: Sociological and Psychological Perspectives. Polity Press, Cambridge (2014)

10. Grundfelder, J., Rispling, L., Norlén, G. (eds.): State of the Nordic Region 2018. Theme 1: Demography [e-publication]. Nordic Council of Ministers (2018). https://norden.diva-portal.org/smash/get/diva2:1180256/FULLTEXT01.pdf

11. Haddon, L.: Domestication analysis, objects of the study, and the centrality of technologies in everyday life. Can. J. Commun. **36**, 311–323 (2011)

12. Hutteman, R., Hennecke, M., Orth, U., Reitz, A.K., Specht, J.: Developmental tasks as a framework to study personality development in adulthood and old age. Eur. J. Pers. **28**(3), 267–278 (2014)

13. Kennedy, J., Nansen, B., Arnold, M., Wilken, R., Gibbs, M.: Digital housekeepers and domestic expertise in the networked home. Converg.: Int. J. Res. New Media Technol. **21**(4), 408–422 (2015)

14. Liu, B.S., Rook, K.S.: Emotional and social loneliness in later life: associations with positive versus negative social exchanges. J. Soc. Pers. Relatsh. **30**(6), 813–832 (2013)

15. Nixon, P.G., Rawal, R., Funk, A. (eds.): Digital Media Usage Across the Life Course. Routledge, London (2016)

16. Ono, M.: Digital storytelling and the transnational retirement networks of older Japanese adults. In: Prendergast, D., Garattini, C. (eds.) Aging and the Digital Life Course, pp. 220–335, Berghahn Books, New York (2015)

17. Piper, A.M., Cornejo Garcia, R., Brewer, R.N.: Understanding the challenges and opportunities of smart mobile devices among the oldest old. Int. J. Mob. Hum. Comput. Interact. **8**(2), 83–98 (2016)

18. Prendergast, D., Garattini, C. (eds.): Aging and the Digital Life Course. Berghahn Books, New York (2015)

19. Quan-Haase, A., Guan Ying, M., Wellman, B.: Connected seniors: how older adults in East York exchange social support online and offline. Inf. Commun. Soc. **20**(7), 967–983 (2017)

20. Selwyn, N.: Doing IT for the kids: re-examining children, computers and the information society. Media Cult. Soc. **25**(3), 351–378 (2003)

21. Selwyn, N.: Exploring the role of children in adults' adoption and use of computers. Inf. Technol. People **17**(1), 53–70 (2004)

22. Selwyn, N.: Making sense of young people, education and digital technology: the role of sociological theory. Oxf. Rev. Educ. **38**(1), 81–96 (2012)

23. Tolmie, P., Crabtree, A., Rodden, T., et al.: Making the home network at home: digital housekeeping. In: Bannon, L., Wagner, I., Gutwin, C., Harper, R., Schmidt, K. (eds.) ECSCW 2007: Proceedings of the 10th European Conference on Computer-Supported Cooperative Work. Springer, Paris (2007). https://doi.org/10.1007/978-1-84800-031-5_18

24. Van Rompaey, V., Roe, K.: The impact of computer technology on family life. In: The Impacts of Information and Communication Technologies on Social Realities. Facultat de Ciències de la Comunicació Banquerna, Barcelona, pp. 278–286 (2000)

25. Van Rompaey, V., Roe, K., Struys, K.: Children's influence on internet access at home: adoption and use in the family context. Inf. Commun. Soc. **5**, 189–206 (2002)

The Oldest Olds' Perceptions of Social Robots

Chaiwoo Lee[(✉)], Maryam FakhrHosseini, Julie Miller,
Taylor R. Patskanick, and Joseph F. Coughlin

Massachusetts Institute of Technology, Cambridge, MA 02139, USA
{chaiwoo, shabnaml, jmiller1, trpats, coughlin}@mit.edu

Abstract. Social robots are gaining attention as potential tool for improving older adults' social and emotional well-being. A mixed-method study with a panel of older adults 85 years of age and older explored how the oldest old feels about social robots, as well as new technologies in general. Based on responses to a survey and a set of focus groups, it was found that the panel was generally experienced and comfortable regarding use of new technologies. Responses to questions about social robots, however, suggested that there was a mix of perceptions and attitudes. Many participants were able to envision using one, open to interacting with one, and quick to embrace their potential benefits. On the other hand, apprehension to engaging with a social robot was apparent among some participants. Even with some concerns around trust, privacy and security, however, the group overall had no problem understanding the key capabilities and features of social robots, despite having very little to no prior knowledge. The findings indicate the oldest old, although often stereotyped to be slow to accept new technologies, may be open to the possibility of using a social robot as a companion.

Keywords: Social robots · Older adults · Technology adoption · Aging

1 Introduction

The rapid growth of the older population has brought attention to technologies that may help assist older adults, as well as their families and caregivers, with a variety of tasks. While the demographic trend has fostered discussions and research around using and developing technologies to improve physical and cognitive health outcomes and to assist with functional abilities, the potential for new technological advancements to improve older adults' social and emotional well-being has only recently started gaining interest.

Aging brings a crucial need for social engagement and connectedness. More people are living alone in the United States as well as globally, with approximately 15% of households in the world being solo households [1] and 27% of homes in the US today occupied by a single person [2]. The same trend is apparent among the older population, with 26% of older adults 65 years of age or older living alone today [3]. Living alone can bring complications related to social isolation and loneliness. For example, the American Time Use Survey has found that older Americans that live alone spend significantly more time by themselves compared to those that live with a spouse or a partner [4]. In the United Kingdom, it has been reported that of more than 2 million

© Springer Nature Switzerland AG 2019
J. Zhou and G. Salvendy (Eds.): HCII 2019, LNCS 11593, pp. 405–415, 2019.
https://doi.org/10.1007/978-3-030-22015-0_32

older adults over 75 years of age living alone, over a million of them go for a month without speaking to a family member, friend or neighbor [5]. In addition to factors related to living arrangements, older adults are also more likely to face barriers to social engagement due to the increased likelihood of experiencing declines in physical mobility [6] and issues with cognitive abilities [7]. Social isolation and loneliness can bring tremendous negative effects to one's health and quality of life. For example, it has been stated that social isolation and loneliness are associated with about a 50% increased risk of early death [8].

As a potential solution to improve emotional and social well-being among older adults, researchers have been investigating to use social robots. Social robots are interactive robotic agents designed to interact with people along social and emotional dimensions, and behave according to human psychology and social norms [9–11]. Recent developments in social robotics offer capabilities for users to directly interact with a physically embodied agent by engaging in verbal and non-verbal behaviors [12, 13].

Results of previous studies on people's interactions with social robots showed that users may be able to use social robots to continuously engage in social interactions and experience emotional companionship even when human engagement is not available to them. In a study by FakhrHosseini et al. [14], essential factors for robotic companionship were explored in a session where 21 participants played an online game with help from two humanoid robots: Nao and Darwin. Findings from this study showed that both robot appearance and verbal and emotional expressions influence users' perception of the robot as their companion. In this case, more human-like phrasing and appearance influenced participants' perceived enjoyment, perceived sociability, trust, and accepting robots as their companion [14]. Another study surveyed undergraduate students to understand how people associate physical and visual characteristics of various social robots with personality traits [10]. Barnes et al. [15] focused on elementary school students to explore how children interact with social robots as an application to assist in STEAM (science, technology, engineering, arts and mathematics) education.

A small number of studies have focused on older adults as potential users of social robots. For example, robotic pets have been developed to help older adults with their loneliness and isolation [16]. A study by Alves-Oliveira et al. [17] reported on findings from a focus group that involved older adults and discussed that older adults were able to envision various examples of social robots assisting with different activities of daily living. A long-term user study by Ostrowski et al. [18] compared usage patterns and preferences across generations – between children, adults and older adults – and reported that older adults' interactions with social robots were anchored in their entertainment and social features. A recent meta-analysis of randomized controlled trials concerning health effects of social robots suggested that interacting with social robots may have positive impacts on quality of life and reduce loneliness [19]. The same study, however, also discussed that studies that investigate the potential effects of social robots on older adults' well-being are rather limited, and that the topic needs to be studied further [19].

This study focuses on the oldest old population – people 85 years of age or older – to understand the perceptions of social robots among those most likely to experience age-associated issues affecting social and emotional well-being. While the oldest old population is the most rapidly growing demographic segment [20], research regarding their perceptions and acceptance of various new technologies, including social robots, have not been studied thoroughly. This study aims to further understand older adults' thoughts on social robots by focusing on those most likely to experience age-related changes and needs.

2 Data Collection

In this study, a panel of 20 older adults (10 female), all aged 85 or older, was convened to discuss perceptions, attitudes and experiences around new technologies including social robots. This session was part of an ongoing bimonthly panel of older adults, the MIT AgeLab Lifestyle Leaders, that meets to discuss and deconstruct issues and experiences related to aging. Participants for this session ranged in age from 85 to 99. All of the participants lived independently in the Boston-metro area. The majority of the panel was unmarried by widowhood or divorce, and 6 participants were married or living with a partner. Participants were overall more affluent, educated, and racially-homogenous relative to the US and to other older adults in the Boston-metro area. Due to the skewness in demographic and socio-economic characteristics, this panel is not representative of the 85+ population generally.

Prior to the in-person meeting, the panel was invited to complete a questionnaire, either online or on paper, that included items related to: (1) general technology experience; (2) criteria for choosing to use new technologies; (3) perceptions around possible features that may be offered by social robots; and (4) expectations and concerns around social robots. The in-person meeting began with a brief presentation by a guest speaker about research on social robots and robotic agents. After the presentation, participants were divided into four smaller groups for focus group discussions. The small groups were formed based on the participants' self-assessment of their technology adoption behavior. One group included participants who self-identified themselves as early adopters; one other group included self-rated late adopters; and the two remaining groups included participants who fell in between. The focus groups lasted approximately 60 min and were held concurrently. Moderators asked the participants about: (1) attitudes and experiences related to technology in general, including how they learn about new technologies and how much they trust new systems; (2) expectations and thoughts related to social robots; (3) experiences with and attitudes toward other new technologies- including home systems, mobile devices and vehicle automation. The focus group discussions were recorded and transcribed.

3 Results

The panels' responses were analyzed to gain a better understanding of the oldest olds' experiences and thoughts regarding technology in general, as well as about social robots and related applications.

3.1   General Technology Attitudes and Experience

Participants' responses to survey questions around overall technology use and experience showed that the panel was generally open to and comfortable with new technologies. When asked about overall level of experience with technology in general, only one person indicated being not experienced at all, whereas the majority indicated having some experience (7 participants were somewhat experienced, 4 were quite experienced, and 3 were very experienced). When asked to assess if they would describe themselves as early or late adopters of new technologies, only one person said that s/he avoids new technologies as long as possible. Four participants identified as early adopters and said they would try new technologies as soon as possible, while 3 said they would try after a few other people. When asked about confidence in being able to learn and use new technologies, only one person said that s/he is not at all confident, while the majority indicated being generally confident (4 participants said somewhat confident, 6 said quite confident, and 3 were very confident). The group also indicated that they were generally trusting of technology, with only one person indicating having very low trust in technology. To this question on their overall level of trust in technology, 5 participants said they have medium trust, 4 reported having high trust, and 3 indicated having very high trust. However, the group showed some hesitation when discussing data security and privacy. When asked how much they trust technology to protect and secure their privacy and personal information, 4 participants said that have very low trust, while only one person indicated having very high trust.

The group largely consisted of current technology users, with 13 participants regularly using smartphones. Many also reported using desktop computers (12 participants), laptops (10 participants), tablets (9 participants) and in-vehicle technologies (7 participants). Of those currently using smartphones, 8 were also using voice assistants such as Siri, and 2 participants were using mobile payment services such as Apple Pay. There were a few participants in the panel using different in-home technologies and mobile devices. For example, 2 participants reported using smart speakers such as Amazon Echo/Alexa and one person indicated using an activity tracker such as a Fitbit.

In order to better understand the oldest old population's thoughts and decisions around acceptance and adoption of new technologies, the panel was asked about the characteristics or features they look for when they buy or start using new technologies. For this question, a selection of technology adoption factors described by Lee [21] were used, including practical benefits, ease of learning and use, availability of technical support services, cost/affordability, reputation of company/brand, support from family/friends, emotional benefits, familiarity, ability to work with other things, ability to work over time, and positive social image or associations. A few more features were added to comprehensively cover various technology characteristics, including enabling safety and security, good physical design or appearance, novelty or innovativeness, and prestige. As shown in Fig. 1, the panel indicated that they primarily consider the utility and value when they decide to buy or use new technologies, with 16 participants selecting practical benefits as adoption criteria. Only a few participants indicated that they evaluate the physical appearance, social image, novelty or prestige, further supporting that their decisions around technology adoption are value-driven. Key factors around the effort and/or resources needed were chosen by many participants as well, with 15 participants indicating that they think about ease of learning and use, 13 participants choosing availability of technical support services as one of their main criteria, and 12 participants reporting that they consider cost/affordability. A fair number of participants also sought assurance, with 10 choosing reputation of company/brand and 9 choosing support from family/friends as key factors.

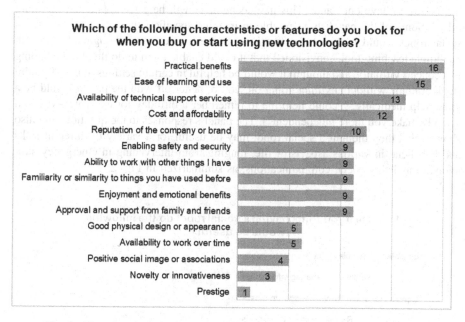

Fig. 1. Key characteristics considered when buying or using new technologies

3.2 Oldest Olds' Perceptions and Acceptance of Social Robots

While the panel generally indicated favorable attitudes and experiences towards new technologies in general, responses specific to social robots showed a mix of positive and negative thoughts and feelings. When presented with the statement "I feel positively about robot technologies", only 2 participants said they strongly agree and 7 said they somewhat agree with the statement. When presented with the statement "I can imagine having a robot in my home", only 2 participants said they strongly agree and 6 said they somewhat agree with the statement, while 4 participants said they strongly disagree. The panel showed a wide range of responses when asked how much they would be willing to pay for a social robot. While 5 participants selected "$0 – I would never buy one", 5 other participants said that they would be willing to pay $500 or more. The sense of hesitation was evident in the focus groups as well. For example, in one of the focus groups with self-identified early adopters, a participant said "As I listened to [researcher's presentation about social robots] I found I was defensive. It threatened my independence."

While the group showed some hesitation around using a social robot, they also indicated that they could envision benefits of having one. For instance, when asked if how much they agree or disagree with the statement "I think social robots would be useful to me", their responses averaged at 3.28 on a scale from 1 for strongly disagree to 5 for strongly agree. Some positive attitudes were observed during the focus groups. For example, in one of the focus groups, a few self-rated early adopters said "I think it'd be fun to have one" and "This new technology will help me appreciate life more fully." Some of the panelists were able to imagine specific situations where having a social robot would be beneficial for them. For example, some thought of it as "an incredible teaching tool," envisioned that it could enable them to do things like "going to a concert virtually, and thought it would be helpful in certain settings (e.g., "if you're stuck at home without anything going on, you're better off with them," "it would be a great help medically," "could help me to remember a birthday for example – it could actually make you more independent"). The panel's responses to the questionnaire also showed that they thought a social robot may be useful for a variety of different tasks and beneficial in various aspects of life, ranging from intervening in emergency situations to assisting social communications, as summarized in Fig. 2.

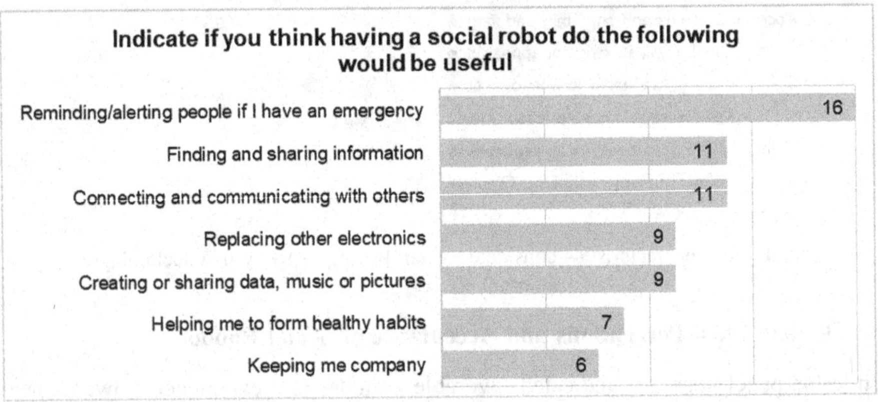

Indicate if you think having a social robot do the following would be useful

Task	Value
Reminding/alerting people if I have an emergency	16
Finding and sharing information	11
Connecting and communicating with others	11
Replacing other electronics	9
Creating or sharing data, music or pictures	9
Helping me to form healthy habits	7
Keeping me company	6

Fig. 2. Responses on potential usefulness of a social robot for various tasks

Participants' positive expectation around a social robot to intervene in case of emergency was echoed in their responses to the question regarding the types of information or actions they would trust a social robot with. While only few participants indicated that they would trust a social robot with information regarding their social relationships, finances and personal beliefs, more participants said that they would trust a social robot regarding home security and personal emergency alerts, as summarized in Fig. 3.

The interest around the potential for a social robot to assist in health-related issues was also apparent in the panel's responses to the question "Which of the following would you want to talk to your social robot about?" As illustrated in Fig. 4, health matters was chosen by the highest number of participants as the topic they would like

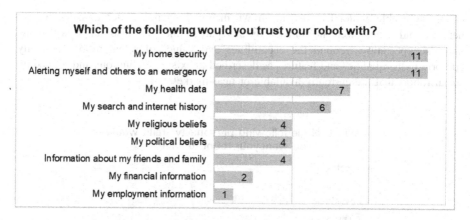

Fig. 3. Responses on trusting a social robot with information and actions

to chat about. However, several participants also chose current events, weather, finances and money, and politics as potential conversation topics that they would like to engage in with a social robot. This suggests that the group expects a social robot to be a casual and informal companion, rather than a healthcare device or an emergency response system. Data summarized in Fig. 4 also hints at the apparent apprehensiveness among some participants, with 4 participants indicating that they would not want to talk with a social robot regardless of the conversation topic.

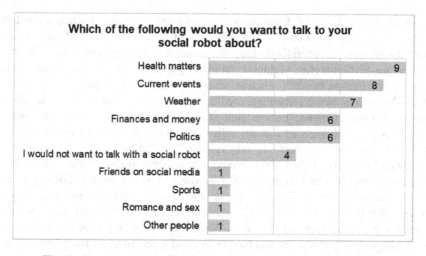

Fig. 4. Responses to possible topics for interactions with a social robot

The panel's responses to a question on preferred personality traits for a social robot further confirmed that they sought informal and easy companionship. While the majority of the panel indicated that they would want a social robot to be respectful, caring, agreeable and/or friendly, as shown in Fig. 5, qualities such as authoritative, neurotic and formal were not chosen by any participant. This also suggests that the group's expectations around the capabilities and values of social robots generally conform to the qualities and features as described in existing definitions and offered by social robots that are currently available or near-market.

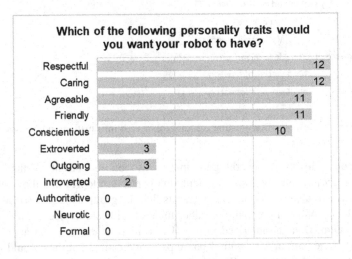

Fig. 5. Preferred personality traits and qualities for a social robot

During the small group discussions, conversations were also formed around the possible physical forms that a social robot could take. Opinions and expectations among the group were generally divided. For example, some preferred a social robot to take a human-like form (e.g., "I think I can identify with it more if it's a person – make it look like a human being"), whereas others favored other forms (e.g., "I think a human-like form is faking something you don't need," "I'd like it to be a little animal. I'd want it to move around.") Some didn't have a clear preference and were open to possibilities (e.g., "It doesn't make any difference. The human animal is very adaptive and you can get used to something very quickly." "What bothers me about robots is that they don't have individual looks. Would it be possible to give different possibilities within one robot? Maybe a teenager? Or a 40-year-old who is more politically aware? Different points of view, different jokes. In some way simulate the diversity of your own real life.") Responses to related questions in the questionnaire also indicated diversity in preferences among the group. When asked what they wanted a social robot to look like, only 2 participants said human-like and 1 person said animal-like, while 5 participants said that they don't care and another 5 preferred it to be more ambient. When asked what they want the robot to sound like, no one chose a female voice or a robotic voice. Responding to this question, 4 participants chose a male voice, 5 said that they didn't care or preferred some other type of sound, while a gender-neural voice was the most popular option with 7 participants choosing it.

4 Conclusion and Discussion

Social robots are posed to deliver multidimensional features and values – including social engagement, emotional attachment and intellectual stimulation – to users across the age spectrum. With capabilities to behave and interact in accordance with human social norms, social robots may be able to serve as social and emotional companions to older adults who are more likely than their younger counterparts to experience social isolation and loneliness.

In this study with a panel of older adults 85 years of age and older, a mixed-method approach was used to better understand how the oldest old view and perceive social robots. An in-person meeting with 20 older adults in the metro Boston area was convened for a set of in-depth focus groups in addition to a questionnaire that was completed prior to the session.

Responses to the questionnaire and the focus group questions revealed that the majority of the panel reported being experienced with technology, confident about learning and using new technologies, and eager to try new technologies before others. When discussing social robots, on the other hand, there was a mix of responses and attitudes, with several participants unwilling to have one or to interact with one. These responses and attitudes can largely be attributed to concerns around trust, security and privacy, as well as to uncertainties around potential impact on independence.

Despite the general sense of apprehensiveness around social robots in comparison to new technologies in general, results also indicated that the group quickly understood the overall concept of social robots as well as some of the key capabilities based only on a brief presentation, with limited to no prior knowledge. In contrast to beliefs around older adults' relative conservatism in willingness to try new technologies, participants in this study were generally open to the possibility of using a social robot as a companion, as well as these robots' abilities to mimic and follow human norms and social conventions. The group indicated that they would value possible practical features, such as intervening in emergency situations and chatting about health matters, which may be more relevant and specific to this demographic group compared to younger generations. However, the panel was also able to imagine social robots being helpful for a variety of situations and user segments, as suggested in the comment, "It's good for everyone."

It should be noted, however, that the panel only included a select group of older adults 85 years and older that is geographically limited and skewed in terms of level of education, physical and cognitive health, and overall wealth. The group was also mostly currently online on a regular basis and relatively technology savvy compared to the general population. While the findings may represent the perceptions and attitudes of the oldest old that fit within these boundaries, they may not apply to a broader group of older adults. A possible direction for future research on the topic would be to gather responses from a more diverse sample to better understand how the oldest old population across various characteristics and backgrounds feel about social robots and new technologies.

Acknowledgment. This work was, in part, supported by an unrestricted grant from the AARP.

References

1. Chamie, J.: The rise of one-person households. Inter Press Service News Agency (2017). http://www.ipsnews.net/2017/02/the-rise-of-one-person-households/. Accessed 29 Jan 2019
2. Vespa, J., Lewis, J.M., Kreider, R.M.: America's families and living arrangements: 2012. United States Census (2013). https://www.census.gov/prod/2013pubs/p20-570.pdf. Accessed 29 Jan 2019
3. Stepler, R.: Smaller share of women ages 65 and older are living alone. Pew Research Center (2016). http://www.pewsocialtrends.org/2016/02/18/smaller-share-of-women-ages-65-and-older-are-living-alone/. Accessed 29 Jan 2019
4. United States Bureau of Labor Statistics. https://www.bls.gov/tus/charts/older.htm. Accessed 15 Oct 2018
5. United Kingdom National Health Service. https://www.nhs.uk/conditions/stress-anxiety-depression/loneliness-in-older-people/. Accessed 29 Jan 2018
6. Rosso, A.L., Taylor, J.A., Tabb, L.P., Michael, Y.L.: Mobility, disability, and social engagement in older adults. J. Aging Health **25**(4), 617–637 (2013)
7. Krueger, K.R., Wilson, R.S., Kamenetsky, J.M., Barnes, L.L., Bienias, J.L., Bennett, D.A.: Social engagement and cognitive function in old age. Exp. Aging Res. **35**(1), 45–60 (2009)
8. Holt-Lunstad, J., Smith, T.B., Layton, J.B.: Social relationships and mortality risk: a meta-analytic review. PLoS Med. **7**(7), e1000316 (2010)
9. Breazeal, C.: Social robots for health applications. In: 2011 Annual International Conference of the IEEE Engineering in Medicine and Biology Society, pp. 5368–5371. IEEE, New York (2011)
10. FakhrHosseini, S.M., Hilliger, S., Barnes, J., Jeon, M., Park, C.H., Howard, A.M.: Love at first sight: Mere exposure to robot appearance leaves impressions similar to interactions with physical robots. In: 26th IEEE International Symposium on Robot and Human Interactive Communication (RO-MAN), pp. 615–620. IEEE, New York (2017)
11. Feil-Seifer, D., Mataric, M.J.: Defining socially assistive robotics. In: 9th International Conference on Rehabilitation Robotics, pp. 465–468. IEEE, New York (2005)
12. Li, J.: The benefit of being physically present: a survey of experimental works comparing copresent robots, telepresent robots and virtual agents. Int. J. Hum.-Comput. Stud. **77**, 23–37 (2015)
13. Thellman, S., Silvervarg, A., Gulz, A., Ziemke, T.: Physical vs. virtual agent embodiment and effects on social interaction. In: Traum, D., Swartout, W., Khooshabeh, P., Kopp, S., Scherer, S., Leuski, A. (eds.) IVA 2016. LNCS (LNAI), vol. 10011, pp. 412–415. Springer, Cham (2016). https://doi.org/10.1007/978-3-319-47665-0_44
14. FakhrHosseini, S.M., et al.: Both "look and feel" matter: essential factors for robotic companionship. In: 26th IEEE International Symposium on Robot and Human Interactive Communication (RO-MAN), pp. 150–155. IEEE, New York (2017)
15. Barnes, J., FakhrHosseini, S.M. Vasey, E., Duford, Z., Jeon, M.: Robot theater with children for STEAM education. In: Proceedings of the Human Factors and Ergonomics Society 2017 Annual Meeting, pp. 875–879. SAGE Publishing, Thousand Oaks (2017)
16. Lazar, A., Thompson, H. J., Piper, A. M., Demiris, G.: Rethinking the design of robotic pets for older adults. In: Proceedings of the 2016 ACM Conference on Designing Interactive Systems, pp. 1034–1046. ACM, New York (2016)
17. Alves-Oliveira, P., Petisca, S., Correia, F., Maia, N., Paiva, A.: Social robots for older adults: framework of activities for aging in place with robots. Social Robotics. LNCS (LNAI), vol. 9388, pp. 11–20. Springer, Cham (2015). https://doi.org/10.1007/978-3-319-25554-5_2

18. Ostrowski, A.K., Singh, N., Park, H.W., Breazeal, C.: Preferences, patterns, and wishes for agents in the home. In: ICSR 2018 Workshop on Social Human-Robot Interaction of Service Robots (2018)
19. Pu, L., Moyle, W., Jones, C., Todorovic, M.: The effectiveness of social robots for older adults: a systematic review and meta-analysis of randomized controlled studies. Gerontologist **59**(1), e37–e51 (2019)
20. Ortman, J.M., Velkoff, V.A., Hogan, H.: An aging nation: the older population in the United States. United States Census (2014). https://www.census.gov/prod/2014pubs/p25-1140.pdf. Accessed 10 July 2018
21. Lee, C.: User-centered system design in an aging society: an integrated study on technology adoption. Doctoral dissertation, Massachusetts Institute of Technology (2014)

Objective Approaches on Urban Soundscape Perception in Night Market Pedestrian Street

Wei Lin[1]([✉]), Yi-Ming Wu[1], Hsuan Lin[2], and Kuo-Liang Huang[3]

[1] School of Architecture, Feng Chia University, Taichung, Taiwan
wlin@fcu.edu.tw, wuyiming2016@gmail.com
[2] Department of Product Design, Tainan University of Technology,
Tainan, Taiwan
te0038@mail.tut.edu.tw
[3] Department of Industrial Design, Sichuan Fine Arts Institute,
Chongqing, China
shashi@scfai.edu.cn

Abstract. In recent years, urban soundscape research, from the typical urban imagery and self-explanatory discussion, infiltrated into the sound field characteristics of the neighborhood street in the pedestrian street space, and explored the perception of the overall urban environment and situation shaping. Urban soundscape description and psychological evaluation are multi-directional and interactive effects. Considering the physical quantity and subjective psychological characteristics of sound energy, it is an important ink for the study of the sound field design of pedestrian streets. The research project focuses on the sound energy distribution of the night market pedestrian system and explores the multi-directionality through factors such as time, energy, space, and perception. The objective measurement results of the field average monitoring with the equivalent average sound level LAeq (dB) are used as the basic prototype of the sound field to draw the regional and acoustic energy distribution map.

Keywords: Urban soundscape · Computer simulation ·
Objective measurement

1 Introduction

After the effective control of the urban acoustic environment, the pursuit of higher quality acoustic environment and urban development environmental characteristics is an important direction of current soundscape research. The sound ecology in urban space has both spatial and temporal characteristics, and these factors influence social development. The high degree of urban development leads to population concentration, and the annoying sounds produced at different stages are regarded as "noise." After entering the 21st century, most international environmental policies focus on noise control and reduce noise in related economic activity materials or social science research. Levels do not necessarily improve the quality of life in the city. The high degree of urban development leads to population concentration, and the annoying sounds produced at different stages are regarded as "noise." After entering the 21st

© Springer Nature Switzerland AG 2019
J. Zhou and G. Salvendy (Eds.): HCII 2019, LNCS 11593, pp. 416–424, 2019.
https://doi.org/10.1007/978-3-030-22015-0_33

century, most international environmental policies focus on noise control and noise reduction in related economic activity data or social science research. It will not improve the quality of life in the city [1–4]. This is why the research on urban soundscape and the environment tends to be complicated. In addition to the record of objective measurement, it pays attention to the actual feelings and listening experience of human senses, the sound diversity record between cultures and customs among different countries, and urban environments. The sound is seen as a "resource" that can be used, not a "pollution." While countries examine the urban development context and future planning, the specific soundscapes can respectively mark the characteristics of a regional community, and more and more soundscape features are not in the homogenized urban scene. In Europe, led by Jian Kang, professor of architecture at the University of Sheffield in the United Kingdom, initiated research and became one of the research topics that the EU values. In North America and East Asia and South Asia, including Australia, Canada, the United States, Japan, China, Hong Kong and Taiwan, considerable attention has been paid to soundscape research. In Europe, the launch of related research, led by Jian Kang, professor of architecture at the University of Sheffield, has become a research topic of importance to EU countries. In North America and East Asia and South Asia, including Australia, Canada, the United States, Japan, China, Hong Kong, and Taiwan, considerable attention has been paid to soundscape research [5]. Leading the research institutes such as the Soundscape of European Cities and Landscapes and the UK Noise futures Network, holds a seminar on the future development of urban acoustic environment in 2009, focusing on solving regional soundscape features of future trends and other issues. Driven by this conference, the city center of Sheffield was classified as a basis for quantitative and qualitative analysis of the soundscape characteristics of public spaces [6]. Waterscapes, bird calls and church bells are the most popular among the public, and the language sound is the main source of discomfort for residents. Relevant research has provided the protection direction of British urban soundscape features. In the urban open space, in addition to effectively controlling the sound source, the common walking sound source is generated by walking on different materials and has an influence on subjective sound perception [7]. There are many good examples for perception of acoustic characteristics in European cities, combined with water feature facilities and noise barrier embedded in the open space of the city, using sound insulation walls to block noise sources and waterscapes mask disturbing background noise. This combination of facilities creates culturally significant connotations such as the Sheffield fountain water and metal noise barriers in the UK, the fountains representing rivers and metals representing the steel industry, and the industrial development and urban planning of Sheffield. Two important historical contexts enhance the enjoyment of residents and tourists in these areas, and rich in human and educational significance. Another example is the soundscape planning of the city of Nauener Platz in Berlin, Germany. By combining space zoning and street furniture design, stone walls are used to protect the park people from the surrounding noise. In addition, the combination of semi-enclosed street furniture can also insolate sound influences [8]. Toshimitsu Musha proposed a study of the subjective taste of sound energy. The research content mainly believes that there are active frequencies of 1/f in nature, and the characteristics of 1/f frequency tend to be positive [9]. One of the concepts of the soundscape is that the sounds in the environment should be the sounds that many people like and accept. In this study, the environmental noise test is used to objectively identify the quality of the environmental sounds and then screen them. How to identify the sound produced in the city as a soundscape is generally a pleasure in listening. Although the sounds produced by the traffic tools are disturbing sounds, the sounds integrated into the city are not all annoying noises. The measurement of the acoustic energy level is very similar to the A-weighted acoustic energy dB (A) in response to the frequency response of the human ear. LAeq and LAmax represent the basic characteristics of average sound energy. The measurement of the physical quantity of environmental acoustic energy mostly uses the sound pressure level of the instrument (or sound pressure level, SPL), and the unit used is decibel (dB), and the decibel indicates the intensity or loudness of the sound. People's hearing and the environment also correspond to the subjective feelings of the decibel standard. Kang [10] notes the current activities and listeners' expectations and their perception of audible sounds, and the visual visibility of the sound source play an important role. Therefore, these concerns are the decisions of urban development and historical culture. This highly recognizable sound, in sequence, organizes its acoustic physics characteristics, predictively gives a positive evaluation, and explores its subjective feeling correspondence. Based on the theory of soundscape, this study takes the night market trail system as an example to explore the sound field energy collection and frequency analysis of the acoustic environment in the urban pedestrian street.

The urban soundscape triangle developed by M. Schafer (1978) includes Sound Mark, Foreground sounds, and Keynote. Through the classification of acoustic measurement and soundscape research, the classification of sound field characteristics is carried out, and all collected sounds are decomposed into many elements for analysis, which is the key basis of research work. The term "Sound mark" is derived from the landmark, indicating the source of the unique sound that is connected or thought of, such as the church bell. The keynote highlights the representative or base of a string of sounds. Although the tone does not require conscious recognition, it abstracts or condenses the characteristics of a string of sounds. Foreground sound is a noticeable and conscious signal that is different from the background sound. Therefore, it is often organized into a voice code to transmit a message [11]. The high degree of urban development, the proximity of transportation facilities and the convenience of the main roads are important choices for the gathering and living of modern urban residents. The pedestrian space with distinctive open sound field is selected which are including three types of sound fields, pedestrian walking space, commercial space and open space sound field. The results of this research can measure whether the characteristics of sound energy are obscuration noise, or can be divided and defined in frequency characteristics. It can provide the next stage of soundscape perception clarification and analysis, which will be the main follow-up work of this research.

2 Night Market Sound Measurement

The study is based on the international sightseeing night market around Feng Chia University in Taichung as the research space for the commercial street walking the sound field. Feng Chia University's night market business district is famous for its diverse snacks and sightseeing night market. In recent years, with the government's tourism promotion, Feng Chia University's business district has become an attractive tourist attraction in Taiwan. Although the walking sound field is attractive, the key indicators affecting it need to be clarified. At present, according to the survey results, the soundscape characteristics of the Fen Chia Night Market can be initially classified. Through the sound measurement and recording to study the sound field of the pedestrian space along the street in the commercial circle market, the data will become an important basic data for sound perception. At the current stage of measurement, the sound energy of the night market in Fen Chia Business Circle can provide a basis for the complete sound field distribution. The measurement time is performed on weekdays and weekends and is divided into three time periods. A total of 49 measurement points are initially used, and each measurement point is evaluated by LAeq (dB). The measurement time is 1 min, which gives an objective evaluation of the regional soundscape. The sound energy result will become an important basis for the exploration of soundscape perception in the next stage. The measurement points and sound field distribution of Feng Chia University's night market business circle are shown in Fig. 1.

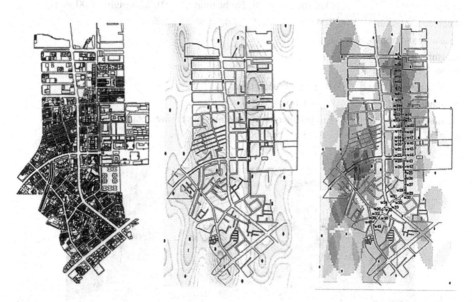

Fig. 1. Map space of Feng Chia University night market walking system (left), peak and off-peak sound field studies (middle) and 49 measuring points distribution (right).

2.1 Measuring Equipment

The environmental noise measurement results with the equivalent average volume LAeq (dB) as the evaluation index and the A-weighted noise intermittently exposed in a certain period of time in the selected position in the sound field are averaged by the energy. The parameter index formula is shown in Eq. 1 below.

$$L_{Aeq} = 10 \, \log \frac{1}{T} \int_{t}^{t+T} \left(\frac{P_t}{P_0}\right)^2 dt \qquad (1)$$

LAeq: A-weighted average energy level dB(A) in period time;

T: measurement time in seconds;

Pt: measure sound pressure in Pa;

P0: reference sound pressure, based on 20μPa;

The study conducted environmental acoustic energy measurements, and the sound energy was measured according to the NIEA P201.96C method. The general conditions of on-site acoustic energy measurement are shown in Table 1. The measurement points and apparatus are located on night mark street. (See in Fig. 2.)

Table 1. List of general conditions of the on-site measurement

Site	Feng Chia night market (Appro. 1 km distance)
Date	12th and 15th Jan. 2019
Time	Day time (16:00), Night time (21:00), Mid-night (1:00 Am)
Weather condition	Temperature: 21C, Humidity: 55–68%
Measurement apparatus	Rion
Measurement point quantities	49 points
Sampling time	10 min for each time
Frequency band	20–20000 Hz
Method	Environmental sound energy measurement according to NIEA P201.96C method

Fig. 2. Photos of Feng Chia Night Market on-site measurement are illustrated

2.2   Results of Room Acoustic Measurement

On site of walking system space in the Feng Chia Night Market, 49 points were selected for measurements, recording at different fixed times and locations. The sound source of the night market walking space is full of changes. Natural sounds and artificial sounds are the main components and interact with each other. All sound sources in this area can be divided into three categories: (1) Natural sound: wind sound, etc.; (2) Equipment sound: car and music sound etc.; and (3) Vocals: footsteps, play and talk. The average noise level of each measurement point is different according to time periods, which are general broadband noise characteristics without obvious significant sound energy. The distribution of LAeq (dB) measurement points is shown in Fig. 3. The measurement time is divided into 16:00 (Starting time), 21:00 (Rush time), and 1:00 am (closing time). The measurement results are 75 dB (A) on average, and the measurement results of each measurement point are shown in the figure.

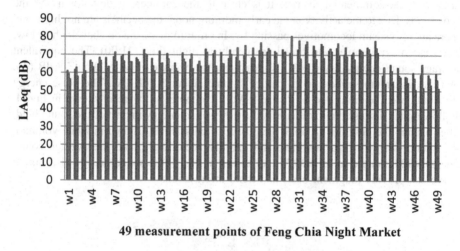

Fig. 3. The distribution results of 49 field measurement points in three periods in Feng Chia Night Market walking space.

3   Computer Simulation

The actual measured sound energy distribution map is analyzed with the software and the distribution curve is drawn. The results can be used to analyze the optimal sound energy of the overall distribution of the sound field. Individual environmental factors are used to validate and hypothesize the model. By implementing the measurement correspondence, the sound pressure level image and the sound field model are further drawn, and the future scene and subjective evaluation benchmarks are predicted computer simulation calculation. The simulation was performed by using the German

NoiseAtWork software package that can handle energy parameters of tracing calculation and was used to validate the schematic concept of using the energy distribution. The calculus method performs grid computing and plots the contours of the sound energy distribution. The results of the sound field environment generated by computer simulation are visually and visually presented, and the sound field environment in which it is located can be evaluated under different conditions. The simulation results provide a lot of information, including the location and strength of the sound energy. In some cases, this method has the effect of trend prediction, especially under stable sound sources, such as fixed noise sources. Multiple sound source measurements can be discussed simultaneously. For different sound sources, the measures to reduce sound energy can also be plotted and sorted according to the size of the sound energy results.

3.1 Results of Computer Simulation

As a result of the simulation, Feng Chia Night Market is located in the narrow and long streets of the commercial district. It is close to the commercial downtown and the crossroads. Due to the activity at the early morning noon, the decibels are not high, and there are also steam locomotives passing by. In order to make the decibels high or low, there are many people who travel frequently at night time (21:00). The equivalent average sound energy LAeq (dB) is measured, the average value is about 75 dB (A), and the maximum sound energy can be LAmax about 80 dB (A). The noise energy distribution curve simulated by NoiseAtWork computer software is shown in Fig. 4. Following the discussion, in order to reduce the sound energy impact of the sound field, after placing the building group at the profile of cross street (shown in white volume), the sound energy will accumulate and amplify accordingly, and the average sound energy will be raised to 75 dB (A). As shown in Fig. 5, the sound energy distribution curve can provide judgment basis and trend information.

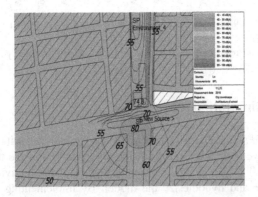

Fig. 4. The computer software simulates the street sound energy distribution

Fig. 5. The computer software simulates the street sound energy the curve distribution after being placed in the building volume.

4 Discussion

Based on the content and methods, this study mainly collects and analyzes the sound environment based on the soundscape related literature. The main target is the commercial pedestrian street along the city recreation space. This study explores the Feng Chia night market in Taiwanese cities, with urban fashion and characteristic business districts, close to high-density residential areas and a large number of crowds, and linear pedestrian streets create linear characteristics of dynamic and static. Acoustic sound source collection includes store street vocals and surrounding environmental humming, including mobile sound sources and fixed sound sources, and draws characteristic sound energy distribution maps, in order to reinterpret the potential characteristics of the pedestrian streets and urban identity. Some preliminary results are abstracted as followed:

(1.) Understand the actual sound energy distribution and changes of the pedestrian street soundscape for the current situation, measure and collect the current state and characteristics of the acoustic environment.
(2.) Explore the impact of sound on environmental behavior, a soundscape analysis model was proposed to provide reference for subsequent research.
(3.) The research results will provide directions for urban planning as a decision-making possibility for the development of tourism and leisure space in the country.

Acknowledgements. The authors wish to thank Chia-Zou Chen, Teamwork Co. Ltd. for the assistant of filed measurements, Professor Wei-Hwa Chiang, Dep. of Architecture, National Taiwan University of Science and Technology the kindly assistances during the survey.

References

1. Alves, S., Est_evez-Mauriz, L., Aletta, F., Echevarria-Sanchez, G.M., Puyana Romero, V.: Towards the integration of urban sound planning in urban development processes: the study of four test sites within the SONORUS project. Noise Mapp. 2(1), 57–85 (2015)
2. Andringa, T.C., et al.: Positioning soundscape research and management. J. Acoust. Soc. Am. 134(4), 2739–2747 (2013)
3. Asdrubali, F.: New frontiers in environmental noise research. Noise Mapp. 1, 1–2 (2014)
4. van Kempen, E., Devilee, J., Swart, W., van Kamp, I.: Characterizing urban areas with good sound quality: development of a research protocol. Noise Health 16(73), 380–387 (2014)
5. Kang, J., et al.: Ten questions on the soundscapes of the built environment. Build. Environ. 108, 284–294 (2016)
6. Kang, J.: Noise management: soundscape approach. In: Reference Module in Earth Systems and Environmental Sciences, Encyclopedia of Environmental Health, pp. 174–184 (2011)
7. Aletta, F., Kang, J., Astolfi, A., Fuda, S.: Differences in soundscape appreciation of walking sounds from different footpath materials in urban parks. Sustain. Cities Soc. 27, 367–376 (2016)
8. Schulte-Fortkamp, B.: The daily rhythm of the soundscape "Nauener Platz" in Berlin. J. Acoust. Soc. Am. 127, 1774 (2010)
9. Musha, T., Katsurai, K., Teramachi, Y.: Fluctuations of human tapping intervals. IEEE Trans. Biomed. Eng. BME-32, 578–582 (1985)
10. Kang, J.: On the diversity of urban waterscape. In: Proceedings of the Acoustics 2012 Conference, Nantes (2012)
11. Schafer, R.M.: The Vancouver Soundscape. ARC Publications (1978)

The Penguin – On the Boundary Between Pet and Machine. An Ecological Perspective on the Design of Assistive Robots for Elderly Care

Emanuela Marchetti[1]([⊠]) [iD], William Kristian Juel[2] [iD],
Rosalyn Melissa Langedijk[3] [iD], Leon Bodenhagen[2] [iD],
and Norbert Krüger[2] [iD]

[1] Media Studies, Department for the Study of Culture,
University of Southern Denmark, (SDU), Odense, Denmark
emanuela@sdu.dk
[2] The Maersk Mc-Kinney Moller Institute, SDU Robotics,
University of Southern Denmark, (SDU), Odense, Denmark
{wkj,lebo,norbert}@mmmi.sdu.dk
[3] Department of Design and Communication, University of Southern Denmark,
(SDU), Sønderborg, Denmark
rla@sdu.dk

Abstract. Following current demographical trends, the aging population has emerged as a main target group for the development of assistive robots [16]. In current studies, assistive robots are seen as assistants, butlers or companion pets [2, 5]. These roles seem to assume an anthropomorphic or zoomorphic metaphor for the role of robots, acknowledging them intelligence and independence in performing daily tasks. In this paper we wish to reflect on the roles that assistive robots could play in elderly care, building on results gathered from a research through design investigation that we conducted as part of the SMOOTH (Seamless huMan-robot interactiOn fOr THe support of elderly people: www.smooth-robot.dk (Last seen 15/02/2019)) project. Our results suggest that the participants to our study seemed divided between understanding our robot as a tool but also as an intelligent being capable of social interaction. Therefore, we propose that assistive robots might be playing an ambiguous, evolving role in between that of a tool with a specific purpose and an intelligent being, like a pet, not equal and unthreatening to their human counterparts.

Keywords: Assistive robots · Elderly care · Ecology · Anthropomorphism

1 Introduction

In this paper we explore the role of assistive robots within elderly care. Taking an ecological perspective [13, 15] we analyze elderly care as a network of artefacts and human actors participating in a set of practices, aimed at securing conditions for successful aging [11] for elderly individuals. By successful aging we mean a positive understanding of aging within elderly care centers, in which residents and caregivers

© Springer Nature Switzerland AG 2019
J. Zhou and G. Salvendy (Eds.): HCII 2019, LNCS 11593, pp. 425–443, 2019.
https://doi.org/10.1007/978-3-030-22015-0_34

daily engage in practices aimed at securing the residents' well-being and individual dignity.

In current literature assistive robots are seen as assistants or companions [2, 3, 16], translated in future visions of human or pet-like robots replacing living beings in our lives. We aimed at challenging such visions through a research through design inquiry [22], in which we designed and tested a low-fidelity prototype to explore the role of assistive robots in future elderly care. This inquiry was part of the SMOOTH project, which was conducted in cooperation with Ølby elderly care center, located in Køge (Denmark). Our design process started with an ethnographic user study, continuing with a co-design workshop and a formative evaluation of a low-fidelity prototype, which we call the Penguin and more specifically "Casper[1]", as the famous character "Casper, the friendly ghost", but also a common male name in Denmark. Currently a high-fidelity prototype is under development.

During the making of the prototype we targeted three main scenarios, defined together with caregivers, in which our robot would: transport dirty and clean laundry, collect the garbage, and guide the residents to common areas for meals or social events. These scenarios (as in [19]) provided meaningful grounding for explore and challenge what could be accepted regarding cultural values, future functionalities, affordances, and interactions with the Penguin in elderly care ecology.

In the following Sect. (2) we present a literature review and the theoretical framework of our study, the methods adopted in the study are discussed in Sect. 3, while Sects. 4 and 5 respectively present results from the evaluation and conclusions.

2   On Role of Assistive Robots in the Ecology of Elderly Care. A Literature Review

In this section we present a literature review grounded on an ecological understanding of elderly care, to identify knowledge gaps and inspirations for our case study. In the first sub-section we discuss the theoretical foundation of our study (Sect. 2.1), in the second we reflect on the definition of assistive robots in relation to the needs of the aging population as it is discussed in literature (Sect. 2.2); in the third we reflect on the role of robots and the use of metaphor in design (Sect. 2.3).

2.1   An Ecological Perspective on Assistive Robots

Based on current literature and preliminary data gathering, we approach elderly care as an ecology [13], a complex set of practices taking place within elderly care centers, such as: medical care, meals, physical exercise and leisure activities like boardgames or movies.

The notion of ecology in the study of technologies is not new and it is intended as a biological metaphor aimed at evoking a complex organic whole composed of relationships among people, their practices, and the artefacts involved. Ecologies have

---

[1] https://en.wikipedia.org/wiki/Casper_the_Friendly_Ghost (Last seen 15/02/2019).

been defined as systems [13], assemblages [10], and networks [6, 15]. We find that these terms are in general equivalent yet embodying subtle differences in meaning. The term assemblages is extensively used by Latour [6, 10], and seems to evoke a messier and more dynamic unit than a system or a network. In his book *Reassembling the Social (2005)*, Latour argues that he aims at analyzing the "social" element in sociological studies as a moving target, an ever-changing element, which needs to be constantly analyzed and explained. System and networks seem to evoke respectively a more technological understanding of ecologies, as in [13]. From our side, we aim at exploring how caregivers and residents of elderly care centers perceive the role of assistive robots, as a human or pet companion, within their ecology, in relation to their values and the different practices they engage in.

According to Nardi and O'Day [13] an ecology is always placed within an environment, composed of artefacts an embodying values and expectations pertaining the practices taking place in it. In this sense, the environment is seen as participating in the relationships and practices in which each species (humans and non-humans) engage in. Regarding our study, we refer specifically to the practices taking place within a Danish elderly care center, which provides a significantly different context for elderly care than private home, as in [11]. For instance, according to the caregivers, in Denmark people retire to the care center when physical or cognitive frailty occurs. Therefore, our study addresses a specific segment of the elderly population, including people who in most cases cannot take care of themselves. Our robot has to act inside the care center, hence the physical layout of the center will set requirements regarding the physical features, as our robot should be able to walk through the corridors together with residents without taking too much space, pass smoothly through doors, and interact with available artefacts such as laundry and garbage bins.

Finally, referring to Trasmundi [19] and Enquist [6] we see our robot as a distributed system relying on affordances, interbodily dynamics, wordings and other artefacts present in the environment, such as doors, laundry and garbage bins, and other objects with which it will have to interact. All these functionalities will act as *perceived affordances* [6], which will be interpreted by different users in personal ways. This aspect becomes central when dealing with elderly, in relation to technological acceptance [2] and cognitive challenges caused by conditions like dementia. Critical questions emerge, therefore, in terms of sensibly framing the design process, to support key values in successful aging such as well-being, safety and life quality.

2.2 Assistive Robots and Their Users

Assistive robots are generally defined as "technologies directed to assist the elder population in a variety of tasks" [8, p. 28]. Two main types of robots are typically identified: service type robots targeting practical tasks [3] and social assistive robots playing an affective role as companions in the life of their users [3, 5]. Service type robots are aimed at supporting an independent life style, while social assistive have also been designed to support physical rehabilitation, however, both are expected to have an emotional impact in the life of their users [3]. Social assistive robots are expected to communicate in a natural and intuitive way with people, eliciting positive feelings

[5, 11]. Other studies [2, 11, 16] do not provide a specific definition of assistive robots, nonetheless they provide a value-based perspective, arguing that assistive robots should enable their users to have an independent life style and to keep their dignity as human beings.

Similarly to Forlizzi et al. [8], our study is framed within an ecology of elderly care, specifically localized within the walls of elderly care centers as in [2]. These care centers share distinctive characteristics that are different from personal homes. First of all, the residents are in close and constant contact with specialized caregivers and conduct a less independent and dangerous life style than if they were alone in their home. Second housing and medical facilities are explicitly designed for the care of elderly, meaning that doors and rooms are wide enough to enable them to move freely with rollators and wheelchairs. Third, building on [10, 13] we find that elderly center are dynamic ecologies, welcoming people with different stories and sociocultural backgrounds, including different experiences with technologies. At the same time, caregivers are bringing their own experiences too, having passed through ever changing trainings with old and new technologies. As a result, new practices and sociocultural values are challenging old ones, creating dynamic tensions and eventually leading to new practices.

Current research has tried to analyze the experience of aging, to identify requirements for the design of assistive robots and to justify the need of creating such robots. At the very start of their study Forlizzi et al. [8] claim that elderly people are rapidly increasing in the USA and that it is has been estimated that "there will be about 12 million people over age 85 in 2040" [8, p. 26]. Similarly, Broekens et al. [3] and Broadbent et al. [2] argue that as the elderly population is increasing in the world, so is the need for advanced technologies that could provide them with assistance, compensating for the insufficient number of professional caregivers. According to both studies [3, 8], people appear to live more meaningful lives in their homes than in elderly care centers, therefore, assistive robots should be designed to enable people to live in their homes for a longer time. On the other hand, Broadbent et al. [2] argue that in general elderly people living in care centers are generally positive towards a future with assistive robots. However, lack of knowledge might generate feelings of embarrassment and mistrust, leading towards a rejection of assistive robots. Lee and Riek argue that the products designed for the elderly embody negative stereotypes of aging, hence leading people to refuse otherwise valuable aids, disregarding that aging means that "people are living longer, active lives" [11, p. 1]. In alternative, Lee and Riek propose a "successful aging" perspective, in which the design of assistive robots should be grounded on a holistic and positive approach to aging emphasizing the interrelation between "physical functions, social engagement and self-confidence" [11, p. 2]. The perspective of successful aging seems to give a more concrete foundation to the claims of Broadbent et al. [2] and Forlizzi et al. [8], who argue for human dignity as a target value for the design of assistive technologies; so defined successful aging provides a main target for our study.

2.3 The Role of Assistive Robots in Elderly Care Ecology

Different metaphors have been used in reflecting on the role of new technologies, such as those of tools, texts and systems [6, 13]. From our perspective we wish to include in this discussion, anthropomorphic and zoomorphic perspectives, which have been applied specifically to assistive robots [3]. These metaphors provide straightforward perspectives, to analyze the role of new technologies within the ecologies they were designed for [13]. However, metaphors can limit our understanding of technologies within the ever-changing social dynamics internal to ecologies of practice [10, 13], so that metaphors can provide only a starting point for our analysis.

The tool metaphor represents an obvious way to look at technologies, intended as artefacts designed to achieve a certain goal [13]. Tools are associated also with "tactics" and selection [13, p. 29], this means that a tool is accurately chosen for a task and users must learn how to master them. Hence the tool metaphor embodies meanings of specialization, skills, and learning [6, 13]. From the perspective of design practice, looking at technologies as tools enables designers to go beyond pure aesthetics and forces them to focus concretely on their target users and practices, hence fitting well an ecological framework on practices and technologies. In the case of elderly care, the tool metaphor can enable designers to consider how their newly designed technology can fit the goals, values, and skills of the users, in relation to professional caregivers and elderly residents. However, as in [6] the tool metaphor can anchor the designers to consider only one specific function, predetermined and unchangeable [10], forgetting users' roles in determining the use of tools, a critique often addressed to the design of assistive robots [8, 11].

On the contrary, the text metaphor emphasizes the communication aspect of design practice and it has been adopted by theorists like Latour [10] in analyzing the active role to users in the process of constructing meaning by engaging with artefacts. This metaphor also acknowledges how the affordances offered by an artefact are not immutable, but subjectively determined by each user, a notion defined as *perceived affordances* [6].

Analyzing technology as a system provides "the richest, most troubling, and most mind-altering perspectives" [13, p. 33], in connection to provocative perspectives of the pervasive influence of technology on human life. Adopting this metaphor, technologies are seen as something independent from people, yet deeply affecting people by reframing systems of values in the name of efficiency. The system metaphor is often associated with negative feelings and skepticism towards technologies [6]. In relation to assistive robots, a system perspective might emphasize the downside of having robots instead of caregivers interacting with residents, subtracting human touch and empathy from a sensitive user group. However, in [13] it is suggested that local perspective on ecologies might suggest more constructive views on technologies, inspiring to investigate how skilled and knowledgeable professionals, like caregivers in elderly care ecologies, can ethically and empathically reframe technologies according to the needs of the elderly.

Assistive robots have been investigated as assistants, mediating between caregivers and residents [2]. Broekens et al. [3] discuss the role of robots as companions, exploring a zoomorphic metaphor for pet-like robots such as Aibo. The terms assistant and companion implicitly embody anthropomorphic and zoomorphic metaphors, suggesting functional and relational values. Following this notion [7, 18] it is argued that people tend to interact with their technologies based on tacit expectations origi- nated by the way in which they interact with each other. Moreover, it has become a common belief that people would prefer to interact with a robot resembling a person or a pet, in looks and interactive capabilities, providing a more intuitive and emotionally appealing interaction style [4, 20]. In this sense, anthropomorphism and zoomorphism have been discussed also as strategies to increase acceptance of assistive robots among the elderly [7].

Disturbing concerns emerge from the anthropomorphic perspective, envisioning robots as "autonomous machines" with the ability of assisting or replacing human beings in specific tasks [20, p. 8]. In [2] it is argued that caregivers from an elderly care center expressed worries regarding the safety of their own jobs, fearing to be replaced by assistive robots in the near future. Furthermore, it has been found that the more human a robot looks like, the more disturbing or scary it might be perceived by users, a phenomenon called the *uncanny valley* [2, 5]. In this regard, studies like Wu et al. [20] claim that no matter how pleasant a robot can be, people are sensitive to the fact that robots are not truly sentient or emotional and are not positive towards the scenario of entirely substituting humans or pets with robots. Hence, Wu et al. warn us against adopting a functional approach to companionship, interpreting it as simply an inter- action with something.

Taking these insights into account, we aim at reflecting on the role of assistive robots acting as assistants and companions in elderly care centers. We refer to anthropomorphism and zoomorphism as metaphors, enabling us to analyze concretely functional and ethical aspects of future scenarios for the use of assistive robots in elderly care.

3   Methodology – Design Process and Data Gathering

In this study, which is connected to the SMOOTH project, we followed a research through design approach [22], so that we conducted our scientific inquiry through a participatory design process, involving our target group of users and stakeholders as co-designers [1]. Being a scientific inquiry, the output or our design process takes the form of artefacts, embodying our understanding and acting as exemplars of a reflective solution for the problem investigated [21]. The testing of our prototype was undertaken as a scientific experiment, to validate the researchers' theoretical results from the study.

We adopted a qualitative approach, leveraging on ethnography, interviews and video analysis, with the goal of exploring needs and values related to the future use of assistive robots in the ecology of elderly care. We aimed also at giving a voice to users and stakeholders regarding their own future, in line with [1].

Our process was scenario-based as it was grounded on a series of scenarios for the use of our robot, which we defined together with the care center and the municipality of Køge early in the process. We formulated 3 main scenarios: transportation of dirty and clean laundry, transportation of garbage, and guiding guests to common areas for meals and social events. An additional scenario was also tested and discussed, in which the robot was supposed to serve drinks to the residents during meals and social arrange-ments. These scenarios provided a main source of inspiration through the process to design functionalities, features, and interaction abilities for the robot. As in Trasmundi [19], the three scenarios provided a concrete framework to explore possible roles for the robots, regarding how it will fit within the cultural values embodied in elderly care ecology, also challenging what could be accepted regarding functionalities, affor-dances, and interactions. The scenarios were literally used as resources for an embodied dialogue, which culminated during our evaluation, when residents and caregivers were invited to enact the scenarios, exploring how they imagined interacting with our pro-totype, which was controlled by one of the researchers.

Our process started with an ethnographic user study, supported by video recordings of interviews and observations with caregivers and residents. Our goal was to make sense of the practices going on at the center. We also conducted a series of three workshops with the project consortium, which included representatives from the research team, from the companies involved in the project, from the caregivers and stakeholders like the administration of the center and the municipality of Køge. During these workshops, we shared our findings from the observations we conducted at the center and we discussed the design of the robot, with the goal of integrating our findings on user needs with the technical expertise provided by the companies.

In the end, we held a formative evaluation with a low-fidelity prototype [14], a simple polystyrene representation of the robot. Two male residents and three employees (2 caregiver and 1 administrator) participated to the evaluation. Our eval-uation aimed at exploring how our prototype could fit within the three scenarios and to gather new requirements to design the final prototype. More details are discussed in Sect. 4.

3.1 The Design of Casper, the Penguin

The making of the prototype included three main stages:

1. A participatory design workshop at the elderly care center,
2. A sketching phase combined with two workshops within the consortium,
3. The making of a low-fidelity prototype, a simple mock-up make of polystyrene, which we used in a formative evaluation at the center.

The participatory workshop was held in June 2017, at Ølby elderly care center, it was conducted early in the project, to gain meaningful requirements for the design of the robot from aesthetic and functional perspectives, and also to increase the users' excitement about the future robot.

We started the workshop with an informal interview with caregivers and residents about developing specific ideas, hopes, needs, and fears regarding the implementation and design of our robot. After the interview, we engaged in a collaborative prototyping session. We divided the participants into three groups and we provided each of the groups with designing materials like: cardboard, paper, scissors, tape, plastic crumbs, straws, rulers, egg trays, Lego bricks and more. The groups were encouraged to reflect on central aspects for the development such as: preferred behaviors and interactions with the robot, its appearance, and what kind of verbal and physical feedback the robot should provide to human input. Since we could not gather permission from all the participants, we did not videorecorded this session, but we took pictures of the final prototypes to gain relevant documentation and inspiration.

At the end of the co-design workshop the groups presented their prototypes, as visible in Figs. 1, 2 and 3. The first two robots (Figs. 1 and 2) were focused on empathy and serving. They both have trays on the front and anthropomorphic features, showing an expressive face to elicit an intuitive interaction and communicate on an emotional level with the residents. The lively colors of the second prototype (Fig. 2), seem aimed at enhancing its expressive value. The third prototype (Fig. 3) is instead designed to look like a machine with arms aimed at solving practical tasks. Almost no effort was made to create an anthropomorphic appearance, there are no anatomical features, like the expressive faces displayed by the first two. Interestingly the first and third prototypes are mainly constructed in cardboard, in the first markers are used to draw specific features, like the face and buttons, and plastic glasses were used to represent the feet. In the third, plastic rulers and forks were used to create the arms.

Fig. 1. Serving robot made of cardboard with expressive face and front platform.

Fig. 2. Robot made of Lego bricks with expressive face, front platform and wheels.

Fig. 3. Robot made in cardboard, designed for practical tasks with arms but without face or anthropomorphic features.

The second prototype (Fig. 2) was entirely made of Lego Bricks, the body is shaped in a parallelepipedal, geometric form, but head and eyes are round, maybe to suggest a softer, human-like appearance. In particular, its large eyes seem to suggest a need for expressivity. Wheels were attached to the base of this prototype, suggesting that the designers explored options for the movement of the robot.

The workshop ended with a plenum discussion, during which we identified three emerging themes on the features of the robot, such as:

- Social interaction: Polite voice, human-like voice;
- Technical constraints: Global call system, be safe around humans, collect garbage and laundry one room at the time, lift outside garbage container lids, wheels for fluid movement;
- Appearance: Appealing design, no sharp edges, hygienic, friendly shape and look.

As we discussed in a previous study [9], the following design process was based on the outcome from this workshop. However, since our final prototype had to be marketable, functional, affordable, and safe, we had to rely on the off-the-shelf technologies provided by the partner companies. We, therefore, tried to combine user's needs and technical constraints in a creative way, to enrich the users' experience, our main priority. Because of technical constraints we had to re-elaborate the prototypes made through the workshops, the front platform present in the first two prototypes had to be replaced with a back platform. The use of the front platform would have required extra sensors to enable the robot to sense people while carrying stuff, causing safety issues as well as higher costs. The arms of the third prototype had to be eliminated, as the companies claimed that for legal and safety issues they cannot design robots with movable arms for healthcare facilities. We, therefore, conceptualized the back platform capable of lifting things to compensate for the loss of arms. Moreover, to guarantee stability, the robot had to move on a wide tricycle base, resembling the wheels attached to the second prototype.

As we were told during the workshop that the robot had to be cute and nice to interact with, we experimented with the concept of the robot as an assistant trying to create a funny looking character. According to the caregivers, the main role of the robot would be to "help with practical tasks", leaving the caregivers free to dedicate more time to the residents. Therefore, we approached the robot as a future mediator [10], acting in between residents and caregivers.

Early versions of the robot included the "Dyno", (Fig. 4) a name which emerged from the shape of robot which included the basic features established with the companies: a wide tricycle base and back platform for lifting and carrying stuff. The Dyno was a very simple prototype to foster discussion and it was presented at a consortium workshop. It was criticized for not being cute enough and elicited comments on the functional features. The Dyno inspired us to explore an animal theme through simple 2-D digital drawings and 3-D models, playing with different sizes and shapes.

Fig. 4. Early design, the "Dyno". 3D model courtesy of Frederik Haarslev.

After the workshop we went on to design the "Butler", which provided a meaningful anthropomorphic metaphor, suggesting a serving-mediating role, in which caregivers would be in charge and the butler would mediate between them and the residents. The Butler was re-elaborated further in an elongated and a shorter version, which were called the "Swan" and the "Penguin" (Fig. 5) [12]. The Swan was a slightly taller design, whose head was supposed to reach the shoulder of an average person, with arms-like wings to grab things but less dangerous and mobile than arms. The elongated version was also re-elaborated in a few colors and into a different robot named the Giraffe. The Penguin emerged as a chubbier character, inspired by pop-culture analogy between a penguin and the black-and-white clothed butlers[2]. A smaller robot was also designed, called the Mouse, which was directly made into a 3D model. These smaller robots were supposed to be less intimidating and modular than the taller ones. These sketches were exchanged by email across the participants to the consortium, initially the Swan, the Mouse, and the Penguin were chosen [12].

---

[2] https://disney.fandom.com/wiki/Penguin_Waiters (last seen 15/02/2019).

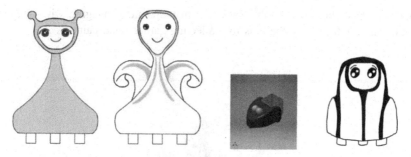

Fig. 5. Different sketches of our robot, from left: Giraffe, Swan, Mouse and the Penguin. 3D model of the Mouse courtesy of Frederik Haarslev.

In the end the Penguin was selected as a basis for developing the prototype to test at Ølby [9]. The Swan appeared a bit bulky and being taller it might also become more unstable, unless it had a larger base, which might not fit well corridors and narrow spaces in the center. The little size of the mouse was potentially dangerous, eventually causing people to trip on it as it might be difficult to see it at a close distance. Finally, the notion of the Penguin elicited some funny remarks, appearing as a funny, cozy character, the Penguin provided the main inspiration for the low-fidelity prototype.

4 Evaluation and Discussions

Based on the design of the Penguin, we made a physical low-fidelity mock-up [14], a simple and cheap prototype which was named Casper (see Fig. 6), which was tested during a formative evaluation at the elderly care center, three caregivers and 2 residents participated in the test. Our test aimed at gathering feedback and inspiration on our prototype to be used in our new design iteration, regarding: functionalities, aesthetics and experience, and emerging challenges.

The evaluation started with an informal conversation accompanied by coffee and tea, during which we presented the plan for the test, which all together took about two hours.

After the conversation we proceeded with enacting the scenarios, the first scenario to be tested was the guiding scenario, also the only one in which the residents are supposed to directly interact with Casper. The residents were invited to walk along the corridor to the dining area together with the mock-up pretending it was a finished robot. Our mock-up was placed on an office chair, so that it could be pushed around by one of the researchers, to give the illusion that the robot was moving on its own. Afterwards we tested the garbage and laundry scenarios, which require the caregivers to interact with Casper. We also tried a fourth scenario, in which the robot had to serve drinks in the dining area. At the end of the test, we had another informal conversation sharing a cake, during which we presented a series of videos representing how we imagined the scenarios in the start, to foster comparisons and reflections with the experience from the test. The video scenarios, which were edited with a combination of video footage and digital drawings, showed the robot in action in the center, engaging with imaginary residents and artefacts, like the bins for collecting garbage and laundry.

Fig. 6. Mock-up of Casper during testing.

On a general level both residents and caregivers welcomed us with a positive attitude and the prototype was commented positively. As for functionalities, one of the caregivers asked why the robot had no arms. We explained about the companies' legal restrictions for safety and its accepted to rely on the back platform for transportation tasks. The lack of arms was found limiting especially while enacting the fourth scenario (drinks serving), as it showed that the robot had to be loaded by caregivers, unless it could rely on specifically designed artefacts. For instance, for the laundry and garbage scenario, it was discussed that the center should adopt trash and laundry bins with wheels to be pushed by Casper along the corridors of the center. These changes were found a doable and valuable investment to support caregivers and residents. Movable carts could be made available to enable the robot to transport different items around the center. Practical and ethical issues emerged enacting the drinking scenario, as in elderly care ecology center drinks have medical meaning. All the residents have some medical condition, such as diabetes or hypertension and they are given individual juices containing medicines and supplements. Moreover, residents affected by dementia need constant help by the caregivers as they tend to forget to eat or drink, or might refuse their drink preferring another one, potentially endangering themselves if taking the wrong drink. Although a simple assistive task, which could be easily performed by a robot in other contexts, serving drinks becomes dangerous within elderly care ecology, posing ethical questions in relation to the role of Casper in case residents would opt for another drink or refusing to drink at all. It was suggested that in this scenario, the robot could act as a self-moving cart, carrying the glasses for the caregivers, who will be in charge of distributing the right drink to the right resident. It was instead suggested that the robot could remind the residents to take their medicines or call them out for social events. Finally, one of the caregivers asked if the robot could lift a wheelchair, a typical scenario for future assistive robots [16]. However, we did not work with that scenario in mind, because we were told during consortium workshops that the residents should be able to move on their own for physical exercise. Moreover, it would require a more expensive technology to secure the safety of the residents, but it is an interesting scenario that will be considered as future work.

Moving towards the aesthetic and experience aspects, it was decided since the start that the robot would interact mainly vocally. During the evaluation, the participants talked to the prototype in a natural way, calling it by name: "Casper!" It was proposed that the robot could respond: "I am coming!", informing the users that the call was heard by the robot. The physical movement of the robot generated safety concerns, it was proposed that it should keep a safety distance from the residents while moving around in the corridors, eventually producing a beeping sound while approaching, to alert residents and avoid accidents. The aesthetic of the penguin, a chubby robot shorter than humans, called Casper was found amusing. However, critical feedback was provided in relation to the face, especially regarding the perceptual capabilities of residents with advanced dementia. A caregiver said pointing at her own face: "They do not know what they see, they need eyes, nose, a face!" The physical prototype had two round big eyes and a sketched mouth (Fig. 6). We were wondering if the face should have been physical or represented in a small screen, enabling for slightly dynamic facial expressions, like smiles. The caregivers instead emphasized the need for a static smiling face, with large expressive eyes and a nose. Dynamically changing facial expressions had to be avoided, as these might be perceived unsettling, hence the caregivers suggested us to check Ruben's dolls[3] (Fig. 7), which are successfully used in the center for the therapy of residents affected by dementia.

Fig. 7. A Ruben's doll used at Ølby center.

---

[3] https://www.rubensbarn.com/ (last seen 15/02/2019).

Caregivers and residents also advised us to use neutral colors, like grey or pastels, as strong colors, like black or red, cause distress in the residents affected by dementia.

Regarding the look of the penguin as a type of assistive robot, a resident said with decision: "It has to look like a machine!" and caregivers nodded agreeing with him. The robot had to be clearly a tool for a practical purpose, a robot imitating a human or zoomorphic shape would be perceived as confusing, unsettling, and even threatening for the residents affected by dementia; nonetheless it might feel like disrespectful for the others, who are not interested in a machine pretending to be a living being, as in [5, 20]. Interestingly this resident said to be fond of science-fiction and to have read Asimov's robots stories, in which in fact robots might have anthropomorphic features, to interact comfortably in human-made environments, however, Asimov's robots are not imitation of humans, their intelligence is different and do not have emotions. He argued that being fond of science-fiction, he is readier than others to embrace assistive robots in his future, saying: "Making a robot is a technical problem, but many old people might not want them!" an issue acknowledged in current research [2].

Interestingly, as it was stated that Casper had to look like a machine, we found a slightly contradiction as during the enactment of the guiding scenario, the residents addressed our prototype politely, engaging in small talk with the researcher controlling the prototype (Fig. 8).

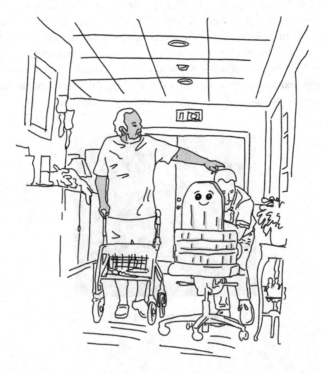

Fig. 8. Sketch taken from our videorecordings, representing a resident chatting with our prototype, Casper, pointing outside at cigarette buds in the garden.

Here is an excerpt of a conversation:

Resident:"Good morning, how are you?"
Researcher:"Good morning, fine thank you, how are you?"
Resident:"Fine, thanks!"
Researcher:"Have you slept well?"
Resident:"Yes, thank you!"
Researcher:"Should you have anything for lunch today?"
Resident:"Yes, I would like that. But look at there!"
Pointing a finger and gazing at the large window on their left
    "They are throwing cigarette buds there! Isn't it bad!"
Researcher:"Sure, ahhh .... that's really bad!"

Residents and researcher-Casper chatted in a friendly way until they reached the seat of the residents in the dining area.

While enacting the laundry scenario, the caregivers called aloud "Caaaasper!" while giggling. They seemed amused by this role-play activity and were calling the robot with an intention that is typically associated to calling a small child or an animal, not certainly an adult or a colleague. A need for a cheerful, human-like interaction also emerged while enacting the drinking scenario. It was suggested that after having delivered all the drinks, Casper could say: "Cheers!", as the caregivers usually do to elicit a feeling of conviviality in relation to a medical care practice. It was also suggested by the residents that the robot could engage in small talk, acting as a mascot, during meals. At the same time, the caregivers claimed that the robot should only be in the common areas and never access the residents' rooms on its own, for safety and hygiene reasons. While not being active, the robot should stay in a service area, isolated enough not to be a bother, but still accessible enough to be called, always available as a butler.

4.1 Which Role for Caper?

Our data from the evaluation suggest that assistive robots are perceived as an ambiguous, mediating species within the ecology of elderly care, placed in between a tool and a pet. Regarding the metaphors used in the study of the technologies, we find that observations and interviews seem to point towards different directions.

The tool metaphor [6, 13] clearly emerged through interviews, which suggest that on a conscious level residents and caregivers like to look at Casper as a tool, a "machine" with a practical purpose. In line with [20] it seems that the users of assistive robots want to keep a clear separation in their mind regarding the living and non-living beings they encounter. A robot imitating a living being could also be perceived as a disrespectful deception towards the residents, especially those affected by cognitive impairments, hence going against the principles of successful aging and dignity [8, 11] that we want to follow in our study.

The text metaphor emerged in our final conversation when the caregivers discussed how residents, especially those affected by dementia, might "read" Casper, eventually projecting malevolent intentions. According to the caregivers, Casper must communicate that being a tool it does not have feelings and that it cannot have the will of causing arm. The caregivers argued that a robotic face able of reproducing dynamically changing feelings, for instance shifting from a neutral to a smiling face, could be interpreted as unpredictable or provoking, as if the robot might shift from having good or bad intentions towards the residents. Therefore, the caregivers insisted on Casper showing an immutable, serene facial expression.

However, during the enactment of the guiding scenario the participants showed a desire for interacting socially with the prototype. Casper was expected to show a certain degree of intelligence: being able to move around in the center, being aware of where to go and of the people in the room, being able to intelligently respond to calls and to perform specific tasks without direct supervision. On the other hand, Casper is not supposed to enter the private rooms of the residents and to initiate a conversation. Casper is also supposed to keep a safety distance from the people moving in the center and to signal its presence to avoid incidents. In this respect, Casper is supposed to act as a sensing being, able to intelligently sense the world through its body and act accordingly [17, 19]. Casper is also envisioned as capable of relying on affordances, wordings and interbodily dynamics with humans and available artefacts, to act as expected by the human actors according to the present circumstances. The interaction with the robot is characterized as bodily dialogue, in which the robot approaches physically when called, turns its gaze towards their interlocutors or at the direction indicated by their interlocutors, as it was enacted by the resident during the guiding scenario (Fig. 8). In this sense, Casper was expected to pay attention and to display empathy, answering politely to the residents' attempts to engage in dialogue. At the same time, Casper had to be kept under control, as if it was a child or helping pet, potentially causing troubles. Interestingly the caregivers called Casper with a loud and amused tone of voice, prolonging the "a" in Casper, as if addressing an intelligent being with a sort of affection, but considered as non-equal in intelligence and status, someone like a child or a pet. According to the caregivers the robot could interact with the residents eliciting a positive mood for the coming activity, for instance discussing the daily menu while guiding them to their meals. However, the caregivers should decide which residents should be guided by the robot, according to their physical and mental condition. These limitations were clearly showed during the drinks-serving scenario, Casper cannot perform this task as an autonomous, responsible being, as functionally Casper cannot identify a specific drink and associate it with the intended resident. But even if Casper was functionally capable to associate a drink and its intended resident, it was too awkward to discuss what would be an acceptable behavior for Casper in case of conflicts, when for instance a resident would refuse his-her destined drink to get another one or nothing at all. The caregivers were not ready to delegate this responsibility to an assistive robot, expressing concerns for the residents' safety and dignity saying: "It would be a disaster if a resident gets the wrong drink..." and "It cannot do it!".

These insights show that caregivers and residents do not want assistive robots to play an actual anthropomorphic role as human assistants, which would be capable of taking responsibilities and ideally equal to human actors. Casper should be hierarchically inferior, being told what to do and act accordingly. This controlling attitude towards assistive robots is confirmed by the need expressed by the caregivers to restrain the future robot socially and physically in ways, which would not be not acceptable for human assistants.

Taking all these insights into consideration, a robot replacing the caregivers would not be acceptable, as this would generate a scenario in which the robot would be in control of the well-being of the residents for better or worse, a dystopian scenario typically embodied in the system metaphor [13], in which technologies are perceived as out of human control and potentially threatening.

Our data suggest instead that the participants would like a robot playing an ambiguous or dynamic role, placed in a dynamic balance between a machine and an intelligent being: unthreatening and non-equal to humans, unable to take responsibility, and easily disposable, but gifted of a certain intelligence, likable, and capable of social interaction. Therefore, we propose that assistive robots, acting in ecologies of elderly care, are envisioned by potential users as playing a role in between that of a machine and a pet. This does not imply the imitation of a pet, as it was explored for robot-companions like Aibo [3], we propose instead the notion of a dynamic machine-pet role, defined as a moving target within a spectrum, confirming the notion that the social interactions in information ecology are in continuous co-evolution, being dynamically negotiated by the participating species [10]. In our scenario, the role of assistive robots would have to be dynamically placed in between a tool and a pet, according to the evolving needs of the users, who will be deciding each time the degree of autonomy and social participation granted to the robot according to the given circumstances. We depict here a complex picture in need for further clarification, for instance on how to concretely explore this spectrum through forms of sociomaterial and playful interactions.

5 Conclusion

Different metaphors have been applied to discuss the role of assistive robots in supporting elderly care practices, such as classical metaphors of tool, text and system, but also anthropomorphic and zoomorphic metaphors. Anthropomorphic metaphors are based on the assumption that people interact with technologies, based on the way they interact with each other [18]. In this way, anthropomorphism has been presented as a strategy to increase the acceptance of assistive robots by elderly people, who are typically seen as reluctant to adopt new technologies [2, 20]. These metaphors are applied as sharp images suggesting aesthetic and functional features of assistive robots.

As part of the SMOOTH project [9], we explore the role of future assistive robots within the ecology of elderly care, seen as a set of individuals (mainly residents and caregivers), tools and practices placed within elderly care centers [6, 10, 13].

Empirical data were gathered through a participatory design process supported by ethnographic methods, in collaboration with Ølby center in Køge (Denmark) and local robotics companies. Our design process was based on three pre-established scenarios in which our robot was supposed to transport laundry, collect garbage, and guide residents to the dining area. An additional scenario was also discussed, in which the robot was supposed to serve drinks to the residents. A low-fidelity prototype was evaluated with caregivers and residents in the center, revealing a complex picture in which our participants claim to want a tool that could support specific tasks. However, during observations we noticed a need for a more intelligent being, able to communicate socially and empathically, but non-equal to the human actors around.

The role played by our robot emerged as that of a sophisticated distributed system [19], able to engage in a bodily dialogue with users, relying on wording and interbodily dynamics to perform practical tasks and to act as a social being. However, the participants to our study are not willing to approach assistive robots as equal anthropomorphic beings capable of taking responsibilities and to tell humans what to do, for instance in case a resident would refuse to take his-her drink. This scenario would be perceived as potentially humiliating and going against the principles of successful aging and human dignity that we want to follow in our study [11].

We propose, therefore, that assistive robots might play a role in between that of a machine and a pet combining a need for functionality and social interaction. An anthropomorphic role, as often implied by current literature discussing the role of assistive robots as assistants or companions [5], eventually replacing specialized caregivers [2], would not be desirable. At the same time, assistive robots imitating humans or pets are seen as a deception, going against the need of people distinguish between the living and non-living beings they encounter [20].

We, therefore, define the role of assistive robots as a dynamic role between a pet and a tool. As in [10], we see the role of assistive robots as a moving target within a spectrum, in which users will decide according to circumstances how much autonomy and social participation to grant to the robot, hence seeing it more as a tool or a pet. The role of assistive robots in elderly care ecology is configured here as the result of a continuous co-evolution among the actors involved [10, 13].

In this respect, open questions emerge in relation to sociomaterial and eventually playful forms of interactions which could be explored in the elderly care center, which we will explore as future works.

References

1. Björgvinsson, E., Ehn, P., Hilgren, P.: Participatory design and "democratizing innovation". In: Participatory Design Conference, pp. 41–50. ACM (2010)
2. Broadbent, E., Tamagawa, R., Patience, A., Knock, B.: Attitudes towards health-care robots in a retirement village. Australas. J. Ageing 31(2), 115–120 (2012)
3. Broekens, J., Heerink, M., Rosendal, H.: Assistive social robots in elderly care: a review. Gerontechnology 8(2), 94–103 (2009)
4. Chastagnol, C., Clavel, C., Courgeon, M., Devillers, L.: Designing an emotion detection system for a socially intelligent human-robot interaction. In: Mariani, J., Rosset, S., Garnier-Rizet, M., Devillers, L. (eds.) Natural Interaction with Robots, Knowbots and Smartphones, pp. 199–211. Springer, New York, NY (2014). https://doi.org/10.1007/978-1-4614-8280-2_18
5. Dautenhahn, K., Woods, S.N., Kaouri, C., Walters, M.L., Koay, K.L., Werry, I.P.: What is a robot companion - friend, assistant or butler? In: IEEE/RSJ International Conference on Intelligent Robots and Systems, pp. 1192–1197 (2005)
6. Enquist, H.: A socio-material ecology of the distributed self. Des. Philos. Pap. 6(2), 123–140 (2008)

7. Fink, J.: Anthropomorphism and human likeness in the design of robots and human-robot interaction. In: Ge, S.S., Khatib, O., Cabibihan, J.-J., Simmons, R., Williams, M.-A. (eds.) ICSR 2012. LNCS (LNAI), vol. 7621, pp. 199–208. Springer, Heidelberg (2012). https://doi.org/10.1007/978-3-642-34103-8_20

8. Forlizzi, J., DiSalvo, C., Gemperle, F.: Assistive robotics and an ecology of elders living independently in their homes. Hum.-Comput. Interact. **19**, 25–59 (2004)

9. Juel, W.K., et al.: The SMOOTH robot: design for a novel modular welfare robot. J. Intell. Rob. Syst. (Submitted)

10. Latour, B.: Reassembling the social. In: An Introduction to Actor-Network-Theory. Oxford University Press (2005)

11. Lee, H.R., Riek, L.D.: Reframing assistive robots to promote successful aging. **1**(1), 1–23 (2018). Article 1

12. Marchetti, E.: If it looks like a duck: names as shared signifiers for discussing "cuteness" in healthcare robotics. In: 9ICOM International Conference on Multimodality Moving the Theory Forward, Odense, Denmark (2018)

13. Nardi, B., O'Day, V.: Information Ecologies. Using Technology with Heart. MIT Press, Cambridge (1999)

14. Preece, J., Rogers, Y., Sharp, E.: Interaction design. In: Beyond Human Computer Interaction. Wiley (2015)

15. Raptis, D., Kjeldskov, J., Skov, M.B., Paay, J.: What is a digital ecology? Theoretical foundations and a unified definition. Aust. J. Intell. Inf. Process. Syst. **13**(4), 5 (2014)

16. Riek, L.: Healthcare Robotics. Commun. ACM **60**(11), 68–78 (2017)

17. Sheridan, T.B.: Human-robot interactions: status and challenges. Hum. Factors **58**(4), 525–532 (2016)

18. Suchman, L.: Human-Machine Reconfigurations. Plans and Situated Actions, 2nd edn. Cambridge University Press, Cambridge (2007)

19. Trasmundi, S.B., Steffensen, S.V.: Meaning emergence in the ecology of dialogical systems. Psychol. Lang. Commun. **20**(2), 154–181 (2016)

20. Wu, Y., Cristancho-Lacroix, V., Fassert, C., Faucouneau, V., de Rotrou, J., Rigau, A.: The attitudes and perceptions of older adults with mild cognitive impairment toward an assistive robot. J. Appl. Gerontol. **35**(1), 3–17 (2016)

21. Zimmerman, J., Forlizzi, J., Evenson, S.: Research through design as a method for interaction design research in HCI. In: CHI Design Theory, pp. 493–502. ACM (2007)

22. Zimmerman, J., Forlizzi, J.: Research through design in HCI. In: Olson, J.S., Kellogg, W.A. (eds.) Ways of Knowing in HCI, pp. 167–189. Springer, New York (2014). https://doi.org/10.1007/978-1-4939-0378-8_8

Interactive Drinking Gadget
for the Elderly and Alzheimer Patients

David A. Plecher[1]([⊠]), Christian Eichhorn[1], Martin Lurz[2], Nadja Leipold[2],
Markus Böhm[2], Helmut Krcmar[2], Angela Ott[3], Dorothee Volkert[3],
and Gudrun Klinker[1]

[1] Chair for Computer Aided Medical Procedures and Augmented Reality,
The Technical University of Munich, Munich, Germany
{plecher,klinker}@in.tum.de,
christian.eichhorn@tum.de
[2] Chair for Information Systems, The Technical University of Munich,
Munich, Germany
{Martin.Lurz,Nadja.Leipold,Markus.Boehm,Krcmar}@in.tum.de
[3] Institute for Biomedicine of Aging, Friedrich-Alexander-Universität
Erlangen-Nürnberg, Nürnberg, Germany
{Angela.Ott,Dorothee.Volkert}@fau.de

Abstract. With this contribution we want to give insights into the
development of a drinking gadget which is useable by the elderly and
dementia patients with the goal to create an automated drinking protocol. Through the literature and available smart cups, we deduced important strategies for the design of a drinking aid. Our natural solution is
integrated into the daily workflow, hence enables the caregivers to react
to the needs of the elderly without additional burden. Therefore, we
identified some key requirements for both user groups. Furthermore, we
integrated aspects of expandability with software, a vision of rich interaction between user/gadget and focused on the convenience during the
daily usage to reach the elderly and caregivers alike.

Keywords: Dementia · Alzheimer patients · Games for elderly ·
Gadgets for elderly · Drinking detection · Dehydration · Caregivers ·
Retirement home

1 Introduction

Reduced fluid intake is an often occurring side effect of aging [1], partly because
older persons tend to forget their daily drink. This increases with diseases such
as Alzheimer. The result is a threatening and often overlooked risk of dehydration, leading to a higher demand for nursing care. In combination with the
shortage of care personnel, missing innovation in the field of elderly care and the
demographic change it contributes to the much discussed care crisis [2].

This paper presents various gadgets to motivate and remind the elderly
to drink, thereby decreasing the workload of the nursing staff (see Fig. 1).

© Springer Nature Switzerland AG 2019
J. Zhou and G. Salvendy (Eds.): HCII 2019, LNCS 11593, pp. 444–463, 2019.
https://doi.org/10.1007/978-3-030-22015-0_35

Usability?   **Advantage?**

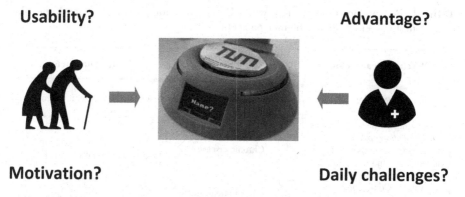

Motivation?   **Daily challenges?**

Fig. 1. Gadgets for supporting the elderly and the caregivers

The drinking behaviour is improved by the integrated use of these smart gadgets with games designed especially for elderly people. We developed a combination of smart sensors and feedback mechanisms to build up a detailed protocol of the patients' fluid intake. Our method detects and internally counts the amount of liquid consumed by patients, thereby providing an overview of the hydration state for the nursing staff. Several gadgets for elderly people have been developed at chairs from the Technical University of Munich (TUM), supported by chairs from the Friedrich-Alexander-Universität Erlangen-Nürnberg (FAU) as part of the project *enable* [3].

2   Reasons for Dehydration of Elderly People

In 2016, 120.107 people in Germany (all age groups) had to be treated in hospital because of dehydration and 5.217 died during their stay [4]. The number of cases increased drastically since the year 2000 and a high percentage of those people are older adults [5]. There are many known reasons for this situation. Table 1 lists such reasons, classified into *Psychological factors*, the *Aging process* and *Situational factors*. Since this can be a cause of death, generating a better understanding is important [6,7].

Impaired vision [8], functional impairment [9] and cognitive impairment [9] through typical, age-related diseases like Alzheimer's are influencing the drinking behavior noticeably [5,10]. Crawley and Hocking [11] wrote a guide for elderly care listing influencing factors due to which dementia patients can be malnourished. Sufficient liquid is needed to have a balanced blood flow such that it can carry away waste and transport nutrition. Furthermore, there are cancer types (e.g. bladder cancer) which occur more frequently when people do not drink enough [12,13]. To support the liquid intake, fluid rich nutrition sources such as yoghurts, soups, vegetables and fruits should be incorporated in the daily meal menu [11].

For elderly people, two main reasons exist for insufficient water intake [5]:

Table 1. Reasons for dehydration, white background for elderly in general and blue background especially for Alzheimer patients

Psychological factors	Aging process	Situational factors
Depression	Diminishing thirst sensation due to decrease in taste and smell [5]	Wounds (e.g. after an operation)
Forgetting the task: *Doorway effect/location updating effect,* entering a new room/performing another task and forgetting the first one [5]	Chronic disease	Medication: Excreting additional water [6]
Anxiety/Confusion: E.g. Worrying about money, fear of incontinence [7]	Functional impairment: Chewing and swallowing	Communication to caregivers
Changing mood: Skipping multiple meals	Limited mobility	Climate change: Heat waves [7]
Distraction, then leaving the table without reason	Decrease in kidney function	Diabetes mellitus
Appetite changes rapidly and changes aren't communicated to the caregivers	Natural decline in memory capabilities	

1. They forget the intention to drink because their prospective memory is unable to connect properly with other necessary brain areas to remember the action.
2. The sensation of thirst may be altered, as during the aging process or disease development, the responsible area in the brain may not function the same way as before.

In summary, dehydration is a cause of morbidity, resulting in increased mortality rates [5,6]. In consequence, drinking protocols were introduced in nursing homes.

3 Drinking Protocols in Nursing Homes and the Requirements for Change

To ensure a healthy daily drinking volume, the German law demands for the documentation of the liquid intake in the form of a drinking protocol in nursing homes. Yet, thus far, there are no regulations on how to measure the liquid intake [6]. The drinking protocols are still handwritten in most cases and the liquid intake is just estimated. This leads to multiple issues. Kreutzer et al. [6] have researched the accuracy of estimating the water intake by the care personnel in a nursing home environment. Even when focusing only on care personnel with experience in measuring liquid levels on a daily basis, the measured volume was by 10% off on average. Taking a sequence of unfavourable estimations into consideration, improvement is urgently necessary. As the number of patients per caregiver in nursing homes is growing and people start to be aware of the disadvantages of handwritten, estimation-based drinking protocols, the need for higher efficiency and automated documentation to maintain the necessary healthcare [14] is growing. Automating the drinking protocols opens new opportunities, such as more time available for interacting with the elderly or instant feedback, e.g. when there is a critical shortage in fluid intake.

A number of basic requirements exist. Studies show a deficit of assistive technology, suited to the daily life of those being assisted. Automation requires gadgets capable of measuring the fluid intake. Many disabled people don't own the necessary equipment for their personal needs [15]. Appropriate infrastructure needs to be ubiquitously available, integrated into the daily routine. It must be distributable and affordable. Furthermore, it must be understandable and acceptable. New technology allows to solve challenges, but constantly adapting to this ever occurring change is hard for some groups of society like the elderly [16]. There must be motivating incentives for the elderly wanting to use the technology.

4   Assistive Technology for Activities of Daily Living

Personal assistance via caregivers and technological assistance through equipment are the two options to counter age-related decline symptoms, which hinder continuing the Activities of Daily Living (ADLs). Assistive Technology (AT) is used to maintain or improve capabilities of cognitive, physical or communication for disabled people [17,18]. In the form of smart devices and *Environmental Interventions (EIs)* such as modifications of objects in the home environment, AT can reduce the burden on caregivers, lower care costs and most importantly improve the independence of the elderly [15,19]. Over time various concepts and devices have been developed, but only a small number of them focuses on drinking and eating habits [19]. Furthermore, many AT devices deal with ADLs, but leave out modern technology based solutions or focus just on monitoring movement [2]. Many forms of AT exist.

Assistive Technology for Information and Communication Technologies (AT ICT) is defined as devices that help a person with disability to process information in various forms. These can be devices to overcome perceptual decline like seeing aids or to support ADLs such as calling a person for support with the overall focus on using some sort of information and communication processing unit [20].

Intelligent Assistive Technology (IAT) extends AT with an integrated computing capability and the option to transmit information in a network (similar to AT ICT). An IAT device is most often used to sense the environment, process the data and inform the user, if there is a benefit (*intelligent decision making*). To maximize the adoption of IAT, a user-centered design approach is beneficial. Through this approach, the needs, preferences and limitations of patients are the foundation of design decisions and extensive testing is performed over the entire development process. Ienca et al. [17] categorized existing IAT with respect to six points of interest: *Technology type, application, function assisted, user-centered design, primary target-user population* and *evidence of clinical validation*. The most common form of IAT with 148 findings in their study, was technology designed to support dementia patients with ADLs. They identified, that only around 40% of the identified IAT is based on user-centered concepts. Missing user focus, high observed drop-out rates and small sample-sizes, which lead to a slow translation of IAT into the actual usage. Another common area of IAT development found by Ienca et al. [17] were robots. Besides daily support with household activities, social and emotional support in the form of assistive companions could be identified as a trend in future IAT development. Because of various, changing needs, "a holistic and multi-level support" [17, p. 1336] for the users is beneficial. IAT can become an ubiquitous trend in dementia care. There is an urgent need to translate innovative technology to *care-oriented IAT* to benefit the elderly and their caregivers alike.

Brain-Computer-Interaction (BCI) can be categorized into three application types: *Communication, functional control* and *entertainment*. Since disabled people and the elderly cannot fully benefit from traditional AT due to motor disabilities, BCI can be extended to generate hybrid systems by combining it with traditional AT, thereby creating hBCI systems. Those intelligent, interactive concepts should be based on helping people to interact with the system, motivating them to use the system by integrating enjoyable experiences. Through *self-adaption* the user can choose when to interact with the system and what kinds of interactions are necessary. Millán et al. [20] experimented with BCI to support disabled people with new interaction possibilities by incorporating the outside world.

Wearables are technology directly worn by users (not just carried), possibly integrated into their clothes. They hence represent the most closed-up form of non-invasive human-computer interaction [17]. A recent example is the use smartwatches to monitor users' health parameters and behavior at home [21]. This concept is quite frequently used to support dementia patients by combining multiple devices and an intelligent computing unit (IAT) to a wireless sensor network (smart home applications). This allows to give feedback for actions and improves the orientation and safety of the person [21]. Other concepts focus mainly on measuring health parameters or detecting tumbles by the elderly [2]. Lutze et al. [22] detected various parameters with a smartwatch to categorize ADLs and react with feedback if necessary. A similar concept was used by Zimmermann et al. [10] who used Internal Measurement Units (IMUs) with acceleration and gyroscope data to classify the movement. Their goal was to detect the drinking activity and the amount which has been drunk with the help of a smart cup. Vidya et al. [23] even suggest a cup which can compensate for the handshaking of Parkinson patients.

Biomedical and Health Informatics (BMHI): The goal is to optimally use the available medical information acquired directly from the patient (biomedical signals), often in combination with a ubiquitous solution (e.g. wearables such as smartwatches). Providing this kind of assistance at home is still a challenge due to the limited availability of devices with interfaces usable for the elderly or disabled. For that reason, during the development of so called *Digital City Frameworks* the target is to create technologically-supported environments for assistance of the elderly [24].

Serious Games are games that convey more than only entertainment content. They are complemented by concepts of Gamification which add gaming elements to non-game applications [26]. For the elderly, recent concepts focus on teaching the elderly to use mobile devices and apps. Therefore, various *Serious Games* were developed with custom interfaces, personalized concepts and additional motivating elements [27]. The concept of providing "fun" through a game (including challenge, curiosity and fantasy), pertains to the goal of immersing the elderly in the *game flow*. The theory of *flow* by Csikszentmihalyi [28] focuses on the level of engagement, hence the absorption in the current activity, which results in enjoyment without the need of future benefit [20]. With the objective to benefit the elderly in health related challenges or ADLs such as liquid intake, *Serious Games* can become a form of AT, especially, as the mobile devices on which they are running, can be easily extended with additional sensors or wearables.

Prototyping and Do-It-Yourself 3D Printing: With the availability of 3D printers for home usage, the *Prototyping* section for AT purposes increased noticeably [18]. With the advance of 3D printing technology, patient-specific medical aids can be developed [29]. Expensive technologies such as artificial hands can be accessible through 3D printers for more users worldwide. However, in terms of assistive devices for ADLs, drinking gadgets are rarely found. There is only a noticeable interest on printable everyday items, such as pill boxes [18].

The field of AT is diverse. But getting an understanding of the input of calories and amount of liquid intake is up until today a challenge. Obstructive approaches, such as using electrodes in the food or beverage, or the need to constantly wear hardware on the body like cameras, limits the possibilities for a target group like the elderly [31]. A new view on drinking aids seems to be necessary, hence the question for a useful sensor strategy must be researched.

5   Approaches to Liquid Level Sensing

Liquid level sensing is an important challenge with varying requirements in multiple industrial areas. For example, a car fuel tank has strict security regulations and needs to be precise in every situation. On the other hand, a water tank will need an approach which doesn't involve endangering hygiene when having contact with the water. Multiple solutions have been developed and researchers such as Kreutzer et al. [14], Hambrice and Hopper [32] and Lanka and Hanumanthaiah [33] documented their usage. We have structured the most relevant ones into four identifiable strategies:

1. **Movable objects:** A common example would be a floating swimmer. The floating object is attached to a string and swims on top of the liquid. The approach is quite simple with high repeatability, but unreliability and the risk of

a short lifetime because of moving parts. These approaches rely on an object directly moving in the liquid to calculate the liquid level, hence are quite troublesome for the usage in a drinking cup scenario because of hygiene concerns or the danger of swallowing the swimming object.

2. **Distance measurement:** More precisely described, it is the measurement of the delay of the Round-Trip Time for the used waves to travel to the surface and back. A typical example would be an ultrasound sensor. A pulse is sent which hits the surface, bounces back to the emitter as echo and the time needed is measured. A potential challenge is the tilting of the cup which needs to be detected to avoid measuring false values. On top of that, the min/max distance to the surface of the specific module to work correctly needs to be taken into consideration. In terms of usage in a drinking cup, a solution would be to mount it in an extension of the handle cup. But the sensor can come in the way when drinking because of its placement.

3. **Liquid feature:** Liquids have various specific features, which can be utilized or manipulated to measure the liquid level. For example, because liquids are typically conductive, two electrodes inside of the container can measure the conductivity, which increases with a higher liquid volume. This approach usually has a high level of precision [34]. One downside would be the potential issue of varying behavior of the sensor readings with different liquids. These approaches aren't based on moving parts in the liquid, but can be influenced by the liquid in the human body when touching the cup. Liquid flow measurement can be a solution too, as shown by Kreutzer et al. [30].

4. **Weight measurement:** A strategy with various types of sensors which all utilize the weight of the liquid, e.g. load cell, where the deformation of the strain gauge can be measured. This category has an advantage because of the fact that there is in general no contact with the liquid itself and any type of cup can be placed on the sensor.

After structuring the found approaches, we further want to compare the various concepts with a focus on using them in a drinking cup scenario. We have chosen *Contact with liquid* as important point because of the hygiene requirement. *Usage of own cup* is based on our experiences in the retirement home, where the elderly people often want to use their own cups or different varieties over the whole day. Another issue is stigmatization, a *Visible modification of the cup* can lead to rejection as the elderly people who still can use common cups, don't want to be seen as requiring help. For that reason, we have created an overview table (see Table 2):

When looking at the various concepts, a "winning strategy" should have no contact with the liquid, the usage of an own cup is recommendable and the modification for the measurement should be as small and inconspicuous as possible. The weight strategy section offers some promising concepts.

Table 2. Liquid level sensing methods

	Measurand	Contact with liquid	Usage of own cup	Visible modification of the cup
Movable objects				
Floating swimmer	Height	X	-	X
Magnetic float gauge	Height	X	-	X
Distance measurement				
Ultrasonic sensing	Delay	X	X	?
Magnetostrictive level transmitter	Delay	X	-	X
Laser	Delay	-	X	?
Radar	Delay	-	-	?
Optical sensor	Current	X	-	X/?
Guided microwave	Delay	X	-	X
Liquid feature				
Conductivity	Voltage	X	-	-
Capacity	Capacity	X/-	X/-	-
Hydrostatic devices	Water pressure	X	-	X
Flow meter	Volume	X	X	X
Vibration	Frequency	X	-	X
Radioactive radiation, obviously not usable	Current	X	-	X
Weight measurement				
Hydrostatic pressure	Pressure	-	X	-
Load cell	Mass	-	X	-
Force Sensing Resistor	**Force**	-	X	-

6 Smart Cups on the Market

Already existing smart cups on the market (see Table 3) are not designed for the elderly or the care environment. They are not easy to use for the elderly, the displays are often too small, and they are not expandable (closed systems). Additionally, most cups are focused on benefitting the user as individual products. They do not provide remote data access and thus cannot be integrated into a nursing infrastructure.

In consequence, we designed our own gadget that is usable by the elderly and can be integrated into our games and apps for motivation purposes. It is open for integration into a diverse ecosystem of gadgets, developed not only by us, but also by external developers.

Table 3. Smart cups on the market

Name/Manufacturer	Selling point	Liquid leveling	Interactive/ Motivating	Suitable for Elderly
Smart Water Cup (VSON)	Reminder, Display, LED	Load cell, Accelerator sensor	Display, App	Display too small
HeyDo (ILOOF)	Reminder, water analyzer, thermometer	Weight	Display	Too big, complicated, hygiene
SPE Hydrogen Generator (AlkaVoda)	Water ionizing	-	Display, App	Too small display for interaction
Ceramic mug (ember)	Heating drinks	-	LED, App	√
Cup (GYENNO)	Reminder	Yes?	Display, App	√ Big screen
Java+ (Ozmo)	Reminder, coffee heater	Yes, Weight	LEDs, gamified app	Too complicated, too big
Smart CUP	Measuring liquid intake	Load cell	Own cup, sound, LED, App	√ made for the elderly
Tumbler (Droplet)	Reminder, measuring drinking frequency	-	Changeable cup, LEDs, sound messages	√ made for the elderly
OBLI	Reminder with app and colorful LEDs	Weight	LEDs, sound, App	√

7   Prototypes

Prototype 1: Cup with an Accelerometer. We used the Development Platform *MetaWear* CPRO by MBientLabs in combination with a 3-axis accelerometer to detect only the drinking gesture. The sensor data was sent to an Android app to compute the tilting angle. Based on threshold of tiltedness we assumed a drinking event. The technical equipment was stored in a double-layered base and had no contact with the liquid (see Fig. 2).

Prototype 2: Cup with an Ultrasound Sensor. We used the ultrasound HC-SR04 module to measure the distance to a surface. The minimum measuring distance for useful values is 2 cm and the maximum distance is up to 4 m with an overall good precision. The sensor was placed at the top of the cup. Furthermore, to

Fig. 2. Prototype 1: Cup with Development Platform *MetaWear* CPRO [25] and an accelerometer

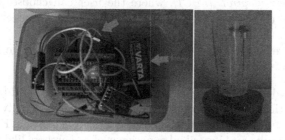

Fig. 3. Prototype 2: Arduino Nano, extension board, Bluetooth module, battery and cable management for the ultrasound sensor and tilt sensor

reliably detect the drinking behavior in contrast to the standing cup situation, a tilt sensor has been integrated (see Fig. 3).

8   The Smart and Interactive Drinking Platform for the Elderly

Based on experiences made with prototypes 1 and 2 during real-world testing in retirement home environments, we derived a set of requirements (see Fig. 4),

Fig. 4. Requirements for the drinking platform and the challenges which needed to be addressed

resulting in a further prototype. It should have a high level of *Expandability* for the hardware (common microcontroller) and also an open system approach (Bluetooth) for future usage in various applications. We chose a user-centered design approach with the goal of developing an *IAT* solution. The platform should benefit the elderly and additionally, with intelligent design choices, it should be able to support the caregivers in their *Daily Challenges* [17]. More importantly, as described by Ienca et al. [17], only a small amount of *IAT* projects for dementia patients (a substantial focus group for our evaluation) has targeted the reduction of isolation and offered social *Interaction*. We see a unique opportunity for such a drinking gadget (*Expandability*) by incorporating our developed *Serious Games* to further enhance motivation and life quality [27]. We want to utilize BCI concepts to help the elderly people to interact with the system by creating enjoyable experiences (*entertainment*). Another core concept of *BCI* is connected to *self-adaption (hBCI)*, where the user can choose when and how to interact with the games. We extend this with incentives, such as showing a banner now and then to remind the person to drink [20].

For this concept we tackled three base requirements for the design and sensor approach:

- **Hygiene:** Elderly people are very susceptible to disease and hence there are harsh regulations on products designed for the elderly. A daily used drinking cup needs to fulfill the precondition of begin dishwasher safe. From our previous project results and described experience of researchers like Kreutzer et al. [30], we think no sensor contact with the liquid should be an important point when choosing the sensor approach (exclusion of most *Liquid feature*-based and *Movable objects*-based approaches, see Table 2). Sensors inside the liquid, such as electrodes (e.g. conductivity measurement), will be a risk factor for mold and deposits. And as demonstrated by Kreutzer et al. [14], designing a cup with integrated sensors to be dishwater safe, will always be a challenge.
- **Usage of the own cup:** When experiencing the daily routines in a retirement home, it became soon clear, there is a given, small selection of cups and tumblers in use. Furthermore, elderly people are preferring their own drinking cup over a given one, especially if the given cup is different in shape and look than the others. The most obvious reason for that rejection is the perceived stigmatization by the elderly people, e.g. when using plastic cups over regular ones. In terms of usability, the typical smart travel cup concepts (see Table 3) are too big and bulky to be used anyway for the elderly. On top of that, the elderly people have issues to adapt to new behavior and approaches. For those reasons, we want to aim for an approach which incorporates existing cups/drink glasses for a natural approach (understanding of *EIs*), hence strategies which need a more substantial modification of a cup, such as described in *Distance measurement* strategies (see Table 2), are not suitable.
- **Safety:** Another point to consider would be the overall safety for the elderly. Therefore, strategies such as *Movable-objects* in the liquid are not suitable as parts could accidentally be swallowed. Because elderly people often suffer from

motor decline like shaking, they are not able to pick up/put down the cup on a too high platform. Furthermore, the solution should add no additional risk of dropping the glass, e.g. by encouraging a slippery grip around the glass.

With these main requirements in mind, we came to the conclusion to choose an approach with a 3D printed platform (*Prototyping*), where the user will put his glass or cup on top of a sensor stand. This means choosing a *Weight measurement* approach, which would allow us to have no sensor contact with the liquid, people can use their own cups and an inconspicuous design can be created by imitating a traditional beermat. For most elderly people putting the glass on a beermat is a natural way of positioning it on the table, hence we are just extending an existing, socially accepted solution with additional functionality (*EIs*).

Besides these core design choices, the following non-functional requirements exist for the platform:

- **Size of the sensor and components:** A typical glass with a volume of 0.2l has a very limited surrounding for fitting sensors and other parts. Therefore, the resulting solution must be as compact as possible and easy to handle even when the elderly person has to reposition the platform.
- **Appearance of the platform:** To build up some confidence and not to disturb the elderly in their daily life, the platform should be inconspicuous (beermat) and more importantly, only actively interacting when needed.
- **Multiple platforms, one mobile device:** In the retirement home scenario many people are sitting around the table. Therefore, the software part of the platform should support such a situation. To achieve this, we want to have a strategy with a mobile device being responsible to collect the data from multiple stations at once.

When looking at the different sensor choices for our smart beermat, the following approach stands out.

9   A Force Sensing Resistor to Measure Liquid Intake

Inspired by Zhou et al. [31], we chose a Force Sensing Resistor (FSR) to measure the weight changes of a drinking glass. They implemented a dining monitoring system with the goal to pervasively measure parameters like calorie intake. Their approach is based on monitoring the dinning activities through pressure changes on a fabric-based pressure matrix in combination with FSR sensors. Thereby the FSR sensors deliver information about the weight changes. This allowed a detailed composition of the eating activity in comparison to other food measuring techniques, e.g. image-based approach. Overall in their study the pressure measuring concept showed high reliability and usability. For us this approach (see Fig. 5) allows a combination of stability and thinness (with the help of a 3D printed stand and a cardboard beermat on top of it). The sensor's height is only 2 mm and if correctly calibrated, the results can be quite accurate. For that reason, we looked at the sensor data under pressure and when no object is being placed on top of it and plotted one function for each case.

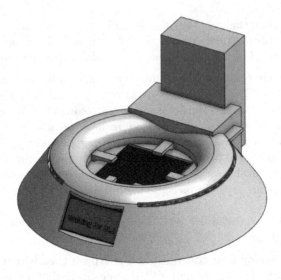

Fig. 5. CAD model with components

10   Situation in the Retirement Home and Platform Integration in the Workflow

To prevent dehydration, a common reason for hospitalization of the elderly [12], a drinking gadget should incorporate typical daily situations in a retirement home.

Day-to-day, elderly people will meet in a living area for eating, entertainment or having a talk with each other (see Fig. 6). There is no room for items which can be damaged through spilled water or accidental force as such incidents will happen frequently. Furthermore, a drinking gadget should be integrated into the environment *(EIs)* in a natural way to enhance the acceptance of the elderly target group. On the other hand, the device should be able to inform the elderly person and/or the caregiver if there is an issue. We thus want to utilize information and communication technology for assisting purposes *(AT ICT)*. Another requirement would be to support the caregivers in their workflow, instead of adding additional workload.

For that reason, we will assign one platform to one elderly person for the whole day to collect information about the liquid intake. Thus, as long as the drinking cup or glass stays the same, the weight loss or gain will always resemble the drunken volume by the person. No pre-calibration is necessary. One mobile device (e.g. tablet) is needed as control unit, to which all the individual gadgets connect and send their data. The caregiver can surveillance the drinking volume per station and act if necessary. To incorporate the *hBCI* ideas [20], additional mobile devices can be situationally integrated to increase the mood of a person or sharpen his/her sense for drinking enough liquid with the help of entertaining

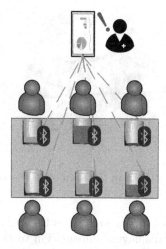

Fig. 6. Multiple cups connected to one device, transmitting data in the background

Serious Games. A trigger for that could be a notification for the caregivers when a person is behind with the liquid intake.

11   Features of the Platform

As described above with this platform approach we want to tackle some challenges found in previous attempts. The result should be an on daily usage focused, interactive gadget which can be integrated in various projects, e.g. *Serious Games.*

11.1   Expandability

We wanted to use a standardized microcontroller and have chosen the Arduino Nano platform. This allows us to extend the gadget with the necessary components and by using the Adafruit Feather nRF52832, there is already a Bluetooth module integrated in combination with a dedicated port for power delivery. With the open nature of the Bluetooth implementation, it is possible to integrate the gadget into various app projects. This often overlooked aspect in commercially available smart cups, can be used to expand the functionality above the predefined one with the help of software developed for mobile devices.

11.2   Interaction

One core aspect, which we wanted to address with this concept, is to create a vision for interaction in two directions. First, by informing the user about an important issue (device $\Rightarrow$ human) and secondly by providing interaction opportunities (human $\Rightarrow$ device):

Fig. 7. Interaction methods in the form of LED stripes and a display

- **LED stripes:** On each side one stripe has been integrated (see Fig. 7), with the specific purpose of displaying information to the elderly with simplistic light patterns. For example, a rainbow pattern is displayed when the glass is taken off the station. The idea behind this is to remind the person of putting the glass back on its place when the drinking process is finished. During the entire process, the pattern will be constantly visible to the person.
- **Display:** The display is a further communication facility of the device (see Fig. 7). It can show information about the status of the gadget. Because of the small screen size, it is suitable rather to the care givers than to the elderly.
- **Serious Games:** The second type of interaction (initiated by the elderly person) occurs through our *Serious Games*. In such games, we pop up a banner which reminds the elderly person of drinking. The gadget then acts as control element and the banner on the screen will only disappear when the weight of the glass decreases, hence the person has drunk. This combination of *game flow* [28] and drink reminder proved to be an interesting incentive for most elderly people in our first study [35].

Conforming to our demand for *Expandability*, the display and LED stripes can be separately accessed via Bluetooth and offer developers the opportunity to send individual commands to the platform.

Fig. 8. FSR sensor with mounting solution for the beermat and holes to remove spilled water

11.3 Daily Usage

Besides our focus on the usage of the gadget by the elderly people, we are aware of the routines of the caregivers in a retirement home. Through our experiences, we identified an issue where the elderly people are sitting around the table (see Sect. 10) and over time are changing places. New drinking cups are handed out frequently. In that situation it is difficult to identify the exact drunken volume for each person. We want to solve this issue by not only creating an automated, digital documentation in the background, but also actively assigning one gadget to one elderly person and showing his or her name on the display. This information is more useful for the caregivers, who are normally repositioning the cups and stations for the elderly.

Another concept is to incorporate aspects of security by e.g. having holes at the top of the drinking platform which avoid a flooding of the internal space (see Fig. 8). The loading process of the battery is focused on ease of use with standardized parts to minimize downtime. Three AAA sized, rechargeable batteries are providing all the energy for at least one whole day of continuous usage. The whole gadget has only one physical switch which turns it on and off. When turned on and the mobile device app is open, the connection will be automatically established without the need of doing anything else.

12   Future Work

For the future we want to focus on various aspects to expand our vision of an interactable, smart drinking gadget:

- **Intelligent decision making:** When looking at the understanding of an *IAT* device, the platform already allows us to sense the environment (liquid intake) and to some extend to process the data (safe the data in a structured table). We want to extend this capability with a smart app, which can visualize the information (e.g. graphs), makes decisions and then informs the user, if there is a *care-oriented* benefit [17].
- **Hardware optimization:** Currently the FSR outputs realistic measurements, but it does take 10 s to do so and because of the nature of this sensor, environmental factors can influence the results, e.g. temperature. With the help of a mathematical model behind the sensor readings, more reliability in terms of outliers can be achieved. One particular possibility would be the Kalman-Filter, which can reduce some of uncertainty in the values.
- **Wide-range evaluation:** We already conducted a first study in a retirement home with dementia patients with interesting and promising results [35]. In this scenario we visited the elderly people for some hours per day and played a selection of *Serious Games* while monitoring their liquid intake. We want to conduct a wide-range evaluation with the help of our project *enable* partners from FAU. An important goal would be to satisfy the need of "a holistic and multi-level support" [17, p. 1336] for our device, which should be beneficial for the majority of elderly people.

- **Framework for developers:** For the integration in the developed *Serious Games*, we already created basic functionality to connect to the platform in Unity and access the LED stripes and the display. As we see the importance behind the vision of an expandable gadget, we want to extend the possibility to integrate the gadget in more applications. For that reason, we will develop additional support for more platforms and expand the functionality of the gadget in future iterations.
- **Combining the platform with further AT:** In another line of research of project *enable*, we investigate aspects of the life of elderly people to develop technologically-supported environments [24]. We want to utilize AT, such as wearables, AR and smart home concepts to achieve this. Wearables can collect health parameters (e.g. heart rate) and those can be combined with lifestyle information (e.g. drinking volume) to achieve a better understanding when health issues occur (*BMHI*). Thereby a useful combination of gadgets and software solutions, which combine all the data, can result in a powerful platform. This has the potential to improve the life quality of the elderly and their caregivers alike, the understanding of *care-oriented IAT* [17].

13   Conclusion

Existing smart drinking cups are not suitable for the elderly and on top of that, waste potential by only providing a closed-up system with no option to access the data outside the delivered app. With the help of AT projects in the literature, we identified interesting focus points for the development of such a gadget. We then experimented with various prototypes to gain our first experiences with a new view on drinking aids. The result was a clear vision of daily requirements (*hygiene, usage of the own cup, safety*) and the perceived need of interaction and expandability. We chose a weight measurement approach with an FSR to automatically document the liquid intake of the elderly person. For the design we created a 3D printed platform which mimics a beermat as natural way of placing the glass on the table. In the gadget design we incorporated two LED stripes to signal an elderly person to put the glass/cup back after drinking. A display provides the caregivers with the name of the current elderly person assigned to the cup, hence reducing the work of distributing new ones. We provide Bluetooth access for further interaction possibilities and benefit with motivation concepts in the form of *Serious Games*, which have been overseen in most other drinking gadget projects. When looking at our user study in a retirement home, we can identify the potential of hardware and software being combined to a powerful platform, which is integrated in the surrounding to support elderly and caregivers alike [35].

Acknowledgments. The preparation of this paper was supported by the enable cluster and is catalogued by the enable steering committee as enable 37 (http://enable-cluster.de). This work was funded by a grant of the German Ministry for Education and Research (BMBF) FK 01EA1409H.

The 3D shape has been designed in Onshape (https://www.onshape.com) with an Education license. Thank you to the support team for the permission to publish it. Thank you to the developer team of PDF3D (https://www.pdf3d.com) who made the interactive experience with the 3D model possible.

References

1. Volkert, D., Kreuel, K., Stehle, P.: Fluid intake of community-living, independent elderly in Germany-a nationwide, representative study. J. Nutr. Health Aging **9**(5), 305–309 (2005)
2. Megalingam, R.K., Radhakrishnan, V., Jacob, D.C., Unnikrishnan, D.K.M., Sudhakaran, A.K.: Assistive technology for elders: wireless intelligent healthcare gadget. In: 2011 IEEE Global Humanitarian Technology Conference (GHTC), pp. 296–300, October 2011
3. Projekt Enable (2018). http://www.enable-cluster.de/index.php?id=217&L=1. Accessed 21 Sept 2018
4. Gesundheitsberichterstattung des Bundes (2018). Diagnosedaten der Krankenhäuser ab 2000 (Eckdaten der vollstationären Patienten und Patientinnen). http://www.gbe-bund.de/. Accessed 02 Apr 2018
5. Lehman, S., Graves, J., Mcaleer, C., Giovannetti, T., Tan, C.C.: A mobile augmented reality game to encourage hydration in the elderly. In: Yamamoto, S., Mori, H. (eds.) HIMI 2018. LNCS, vol. 10905, pp. 98–107. Springer, Cham (2018). https://doi.org/10.1007/978-3-319-92046-7_9
6. Kreutzer, J.F., Pfitzer, M., D'Angelo, L.T.: Accuracy of caring personnel in estimating water intake based on missing liquid in drinking vessels. In: 2013 35th Annual International Conference of the IEEE Engineering in Medicine and Biology Society (EMBC), pp. 4682–4685. IEEE, July 2013
7. Schols, J.M.G.A., De Groot, C.P.G.M., Van Der Cammen, T.J.M., Rikkert, M.O.: Preventing and treating dehydration in the elderly during periods of illness and warm weather. JNHA-J. Nutr. Health Aging **13**(2), 150–157 (2009)
8. Hodgkinson, B., Evans, D., Wood, J.: Maintaining oral hydration in older adults: a systematic review. Int. J. Nurs. Pract. **9**(3), S19–S28 (2003)
9. Bunn, D., Jimoh, F., Wilsher, S.H., Hooper, L.: Increasing fluid intake and reducing dehydration risk in older people living in long-term care: a systematic review. J. Am. Med. Dir. Assoc. **16**(2), 101–113 (2015)
10. Zimmermann, C., Zeilfelder, J., Bloecher, T., Diehl, M., Essig, S., Stork, W.: Evaluation of a smart drink monitoring device. In: 2017 IEEE Sensors Applications Symposium (SAS), pp. 1–5. IEEE, March 2017
11. Crawley, H., Hocking, E.: Eating Well: Supporting Older People with Dementia. Practical Guide. The Caroline Walker Trust, London (2011)
12. Collins, C.: WATER Foundation of Life: Senior Wellness Series. Fact Sheet. Cooperative Extensions. University of Nevada (2016). https://www.unce.unr.edu/publications/files/hn/other/fs9930.pdf. Accessed 02 Apr 2018
13. Juan, W., Basiotis, P.P.: More than one in three older Americans may not drink enough water. Fam. Econ. Nutr. Rev. **16**(1), 49 (2004)
14. Kreutzer, J.F., Ramesberger, S., Reimer, S.M., Entsfellner, K., Lueth, T.C.: Automatically detecting fluid intake using conductivity measurements of beverages in a cup. In: Automation Science and Engineering (CASE), pp. 1546–1551. IEEE, August 2015

15. Hoenig, H., Taylor Jr., D.H., Sloan, F.A.: Does assistive technology substitute for personal assistance among the disabled elderly? Am. J. Public Health **93**(2), 330–337 (2003)
16. Saracchini, R., Catalina-Ortega, C., Bordoni, L.: A mobile augmented reality assistive technology for the elderly. Comunicar **23**(45), 65–74 (2015)
17. Ienca, M., et al.: Intelligent assistive technology for Alzheimer's disease and other dementias: a systematic review. J. Alzheimer's Dis. **56**(4), 1301–1340 (2017)
18. Buehler, E., et al.: Sharing is caring: assistive technology designs on thingiverse. In: Proceedings of the 33rd Annual ACM Conference on Human Factors in Computing Systems, pp. 525–534. ACM, April 2015
19. Mann, W.C., Ottenbacher, K.J., Fraas, L., Tomita, M., Granger, C.V.: Effectiveness of assistive technology and environmental interventions in maintaining independence and reducing home care costs for the frail elderly: a randomized controlled trial. Arch. Fam. Med. **8**(3), 210 (1999)
20. Millán, J.D.R., et al.: Combining brain-computer interfaces and assistive technologies: state-of-the-art and challenges. Front. Neurosci. **4**, 161 (2010)
21. Biswas, J., et al.: Health and wellness monitoring through wearable and ambient sensors: exemplars from home-based care of elderly with mild dementia. Ann. Telecommun.-annales des télécommunications **65**(9–10), 505–521 (2010)
22. Lutze, R., Baldauf, R., Waldhör, K.: Dehydration prevention and effective support for the elderly by the use of smartwatches. In: 2015 17th International Conference on E-health Networking, Application & Services (HealthCom), pp. 404–409. IEEE (2015)
23. Vidya, V., Poornachandran, P., Sujadevi, V.G., Dharmana, M.M.: IMU sensor based self stabilizing cup for elderly and parkinsonism. In: 2017 International Conference on Advances in Computing, Communications and Informatics (ICACCI), pp. 2264–2269. IEEE (2017)
24. Doukas, C., Metsis, V., Becker, E., Le, Z., Makedon, F., Maglogiannis, I.: Digital cities of the future: extending@ home assistive technologies for the elderly and the disabled. Telematics Inform. **28**(3), 176–190 (2011)
25. Development Platform MetaWear CPRO. montreal.wearhacks.com
26. Deterding, S., Khaled, R., Nacke, L.E., Dixon, D.: Gamification: toward a definition. In: CHI 2011 Gamification Workshop Proceedings, vol. 12, Vancouver BC, Canada, May 2011
27. Eichhorn, C., et al.: Innovative game concepts for Alzheimer patients. In: Zhou, J., Salvendy, G. (eds.) ITAP 2018. LNCS, vol. 10927. Springer, Cham (2018). https://doi.org/10.1007/978-3-319-92037-5_37
28. Csikszentmihalyi, M.: Flow and the Psychology of Discovery and Invention, p. 39. HarperPerennial, New York (1997)
29. Hein, C.M., Maroldt, P.A., Brecht, S.V., Oezgoecen, H., Lueth, T.C.: Towards an ergonomic exoskeleton structure: automated design of individual elbow joints. In: 2018 7th IEEE International Conference on Biomedical Robotics and Biomechatronics (Biorob), pp. 646–652. IEEE, August 2018
30. Kreutzer, J.F., Flaschberger, J., Hein, C.M., Lueth, T.C.: Capacitive detection of filling levels in a cup. In: 2016 IEEE 13th International Conference on Wearable and Implantable Body Sensor Networks (BSN), pp. 31–36. IEEE, June 2016
31. Zhou, B., et al.: Smart table surface: a novel approach to pervasive dining monitoring. In: 2015 IEEE International Conference on Pervasive Computing and Communications (PerCom), pp. 155–162. IEEE (2015)

32. Hambrice, K., Hopper, H.: A dozen ways to measure fluid level and how they work (2004). http://www.sensorsmag.com/sensors/leak-level/a-dozen-ways-measure-fluid-level-and-how-they-work-1067. Accessed 17 Jan 2019
33. Lanka, S., Hanumanthaiah, S.: How to implement liquid-level measurement using capacitive sensing technology (2016). http://core.cypress.com/article/how-to-implement-liquid-level-measurement-using-capacitive-sensing-technology-2/. Accessed 21 Aug 2016
34. Kreutzer, J.F.: Messmethoden für die Detektion der Flüssigkeitsaufnahme zur Prävention von Dehydratation. Doctoral dissertation, Technische Universität München (2017)
35. Eichhorn, C., et al.: The Innovative Reminder in Senior-focused Technology (THIRST) - Evaluation of Serious Games and Gadgets for Alzheimer Patients. In: Zhou, J., Salvendy, G. (eds.) HCII 2019. LNCS, Part II, vol. 11592, pp. 135–154 (2019)

Development and Comparison of Customized Voice-Assistant Systems for Independent Living Older Adults

Shradha Shalini[1(⊠)], Trevor Levins[1], Erin L. Robinson[2], Kari Lane[3], Geunhye Park[2], and Marjorie Skubic[1]

[1] Electrical Engineering and Computer Science, University of Missouri, Columbia, MO, USA
{ss9cw, trevorlevins}@mail.missouri.edu,
skubicm@missouri.edu

[2] School of Social Work, University of Missouri, Columbia, MO, USA
robinsonel@missouri.edu, gpmdm@mail.missouri.edu

[3] Sinclair School of Nursing, University of Missouri, Columbia, MO, USA
laneka@missouri.edu

Abstract. Voice-controlled in-home personal assistants have a great potential to assist older adults. This paper explores the aspects of a human-computer interface design, specifically a voice assistant, to help older adults manage their personal health, especially in the case of chronic health conditions. In our previous work, we have built a web interface for caregivers to monitor older adults' health changes based on in-home sensor data from motion sensors, bed sensors and depth sensors. Data collected from these sensors are stored in servers and processed using several algorithms to obtain health and activity parameters including gait, motion patterns, sleep, heart rate, and respiration rate, as well as to generate health alerts. The sensor system with automated health alerts and care coordination has been shown to help seniors maintain better functionality. In our current research project, we focus on developing a consumer interface for older adults and their family members that can provide health information on-demand, based on spoken queries. The health information is presented as both audio and visual displays and uses graphical visualizations and linguistic summaries of the sensor data trends and changes. The goal is to present data in a form that is simple to understand. To accomplish our objective of creating an easy-to-use-and-understand health data interface for older adults, we explore voice-controlled, in-home personal assistants as a solution. Two voice assistant platforms with displays have been selected for implementation and testing, namely, the Amazon Echo Show and the Lenovo Smart Display with Google Assistant.

Keywords: Voice-assistant · Older adults · Google Assistant · Google Home · Amazon Echo show · Alexa · Human-Computer Interaction · Speech recognition

© Springer Nature Switzerland AG 2019
J. Zhou and G. Salvendy (Eds.): HCII 2019, LNCS 11593, pp. 464–479, 2019.
https://doi.org/10.1007/978-3-030-22015-0_36

1 Introduction

With the emerging of various health tracking systems, such as smart watches and smart phone apps that provide continuous health information on-demand, there is a great potential for health tracking systems, specifically designed for older adults to monitor their own health. Voice-controlled in-home personal assistants can be leveraged to assist older adults in an easier, hands-free voice interaction that can provide their health information. Our proposed method is to provide continuous, on demand health information to independent living older adults using a voice-assistant system.

Several independent living older adults at Tigerplace (an independent living facility for older adults with tiered levels of skilled care available to allow older adults to age in place) have in-home sensors, such as depth sensors, bed sensors and motion sensors to track their daily activities and health [1, 2]. The sensor data are analyzed through various algorithms to generate health alerts for the clinicians [3]. Studies show that the automated health alert system enhances the registered nurse care coordination care delivery model at Tigerplace, increasing the length of stay of the older adults living with sensor systems nearly twice as compared to the older adults who do not live with a sensor system [4]. In this study, we are exploring how these health data and alerts can also be represented in a simpler and more accessible form to the older adults and their family members. The voice-assistant system has been designed such that the older adult's health information can be accessed by themselves as well as by designated family members. The health information is presented in the form of audio, text, and graphical visualizations. The text messages are developed using linguistic summaries based on trends in the sensor data [5]. This could possibly help the older adults to manage their own chronic health conditions and have a healthier aging trajectory.

In this study, we have used two different voice assistant devices with built-in displays: Amazon Echo Show and Lenovo Smart Display that provide health information through voice responses, text messages displayed on the screen, and data visualization graphs. Considering the health literacy appropriate for an aging population, shorter and simpler messages were created to prevent an overburden of information to the older adults. Therefore, to deliver useful health information in an easy to interpret format, the voice responses were made slower and the data visualization graphs were made simpler.

This paper provides an overview of the development of the two voice assistant systems and a preliminary comparison of their performance in recognizing voice commands. In Sect. 3, we discuss initial older adult input from a focus group study. In Sect. 4, we describe the comparative study of the two voice assistant prototypes for personal health, including a brief description of the voice-assistant platforms, a comparison of the speech recognition capabilities of the two devices, and test scenarios for using the voice-assistant app. In addition, we describe the app development process for the two devices and discuss the advantages and limitations of each platform. Section 5 includes conclusions and future work on voice-assistant systems for older adults.

2 Related Work

Studies have shown that designing user interfaces for older adults bring unique challenges. The information provided through these interfaces must be simple to understand by the older adults [6]. Previous studies have explored the human-computer interaction (HCI) challenges in developing different user interface options for older adults and their family members. In [7], Skubic et al. have presented challenges in two user interfaces for consumer health applications. The first is to provide sensor data information for detecting early signs of health detection, and the second is an interactive remote physical therapy (PT) system that can be used for remote PT sessions between a client and a therapist. The study provides insights for developing interactive user interface systems that can be used to engage older adults effectively to manage their health conditions.

There have been studies on voice-assistant interfaces for older adults [8–11]. König et al. and Riva et al. have explored custom designed voice assistants for older adults [8, 9]. Alexenko et al. have discussed the benefits of using voice-assistive technology to control an assistive robot and conducted a speech recognition accuracy test for younger versus older adults [10]. In [11], Schlögl et al. have shown that voice-assistant devices can be used effectively by older adults, though an adequate fall back modality is a necessity should errors arise. Several studies have also explored the usability of voice-assistive technologies in different fields of healthcare and health management [12–14]. In [12], Carroll et al. have designed a routine management system using the Amazon Alexa. They found that the system was simple yet effective for individuals with early and middle stage dementia. In [13], Pradhan et al. show the effectiveness of the voice-assistant Amazon Echo for users with a range of disabilities.

In the recent years, there has been a significant growth in natural language processing technologies that has enabled the development of several voice-assistant devices for consumers, such as, Google Home and Amazon Echo [15, 16]. There have been several studies in developing interactive user interfaces for older adults using the voice-assistant devices [17–20]. Ma et al. have developed a personalized healthcare application using Amazon Alexa [17]. The voice-assistant application provides health information collected through a wearable sensor. In this study, the authors have also performed a speech recognition accuracy test. In [18], Ennis et al. have designed a smart cabinet system that includes an Amazon Echo device and a bathroom cabinet. The system can track objects in the cabinet and provide relevant information upon asking with a voice command. Their findings show that the system received a positive usability score. However, they have highlighted a few limitations of using an off the shelf voice-assistant, e.g., Amazon Echo cannot proactively speak. In [19], Cheng et al. have explored the potential and limitations of using a Google Home application for diabetes self-management for older adults when compared to a mobile application. Results show that the participants were inclined towards using the Google Home application over the mobile application.

In [20], Choi et al. have conducted a study with nineteen older adult participants (age: 65+) over a two month time period to explore the feasibility of using voice-assistant devices to support aging in place. The authors have conducted semi-structured interviews to gather their overall attitude towards using the voice-assistant devices. Results show that the participants had a positive experience using the voice-assistant devices and expressed their interest in using this technology as a health management device to keep track of their health data, such as, blood pressure or blood sugar.

3   Initial Feedback from Focus Groups

As an initial study, twenty-three older adult participants (Mean age = 80; 85% female) and five family members (Mean age = 64; 100% female) were recruited to get their feedback on different possible platforms that could be used to show their health information and health messages, or those of their family member [21]. The participants were informed about the health and wellness system that the University of Missouri Center for Eldercare and Rehabilitation Technology (CERT) has developed to track the health of older adults. The system primarily includes three different sensor systems, including a depth sensor system to track gait and fall risk and detect falls, a noninvasive bed sensor system to track heart rate, respiration rate, sleep patterns, and restlessness in bed, and a motion sensor system to track daily activity patterns. Sensor information is accessible via a web portal for the clinical staff in senior housing sites [7]. The participants of this focus group study were then asked about the idea of using a personal health system, specifically designed for older adults and their family members to visualize the same sensor data in a format designed for them.

In this focus group study, different interface platforms were explored. These platforms included smart phones, computers, televisions, tablets, voice-assistant devices, and smart watches. Focus group participants were shown prototypes of smart phones, voice-assistant systems, and tablets that were connected to our research database containing data from an in-home sensor system for older adults living independently at Tigerplace [1]. The participants were informed about different health data presentation options for each platform, which include voice messages, text messages displayed on a screen, and text plus voice messages with data visualization graphs. Their comments were noted for each platform.

In the case of data visualization graphs, the participants preferred a simpler data graph that represents their health changes. However, they did not want to forgo important information about their health for simplicity sake. Most participants preferred a line graph as compared to bar graphs and risk meter visualizations showing their health risk level in the form of a thermometer gauge.

The focus group participants preferred to interact with the sensor-generated health information using smart phones. Smart phone and computer use were highly preferred, but a combination of technology interfaces was desirable. Both older adult and family member participants preferred options in interacting with health information and receiving health messages, e.g., emergency health alerts sent via text message and other health information accessible via computer. Most participants did not prefer a television as a medium to get their health information. From their options of voice assisted technology, they preferred a voice assistant with a visual display. However, since investigating the feasibility of using a voice-assisted device with this population group was not the main aim of the focus group study, our results are limited. In addition, since the voice assisted platforms are relatively new and many participants had no prior experience with them, a more in-depth study was planned to investigate this further.

This initial focus group study helped us to understand the preferences of older adults and family members in receiving their health messages and other health information based on the sensor data. The voice assistant systems described in this paper were designed based on the input received from the focus group participants. The voice assistant platforms show the data in the form of simple line graphs with adequate information and simple text messages that summarize the data trends.

4   Voice Assistant Prototypes for Personal Health

Google Assistant and Amazon Echo voice assistant platforms were used to conduct this study. For evaluation of the voice assistant systems, four different test scenarios were designed. The details of the test scenarios are provided in Sect. 4.3. A common prototype voice-command app was developed for both platforms based on these test scenarios. The study aims at recruiting older adults and family members in dyads for interviews to get their overall feedback towards these voice-assistant systems. In a typical interview session, participants interact with the voice-assistant systems using the test scenario scripts listed in Tables 3, 4, 5 and 6, and provide feedback based on their experience. To make the voice-assistant interaction process easier for the participants, we placed a note with the app activation command on top of each device. The activation command can be followed by a set of health questions listed in the scenario tables. Figures 1 and 2 show the voice assistant devices in use during the interview sessions. Speech recognition accuracies are compared for both systems.

4.1   Platforms

In this study, two-leading consumer-based voice-assistant platforms with displays were used: the Amazon Echo Show with a 10-inch display and the Lenovo Smart Display with Google Assistant, which also has a 10-inch display. These platforms were selected because they have comparable displays and offer a multi-modal interaction between the voice assistant system and the older adult user. Table 1 shows the physical dimensions and specifications of the Amazon Echo Show and Lenovo Smart Display.

Table 1. Device specifications for Amazon Echo Show and Lenovo Smart Display.

Device	Specification
Amazon Echo Show (2nd Generation) Display Resolution: 1280 × 800	10.1″
Lenovo Smart Display Display Resolution: 1920 × 1200	10.0″

Both the devices function by staying in an always-listening mode once plugged in. The devices activate by listening to specific wake words. A user can ask a specific question to the voice-assistants by first speaking the wake word. The words spoken after the wake word are processed and a voice response is delivered to the user. The built-in displays are used in both devices to display the text of the device's response as well as data visualization graphs as necessary.

Lenovo Smart Display with Google Assistant. By default, the wake word for Google Assistant powered devices is "Ok Google" or "Hey Google". The google assistant transcribes the question asked by the user and displays it on the screen. Figure 1 shows a Lenovo Smart Display Device running the health app.

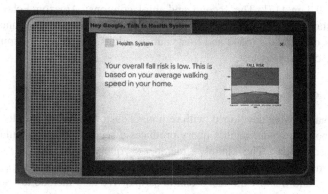

Fig. 1. Lenovo Smart Display with built-in Google Assistant showing fall-risk information within the Health System App.

Amazon Echo Show with Alexa. By default, the wake word for Alexa powered devices is "Alexa"; however, this can be changed to "Echo", "Amazon", or "Computer". The Amazon Echo device does not transcribe the question text as is done with the Google Assistant device. Figure 2 shows a picture of the Amazon Echo Show display running the health app.

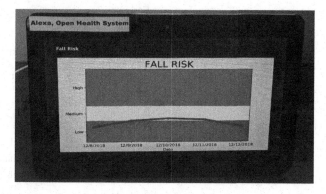

Fig. 2. Amazon Echo Show with built-in Alexa showing fall-risk information within the Health System App.

4.2 Speech Recognition

We tested the speech recognition accuracy of both voice-assistants by using the "repeat after me" feature of Google Assistant and the "copycat" skill of Amazon Echo Show, to determine which platform could recognize the voice better. Twelve different sentences were used in this test, with each sentence having a different combination of words. We found that some of the words in the sentences were incorrectly recognized by Alexa while Google Assistant recognized and repeated all the words correctly. Table 2 shows a comparison of voice recognition performance between the Amazon Echo Show and the Google Assistant. In the first column: Amazon Echo (2016), we have included results provided in [17]. The second and third columns: Amazon Echo Show and Google assistant, show the misinterpreted words by the two voice-assistants using test data from six older adults (65+) and four younger adults. These are preliminary results based on the comparison test.

4.3 Test Scenarios

Two test scenarios were developed, with responses customized for the older adult and a family member. The older adult's query produces a second person singular response, e.g., you or your. The family member's query produces a third-person masculine/feminine singular response referring to the older adult, e.g., he or she. Tables 3, 4, 5, and 6 show the test scenario scripts. We also include test scenarios for husbands and wives to query health data of each other.

Table 2. Speech recognition test results with word-list and misinterpretations.

Words/Phrases	Misinterpreted as		
	Amazon Echo (2016) Based on [17]	Amazon Echo Show (2018)	Google Assistant (2018)
Health	Hill; How; House; Hail	Heart	*
Pulse	Pause	Pearls; #; Pets	*
Was	Or; Have; Is	*	*
An hour	In our	End our	*
Vacation	Location	Location; $	*
Rearview	*	Review; View	*
Early	*	Hurly	*
Shut eye	*	Shark; Shut up; $	Shut up
On	*	#	*
On account of	*	$	*
Your	*	$	*
Am I	*	*	I am I
Will enhance	*	Without $	One hand catch
Hang	*	Hang in	Hey there
The	*	#	*
On numerous	*	No worse	*
To	*	#	*

(*continued*)

Table 2. (*continued*)

Words/Phrases	Misinterpreted as		
	Amazon Echo (2016) Based on [17]	Amazon Echo Show (2018)	Google Assistant (2018)
She	*	Are	*
Strenuous	*	Strangers	*
Do strenuous	*	Two words	*
Body	*	Bot	*
An hour of	*	In our daily	*

* Interpreted correctly
\# Did not repeat the word
\$ Illegible word

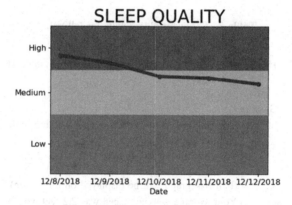

Fig. 3. Sample data visualization for sleep quality.

Table 3. Script for older adults for sleep quality.

Older adult	Voice assistant
Hey Google, talk to Health System Or Alexa, open Health System	Hi, Welcome to your personal Health System. How can I assist you today?
Tell me about my sleep quality	Your sleep quality has been decreasing over the past few days. Would you like to know more?
Tell me more	This is what your sleep quality graph looks like. This graph uses several pieces of data to determine your overall quality of sleep. Overall, your sleep quality has been decreasing over the past few days (Sleep quality graph will be displayed on the screen) (see Fig. 3)
How is my sleep quality calculated?	Your sleep quality is calculated by comparing your non-restlessness time in bed to your total time in bed
How long was I restless?	You were restless for 1 h 34 min and spent 7 h and 20 min in bed

Table 4. Script for family members for sleep quality.

Family member	Voice assistant
Hey Google, talk to Health System Or Alexa, open Health System	Hi, Welcome to your personal Health System. How can I assist you today?
Tell me about my mom's sleep quality	Your mom's sleep quality has been decreasing over the past few days. Would you like to know more?
Tell me more	This is what her sleep quality graph looks like. This graph uses several pieces of data to determine her overall quality of sleep. Overall, her sleep quality has been decreasing over the past few days (Sleep quality graph will be displayed on the screen) (see Fig. 3)
How is her sleep quality calculated?	Your mom's sleep quality is calculated by comparing her non-restlessness time in bed to her total time in bed
How long was she restless?	She was restless for 1 h 34 min and spent 7 h and 20 min in bed

Table 5. Script for older adults for fall risk.

Older adult	Voice assistant
Hey Google, talk to Health System Or Alexa, open Health System	Hi, Welcome to your personal Health System. How can I assist you today?
Do I have any risk of falling?	Your fall risk is low. Your overall walking looks good. Would you like to know more?
Tell me more	Your overall fall risk is low. This is based on your average walking speed in your home (Fall risk graph will be displayed on the screen) (see Fig. 4)
What is my walking speed?	Your average walking speed was 2.2 feet per second
How is the walking speed measured?	Your walking speed is measured using a sensor that is mounted on the wall in your home

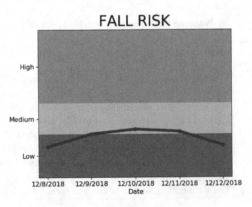

Fig. 4. Sample data visualization for fall risk.

Table 6. Script for family members for fall risk.

Family member	Voice assistant
Hey Google, talk to Health System Or Alexa, open Health System	Hi, Welcome to your personal Health System. How can I assist you today?
Does my mom have a fall risk?	Your mom's fall risk is low. Her overall walking looks good. Would you like to know more?
Tell me more	Your mom's overall fall risk is low. This is based on her average walking speed in her home (Fall risk graph will be displayed on the screen) (see Fig. 4)
What is my mom's walking speed?	Her average walking speed was 2.2 feet per second
How is the walking speed measured?	Her walking speed is measured using a sensor that is mounted on the wall in her home

4.4   Ease of Development

In this section, we describe the ease of programming and development on the Alexa platform and on the Google Assistant platforms. We also describe development methods on these platforms with the goal of accommodating older adults. While voice assisted technology may be accessible and easy to use for younger adults, there are several changes that must be made to give older adults a more accessible experience with the technology. Development of user interfaces for data visualization to present health data to older adults was done based on focus group results and recommended guidelines [6]. Guidelines for designing technology for older adults indicate that some fonts are more easily readable than others [6]. Sans-Serif font has been noted as preferred by older adults and perceived as more legible when compared to a Serif font. The default font family used for our data visualizations is Sans-Serif to ensure legibility. In addition, the same guidelines specify that brighter and clearer colors tend to stick out and bring attention to themselves, which in turn result in less effort to focus on a specific image. By enhancing the contrast on the screen, a viewer may begin to use pre-attentive processes of searching for information. In pre-attentive searching, a bright and high contrast combination of colors bring attention to themselves and alleviate the user of using more effort to view the screen. As this type of searching helps older and younger adults, the data visualizations have been created with bright colors that offer a contrast to take advantage of pre-attentive searching. As a result, the line in the line graph is clearer to see, and the separations between each boundary on the graph are well known to a viewer. The contrasting colors utilized are commonly associated with other day to day phenomenon, such as a bold red for a stop sign being used to indicate a higher fall risk. In the earlier focus group study, the participants have preferred a simpler graph when shown several types of data visualizations. Therefore, the graphs used in the health app are simple. Also, the graphs have contrasting colors and the text messages are bigger [6].

The two health apps were configured on both the devices with a set of training phrases (Google)/Sample utterances (Amazon) listed in Tables 7 and 8. The apps were also trained with follow-up questions. Synonym and similar pronouncing words were included for better performance of the app, e.g., mom and mum for mother, and dad for father. More training data will be added to the apps based on the information collected in the dyad interviews.

Finally, a third method of accommodation for older adults was done by slowing down the speed of the audio response on the voice-assistant devices. Both devices supported SSML tags to modify various aspects of an audio response. In this study, we elected to slow the rate of speech with SSML tags. The user interface development guidelines for older adults indicate that as aging occurs, it becomes difficult to process faster rates of speech, and that slower rates of speech are generally favored by older adults. In addition to the previous studies, our results from the initial focus group study show that older adults preferred a slow speech response.

Table 7. Training phrases (Google)/sample utterances (Amazon) for sleep quality.

Older adult's query	Family member's query
Tell me about my sleep quality	Tell me about my mom's sleep quality
Tell me about my sleep	How did mom sleep?
How did I sleep?	Did my mom sleep well?
How was the quality of my sleep?	How's the sleep quality of my mom?
Did I sleep well?	Tell me about my mother's sleep quality
How did I sleep last night?	How did my mother sleep?
	Did my mother sleep well?
	How's the sleep quality of my mother?
	Tell me about my mum's sleep quality
	How did my mum sleep?
	Did my mum sleep well?
	How's the sleep quality of my mum?
Tell me more	Tell me more
Yes	Yes
Sure	Sure
How is my sleep quality calculated?	How is my mom's sleep quality calculated?
How is my sleep quality estimated?	How is my mom's sleep quality estimated?
How is my sleep quality measured?	How is my mom's sleep quality measured?
How is my sleep quality captured?	How is my mom's sleep quality captured?
How is the sleep quality calculated?	How is her sleep quality calculated?
How is the sleep quality estimated?	How is her sleep quality estimated?
How is the sleep quality measured?	How is her sleep quality measured?
How is the sleep quality captured?	How is her sleep quality captured?
	How is the sleep quality calculated?
	How is the sleep quality estimated?

(*continued*)

Table 7. (*continued*)

Older adult's query	Family member's query
	How is the sleep quality measured?
	How is the sleep quality captured?
How long was I restless?	How long was my mom restless?
How long did I sleep?	How long did my mom sleep?
For how long I was restless?	How long was my mom in bed?
	How long was my mother restless?
	How long did my mother sleep?
	How long was my mother in bed?
	How long was my mum restless?
	How long did my mum sleep?
	How long was my mum in bed?
	How long was she restless?
	How long did she sleep?
	For how long she was in bed?

Table 8. Training phrases (Google)/sample utterances (Amazon) for fall risk.

Older adult's query	Family member's query
Tell me about my fall risk	Tell me about my mom's fall risk
Tell me about my walking data	Tell me about mom's walking data
Do I have any risk of falling?	Does my mom have a fall risk?
What does my fall risk look like?	How does my mom's fall risk look like?
How does my fall risk look like?	Tell me about my mother's fall risk
Tell me about my walking	Tell me about mother's walking data
How's my walking?	Does my mother have a fall risk?
	How does my mother's fall risk look like?
	Tell me about my mum's fall risk
	Tell me about mum's walking data
	Does my mum have a fall risk?
	How does my mum's fall risk look like?
Tell me more	Tell me more
Yes	Yes
Sure	Sure
What is my walking speed?	What is my mom's walking speed?
What is my average walking speed?	What is my mom's average walking speed?
	What is the walking speed of my mom?
	What is the average walking speed of my mom?
	What is my mother's walking speed?
	What is my mother's average walking speed?

(*continued*)

Table 8. (*continued*)

Older adult's query	Family member's query
	What is the walking speed of my mother?
	What is the average walking speed of my mother?
	What is my mum's walking speed?
	What is my mum's average walking speed?
	What is the walking speed of my mum?
	What is the average walking speed of my mum?
	What is her walking speed?
How is the walking speed calculated?	How is my mom's walking speed calculated?
How is the walking speed estimated?	How is my mom's walking speed estimated?
How is the walking speed measured?	How is my mom's walking speed measured?
How is the walking speed captured?	How is my mom's walking speed captured?
	How is my mother's walking speed calculated?
	How is my mother's walking speed estimated?
	How is my mother's walking speed measured?
	How is my mother's walking speed captured?
	How is my mum's walking speed calculated?
	How is my mum's walking speed estimated?
	How is my mum's walking speed measured?
	How is my mum's walking speed captured?
	How is the walking speed calculated?
	How is the walking speed estimated?
	How is the walking speed measured?
	How is the walking speed captured?

Google Assistant. The google assistant app was developed using Google's Dialogflow API V2 platform. This technology is developed by Google and supports natural language conversations through devices with Google Assistant enabled. The platform can be used to develop voice-assistant applications that can provide two-way continuous conversation between the Google Home device and the user, until the user's intent is fulfilled, or the conversation is finished. The Dialogflow platform uses "Intents" as the unique identifiers that correspond to specific user utterances. Each intent has a set of training phrases. The training phrases consist of the many possible variations of a query that have the same intent. Each intent has a dedicated response to it. There are several types of responses to choose from [22]. In addition, each intent can have a set of follow-up intents. The device sends the user's utterance to the Google Assistant, which routes it to the fulfillment service via HTTP POST requests. The fulfilment for this application is developed using Node.js 8 programming. Several platforms were explored for deploying the fulfilment, including a University of Missouri server, the Inline Editor provided by the Dialogflow platform and the Heroku web platform. The prototype code was written in the Dialogflow Inline Editor, which is powered by the cloud functions for Firebase.

Alexa. An Amazon Echo application, or "skill" is comprised of "intents" that each perform specific actions within the skill. An intent represents an action that can be performed by the skill and may contain optional "slot" values to accomplish more specific tasks requested of it by the user of the device. To utilize an intent, the user speaks to the device, and the device matches the spoken words to an intent via an "utterance". Utterances are phrases that contain words that Amazon looks for when deciding which intent to select after determining the words spoken by the user and may contain spots for slot values to be inserted. When the user of an Echo device speaks to the device, Amazon determines which intent to select by comparing the words it understands to the utterances of each intent. When an intent is successfully determined, the code written to handle that intent is run.

Development for Amazon Alexa was done in Node.js version 8.10. Amazon's APL was used alongside Node.js 8.10 to deliver full-screen data visualizations. Additionally, Amazon's AWS Lambda service was used to host the code required for the Alexa skill. Code uploaded to Lambda was done so in the form of a zip file containing the Node.js code to handle each intent and the imported modules that the code requires. At the current time of prototype implementation, Amazon's Alexa Presentation Language (APL), a JSON object used to format images, is in a public beta release and is utilized by our Show devices to present full screen data visualizations.

4.5   Discussion

While the idea behind both the Echo Show and the Lenovo Smart Display is the same, each has several advantages and disadvantages when compared to the other. For example, we have shown that Google Assistant scores better in speech recognition tests than Alexa does. However, in designing displays with images, currently, Google Assistant cannot display full screen images like Alexa can [22]. If developing an application that requires an image to be easily seen or displayed across the screen, working with Amazon's Alexa may prove easier. In addition, Google Assistant at this point in time lacks the ability to change its wake word to any other option than "Hey Google", while Alexa can be changed from "Alexa" to "Computer", "Amazon", or "Echo".

So far, we have interviewed 4 dyads of people aged 65+ and one of their family members. In these preliminary interviews, some of the older adult participants have preferred the Google Assistant, as they thought the voice of the Google Assistant is more natural. However, some of the other older adults preferred Amazon Echo, as they thought the wake word – "Alexa" is easier to use than "Hey Google" for the Google Assistant. Also, they preferred the larger graphs in the Amazon Echo Show as compared to the Google Assistant. Thus far in this dyad interview study, all 8 dyad participants liked the technology and they mentioned that they would like to use it.

Although preliminary, the study illustrates the potential of voice assistant platforms as a user interface for older adults, as well as the tradeoffs between the two platforms investigated. The preliminary results show that our target users are enthusiastic about the voice assistant technologies as a healthcare information interface.

5 Conclusion and Future Work

In this study, we have developed a voice-assistant app for the Google Assistant and Amazon Echo platforms, based on feedback provided in an earlier focus group study and previous literature. The applications can provide on-demand health information, such as sleep quality and fall risk to independent living older adults and their family members. Four different test scenarios were designed to get the feedback of older adults and their family members on the usability of the voice-assistant devices for managing and tracking health.

The speech recognition capabilities of the two voice assistant devices were also compared. Preliminary results show that Google Assistant performs better than Amazon Echo in accurately recognizing speech.

Currently, we are actively recruiting dyad participants of people aged 65+ and one of their family members for testing and getting feedback on the two devices and the health app.

References

1. Senior Living in Columbia, MO—TigerPlace - Americare Senior Living. https://www.americareusa.net/senior-living/mo/columbia/tiger-place/. Accessed 31 Jan 2019
2. Phillips, L.J., et al.: Using embedded sensors in independent living to predict gait changes and falls. West J. Nurs. Res. **39**(1), 78–94 (2017)
3. Skubic, M., Guevara, R.D., Rantz, M.: Automated health alerts using in-home sensor data for embedded health assessment. IEEE J. Transl. Eng. Health Med. **3**, 1–11 (2015)
4. Rantz, M., et al.: Enhanced registered nurse care coordination with sensor technology: impact on length of stay and cost in aging in place housing. Nurs. Outlook **63**(6), 650–655 (2015)
5. Jain, A., Keller, J.M.: Textual summarization of events leading to health alerts. In: 2015 37th Annual International Conference of the IEEE Engineering in Medicine and Biology Society (EMBC), pp. 7634–7637 (2015)
6. Pak, R., McLaughlin, A.: Designing Displays for Older Adults, 1st edn. CRC Press, Boca Raton (2010)
7. Skubic, M., et al.: HCI challenges for consumer-based aging in place technologies. In: Zhou, J., Salvendy, G. (eds.) ITAP 2016. LNCS, vol. 9754, pp. 105–116. Springer, Cham (2016). https://doi.org/10.1007/978-3-319-39943-0_11
8. König, A., Malhotra, A., Hoey, J., Francis, L.E.: Designing personalized prompts for a virtual assistant to support elderly care home residents. In: Proceedings of the 10th EAI International Conference on Pervasive Computing Technologies for Healthcare, pp. 278–282. ICST (Institute for Computer Sciences, Social-Informatics and Telecommunications Engineering), Cancun (2016)
9. Riva, G.: ALFRED: a personalized, fully interactive, and mobile assistant for independent living. Cyberpsychol. Behav. Soc. Netw. **21**(3), 212–213 (2018)
10. Alexenko, T., Biondo, M., Banisakher, D., Skubic, M.: Android-based speech processing for eldercare robotics. In: Proceedings of the companion publication of the 2013 international conference on Intelligent User Interfaces Companion, Santa Monica, pp. 87–88 (2013)

11. Schlögl, S., Chollet, G., Garschall, M., Tscheligi, M., Legouverneur, G.: Exploring voice user interfaces for seniors. In: Proceedings of the 6th International Conference on Pervasive Technologies Related to Assistive Environments, pp. 1–2. ACM, Rhodes (2013)

12. Carroll, C., Chiodo, C., Lin, A.X., Nidever, M., Prathipati, J.: Robin: enabling independence for individuals with cognitive disabilities using voice assistive technology. In: Proceedings of the 2017 CHI Conference Extended Abstracts on Human Factors in Computing Systems, pp. 46–53. ACM, Denver (2017)

13. Pradhan, A., Mehta, K., Findlater, L.: "Accessibility Came by Accident": use of voice-controlled intelligent personal assistants by people with disabilities. In: Proceedings of the 2018 CHI Conference on Human Factors in Computing Systems, pp. 1–13. ACM, Montreal (2018)

14. Hassoon, A., et al.: Increasing physical activity amongst overweight and obese cancer survivors using an Alexa-based intelligent agent for patient coaching: protocol for the physical activity by technology help (PATH) trial. JMIR Res. Protoc. 7(2), e27 (2018)

15. Google Home - Smart Speaker & Home Assistant. https://store.google.com/us/product/google_home?hl=en-US. Accessed 29 Jan 2019

16. Echo & Alexa - Amazon Devices - Amazon Official Site. https://www.amazon.com/Amazon-Echo-And-Alexa-Devices/b?node=9818047011. Accessed 29 Jan 2019

17. Ma, M., Skubic, M., Ai, K., Hubbard, J.: Angel-Echo: a personalized health care application. In: Proceedings of the Second IEEE/ACM International Conference on Connected Health: Applications, Systems and Engineering Technologies, pp. 258–259. IEEE Press, Philadelphia (2017)

18. Ennis, A., et al.: A smart cabinet and voice assistant to support independence in older adults. In: Ochoa, S.F., Singh, P., Bravo, J. (eds.) Ubiquitous Computing and Ambient Intelligence, UCAmI 2017. LNCS, pp. 466–472. Springer, Cham (2017). https://doi.org/10.1007/978-3-319-67585-5_47

19. Cheng, A., Raghavaraju, V., Kanugo, J., Handrianto, Y.P., Shang, Y.: Development and evaluation of a healthy coping voice interface application using the Google home for elderly patients with type 2 diabetes. In: 2018 15th IEEE Annual Consumer Communications & Networking Conference (CCNC), Las Vegas, NV, USA, pp. 1–5 (2018)

20. Thompson, H., Choi, Y., Demiris, G.: Feasibility of smart speaker use to support aging in place. Innov. Aging 2(Suppl_1), 560 (2018)

21. Robinson, E.L., et al.: Creating a tailored, in-home, sensor system to facilitate healthy aging: the consumer perspective. Innov. Aging 2, 912 (2018)

22. Responses—Actions on Google—Google Developers. https://developers.google.com/actions/assistant/responses. Accessed 31 Jan 2019

Interaction Design in the Active and Assistive Living Field of Practice

Miroslav Sili[(✉)], Johannes Kropf, and Sten Hanke

AIT Austrian Institute of Technology GmbH, Center for Health & Bioresources,
Vienna, Austria
miroslav.sili@ait.ac.at

Abstract. The design process of interactive systems is a multifaceted process
that can lead to various forms of manifestations. Designers can draw on different
interaction design styles to realize the intended, to-be designed interactive
system and the corresponding HCI artifacts. This work identifies and investigates different interaction design styles based on concrete prototypes that have
been designed, developed and evaluated in co-funded research project in the
Active and Assisted Living domain. In total, the work presents 12 concrete
prototypes which have been implemented between 2011 and 2018 and list 8
designable interaction design styles. The work lists identifies main characteristics and elaborates their relationships and dependencies which serve as basis for
the future extensive research work that questions the impact of different interaction design styles on the targeted end users supposed to use the intended, to-be
designed interactive system.

Keywords: Interaction design · IxD · User centered design process · UCD ·
Active assisted living · AAL · Maslow's pyramid of needs

1 Introduction

Human Computer Interaction (HCI) is a multidisciplinary field including, among some
others, computer science, cognitive and behavioral psychology, anthropology, sociology, ergonomics, industrial design [1]. Moreover, HCI addresses a broad range of
topics and has various forms of manifestations. This also applies to people that use HCI
artifacts. They have different needs, different expectations, different preferences and
different habits. Unfortunately, these individual characteristics are usually considered
only superficially during the design process of interactive systems. This very often
results in dissatisfaction and frustration in latterly use of these systems. Even if the
provided functionality is perceived as valuable, user might reduce the usage time or
stop using the offered systems because they leak to support individual aspects. Thus,
interactive systems that target the long-standing engagement with the user are requested
to address these individual aspects in order to reach the aimed goal.

The User Centered Design (UCD) process [2] contributes towards this goal and
involves the user at the very early stage of the design process. Moreover, some UCD
methods, for instance, the participatory design method, involve the user on such a deep
level, that users become co-designers during the design phase. This in fact, can increase

J. Zhou and G. Salvendy (Eds.): HCII 2019, LNCS 11593, pp. 480–492, 2019.
https://doi.org/10.1007/978-3-030-22015-0_37

users' satisfaction about the final product, but consequently this approach, at the same time, also increases the required efforts during the development process in terms of time, costs and management.

Situated in the Active and Assisted Living (AAL) field of practice, we have been utilized the UCD process in several research projects during the development of various interactive systems. Consequently, we expected an increase of users' satisfaction and a long-standing user engagement with the offered prototype. Long-term user evaluation results, gained from these research projects, highlighted that even an increased user involvement and the linked increase of design and development efforts had some drawbacks. It was noticeable that many projects had a significant number of unsatisfied users which reduced the usage time of the developed prototype. Moreover, some users stopped using the offered solution before the end of the project period.

This represents a contradiction to the concept of the UCD approach since users have been involved from the early stage of the project. They have been involved in the user requirements analysis, in the mock-up testing, in the testing of the first functional prototype and very often also into the testing of the second functional prototype before the release of the final prototype. Since users were involved from the early stage of the project and even in the identification process of their needs, it is precluded that the functionality of the offered solution failed. Functional aspects have been explicitly requested by the users. Also, since users were involved in several design, evaluation and improvement cycles, it is precluded that the usability of the offered solution failed. The improvement of the usability was one of the key elements of every iteration step. These two aspects highlight that the applied approach could address basic user needs (in terms of problem identification and problem-solving utilizing functionality and usability) but also that the applied approach did not reach all targeting users on the individual level, considering their inner and very often unconscious values, wishes and needs.

This work contributes to the alleviation of the problem stated and represents the starting point of an extensive work that investigates whether and how far the utilized interaction design style influences the users' acceptance rate of the offered interactive system. In this work the focus is on the identification of different interaction design styles (hereinafter called as Interaction Design Opportunities - IxDOs) and on the elaboration of their characteristics, relationships, and dependencies. Future work will build upon this work and will focus on possibilities to reflection the user on the individual level. These two research areas build conclusively the basis for mentioned overall research goal, namely the investigation of the impact of different IxDOs on user's system acceptance rate. Figure 1 illustrates the workflow of the overall research and highlights in red the contribution of this work.

Fig. 1. The workflow of the overall research and the contribution of this work highlighted in red. (Color figure online)

The work is structured as follows: Sect. 2 summarizes the identified IxDOs, their key characteristics, and the corresponding prototypes in the AAL field of practice. Section 3 presents the so-called Interaction Design Opportunity Research Grid that supports the investigation of the identified IxDOs in a structured manner. Section 4 discusses the arrangement of the identified IxDOs based on their main purposes and user needs and based on dependencies that IxDos build upon each other. These results serve as the basis for the further work which is outlined in Sect. 5.

2   Interaction Design Opportunities

As pointed out before, the synthesis of different IxDOs emerged out of the AAL context and the fact that the UCD process in various research projects led to the development of different prototypes, each assignable to a specific IxDO class. This work is based on 12 concrete prototypes which have been implemented between 2011 and 2018. In total, we were able to identify eight different IxDO classes. The following section summarizes the key characteristics of these eight IxDOs in respect to the underlying AAL application field and the corresponding projects and prototypes, respectively.

2.1   Application IxDO

Application IxDO (App-IxDO) focuses on interaction designs that target the use of one primary interaction device and represents the classical and minimal setting that covers basic user needs regarding functionality and usability. A smartphone, a tablet device, or a wearable represent such a primary interaction device. However, the primary device aspect does not limit the number of usable devices within the system, but the interaction design opportunity rather characterizes the concept where the full functionality set of the intended application, and thus all possible interaction steps, are provided via- and accessible by one single device. In our AAL field of practice, App-IxDO was utilized in the large-scale pilot project moduLAAr [3]. The main objective of the project was to equip at least 50 flats with an AAL solution that can be adapted to the individual needs of the residents in assisted living homes. Further, App-IxDO was utilized in the project DOREMI [4, 5]. The aim of the project was to devise ICT-based home care services for aging people to contrast cognitive decline, sedentariness and unhealthy dietary habits. Both prototypes have been realized as Android applications and rendered on tablet devices.

2.2   Multi-Application IxDO

Multi-Application IxDO (MApp-IxDO) enhances the App-IxDO and offers users the opportunity to experience seamless interactions between multiple devices. The primary goal is to exploit synergies between complementary modalities used on multiple devices and to offer optimized interactions for the end user and the concrete use case. The seamless interaction aspect allows users to interrupt an existing interaction on one device and seamlessly continue the same interaction on another device. This approach contributes towards an enhanced comfort. Similarly, complement modalities targets the increase of accessibility as well as the increase of error tolerance because users can change the interaction modality if the chosen one is inaccurate or does not fit their requirements. In our AAL field of practice, MApp-IxDO was utilized in the national co-founded project ibi [6, 8]. The main objective of the project was to develop a communication system that connects older adults in need of care, their relatives, and the formal caregivers. The prototype provided a seamless multi-device interaction experience between the used tablet device and users' TV device. Similar approach was also realized in the project YouDo [7]. The project objective was the development of a modular, extensible, and user adaptable multimodal information and training platform for informal caregivers. Again, YouDo provided a seamless multi-device interaction between users' PC, a tablet device, and user's TV device.

2.3 User Group Tailored IxDO

User Group Tailored IxDO (UGT-IxDO) focuses on optimization of traditional HCI techniques. The primary goal is to fulfill the users' wishes and meet their needs by increasing accessibility and usability. The former is related to aspects that provide equivalent user experience for people with disabilities, including people with age-related impairments, and the latter is related to the design process towards effective, efficient, and satisfying products. UGT-IxDO utilizes App-IxDO or MApp-IxDO and modifies either existing interaction techniques or generates new interaction techniques according to the users' needs. In our AAL field of practice, UGT-IxDO was utilized in the project ION4II [9]. The aim of the project was to develop an assistive system for visually impaired or blind older adults living in a care and residential facility. The prototype utilized the App-IxDO (a classical smartphone application) and modified the preexisting interaction technique (the graphical and touch-based UI) towards special user needs. The tailoring process was conducted of functionality reduction and the provision of tactile and acoustical interaction feedback for this target group.

2.4 Adaptive IxDO

Adaptive-IxDO has an analogy to the UGT-IxDO but a stronger focus on users' individuality. Adaptive-IxDO can react to changing conditions timely since the adaption process takes place during the operational and rendering time. In our AAL field of practice, Adaptive-IxDO was utilized in the project AALuis [10]. The aim of the project was to develop a middleware UI generation layer that can automatically adapt the user interface according users' wishes and needs.

2.5 Ambient Intelligence IxDO

Ambient Intelligence IxDO (AmI-IxDO) focuses on interactions that are supported by- and embedded in digital equipped environmental settings. As indicated in the work of Augusto and McCullagh [11], AmI is a concept that refers to a digital environment that pro-actively, but sensibly, supports people in their daily lives. From this point of view, AmI-IxDO represents a specialization of the mentioned Adaptive-IxDO with the focus on the environmental setting. In our AAL field of practice, AmI-IxDO was utilized in the project RelaxedCare [12]. The aim of the project was to develop a supportive solution for informal caregivers. The goal was to reduce their burden by providing the overall wellbeing information of the person in need of care.

2.6   Personal Assistant-Based IxDO

Personal Assistant IxDO (PA-IxDO) focuses on the design of computer generated personal assistants. The focus is on the instant, direct, and personalized end user support, and on the representation of an independent and personal entity. PA-IxDO encourages a level of personality that can be uniquely named, and that people can become familiar with. Especially this characteristic, namely the aim to establish a trustful relationship with the user, shapes the PA-IxDO and differs from others. In our AAL field of practice, PA-IxDO was utilized in the project CogniWin [13, 15]. The aim of the project was to develop an integrated framework that provides personalized support to overcome eventual age-related memory degradation and gradual decrease of other cognitive capabilities. Furthermore, PA-IxDO is used in the current running project vCare [14]. The Project targets the development of a smart coaching solution grounded on personalized care pathways.

2.7   Companion IxDO

Companion-IxDO utilizes PA-IxDO techniques and enhances the previously mentioned independent entity towards a so-called artificial companion. The primary focus is on the design of virtual beings, able to support the user but also able to bear company to the user. Companion-IxDO employs activating and pleasant core affects such as curiosity, eagerness, desire, joyfulness, satisfaction to engage the user with the system, and to establish a kind of companionship with the user. In our AAL field of practice, Companion-IxDO was utilized in the project CompanionAble [16]. The aim of the project was to provide a new AAL solution through the combination of a service robot that is perceived as a companion and the seamless integration into the smart home environment. Furthermore, Companion-IxDO was also utilized in the project Miraculous-Life [7, 17]. In contrast to CompanionAble, the project used a virtual avatar as the embodied conversational agent and not a physical robot. However, both projects aimed at the same goal, namely the enhancement of PA-IxDO techniques towards an individual entity with a friend-like character.

2.8   Tangible IxDO

Tangible-IxDO focuses interactions that use physical and graspable components as the main interaction medium. As noted in [18] tangible user interfaces provide a physical representation of digital information and computation, facilitating the direct manipulation of bits. In our AAL field of practice, Tangible-IxDO is utilized in the ongoing project KithNKin [19]. The project tackles the problem of the progressive social isolation of older adults living alone and in far distance from their family members. It aims to foster the communication and interaction with family members and friends utilizing tangible interaction objects which extend interaction capabilities of a standard tablet device.

3 Interaction Design Opportunity Research Grid

The goal of this work is the identification of different IxDOs and the elaboration of their characteristics, relationships, and dependencies. These results, in turn, serves as the foundation and the starting point for the before-mentioned overall research goal that investigates the impact of different IxDOs on users' system acceptance rate. Section 2 presented the identified IxDOs and sketched their main characteristics in decoupled manner. To draw conclusions regarding IxDOs impact on users' acceptance it is necessary to elaborate them in a structured manner. This task is accomplished by the so-called Interaction Design Opportunity Research Grid (IxDO-RG). Figure 2 illustrates the basic concept and structure of the IxDO-RG.

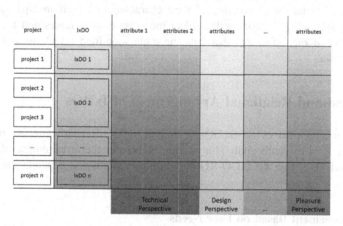

Fig. 2. IxDO-RG structure depicting the concept of information processing based on a research grid including the IxDOs, the corresponding projects and the IxDOs attribute clustered based on different perspectives.

The IxDO-RG is based on the Design Case Study Research Framework methodology which is presented in [20]. The first column of the IxDO-RG summarizes the involved projects followed by the corresponding IxDOs. The remaining columns represent co-called cross-cutting issues which highlight IxDO attributes clustered by thematic affiliations.

The IxDO-RG utilizes three cross-cutting issues, namely the technological perspective, the design perspective, and the pleasure-oriented perspective. The technological perspective characterizes IxDOs in terms of technological aspects such as software models, system architecture approaches, and concrete tools and frameworks that contribute towards the manifestation of these IxDOs. The design perspective characterizes IxDOs in terms of interaction design purposes referred from the literature such as design for flow, design for the fast, design for the slow, design for the need, design for the pleasure [21, 22]. Finally, the pleasure perspective targets the reflection of end user experiences in respect to different IxDOs. As the name already suggests, the perspective focusses primarily on the evocation of different pleasure types as indicated in [23].

These cross-cutting issues have been developed in a successive process, started from the technological perspective in the AAL field of practice, over the design perspective to the pleasure-oriented perspective. Design results from the technological perspective (in form of dedicated arrangement of involved technological aspects) have been used for the development of the design perspective. Results from the design perspective (again in form of dedicated arrangement of interaction design purposes), have been used for the development of pleasure-oriented perspective. The pleasure-oriented perspective represents the basis for the future work that focusses on the reflection the users on their individual level. These threefold process sketches already the roadmap of the future work towards the final research goal.

However, since this work targets the first research step, namely the identification of different IxDOs and the elaboration of their characteristics, relationships, and dependencies the following Sections will neglect the cross-cutting issues and focus on the main column of the IxDO-RG that lists the eight identified IxDOs in a logical and relational order.

4   Logical and Relational Arrangement of IxDOs

The right arrangement of the IxDOs within the IxDO-RG structure is crucial step towards the final research goal. This section elaborates the arrangement of the eight identified IxDOs within the IxDO-RG based on user needs and dependencies between the IxDOs.

4.1   Arrangement Based on User Needs

In Sect. 2 it was stated that IxDOs can be described by individual sets of characteristics which form the main purpose of the IxDO. These main purposes address certain user needs that have been used for the initial arrangement within the IxDO-RG. The Table 1 summarizes the main purposes of the eight identified IxDOs and the corresponding key characteristics.

As indicated in Table 1, the App-IxDO represents the classical and minimal setting for the design of interactive systems. Thus, the App-IxDO can be used as the initial candidate for the order of IxDOs. The remaining seven IxDOs are arranged according their main purposes and the satisfaction of the underlying user needs that they aim at. This task is supported by Maslow's pyramid of needs [24].

Maslow's pyramid of needs was introduced 1943 and is based on believe that people are motivated to achieve certain needs. Maslow distinguishes between five different classes of needs which are arranged in a hierarchical order. Maslow assumed that a person needs to fulfill a lower ranked need before she or he can seek for a higher one. The

Table 1. Main purposes of the eight identified IxDOs and their key characteristics.

IxDO	Main purpose	Key characteristics
App-IxDO	Classical setting	Covers basic needs regarding functionality and usability
MApp-IxDO	Comfort setting	Targets the enhancement of usability aspects such as accessibility and error tolerance
UGT-IxDO	Supportive setting	Targets the enhancement of accessibility aspects for target groups with special needs
Adaptive-IxDO	Dynamical supportive setting	Targets the dynamic adjustment of the system according to the changing users' wishes and needs
AmI-IxDO	Environmental setting	Targets the support of users in managing daily life routines via utilization of their living environments
PA-IxDO	Assistive setting	Targets the personal and cognitive support of daily life activities
Companion-IxDO	Friendship setting	Targets the evolvement of the PA-IxDO toward individual entity with a friend-like character
Tangible-IxDO	Graspable setting	Targets the inclusion and emphasis of graspable artifacts in user-system interaction

classical illustration of Maslow's pyramided of needs with sharp borders is illustrated in Fig. 3 on the left. These sharp borders are often used as an aspect against the theory since it is understood (as it is in this work) that an entity, such as a software application, can satisfy several needs at once. This led to the developed of alternative versions with dynamic borders as depicted in Fig. 3 on the right [26]. These dynamic borders form overlapping need areas and highlight that the personal development is a continuous process and that users seek to fulfill more than one need at a certain point of time.

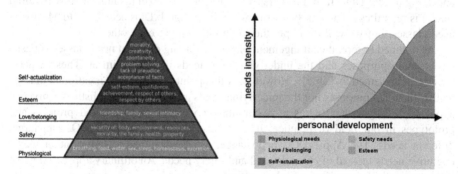

Fig. 3. Maslow's pyramid of needs highlighting distinguishable levels of user needs with sharp borders between levels on the left [25] and the needs with dynamic and overlapping levels [26].

Maslow's pyramid of needs was, beyond the mentioned sharp border problem, discussed controversially. Abulof Uiel presents in his work "Introduction: Why We Need Maslow in the Twenty-First Century" [25] an excerpt of the controversial debate.

However, regardless the controversial discussion, the basic concept of different needs matches very well the listing of main IxDO purposes and the satisfaction of user needs they are aiming at. Thus, it is reasonable to arrange IxDOs according to user need classes as defined by Maslow.

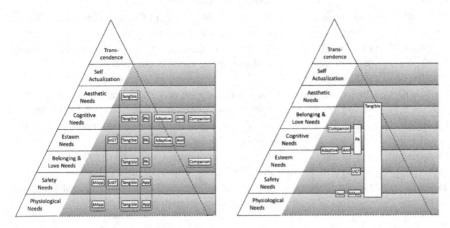

Fig. 4. Initial arrangement of IxDOs within Maslow's classes of need on the left and the simplified version on the right.

However, even if we use these Maslow's classes of need it is not wise to adapt the prioritization concept where users need to fulfill the lower ranked needs before they can seek for higher ranked needs. Following argumentation justifies this decision. From the end user perspective, the overall goal of an interactive system is the right treatment of the current appearing problem and consequently the right treatment of the current appearing needs. Thus, from this perspective the priority level (as indicated by pyramid shape) is regardless. Thus, in this work we will arrange IxDOs according to Maslow's need classes, but we will decouple their relations among each other.

As outlined before, the arrangement of IxDOs among different need classes is based on the main purposes and the underlying user needs that they aim at. These aspects have been presented in Table 1. However, at this point it needs to be mentioned that the neither the main purposes nor the underlying needs are meant to be holistic or universal applicable. They rather represent a cumulative view of the presented projects and prototypes in our field of practice. It is understood that different IxDOs can target different needs. The App-IxDO, for instance, can be designed to target rather users' cognitive needs instead of physiological and safety needs. An ordinary app-based game is a stereotypical example for such a setting.

Figure 4 illustrates the initial arrangement of IxDOs within the pyramid classes to the left. It is noticeable that certain IxDOs can be assigned to several classes. App-IxDO, for instance, can be assigned to the physiological need class as well as to the safety need class. Similar applies for other IxDOs. To reduce the complexity of the illustration, this initial setting can be rearranged. The following two actions provide a simplified version: (a) IxDOs can be placed between need classes. This is valid since needs do not have a sharp border as depicted in the Fig. 3 to the left but rather fuzzy borders as depicted in Fig. 3 to the right, and (b) need classes within the pyramid can be rearranged. This is also valid since the need levels build not upon each other as argued before. The simplified arrangement is illustrated in Fig. 4 to the right. As one can see, two need classes ("esteem needs" and "belonging & love needs") swapped their places. Moreover, it is noticeable that the PA-IxDO and Tangible-IxDO span multiple need classes. This highlights that these IxDOs target the satisfaction of multiple needs. Conclusively, the arrangement within the pyramid of needs provides the following ranking: App-IxDO, MApp-IxDO, UGT-IxDO, Adaptive-IxDO, AmI-IxDO, PA-IxDO, Companion-IxDO, and in parallel to this listing the Tangible-IxDO that over spans all other IxDOs. This ranking is also influenced by the dependency structure of IxDOs as described in the following section.

4.2   IxDO Dependencies

The arrangement of IxDOs based on Maslow's pyramid of needs was performed in respect to their dependency structure. As indicated in Sect. 2, IxDOs build dependencies upon each other. They build dependencies on the technological complexity level, but they also inherit from each other on the conceptual level. Dependencies on the technological complexity level derive from the fact that more complex IxDOs utilize and extend technological concepts and methods that are used in less complex IxDOs. Inheritance on the conceptual level results from the continuous reuse of IxDO concepts. This is comparable to generalization and specialization of classes in the Object-Oriented Paradigm (OOP). Using this analogy leads to argumentation that higher ranked IxDOs specialize lower ranked IxDOs. Table 2 summarizes this concept applied on all eight IxDOs including their specialization and their inheritance.

Table 2. Specialization of IxDOs on the conceptual level highlighting the specialization attributes and the lower ranked IxDOs that serve as the source for the inheritance.

IxDO	Specialization	Inheritance from...
App-IxDO	–	–
MApp-IxDO	Collective	App-IxDO
UGT-IxDO	Tailored	App-IxDO or MApp-IxDO
Adaptive-IxDO	Re-adjustable	UGT-IxDO
AmI-IxDO	On demand	Adaptive-IxDO
PA-IxDO	Supportive	AmI-IxDO or Adaptive-IxDO
Companion-IxDO	Personality enriched	PA-IxDO
Tangible-IxDO	Physical	App-IxDO, MApp-IxDO, UGT-IxDO, Adaptive-IxDO, AmI-IxDO, PA-IxDO or Companion-IxDO

Figure 5 illustrates the final dependency structure of the eight identified IxDOs including Maslow's classes of need (to the right), including the dependencies on the technological complexity level (to the left) and including IxDOs inheritance on the conceptual level (arrows between IxDOs). It is noticeable that three IxDOs over span multiple technology complexity levels, namely the UGT-IxDO, the PA-IxDO, and the Tangible-IxDO. This is in line with the ranking based on Malsow's classes and based on the inheritance on the conceptual level as presented in Table 2.

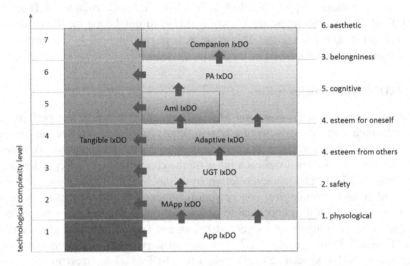

Fig. 5. Dependency structure of the eight identified IxDOs

This dependency structure represents the preliminary result of this work that can be used within the IxDO-RG.

5 Summary and Outlook

This work emerged out of the Active and Assisted Living (AAL) context and the awareness that prototypes developed in various research projects shared similarities regarding their interaction design styles. This led to the development of the overall research question which targets the investigation whether and how far different inter-action design styles impact users' system acceptance rate. This work contributes towards answering this research question and represents the starting point of future research work.

The aim of this work was the identification of different interaction design styles which we further named as Interaction Design Opportunities (IxDOs), and the elaborate of their characteristics, relationships, and dependencies. In Sect. 2 the focus was on the identification of the eight IxDOs. Section 3 presented the so-called Interaction Design Opportunities Research Grid (IxDO-RG) that builds the working space for the iden-tified IxDOs with the aim to investigate their characteristics from different perspectives.

These perspectives have been further named as cross-cutting issues. The Sect. 4 focused on the development of the logical and structural arrangement of IxDOs within the IxDO-RG. This represents the ground work for the further elaboration of the cross-cutting issues.

As pointed out earlier, this work is the starting point of an extensive research. The future work will focus on the development of a dynamic user model that considers users' inner values, wishes and needs. The IxDO-RG combined with this dynamic user model will build the research framework and the toolset that targets the investigation of the overall research question, namely whether and how far different IxDOs impact users' acceptance of the offered interactive system.

Acknowledgements. This work summarizes individual aspects of the PhD thesis of Miroslav Sili with the title "UX in the AAL Field of Practice - Interaction Design Framework Targeting Long-Standing User Engagement with Interactive Systems". The aspects have been revised and extended in collaboration with the co-authors in order to form a compact and self-contained representation of the dedicated research task within the overall PhD work.

References

1. Franklin Waddell, T., Zhang, B., Sundar, S.: Human–Computer Interaction. The International Encyclopedia of Interpersonal Communication (2016)
2. Abras, C., Maloney-Krichmar, D., Preece, J.: User-centered design. In: Bainbridge, W. (ed.) Encyclopedia of Human-Computer Interaction, vol. 37, no. 4, pp. 445–456. Sage Publications, Thousand Oaks (2004)
3. Siegel, C., Prazak-Aram, B., Kropf, J., Kundi, M., Dorner, T.: Evaluation of a modular scalable system for silverager located in assisted living homes in Austria - study protocol of the ModuLAAr ambient assisted living project. BMC Publ. Health **14**(1), 736 (2014)
4. Scase, M., Marandure, B., Hancox, J., Kreiner, K., Hanke, S., Kropf, J.: Development of and adherence to a computer-based gamified environment designed to promote health and wellbeing in older people with mild cognitive impairment. Stud. Health Technol. Inform. **236**, 348–355 (2017)
5. Bacciu, D., et al.: Smart environments and context-awareness for lifestyle management in a healthy active ageing framework. In: Pereira, F., Machado, P., Costa, E., Cardoso, A. (eds.) EPIA 2015. LNCS (LNAI), vol. 9273, pp. 54–66. Springer, Cham (2015). https://doi.org/10.1007/978-3-319-23485-4_6
6. Sili, M., Gira, M., Müllner-Rieder, M., Mayer, C.: Interaction model-based user interfaces: two approaches, one goal - comparison of two user interface generation approaches applying interaction models. In: Helfert, M., Holzinger, A., Ziefle, M., Fred, A., O'Donoghue, J., Röcker, C. (eds.) Information and Communication Technologies for Ageing Well and e-Health. CCIS, vol. 578, pp. 185–197. Springer, Cham (2015). https://doi.org/10.1007/978-3-319-27695-3_11
7. Sili, M., Bobeth, J., Sandner, E., Hanke, S., Schwarz, S., Mayer, C.: Talking faces in lab and field trials. In: Zhou, J., Salvendy, G. (eds.) ITAP 2015. LNCS, vol. 9193, pp. 134–144. Springer, Cham (2015). https://doi.org/10.1007/978-3-319-20892-3_14
8. Hanke, S., Tsiourti, C., Sili, M., Christodoulou, E.: Embodied ambient intelligent systems, vol. 20, pp. 65–85 (2015)

9. Sili, M., Gira, M., Mayer, C.: Usability matters. In: Kurosu, M. (ed.) HCI 2017. LNCS, vol. 10271, pp. 384–394. Springer, Cham (2017). https://doi.org/10.1007/978-3-319-58071-5_29

10. Mayer, C., et al.: Avatar enriched user interfaces for older adults. In: GLOBAL HEALTH, pp. 1–4 (2013)

11. Augusto, J.C., McCullagh, P.: Ambient intelligence: concepts and applications. Comput. Sci. Inf. Syst. **4**(1), 1–27 (2007)

12. Morandell, M.: RelaxedCare: how informal caregivers stay informed and connected in a really easy way. Alzheimer's Dementia J. Alzheimer's Assoc. **12**(7), 157 (2016)

13. Portugal, D., et al.: CogniWin: An Integrated Framework to Support Older Adults at Work. In: UMAP (Extended Proceedings) (2016)

14. vCare Consortium: vCare Project (2019). https://vcare-project.eu/

15. Hanke, S., Samaras, G., et al.: CogniWin – a virtual assistance system for older adults at work. In: Zhou, J., Salvendy, G. (eds.) DUXU 2015. LNCS, vol. 9194, pp. 257–268. Springer, Cham (2015). https://doi.org/10.1007/978-3-319-20913-5_24

16. Renteria, A., Pastor, C., Gaminde, G.: Intelligent homes to assist elderly people. In: Proceedings of International Workshop on Ambient Assisted Living, Spain (2010)

17. Hanke, S., Sandner, E., Kadyrov, S., Stainer-Hochgatterer, A.: Daily life support at home through a virtual support partner (2016)

18. Ishii, H., Ullmer, B.: Tangible bits: towards seamless interfaces between people, bits and atoms. In: Proceedings of the ACM SIGCHI Conference on Human Factors in Computing Systems, pp. 234–241. ACM (1997)

19. Koscher, A., Dittenberger, S., Stainer-Hochgatterer, A.: ICT inexperienced elderlies: what would attract elderlies to use items of technology? In: Harnessing the Power of Technology to Improve Lives (2017)

20. Wulf, V., Rohde, M., Pipek, V., Stevens, G.: Engaging with practices: design case studies as a research framework in CSCW. In: Proceedings of the ACM 2011 Conference on Computer Supported Cooperative Work, pp. 505–512. ACM (2011)

21. Leech, J: Psychology for Designers. Mrjoe Press, Bristol (2017)

22. Spool, J: Building a winning UX strategy using the Kano model (2016). https://blog.usievents.com/building-a-winning-ux-strategy-using-thekano-model-ou-comment-aboutir-a-une-experience-utilisateur-optimiseepar-jared-spool

23. Jordan, P.: The four pleasures. In: Designing Pleasurable Products, pp. 11–57 (2000)

24. McLeod, S.: Maslow's hierarchy of needs. https://www.simplypsychology.org/maslow.html. 24 May 2019

25. Factoryjoe: Maslow's Hierarchy of Needs - What Matters_Maslow's Hierarchy of Needs (2018). https://commons.wikimedia.org/wiki/File:MaslowHierarchy_of_Needs.svg

26. Guttmann, P.: Dynamic hierarchy of needs - Maslow - Maslow's hierarchy of needs (2019). https://upload.wikimedia.org/wikipedia/commons/e/ef/Dynamic_hierarchy_of_needs_-_Maslow.svg

Aging, Motion, Cognition, Emotion and Learning

Trends in the Decline in Gait and Motor Ability of Older Adults: A Case Study Based on SHARE Data

Ruoyu Chen and Jia Zhou[✉]

Department of Industrial Engineering, Chongqing University,
Chongqing 400044, China
chenruoyu2013@gmail.com, zhoujia07@gmail.com

Abstract. This study analyzed data from the SHARE study to compare the gait speed of older adults in European countries and China and to explore the association of gait speed with other physical abilities. Given that the motor development of children follows a cephalocaudal and proximodistal trend, the declining trend of older adults' physical abilities was also analyzed. The results showed that, on average, older adults in China walked faster than older adults in European countries. Slower gait speed and weaker grip strength were observed for older adults with worse motor abilities. Furthermore, this study found that the decline in motor abilities of older adults accelerated with age. The participants' lower-extremity abilities showed earlier and more rapid decline than the abilities of the upper extremities and hands. This study helps to better understand the health condition and aging process of older adults.

Keywords: Older adults · Gait · Motor ability · Decline trend

1 Introduction

Aging often leads to degeneration of both the cognition function and physical function of the elderly. It is well known that these two functions are inter-related, both playing roles in the decline in mobility in activities such as walking. The lower cognitive function and weak muscle power observed in older adults are associated with slower gait speed [1–6]. Gait speed is used to predict the risk of disability, cardiovascular disease, dementia and even mortality of older adults [7, 8].

The dynamic systems theory of motor development suggests that the behavior of walking is not a single motor skill. It is a dynamic system consisting of various single motor abilities like crawling, standing, arm-reaching movements and stepping [9]. Moreover, studies focused on the motor development of children found that the organization and direction of motor development in infants shows a significant cephalocaudal trend and proximodistal trend [10]. The cephalocaudal trend refers to earlier control of the head than the arms, and earlier control of the arms and torso than the legs. The proximodistal trend refers to earlier control of the head, torso and arms than coordination of the hands and fingers. This raises the interesting possibility that the decline in motor ability of older adults might follow a similar trend.

© Springer Nature Switzerland AG 2019
J. Zhou and G. Salvendy (Eds.): HCII 2019, LNCS 11593, pp. 495–505, 2019.
https://doi.org/10.1007/978-3-030-22015-0_38

Furthermore, cultural differences in infant-raising methods are also known to influence the development of motor skills [11–13]. Thus, we can assume that these cultural differences might also influence the gait speed of older adults. Therefore, this study aimed to (1) compare the gait speed of several European countries and China, (2) explore whether the relationship between gait speed and motor abilities differs due to changes in the abilities of different body parts, and (3) explore the declining trend in motor ability of older adults and identify when this decline begins to accelerate. The results from this study will provide a better understanding of the physiology and aging process of older adults.

2 Methodology

2.1 Study Population

The Survey of Health, Aging and Retirement in Europe (SHARE) collects data on the health, socioeconomic status and social and family networks of people aged over 50 years. The survey started in 2004, and five panel waves (waves 1, 2, 4, 5 and 6, shown in Table 1) [14–18] and one retrospective life history wave (wave 3) have been conducted, covering more than 120,000 individuals across 27 European countries and Israel. Computer-assisted personal interviewing (CAPI) was used for the main interviews, in addition to paper and pencil surveys for drop-offs. The CAPI questionnaire has remained almost the same over the subsequent waves. Detailed and rigorous instruction about the questionnaire and interviewing process guarantees the reliability of the data.

Table 1. Year, number of respondents and data collected in SHARE study waves 1, 2, 4, 5 and 6.

	Wave 1	Wave 2	Wave 4	Wave 5	Wave 6
Year	2004	2006	2011	2013	2015
Number of respondents	30,434	37,174	58,184	66,221	68,231
Gait speed	√	√			
Chair stand		√		√	
Grip strength	√	√	√	√	√
Motor ability	√	√	√	√	√

Note: √ indicates that the module was measured in the wave.

To analyze the gait speed of participants from different countries, the data from wave 2 was used. Individuals from the only non-European country, Israel, were excluded. A total of 3479 individuals aged 50 or older from 13 countries who successfully finished the walking test were included in the analysis sample. The gait speed data of older Chinese adults was obtained from a study by [19], which included 50 adults aged over 50 years from Beijing. For analysis of the declining trend, individuals who did not participate in the follow-up waves were excluded from the baseline wave 1 when corresponding factors were analyzed.

2.2   Gait Speed

Participants in the SHARE study conducted two walking tests on the premise of walking without the help of another person or using support, as well as feeling safe to walk. The respondents walked 2.5 m two times in the condition of available space. The time taken to complete each walking test was recorded in seconds. Respondents whose time for any walking test was less than 1.5 s which might not be a comfortable speed [20] were excluded. The gait speed for each test was calculated by dividing the time by 2.5 m, and gait speed was expressed as meters per second. Participants in the study by [19] were instructed to walk 10 m at a comfortable speed while wearing a smart bracelet. The average gait speed under this condition was taken into consideration.

2.3   Measurement of Motor Abilities

Self-reported mobility difficulties while performing 10 activities were recorded (walking 100 m, sitting for about 4 h, getting up from a chair, climbing several flights of stairs, climbing one flight of stairs, stooping, reaching arms, pulling or pushing objects, lifting or carrying objects, and picking up a coin). Considering the motor development trends of children, the motor abilities of older adults were categorized into the abilities of the hands, upper extremities and lower extremities [21]. The upper-extremity ability was defined as a binomial variable where the respondent reported having no difficulty or difficulty in at least one of the following activities: reaching arms, pulling or pushing objects, lifting or carrying objects, and sitting for about 2 h. The lower-extremity ability was defined as the respondent having no difficulty or difficulty in at least one of the following activities: climbing several flights of stairs, climbing one flight of stairs, stooping, kneeling or crouching, getting up from a chair, and walking 100 m. The hand ability refers to whether the respondent reported difficulty in picking up a coin.

The grip strength was analyzed as a continuous variable, indicating the respondent's hand-related ability. Both hands of each respondent were measured two times using a handheld dynamometer. The maximum value from the four measurements was used in the analysis [22]. The chair stand activity, representing lower-extremity ability, was measured by instructing respondents to stand from a chair five times, and the total time was recorded in seconds.

2.4   Confounders

The demographic information of respondents, including age and gender, were treated as potential confounders. Age was classified into four groups based on the respondents' age range: 50–60, 61–70, 71–80, 81–90, and 91–100 years. In addition, the current health condition of participants, consisting of smoking, alcohol consumption and physical activity, was also included. The smoking status was classified into three levels: never, former, and current [7, 22]. Alcohol consumption was measured by asking respondents how often they had consumed any alcoholic drinks during the past 3 months, with seven levels of response: almost every day, five or six days a week, three or four days a week, once or twice a week, once or twice a month, less than once a month, not at all in the past 3 months. Physical activity was measured by asking the respondent how often they engage in vigorous physical activity such as sports, heavy housework or a job that involves physical labor, which was recorded in four levels: more than once a week, once a week, one to three times a month, and hardly ever or never [23, 24].

2.5 Statistical Analysis

Means and standard deviations were used to describe the gait speed and grip strength of respondents in wave 2. Factorial analysis of variance (ANOVA) was used to analyze differences between two measurements in groups with different characteristics. Three samples were extracted: the sample including 1272 individuals who completed the walking test in both wave 1 and wave 2, the sample including 9947 individuals who completed the chair stand measurements in both wave 2 and wave 5, and the sample including 5069 individuals who completed the grip strength measurement in all five waves. Factorial repeated-measures ANOVA was used to analyze the variation in gait speed, chair stand time, grip strength and motor abilities across waves for each age group. The variation in extremity abilities for each age group across waves was determined by comparing the proportion of respondents who reported difficulty in extremity ability relative to the total number of respondents in each group. All statistical analyses were performed using R 3.5.1 software.

3 Results and Discussion

3.1 Comparison of Gait Speed Between Countries

The average age of respondents in wave 2 was 79.65 years (SD = 4.17), and the average gait speed was 0.68 m/s (SD = 0.30). As shown in Table 1, the gait speed differed significantly across countries ($F_{(13,3465)}$ = 27.855, $p < 0.001$). Moreover, post hoc tests revealed potential regional differences [25]. The gait speed in three southern European countries, Italy, Spain and Greece, did not show any significant differences (Spain-Italy, t = −3.233, p = 0.054; Spain-Greece, t = −1.574, $p < 0.001$; Italy-Greece, t = 1.784, $p < 0.001$). However, the gait speed of respondents from these countries was lower than those in Germany, which is in central Europe (Germany-Italy, t = 2.633, p = 0.32; Germany-Spain, t = 5.483, $p < 0.001$; Germany-Greece, t = 4.27, $p < 0.01$), and the gait speed of participants in Germany was slower than those in Denmark and Sweden, which are northern European countries (Germany-Denmark, t = −5.234, $p < 0.001$; Germany-Sweden, t = −4.289, $p < 0.01$). The gait speed of older adults in Beijing, China, was faster than all European countries. Another two studies that measured the average gait speed of older adults in Hong Kong [26] and Chongqing [27] reported gait speeds of 0.78 m/s (SD = 0.214) and 0.86 m/s (SD = 0.14) respectively, which were also faster than most European countries evaluated in the SHARE study.

Table 2. Gait speed and grip strength according to the selected measure.

Selected measure	Gait speed (m/s)			Grip strength (kg)	
	N	Mean (SD)	p	Mean (SD)	p
Age (years)			<0.01		<0.01
58–70	4	0.65 (0.28)		28.75 (3.50)	
71–80	2231	0.71 (0.31)		28.96 (9.59)	
81–90	1187	0.63 (0.29)		25.63 (9.08)	
91–100	57	0.52 (0.29)		20.75 (7.55)	
Sex			<0.01		<0.01
Male	1637	0.71 (0.31)		34.52 (8.20)	
Female	1842	0.65 (0.30)		21.62 (5.96)	
Country			<0.01		<0.01
Austria	122	0.64 (0.32)			
Germany	157	0.67 (0.28)			
Sweden	365	0.78 (0.29)			
Netherlands	295	0.71 (0.29)			
Spain	251	0.51 (0.30)			
Italy	248	0.59 (0.25)			
France	313	0.71 (0.29)			
Denmark	349	0.81 (0.31)			
Greece	292	0.54 (0.31)			
Switzerland	195	0.76 (0.28)			
Belgium	412	0.70 (0.34)			
Czech Republic	213	0.71 (0.34)			
Poland	176	0.55 (0.25)			
Ireland	91	0.65 (0.30)			
China (Beijing)	50	1.33 (0.07)			
Lower-extremity ability			<0.01		<0.01
No difficulty	1405	0.76 (0.31)		30.46 (9.45)	
Difficulty in at least one activity	2074	0.62 (0.28)		25.82 (9.22)	
Upper-extremity ability			<0.01		<0.01
None difficulty	2105	0.74 (0.30)		30.22 (9.40)	
Difficulty in at least one activity	1374	0.59 (0.28)		23.81 (8.52)	
Hand ability			<0.01		<0.01
No difficulty	3332	0.68 (0.30)		27.92 (9.55)	
Difficulty	147	0.54 (0.27)		22.48 (8.94)	
Smoker			0.27		0.36
Former	305	0.70 (0.30)		30.26 (9.47)	
Current	363	0.68 (0.29)		30.17 (9.90)	
Never	2811	0.67 (0.30)		27.09 (9.47)	
Alcohol consumption			<0.01		<0.01
Almost every day	842	0.71 (0.30)		29.92 (9.47)	

(continued)

Table 2. (*continued*)

Selected measure	Gait speed (m/s)			Grip strength (kg)	
	N	Mean (SD)	p	Mean (SD)	p
Five or six days a week	85	0.76 (0.35)		33.84 (10.12)	
Three or four days a week	197	0.77 (0.28)		31.76 (9.50)	
Once or twice a week	462	0.74 (0.30)		29.30 (9.78)	
Once or twice a month	338	0.72 (0.30)		28.03 (9.57)	
Less than once a month	329	0.66 (0.29)		26.25 (9.23)	
Not at all	1226	0.60 (0.29)		24.77 (8.68)	
Vigorous physical activity			<0.01		<0.01
More than once a week	680	0.76 (0.32)		30.75 (9.86)	
Once a week	346	0.76 (0.31)		29.69 (9.53)	
One to three times a month	336	0.69 (0.32)		29.22 (9.79)	
Hardly ever, or never	2117	0.63 (0.28)		26.14 (9.13)	

3.2   Gait Speed and Motor Ability

The differences in gait speed and grip strength according to the respondents' characteristics are shown in Table 2. The average grip strength was 26.68 kg (SD = 9.59). Older adults who reported no difficulty in upper-extremity, lower-extremity and hand abilities walked faster than those who reported at least one difficulty. Furthermore, an interaction of upper-extremity and lower-extremity abilities on gait speed was observed ($F_{(1,3166)}$ = 12.62, p < 0.001). Older adults who reported no difficulty in both the upper and lower extremities had a faster gait speed (0.77 m/s, SD = 0.31) than those who reported at least one difficulty in any ability. Older adults who reported at least one difficulty in upper-extremity ability but no difficulty in lower-extremity ability (0.73 m/s, SD = 0.30) walked faster than those who reported no difficulty in upper-extremity ability but at least one difficulty in lower-extremity ability (0.69 m/s, SD = 0.28). However, superiority in gait speed was not reflected in grip strength. The former had weaker grip strength (25.53 kg, SD = 7.88) than the latter (28.83 kg, SD = 9.16), which indicated that difficulties in different extremities were related to changes in abilities. These benefits infer extremity-related abilities through gait and grip strength, thus further predicting physical limitation and risk of disability rather than predictions based only on measuring activities of daily living or instrumental activities of daily living (ADLs/IADLs) [2].

3.3   Declining Trend

Regarding the decline in gait speed, there was a significant effect of age group ($F_{(2,2538)}$ = 12.67, p < 0.001) and wave ($F_{(1,2538)}$ = 57.81, p < 0.001) on gait speed. As shown in Table 3, respondents in the older group had a slower gait speed. The decreased gait speed of the 71–75-year age group after 2 years was not significant when compared to the other age groups, which indicates that adults aged older than 76 experienced a significant decline in gait speed. However, the decreased gait speed in each age group did not significantly differ after 2 years ($F_{(4,1267)}$ = 0.474, p > 0.05). The gait degeneration and age were negatively related (r = −0.016, p > 0.05), which indicates that gait slowed down, but that the change was slower with increasing age.

Table 3. Gait speed of wave 1 and wave 2

Gait speed (m/s)					
Age group (years)	N	Wave 1	Wave 2	Change	T-test
		Mean (SD)	Mean (SD)		
71–75	67	0.67 (0.26)	0.63 (0.28)	−0.04	t = −0.938, p = 0.352
76–80	739	0.75 (0.28)	0.68 (0.29)	−0.07	t = −0.883, p < 0.001
81–85	336	0.67 (0.26)	0.62 (0.28)	−0.05	t = −3.677, p < 0.001
86–90	105	0.61 (0.30)	0.53 (0.30)	−0.08	t = −3.270, p < 0.01
91–95	25	0.58 (0.26)	0.55 (0.31)	−0.03	
Sum	1272	0.71 (0.28)	0.65 (0.29)		

Regarding the decline in chair stand ability, the main effect of age group ($F_{(4,9969)}$ = 58.12, p < 0.001) and wave ($F_{(1,9969)}$ = 148.74, p < 0.001) on the time to complete five chair stands were significant. Moreover, the increased time after 7 years of each age group differed with each other ($F_{(4,9969)}$ = 4.39, p < 0.01). The increased time for the 66–70 age group was significantly higher than that of the 51–55 age group (t = 2.861, p < 0.05), and the increased time of the 71–75 age group was greater than that of the 51–55 (t = 3.327, p < 0.01) and 56–60 (t = 2.986, p < 0.05) age groups. Given that the increased time to complete the chair stands was positively related to age (r = 0.042, p < 0.001), it was speculated that for older adults, the time required to stand from a chair and the change per year was increased with advancing age, especially for those aged 66 years or older (Table 4).

Table 4. Time to perform five chair stands of respondents in wave 2 and wave 5.

Chair stands (s)					
Age group (years)	N	Wave 2	Wave 5	Change	T-test
		Mean (SD)	Mean (SD)		
51–55	2342	10.52 (6.40)	11.25 (7.51)	0.73	t = 3.793, p < 0.001
56–60	2730	10.81 (6.03)	11.69 (6.83)	0.88	t = 5.392, p < 0.001
61–65	2251	11.13 (6.16)	12.39 (6.97)	1.26	t = 6.926, p < 0.001
66–70	1747	11.98 (7.67)	13.56 (8.82)	1.58	t = 5.972, p < 0.001
71–75	904	12.36 (7.05)	14.32 (8.70)	1.96	t = 5.523, p < 0.001
Sum	9947	11.16 (6.58)	12.31 (7.65)		

When analyzing the decline in grip strength, there was a significant effect of age group ($F_{(7,25302)}$ = 343.23, p < 0.001) and wave ($F_{(4,25302)}$ = 126.31, p < 0.001). As expected, older adults had weaker grip strength, and their grip strength became weaker over time. We also observed that there were significant effects of age group ($F_{(7,21)}$ = 10.18, p < 0.001) and wave ($F_{(3,21)}$ = 1102.75, p < 0.001) on the decrease in grip strength between waves. As shown in Fig. 1, the grip strength of each age group did not decline equally, with a faster decline observed with increasing age. On average, the older age group showed a greater decrease in grip strength per year when compared to the younger age group, demonstrating an accelerated decline trend.

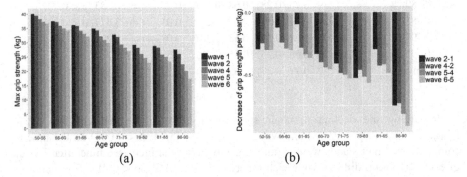

(a)   (b)

Fig. 1. Grip strength of different age groups over subsequent study waves (a), and the decrease in grip strength between waves (b).

For analysis of motor ability decline, the upper-extremity ability, lower-extremity ability and hand ability were measured according to age group and wave number. Figure 2 shows the proportion by age groups and waves. In both the comparison between age groups and the comparison between waves, there was a larger proportion of respondents who had difficulty in motor ability with increasing age. In each age group, the proportion of older adults who had difficulties in their lower-extremity ability was highest, followed by the proportion of those who reported difficulty in their upper-extremity ability. When compared to upper- and lower-extremity abilities, very few older adults reported difficulty in their hand ability. On average, lower-extremity ability declined faster than upper-extremity ability, while hand ability declined the slowest. Although a small improvement was observed between two certain waves [27], the three kinds of motor abilities generally declined with age, especially from 66 years of age. The motor abilities of these older adults showed a faster decline between waves when compared to the younger age groups.

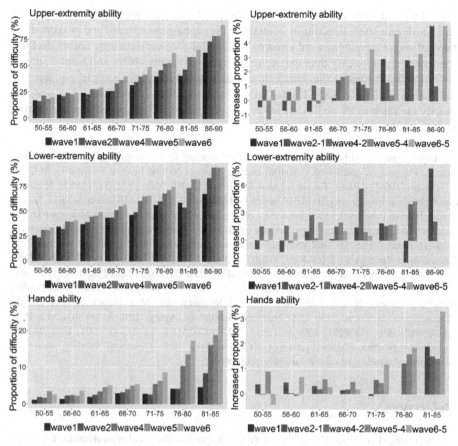

Fig. 2. The proportion of older adults with difficulties in upper-extremity, lower-extremity and hand abilities in each age group across waves and the increased proportion of older adults who had difficulties in the corresponding motor ability compared with last wave.

4 Conclusions

This study analyzed data from the SHARE study in order to compare the gait speed of participants in certain European countries and China. The results showed that older Chinese adults walked 0.31 m/s faster than older adults in Europe, and this difference in gait speed can reveal cultural and regional differences to a certain extent. This study divided the motor ability into upper-extremity ability, lower-extremity ability and hand ability, inspired by the motor development trend of children, and found that the gait speed of respondents differed significantly between those who reported at least one difficulty in upper-extremity ability and those who reported no difficulty. Slower gait speed was associated with worse upper-extremity ability, with a similar effect observed in lower-extremity ability and hand ability.

The longitudinal data for gait speed, chair stand time, grip strength and motor ability showed that the physical abilities of older adults not only declined, but declined at a faster rate after the age of 66 years. The older the participant, the more quickly their motor abilities degenerated. In addition, contrary to the cephalocaudal trend and proximodistal trend of motor development of children, older adults' lower-extremity ability declined sooner and more quickly than the decline in upper-extremity ability and hand ability.

Some limitations of this study should be noted. Firstly, the sample was not representative of older adults in China. Secondly, the methods of measuring gait were not exactly the same in all studies, therefore, the comparison of gait speed across countries requires more in-depth study.

Acknowledgment. This work was supported by funding from Chongqing Municipal Natural Science Foundation (cstc2016jcyjA0406) and the National Natural Science Foundation of China (Grants no. 71661167006). This paper uses data from SHARE Waves 1, 2, 3 (SHARELIFE), 4, 5 and 6 (DOIs: https://doi.org/10.6103/share.w1.611, https://doi.org/10.6103/share.w2.611, https://doi.org/10.6103/share.w3.611, https://doi.org/10.6103/share.w4.611, https://doi.org/10.6103/share.w5.611, https://doi.org/10.6103/share.w6.611), see Börsch-Supan et al. [28] for methodological details. The SHARE data collection has been primarily funded by the European Commission through FP5 (QLK6-CT-2001-00360), FP6 (SHARE-I3: RII-CT-2006-062193, COMPARE: CIT5-CT-2005-028857, SHARELIFE: CIT4-CT-2006-028812) and FP7 (SHARE-PREP: N°211909, SHARE-LEAP: N°227822, SHARE M4: N°261982). Additional funding from the German Ministry of Education and Research, the Max Planck Society for the Advancement of Science, the U.S. National Institute on Aging (U01_AG09740-13S2, P01_AG005842, P01_AG08291, P30_AG12815, R21_AG025169, Y1-AG-4553-01, IAG_BSR06-11, OGHA_04-064, HHSN271201300071C) and from various national funding sources is gratefully acknowledged (see www.share-project.org).

References

1. Atkinson, H.H., et al.: Cognitive function, gait speed decline, and comorbidities: the health, aging and body composition study. J. Gerontol. Ser. A **62**(8), 844–850 (2007)
2. Fitzpatrick, A.L., et al.: Associations of gait speed and other measures of physical function with cognition in a healthy cohort of elderly persons. J. Gerontol. A Biol. Sci. Med. Sci. **62**(11), 1244–1251 (2007)
3. Cuoco, A., Callahan, D.M., Sayers, S., Frontera, W.R., Bean, J., Fielding, R.A.: Impact of muscle power and force on gait speed in disabled older men and women. J. Gerontol. A Biol. Sci. Med. Sci. **59**(11), 1200–1206 (2004)
4. Ferrucci, L., et al.: Subsystems contributing to the decline in ability to walk: bridging the gap between epidemiology and geriatric practice in the inchianti study. J. Am. Geriatr. Soc. **48**(12), 1618–1625 (2000)
5. Holtzer, R., Verghese, J., Xue, X., Lipton, R.B.: Cognitive processes related to gait velocity: results from the Einstein aging study. Neuropsychology **20**(2), 215–223 (2006)
6. Visser, M., et al.: Muscle mass, muscle strength, and muscle fat infiltration as predictors of incident mobility limitations in well-functioning older persons. J. Gerontol. A Biol. Sci. Med. Sci. **60**(3), 324–333 (2005)
7. Newman, A.B., et al.: Association of long-distance corridor walk performance with mortality, cardiovascular disease, mobility limitation, and disability. JAMA **295**(17), 2018 (2006)

8. Studenski, S., et al.: Physical performance measures in the clinical setting. J. Am. Geriatr. Soc. **51**(3), 314–322 (2003)
9. Thelen, E.: The (re)discovery of motor development: learning new things from an old field. Dev. Psychol. **25**(6), 946–949 (1989)
10. Berk, L.: Development Through the Lifespan. Pearson Education India, Bengaluru (2017)
11. Majnemer, A., Barr, R.G.: Influence of supine sleep positioning on early motor milestone acquisition. Dev. Med. Child Neurol. **47**(6), 370–376 (2005)
12. Scrutton, D.: Influence of supine sleep positioning on early motor milestone acquisition. Dev. Med. Child Neurol. **47**(6), 364 (2005)
13. Seymour, S.C., Seymour, S.C.: Women, Family, and Child Care in India: A World in Transition. Cambridge University Press, Cambridge (1999)
14. Börsch-Supan, A.: Survey of Health, Aging and Retirement in Europe (SHARE) Wave 1. Release version: 6.1.1.SHARE-ERIC. Dataset (2018)
15. Börsch-Supan, A.: Survey of Health, Aging and Retirement in Europe (SHARE) Wave 2. Release version 6.1.1. SHARE-ERIC. Dataset (2018)
16. Börsch-Supan, A.: Survey of Health, Aging and Retirement in Europe (SHARE) Wave 4. Release version: 6.1.1 SHARE-ERIC. Dataset (2018)
17. Börsch-Supan, A.: Survey of Health, Aging and Retirement in Europe (SHARE) Wave 5. Release version: 6.1.1. SHARE-ERIC. Dataset (2018)
18. Börsch-Supan, A.: Survey of Health, Aging and Retirement in Europe (SHARE) Wave 6. Release version: 6.1.1 SHARE-ERIC. Dataset (2018)
19. Zhong, R., Rau, P.-L.P., Yan, X.: Application of smart bracelet to monitor frailty-related gait parameters of older Chinese adults: a preliminary study: Smart bracelet for gait assessment. Geriatr. Gerontol. Int. **18**(9), 1366–1371 (2018)
20. Bohannon, R.W.: Comfortable and maximum walking speed of adults aged 20–79 years: reference values and determinants. Age Ageing **26**(1), 15–19 (1997)
21. Verropoulou, G.: Key elements composing self-rated health in older adults: a comparative study of 11 European countries. Eur. J. Ageing **6**(3), 213–226 (2009)
22. Wang, T., et al.: Weak grip strength and cognition predict functional limitation in older Europeans: predictors of functional limitation. J. Am. Geriatr. Soc. **67**(1), 93–99 (2019)
23. de Souto Barreto, P., Cesari, M., Andrieu, S., Vellas, B., Rolland, Y.: Physical activity and incident chronic diseases: a longitudinal observational study in 16 European countries. Am. J. Prev. Med. **52**(3), 373–378 (2017)
24. Marques, A., Peralta, M., Sarmento, H., Martins, J., González Valeiro, M.: Associations between vigorous physical activity and chronic diseases in older adults: a study in 13 European countries. Eur. J. Public Health **28**(5), 950–955 (2018)
25. Ahrenfeldt, L.J., Lindahl-Jacobsen, R., Rizzi, S., Thinggaard, M., Christensen, K., Vaupel, J.W.: Comparison of cognitive and physical functioning of Europeans in 2004–2005 and 2013. Int. J. Epidemiol. **47**(5), 1518–1528 (2018)
26. Chu, L.-W., Chiu, A.Y.Y., Chi, I.: Impact of falls on the balance, gait, and activities of daily living functioning in community-dwelling chinese older adults. J. Gerontol. Ser. A **61**(4), 399–404 (2006)
27. Li, X., Shu, B., Gu, X., Jiang, W., Lv, L.: Temporal-spatial parameters of gait: reference data of normal subjects from Chinese adults. Chin. J. Rehabil. Med. **27**(3), 227–230 (2012)
28. Börsch-Supan, A., et al.: Data resource profile: the survey of health, ageing and retirement in Europe (SHARE). Int. J. Epidemiol. **42**(4), 992–1001 (2013)

The Use of Interactive Tables in Promoting Wellbeing in Specific User Groups

Alice Good[1] , Omobolanle Omisade[1] , Claire Ancient[2(✉)] ,
and Elisavet Andrikopoulou[1]

[1] School of Computing, University of Portsmouth, Portsmouth, UK
{alice.good, omobolanle.omisade,
elisavet.andrikopoulou}@port.ac.uk
[2] Department of Digital Futures, University of Winchester, Winchester, UK
claire.ancient@winchester.ac.uk

Abstract. Dementia is estimated to affect 50 million people worldwide [1].
A significant proportion of residents in residential homes are people with
moderate to severe dementia [2, 3]. Apathy amongst them is a major issue [3–5].
Tovertafel is an interactive table that was designed to reduce apathy and to
facilitate play for people with moderate to severe dementia [6].

This mixed methods study has three aims; firstly to explore the Tovertafels'
impact upon the wellbeing of people with moderate to severe dementia in a
residential care home from the professional carers' perspective; secondly to
explore the impact of Tovertafel on the wellbeing of these carers; and thirdly to
explore whether Tovertafel has any impact on the quality and quantity of visits
by the family of the residents. Semi-structured interviews were conducted with
12 carers and The Work Related Quality of Life Scale (WRQoL) [7] was used to
explore carers' perspective of the extent to which Tovertafel improved their own
wellbeing and the quality of their working life.

Some key findings indicate that visiting families interacted more with their
loved-one when they are using the Tovertafel. Residents do use Tovertafel when
it is switched on, but many needed to be initially prompted by staff. Tovertafel
did have a positive impact upon residents' mood during the time it was used and
a short time after. Tovertafel also had an impact on improving interaction
between carers and residents when it was on. Tovertafel's most successful
games are reported as being the bubbles and puzzles, and carers also stressed the
importance of identifying an appropriate location for the Tovertafel, to enable
optimum usage.

Keywords: Dementia · Wellbeing · Apathy · Mood · Interaction

1 Introduction

Dementia is an umbrella term for a range of progressive conditions that affect the brain.
The most common symptoms of dementia, which tends to develop gradually over time,
are memory loss, mood changes, difficulty with reasoning, and problems with communication [8]. The number of people with dementia is increasing at a rapid rate, and it
is estimated to affect 50 million people worldwide [1]. In the next five years, the

© Springer Nature Switzerland AG 2019
J. Zhou and G. Salvendy (Eds.): HCII 2019, LNCS 11593, pp. 506–519, 2019.
https://doi.org/10.1007/978-3-030-22015-0_39

number of people with dementia in the UK is expected to reach 1 million [1, 2]. For those with dementia aged over 60 years, 55% have mild dementia, 32% have moderate dementia, and 12% have severe dementia [2].

A significant proportion of residents in residential and nursing homes are people living with moderate to severe dementia [2, 3]. Apathy amongst these residents is a major issue [3–5] and is seen as the most common behavioral change experienced by people living with dementia [6]. Research indicates that 90% of nursing home residents with dementia experience apathy, which negatively influences their physical, cognitive, and emotional wellbeing [6, 9]. These findings are worrisome, as the absence of physical activity correlates with the decline of physical health as well as cognitive capacities [6, 10].

Tovertafel (TT) is an interactive table that was designed to stimulate nursing home residents living with moderate to severe dementia with the aim of reducing feelings of apathy [6]. Research suggests that by enabling playful and stimulating activities, apathy can be reduced [8, 11]. The research presented in this paper aimed to explore the potential for TT to improve the wellbeing of people living with moderate to severe dementia. It also explored any impact TT has upon the wellbeing of professional carers working within the residential care homes, as well as potential effect upon the quality or quantity of visits from families of the residents.

This study evaluates TT's impact on wellbeing from a professional carer's perspective in a longitudinal mixed-methods study. Qualitative and quantitative data were generated by conducting both interviews and questionnaires. It is anticipated that the output from this exploratory research will provide increased confidence in the effectiveness of TT to improve the wellbeing of specified target groups and may increase acceptance of the system.

1.1 Aims and Objectives

The research aims to explore whether the TT has the potential to improve the wellbeing of people within three user groups. Firstly, people with moderate to severe dementia residing in residential homes. Secondly, the wellbeing of professional carers, termed as staff, working within the residential care homes. Thirdly, any impact on the quality and quantity of visits from the resident's family.

The results of this research aim to show an improvement in wellbeing for both residents and staff when a TT is in use. The three objectives of this research include:

1. To explore the impact of TT on the wellbeing of people living with moderate to severe dementia in a residential care home from the staff's perspective.
2. To explore the impact of TT on the wellbeing of staff in a residential care home which caters for people living with moderate to severe dementia.
3. To explore the quality and quantity of visits by the family of those who live in the residential care home for people with moderate to severe dementia from the staff's perspective.

2 Method

2.1 Design and Procedure

Based on the aims of this study, we conducted a longitudinal mixed-methods approach using qualitative and quantitative methods [13]. In this study, the quantitative and qualitative methods provide breadth and depth to understand the use of TT in promoting wellbeing in people living with moderate to severe dementia and their professional carers. The participants for this study are carers working at a residential home for people living with moderate to severe dementia in the UK. The qualitative and quantitative data were gathered from the same population. We concurrently surveyed and interviewed professional carers of people living with dementia. This included drawing their opinions on the impact upon wellbeing when TT was not in use and when in use. For this study the people living with dementia are referred to as "residents".

2.2 Measures

The interviews were conducted face-to-face and audio-recorded. Professional carers were asked questions on their own wellbeing, the wellbeing of the residents under their care, and their perspective on the quality and quantity of family visits. These qualitative semi-structured open questions were informed by Qualidem [14], a quality of life observation instrument rated by professional caregivers of persons with mild to very severe dementia living in residential settings. Since this is an exploratory study, we seek to explore the views of professional carers on how they perceive the wellbeing of people living with moderate to severe dementia. Professional carers were asked to provide their opinion on residents' wellbeing retrospectively and currently. This is in relation to a period of TT being turned off for one week and after a week of it being turned on.

Table 1. The six subscales of the WRQoL scale

Subscale	Name	Abbreviation	Measure of:
1	Job and career satisfaction	JCS	Job and career satisfaction
2	General Wellbeing	GWB	Everyday happiness and satisfaction
3	Home-work	HWI	Accommodating family and work commitments
4	Stress at work	SAW	Demands in the workplace
5	Control at work	CAW	Level of control carer feel they have over decisions at work
6	Working conditions	WCS	Physical working environment

The Work Related Quality of Life (WRQoL) scale was used in the current study to measure six factors [7] (as shown in Table 1). This scale was developed for health care workers in England to assess the quality of their working life [15, 16]. The WRQoL scale has robust psychometrics, good reliability and validity when tested with healthcare workers [7]. The WRQoL scale contains 24 items each evaluated on a 5-point Likert scale (1 = strongly disagree to 5 = strongly agree) and produces six subscales which link to the Quality of Working Life [17]. Professional carers were asked to complete the survey after one week of TT being turned off and then again after the TT had been switched on for one week.

2.3   Participants

Participants were professional carers working at a residential home for people living with moderate to severe dementia in Hampshire, a county in the UK. All of the professional carers were given the option to take part in the study, via communication from the manager of the residential home. 12 of the staff voluntarily offered to participate. These participants were asked to complete the WRQoL scale after one week of the TT being turned off and again, after it had been turned on for a week. They were then interviewed on their perspective on whether TT has any impact on wellbeing, for both themselves and residents within the home. Participants were advised that they will be provided with feedback if required and they had the right to withdraw at any time during completing the questionnaire and interview. Once participants read the information sheet and signed the consent form, the questionnaire was completed and the researchers conducted the interviews. Confidentiality of participant's responses and the right to withdraw from the survey were outlined via instructions to the professional carers and in the provided information sheets.

2.4   Analysis

The analysis of qualitative and quantitative data included the following steps

1. Mixed methods data analysis involved analysing the quantitative and the qualitative data
2. Content analysis was used for qualitative analysis;
3. NVivo version 12 was used to support and document the qualitative analysis;
4. Descriptive statistics were used to analyse the quantitative data in Microsoft Excel 2016.

3   Results

3.1   Qualitative Study

Recent literature that informed the design of the qualitative study [3–8] indicated that there could be potential for TT in improving the wellbeing of people living with dementia, their carers, and family. Some of the themes derived from this literature as well as the Qualidem scale [14] include:

- Level of engagement
- Relationship of people living with dementia and their carers
- Mood change

- Restlessness
- Quantity and quality of family visits

Several other themes emerged from the qualitative thematic data analysis [18]. These emergent themes were categorised into: engagement using prompts; limited usage time; TT location; individuality; bubbles, popular games.

All of the 12 carers who agreed to participate in the study were interviewed.

3.2   Engagement

Participants reported positive changes in the engagement of residents when interacting with TT. This indicates that using the interactive table facilitated reduced apathy and helped people living with dementia to interact and concentrate more. This also implies that the provision of a TT system in the home creates the opportunity to keep the residents active and busy. Quotes from professional carers in relation to 'engagement' include:

P06 - "…I would say it changes when it is on because they seem more interested in what you are doing…"
P11 - "…It reduces boredom definitely…"
P12 - "…They have been happy when they play with it" and "…the one that uses it enjoy it…"

3.3   Relationship Between People with Dementia and Their Carers

The use of the TT table helped facilitate a positive relationship between people living with dementia and their carers. Some participants stated that the residents often want to discuss their experience in relation to interacting with the table, after using it. This then helped to create the opportunity to have further discussion, and strengthen the relationship between the carers and the residents. This is evident in some of the comments from the participants.

P07 - "…It is better when it is switched on because you interact with them more…"
P06 - "…They socialise with you a bit better…"
P09 - "…They talk to you about it especially about the puzzle…"

Participants reported that some TT activities and games helped to improve the communication between them and the residents. With these activities, the residents seemed happier, laughed more, and the carers seemed more likely to interact with them. Some of the quotes from the participants include:

P07 - "…The bubble one helps, and the ball one is more enjoyable…"
P09 - "…They talk to you about it especially about the puzzles…"

Interestingly some expressed that the use of TT also facilitates improved interaction for them as carers and subsequent positive effect on the people they are caring for. One comment was:

P05 - "…you are more interactive with the service user when it is on…"

3.4   Mood Change

The findings from this study suggest a positive effect of TT on the mood of the residents. They remained happy after they finished using TT. This, however, was short-lived as expected and in line with previous research on short attention span with people living with dementia [18]. It was commented that when residents take part in the TT activities, they interacted well with both other residents and staff, and appeared happy, however, this did not last all day. Comments from carers include:

P01 - "...They are happy for a short time..."
P03 - "...When we are taking part in it they interact, and they are happy and [Tovertafel] uplifts their mood in that moment, when they walk away, they are still in the uplifting happy mood, but it does not last all day..."

3.5   Change in Restlessness

The carers expressed that the use of TT helped to keep the residents occupied. Consistent feedback indicates that the use of TT helped encourage the residents to be calmer. Residents did not appear to be anxious after sessions using TT. For example, one quote:

P02 - "...They are a bit calmer when the table is on. Not anxious..."

3.6   Quality of Family Visit Changes

There is consistent feedback from all of the participants, which indicates that using TT has a positive effect on the quality of visits from the residents' families. Families interacted more with their loved ones when the TT is switched on. Some of the feedback includes:

P03 - "...when the table is on the families tend to go around it. And when it is not on they notice it was not on..."
P11 - "...They sit with it and play games with it, and they interact with them more, rather than just come and sit there with a cup of tea..."
P03 - "...When the table is on the families, engage more and interact with their family members who are here. I think it is good because it builds up the interaction between families and they have something to do together instead just sitting here..."

Carers also reported that families appear to be happier when TT is switched.

P01 - "...when they visit and see the table on they seem happy..."
P04 - "...It builds up the interaction between families, and they have something to do together..."

Furthermore, families that visit with children would go over to play and interact with TT. This appeared to encourage residents to join their loved ones in engaging with the system.

P05 - "...It brings them together a little bit more..."

3.7   Engagement Using Prompts

Carers reported having to prompt residents to use TT, which subsequently helps keeps the residents engaged. Residents only seemed to be interested when their carers initiate the interactive table activities. This indicates that changes in the quality of engagement of their residents are based on prompts from carers. Comments from carers include:

P01- "...They do engage, no they kind of take-part in it but you have to prompt them to take part in it..."

P08 - "...we encourage them to sit and play..."

P01 - "...we prompt them saying let's play like this, let's do like this..."

P03 - "...you have to prompt them to take part..."

3.8   TT Location

Some of the carers indicated that the TT would not only be used more but also be more effective if it was located in a specific location that was also regularly evaluated to ensure it facilitated optimum usage. In the case of the residential home featured in this study, the TT is located in the dining room. The feedback suggested:

P10 - "...I think it would be better if it were in a different location..."

P05 - "...it would be better if it were in a different location" and "...You have like the pool table in a pool table area, that sort of thing. Just in the dining area, people don't know but if it were sort of in a room where you have soft play or lights and things like that I think it would be used a lot more. Like a sensory room ..."

P06 - "...it should be in a different area because we use this as a dining area sometimes and you don't really associate that with playing. It should be in a sensory room or in one of the lounges..."

3.9   Consistency in Switching the TT on

Carers reported that residents are attracted to the interactive table when it was switched on. In addition, residents' families were also interested in using the table and seemed to notice when it is not in use. Observations from carers include:

P12 - "....I think more residents are attracted to it when it is on..."

P03 - "....when it is on they take part..."

P05 - "...I have to say when the table is on the families tend to go around it. And when it is not on, they notice it was not on..."

P11 - "...When it is switched on they engage..."

P04 - "...When the table first came, and we told them the table was on, they used it..."

3.10   Limited Usage Time

People with moderate to severe dementia find it hard to self-initiate and that their concentration can be poor [18, 19]. This is consistent with our finding in this study that although TT seems to improve the residents' mood, the table is infrequently used by the residents without initiation from carers or loved ones, and sometimes for short durations. An explanation for limited usage time could be because people living with moderate to severe dementia have limited memory capacity and short concentration [19]. Comments include:

> P08 - "....they will only play it for a very short time because their concentration is very short. They will do it for a little while...."
> P09 - "...one minute they are with you and next minute in their mind they are somewhere else. And that's when they just get up and walk away..."

Furthermore, not all carers may be aware of the importance of encouraging residents to use it.

3.11   Individuality

Results from this study suggest that the extent of interaction using TT depends on the individual personality and general preferences of the person living with dementia. This finding resonates with previous research in the technology acceptance and personality domain [20]. A few professional carers shared:

> P04 - "...some of them like the table more, and they do tap it and find it interesting. I think all depends on the resident individually...." and "...it is just a case of each individual liking or not to use the table..."
> P06 - "...it depends on the person though, because you can have an actual conversation with some of them and they will enjoy it, whilst others they get frustrated and they walk away..."

3.12   Popular Games

Carers reported that a few features of TT were more likely to be used and enjoyed than others. Puzzles and games seem to improve the engagement between the carers and residents. Feedback indicates that the most popular games are bubbles, ball and puzzles.

> P11 - "...Some of the games are better than others, and some they enjoy more than others. The bubble one helps, and the ball one are more enjoyable..."

Puzzles also provided a good talking and engagement point, which needed to be initiated by the professional carers.

> P09 - "...I think they engage more with the puzzle ones because you can do more with them..."

Furthermore, families of the residents also appeared to enjoy playing with the TT games, especially the one that displays quotes:

> P05 - "...there are a lot of family members who come in who were with their clients and obviously sit around there and they remember the quote of them being children..."

3.13   Professional Carers Wellbeing

Although the majority of the professional carers did not notice any impact upon their own wellbeing when using TT, a few did highlight a positive mood change. For example:

P06 - "…We had a giggle playing the games, and this is a good thing. Keeps you thinking…"

This indicates that carers were more likely to interact and engage more with residents when TT is switched on. Feedback from carers included:

P07 - "…It is better when it is switched on because you interact with them more…"
P06 - "….they socialise with you a bit better…."
P05 - "…It is a little more engagement with people. You get together a bit more…."

3.14   Results Based on the WRQoL Scale

Whilst there were 12 carers who agreed to participate in the study, only 8 attempted to take part in the quantitative study using the WRQoL scale. Of the eight participants, five responses were not appropriate for the factor analytical technique as they had a least one missing value and were removed from the dataset. Whilst the numbers for the quantitative study are very low, the results were analysed for exploratory purposes.

As previously mentioned, the WRQoL scale can be used to measure the overall work-related quality of life, and this was adopted in this study [17]. All the responses across all six subscales were recorded on a five-point Likert-type scale. Responses to the WRQoL scale measured within this study shows the effect of the TT on the quality of life and wellbeing of the professional carer when it is switched on or off. Carers reported that their work-life balance and the extent to which they receive support from their employer regarding their home life increased when the TT is on. Their physical working environment is satisfactory with the provision of the TT at the residential home. The carers also reported that the level of control they have increased when the TT is on. Similarly, carers reported that there is a balance with the demand at workplace when the TT is switched off or on (Table 2).

Table 2. Summary of changes to WRQoL Subscales when TT is switched off and on

Subscale	TT off	TT on
GWB	4.17 (SD = 0.10, N = 3)	4.14 (SD = 0.17, N = 3)
HWI	4.33 (SD = 0.31, N = 3)	4.38 (SD = 0.32, N = 3)
WCS	4.10 (SD = 0.25, N = 3)	4.10 (SD = 0.25, N = 3)
CAW	3.76 (SD = 0.24, N = 3)	3.90 (SD = 0.21, N = 3)
SAW	3.00 (SD = 0.35, N = 3)	2.86 (SD = 0.32, N = 3)

The differences are generally minor, and 3 had almost identical scores during the time TT was off and when it was switched back on. The most noticeable difference between the times TT was on and off was in CAW and SAW factors. This might be explained in that carers who identified differences in these two factors, also mentioned the themes of mood changes and quality of family visit changes. There were no overall noticeable changes regarding the GWB and HWI factors. There are subtle differences in the rest of the factors JCS, WCS and the overall score, which are not considered substantial enough to provide a sound conclusion.

4   Discussion

The purpose of this study is to explore TT's impact upon the wellbeing of people living with moderate to severe dementia residing in residential homes and, furthermore, the wellbeing of professional carers working within these homes. In addition to the collated 'themes' that informed the structure of the interview, several other themes emerged from the study. Recommendations in relation to using TT to improve the wellbeing of people with dementia, and their professional carers will be discussed.

During the interviews, carers reported that TT has a positive impact on the level of engagement of the people living with dementia. This was seen to be a result of the varieties of play and activity available within the system. The analysis from the interviews consistently suggest that residents interact more with their loved-ones when they are sat around the TT. This finding supports the original research behind TT in that it facilitates engagement and improves play activity [6]. Findings from the study presented here, also suggest that residents would discuss their experience using TT afterwards and this subsequently creates the opportunity to engage in further discussion with carers, which helps in building on engagement and improving the carer-resident relationship. Analysis of the interviews suggest that the families of the residents should be encouraged to use the table more often given the quality of interaction observed. Furthermore, the analysis indicates that families who visit with children would go over to play and interact with the interactive table. This encouraged residents to join their loved ones in engaging with the TT. Engaging in activities has a positive impact upon the psychological wellbeing of people with dementia [21, 22]. Similarly, literature indicates that involvement with activities is associated with reduced risk and slower progression of dementia [23].

The use of "prompts" seems to be an important factor given carers suggested that residents mostly engage when they are prompted to take part in TT activities. Research suggests that people with dementia are highly dependent on the use of prompts and cue facilitations by their carer or family [24–26]. This is explained by impaired cognitive ability, given the difficulty remembering appropriate sequence of actions [24–26]. Other research shows that reminders or prompts seem to be particularly effective for elderly patients, especially those with dementia [19, 20]. It is suggested that to enable optimum impact from TT, residents should be regularly prompted to interact with TT.

People living with dementia often have shorter attention spans [18]. The carers included within this study also mention this difficulty for the person living with dementia to maintain concentration for a significant period of time. This, coupled with the comments that the positive emotional effects of TT do not persist, suggests that the TT should be switched on regularly for short periods of time throughout the day. This may support the maintenance of positive emotions during the course of the whole day.

The location of TT also emerged as an important factor with comments from the interviews suggesting that having the system in a specially designated area could facilitate cues for the residents that it relates to a specific activity. In the residential home used in this study, the TT is located in the dining area. Residents sometimes confused activity time for tea/lunch time. Carers suggested moving the TT to either a sensory area that could potentially include further games and objects or to move it to a designated area. Increased use of activity spaces improves social interaction amongst residents [24, 25]. It is suggested that TT should be situated in a specifically designed activity environment to encourage increased acceptance and usage.

Furthermore, there is some potential in encouraging carers to engage in the TT. It was identified that TT is used predominantly when a resident and a carer are using it together as a one-to-one form of interaction. Therefore, if the residential home encourages their professional carers to use TT, this subsequently could encourage residents to participate.

The results do show that TT had some impact upon carers' wellbeing. Using the WRQoL scale, carers did not report significant differences in their own wellbeing when the TT was switched on or off, however the sample size was very small. The interviews with a much larger sample size did indicate positive impact upon wellbeing during the interactions with residents. Caring for people with dementia can be stressful, and research suggests that carers have less time and opportunity to engage in wellbeing activities [26]. Carers may not have seen TT as an opportunity to engage in a wellbeing activity, nor might that TT have any positive impact upon their own wellbeing. Engaging in activities has been associated with an increase in positive mood, lowering the risk for chronic illness and increased stamina, which may improve carers' overall health and ability to perform their caregiving duties. Furthermore, research shows a correlation between caregivers' health and wellbeing with job satisfaction and retention [27, 28]. It is therefore recommended that carers should be prompted to engage with TT due to the potential positive impact on their own wellbeing.

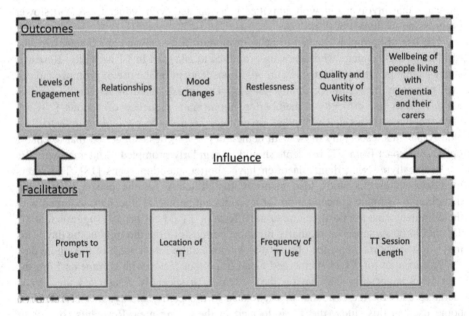

Fig. 1. Proposed TT influence model

The findings from this study informed the development of a proposed TT influence model (Fig. 1). This model suggests a two-layered approach with facilitators that could help encourage increased usage and may inform a subsequent improvement wellbeing of people with dementia and their professional carer. For example, to increase levels of engagement facilitated by the use of TT, there is a need to establish if users are prompted to use the system and it is in the right location. It is also important to ensure that the system is frequently switched on and the usage time is appropriate for the people living with dementia. This could also be applied with improving the wellbeing of the professional carers, the relationship of people with dementia, their mood, restlessness and the quality and quantity of family visits.

5 Conclusion

This study contributes to the body of knowledge that TT has a positive effect upon the wellbeing of people living with moderate to severe dementia in residential homes, by improving their mood, reducing apathy and restlessness, as well as increasing levels of engagement. Furthermore, TT helped improve relationships between professional carers and these residents by facilitating playful activities. TT also facilitated increased quality of family visits when they are actively using the TT to interact with their loved ones. This research also indicates that TT can improve carers' overall health and ability to perform their caregiving duties, as well as increasing positive mood, lowering the risk for chronic illness and increasing stamina.

The results of this study were distilled into a potential TT Influence Model, which hopes to inform the facilitators and outcomes of effective use of TT. Future research should investigate whether this model contains all the relevant factors, and if it is effective at demonstrating how facilitators influence positive outcomes when using TT.

In this study a convenience sample of professional carers caring for people with moderate to severe dementia was utilised. The sample size and findings may not reflect professional carers of people with moderate to severe dementia in general, however, there are no specific rules for sample size in qualitative inquiry. Sample size depends on what you want to know, the purpose of the inquiry, what's at stake, what will be useful, what will have credibility, and what can be done with available resources [29]. The sample size of the qualitative study was deemed appropriate for an exploratory study. The quantitative study using the WRQoL scale was recognised as having a very small sample size however the results indicate that there is potential for carrying out further research to explore these findings further. As with all research of subjective experiences, there is a possibility of recall bias. Moreover, there is very little data that supports benefit to carers. This, however, is an exploratory study, which generated some positive findings and should therefore be viewed as a prelude to further research with an extended sample size.

In conclusion, there is a need to further explore the impact TT has on the professional carers and other staff of nursing homes in a larger study. Additional observational studies with both the professional carers, family and residents interacting with TT could help provide increased evidence on TT's impact upon wellbeing.

Acknowledgements. This research was supported by Shift8.

Ethics. This study was given a favourable opinion by the Faculty of Technology ethical review committee at the University of Portsmouth.

References

1. Frankova, H.: Dementia is a disease and diseases can be treated. Nurs. Resid. Care **19**(8), 464–466 (2017)
2. Prince, M., et al.: Dementia UK: Update, 2nd edn., vol. 91 (2017). https://www.alzheimers. org.uk/sites/default/files/migrate/downloads/dementia_uk_update.pdf
3. Alzheimer Scotland: Activities: a guide for carers of people with dementia (2005). https:// www.alzscot.org/assets/0002/9343/AlzScot_Activities_Booklet_WEB.pdf
4. Brodaty, H., Burns, K.: Nonpharmacological management of apathy in dementia: a systematic review. Am. J. Geriatr. Psychiatry **20**(7), 549–564 (2012). https://doi.org/10. 1097/JGP.0B013E31822BE242
5. Holmén, K., Ericsson, K., Winblad, B.: Social and emotional loneliness among non-demented and demented elderly people. Arch. Gerontol. Geriatr. **31**(3), 177–192 (2000). https://doi.org/10.1016/S0167-4943(00)00070-4
6. Anderiesen, H.: Playful design for activation: co-designing serious games for people with moderate to severe dementia to reduce apathy (2017). https://doi.org/10.4233/UUID: EBEEF0FA-46FE-4947-86C1-C765A583770A
7. Van Laar, D., Edwards, J.A., Easton, S.: The work-related quality of life scale for healthcare workers. J. Adv. Nurs. **60**(3), 325–333 (2007). https://doi.org/10.1111/j.1365-2648.2007. 04409.x
8. Dyer, S.M., Harrison, S.L., Laver, K., Whitehead. C., Crotty, M.: An overview of systematic reviews of pharmacological and non-pharmacological interventions for the treatment of behavioral and psychological symptoms of dementia. Int. Psychogeriatr. [Internet] **30**(3), 295–309 (2018). https://www.cambridge.org/core/article/an-overview-of-systematic-revi ews-of-pharmacological-and-nonpharmacological-interventions-for-the-treatment-of-behavi oral-and-psychological-symptoms-of-dementia/DCA87B8BC78047977CB92427BF3F4FC3
9. Kolanowski, A.M., Litaker, M., Buettner, L.: Efficacy of theory-based activities for behavioral symptoms of dementia. Nurs. Res. **54**(4) (2005). https://journals.lww.com/nursin gresearchonline/Fulltext/2005/07000/Efficacy_of_Theory_Based_Activities_for_ Behavioral.3.aspx
10. Colcombe, S., Kramer, A.F.: Fitness effects on the cognitive function of older adults: a meta-analytic study. Psychol. Sci. **14**(2), 125–130 (2003). https://doi.org/10.1111/1467-9280.t01-1-01430
11. Blondell, S.J., Hammersley-Mather, R., Veerman, J.L.: Does physical activity prevent cognitive decline and dementia?: A systematic review and meta-analysis of longitudinal studies. BMC Public Health **14**, 510 (2014). https://doi.org/10.1186/1471-2458-14-510
12. Heyn, P., Abreu, B.C., Ottenbacher, K.J.: The effects of exercise training on elderly persons with cognitive impairment and dementia: a meta-analysis. Arch. Phys. Med. Rehabil. **85**(10), 1694–1704 (2004). https://doi.org/10.1016/J.APMR.2004.03.019
13. Creswell, J.W., Plano Clark, V.L.: Designing and Conducting Mixed Methods Research. SAGE, Los Angeles (2017). http://search.ebscohost.com/login.aspx?direct=true&db=cat 01619a&AN=up.1260349&site=eds-live

14. Ettema, T.P., Dröes, R.-M., de Lange, J., Mellenbergh, G.J., Ribbe, M.W.: QUALIDEM: development and evaluation of a dementia specific quality of life instrument—validation. Int. J. Geriatr. Psychiatry [Internet] **22**(5), 424–430 (2007). http://doi.wiley.com/10.1002/gps.1692

15. Danna, K., Griffin, R.W.: Health and well-being in the workplace: a review and synthesis of the literature. J. Manag. **25**(3), 357–384 (1999). https://doi.org/10.1177/014920639902500305

16. Zeng, X., et al.: Work-related quality of life scale among Singaporean nurses. Asian Biomed. **5**(4), 467–474 (2011)

17. Easton, S., van Laar, D.: User Manual for the Work-Related Quality of Life (WRQoL) Scale. [Electronic Resource] : A Measure of Quality of Working Life. University of Portsmouth, Quality of Working Life, Portsmouth (2018). http://search.ebscohost.com/login.aspx?direct=true&db=cat01619a&AN=up.1276003&site=eds-live

18. Braun, V., Clarke, V.: Using thematic analysis in psychology. Qual. Res. Psychol. **3**(2), 77–101 (2006). http://eprints.uwe.ac.uk/11735

19. Lyketsos, C.G., Steinberg, M., Tschanz, J.T., Norton, M.C., Steffens, D.C., Breitner, J.C.S.: Mental and behavioral disturbances in dementia: findings from the cache county study on memory in aging. Am. J. Psychiatry [Internet] **157**(5), 708–714 (2000). https://ajp.psychiatryonline.org/doi/abs/10.1176/appi.ajp.157.5.708

20. Svendsen, G.B., Johnsen, J.A.K., Almås-Sørensen, L., Vittersø, J.: Personality and technology acceptance: The influence of personality factors on the core constructs of the technology acceptance model. Behav. Inf. Technol. **32**(4), 323–334 (2013)

21. Harmer, B.J., Orrell, M.: What is meaningful activity for people with dementia living in care homes? A comparison of the views of older people with dementia, staff and family carers. Aging Mental Health **12**(5), 548–558 (2008)

22. Marshall, M.J., Hutchinson, S.A.: A critique of research on the use of activities with persons with Alzheimer's disease: a systematic literature review. J. Adv. Nurs. **35**(4), 488–496 (2001)

23. Saczynski, J.S., et al.: The effect of social engagement on incident dementia: the Honolulu-Asia Aging study. Am. J. Epidemiol. **163**(5), 433–440 (2006)

24. Kovach, C., Weisman, G., Chaudhury, H., Calkins, M.: Impacts of a therapeutic environment for dementia care. Am. J. Alzheimer's Dis. **12**(3), 99–110 (1997)

25. Volicer, L., Simard, J., Pupa, J.H., Medrek, R., Riordan, M.E.: Effects of continuous activity programming on behavioral symptoms of dementia. J. Am. Med. Dir. Assoc. **7**(7), 426–431 (2006)

26. Orgeta, V., Miranda-Castillo, C.: Does physical activity reduce burden in carers of people with dementia? A literature review. Int. J. Geriatr. Psych. **29**(8), 771–783 (2014)

27. Perry, L., Gallagher, R., Duffield, C., Sibbritt, D., Bichel-Findlay, J., Nicholls, R.: Does nurses' health affect their intention to remain in their current position? J. Nurs. Manag. **24**, 1088–1097 (2016)

28. Duggleby, W., Cooper, D., Penz, K.: Hope, self-efficacy, spiritual well-being and job satisfaction. J. Adv. Nurs. **65**, 2376–2385 (2009). https://doi.org/10.1111/j.1365-2648.2009.05094.x

29. Marshall, B., Cardon, P., Poddar, A., Fontenot, R.: Does sample size matter in qualitative research?: A review of qualitative interviews in IS research. J. Comput. Inf. Syst. **54**(1), 11–22 (2013)

The Golden Age of Silver Workers?

The Role of Age in the Perception of Increasing Digital Work Environments

Johanna Kluge[✉], Julian Hildebrandt, and Martina Ziefle

Chair of Communication Science, Human Computer Interaction Center,
RWTH Aachen, Campus-Boulevard 57, 52074 Aachen, Germany
kluge@comm.rwth-aachen.de

Abstract. Digitization is progressing intensively, in particular in the world of work. Thereby, intelligent systems, mobile devices, cloud computing, and social media change the development of work and employment by (in parts) replacing employees or changing ways of production. In line with demographic change and in order to face economic, societal, and demographic challenges of a future labor market, it is necessary to consider the integration of aging employees. Therefore, this paper investigates the perception of motivational factors and stress factors triggered by technology in the working context. In addition, factors influencing the individual perception of strains are analyzed. For this purpose, an online survey was conducted (N = 507) asking for agreement to motivational and stressing factors in the context of increasing digital working environments. The results show that the overall motivational factors received a similar evaluation pattern for younger and older participants. However, the younger employees showed stronger agreements to all motivational aspects. Additionally, the results show that the perception of techno-stress factors was significant lower in the older aged group compared to the younger aged group. The study's findings highlight the importance of user diversity for a successful and healthy transformation to a digital work environment putting employees needs and requirements into the center.

Keywords: Digitization · Future of work · Age · Ageing workforce · Techno-stress

1 Introduction

Today we experience a fundamental change of work environments. The turn from industrial work to knowledge based tasks is attended by technological progress. The digitization of the world of work is progressing at a rapid pace. Mobile devices, big data, cloud computing and social media change the development of work and employment fundamentally. Intelligent systems will replace employees, productions will change, professions have to be redefined. This fundamental change leads to challenges for employment, organizational structures, education and social and societal systems. The greatest challenge but also opportunity lies in the shaping of this industrial revolution. In the light of that, research about the rapid changes in the work

© Springer Nature Switzerland AG 2019
J. Zhou and G. Salvendy (Eds.): HCII 2019, LNCS 11593, pp. 520–532, 2019.
https://doi.org/10.1007/978-3-030-22015-0_40

environment is necessary to put the human into center of discussion. Additionally the demographic change will lead to a shift of the population structure, what will additionally influence the future of work. There are more and more people of an advanced age in the working world and less younger people. This leads to several necessary changes in the organization of an aging society, for example with regard to care work, public pension systems but also employment environments. To integrate qualified older workers into organizational structures and planning offers a great potential for society and economy. The strategy to replace older workers by qualified younger workers, as it was and is predominant in economy, is not a functional model for the future of work, if the average age of the workers keeps rising. Although industry already changed partly its view on the potential of advanced aged employees, a focus on the integration of aging employees is necessary, when facing the economic, societal and demographic challenges of a future labor market. Following that it is necessary to understand motivational factors and psychological strains for older employees in the working context – especially with regard to digitization. While in an digitized workspace physical stress factors decrease, psychological stress factors increase. Thus, we will focus in this paper on factors influencing the individual perception of strains by investigating perception of motivational factors and stress factors triggered by technology in the working context.

2 Aging Workforce and the Future of Work

Age and its role in the future of work is coming increasingly into the focus of research. Prejudices about older workers, such as them being no longer productive or having longer absences due to physical limitations in contrast to younger workers, are repeatedly refuted. Studies were able to show that older employees have not more physical issues than younger colleagues in average [1, 2].

Although memory or cognitive processing limitations occur with increasing age, research shows that these be offset by professional experience, acquired knowledge, and learned problem-solving strategies. Studies showed, there is no negative relationship between job performance and age. Additionally, older workers have better strategies to cope with different forms of age related stress [3]. Thus, there is no disadvantage of an older workforce compared to a younger workforce.

On the contrary, it could be shown that older workers tend to have a stronger commitment to the employer organization and additionally tend to have a better relationship with coworkers [4].

Coping with stress, social skills, expert knowledge and a strong commitment to the employer are vital characteristics when facing the future of work.

Demographic change is exacerbating a shortage of skilled workers in the future of work, a fact, which is already noticeable today. Experienced employees are therefore of great importance. And since they are becoming scarce, employee retention is important for successful companies. Moreover, in a globalized world, future work teams will become increasingly heterogeneous, which will increase the demands on employees' social skills [e.g. 5].[1]

In addition to physical, mental and cognitive age-related changes in work, studies have also found motivational changes related to age. With increasing age, employees are less driven by motives like career opportunities and personal development. Motivating factors such as a good working environment, security and a good relationship with colleagues and supervisors become more important [6, 7]. This means that the incentives and support measures for employees in the company should vary according to age. Kooij et al. suggest, that because of the more intrinsic motives in job performance, older workforces may appreciate an enrichment of their work tasks by being a mentor, for example [7, 8].

Thoughts about the future of work must always include considerations about the use of technology in the work process and the associated changes for the employee. The role of age and technology adoption has been examined a lot. Studies found, a difference in adoption and use of technology between younger and older adults. Especially the self-evaluation of older people regarding learnability and ability to use, as well as using confidence proved to be less in contrast to younger people.

Elderly people had the perception of needing more time to learn how to handle a technical system and assumed they would have more difficulties than younger persons [9, 10]. They frequently stated they felt uncomfortable with technical systems and were insecure in dealing with it [e.g. 11]. Studies suggest age has a negative relationship with computer knowledge and interest – both aspects that are positively related to confidence in using technology. Additionally age correlates positive with computer anxiety which in turn is correlating negatively with computer knowledge and interest [12].

The differences in attitude and self-perception of technology use between younger and older adults suggest giving older people special training for the use of technology. This will lower anxiety in dealing with technology and reduce stress for older workers [9, e.g. 13, 14].

2.1 Techno-Stress

Looking at the future of work, we see growing chances and changes due to digitization. Physical stress factors will decrease and psychological stress – especially in the transformation phase – will increase. Mental load such as work related-stress is a major factor influencing health at the future workplace. As studies in the past could show, the use of technology to support work processes can lead to stress in the workforce if the user is not taken into account (e.g., [15]). Stress has negative consequences for the employee him- or herself but also to his/her performance at work [16].

---

[1] It is important to correctly classify all these results on the role of age in the work context. Ageing is a very individual process with many different influencing factors. It is particularly important to keep in mind that individual differences increase with age [e.g. 4].

Stress is a physical and psychological reaction to a situation in which he/she feels or is unable to cope with the task. Techno-Stress describes the inability to find a healthy way to adopt a new technology. This includes the way technology is used, but also the way in which technology changes one's own habitual behavior and environment [17]. For example, the introduction of service mobile phones requires new rules for dealing with accessibility. Employees easily get the feeling they always have to be reachable, because accessibility has become unconnected from the actual working time. The boundaries between leisure time and working time becomes blurred. This is one possible example of techno-stress. It shows oversimplified, that the change of work processes (increased availability for customers, supervisors and colleagues) changes work related rules (times of availability), cultures (is it expected to be available at weekends and evenings or holidays?) and the role of the individual in his working environment (can call customers from home, has to decide when or if to pick up the phone in their leisure time).

The use of technology will make change faster and far more complex in the future. Thus, the study of techno-stress and its effects is of most importance for the perspective of workers (e.g. impairment of well-being and health) and employers (e.g. impairment of productivity and performance).

As explained above, older workers often show better management of work-related stress situations. It has also been shown in relation to technology-induced stress that older people experience less techno-stress than young people in relation to new information and communication technologies in their work environment [17]. Research found that factors as computer knowledge and gender are more relevant for the emergence of techno-stress than age. However, the question is whether this is also similar with regard to the future of work and the associated digitalization, or whether a general digital change has a different effect on stress perception through technology than the introduction of information and communication technologies at the workplace.

Thus, this paper raises the question whether there is a difference between younger and older employees with regard to the perception of techno-stress but also with regard to the perception of motivational factors in relation to the digitalization of the world of work.

3 Methodology

In the following section the methodological approach will be presented. The sample is described hereafter.

3.1 Online Survey

A questionnaire was conducted, including demographics (age, gender, education), perceived techno-stress and motivational aspects of the digitization of the workplace.

Techno-stress was measured by four subscales developed by Tarafdar and colleagues [17]:

Table 1. Overview of used dimensions of techno-stress and their meaning

Dimensions of techno-stress	Creators of techno-stress
Techno-overload	The use of technology at the workplace means more work must be done faster in a shorter time
Techno-invasion	the use of digital work equipment blurs the boundaries between private and professional life
Techno-complexity	learning how to use digital tools is time consuming and complicated
Techno-insecurity	digital work tools and changed processes trigger the concern of not being good enough in the job and perhaps being replaced because of it

In addition, motivational aspects of the digitization of the workplace, based on motivational aspects found in literature, were surveyed.

They have been grouped into seven main aspects, each of which consists of two items. These can be found in the table below. The motivational aspects include aspects of the own performance and work area related quality increase, flexibility of working hours and increase of the work life balance, security of the workplace with changing circumstances (economic or private), as well as communicative aspects such as an improved exchange among colleagues and a faster information flow at the workplace (Table 2).

Table 2. Overview of summarized motive variables

Variable	Cronbachs α
Productivity	.91
Quality	.89
Flexibility	.79
Security	.81
Work life balance	.89
Exchange between colleagues	.81
Flow of information	.85

Items to motivational aspects as well as techno-stress could be answered on a Six-Point Likert scale from 1 = *I totally disagree* to 6 = *I totally agree*. The respondents were asked to relate all questions to the digitization of the world of work.

3.2   Sample

507 working participants aged between 19 and 66 years (M = 46.18 years, SD = 11.82) took part in the survey. The participants were divided into three age groups: Young professionals with an age range from 18 to 35 years (n = 109), experienced workers with an age range from 36 to 55 years (n = 277) and silver workers with an age range from 56 to 66 years (n = 121). The sample consisted of 254 women and 253 men. All respondents live in Germany. The survey was conducted from may to august 2018 by an online questionnaire.

4   Results

Results were analyzed descriptive with mean values. Non-parametric Kruskal-Wallis-Tests were used for the analysis of group differences. Level of significance was set at p < .05.

4.1   Motivational Aspects

Overall, the results show medium agreement on the motivational aspects of a digital workplace (Fig. 1).

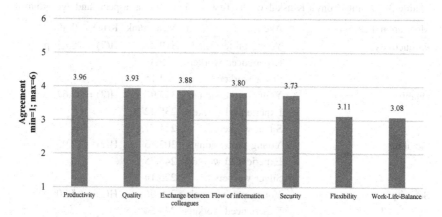

Fig. 1. Mean of overall agreement to motivational aspects

The digitization of the workplace to increase one's own work performance (M = 3.96; SD = 1.47) and its quality (M = 3.93; SD = 1.44) receives the most approval. The least agreed is that the use of digital means in the workplace increases flexibility (M = 3.11; SD = 1.47) and the work-life balance (M = 3.08; SD = 1.39). This shows that overall the advantages play less of a role in areas of private life design, such as one's work-life-balance. The advantages of an optimal work design are most clearly seen by the participants.

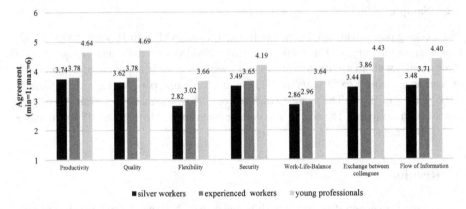

Fig. 2. Mean of agreement to motivational aspects in age-groups, based on mean values

Figure 2 shows a comparison of the assessment of the motivational aspects of digitising the workplace by age group. It can be seen that the order in which the individual aspects are assessed in each age group is the same as in the overall sample. However, it can also be seen that agreement decreases overall with increasing age.

Table 3. Results from a Kruskal-Wallis-Test for motivational aspects and age group

Motivational aspect	Age group	Mean rank	Kruskal-Wallis
Productivity	Young professionals	319.37	H(2) = 28.83; p = 0
	Experienced workers	235.3	
	Silver workers	234.15	
Quality	Young professionals	332.9	H(2) = 42.67; p = 0
	Experienced workers	235.42	
	Silver workers	221.77	
Flexibility	Young professionals	302.75	H(2) = 17.93; p = 0
	Experienced workers	245.75	
	Silver workers	225.14	
Security	Young professionals	299.96	H(2) = 15.20; p = 0
	Experienced workers	244.54	
	Silver workerss	230.38	
Work Life Balance	Young professionals	306.09	H(2) = 19.28; p = 0
	Experienced workers	242.84	
	Silver workers	228.78	
Exchange between colleagues	Young professionals	305.4	H(2) = 22.71; p = 0
	Experienced workers	249.25	
	Silver workers	214.79	
Flow of information	Young professionals	315.76	H(2) = 26.99; p = 0
	Experienced workers	241.22	
	Silver workers	223.86	

To get deeper insights about the perception of motivational aspects regarding age differences a Kruskal-Wallis-Test was performed. Results show the difference in agreement to the motives is significant for each aspect, as shown in Table 1 below.

Results show the overall ranking of motives is the same over all age groups. However, consent to the motivational aspects varies significantly depending on the age group. While young professionals see a stronger support for the motives for the digitalization of the working world, the older participants agree less with the motives.

4.2   Techno-Stress

To investigate techno-stress, techno-stress perception was first considered in the entire sample (Fig. 3).

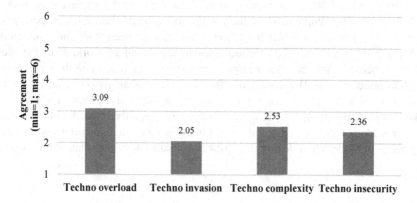

Fig. 3. Perceived techno-stress

The overall perception of techno-stress in the sample is low. The perception that by implementing technology in the work process more work has to be done in shorter time and that thus the individual workload gets too much, is most pronounced (Techno-overload: M = 3.08; SD = 1.27). The feeling that the use of technology in the workplace blurs the line between work and leisure time, e.g. through accessibility, is the least pronounced (Techno-invasion: M = 2.05 SD = 1.20).

To investigate the relationship between age and techno-stress, a Kruskal-Wallis-Test was performed (Table 4).

Table 4. Results from Kurskal-Wallis-Test for age and techno-stress

Dimensino of techno-stress	Age group	Mean rank	Kruskal-Wallis
Techno-overload	Young professionals	263.23	H(2) = 2.88; p = 0.24
	Experienced workers	258.87	
	Silver workers	234.55	
Techno-invasion	Young professionals	303.54	H(2) = 22.06; p = 0.00
	Experienced workers	251.15	
	Silver workers	215.91	

(*continued*)

Table 4. (*continued*)

Dimensino of techno-stress	Age group	Mean rank	Kruskal-Wallis
Techno-complexity	Young professionals	243.21	H(2) = 0.98; p = 0.61
	Experienced workers	254.66	
	Silver workers	262.2	
Techno-insecurity	Young professionals	280.14	H(2) = 10.92; p = 0.004
	Experienced workers	259.08	
	Silver workers	218.82	

As Table 3 shows, there is a significant difference in the perception of techno-stress between the age groups at the dimensions Techno-invasion (H(2) = 22.06; p = 0.00) with a mean rank of 303.54 for young professionals, 251.15 for experienced workers and 215.91 for silver workers. Thus, the young professionals show a higher perception of the stress triggered by the blurring of the boundaries between work and professional life through the use of modern technologies in the world of work, than the older workers. It became apparent that the age groups differ significantly in their perception of techno-insecurity (H(2) = 10.92; p = 0.004) with a mean rank of 280.14 for the young professionals, 259.08 for the experienced workers and 218.82 for the silver workers. Again, the group of young workers is more sensitive than the older groups. Younger workers who are worried about not being good enough in comparison to their competitors or worry about losing their jobs as a result rate higher than older workers.

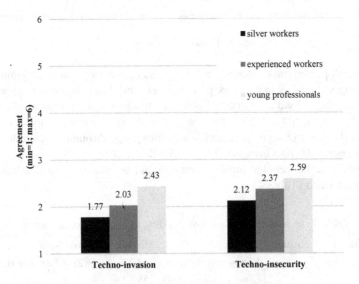

Fig. 4. Age Difference in the perception of techno-stress, based on mean values

Figure 4 shows the mean of techno-invasion and techno-insecurity for all three age groups and makes it clear that stress and strain factors induced by technology and related to work are perceived weaker with increasing age than in younger years.

Results show, that the perception of techno-stress in general is not very pronounced. Nevertheless, the examination of techno-stress in the different age groups showed a significant difference in perception between older and younger employees.

5 Discussion and Future Work

The inexorable changes in the world of work have already begun. A major challenge is demographic change and the resulting shortage of skilled workers. Experienced employees are an important and essential resource for competitive companies. Understanding this particular group of workers and investigating the needs and requirements of older workers is therefore of particular relevance. This paper focuses on the question of how differences in the perception of motivational and stressful factors in connection with the digitization of the workplace are related to age.

The results of the empirical study showed that the motives were assessed similarly, regardless of age, but that this assessment was stronger in the younger age group than among older employees. Other studies examining age differences in work-related motives found that the type of motivation changes with age. While younger workers focus on aspects such as career development, older workers are looking for a good working environment and job security [7]. The results presented here, showed that focus on growth like the increased productivity and quality of work in particular, are seen by the test persons as the strongest motivational aspects associated with digitization. However, this is the strongest aspect for all age groups – even if the younger group gives it stronger support than the silver workers and also the experienced group. So there is no difference here in the weighting of the individual motives between the age groups, but nevertheless in the intensity of the endorsement. The younger group may associate greater enthusiasm with the potential of a digital workplace because they were at the beginning of their career. However, the results indicate that there are no differentiated motivational assessment patterns between the age groups with regard to the digitization of the workplace. Companies that introduce digitization measures should therefore respond to positive aspects of the changes – such as improved work processes that enable the individual to achieve a quality increase of work – in order to raise motivation.

The results concerning the perception of techno-stress showed that the group of silver workers feel significantly less techno-stress than young professionals. This is in line with the results of Tarafdar et al. [18]. They assume that older employees are in a better position to compensate for technical innovations and the associated changes because they are equipped with more experience and knowledge [18]. With regard to techno-invasion, it is precisely this wealth of experience and formal and informal knowledge acquired, such as accessibility rules, that could mean greater serenity for silver workers than for inexperienced newcomers to the profession. In terms of techno-insecurity, too, awareness of one's own abilities and one's own standing in the work environment and in comparison with colleagues seems to lead to increased insensitivity to stress. Kooij et al.

suggest, that because of the more intrinsic motives in job performance, older workforces may like to have an enrichment of their work tasks by e.g. being a mentor [7, 8]. In line with that, the here presented results indicate a mentoring program between younger and older workers as a measure for transformation processes to a digital work environment. This could lead to a healthy and social work environment as a base for innovation, commitment and healthiness. Job enrichment by mentoring etc. might be the best solution to use potential, knowledge and experience from older workforce and at the same time may provide better job satisfaction for employees – both, younger and older.

The results imply it makes sense to design measures and strategies oriented towards the transformation of work processes and structures, taking into account the age structure of the employees and offering differentiated options of training, learning teams and mentorship programs designed to meet the complex requirements of the future of work.

Following studies showing the potential of older workers for the labor market of the future (e.g. through loyalty, expert knowledge, social competence) [4], the potential high value of older workers for sustainable enterprises could also be pointed out here. This study gives an indication that the motivational aspects of the digitization of the workplace are perceived similarly by young professionals and silver workers, even if the young people give a little more emphasis to this assessment. In principle, however, the assessment of motivational aspects does not drift apart between young and old, from which it can be concluded that the implementation of digitalization does not require a special address for older employees. On the other hand, the silver workers show themselves to be more relaxed and stress-resistant with regard to stress caused by technology, which indicates less susceptibility to the consequences of psychological stress in the work context. Against the background of a changing world of work, a lack of skilled workers and demographic change, the present study thus provides further indications that older workers are becoming a sought-after group of employees and that golden times for silver workers in the sense of sought-after skilled workers are imminent on the labor market of the future.

6 Limitations

In the present study age was measured by chronological age. Since the differences in the physical and mental aging processes are very individual, future studies must take this into account in order to obtain reliable information about the effects of aging. In addition, no relationship was established between age group and type of occupation. But especially when it comes to aspects such as experience, this plays a role. For example, the entry age of an academic into a profession is usually higher than that of a person with vocational training, which in turn can have an effect on stress management and coping strategies.

Similarly, the nature of the profession plays a role in the assessment of digitization and positive aspects and should therefore be included in future analyses. Thus, other patterns of evaluation of motivational aspects will probably emerge (e.g., comparison of physical work and knowledge work).

In this study, the subjects were introduced to a rather rough scenario of digitization on the basis of which they were to answer the questions. In a first step, this was important to capture general trends. in a next step, however, more specific scenarios should be queried in order to obtain more concrete results for individual aspects.

Acknowledgements. This research was funded by the Project SiTra 4.0 (German Ministry for research and education, reference no. 02L15A000-02L15A004). We thank all participants for taking part in the study and sharing their opinion with us. Special thank goes to Mona Frank for research assistance.

References

1. Ng, T.W., Feldman, D.C.: The relationship of age to ten dimensions of job performance. J. Appl. Psychol. **93**, 392 (2008)
2. Ng, T.W., Feldman, D.C.: Evaluating six common stereotypes about older workers with meta-analytical data. Pers. Psychol. **65**, 821–858 (2012)
3. Shirom, A., Shechter Gilboa, S., Fried, Y., Cooper, C.L.: Gender, age and tenure as moderators of work-related stressors' relationships with job performance: a meta-analysis. Hum. Relat. **61**, 1371–1398 (2008)
4. Zacher, H., Kooij, D.T.A.M., Beier, M.E.: Active aging at work. Organ. Dyn. **47**, 37–45 (2018)
5. Schermuly, C.C.: New Work-Gute Arbeit gestalten: Psychologisches Empowerment von Mitarbeitern. Haufe-Lexware (2016)
6. Kooij, D.T.A.M., Guest, D.E., Clinton, M., Knight, T., Jansen, P.G.W., Dikkers, J.S.E.: How the impact of HR practices on employee well-being and performance changes with age: how the impact of HR practices changes with age. Hum. Resour. Manag. J. **23**, 18–35 (2013)
7. Kooij, D.T., Jansen, P.G., Dikkers, J.S., De Lange, A.H.: The influence of age on the associations between HR practices and both affective commitment and job satisfaction: a meta-analysis. J. Organ. Behav. **31**, 1111–1136 (2010)
8. Kooij, D.T.A.M., De Lange, A.H., Jansen, P.G.W., Kanfer, R., Dikkers, J.S.E.: Age and work-related motives: results of a meta-analysis. J. Organ. Behav. **32**, 197–225 (2011)
9. Czaja, S.J., et al.: Factors predicting the use of technology: findings from the Center for Research and Education on Aging and Technology Enhancement (CREATE). Psychol. Aging **21**, 333 (2006)
10. Umemuro, H.: Computer attitudes, cognitive abilities, and technology usage among older Japanese adults. Gerontechnology **3**, 64–76 (2004)
11. Tacken, M., Marcellini, F., Mollenkopf, H., Ruoppila, I., Szeman, Z.: Use and acceptance of new technology by older people. Findings of the international MOBILATE survey: 'Enhancing mobility in later life'. Gerontechnology. **3**, 126–137 (2005)
12. Ellis, R.D., Allaire, J.C.: Modeling computer interest in older adults: the role of age, education, computer knowledge, and computer anxiety. Hum. Factors **41**, 345–355 (1999)
13. Arning, K., Himmel, S., Ziefle, M.: You can('t) teach an old dog new tricks: analyzing the learnability of manufacturing software systems in older users. In: Zhou, J., Salvendy, G. (eds.) ITAP 2016. LNCS, vol. 9755, pp. 277–288. Springer, Cham (2016). https://doi.org/10.1007/978-3-319-39949-2_27
14. Hayslip Jr., B., Maloy, R.M., Kohl, R.: Long-term efficacy of fluid ability interventions with older adults. J. Gerontol. B Psychol. Sci. Soc. Sci. **50**, P141–P149 (1995)

15. Nelson, D.L., Kletke, M.G.: Individual adjustment during technological innovation: a research framework. Behav. Inf. Technol. **9**, 257–271 (1990)
16. Kahn, R.L., Wolfe, D.M., Quinn, R.P., Snoek, J.D., Rosenthal, R.A.: Organizational stress: studies in role conflict and ambiguity (1964)
17. Tarafdar, M., Tu, Q., Ragu-Nathan, B.S., Ragu-Nathan, T.S.: The impact of technostress on role stress and productivity. J. Manag. Inf. Syst. **24**, 301–328 (2007)
18. Tarafdar, M., Tu, Q., Ragu-Nathan, T.S., Ragu-Nathan, B.S.: Crossing to the dark side: examining creators, outcomes, and inhibitors of technostress. Commun. ACM **54**, 113 (2011)

Effect of Gamification of Exercise Therapy on Elderly's Anxiety Emotion

Xiaozhou Li[1], Ruoyu Li[2], and Ting Han[1(✉)]

[1] School of Design, Shanghai Jiao Tong University, No. 800 Dongchuan Road, Shanghai 200240, China
{xiaozhouli,hanting}@sjtu.edu.cn
[2] Department of Computer Science, Columbia University, 116th St & Broadway, New York, NY 10027, USA
rl2929@columbia.edu

Abstract. The anxiety of the elderly has been one of the most common psychological disorders, which will lead to increased mortality and economic loss. Exercise therapy has been shown to alleviate anxiety in the elderly. This study aims to compare the impact of simple exercise therapy and gamified exercise therapy on the elderly's anxiety. For the elderly, this research developed a prototype system which allows players to control the video game Tetris by hitting the punch bag to gamify the process of exercise. The study recruited 14 subjects with an average age of 66 years (60–75). The participants were divided into a control group with only simply punching and an experimental group with gamification intervention. This study used The State Trait Anxiety Scale and the Rating of Perceived Exertion. The game score changes in the experimental group were recorded. The results show that compared with simple exercise therapy, gamified exercise therapy has a more significant mitigation effect on the state anxiety of the elderly. The degree of exercise fatigue of both groups is consistent. It is shown that such simple gamification is not a big challenge for the cognitive ability of the elderly, and most of the participants felt satisfied with the procedure and expressed initiatives to play the game. This method might be a promising intervention for relieving the elderly's anxiety. In the future work, it is necessary to conduct long-term experiments to verify the effect of gamification of exercise therapy on the trait anxiety of the elderly.

Keywords: Gamification · Exercise therapy · The elderly

1 Introduction

Currently, the aging of population has become a severe social issue to be solved across the world. The entire society is under pressure to achieve a goal of active and healthy aging among the elderly. Elderly people are facing a variety of stress from health, family, income, interpersonal relationships, social obligations and role transition, which may increase the burden of and even cause harm to the elderly's mental health, and lead to frequent negative emotion such as depression and anxiety [1]. The data reveal that the rate of suffering anxiety disorder among aged citizens in China is as high as 22.11% [2]. In five European countries and Israel, the prevalence rate of elderly anxiety

© Springer Nature Switzerland AG 2019
J. Zhou and G. Salvendy (Eds.): HCII 2019, LNCS 11593, pp. 533–544, 2019.
https://doi.org/10.1007/978-3-030-22015-0_41

disorder is reaching 17.2% [3], which has been one of the most common psychological disorders. Elderly anxiety disorder increases the mortality and brings about large economic loss [4, 5].

Existing research has proved that exercise therapy can effectively reduce the level of anxiety emotion [6], and physical exercise can increase the resilience of the emotion when people are dealing with stress. According to some data analysis, the people who frequently participate in physical activities show less anxiety and depression and more extraverted than those who do not exercise [7].

Gamification is defined as using the elements of games under a non-game circumstance [8]. It can be used as a tool to improve the motivation and participation of different activities and tasks. Gamification has been widely applied in the field of military, education, treatment and healthcare [9]. A gamified application consists of the elements of games [9]. Reeves and Read once summarized ten elements of a great game: "self-representation with avatars, three-dimensional environments, narrative context, feedback, reputations & ranks & levels, marketplaces and economies, teams, parallel communication systems that can be easily reconfigured, time pressure" [10].

Gamification has widespread use in healthcare. Some research indicates that gamification and the serious game helps prevent and treat children's chronic diseases by changing children's behaviors. For instance, Kharrazi et al. [11] proposed that Theory of Planned Behavior-based serious game can enhance the treatment adherence of adolescent Type 1 Diabetes (T1D) patients; educational games effectively reduce the risk of hypoglycemia when adolescents with T1D are driving. Knöll et al. [12] discussed how the popularization of the prevention and treatment of chronic diseases benefits from the design strategy of city games, integrating gameplay with daily healthcare of adolescent diabetes patients. Hassan et al. [13] put forward a digital storytelling concept-based personalized game that helps autistic children between 9 and 14 establish a concept with money. For common diseases in the elderly, gamification and serious game are meaningful for the improvement of Parkinson's patients' mobility [14]. Ko [15] utilized a serious game with Arduino to enhance body's coordination so that the risk of cognitive decline can be decreased. Ma et al. [16] developed and tested a serious game that assists stroke patients in recovering the strength of upper limbs by exercise.

In healthcare, the combination of exercise therapy and gamification also raises some discussion and research. Over all research, many trials intended to prove the positive effects of exergame's or gamification's intervention on physiological monitoring and health care. For example, the study from Mhatre et al. [17] suggests that Nintendo Wii Fit can be an effective form of family intervention for patients with nerve damage with more convenience and less cost. Kempf and Martin [18] conducted a randomized controlled trial to test the effect of the interactive game Wii Fit Plus on the quality of life and physical activity of patients with Type 2 Diabetes Mellitus (T2DM), finding that this game obviously motivates the patients with T2DM to increase the level of physical exercise, glucose metabolism and quality of life. Lange et al. [19] designed a rehabilitation game 'JewelMine' based on Microsoft Kinect that consists of a set of static balance exercise and encourages players to increase the level of balance.

There are many studies trying to figure out the relationship between exergame's or gamification's intervention and people's psychological parameters. Meldrum et al. [20] applied the balance and walking exercise of Nintendo Wii Fit Plus to relieving anxiety and depression of patients with gait and balance damage. The study from Song et al. [21] suggests that the people with body image dissatisfaction (BID) can benefit from exergames with which the feeling of social anxiety is alleviated. Shin et al. [22] proved that the game-based virtual reality rehabilitation combined with occupation therapy has a certain effect on the improvement of upper limb functions and depression of hemiplegia patients with chronic stroke. Knox et al. [23] found that biofeedback-assisted relaxation therapy can effectively reduce the symptoms of adolescent negative emotions. In a recent study, Benzing and Schmidt [24] examined the effect of exergames for cognitive and physical demands on the executive function of children with attention deficit hyperactivity disorder (ADHD), proving that this kind of games has positive impact on executive function and ADHD.

Dori et al. [25] invited 19 older citizens who are suffering sub-syndromic depression (SSD) to participate in a 12-week trial with Wii Sports. The result demonstrates that the retention rate (86%) and compliance (84%) are high, and the symptoms of depression are markedly improved, which comes into conclusion that exergames are practical and acceptable for elderly patients with SSD and might be a new approach to the improvement of elderly depression. Chao et al. [26] investigated the influence of Wii Fit exergame combined with self-efficacy theory upon citizens physiologically and psychologically, conducted a trial and proved that the exergame is an effective method to elevate and maintain elderly's physical and mental health.

Among these exergame or gamification studies for the elderly, most of them concentrate on rehabilitation training or cognitive function. Few of them focus on the prevention of mental disorders; even fewer on the elderly anxiety emotion. Since exercise therapy has been proven to effectively reduce anxiety emotion [6], our study aims at the elderly, gamifying the process of exercise therapy, and proves the usability and effectiveness of the design via a randomized controlled trial. By comparing the normal exercise and game-based exercise, the research investigates the effect of gamification of exercise therapy on elderly's anxiety emotion. Our goal is to design an effective and attractive intervention approach to the relief of the elderly's anxiety.

2   Materials and Methods

2.1   System Design

Before the design of the gamification, the study needs to investigate the physiological and psychological characteristics of the elderly to design. The physiological features of the elderly are as follow [27]:

- Visual acuity: color vision changed; sensitivity to color and shape reduced; descending capacity to adapt lightness and darkness; sensitivity to glare increased.
- Hearing: auditory system suffering degeneration; suffering hearing loss.

- Touch sensation: aging skin; sense of touch relatively declined.
- Brain: decreasing nerve cells; blood flow getting slow; ability to memorize, analyze and judge weakened.
- Skeleton and muscle: low bone density, high bone fragility; vulnerable to bone fractures and calcifications; suffering muscle atrophy; muscle strength lost; slowed response; athletic ability and strength declined; slow movements

As the physical decline with age and maladaptive role transition arise after the retirement, the elderly's psychological characteristics are also changed, such as cognitive decline; negative emotions caused by physical functions and external environment like anxiety, depression and loneliness [28]; nostalgia; habitual psychology; the pursuit of internal value [29].

Therefore, researchers can follow some design strategies that are suitable for the aged when gamifying the exercise therapy (see Table 1).

Considering the uncertainties and other uncontrollable factors of the outdoor activity, the study determined indoor punching on punch bags as exercise. This study integrated the height-adjustable punch bags with some pressure sensors on the surface, using pressure as a signal input to control the game Tetris in the computer. When a user hits the punch bag, it triggers the movement of Tetris in the computer. The game interface is projected from the computer onto the wall in front of the user through a projector so that the elderly user can clearly watch the projected interface and play the game. The Tetris game was chosen because of its high popularity, which reduces the cost of learning new things for the elderly and is simple to operate. Considering the various characteristics of the elderly mentioned above, the interface of the Tetris was redesigned with high contrast and low-light colors, enlarged game elements, and when each Tetris brick is falling, a transparent brick is displayed at the bottom so that the elderly can be informed of the expected whereabouts.

This prototype used the Arduino UNO and pressure sensors to create the hardware part of the project and developed the software in C and Python. Arduino UNO [30] is an open-source microcontroller board developed by Arduino.cc. It is based on the microchip ATmega328P and equipped with a set of analog and digital I/O interfaces to connect with other circuits. Via the Arduino, the pressure signal can be converted into the keystroke signal of the computer. The three film pressure sensors replace the function of the left arrow, right arrow and space key of the computer. The left arrow represents the leftward movement of the Tetris; the right arrow represents the rightward movement of the Tetris; the space key represents the deformation of the Tetris. Researchers fixed the three film sensors on the three punch bags respectively. The elderly will hit these three punch bags with gloves to control the Tetris in the computer, and the game interface will be projected on the wall. The elderly can achieve the goal of exercise by the movement of the upper limbs and body.

The study used some gamification elements to motivate the elderly to exercise (see Fig. 1). In the sidebar of the redesigned game interface, there is a scorer which shows the score of the current game and the highest record. Every time a line of Tetris bricks is eliminated, the score will increase and positive feedback sound will be given.

The game has three difficulty levels, each of which is related to the falling speed of the brick, and the user can select the level according to his or her own need. The game maintains a hierarchy. When the user's playtime reaches a certain amount, the game can get into a higher level. Within different levels, the user can obtain different game titles and badges.

Table 1. The design strategy for the elderly

Characteristic	Manifestation	Strategy
Visual acuity	Color vision changed; sensitivity to color and shape reduced; descending capacity to adapt lightness and darkness; sensitivity to glare increased	High contrast color; fewer visual elements; large screen; large font size
Hearing	Auditory system suffering degeneration; suffering hearing loss	High feedback volume
Touch sensation	Aging skin; sense of touch relatively declined	Appropriate texture
Brain	Decreasing nerve cells; blood flow getting slow; ability to memorize, analyze and judge weakened	Relatively simple rules and flows; adjustable game speed; handy operations
Skeleton & muscle	Low bone density, high bone fragility; vulnerable to bone fractures and calcifications; suffering muscle atrophy; muscle strength lost; slowed response; athletic ability and strength declined; slow movements	Appropriate exercise intensity; protective measures; adjustable height
Psychology	Cognitive decline; negative emotions caused by physical functions and external environment like anxiety, depression and loneliness [28]; nostalgia; habitual psychology; the pursuit of internal value [29]	Simple rules; clear objectives; clear feedback; motivations; fewer new things

2.2 Participants

In order to verify the impact of gamification of exercise therapy on elderly's anxiety, this study recruited 14 participants of different backgrounds with an average age of 66 (ranging from 60 to 75). All participants were asked to sign a consent and fill out a subjective basic information questionnaire. The inclusion criteria are as follow: (a) clear consciousness and communication with people; (b) autonomous mobility, no physical diseases that may cause serious discomfort due to exercise, such as heart disease and cerebral infarction; (c) no large amount of food or alcohol consumption 1 hour before the experiment; (d) no large amount of exercise 1 hour before the experiment.

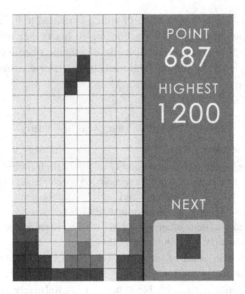

Fig. 1. Game interface

2.3   Procedure

First of all, a training session was given to all participants in order to familiarize our equipment, user interface and the correct method and strength of punching on the punch bag. After the training session, each participant was expected to reach a status of self-use of the equipment. Researchers sequenced 14 participants sequentially, and then used a pseudorandom number generator to generate the serial number. The first 6 participants were selected into the control group and the last 8 participants were selected into the experimental group. The control group only performed single punching on the punch bag, while the experimental group engaged in the game intervention during the punching. The experiment lasted for 20 minutes.

2.4   Measurements

The study mainly measures the following aspects: anxiety level, fatigue level, satisfaction and design efficacy.

- Anxiety level—Anxiety level is tested by using the State-Trait Anxiety Inventory (STAI). The STAI consists of two subscales which evaluate two different types of anxiety for a total of 40 items. The State Anxiety Scale (S-AI) primarily assesses an individual's immediate emotional experience or feelings. The Trait Anxiety Scale (T-AI) is used to assess more stable anxiety and tense personality, i.e., emotional sensations in a near period of time [31]. The higher the score is, the higher the anxiety level is. In order to verify the influence of gamification of exercise therapy on the anxiety of the elderly, the control group and the experimental group need to fill out the scale before and after the experiment.

- Fatigue level—The Rating of Perceived Exertion (RPE) [32] is used to assess the perceived amount and intensity of exercise in order to investigate the fatigue level of gamified exercise.
- Efficacy indicators—The change in scores of each task is recorded and compared by the researchers.

3 Results

3.1 STAI

After an F-test, this study used a two-sample homoscedastic T-test to evaluate whether the baselines of the two groups were consistent. The result of the T-test shows no significant difference between the baseline of the S-AI in the experimental group and the control group (p = 0.95 > 0.05) and the baseline of the T-AI (p = 0.08 > 0.05) (See Table 2). Therefore, the samples have statistical significance.

Table 2. STAI score baseline

Scale	EG (Mean ± SD)	CG (Mean ± SD)	F test (p)	Homoscedastic T-test (t)	Homoscedastic T-test (p)
S-AI	40.00 ± 9.97	40.33 ± 10.91	0.35	2.18	0.95
T-AI	45.50 ± 6.30	39.50 ± 5.01	0.14	2.18	0.08

Table 3. Paired T-test of baseline and post-intervention STAI of experimental group

Scale	S-AI		T-AI	
	Baseline	Post-intervention	Baseline	Post-intervention
Mean	40.00	27.88	45.50	37.38
Variance	99.43	55.55	39.71	81.41
Person correlation coefficient	0.52		0.29	
t Stat	3.89		2.44	
P(T <= t)	0.006		0.044	
t	2.36		2.36	

The study used a paired T-test to evaluate the difference in values between the experimental and control groups before and after the experiment. The T-test shows that the S-AI of the experimental group is significantly different before and after the experiment (p = 0.006 < 0.01), while the T-AI has some differences before and after the experiment but not obvious (0.01 < p = 0.044 < 0.05) (See Table 3). The S-AI of the control group shows some differences before and after the experiment but it is not obvious (0.01 < p = 0.029 < 0.05), and the T-AI does not differ before and after the experiment (p = 0.65 > 0.05) (See Table 4). This proves that the gamification of exercise therapy has a significant effect on reducing the state anxiety of the elderly compared with the simple exercise therapy, and has a certain effect on relieving the trait anxiety of the elderly but is not obvious.

Table 4. Paired T-test of baseline and post-intervention STAI of control group

Scale	S-AI		T-AI	
	Baseline	Post-intervention	Baseline	Post-intervention
Mean	40.33	34.00	39.50	36.67
Variance	119.07	180.80	25.10	243.07
Person correlation coefficient	0.93		0.38	
t Stat	3.03		0.48	
P(T <= t)	0.029		0.65	
t	2.57		2.57	

3.2 RPE

The study used a two-sample heteroscedastic T-test to detect differences in RPE between the experimental and control groups. The data shows no obvious difference in RPE between the two groups ($p = 0.08 > 0.05$) (See Table 5).

Table 5. RPE score

Scale	EG (Mean ± SD)	CG (Mean ± SD)	F test (p)	Heteroscedastic T-test (t)	Heteroscedastic T-test (p)
RPE	11.13 ± 2.42	13.00 ± 1.10	0.059	2.23	0.080

The mean of RPE in the experimental group is 11.13, and that in the control group is 13.00. According to Scherr et al. [33], for individuals with less exercise, the fatigue level of 11–13 is recommended. In this experiment, most of the participants in both the experimental group and the control group obtained a relatively comfortable exercise experience.

3.3 Efficacy Indicators

All participants in the experimental group were able to quickly master the skills of our equipment and game after a brief training by the researchers. Most of the game scores in the experiment rose during the procedure (See Fig. 2). In the experimental group's game, only a small number of participants required researchers to perform very little verbal intervention, and most participants did not need verbal intervention. The operation of all participants became more and more skilled in 20 minutes.

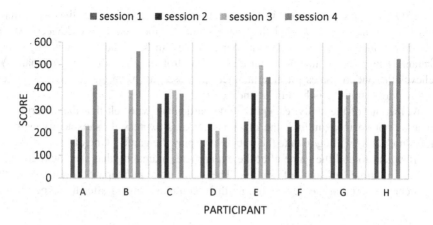

Fig. 2. Tetris score obtained in the first four sessions

3.4 Qualitative Feedback

Among the participants, the most popular exercise is walking; the second popular exercise is Tai Chi, gymnastic exercise and dance, followed by basketball, table tennis and cycling. All participants stated that they exercised for the health of the body and relief from mental fatigue. One participant said that in addition to the above reasons, she also had physical exercise to alleviate dementia.

As for the incentives for physical exercise, except that two participants said that physical exercise was carried out only when a friend invited, other participants said that they would take the initiative to carry out sports activities.

In the choice of sports locations, most of the participants prefer inside the community. The second popular is the park or plaza in the neighborhood. The third is on campus near the home. A small part of people exercise at home.

In the number of years of persistence in physical exercise, the proportion of participants who persisted for less than 5 years accounted for 21%. The proportion of participants who adhered to 5 years to 10 years accounted for 21%, and the proportion of participants who persisted for more than 10 years accounted for 58%.

In terms of anxiety, 50% of the participants said they often feel anxious. 28% said they have occasional anxiety. 22% said they never feel anxious. The main cause of their anxiety is family reasons, followed by work issues, and a fraction of the people felt anxious for economic and physical reasons. The most popular way among them to cope with anxiety is by exercising to ease negative emotions, followed by entertainment and reading. Only a small number of participants did not know how to handle the emotion when they were anxious.

In terms of contact with video games, 14% of participants said that they never have any experience, 28% said they play regularly, 16% said they play occasionally, and 42% said they played before but they do not play recently. One participant introduced himself as a result of excessive addiction to video games, once leading to periarthritis of the shoulder and cervical spondylosis. They mainly play games in casual and chess. 28% of people said that they have never downloaded a game in their electronic devices, and 28% said they had games in their electronic devices before but they don't have them. The remaining 44% said they have games in their electronic devices. At the attitude of video games for entertainment purposes, most of the elderly are open and tolerant. They believe that it is harmless to control the time of play. A small part believes that video games for entertainment purposes are harmful. For serious games, all the elderly think it is beneficial and acceptable.

At the end of the study, except for one participant who felt that the experimental process "not so meaningful", the other participants expressed "satisfactory with the procedure" and "willing to take the initiative to play the game". One of the participants was reluctant to end the game after the experiment, indicating that she could continue to play multiple sessions of games. The other two participants even asked the researchers to reopen the device and let them continue playing after the experiment.

4   Discussion and Conclusion

The results show that under a 20-minute experiment, the gamification of exercise therapy has a significant mitigation effect on the state anxiety score of the elderly compared with the simple exercise therapy, and has a certain influence on the trait anxiety value, although it is not obvious. The simple exercise therapy has a certain relief effect on the state anxiety value of the elderly, which is not obvious, and has no impact on the trait anxiety value. The reason might be that the trait anxiety value reflects the emotional feeling of the subject in the near future. Thus the short-term experiment has little effect on it. The effect of gamified exercise therapy on anxiety is not much differentiated between genders.

Through the results of the RPE measurement, it can be proved that the gamification of exercise therapy has no significant effect on the level of the elderly's fatigue and exercise intensity compared with the simple exercise therapy. And during the 20-minute experiment, both sides can obtain a more comfortable exercise experience with time. This study is at low cost of learning for the elderly since the elderly can master and use the device in a short time, which proves that in the face of simple video games, their cognitive ability is not a big challenge, and through the qualitative feedback, most of the participants felt satisfied with the procedure and expressed initiatives to play the game, and were positively optimistic about physical exercise and video games. Therefore, the use of gamification to promote exercise therapy is achievable and encouraged.

The limitations of this study include a small sample size that falls within a small experimental range, and it belongs to a short-term experiment, which can only test the influence of the gamification of exercise therapy and simple exercise therapy on the state anxiety of the elderly, but cannot reveal the impact on the long-term trait anxiety. In the future work, it is necessary to have a larger sample size and long-term trial of the experiment. In the meanwhile, it is also important to study further the changes in the anxiety of the subjects after the stop of the treatment for a period of time.

In conclusion, this study initially shows that the gamification of exercise therapy has a more significant mitigation effect on the elderly's anxiety than simple exercise therapy. This might be a more promising intervention method for the anxiety of the elderly.

Acknowledgement. The research is supported by National Social Science Fund (Grant No. 18BRK009).

References

1. Zhang, C., Hong-yu, M.A.: The influence of four fitness qigongs' exercise on emotional health of senior citizens. Chin. J. Clin. Psychol. **19**, 407–409 (2011). (in Chinese)
2. Liang, S., Cai, Y., Shi, S., Wang, L.: A meta analysis of prevalence in anxiety disorders of elderly people in China. J. Clin. Psychiatry **21**, 87–90 (2011). (in Chinese)
3. Canuto, A., et al.: Anxiety disorders in old age: psychiatric comorbidities, quality of life, and prevalence according to age, gender, and country. Am. J. Geriatr. Psychiatry **26**, 174–185 (2018)
4. Smit, F., Cuijpers, P., Oostenbrink, J., Batelaan, N., De, G.R., Beekman, A.: Costs of nine common mental disorders: implications for curative and preventive psychiatry. J. Mental Health Policy Econ. **9**, 193 (2006)
5. Beekman, A., De, B.A., Deeg, D., Van, D.R., Van, T.W.: Anxiety and depression in later life: co-occurrence and communality of risk factors. Am. J. Psychiatry **157**, 89 (2000)
6. Petruzzello, S.J., Landers, D.M., Hatfield, B.D., Kubitz, K.A., Salazar, W.: A meta-analysis on the anxiety-reducing effects of acute and chronic exercise. Sports Med. **11**, 143–182 (1991)
7. Moor, M.H.M.D., Beem, A.L., Stubbe, J.H., Boomsma, D.I., Geus, E.J.C.D.: Regular exercise, anxiety, depression and personality: a population-based study. Prev. Med. **42**, 273–279 (2006)
8. Deterding, S., Sicart, M., Nacke, L., O'Hara, K., Dixon, D.: Gamification. using game-design elements in non-gaming contexts. In: CHI 2011 Extended Abstracts on Human Factors in Computing Systems, pp. 2425–2428. ACM (2011)
9. Deterding, S., Dixon, D., Khaled, R., Nacke, L.: From game design elements to gamefulness: defining gamification. In: International Academic Mindtrek Conference: Envisioning Future Media Environments (2011)
10. Reeves, B., Read, J.L.: Total Engagement: How Games and Virtual Worlds are Changing the Way People Work and Businesses Compete. Harvard Business Press, Boston (2009)
11. Kharrazi, H., Faiola, A., Defazio, J.: Healthcare game design: behavioral modeling of serious gaming design for children with chronic diseases. In: Jacko, J.A. (ed.) HCI 2009. LNCS, vol. 5613, pp. 335–344. Springer, Heidelberg (2009). https://doi.org/10.1007/978-3-642-02583-9_37
12. Knöll, M.: Diabetes city: how urban game design strategies can help diabetics. In: International Conference on Electronic Healthcare, pp. 200–204. Springer (2008)
13. Hassan, A.Z., et al.: Developing the concept of money by interactive computer games for autistic children. In: 2011 IEEE International Symposium on Multimedia, pp. 559–564. IEEE (2011)
14. van der Meulen, E., Cidota, M.A., Lukosch, S.G., Bank, P.J., van der Helm, A.J., Visch, V. T.: A haptic serious augmented reality game for motor assessment of Parkinson's disease patients. In: 2016 IEEE International Symposium on Mixed and Augmented Reality (ISMAR-Adjunct), pp. 102–104. IEEE (2016)
15. Ko, J.-W., Park, S.-J.: Serious Game of increase Cognitive Function for Elderly using Arduino. J. KIIT **13**, 111–119 (2015)

16. Ma, M., Bechkoum, K.: Serious games for movement therapy after stroke. In: IEEE International Conference on Systems, Man and Cybernetics. SMC 2008, pp. 1872–1877. IEEE (2008)

17. Mhatre, P.V., et al.: Wii Fit balance board playing improves balance and gait in Parkinson disease. PM & R J. Injury Funct. Rehabil. **5**, 769–777 (2013)

18. Kempf, K., Martin, S.: Autonomous exercise game use improves metabolic control and quality of life in type 2 diabetes patients - a randomized controlled trial. BMC Endocr. Disord. **13**, 57 (2013)

19. Lange, B., et al.: Interactive game-based rehabilitation using the Microsoft Kinect. In: 2012 IEEE Virtual Reality Workshops (VRW), pp. 171–172. IEEE (2012)

20. Dara, M., et al.: Effectiveness of conventional versus virtual reality-based balance exercises in vestibular rehabilitation for unilateral peripheral vestibular loss: results of a randomized controlled trial. Arch. Phys. Med. Rehabil. **96**, 1319–1328 (2015)

21. Song, H., Kim, J., Lee, K.M.: Virtual vs. real body in exergames: reducing social physique anxiety in exercise experiences. Comput. Hum. Behav. **36**, 282–285 (2014)

22. Shin, J.-H., Park, S.B., Jang, S.H.: Effects of game-based virtual reality on health-related quality of life in chronic stroke patients: a randomized, controlled study. Comput. Biol. Med. **63**, 92–98 (2015)

23. Knox, M., Lentini, J., Ts, C., Mcgrady, A., Whearty, K., Sancrant, L.: Game-based biofeedback for paediatric anxiety and depression. Ment. Health Fam. Med. **8**, 195–203 (2011)

24. Benzing, V., Schmidt, M.: Cognitively and physically demanding exergaming to improve executive functions of children with attention deficit hyperactivity disorder: a randomised clinical trial. BMC Pediatr. **17**, 8 (2017)

25. Dori, R., et al.: Exergames for subsyndromal depression in older adults: a pilot study of a novel intervention. Am. J. Geriatr. Psychiatry Official J. Am. Assoc. Geriatr. Psychiatry **18**, 221–226 (2010)

26. Chao, Y.Y., Scherer, Y.K., Montgomery, C.A., Wu, Y.W., Lucke, K.T.: Physical and psychosocial effects of Wii Fit exergames use in assisted living residents: a pilot study. Clin. Nurs. Res. **24**, 589 (2014)

27. Wu, P.: A study on the product design and development strategy for the elderly based on their physiological characteristics. Art Des. 129–131 (2013). (in Chinese)

28. LIU Bi- ying: Mental health protection in the old people. Chin. J. Clin. Psychol. **13**, 373–374 (2005). (in Chinese)

29. Meng, F., Jiang, X.: The inspiration of elderly psychological need for design. Dazhong Wenyi 61 (2012). (in Chinese)

30. Wikipedia: Arduino Uno. https://en.wikipedia.org/wiki/Arduino_Uno. Accessed 14 Feb 2019

31. Spielberger, C.D.: State-Trait anxiety inventory. The Corsini encyclopedia of psychology, p. 1 (2010)

32. Dawes, H.N., Barker, K.L., Janet, C., Neil, R., Oona, S., Derick, W.: Borg's rating of perceived exertion scales: do the verbal anchors mean the same for different clinical groups? Arch. Phys. Med. Rehabil. **86**, 912–916 (2005)

33. Scherr, J., Wolfarth, B., Christle, J.W., Pressler, A., Wagenpfeil, S., Halle, M.: Associations between Borg's rating of perceived exertion and physiological measures of exercise intensity. Eur. J. Appl. Physiol. **113**, 147–155 (2013)

Analyzing Cognitive Flexibility in Older Adults Through Playing with Robotic Cubes

Margarida Romero[✉]

Laboratoire d'Innovation et Numérique pour l'Éducation,
Université Côte d'Azur, Nice, France
Margarida.romero@univ-cotedazur.fr

Abstract. Cognitive flexibility is an important ability to adapt to changing situations. We consider the evolution of technologies in the digital era as a changing situation requiring the individuals to maintain a certain cognitive flexibility. Across the lifespan, cognitive flexibility is an essential ability to adapt to a continuous evolution of human-computer interactions (HCI). In this study, we observe older adults in a playful robotic task aiming to observe their cognitive flexibility in order to consider if older adults shows an adequate level of cognitive flexibility to solve a problem solving task with unknown robotic cubes. The playful robotic task engages the participants individually in problem solving a puzzle-based challenge with modular robotics.

Keywords: Cognitive flexibility · Robotics · Lifelong learning ·
Human-computer interactions · Problem solving

1 Introduction

The evolution of technologies in the digital era engages the citizens in a never-ending situation of novelty which requires a certain degree of cognitive flexibility to adapt to new or changing technologies and their interfaces. Human-computer interaction (HCI) has changed along the evolution of the different forms of technologies that has been developed in the last decades. The changes in the technologies requires citizens to maintain a certain cognitive flexibility in their ability to adapt to a continuous evolution of HCI. While elderly oriented screen based applications are often designed according the important corpus of knowledge in the HCI field [1, 2] we lack of a so extensive corpus when we consider robotic technologies. Robotic technologies have evolved into a wide diversity of forms and when we use the term robot we should consider an important diversity of devices that corresponds to the definition of what is a robot. While some robots are human shaped and integrate vocal based interactions like the Nao robotic robot in which the user can engage in turn-taking like in human-to-human interactions [3], other robots such the Cubelets kit [4] are composed of basic robotic cubes with basic interaction capacities. In the case of this robotic kits, the user can just manipulate and assemble the cubes to create a robot capable of very basic interactions. The diversity in robotic technologies should be considered when analyzing the type of Human Robot Interactions (HRI). In this study we focus on the use of the Cubelets modular robots to understand the

© Springer Nature Switzerland AG 2019
J. Zhou and G. Salvendy (Eds.): HCII 2019, LNCS 11593, pp. 545–553, 2019.
https://doi.org/10.1007/978-3-030-22015-0_42

cognitive flexibility that could be observed among elderly engaged in the interactions with this robotic technology when solving a puzzle-based task.

2 Diversity Within Human Robot Interactions (HRI)

Robots are defined as "an autonomous system existing in the physical world that can detect the environment and take action to achieve the goal" [5]. They have a physical existence including the sensors to detect different signals from the environment but also processing units to take actions through the actuators. Thereby, from a technological perspective, Munich, Ostrowski and Pirjanian [6] define a robot "as a system that has a number of sensors, processing units (e.g., computer), and actuators". The type of technologies responding to these characteristics is very diverse, but the social representation of robots is not based in these features but on the representation influenced by science fiction and robots highlighted in mass media, most of them, having a humanoid form. But humanoid robots are only a type of robotic technologies. A wide diversity of robotic technologies has smaller and more abstract features than the humanistic ones. The robotic technologies embedded in our lives could not easily recognized by the user as robots because of the gap between the metal representation of a robot, often associated to a humanoid robot, and the robotic technologies that could be small and very diversity shaped (Fig. 1).

Fig. 1. Poppy humanoid robot.

Humanoid robots have an anthropomorphic appearance that corresponds to the social representation of robots. When people are interacting with humanoid robots, some of their characteristics such the head's dimension and the number of facial features influences the humanness perception of the robot [7]. Within the educational robots, Nao and Poppy are two popular robots that has been designed to have a humanoid look and feel. Poppy humanoid robot [8, 9] has multiple sensors, a complex software being able to create different types of reactions according to the programs integrated in the Poppy robot. Finally, the actuators make Poppy able to move in different ways and generate sounds and images.

Fig. 2. Robot created with Cubelets modular robotic cubes.

Users with no knowledge in robotic technologies does not perceive not humanoid robots as robots. When facing robotic solutions such the Cubelets [4], they consider them as electronic toys without considering them as robots [10]. In Fig. 2, the robot is created by the user by assembling a sensor (a light sensor integrated in the black cube), a battery making the system able to react, and a wheel which serves as actuator when the light signal is transformed into a signal for the motor moving the wheels. All the components of a robot are present but the look and feel and the simplicity of the system makes the users perceive it as an electronic toy instead of a robot.

In the diversity of Human Robot Interactions (HRI), Yanco and Drury [11] develops a taxonomy for considering the different types of interactions humans can develop individually or in team when engaged with a robot. In the updated taxonomy later by Yanco and Drury [12] they expand the categories for classifying HRI to integrate the social nature of the task by considering the different types of human and the human-robot proximity. The taxonomy could fit the HRI for the use of robots in the professional field, but should be expanded to consider the design, the programming and the building phase of educational robots. In education, robots are not only pre-existing technologies to be interacted, but could be also be a set to build engaging the learner in a designing, programming and building process through the robot creation such in the case of Cubelets modular robotic kit [10].

3 Robotic Technologies for the Elderly

Robots for the elders has been designed in the field of service, in some cases with a focus on healthcare and in other cases on social interaction [13–15]. Most of the uses has been developed in the domestic arena by introducing robots at elderly's home. The importance of technology acceptance in a healthcare relationship has led to consider humanoid robotics as key aspect in the design of robotic technologies for the elderly. Human robot interaction (HRI) for the elders has also focus strongly on humanoid robotic systems aiming to mimic socio-emotional traits of humans. In elderly care robotic systems, the appearance of humanoid robots has an influence in their acceptance, but also can cause some confusion among elderly with cognitive decline [13]. The use of not humanoid robots with the elderly has been less explored, except for robotic pets which pretends, as humanoid robots, be as close as possible of the pets they represent such in the case of the AIBO robotic dog [16, 17]. Beyond humanoid robots and robotic pets, the use of other robotic technologies has been rarely studied or just proposed to the elders as final users without engaging them in the robotic design [18]. In this study we engage elders not in the role of robotic technologies consumers, but as robot designers with educational robotic solutions. For this objective, we engage them in the CreaCube task, in which they should analyse the use of the robotic cubes and create a robot.

4   CreaCube Task, a Playful Robotic Activity for All the Lifespan

Modular robotics engages the users in assembling a set of robotic components into a robot. Among the most known robotic kits, LEGO Mindstorms engages the player in creating, building and programming a robot [18, 19]. In order to analyse the cognitive flexibility, we designed the CreaCube task [10, 20] in which the player should create a robot able to go from a point to another in an autonomous way. Cubelets are modular robotic cubes which are not initially recognized as robotic technologies, neither as a robot [10]. In this study we focus on elders' exploration of these robotic technologies which are unknown for them. For succeeding in the CreaCube task the participants are proposed to use four Cubelets robotic modular cubes to solve a robot creation challenge in which they should build a vehicle able to move from an initial red point to a final black point (Fig. 3).

Fig. 3. Participant exploring the cubes.

The CreaCube task requires the participant to explore the robotic cubes in order to figure out the way the behave. This initial exploration is required before engaging in a building activity requiring an important cognitive flexibility to adjust the intermediate solutions to achieve the solution. The novelty of the task and the technology manipulated by the participants could impact their cognitive flexibility in the problem solving CreaCube task. Cognitive flexibility, understood as the human ability to adapt cognitive processing strategies to face new and unexpected conditions, has pointed as intrinsically linked to attentional processes in problem solving tasks [21].

We observe older adults in a playful robotic task aiming to observe their cognitive flexibility. The playful robotic task engages the participants individually in problem solving a puzzle-based challenge with modular robotics. Modular robotics are an unknown technology for most of the participants; in particular older ones which has not played with this type of technologies [22]; older adults does not associate it to the electronic games younger participants evoke when interacting with the robotic cubes. Elderly engaged in the CreaCube task observes the cubes and grasp them to touch the metallic parts. Once they observe the cubes are magnetic and could be assembled, the participants engage in a, reflexive analysis of the errors and cognitive flexibility is required to change the different building solutions until finding a correct solution. CreaCube is an ill-defined robotic task in which the initial complexity engages the participant in a series of unsuccessful prototypes. When observing the problems appearing in each prototype the participant has the possibility to understand the features of each robotic cube and be potentially able to acquir3e the enough knowledge to complete the CreaCube task. Cognitive flexibility is therefore important to be able to develop different solutions with the robotic cubes and analyze the errors in each of the phases. In each prototype testing, we can observe cognitive flexibility as how the person changes its solution "selectively in response to appropriate environmental stimuli" [23]. In a similar way, cognitive flexibility is for Krems [24] the "person's ability to adjust his or her problem solving as task demands are modified" (p. 202), a set of modifications which in the CreaCube appears at each new combination of the robotic cubes.

4.1 Cognitive Flexibility

When engaged in problem solving activities, the participants should be able to generate different ideas in order to explore the best solution for the problem. Within this context, cognitive flexibility is a key executive function to generate and decide the best idea. Cognitive flexibility is part of the important executive functions making possible to the individuals to understand a problem, generate hypotheses to solve it and evaluate the relevance of each of these hypotheses to find the most appropriate solution. If the first hypothesis tested is not the right one, then it will be necessary to be able to disengage from this solution to seek a new and more suitable resolution mode [25].

Cognitive flexibility is expected to be better developed in adulthood [26] when the prefrontal cortex is already mature [27]. From the observations we have started to develop through the CreaCube task we observe kids younger than 10 years to have difficulties to keep in mind the task objective, while older kids and adults are able to keep in mind the objectives. Among older adults, cognitive flexibility could decline [28], which could be explained with a reduction of dopamine levels [29]. Through the CreaCube task we observe cognitive flexibility in relation to the iterative prototypes proposed to solve the task.

5   Results

Four older adults were voluntarily engaged in the CreaCube task within a community center environment in a peripherical neighbourhood of a small city. Participants engaged in the CreaCube tasks are healthy and socially active older adults, but they self-declare themselves as less knowledgeable than other adults which could be analysed as a low self-steem in relation to academic tasks. We analyse cognitive flexibility in relation to the different shapes and cubes moves made during the CreaCube tasks.

We can observe all the four adults to focus on a single shape for the construction instead of creating different shapes. The shape used by the older adults is the "train", which combine the four cubes in a row (Fig. 4).

Fig. 4. Participant assembling the cubes in a "train" shape.

Adults and younger participants created different shapes during their problem-solving activity demonstrating a higher cognitive flexibility in terms of shapes imagined solving the CreaCube task (Fig. 5).

Fig. 5. Adult participant assembling the cubes in a "S" shape.

The problems faced by the older participants during the CreaCube task are also informative about their difficulties within this task.

In Fig. 6, we observe the difficulties of an elderly participant along the CreaCube task. The elderly engages in the task 9:30 min. Until 9:15, the participant fails to make move the robot, and thereafter the sense of advancements of the robot is inversed. The duration of these problems could be analysed as a difficulty to propose other solutions which can overcome the problem.

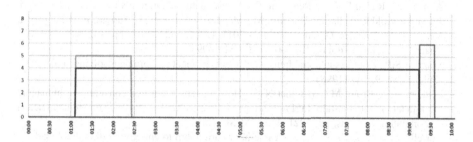

Fig. 6. Elderly participant problems during the CreaCube task.

6   Conclusion, Limitations and Implications

Older participants appear to be less cognitive flexible in the CreaCube task. The task is characterized by its novelty and its ill-definition. Elderly focus on a single shape for the solution despite the persistence of the problems when they test their solution. Younger participants react with a higher cognitive flexibility to problems appearing during the CreaCube task. The error tolerance of participants facing the assembling problems during the process of solving the CreaCube task is invoked by the activity [30]. When facing a problem, the participants with higher cognitive flexibility considers an array of different solutions that could be tested to verify the hypothesis generated during the problem-solving process.

We should consider the possibility that the context of the task could have led to frustration in a context where the older adults are not familiar with the researchers engaging them in the CreaCube task and they feel evaluated. Additional tests of the CreaCube tasks would consider the social connection with the researchers to consider the possibility that creating a more relaxed condition for the CreaCube test could help the older participants to better cope with the frustrations generated by the errors in the intermediate solutions. Another possibility to better manage the stress of the task developed in individual settings is the possibility to evaluate the collaborative problem-solving processes when participants are engaged in same-age groups or intergenerational teams. In addition to better managing the situation, the CreaCube task should be developed with a higher number of participants in order to analyse the standardised ways of solving the task and better situate each of the participants within a certain level of cognitive flexibility. The advancement on this research axes is integrated in the ANR CreaMaker project which will finish in 2022 with the early results on the collaborative problem-solving favors and cons.

Acknowledgments. This work benefited from the support of the project ANR CréaMaker of the French National Research Agency (ANR).

References

1. Ahmad, B., Richardson, I., Beecham, S.: A systematic literature review of social network systems for older adults. In: Felderer, M., Méndez Fernández, D., Turhan, B., Kalinowski, M., Sarro, F., Winkler, D. (eds.) PROFES 2017. LNCS, vol. 10611, pp. 482–496. Springer, Cham (2017). https://doi.org/10.1007/978-3-319-69926-4_38
2. Wagner, S.P.: Robotics and children: science achievement and problem solving. J. Comput. Child. Educ. **9**, 149 (1998)
3. Pelikan, H.R., Broth, M.: Why that Nao?: How humans adapt to a conventional humanoid robot in taking turns-at-talk. In: Proceedings of the 2016 CHI Conference on Human Factors in Computing Systems, pp. 4921–4932. ACM (2016)
4. Correll, N., Wailes, C., Slaby, S.: A one-hour curriculum to engage middle school students in robotics and computer science using cubelets. In: Ani Hsieh, M., Chirikjian, G. (eds.) Distributed Autonomous Robotic Systems. STAR, vol. 104, pp. 165–176. Springer, Heidelberg (2014). https://doi.org/10.1007/978-3-642-55146-8_12
5. Matarić, M.J., Arkin, R.C.: The Robotics Primer. MIT Press, Cambridge (2007)
6. Munich, M.E., Ostrowski, J., Pirjanian, P.: ERSP: a software platform and architecture for the service robotics industry. In: 2005 IEEE/RSJ International Conference on Intelligent Robots and Systems, (IROS 2005), pp. 460–467. IEEE (2005)
7. DiSalvo, C.F., Gemperle, F., Forlizzi, J., Kiesler, S.: All robots are not created equal: the design and perception of humanoid robot heads. In: Proceedings of the 4th Conference on Designing Interactive Systems: Processes, Practices, Methods, and Techniques, pp. 321–326. ACM (2002)
8. Lapeyre, M., et al.: Poppy: open source 3D printed robot for experiments in developmental robotics. In: ICDL-EPIROB, pp. 173–174 (2014)
9. Noirpoudre, S., et al.: Poppy education: un dispositif robotique open source pour l'enseignement de l'informatique et de la robotique. In: Environnements Informatiques pour l'Apprentissage Humain, EIAH 2017, p. 8 (2017)
10. Romero, M., David, D., Lille, B.: CreaCube, a playful activity with modular robotics. In: Games and Learning Alliance, Palermo, IT (2011)
11. Yanco, H.A., Drury, J.L.: A taxonomy for human-robot interaction. In: Proceedings of the AAAI Fall Symposium on Human-Robot Interaction, pp. 111–119 (2002)
12. Yanco, H.A., Drury, J.: Classifying human-robot interaction: an updated taxonomy. In: 2004 IEEE International Conference on Systems, Man and Cybernetics, pp. 2841–2846. IEEE (2004)
13. Wu, Y.-H., Fassert, C., Rigaud, A.-S.: Designing robots for the elderly: appearance issue and beyond. Arch. Gerontol. Geriatr. **54**, 121–126 (2012)
14. Broekens, J., Heerink, M., Rosendal, H., et al.: Assistive social robots in elderly care: a review. Gerontechnology **8**, 94–103 (2009)
15. Kidd, C.D., Taggart, W., Turkle, S.: A sociable robot to encourage social interaction among the elderly. In: Proceedings 2006 IEEE International Conference on Robotics and Automation, ICRA 2006, pp. 3972–3976. IEEE (2006)
16. Tamura, T., et al.: Is an entertainment robot useful in the care of elderly people with severe dementia? J. Gerontol. A Biol. Sci. Med. Sci. **59**, M83–M85 (2004)

17. Banks, M.R., Willoughby, L.M., Banks, W.A.: Animal-assisted therapy and loneliness in nursing homes: use of robotic versus living dogs. J. Am. Med. Dir. Assoc. **9**, 173–177 (2008)
18. Al-Halhouli, A., Qitouqa, H., Malkosh, N., Shubbak, A., Al-Gharabli, S., Hamad, E.: LEGO mindstorms NXT for elderly and visually impaired people in need: a platform. Technol. Health Care **24**, 579–585 (2016)
19. Cruz-Martín, A., Fernández-Madrigal, J.A., Galindo, C., González-Jiménez, J., Stockmans-Daou, C., Blanco-Claraco, J.L.: A LEGO mindstorms NXT approach for teaching at data acquisition, control systems engineering and real-time systems undergraduate courses. Comput. Educ. **59**, 974–988 (2012)
20. Romero, M., DeBlois, L., Pavel, A.: Créacube, comparaison de la résolution créative de problèmes, chez des enfants et des adultes, par le biais d'une tâche de robotique modulaire. MathémaTICE (2018)
21. Canas, J., Quesada, J., Antolí, A., Fajardo, I.: Cognitive flexibility and adaptability to environmental changes in dynamic complex problem-solving tasks. Ergonomics **46**, 482–501 (2003)
22. Romero, M., Loos, E.: Playing with robotic cubes: age matters. In: Britesa, M.J., Amaral, I., Patrício, R., Pereira, L. (eds.) Intergenerationality in a Digital World: Proposals of Activities, pp. 55–56. Edições Universitárias Lusófonas (2018)
23. Scott, W.A.: Cognitive complexity and cognitive flexibility. Sociometry, 405–414 (1962)
24. Krems, J.F.: Cognitive flexibility and complex problem solving. Complex Probl. Solving Eur. Perspect., 201–218 (1995)
25. D'zurilla, T.J., Goldfried, M.R.: Problem solving and behavior modification. J. Abnorm. Psychol. **78**, 107 (1971)
26. Davidson, M.C., Amso, D., Anderson, L.C., Diamond, A.: Development of cognitive control and executive functions from 4 to 13 years: evidence from manipulations of memory, inhibition, and task switching. Neuropsychologia **44**, 2037–2078 (2006)
27. Dennis, J.R.: Computer classification of triangles and quadrilaterals–a challenging application. Ill. Ser. Educ. Appl. Comput. 19 (1976)
28. Johnco, C., Wuthrich, V., Rapee, R.: The role of cognitive flexibility in cognitive restructuring skill acquisition among older adults. J. Anxiety Disord. **27**, 576–584 (2013)
29. Berry, A.S., et al.: Aging affects dopaminergic neural mechanisms of cognitive flexibility. J. Neurosci. (2016). 0626–16
30. Dörner, D.: The Logic of Failure: Recognizing and Avoiding Error in Complex Situations. Addison-Wesley Pub, Reading (1997)

Is the Eye Movement Pattern the Same? The Difference Between Automated Driving and Manual Driving

Qiuyang Tang[✉] and Gang Guo

College of Automotive Engineering, Chongqing University, Chongqing, China
qiuyang.tang@foxmail.com

Abstract. This driving simulator study was conducted to investigate the drivers' eye movement pattern in automated and manual driving condition, and examine which ocular metrics are effective to evaluate the vigilance (response task) of drivers when they in a state of fatigue. Images of drivers' eye movement were recorded in both conditional automated and manual driving conditions. Ocular metrics such as horizontal eye activity, vertical eye activity, PERCLOS and time of each eye closure (TEEC) were obtained from the images, and the metrics were averaged in a 5-min period with the label of fatigue level (Karolinska Sleepiness scores). Using a within-participant design, twenty participants experienced automated and manual driving with response tasks. Results of the study showed that drivers' horizontal and vertical eye activity were generally higher than that observed during manual driving when drivers in some signs of sleepiness. However, with the deepening of fatigue, drivers' eye activity decreased significantly in automated driving condition, but a sustainable effect was found in manual driving. Interestingly, the ocular metric of TEEC seems more accurate to evaluate the vigilance of drivers than PERCLOS in automated driving condition. Therefore, decreasing the time of each eye closure seems a useful way to increase the vigilance of drivers.

Keywords: Automated driving · Manual driving · Fatigue · Eye movement

1 Introduction

Nowadays, highly-automated vehicles that can drive autonomously in specific scenario are conceivable. Drivers in highly-automated vehicle are free from operating the steering wheel, accelerator, or brake, but are requested to supervise the automated driving system and regain control authority when vehicle meets its system limitations such as extremely weather, sensor failure or unpredictable events (International 2016). However, it is highly monotonous for drivers to detect and response to rare and unpredictable events during automated driving, and it requires drivers to keep vigilance for a long time (Hancock 2017). Due to the monotonous process of monitoring, drivers in highly automated vehicle have been shown to become fatigue faster than manual drivers (Schömig et al. 2015; Vogelpohl et al. 2018). Consequently, drivers' vigilance and the ability of drivers to response to takeover request reduced due to the increase of fatigue level (Greenlee et al. 2018; Körber et al. 2015; Saxby et al. 2013). In addition,

© Springer Nature Switzerland AG 2019
J. Zhou and G. Salvendy (Eds.): HCII 2019, LNCS 11593, pp. 554–563, 2019.
https://doi.org/10.1007/978-3-030-22015-0_43

low mental workload will impair the performance of driver. Previous studies demonstrated that drivers' attention resource pools decreased with the reduction in mental workload, and drivers might not aware of the decrease of performance if they were in a state of fatigue (Matthews and Desmond 2002; Young and Stanton 2002). In practice, many methods have been used to detect driver fatigue and drowsiness. In the study of Saito et al. (2016) vibration of vehicle's lateral position and steering wheel angle were found increasing significantly when the drivers became extremely drowsy. Physiologically, ECG and EEG are widely used to evaluate the fatigue of drivers (Mahachandra et al. 2015; Schmidt et al. 2017). Eye movement metrics were also highly related to the fatigue of drivers. PERCLOS (The percentage of time that the eyelids were closed) was found to be sensitive to driver fatigue (Kozak et al. 2005). In the study of McKinley et al. (2011), an indicator of approximate entropy (ApEn) was found to be more sensitive to evaluate vigilance than PERCLOS. Pupil diameter, blink frequency and closure time were also used to evaluate driver fatigue and vigilance (Abe et al. 2011; Bradley et al. 2008). The studies mentioned above were conducted in the condition of manual driving. However, shortcomings in pilot's automation monitoring strategies and performance was found based on eye tracking analysis (Sarter et al. 2007). In conditional automated driving condition, drivers are still requested to maintain vigilance for potential dangers and takeover control authority if the automated system meets its system limitations. Due to the totally different driving condition, the eye movement results obtained from manual driving condition may not appropriate for automated driving condition.

Therefore, the eye movement pattern of drivers in conditional automated vehicle is critical for evaluation of driver fatigue and vigilance, and should be explored for better design of in-vehicle HMI. In this study, a driving simulator experiment was conducted in the condition of automated and manual driving.

2 Method

2.1 Participants

Twenty participants (12 men and 8 women) taken part in this experiment had a mean age of 28.5 years (SD = 6.0). The mean driving experience of participants was 5.1 years (SD = 2.7). The participants were students and teachers of the College of automotive engineering, Chongqing University, and all of them had the knowledge of automated driving and driving simulator. All participants received monetary compensation for taking part in the experiment. Participants were instructed to keep their sleep schedule for one week before the experiment, and avoid tea or caffeine on the day of experiment.

2.2 Apparatus

In this experiment, a fixed-base driving simulator (Realtime Technology SimCreator, USA) with automated driving function was adopted. The 180° horizontal field of view was projected by three faceted front screens (1,920 × 1,080 resolution), and the rear views were displayed by three LCD screens. The road noise, engine sound and vehicle vibration were simulated by a series of speakers around the simulator.

The eye movement images of participants were recorded and analyzed through a Dikablis Professional eye tracker (Ergnoeers, Germany). Two infrared cameras were used to record the images of left eye and right eye respectively. The eye movement indicators adopted in this study were calculated by eye movement analysis software D-Lab (Ergnoeers, Germany) based on the images that recorded by the eye tracker.

2.3 Procedure

The study employed a within-subject-design, participants were requested to travel on a monotonous highway with two driving conditions: automated and manual. Before the formal experiment, participants were allowed to familiar themselves with the driving simulator and the automated driving system for 5 min. After that, participants were traveling on a bi-directional four-lines motorway in one of the two conditions. In order to elicit the fatigue of driver, the experiment was conducted in a dark room with dim lights.

Participants were required to monitor the vehicle condition and driving environment, and press a button on the steering wheel immediately when a yellow light on dashboard started to flicker. The time from the light starting to flicker to participants pressing the button was regarded as reaction time. The hint will be displayed on the dashboard for five seconds. In case a participant missed the hint, the reaction time will be regarded as 5 s. The yellow light on dashboard would flicker with an interval of 5 min. After the participants had made response to the yellow light, the subjective fatigue would be evaluated immediately through the Karolinska Sleepiness Scale (KSS) (Åkerstedt and Gillberg 1990). Simultaneously, the data of eye movement in the 5-min period will be averaged. In both automated and manual driving condition, the traffic speeds are restricted to 120 km/h, and the traffic density is 13 vehicles per kilometer. The duration of the experiment was not limited, and it ended until the drivers reached fatigue level of 8. For each participant, the interval of the two experiment is at least one day, and the order was randomized to counterbalance the bias.

2.4 Data Analysis

With the eye movement analysis software D-Lab (Ergnoeers, Germany), evidence values for diverse eye movement could be extracted. In the D-lab, the indicator of percentage of eyelid closure time (PERCLOS) was adopted in this study, which was of interest for objective fatigue evaluation. In addition, the indicator of time of each eye closure (TEEC) were calculated based on the image that recorded by the infrared cameras. The indicators of horizontal eye activity and vertical eye activity were utilized to evaluate the vigilance of drivers. The continuous recording data of eye movement were averaged for each period, and the data of the left and right eye were averaged before further analysis.

A two-factor ANOVA with repeated measures was adopted to analyze the variables separately. One factor is driving condition (two levels) and the repeated measures factor is KSS score: 6, 7 and 8 (K6, K7 and K8). Degrees of freedom were Greenhouse-Geiser corrected, if Mauchly's test for sphericity showed violated. Post-hoc tests with Bonferroni correction were performed for any statistical significant differences. Statistical significance was noted when p-values were less than 0.05.

3 Results

We measured drivers' fatigue and vigilance based on subjective and objective metrics. Prior to any inferential analyses, data of eye movement were averaged for the three fatigue levels: K6, K7 and K8.

3.1 Measures of Eye Movement

Horizontal Activity. The result of horizontal activity was shown in Fig. 1. There was a significant interaction effect between driving condition and fatigue level on horizontal activity $(F(2,38) = 3.306, p = 0.047)$. As for the fatigue level the horizontal activity has no significant difference between the two conditions $(F(1,19) = 1.132, p = 0.301)$ for K6, $F(1,19) = 0.057, p = 0.814$ for K7 and $F(1,19) = 1.622, p = 0.218$ for K8). However, in automated driving condition the horizontal activity decreased significantly with the increase of fatigue level $(F(1.312,24.937) = 23.381, p < 0.001)$, Post hoc pairwise comparisons indicated that horizontal activity in K7 was significantly lower than K6 $(p = 0.023)$ and K8 was significantly lower than K7 $(p < 0.001)$. In the manual driving condition, the results of ANOVA show that fatigue level had no significant effect on horizontal activity $(F(2,38) = 0.146, p = 0.865)$.

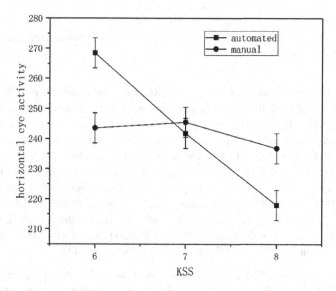

Fig. 1. Horizontal eye activities as a function of KSS score for the two driving conditions, error bars (± 5) represent standard deviations.

Vertical Activity. The result of vertical activity was shown in Fig. 2. The interaction effect between condition and fatigue level was not significant ($F(1.407,26.728) = 2.981, p = 0.083$). The results of ANOVA analysis demonstrated that drivers' vertical eye activity had no significant difference between automated and manual driving ($F(1,19) = 0.333, p = 0.571$). However, vertical activity indeed changed with fatigue level ($F(1.450,27.555) = 6.257, p = 0.011$). Post hoc pairwise comparisons indicated that vertical activity in K8 was significantly lower than K6 ($p = 0.025$) and K7 ($p = 0.001$).

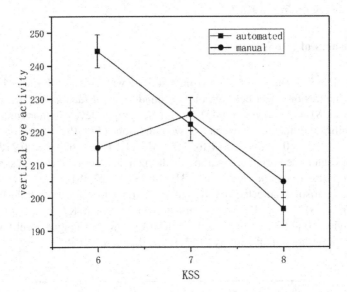

Fig. 2. Vertical eye activities as a function of KSS score for the two driving conditions, error bars (± 5) represent standard deviations.

PERCLOS. Figure 3 shows the results of PERCLOS. The results of ANOVA analysis indicate that driving condition and fatigue level have a significant interaction effect on PERCLOS ($F(1.400,26.594) = 46.553, p < 0.001$). In the three fatigue levels, the PERCLOS in automated driving condition was all greater than manual driving condition ($F(1,19) = 9.452, p = 0.006$) for K6, $F(1,19) = 31.362, p < 0.001$ for K7 and $F(1,19) = 181.843, p < 0.001$ for K8). In automated driving condition, the PERCLOS increased significantly with the deepening of the fatigue ($F(1.240,23.555) = 57.147, p < 0.001$). Post hoc pairwise comparisons indicated that PERCLOS in K8 was significantly greater than K7 ($p < 0.001$) and K7 was significantly greater than K6($p < 0.001$). However, in manual driving condition, the PERCLOS seems was not affected by fatigue level ($F(1.507,28.639) = 1.056, p = 0.343$).

TEEC. The results of TEEC was shown in Fig. 4. An ANOVA revealed that period of driving condition and fatigue level had no interaction effect on TEEC ($F(1.115,21.951) = 0.289, p = 0.629$). However, significant difference of TEEC was found between the two conditions $(F(1,19) = 19.675, p < 0.001)$. As the Fig. 4 shows, the TEEC increased with the deepening of fatigue in both automated and manual driving condition, but no significant effect was reported $(F(2,38) = 3.009, p = 0.061)$.

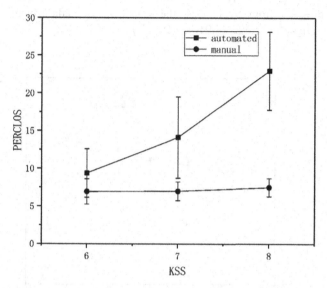

Fig. 3. PERCLOS as a function of KSS score for the two driving conditions, error bars represent standard deviations.

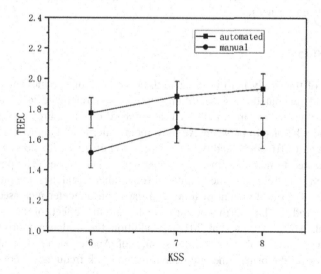

Fig. 4. TEEC as a function of KSS score for the two driving conditions, error bars represent standard deviations.

Reaction Time. As can be seen in Fig. 5, the reaction time presents out the same change trend with TEEC in both automated and manual driving condition. No interaction effect between driving condition and fatigue level was found ($F(2,38) = 0.945$, $p = 0.397$). The results of analysis revealed a significant main effect of driving condition, drivers in automated condition indeed made response to hints slower than manual driving ($F(1,19) = 18.485, p < 0.001$). However, the results of ANOVA found that, different from hypothesis, the reaction time didn't increase with the deepening of fatigue ($F(1.522,28.910) = 2.322, p = 0.127$).

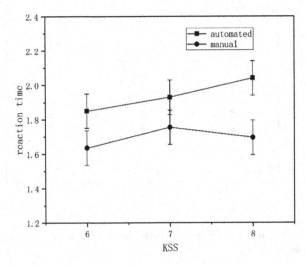

Fig. 5. Reaction time as a function of KSS score for the two driving conditions, error bars represent standard deviations.

4 Discussion

The purpose of this study is to investigate the difference of eye movement pattern in automated and manual driving condition, and provide reference to in-vehicle HMI design for better safety in conditional automated driving. Previous studies had researched the relationship between eye movement pattern and fatigue level. The study of Jackson et al. (2016) indicated that, the proportion of time with slow eyelid closure was highly related to reaction time, attentional lapses and crashes. The pupil diameter was also found to be related to the fatigue. In some other researches, the pupil diameter decreased with the development of time, and the pupil diameter increased when participants received a short-term cooling which had the effect of relieving fatigue (Schmidt et al. 2017; Schmidt et al. 2017). In addition, the vigilance of driving was also related to the behavior of eyes. In the studies of Abe et al. (2011), increasing in percentage of eyelid closure time and decreasing in blink frequency were observed as the consecutive missed responses increased. However, the studies mentioned above were conducted in manual driving condition. In the research of Abe et al. (2011) the participants were free from driving task, but the event rate was relatively high. The interval between two events was 3 s, and the test will end when closing eyes more than 21 s. However, our experiment was conducted based on the background of conditional automated driving. Actually, the frequency of drivers encountering potentially dangerous events in conditional automated vehicle is quite low. Therefore, the interval between two events in this experiment is 5 min. Due to the monotonous automated driving and underload, drivers got fatigued very soon. In addition, most participants reported that they lost track of time due to the monotonous monitoring task. Therefore, the participants couldn't be prepared for the next event.

As the results of horizontal eye activity show, when drivers in a state of some signs of sleepiness (K6) the horizontal eye activity is slightly higher in automated driving condition compared with manual driving condition, which is in consistent with the research of Louw and Merat (2017). Drivers in conditional automated driving condition were free from driving tasks, so they had more attention resource for monitoring tasks. In this experiment, participants were driving on a monotonous highway, and the traffic density was 13 vehicles per kilometer. Therefore, the event rate of overtaking was quiet low, which resulted in gazing on the road center. However, despite the drivers seemed to ignore the vehicle dashboard, but they could still make response to the hints on dashboard.

However, a significant decrease in horizontal activity was found with the deepening of fatigue in automated driving condition, but no significant effect was found in manual driving condition. The results of ANOVA demonstrated a significant interaction effect between driving condition and fatigue level. Presumably, drivers can easily see the hint on dashboard and believe they can takeover control authority from automation rapidly.

As for vertical eye activity, no difference was found between the two driving condition. In both automated and manual driving condition, drivers generally check the rearview mirror, and drivers' attention will be attracted by the vehicles that overtake their vehicle. In spite the fact that the alarm light was placed on the dashboard, drivers were still seldom lowered their gaze to check the alarm light. The main course may be that, the alarm light is in their sight, drivers could still notice the change of alarm light even they didn't gaze at it.

In this experiment, the PERCLOS and the TEEC in automated driving condition were found significantly higher than manual driving condition in K6, K7 and K8. The indicator of PERCLOS was found to be highly correlated to vigilance while performing visual vigilance tasks (Wierwille and Ellsworth 1994). Additionally, the results of Abe et al. (2011) has shown that the response time increased significantly with the increasing of PERCLOS levels. However, in the automated driving condition experiment of this study, no significant correlation was reported between PERCLOS and reaction time ($p = 0.636$). Interestingly, a Pearson correlation analysis revealed that the eye movement indicator of TEEC was highly related to the reaction time ($p < 0.001$). In the study of Schmidt et al. (2017), drivers were driving manually, so it is dangerous for drivers to close their eyes for a long period of time. However, this experiment was conducted based on the background of conditional automated driving. Actually, the frequency of drivers encountering potentially dangerous events in conditional automated vehicle is quite low. The reaction time, PERCLOS and the TEEC were increasing simultaneously from the with the deepening of fatigue. However, with the deepening of fatigue, drivers adopted different monitoring strategies for potentially system failure. Participants tended to close their eyes more frequently, instead of prolonging the duration of each eye closure. They tended to take a glance at the driving environment after several seconds of eye closure. This kind of eye movement behavior will increase the PERCLOS rapidly, but the time of each eye closure (TEEC) seemed unaffected. Which is perhaps why, despite the deepening of the fatigue, the driver's reaction time did not increase significantly with the deepening of fatigue. The study of Lu et al. (2017) concluded that observers could reproduce the layout of a situation in a short period of time. In this experiment, the driving environment and the tasks were both relatively simple. Therefore, taking a glance at driving environment may be sufficient for drivers to keep situation awareness and vigilance for a few seconds.

5 Conclusion

Drivers eye movement pattern in automated and manual driving conditions are different. The eye movement activity of drivers in automated driving vehicle will decrease with the development of fatigue, which results in deteriorated situation awareness and longer reaction time. In addition, the indicator of TEEC is more effective in evaluation of vigilance in conditional automated driving, especially for drivers in extremely sleepy.

References

Abe, T., Nonomura, T., Komada, Y., Asaoka, S., Sasai, T., Ueno, A., et al.: Detecting deteriorated vigilance using percentage of eyelid closure time during behavioral maintenance of wakefulness tests. Int. J. Psychophysiol. **82**(3), 269–274 (2011)

Åkerstedt, T., Gillberg, M.: Subjective and objective sleepiness in the active individual. Int. J. Neurosci. **52**(1–2), 29–37 (1990)

Bradley, M.M., Miccoli, L., Escrig, M.A., Lang, P.J.: The pupil as a measure of emotional arousal and autonomic activation. Psychophysiology **45**(4), 602–607 (2008)

Greenlee, E.T., DeLucia, P.R., Newton, D.C.: Driver vigilance in automated vehicles: hazard detection failures are a matter of time. Hum. Factors **60**(4), 465–476 (2018)

Hancock, P.A.: On the nature of vigilance. Hum. Factors **59**(1), 35–43 (2017)

SAE International. Taxonomy and Definitions for Terms Related to Driving Automation Systems for On-Road Motor Vehicles (J3016) (2016)

Jackson, M.L., Kennedy, G.A., Clarke, C., Gullo, M., Swann, P., Downey, L.A., et al.: The utility of automated measures of ocular metrics for detecting driver drowsiness during extended wakefulness. Accid. Anal. Prev. **87**, 127–133 (2016)

Körber, M., Cingel, A., Zimmermann, M., Bengler, K.: Vigilance decrement and passive fatigue caused by monotony in automated driving. Procedia Manuf. **3**, 2403–2409 (2015)

Kozak, K., Curry, R., Greenberg, J., Artz, B., Blommer, M., Cathey, L.: Leading indicators of drowsiness in simulated driving. Proc. Hum. Factors Ergon. Soc. Annu. Meet. **49**(22), 1917–1921 (2005)

Louw, T., Merat, N.: Are you in the loop? using gaze dispersion to understand driver visual attention during vehicle automation. Transp. Res. Part C **76**, 35–50 (2017)

Lu, Z., Coster, X., de Winter, J.: How much time do drivers need to obtain situation awareness? a laboratory-based study of automated driving. Appl. Ergon. **60**, 293–304 (2017)

Mahachandra, M., Garnaby, E.D.: The effectiveness of in-vehicle peppermint fragrance to maintain car driver's alertness. Procedia Manuf. **4**, 471–477 (2015)

Matthews, G., Desmond, P.A.: Task-induced fatigue states and simulated driving performance. Q. J. Exp. Psychol. Sect. A **55**(2), 659–686 (2002)

McKinley, R.A., McIntire, L.K., Schmidt, R., Repperger, D.W., Caldwell, J.A.: Evaluation of eye metrics as a detector of fatigue. Hum. Factors: J. Hum. Factors Ergon. Soc. **53**(4), 403–414 (2011)

Saito, Y., Itoh, M., Inagaki, T.: Driver assistance system with a dual control scheme: effectiveness of identifying driver drowsiness and preventing lane departure accidents. IEEE Trans. Hum.-Mach. Syst. **46**(5), 660–671 (2016)

Sarter, N.B., Mumaw, R.J., Wickens, C.D.: Pilots' monitoring strategies and performance on automated flight decks: an empirical study combining behavioral and eye-tracking data. Hum. Factors: J. Hum. Factors Ergon. Soc. **49**(3), 347–357 (2007)

Saxby, D.J., Matthews, G., Warm, J.S., Hitchcock, E.M., Neubauer, C.: Active and passive fatigue in simulated driving: discriminating styles of workload regulation and their safety impacts. J. Exp. Psychol.: Appl. **19**(4), 287–300 (2013)

Schmidt, E., Decke, R., Rasshofer, R., Bullinger, A.C.: Psychophysiological responses to short-term cooling during a simulated monotonous driving task. Appl. Ergon. **62**, 9–18 (2017)

Schmidt, J., Dreißig, M., Stolzmann, W., Rötting, M.: The influence of prolonged conditionally automated driving on the take-over ability of the driver. Proc. Hum. Factors Ergon. Soc. Annu. Meet. **61**(1), 1974–1978 (2017)

Schömig, N., Hargutt, V., Neukum, A., Petermann-Stock, I., Othersen, I.: The interaction between highly automated driving and the development of drowsiness. Procedia Manuf. **3**, 6652–6659 (2015)

Vogelpohl, T., Kühn, M., Hummel, T., Vollrath, M.: Asleep at the automated wheel—sleepiness and fatigue during highly automated driving. Accid. Anal. Prev. **126**, 70–84 (2018)

Wierwille, W.W., Ellsworth, L.A.: Evaluation of driver drowsiness by trained raters. Accid. Anal. Prev. **26**(5), 571–581 (1994)

Young, M.S., Stanton, N.A.: Malleable attentional resources theory: a new explanation for the effects of mental underload on performance. Hum. Factors **44**(3), 365–375 (2002)

Augmented Walking Suit for Elderly Farmers in Agricultural Environment

Chetan Thakur[✉] and Yuichi Kurita

Graduate School of Engineering, Hiroshima University, 1-4-1, Kagamiyama,
Higashi-Hiroshima 739-8527, Japan
{chetanthakur,ykurita}@hiroshima-u.ac.jp
http://www.bsys.hiroshima-u.ac.jp

Abstract. Aging impacts muscle function and reduces one's ability to perform daily tasks comfortably. Elderly people face various challenges due to such condition to continue perform their work. Elderly farmers or workers are often expose to accidents or muscle injuries due to stressful work condition and can easily get tired. Elderly people find it difficult to use or adapt current set of human augmentation devices mainly due to the size, weight and ability to use it in agricultural environment. Previously developed a soft wearable and lightweight augmented walking suit (AWS) assists swing phase of the walking gait. Evaluation showed reduced muscle efforts and no major change in gait kinematics. To understand the requirement, usability and usefulness of the AWS in real life situation we conducted survey and pilot trial with farmers in rural areas. In this paper we discussed the feedback and requirements received through survey and pilot trials. The survey and subjective evaluation from these trials suggests the elderly people prefers lightweight and wearable assistive devices to reduce the required muscle efforts of similar tasks.

Keywords: Wearable assistive suit · Elderly assist design ·
Pilot trial · Soft actuators

1 Introduction

Quality of life and aging gracefully is directly linked with one's ability to easily performs his daily routine tasks. In 2018, Japan's elderly population was 28% of the total population [1] out of which 79% and 56% of elderly in the age group of 60 to 64 and 65 to 69 are engaged in work respectively [2]. As per japan industrial safety and health association (JISHA) [3] 25% of all the critical accidents involves people aged 60 and above. Most common reason for such accidents is occupational injuries, weak muscle or related to workspace management. To address these concerns researchers developed augmentation devices such as exoskeletons or exosuits for agricultural assistance or factory worker assistance devices [4–7]. Human augmentation devices are developed to enhance

© Springer Nature Switzerland AG 2019
J. Zhou and G. Salvendy (Eds.): HCII 2019, LNCS 11593, pp. 564–574, 2019.
https://doi.org/10.1007/978-3-030-22015-0_44

one's physical ability to perform certain tasks. Exoskeletons greatly augment human ability, exosuits address wearability of exoskeletons and yet augments human motions it is designed for. The third category is assistive suit which uses wearable design and soft wearable actuators for human augmentation. These assistive suit augments human motion by reducing required muscle effort for certain tasks.

These recent advancement in the exoskeleton technology allows people working in factories and warehouses reduce stress and muscle fatigue. Yet, elderly find it difficult to use such devices mainly due to size and weight of such devices. Development of lightweight and wearable and easy to use devices is essential for elderly people involve in work.

To address one such concern about walking augmentation, herein in Sect. 2, we briefly discuss the previously developed augmented walking suit (AWS) and its effect in the muscle activation pattern during walking. In Sect. 3, we discuss the outcomes of survey and pilot trials conducted with farmers in rural area. The results, conclusion and future work involves are discussed in the following sections.

2   Augmented Walking Suit

AWS is designed to overcome the challenges of currently available walking assist devices which are wearable, portable and easy to use. Together these are missing in most of the devices [8]. In our research we addressed this by developing pneumatic gel muscle (PGM) [9] which is low pressure driven soft artificial muscle. In AWS we used PGM for generating assistive force.

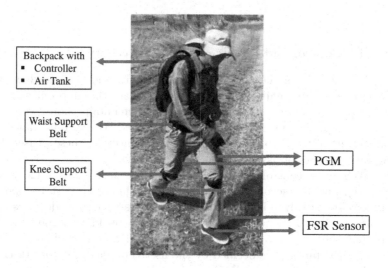

Fig. 1. Configuration of AWS as being used by elderly farmer.

Figure 1 shows the elderly user wearing AWS. AWS consist of PGM to provide assistive force. PGM is low pressure driven soft actuator [9]. Actuation unit consists of pneumatic solenoid valves, force sensors in the shoe to detect gait events, controller, battery and portable air tank required for actuation of PGM. The objective of the AWS is to reduced muscle activity during walking gait by assisting forward motion of lower limb in swing phase of the gait cycle, as shown in Fig. 2. The assistance provided with PGM start from initial swing phase until just before the terminal swing. Assisting swing phase reduces muscle efforts required for hip flexion and knee extension as shown in Fig. 2.

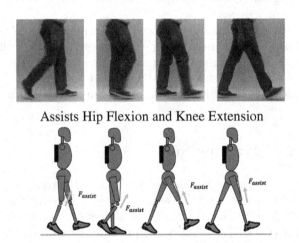

Assists Hip Flexion and Knee Extension

Fig. 2. Objective of AWS, figure shows swing phase of the gait cycle where assistance is provided.

2.1   Assist Control and Effects on Muscle Activity

Walking is synchronous activity of both lower limbs and is divided in stance and swing phase of the gait cycle. In the swing phase the limb makes forward movement at the same time other limb in stance maintains body weight [11]. Chen et al. [12] in his review identified that the time of the limb in stance phase is equal to time of the limb in swing phase and identifying these phases during walking various types of assist control can be achieved.

The AWS assist control is twostep process, the gait phase is identified in the first step and the second step decides which limb to assist by operating pneumatic solenoid valve. The magnitude of the assistive force depends on the supply air pressure. In case of AWS it is between 60 kPa to 200 kPa which is supported operating air pressure range of PGM as reported in [9]. In the current implementation it is decided by the user through regulator attached to the portable air tank.

$$Stance_{phase} \text{ if } FSR \geq FSR_{ref} \tag{1}$$

$$Swing_{phase} \text{ if } FSR < FSR_{ref} \tag{2}$$

$$Right_{Limb}/\text{Left}_{Limb} = \begin{cases} 1, & \text{if } Stance_{phase} \\ 0, & \text{if } Swing_{phase} \end{cases} \tag{3}$$

In the first step FSR sensors in the shoes detects stance and swing phase of the limb as described in Eqs. 1 and 2 assuming normal healthy gait cycle. FSR is real time sensor value and FSR_{ref} is the reference value which decides if the limb is in stance or swing phase. Both the limbs are set either 1 or 0 to signify stance and swing phase respectively as shows in Eq. 3. Based on this in second step, by considering the state of both limb we decide controller action. Table 1 shows the controller action based on phase of right and left limb as set in first step.

Table 1. Assist control actions based on phase detected for both legs

Controller action	RightLimb	LeftLimb
Assist right swing	0	1
Assist left swing	1	0
No assist	1	1
No assist	0	0

2.2 Effects on Muscle Activity

In [8] AWS was evaluated to observe the difference in the muscle activities of assisted and unassisted walking. The experiment involved measuring surface EMG (SEMG) of eight muscles of lower limb which superficially available for recording sEMG, in assisted and unassisted walking. The experiment was conducted on seven healthy subjects. Figures 3 and 4 shows the results of this experiment comparing assisted walking at 100 Kpa assistive air pressure supply and unassisted walking.

In Fig. 3 shows overlapped sEMG signal of eight muscles of lower limb comparing difference in muscle actuation. From these two figures we observe that tibialis anterior, soleus, gastrocnemius (medial and lateral), rectus femoris and biceps femoris muscles which contributes to the swing phase of the gait cycle shows significant reduction. Vastus medialis and vastus latralis shows no change. Figure 4 shows comparison of average of sEMG signals and the significance of the change for each muscle. From these graphs we also observe that assisting swing phase of the gait cycle along hip flexors reduces muscle effort not just in the swing phase but in stance phase as well. This proves that the AWS designed to overcome limitation of traditional exoskeletons can augment human walking by reducing the required muscle activities of the lower limb muscles.

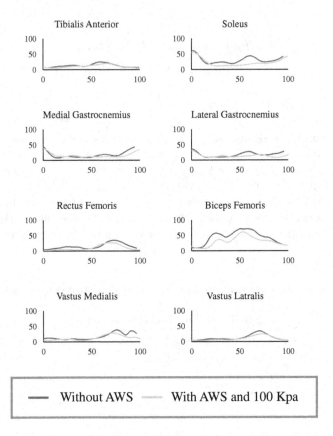

Fig. 3. Comparison of normalized average sEMG signal for unassisted and assisted walking with AWS. The signal in the figure are swing phase to swing phase of gait cycle.

3   Pilot Trials of AWS

The objective of the pilot trial was to study the effectiveness, suitability, usefulness and improvements required for AWS to be used as wearable assistive device for elderly and others. Figure 5 illustrate overview of pilot study and expected outcome.

As shown in Fig. 5, this study was conducted in two parts, in first part we conducted survey about the lifestyle and problem faced due to health issues in agricultural activities. In second part, information related to AWS and its evaluation results, contents of the experiment and its objective were shared with the various prospective participants in the rural region including young and elderly.

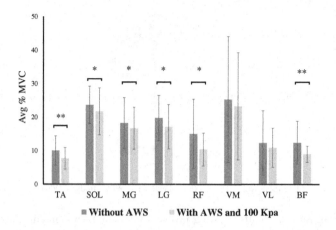

Fig. 4. Comparision of average of normalized sEMG signal for unassisted and assisted walking with AWS.

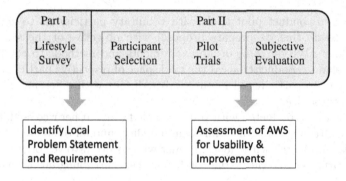

Fig. 5. Overview of pilot study and expected outcome

3.1   Survey

The survey was distributed through the leader of various settlements in the rural areas. Each settlement includes 10 to 15 household. Total 63 people responded to our survey, average age of respondents was 65.31 (min = 28 and max = 85) and 95% were farmers. The survey targeted to identify the nature of work, agricultural practice, common problems faced during farming, are they open to use of assistive devices such as exoskeletons or wearable suit and their view on such technologies. Figure 6 shows physical limitation or problem faced during farming activity and Fig. 7 shows various factors that might affect for adopting to assistive devices. It shows 21% face difficulty or fatigue in their upper limb, 11% face back pain, 17% faces stress in legs and 40% said whole body pain. From Fig. 7 we also observed that most people would want to use newer assistive devices such as exoskeleton or assistive suit provided they are easy to use, safe and affordable. For some respondents its weight and portability is important for adopting to such devices.

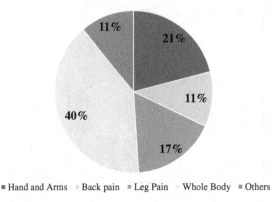

Fig. 6. Survey results showing problem faced by people in rural area.

3.2   Pilot Trials

We decided to conduct pilot trials with voluntary participants to get genuine feedback. To do this we prepare proposal with objective of the study, information about AWS outcome of lab experiments and methods to conduct pilot trials. We plan to conduct trials at the workspace of respective participants. Four people agreed to participated in our study. All four with different age, sex and agricultural practice.

First trial was conducted with young female farmer at her rice field. Her work involves maintenance of poultry farm and rice field and all the related work. The second trial conducted with elderly farmer who's work involves organic rice and vegetable farming. The third trial conducted with two young farmer who's work

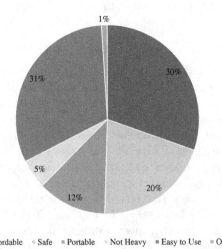

Fig. 7. Factors affecting adoption of assistive devices.

involves rice farming from growing seedlings to processing and packaging rice. Figures 8 and 9 shows volunteers wearing AWS and elderly farmer testing it while performing various activities near his workplace respectively.

Fig. 8. Volunteers trying to AWS.

Fig. 9. Elderly farmer trying AWS performing various daily farming related activities.

After AWS trials, feedback from all the participants were collected using questionnaire and open-ended interview. Figure 10 shows important aspect from questionnaire. The answer to the question is in the range of 1 to 5, where 1 is least likely and 5 is highly likely. From these feedbacks we observed that participants could feel the assistance during walking, it did not interfere regular tasks and was comfortable to walk and they can differentiate between walking with and

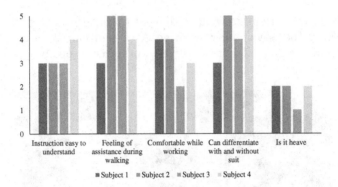

Fig. 10. Feedback received through questionnaire after trials of AWS.

without assistive suit. All participants feel the suit is not heavy and moderately easy to use.

From open-ended interview with each volunteer after trial all said, walking with AWS feels easy as compared to without AWS. The suit is lightweight and does not disturbs the individual workspace or motion. The young female tested the suit for asks such as loading and unloading food packets for chicken in poultry farm, surveying the rice field and farm while walking up and down the slope. Whereas the young male tested the suit in the rice factory. During this he walked around factory, climbing up and down the stairs. He did not find difficulty in using the suit as he felt assistance during walking, and it did not interfere with his regular tasks.

The trial with elderly farmer was conducted at his rice field. The surface at this location was uneven with slopes. The elderly felt assistive force while walking on different type of surfaces doing various tasks involved in his daily farming routine. He felt less effort were required when walking with AWS as compared to without AWS on various surfaces.

From the subjective feedbacks in all the trials we observed that walking with AWS was easier compared to unassisted walking, which complements the results obtained in the evaluation experiment conducted in laboratory. Along with this, volunteers provided additional feedback, where, for young farmers just assisted walking is not enough. They face difficulties in lifting tasks e.g. pick and place of various objects. Use of machineries are not possible due to expensive tools and small workspace. On the other hand, have elderly farmers finds assistive walking useful, because his work involves lot of walking in his rice fields. But he finds the backpack for controller and air tank disturbing while driving the truck to go from one farm to another. Modifying placement of controller and air tank will allow them to keep the suit on while driving and save time when need to use next place.

4 Conclusion and Future Work

From the subjective feedback received from the pilot trials we observed that the assisted walking was very helpful for elderly farmer while walking around agricultural field on various surfaces and doing daily routine tasks. He could identify the difference between muscle stress with and without assistive suit found it useful. For young lady and male farmers, the walking assist force was not so significant, but they found it useful for couple of tasks which requires longer duration of walking or standing activity in agricultural lifestyle. The AWS did not intervene in the workspace while doing various daily routines during trials. All the participants suggested that having lumbar support in addition to the walking assist will be greatly useful. Moving the controller and air tank to the lower limb will make the suit more wearable.

From these feedbacks, we believe that AWS has possibility to be used as assistive device for elderly and others. To improve the usability of the device, we are currently working on improving the wearability of the device. The changes in muscle activation and lower limb kinematics on various types of surfaces are to be identified and evaluated in near future. In addition to this, it is also possible to implement autonomous control for AWS to detect and change assistance based on the user intention. One of the limitations to the device is the portable air tank which lasts for actuation, the technique needs to devised for tank to last longer than current implementation.

Acknowledgments. The authors take this opportunity to thank members of Biological Systems Engineering lab at Graduate School of Engineering in Hiroshima University, Japan for participating in the performance evaluation of the AWS. We also like to thank Daiya Industries for development and support of low pressure driven pneumatic gel muscle i.e. PGM. We also thank all volunteers participated in the pilot trial of AWS and provide their constructive feedback. We would also like to thank Associate Prof. Toshiaki Kondo of Graduate School for International Development and Cooperation, for coordination and support during pilot trials.

This research was partially supported by the Japan Science and Technology Agency as part of the Japan-Taiwan Collaborative Research Program.

The author Chetan Thakur was supported through the Hiroshima University TAOYAKA Program for creating a flexible, enduring, peaceful society, funded by the Program for Leading Graduate Schools, Ministry of Education, Culture, Sports, Science and Technology.

References

1. Stastics Japan: estat. 22 January 2019. http://www.stat.go.jp/data/jinsui/pdf/201901.pdf
2. Stastics Japan: estat, 22 January 2019. http://www.stat.go.jp/english/data/shugyou/pdf/sum2017.pdf
3. JISHA: JISHA:OSH Statistics in Japan, 20 October 2018. https://www.jisha.or.jp/english/statistics/index.html

4. Toyama, S., Yamamoto, G.: Development of wearable-agri-robot mechanism for agricultural work. In: 2009 IEEE/RSJ International Conference on Intelligent Robots and Systems, pp. 5801–5806, October 2009
5. Ikeuchi, Y., Ashihara, J., Hiki, Y., Kudoh, H., Noda, T.: Walking assist device with bodyweight support system. In: 2009 IEEE/RSJ International Conference on Intelligent Robots and Systems, pp. 4073–4079, October 2009
6. Noritsugu, T., Sasaki, D., Kameda, M., Fukunaga, A., Takaiwa, M.: Wearable power assist device for standing up motion using pneumatic rubber artificial muscles. J. Rob. Mechatron. **19**(6), 619–628 (2007)
7. Malcolm, P., Derave, W., Galle, S., De Clercq, D.: A simple exoskeleton that assists plantarflexion can reduce the metabolic cost of human walking. PLoS ONE **8**(2), e56137 (2013)
8. Thakur, C., Ogawa, K., Tsuji, T., Kurita, Y.: Soft wearable augmented walking suit with pneumatic gel muscles and stance phase detection system to assist gait. IEEE Rob. Autom. Lett. **3**(4), 4257–4264 (2018)
9. Ogawa, K., Thakur, C., Ikeda, T., Tsuji, T., Kurita, Y.: Development of a pneumatic artificial muscle driven by low pressure and its application to the unplugged powered suit. Adv. Rob. **31**(21), 1135–1143 (2017)
10. Thakur, C., Ogawa, K., Kurita, Y.: Active passive nature of assistive wearable gait augment suit for enhanced mobility, 1–12 (2018)
11. Perry, J., Burnfield, J.: GAIT normal and pathological function. J. Sports Sci. Med. **9**(2), 551 (2010)
12. Chen, S., Lach, J., Lo, B., Yang, G.Z.: Toward pervasive gait analysis with wearable sensors: a systematic review. IEEE J. Biomed. Health Inf. **20**(6), 1521–1537 (2016)

Integration of Augmented Reality with Pressing Evaluation and Training System for Finger Force Training

Jayzon Ty[1(✉)], Naoki Inoue[1], Alexander Plopski[1], Sayaka Okahashi[2], Christian Sandor[1], Hsiu-Yun Hsu[3], Li-Chieh Kuo[3], Fong-Chin Su[3], and Hirokazu Kato[1]

[1] Nara Institute of Science and Technology, Ikoma, Japan
jayzon.ty.jn8@is.naist.jp
[2] Kyoto University, Kyoto, Japan
[3] National Cheng Kung University, Tainan, Taiwan

Abstract. One major concern for the elderly is the decline in their ability to control their hands, which can significantly affect their ability to perform activities of daily living. One of the important hand functions that deteriorate over time is the ability to control finger force exertion, due to the gradual decrease in finger muscle strength as people age. Previous studies have shown that with proper training, it is possible to regain finger strength. However, when designing training systems for finger force control, visualization of the finger forces plays an important role in its effectiveness. In this paper, we describe the development of the augmented reality pressing and evaluation system (AR-PETS), an augmented reality based prototype system for finger force control training. We discuss the development of the system, as well as the design considerations during the development of the system.

Keywords: Augmented reality · Finger force training · Gamification · Pressing evaluation and training system

1 Introduction

People experience a decline in their capability to control different parts of their bodies as they age. One major cause for concern for the elderly is the decline in their ability to control their hands, which can manifest in the form of reduced finger dexterity, strength, coordination and sensation [1,2]. This can significantly affect their capability to perform activities of daily living (ADLs) that require precise control of their fingers, such as grasping and picking up items.

However, studies have shown that with proper training, regaining control of the hands to a certain extent is possible [3–6], thus enabling the elderly to recover their ability to perform ADLs. Because of this, various training programs for different aspects of hand control have been devised to assist the elderly.

© Springer Nature Switzerland AG 2019
J. Zhou and G. Salvendy (Eds.): HCII 2019, LNCS 11593, pp. 575–587, 2019.
https://doi.org/10.1007/978-3-030-22015-0_45

One particular training that they perform is finger strength training, wherein the tasks usually involve controlling and sustaining the amount of force they exert with their fingers over a period of time. To ensure accurate finger force production, proper feedback is necessary, and previous studies have shown that the lack of feedback during finger strength training can have a negative impact in force control ability [7–9].

Considering the medium for displaying the visualizations representing the finger forces is also important. Usually, training systems display visualizations with a monitor. However, this results in divided attention to two different places, potentially increasing cognitive load. In recent years, augmented reality (AR) technology is re-surfacing as a way of displaying virtual information. AR provides us with the ability to superimpose virtual objects onto the real world, enhancing our perception of and interaction with the real world [10]. In the context of training, we can potentially reduce the cognitive load placed onto the user by placing the finger force visualizations directly on top of the fingers. This allows users to see their hand together with the visualizations, making it easier for them to map a finger with its corresponding visualization.

Based on the above considerations, we developed AR-PETS, a system for finger strength training that integrates augmented reality with the pressing evaluation and training system (PETS), a device specifically built for measuring finger force. In this paper, we discuss the different components of the system, as well as the design considerations during the development of the system.

2   Related Work

2.1   Traditional Hand Rehabilitation Methods

Traditional methods for training hand functions usually involve training with a device specifically built for hand training. For example, a study by Olafsdottir et al. [4] used a hand training device (Digi-Flex) to administer finger strength training to elderly participants. The device can be set to generate different levels of force resistance, and participants train by squeezing the device with their fingers through different levels of resistance. Parikh and Cole [11] asked participants to perform tasks that involve picking up a custom-built object and moving it to different positions and orientations. The custom-built object contains force sensors that measure the force exerted by the participants while grasping the object, and was used as a way to evaluate hand strength and dexterity. One common limitation of these traditional methods is the lack of real-time feedback regarding their performance during the training, e.g., the correctness of their motion, or the amount of force they are exerting with their fingers. Previous studies have shown that the lack of real-time feedback during training can lead to a slow decline in their performance during training, especially in tasks involving accurate finger force production [7–9].

2.2   Multimodal Approach to Hand Rehabilitation Feedback

To address this problem in traditional methods for training hand functions, current systems utilize different modalities to convey a variety of information in real time during training. For example, there are training systems that use auditory displays to convey information to the trainees. Wallis et al. [12] encoded arm movement information into musical notes, and administered training by asking the trainees to move their arms in such a way that they produce pleasing music. Järveläinen et al. [13] encoded finger force into note pitch, and instructed trainees to associate the pitch of the note that they hear and the amount of force they are exerting with their finger.

Training systems commonly present feedback visually, using different forms of media. For example, the systems introduced in [7–9,14,15] use monitors to display visual feedback regarding the amount of force exerted by the trainees onto a force measurement device. Taheri et al. [16,17] and Friedman et al. [18] developed gamified training systems that display both visual and audio feedback for finger movement training. Immersive virtual reality (VR) is also being used for training, where trainees are immersed in a completely virtual environment to make the training tasks more engaging. For example, immersive VR games were developed to promote engagement when undergoing rehabilitation for upper limb movement, such as those done by Elor et al. [19] and Baldominos et al. [20].

2.3   Augmented Reality in Hand Rehabilitation

In recent years, augmented and mixed reality is also being used in rehabilitation programs to enhance motivation and enjoyment of patients while undergoing training. Luo et al. [21] integrated augmented reality with special gloves designed for hand opening rehabilitation to display virtual objects for reach-and-grasp task training. They conducted a preliminary study with three participants, and found general improvements in patients' performance during standard functional tests. Burke et al. [22] described the design principles for creating AR games for rehabilitation, and developed various examples of AR games for rehabilitation using those design principles. Hondori et al. [23] investigated the impact of interface choice on patients' performance during rehabilitation for hand and arm movement. They developed a desktop and projector-based AR version of a popular game "Fruit Ninja" to be used for rehabilitation, and evaluated how patients performed for each version. They found that patients generally had faster reaction times and more targeted movement in the AR version as opposed to the desktop version. They attribute these results to higher cognitive demand for the desktop version since patients need to consider hand-eye coordination. Colomer et al. [24] described the use of a mixed-reality tabletop system as a rehabilitation tool for upper limb rehabilitation. The system presented the users with different mini-games that require the use of different kinds of arm and hand movements to complete. They recruited 30 participants who are recovering from stroke, and found significant improvements in their performance after the training.

They also reported that the system had a positive effect on participants' enjoyment and motivation towards the training.

While the aforementioned systems utilized augmented reality for hand rehabilitation, they focus more on hand and finger movement training, rather than training for accurate finger force production. The closest work with this current study is done by Plopski et al. [25], who developed the original idea of AR-PETS. In their study, they used a haptic device as a substitute for a PETS device to measure finger force, and a video-see-through head-mounted display to display the force visualizations next to the trainees' fingers through augmented reality. They conducted a user study with 18 students, and while they found no significant improvement in performance due to AR, participants expressed their preferences towards AR. The current study extends the training system developed in the previous study by replacing the AR display from a video-see-through head-mounted display to an optical-see-through head-mounted display (Microsoft HoloLens [26]), and by using an actual PETS for the training.

3   AR-PETS Prototype

3.1   System Overview

Figure 1 shows a diagram of how AR-PETS generally work. From this point on, we will refer to the person undergoing the training as the "trainee", while the person administering the training as the "trainer". The trainee, who is wearing the HoloLens, exerts force onto the PETS, which is captured by the PETS as voltage signal. The voltage signal is then sent to the computer, where it will be sampled and filtered. The sampled data is then sent to the HoloLens, which updates and renders the force visualizations back to the trainee.

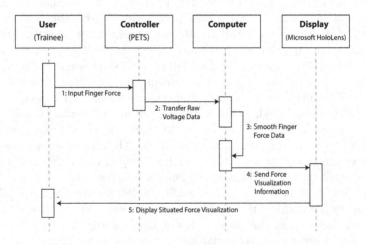

Fig. 1. Overview of AR-PETS.

The AR-PETS consists of the following components: the PETS that measures the finger forces, a software for acquiring and processing raw data from the PETS, a control panel application for controlling parameters related to the training, and a HoloLens application that displays the training program on top of the real-world using the AR capabilities of the HoloLens. Figure 1 shows a diagram describing the prototype system.

Pressing Evaluation and Training System. PETS is a device for measuring the amount of force exerted by a person's fingers through the 5 force plates that are built into the device (Fig. 2). Trainees rest their hand on the device such that all five fingers are touching the force plates, and they press down the force plates with their fingers to exert the specified amount of forces during the training. The position and height of each force plate can all be adjusted as necessary to fit the trainee's hand. The configuration of the force plates can also be rearranged to support training for both left and right hands.

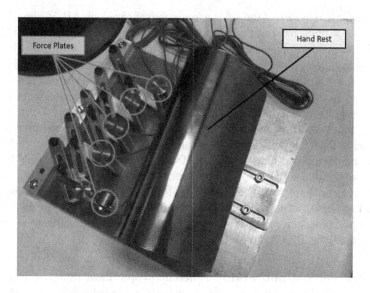

Fig. 2. Pressing evaluation and training system.

Data Acquisition and Processing Application. A data acquisition application based on LabWindows/CVI [27] acquires raw force data measured by the PETS. Upon receiving new data from PETS, the application attempts to reduce noise from the data using a simple moving average filter, where it takes the average of the last 5 samples. The resulting filtered data is then delivered via the UDP networking protocol for external programs to use and process. In the case of AR-PETS, the data is sent locally to a separate application that manages the training program itself.

Training Control Panel Application. The training control panel application based on Unity [28] provides a user interface for controlling the training program. The application allows the trainer to choose from different training modes for the trainees to perform, and to adjust different parameters related to the training modes. A detailed description of the different training modes can be found in Sect. 4.2. The application also shows a representation of the trainee's progress through the training mode.

HoloLens Application. The HoloLens application is a separate Unity-based application that displays the different virtual information needed for the training to the trainee wearing the HoloLens. The HoloLens application receives different commands from the training control panel application, and updates the virtual information that the trainee sees accordingly.

3.2   Calibration

Position Calibration. One of the main advantages of AR is the ability to superimpose virtual information on top of the real world in such a way that the virtual information appears to be integrated with the real world. To do so, the AR system requires a specific location in the real world to overlay the information onto. Thus, for this application, we perform a manual calibration procedure to provide the HoloLens application with real world position information of the finger force plates. This allows the HoloLens application to accurately place the corresponding visualization for each finger. The calibration procedure consists of positioning an AR marker on the location of each finger force plate, then letting the HoloLens detect the marker using its front camera and the Vuforia AR library (Fig. 3). We created a 3D-printed stand for the AR marker for this purpose. We repeat this procedure for all 5 fingers. After calibrating all 5 finger positions, the HoloLens saves these position data internally. This allows the HoloLens to reuse the positions across sessions, eliminating the need to calibrate every time, assuming that the PETS device is not moved.

Maximum Force Calibration. Different people have different amounts of maximum force that they can exert with each finger, also known as the maximum voluntary contraction (MVC). Thus, this prototype system also provides a calibration routine to measure the MVC of each user. During calibration, we ask trainees to exert as much force as possible for each finger, one finger at a time. Upon completion, the measured maximum forces can now be used as a basis for the different training modes, which are described in the next section.

4   AR-PETS Training

In this section, we first describe the different finger training patterns that we used as basis for designing the training modes. We then follow this with a description of the different training modes that the AR-PETS can possibly provide.

Fig. 3. Position calibration using an AR marker attached to a stand (left). The calibrated positions of the finger force plates are then visualized after the calibration procedure (right).

4.1 Finger Pressing Patterns

The hand is capable of performing different kinds of force exertions, e.g., single and multiple digit exertions [29]. Based on this idea, we considered 4 patterns for finger force training, namely: single digit pressing, synchronous pressing, rhythmical pressing, and pressing with force variation. Figure 4 provides a summary of these 4 training patterns. In single digit pressing, the trainee presses down the force plates with a predetermined force one finger at a time. This pattern enforces the trainee to sustain the force they exert with one finger. In synchronous pressing, the trainee presses with two or more fingers at the same time, also with a predetermined amount of force for each finger. The goal for this is to sustain the force they exert with multiple fingers at a time. In rhythmical pressing, the trainee presses with their fingers in a certain rhythm, which trains the trainee's ability to control fingers at will, and as well as stamina. Finally, force variation makes the trainee's fingers press the force plates with varying amounts of force over time, which trains the control of the amount of force exerted with the fingers over time. These 4 training patterns become the basis for designing the training modes in AR-PETS, which will be described in the next section.

4.2 Training Modes

AR-PETS offers four training modes for the trainees to choose from, namely: sequential force pressing, dynamic force tracking, rhythm game, and obstacle avoidance game. Each training mode implements one or more of the finger force training patterns outlined in the previous chapter. For the modes regarding games, we refer to the trainee as the player. The following sections describe each training mode in more detail.

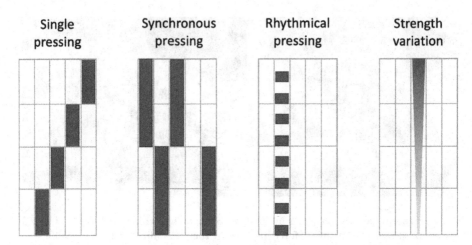

Fig. 4. The 4 training patterns for finger force training.

Sequential Force Pressing. In this mode, we ask the trainee to exert a certain amount of force for each finger, and sustain it for a certain amount of time. The trainee performs the task one finger at a time, in a specific order. This training mode implements the single digit pressing training pattern, and is geared towards training the ability to maintain the force exerted by each individual finger within a certain duration.

While wearing the HoloLens, this mode presents trainees with 5 bar graphs (one for each finger) that are rendered on top of the finger force plates. The bar graphs show the amount of force they are exerting with each finger, and also the amount of force they need to exert for each finger. The trainee must fill up the bar graph and reach the target force. The target force for each finger is based on percentages of the MVC for each finger, which can be set by the trainer via the training control panel application. Finally, an indicator displayed on top of the bar graphs notifies the trainee which finger to press, and this indicator moves through each finger in a specific order, which can also be set via the control panel application.

Dynamic Force Tracking. In this mode, the trainee is asked to exert variable amounts of force with their fingers over time, either with a single finger or a combination of fingers. This training mode implements the single pressing, synchronous pressing, and force variation training patterns, and is designed for training the trainee's ability to dynamically adjust the amount of force they exert with their fingers (Fig. 5).

With the HoloLens, the trainee is presented with a line graph, with the x- and y-axis representing time and force respectively. The graph contains a red line representing the force that the trainee is exerting, as well as a green line representing the amount of force needed to be exerted over time (Fig. 6). The trainee should match the green line as closely as possible by exerting the

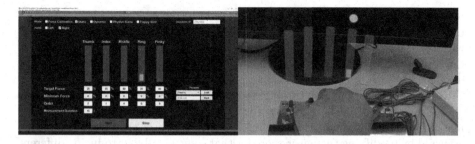

Fig. 5. Trainer's view (left) and trainee's view (right) of the sequential force pressing training mode.

necessary amount of force with the specified finger/s, which are indicated with green circles rendered on top of the fingers. The fingers the trainee needs to use can be specified by the trainer using the desktop control panel application.

The target force line consists of five phases: resting phase, rising phase, plateau phase, falling phase, and another resting phase. The initial resting phase serves as the time for the trainee to prepare, while the later resting phase signals the end of the session. The plateau phase represents the maximum force that the trainee needs to exert for that session, and is decided based on a percentage of the MVC (or the sum of MVCs) of the specified finger/s. The rising phase requires the trainee to gradually increase the force until they reach the plateau phase, and the falling phase requires the trainee to gradually decrease the force until the resting phase. The amount of time the trainee spends on each phase can also be controlled using the desktop control panel application.

Fig. 6. Trainer's view (left) and trainee's view (right) of the dynamic force tracking training mode. (Color figure online)

Music Game. Previous studies have shown that incorporating music games into rehabilitation programs can increase the motivation of rehabilitation patients to undergo the training [18]. With this in mind, we added a training mode that incorporates music game mechanics. In this mode, players must press with their fingers in time with a music (Fig. 7). Musical notes descend onto each finger's position, giving an indication to the player of which fingers to press. The height of musical notes determines how long the player must press with the finger, and the width determines how much force is needed to exert for the corresponding finger, which can either be constant or varying throughout the duration of the note. This training mode implements all of the training patterns.

Song selection is possible through the training control panel application. This allows the trainee to choose songs that they like, potentially enhancing their motivation to go through the training. The difficulty of the song can also be adjusted by modifying the music score for that song, e.g., by introducing different note patterns such as double notes or notes that vary in force over time, or by introducing big variations in terms of the target force between each note.

Fig. 7. Trainer's view (left) and trainee's view (right) of the music game training mode.

Obstacle Avoidance Game. In this mode, the trainee as a player plays a rendition of the game "Flappy Bird" [30], where the goal is to guide an avatar to avoid as many obstacles as possible (Fig. 8). The player controls an avatar that automatically scrolls to the right, while avoiding obstacles that appear in certain time periods as they scroll to the left. The obstacles consist of two pillars (top and bottom) with a gap in between, and the player needs to guide the avatar through these gaps. When the avatar touches the pillars, the game ends and the player is given the option to start over. Since the avatar automatically moves from left to right, the player can only control the vertical position of the avatar, which is done by pressing with the designated fingers. The vertical position of the avatar is based on the amount of force relative to the sum of the MVCs of the designated fingers. When no force is exerted, the avatar is positioned in the lower bound of the game area. Exerting 50% of the sum of MVCs puts the avatar in the middle, and exerting 100% of the sum of MVCs puts the avatar in the upper bound of the game area, which also results in game over.

The difficulty adjustment of the game is also possible through the training control panel application, as certain parameters can be modified to affect how the obstacles are generated or spawned. One such parameter is the time between two obstacle spawns. A shorter time between obstacle spawns means that the obstacles are closer to each other, requiring the user to adjust the force quickly, while a longer time between obstacle spawns means the obstacles are farther away from each other, giving the player more time to adjust the force they are exerting. Another parameter is the height of the gap of the obstacles. A smaller gap for the obstacles requires the player to be more precise with the force they exert, while a larger gap gives more leeway for the player.

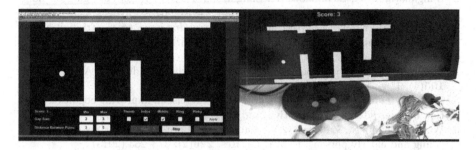

Fig. 8. Trainer's view (left) and trainee's view (right) of the obstacle avoidance training mode.

5 Conclusion and Future Work

In this paper, we introduced AR-PETS, a prototype system that integrates augmented reality and the pressing evaluation and training system to facilitate finger force control training. We hypothesize that using augmented reality as a medium to present the training environment has the potential to reduce the cognitive load of patients undergoing the training by rendering important information about the training directly on top of their fingers. We described the different components that make up the system, the different types of finger force training methods that we considered, and the four training modes included in the system, namely sequential force pressing, dynamic force tracking, music game, and obstacle avoidance game.

We have yet to conduct a formal user study to evaluate the effectiveness of the system for finger force training. However, we plan to further improve the prototype system and eventually conduct a user study to evaluate whether incorporating augmented reality into finger force training can effectively reduce cognitive load of elderly people undergoing rehabilitation, and how the presentation of the different training modes can have an impact on their performance and motivation over time.

Acknowledgements. This research was supported by the Japan Science and Technology Agency and Ministry of Science and Technology of Taiwan as part of the Japan-Taiwan Collaborative Research Program (106-2923-E-006-005-MY3).

References

1. Hackel, M., Wolfe, G., Bang, S., Canfield, J.: Changes in hand function in the aging adult as determined by the jebsen test of hand function. Phys. Ther. **72**(5), 373–377 (1992)
2. Ranganathan, V., Siemionow, V., Sahgal, V., Yue, G.: Effects of aging on hand function. J. Am. Geriatr. Soc. **49**(11), 1478–1484 (2002)
3. Keogh, J., Morrison, S., Barrett, R.: Strength training improves the tri-digit finger-pinch force control of older adults. Arch. Phys. Med. Rehabil. **88**, 1055–1063 (2007)
4. Olafsdottir, H., Zatsiorsky, V., Latash, M.: The effects of strength training on finger strength and hand dexterity in healthy elderly individuals. J. Appl. Physiol. **105**(4), 1166–1178 (2008)
5. Kwok, T., et al.: Effectiveness of coordination exercise in improving cognition function in older adults: a prospective study. Clin. Interv. Aging **6**, 261–267 (2011)
6. Wu, Y., Pazin, N., Zatsiorsky, V., Latash, M.: Improving finger coordination in young and elderly persons. Exp. Brain Res. **226**(2), 273–283 (2013)
7. Li, K., Marquardt, T., Li, Z.: Removal of visual feedback lowers structural variability of inter-digit force coordination during sustained precision pitch. Neurosci. Lett. **545**, 1–5 (2013)
8. Ambike, S., Zatsiorsky, V., Latash, M.: Processes underlying unintentional finger-force changes in the absence of visual feedback. Exp. Brain Res. **233**(3), 711–721 (2015)
9. Jo, H., Ambike, S., Lewis, M., Huang, X., Latash, M.: Finger force changes in the absence of visual feedback in patients with parkinson's disease. Clin. Neurophysiol. **127**(1), 684–692 (2016)
10. Azuma, R.: A survey of augmented reality. Presence: Teleoperators Virtual Environ. **6**(4), 355–385 (1997)
11. Parikh, P., Cole, K.: Handling objects in old age: forces and moments acting on the object. J. Appl. Physiol. **112**(7), 1095–1104 (2012)
12. Wallis, I., et al.: Real-time sonification of movement for an immersive stroke rehabilitation environment. In: Proceedings of the International Conference on Auditory Display, pp. 497–503 (2007)
13. Järveläinen, H., Papetti, S., Schiesser, S., Grosshauser, T.: Audio-tactile feedback in musical gesture primitives: finger pressing. In: Proceedings of the Sound and Music Computing Conference, pp. 109–114 (2013)
14. Kapur, S., Zatsiorsky, V., Latash, M.: Age-related changes in the control of finger force vectors. J. Appl. Physiol. **109**(6), 1827–1841 (2010)
15. Dovat, L., et al.: HandCARE: a cable-actuated rehabilitation system to train hand function after stroke. IEEE Trans. Neural Syst. Rehabil. Eng. **16**(6), 582–591 (2008)
16. Taheri, H., Rowe, J., Gardner, D., Chan, V., Reinkensmeyer, D., Wolbrecht, E.: Robot-assisted guitar hero for finger rehabilitation after stroke. In: Proceedings of the IEEE International Conference on Engineering in Medicine and Biology Society, pp. 3911–3917 (2012)
17. Taheri, H., et al.: Design and preliminary evaluation of the FINGER rehabilitation robot: controlling challenge and quantifying finger individuation during musical computer game play. J. NeuroEng. Rehabil. **11**(1), 10:1–10:17 (2014)
18. Friedman, N., et al.: Retraining and assessing hand movement after stroke using the musicglove: comparison with conventional hand therapy and isometric grip training. J. Neuroeng. Rehabil. **11**(1), 76:1–76:14 (2014)

19. Elor, A., Teodorescu, M., Kurniawan, S.: Project star catcher: a novel immersive virtual reality experience for upperlimb rehabilitation. ACM Trans. Accessible Comput. **11**(4), 20:1–20:25 (2018)

20. Baldominos, A., Saez, Y., Pozo, C.: An approach to physical rehabilitation using state-of-the-art virtual reality and motion tracking technologies. Procedia Comput. Sci. **64**(1), 10–16 (2015)

21. Luo, X., Kline, T., Fischer, H., Stubblefield, K., Kenyon, R., Kamper, D.: Integration of augmented reality and assistive devices for post-stroke hand opening rehabilitation. In: Proceedings of the IEEE Engineering in Medicine and Biology Annual Conference, pp. 6855–6858 (2005)

22. Burke, J., McNeil, M., Charles, D., Morrow, P., Crosbie, J., McDonough, S.: Augmented reality games for upper-limb stroke rehabilitation. In: Proceedings of the International Conference on Games and Virtual Worlds for Serious Applications, pp. 75–78 (2010)

23. Hondori, H., Khademi, M., Dodakian, L., McKenzie, A., Lopes, C., Cramer, S.: Choice of human-computer interaction mode in stroke rehabilitation. Neurorehabilitation Neural Repair **30**(3), 258–265 (2016)

24. Colomer, C., Llorens, R., Noé, E., Alcañiz, M.: Effect of a mixed reality-based intervention on arm, hand, and finger function on chronic stroke. J. Neuroeng. Rehabil. **13**(45), 1–10 (2016)

25. Plopski, A., Mori, R., Taketomi, T., Sandor, C., Kato, H.: AR-PETS: development of an augmented reality supported pressing evaluation training system. In: Zhou, J., Salvendy, G. (eds.) ITAP 2018. LNCS, vol. 10927, pp. 113–126. Springer, Cham (2018). https://doi.org/10.1007/978-3-319-92037-5_10

26. Microsoft: Microsoft Hololens. https://www.microsoft.com/en-us/hololens. Accessed 01 Feb 2019

27. National Instruments: LabWindows[TM]/CVI - National Instruments. http://www.ni.com/lwcvi/. Accessed 22 Jan 2019

28. Unity Technologies: Unity. https://unity3d.com/. Accessed 22 Jan 2019

29. Astin, A.: Finger Force Capability: Measurement and Prediction Using Anthropometric and Myoelectric measures. Virginia Polytechnic Institute and State University (1999)

30. dotGears: Flappy Bird. https://www.dotgears.com/apps/app_flappy.html. Accessed 22 Jan 2019

Strategies to Enhance Technology-Based Learning Experiences in Older Adults: A Field Study

Ana Isabel Veloso[1(✉)], Liliana Vale Costa[1], Célia Soares[2],
and Sónia Ferreira[3]

[1] DigiMedia Research Centre, Department of Communication and Art,
University of Aveiro, Campus Universitário de Santigo,
3810-193 Aveiro, Portugal
{aiv,lilianavale}@ua.pt

[2] Instituto Politécnico da Maia, Avenida Carlos de Oliveira Campos – Castelo da
Maia, 4475-690 Maia, Portugal
csoares@ismai.pt

[3] Instituto Politécnico de Viseu, Escola Superior de Educação de Viseu, R.
Maximiano Aragão, 3504-501 Viseu, Portugal
sonia.ferreira@esev.ipv.pt

Abstract. The aim of this study is to explore the main aspects that affect pre/during and post-learning experiences in later age. Specifically, the study examined the problems adult learners encountered in learning how to use digital technologies, accessibility in learning and strategies to enhance technology-based learning experiences that take into account the ageing process. Eighty-one learners from learning organizations in the North of Portugal (Community-dwelling older adults, Short-time Courses and Universities of Third Age) participated in this study. The participants attended a set of learning sessions related with the use of digital devices and data were collected from observation notes and group interviewing. Results suggest that there is a variety of prominent aspects that can affect pre-/during and post-learning experiences in later age that include the access to technology, time availability for learning and lack of on-demand learning instructions. A set of recommendations to design technology-based learning experience that takes the ageing process into account is proposed and lessons from the study are discussed.

Keywords: Technology-based learning · Learning experiences · Strategies · Older adults · Field study

1 Introduction

Over the past decade, much more information [1, 2] has become available on learning Technologies of Information and Communication in later adulthood. Indeed, the field of 'geragogy' or 'gerontagogy' used to define the science that studies the process of learning in later age [3–5] has become extremely relevant since the access to education

J. Zhou and G. Salvendy (Eds.): HCII 2019, LNCS 11593, pp. 588–601, 2019.
https://doi.org/10.1007/978-3-030-22015-0_46

and training has been a priority of the older adult learner's rights, presented in the second World Assembly on Aging [6].

Similarly, the number of Universities of Third Age has risen dramatically, leading to the need of understanding the learners' context, needs and motivations, aiming at providing a positive learning experience and increasing the learners' sense of wellbeing and quality of life [7–9].

The advent of the Information and Communication Society also brings many challenges that can compromise learning, communication and daily-life routines that are mediated by digital devices. Indeed, there is a need to create inclusive learning environments that fosters info-inclusion and encourages critical thinking skills in the media ecology [9–12].

This paper, therefore, provides guidance for learning practitioners to address effective technology-based instructions that take the adult learners' context and ageing aspects into account. In specific, the research question is 'What strategies can be adopted to enhance pre-/during and post-learning experiences in later age?' and, subsequently, the aim of this paper is to explore the main aspects that can affect these learning experiences in later age, given the difficulties that can emerge and the participants' context.

2 Background

The demographic ageing in the European Union (EU) results from low birth rate, retirement of the post-war baby-boom generation and high life expectancy. The Portuguese case is also identical to the EU-28 and according with the Eurostat [13], the old-age dependency relative to the total population for the EU-28 was 29.9% whereas in Portugal was 32.5% in 2017. In 2080, this old-age dependency is estimated to grow to 52.3% [13].

Beyond this demographic scenario, the ageing process is an individual and complex process that involved physiological, social and psychological changes [14, 15]. For example, many of these changes involve the sensory system, in which the smell and taste can deteriorate, regardless of the ability to perceive the four basic tastes (sweet, sour, bitter and salt) [1, 14, 15].

In terms of older adults' cognition, a cognitive decline is often associated with the ageing process and it is generally characterized by a number of specific changes [1, 17]: (a) increasing difficulty in understanding long and/or complex messages and in recovering specific terms; (b) greater difficulty in reasoning activities involving a logical and organized analysis of abstract or unfamiliar material; (c) repetitive discourse; (d) difficulty in selecting information; (e) reducing the ability to perform new and rapid psychomotor tasks; (f) memory impairment, especially relative to the acquisition of new information and multi-tasking; and finally, (g) difficulties in inductive reasoning, spatial orientation, numerical and verbal skills and perceived speed.

Changes in motor skills due to ageing are also likely to occur and these include: slower response times; decrease in the ability to maintain continuous movements; coordination disorders; loss of flexibility; and less variability in movements [18]. Furthermore, the incidence of chronic conditions, such as arthritis, also affects movements and these changes also have a direct relevance to the use of computers [1].

According to some authors [1, 18], the older adult population embody different age cohorts and cannot be studied as a single target group owing to different changes that tend to appear at different life stages and, therefore, the age cohorts that are the most frequent are the following: young older adults (>65 to 75 years old) and old older adults (>75 years old).

Contradicting techno-ageism [20] and ageism [21], several studies also show that older people are interested in using Information and Communication Technologies (ICT) [1, 14, 19], regardless the limitations of the ageing process. The difficulty or non-existent relationship between older adults and ICT may be due to different aspects: the fear of using computers often associated with the fear of damaging the hardware and/or software; the equipment cost; and unfamiliarity with the language and interface conventions [19, 22] and certain difficulties associated with the ageing process, i.e. short-term memory, vision, motor skills and other physical or psychological changes.

In terms of the benefits of its use by the older adult target group, digitally-mediated learning is suggested to foster social support [24–27] improvements in cognition [21] and well-being [26, 28]; reinforcement of self-realization and self-esteem [23, 29], reduction of the feeling of loneliness [24], increase in quality of life (QL) [21, 23, 30, 31] and reinforcement of self-concept (SC) [21, 23].

Active ageing and healthy lifestyles are also suggested to keep the body and mind healthy, through good nutrition habits, involvement in interesting mind-challenging activities and reinforcement of the importance of social support and self-concept maintenance [23, 28, 32]. In this sense, facilitating access to social, cultural and leisure interaction is essential [28].

Concerning the motivation to learn digital technologies in later adulthood, the information is often contradictory. On the one hand, the older adults are seen as anxious in the use of computers and with little motivation to perform tasks involving technology [33, 34]. On the other hand, technologies are omnipresent in daily life and this target group seems to be interested in new opportunities and functionalities offered [35].

Given the aforementioned implications of the ageing process, the organization of tutorials and/or materials to support ICT's teaching-learning strategy for older adults may follow the fundamental principles of instructional design for meaningful learning [36, pp. 45–51]:

1. Learning occurs when students are involved in solving real-world problems. This principle focuses on the presentation of the problem, its deconstruction in tasks in order to solve it, followed by its operationalization and consequent action of making them feasible;
2. Learning proceeds when prior experiences and knowledge provide a basis for new knowledge. The development of this principle is to identify previous knowledge that can be valued in new learning and structure the way in which the new knowledge and apprenticeships can be used;

3. Learning occurs when students are presented with a set of demonstrative instructions instead of relying solely on information related with the learning goals. The focus of this principle is on demonstration in how to solve a problem and how the tasks can be performed. Different mental models and the generalization of knowledge into different situations should be considered in these demonstrations;

4. Learning is encouraged when learners are required to use new knowledge and problem-solving skills by using examples and real-world problems. Furthermore, feedback is crucial when solving these problems in order to understand, recover and avoid mistakes;

5. The process of learning also happens when there is a general encouragement to transfer and integrate new knowledge or/and skills into everyday life. This principle enables learners moving on different learning stages – i.e. integration, experimentation, creation and reflection until new knowledge is incorporated outside the learning environment and included in the daily routine.

In a nutshell, the design of instructional programs should consider the learner's cognition and in order to address meaningful learning experiences, one should take into account some general instructional strategies, namely, specific learning subtasks and/or tasks; supportive information strategies according with the tasks' difficulty level; the learner's pacing and feedback; timing exposure of the material in the training session; adaptive and simulation training; e-learning and performance assessment [15, pp. 93–106].

3 Method

As mentioned in the Introduction, the intent of this research is to explore the main aspects that can affect pre-/during and post-learning experiences in later age. A goal-oriented training method relying on step-by-step was used owing to the fact that it may be effective by telling participants which steps to perform and order and reducing working memory [37, 38].

Being a step-by-step self-pace learning process [38], such measured tasks as completion time and accuracy metrics are often used to assess the use of digital devices and help in self-judgements about the learning journey, enabling metacognition and adjusting the actual learning performance to the one that is expected. Furthermore, each participant is assigned to a certain goal and feedback is given towards the tasks and that way, fostering repetition and enactive mastery of the learning process and creating awareness towards errors.

Given the aforementioned procedures relative to a goal-oriented method [16, 17], information about the participants' learning context was needed through ongoing participant observation. Although the role of the researchers as primary data collection instrument can bring personal biases at the outset of the study as the relationship established between the participants and the institutions and researchers, our research team has practice on the field throughout at least five years and are aware and sensitive to the challenges and ethical concerns that may be brought to the field.

3.1 Settings

The study was carried out on three places in the North of Portugal: Four community-dwelling centers (Group 1 – G1), University of Aveiro (short-time course Multimedia addressed to older adults) (Group 2 – G2) and two Universities of Third Age (Group 3 – G3). These different learning organizations were purposefully selected in order to focus on different learning contexts that can affect the perception and meaning associated with those experiences expressed by the participants.

3.2 Data Collection and Analysis Procedures

Data was collected from September 2011 to July 2013 at the four community-dwelling centers, from December 2012 to February 2013; University of Aveiro from October 2012 to May 2013; University of Third Age 1 from October 2012 to May 2013; and University of Third Age 2 from October 2015 to December 2016.

Multiple sources of data were gathered in the field (i.e. field notes, surveys, documents…) and participants were observed in the activities within their context. The researchers also lectured the subject 'Multimedia' that was part of the curriculum from the Learning Organizations.

In ensuring internal validity, the following strategies were used: Triangulation of data sources of information (field notes and literature); and Extension of the field work in time. Data were analyzed in terms of the codes: Learning strategies used; Difficulties observed and Learning experiences.

The research safeguards: (a) Participants' informed consent; (b) Voluntary participation; (c) Involvement of the research team in the process; and (d) that the risks of participating in the study do not outweigh the risks associated with the participants' daily lives.

3.3 Participants

Community-Dwelling Participants (Group 1 – G1)

The group of participants from four community-dwelling centers consisted of 22 older adults: 14 females and 8 males, aged between 66 and 90 (M = 81.1, SD = 6.5). Eleven participants opted for the day care center modality whereas 10 are in retirement homes and 1 opted for the home-support service. Furthermore, 16 participants have been in institutions and 1 opted for four years or less than four years. In terms of the reasons that led these participants to join the community-dwelling centers, the majority (11) were recommended by a family member, seven took the initiative, three had a friend's suggestion and one participant was suggested by the Social Portuguese Services.

Given the context of use of Information and Communication Technologies (ICT), 14 out of 22 participants had never used a computer. Seven out of eight older adults, who used a computer had assistance, either in the community-dwelling centers or in ICT sessions and such activities as transcribing information and surfing in the Internet, promoted by the Town Council.

Group of Short-Time Courses in Multimedia Addressed to Older Adults (Group 2 – G2)

The group of participants from the short-time course in Multimedia consisted of 14 older adult learners: 7 females and 7 males, aged between 54 and 78 years old (M = 64.9; SD = 7.97).

Two focus groups with older adults aged between 65–75 years old, who were not in community-dwelling centers and were literate in order to overcome the limitation of the sample size of older adults with low literacy in the use of ICT in daily activities. The added groups were from the following institutions: 'Universidade Sénior de Ermesinde' and a group of 'Encontros com a Ciência' at the University of Aveiro.

Most of the participants in the group of short-time courses in Multimedia addressed to older adults has between 9 years of schooling and a college degree. Given their context of use in ICT, all participants used personal computer for basic tasks (e.g. writing, information searching…).

Group of the Universities of Third Age 1 - UTA (Group 3 – G3a)

The group of participants from the University of Third Age 1 consisted of 12 participants aged between 60 and 83 years old (M = 67.33; SD = 7.33), divided into 5 males and 7 females. Their school qualifications varied between the 6th year of schooling and a college degree. Given their context of use in ICT, all participants had computer at home and similarly to G2, they used personal computer for basic tasks (e.g. writing, information searching…).

Group of the Universities of Third Age 2 - UTA (Group 3 – G3b)

The group of participants from the University of Third Age 2 consisted of 33 participants aged between 55 and 82 years old (M = 67.33; SD = 7.06), divided into 16 males and 17 females. Their school qualifications varied between 10 and 14 years of schooling.

4   Results

4.1   The Case of Community-Dwelling Participants (Group 1 – G1)

These participants (G1) initiated their contact with digital devices in these classes and did not have access to personal computers beyond those used in the classroom. Furthermore, the activities had to be carefully prepared in order to motivate and engage the older target group with no knowledge about the metaphors used, language used and interaction paradigms.

The activities were, therefore, divided into four units: Unit 1. Introduction to computers; Unit 2. Text writing and formatting; Unit 3. Internet browsing; and Unit 4. Communication services: email and instant messaging.

During the sessions related with Units 1 and 2, most of the participants demonstrated the following difficulties:

- Handling the mouse and understanding the pointer position on the screen [1, 29]. As soon as they had reduced hand motricity, they would get frustrated;

- Ongoing difficulty in using the 'Caps Lock' key and other keys simultaneously for punctuation marks and accents;
- Confusion when using the letters 'W' and 'M' or 'O' and '0' and persistent difficulty in distinguishing between the keys 'Enter', 'Space bar' and 'Delete';
- Difficulties in starting the Microsoft Word, opening an existing document and saving it. Such problems as memory and learning impairments are related with changes in the ageing process.

Relative to the units 3 – Internet browsing, the following observations were noted:

- The participants were surprised with the amount and diversity of information provided, leading to difficulties in selecting the information that was provided. One of the changes inherent to the ageing process is the decline in the ability for divided attention, which interferes in Human-Computer Interaction when older adults need to activate selective attention or when many details are shown, and older adults are unable to pay attention to all of them. Moreover, their perception is diminished, i.e. their ability to recognize patterns [29];
- Older participants express their dislike about the way in which information is listed, declaring that it is often disorganized;
- The participants had difficulty in understanding which areas are clickable and lacked the confidence to perform some actions [1];
- In terms of information searching, the topics that were chosen were extremely diverse. They searched information about religion, travelling, crafting, and place in which they were born.

The main findings of this study on older adults' use of communication tools (unit 4 – communication services: email and instant messaging) were the following:

- The participants were afraid of starting new activities, either because they lacked the knowledge or because they feared about making a mistake [29];
- The participants felt great joy in receiving messages from relatives and friends;
- The participants never left messages unanswered. They always answered to the messages, even if it was just to say 'thank you';
- The participants had difficulty in remembering their email address and password. This problem was related to changes in working memory and learning inherent to the ageing process [1, 29, 39];
- The participants had difficulty in completing tasks. For example, participants rarely clicked in 'Sending', after writing a message, whether on *Gmail* or *GTalk*;
- The participants rarely included the subject in the emails they send, justifying it by saying that they didn't understand what they had to write. In other cases, they started to write the message in the subject box;
- The participants were not aware that the messages had attachments;
- The participants found that message feedback was important;
- The participants learned on how to open and answer an email, but rarely did it without checking if they were doing it properly;
- The participants understood the purpose of synchronous communication services, but they expressed that it would be only useful if relatives or friends were available to communicate simultaneously, which does not happen very often.

Despite having only basic knowledge about Information and Communication Technologies, the participants have soon realized their advantages, e.g. enable the exchange of written messages with distant relatives. It became, therefore, clear how much older adults were motivated during the sessions and interested in using ICT in their daily lives.

4.2 The Case of Short-Time Courses in Multimedia Addressed to Older Adults (Group 2 – G2)

The short-time courses in Multimedia were held once a week. A total of 10 sessions were given and each one lasted 90 min, in which the participants (G2) were highly motivated to learn and engage with technological activities.

The strategies adopted for the ICT activities were challenge-based with real-world problems, as recommended in the previous literature [36, 39]. Relative to the activities that were carried out, these were divided into four units: (i) Fundamentals of Computing; (ii) Introduction to Multimedia: Text and Image; (iii) Internet: Information searching and processing; and (iv) Social networks and communication services.

Despite the differences in the participants' skills, age, and level schooling relative to the ones from the community-dwelling centers, the difficulties observed during ICT usage were a transversal to all groups.

After the course sessions, the participants assessed the training course, accordingly with the following criteria: (i) level of satisfaction; (ii) the influence of sessions on their lives; (iii) positive aspects; and (iv) negative aspects. It is important to highlight, however, that there were four withdrawals during the course owing to health reasons.

In terms of the participants' level of satisfaction with the training sessions, the participants were satisfied (42.9%, N = 6) or very satisfied (28.6%, N = 4). Similarly, they reported that these training sessions influenced (42.9%, N = 6) or greatly influenced (28.6%, N = 4) their lives, contributing to a greater computer knowledge, familiarity and computer skills.

The main strengths of this course were the pedagogical capacity, diversified approach, support, contact, teachers' supervision and collaborators. Relative to its weaknesses, the participants mentioned the lack of time and reduced number of sessions.

4.3 Group of the Universities of Third Age 1 - UTA (Group 3 – G3a)

A 35-working session plan was taken over a period of 8 months (once a week), aiming at enhancing the participants' ICT skills and motivation. Indeed, these sessions had the purpose of training to ICT use in a context of information sharing, giving particular emphasis on the use of social networks. Although the first sessions were devoted to the Introduction of Computers and its interface, there was some familiarity with the interface conventions and some functionalities, increasing their motivation to become a regular or advanced user. The learning activities were, therefore, prepared in order to combine the participants' expectations, course goals and motivations to interlink the content to the daily life [7].

The activities that were carried out can be divided into five units: (i) Internet Security and Personal data protection; (ii) Social networks: Facebook; (iii) Image manipulation tools: *Picasa*; (iv) Creating a blog: *Blogger vs Tumblr*; and (v) Video editing tools: *Windows MovieMaker*.

The first module – Internet Security and Personal data protection (6 sessions) expected to clarify any of the participants' doubts relative to e-mail security, passwords, safe websites, *phishing* messages, antivirus and *Malware*. This module aimed at reducing participants' anxiety towards their doubts about security issues, namely in terms of their reported difficulties: (a) Memorizing passwords; and (b) Identifying safe websites through web addresses. In a nutshell, the participants find it hard to trust in the unknown and start using a different tool.

The second module – Social networks: *Facebook* (10 sessions) is one of the most popular and it embodies the following tasks: Learning how to create a User Profile; Adjusting the users' privacy policies; Finding friends; Publishing posts; Commenting on friends' profile; Sending private messages; Sharing photographs and videos; and Playing games. Relative to the difficulties that were found in this module, these were: (a) The insecurity and fear of trying new activities [29, 40], without having to ask someone with more experience; and (b) The inability to concentrate on a specific activity due to information overload and multimodality [1]. In general, the participants seem to not like to reveal their private life and they have shown their concerns on avoiding the expose of private information in a context of sharing.

Relative to the third module – Image manipulation tools – *Picasa* (4 sessions), the participants were taught on how to solve minor problems on manipulating images, organizing them on the computer, sharing images, and identifying the file formats. More specifically, participants found it difficult to:

- Switching between multiple computer applications, particularly when the application they were working on forced them to interact with the operating system;
- Using the cursor and understanding its functionality and accuracy caused frustration in some participants, who had physical limitations [1, 29, 31];

The fourth module – Creating a blog – *Blogger vs Tumblr* (8 sessions) aimed at teaching the participants how to create a blog, using two existing market-oriented platforms. The activities were: (i) Defining the blog theme; (ii) Formatting text (inserting hyperlinks, images and videos) and writing messages. In this module, the participants also explored the notion of *following someone* and defined privacy policies. Moving from *Blogger* to *Tumblr*, the following observations were made:

- There were some difficulties in selecting the information as the ability to recognize disorganized and unmatched patterns and elements without hierarchy affected the participants' whole experience [29];
- The participants had some difficulties in completing certain tasks, for e.g. they wrote the comment but did not publish it [41];
- When using *Tumblr*, the decrease in the number of configuration options and the reasonable amount of information shown in the screen facilitated the participants' interaction with the information provided.

Similarly, the most experienced participants had less difficulties and these were related to the configurations of the digital platforms.

Finally, the fifth module – Video editing tools – *Windows Movie Maker* (7 sessions) had the ultimate goal of capturing and editing videos to be uploaded on *Youtube*. The main subjects covered in this module were: The concept of frames per second, video subtitling, transition effects, different video formats, uploading and sharing videos on Youtube, and publishing the video on a created channel. The main difficulties in this module were: The quantity of steps that were demanded to upload a video on *Youtube* [41] and dual tasking, particularly when inserting images and/or audio files.

4.4   Group of the Universities of Third Age 2 - UTA (Group 3 – G3b)

A total of 34 session course was held at the University of Third Age 2, once a week with an average duration of 2 h per session (1 h per group of 15). There was also some familiarity with the interface conventions and some functionalities by these participants and their motivation to the use of computer-mediated communication and image and video digitalization and editing had implications on the topics that were selected to the course.

Although a module of 'Computer fundamentals' has been given in the first session, these learners wanted the tutor to adopt an 'on-demand' strategy and focus on image and video editing, and social networks. Hence, the modules were: (i) Image and video digitalization and editing; (ii) Internet browsing and bookmarking; and (iii) Communication tools, social networks and privacy.

In the module '(i) Image and video digitalization and editing', the participants learned to transfer their images and videos from their devices (i.e. mobile phone, camera...) to the computer. Furthermore, they learned how to edit their photos with the online photo editor pixlr.com and the videos with the video editor of *Youtube*. The 'bring-your-own device' approach seemed to best strategy to motivate these learners to interlink the information provided with daily-life challenges [7]. By contrast, this approach also brings many challenges to the tutor in order to meet every need and problem encountered in different devices. The tutor had also to find alternative solutions to downloadable content as the majority of the learners in order to express a strong suspicion towards downloadable content [7], regardless of the source's reliability.

Mouse precision was one of the most reported difficulties when editing image and adding transitions to the video, as it was also observed with University of Third Age 1.

In the module '(ii) Internet browsing and bookmarking', the participants learned to browse, filter images by using rights, colour and size, and add the search results to their Favourites. Although the participants were familiar with internet browsing, they were surprised with the options of filtering the information (*e.g.* use of quotation marks to refine their search).

Finally, the module '(iii) Communication tools, social networks and privacy' enabled the participants to learner how to configure their privacy settings in *Facebook*, manage their publications in terms of visibility and videochat. The same difficulties observed in the participants of the University of Third Age 1 were replicated in these participants. Moreover, these participants expected that the social network *Facebook* would work as an online community in the way that it enabled to filter the friends' publications accordingly with their interests and ignoring the posts that are from their friends but do not share the same interests.

It is also worth to notice that co-challenges and co-exercises were not successful as thought in this team because each participant had different, individual and very straightforward needs.

5 Discussion

There is a variety of prominent aspects that can affect pre-/during and post- learning experiences in later age that include the access to technology, time availability for learning and lack of on-demand learning instructions.

Based on the aforementioned cases in the use of technology-based learning experiences and in response to the research question, one may suppose that the following strategies to design such experiences that take into account the ageing process are: (a) facilitate the discourse between learning agents; (b) divide problems and abstract concepts into specific and concrete ones; (c) provide age-friendly learning and non-downloadable services or products; (d) provide step-based feedback; (e) simulate and offer a potential solution to a learning exercise; (f) deliver the learning service on demand and at the learner's pace; and meet the adult learner's previous experience, concrete needs and everyday context.

Relative to the difficulties that technology-based learning may bring and affect the whole experience, these are: (a) Precision in house handling and understanding the pointer position on the screen; (b) Simultaneous actions (e.g. using 'Caps Lock' key and punctuation marks; switching between multiple computer applications; (c) Lack of time and reduced number of sessions to learn and dealing with insecurity and fear of trying new activities, information overload, multimodality and exposition of private information; and (d) difficulties in selecting the information and recognize disorganized and unmatched patterns.

The aspects that may affect pre-learning experiences tend to be the learners' expectations towards the content; their motivations; pre-defined goals and access to technology. The learning experience that occurs *in loco* may be affected by changes in the sensory system and implications in terms of multimodality in learning; changes in cognition and repetitive step by step tasks, discourse and metaphors used, demonstrative instructions and a learning service on demand and at the learner's pace. Finally, the post-learning experience is likely to be affected to the perceived interlink between the learning content and daily tasks and self-judgements about the learning journey and enactive mastery of the learning process. The major limitation of this study is that it relies too heavily on observation and experience of authors in the field. Large randomized controlled trials could provide more evidence of the observed aspects and future work needs to be carried out in order to understand in what way digitally-mediated learning could be embedded and have an impact on daily life decisions and subsequent actions.

Acknowledgements. We thank the Portuguese Community Dwelling Centers: Centro Paroquial de São Bernardo, Centro Social de Santa Joana Princesa, Centro Social do Distrito de Aveiro and Patronato de Nossa Senhora de Fátima de Vilar; the participants from the Multimedia Course lectured at the University of Aveiro; and the Universities of Third Age – Ermesinde and Gafanha da Nazaré for their willingness to embrace this project, enabling a true exchange of know-how and values. A special thanks to all the participants, who engaged in this study and made this possible. We would also like to thank to DigiMedia (University of Aveiro) and Centre for the Study in Education, Technologies and Health (Polytechnic Institute of Viseu). This work was supported by Fundação para a Ciência e Tecnologia and ESF under Community Support Framework III – the project SEDUCE 2.0 nr. POCI-01-0145-FEDER-031696.

References

1. Czaja, S., Sharit, J.: Designing Training and Instructional Programs for Older Adults, 1st edn., pp. 1–325. CRC Press, Taylor & Francis Group, Boca Raton (2012)
2. Sanchez-Gordon, S., Luján-Mora, S.: Web accessibility of MOOCs for elderly students. In: 2013 International Conference on Information Technology Based Higher Education and Training, Antalya, Turkey (2013). https://doi.org/10.119/ithet.2013.6671024
3. Findsen, B., Formosa, M.: Lifelong Learning in Later Life: A Handbook on Older Adult Learning. Sense Publishers, Rotterdam (2011)
4. Lemieux, A., Martinez, M.: Gerontagogy beyond word: a reality. Educ. Gerontol. **26**(5), 475–498 (2000). https://doi.org/10.1080/03601270050111887
5. Peterson, D.: Educational gerontology: the state of the art. Educ. Gerontol. **1**(1), 61–73 (1976). https://doi.org/10.1080/03601277.1976.12049517
6. United Nations: Political Declaration and Madrid International Plan of Action on Ageing. Second United Nations World Assembly on Ageing, Madrid (2002)
7. Costa, L.V., Veloso, A.I.: Demystifying ageing bias through learning. In: Beck, D., et al. (eds.) iLRN 2017. CCIS, vol. 725, pp. 201–213. Springer, Cham (2017). https://doi.org/10.1007/978-3-319-60633-0_17
8. Shapira, N., Barak, A., Gal, I.: Promoting older adults' well-being through Internet training and use. Aging Mental Health **11**(5), 477–484 (2007). https://doi.org/10.1080/13607860601086546
9. Veloso, A.: SEDUCE - utilização da comunicação e da informação em ecologias web pelo cidadão sénior, Edições Afrontamento/CETAC.MEDIA, Porto (2014)
10. Castells, M.: The Internet Galaxy: Reflections on the Internet, Business, and Society. Oxford University Press, Inc., Oxford (2001)
11. Friemel, T.: The digital divide has grown old: determinants of a digital divide among seniors. New Media Soc. **18**(2), 313–331 (2016). https://doi.org/10.1177/1461444814538648
12. Harwood, J.: Understanding Communication and Aging: Developing Knowledge and Awareness. SAGE Publishing, University of Arizon, Thousand Oaks (2007)
13. Postman, N.: Technopoly: The Surrender of Culture to Technology. Random House Digital Inc., New York (1992)
14. EUROSTAT: Record high old-age dependency ratio in the EU. EUROSTAT European Commission (2018). https://ec.europa.eu/eurostat/web/products-eurostat-news/-/DDN-20180508-1?inheritRedirect=true. Acedido em 26 Jan 2019
15. Fisk, A., Rogers, W., Charness, N., Czaja, S., Sharit, J.: Designing for Older Adults. CRC Pres, Taylor & Francis Group, New York (2009)

16. Maddox, G., Douglass, E.: Aging and individual differences: a longitudinal analysis of social, psychological, and physiological indicators. J. Gerontol. **29**(5), 555–563 (1974). https://doi.org/10.1093/geronj/29.5.555
17. Czaja, S.J., et al.: Designing for Older Adults: Principles and Creative Human Factors Approaches, pp. 1–232. CRC Press, Boca Raton (2009)
18. Pak, R., McLaughlin, A.: Designing Displays for Older Adults. CRC Press, Boca Raton (2010)
19. Hertzog, C., Light, L.: Movement control in the older adult. In: Van Hemel, S. (ed.) Technology for Adaptive Aging, pp. 64–92. The National Academies Press, Washington, DC (2004)
20. Zheng, R., Hill, R., Gardner, M.: Engaging Older Adults with Modern Technology: Internet Use and Information Access Needs. Idea Group Global, Harrisburg (2012)
21. Pires, A.: Efeitos dos Videojogos nas Funções Cognitivas da Pessoa Idosa (Master's thesis]. Faculdade de Medicina do Porto, Porto (2008)
22. Angus, J., Reeve, P.: Ageism: a threat to "aging well" in the 21st century. J. Appl. Gerontol. **25**(2), 137–152 (2006). https://doi.org/10.1177/0733464805285745
23. Ferreira, S., Torres, A., Mealha, O., Veloso, A.: Training effects on older adults in information and communication technologies considering psychosocial variables. Educ. Gerontol. **41**(7), 482–493 (2015). https://doi.org/10.1080/03601277.2014.994351
24. White, V., Weatherall, A.: A grounded theory analysis of older adults and information technology. Educ. Gerontol. **26**(4), 371–386 (2000). https://doi.org/10.1080/036012700407857
25. Xie, B.: Multimodal computer-mediated communication and social support among older Chinese internet users. J. Comput.-Mediated Commun. **13**, 728–750 (2008). https://doi.org/10.1111/j.1083-6101.2008.00417.x
26. Miranda, L., Farias, S.: Contributions from the Internet for elderly people: a review of the literature. Interface Comunicação Saúde Educação **13**(29), 383–394 (2009). https://doi.org/10.1590/s1414-32832009000200011
27. Pfeil, U., Zaphiris, P., Wilson, S.: Online social support for older people: characteristics and dynamics of social support. In: Workshop Enhancing Interaction Spaces by Social Media for the Elderly, Vienna (2009)
28. Costa, L., Veloso, A., Loizou, M., Arnab, S.: Games for active ageing, well-being and quality of life: a pilot study. Behav. Inf. Technol. **37**(9), 842–854 (2018). https://doi.org/10.1080/0144929x.2018.1485744
29. Sales, M., Abreu Cybis, W.: Development of a checklist for the evaluation of the web accessibility for the aged users. In: Proceedings of the Latin American Conference on Human-Computer Interaction, Rio de Janeiro, Brazil (2003). https://doi.org/10.1145/944519.944533
30. Leung, L., Lee, P.: Multiple determinants of life quality: the roles of Internet activities, use of new media, social support, and leisure activities. Telematics Inform. **22**(3), 161–180 (2005). https://doi.org/10.1016/j.tele.2004.04.003
31. Kiel, J.: The digital divide: Internet and e-mail use by the elderly. Med. Inform. Internet Med. **30**(1), 19–23 (2005). https://doi.org/10.1080/14639230500066900
32. Sidorenko, A., Walker, A.: The Madrid international plan of action on ageing: from conception to implementation. Ageing Soc. **24**(2), 147–165 (2004). https://doi.org/10.1017/S0144686X03001661
33. Cutler, S., Hendricks, J., Guyer, A.: Age differences in home computer availability and use. J. Gerontol. Ser. B Psychol. Sci. Soc. Sci. **58**(5), 271–280 (2003)

34. Wagner, N., Hassanein, K., Head, M.: Computer use by older adults: a multi-disciplinary review. Comput. Hum. Behav. **26**(5), 870–882 (2010). https://doi.org/10.1016/j.chb.2010. 03.029

35. Rogers, W., Meyer, B., Walker, N., Fisk, A.: Functional limitations to daily living tasks in the aged: a focus group analysis. Hum. Factors J. Hum. Factors Ergon. Soc. **40**(1), 111–125 (1998). https://doi.org/10.1518/001872098779480613

36. Merrill, M.D.: First principles of instruction. Educ. Technol. Res. Dev. **50**(3), 43–59 (2002)

37. Sanders, M.J., O'Sullivan, B., DeBurra, K., Fedner, A.: Computer training for seniors: an academic-community partnership. Educ. Gerontol., 179–193 (2013). https://doi.org/10.1080/ 03601277.2012.700816

38. Hollis-Sawyer, A., Sterns, H.L.: A novel goal-oriented approach for training older adult computer novices: beyond the effects of individual-difference factors. Educ. Gerontol. **25**(7), 661–684 (1999). https://doi.org/10.1080/036012799267521

39. Rogers, Y., Sharp, H., Preece, J.: Interaction Design: Beyond Human-Computer Interaction. Wiley, Chichester (2011)

40. Bates, M.: The invisible substrate of information science. J. Am. Soc. Inf. Sci. **50**(12), 1043–1050 (2000)

41. Wersig, G., Neveling, U.: The phenomena of interest to information science. Inf. Sci. **9**(4), 127–140 (1975)

Predicting Daily Physical Activity Level for Older Adults Using Wearable Activity Trackers

Yaqian Zheng, Junfei Xie[✉], Tri Van Thanh Vo, Byung Cheol Lee, and Toyin Ajisafe

Texas A&M University-Corpus Christi, Corpus Christi, TX 78412, USA
{yzheng1,tvo5}@islander.tamucc.edu,
{junfei.xie,byungcheol.lee,toyin.ajisafe}@tamucc.edu

Abstract. In recent years, there is an increasing trend towards using wearable activity trackers to help monitor and track physical activities (PA) for older adults, with the purpose of motivating regular PA for better health. However, existing activity trackers are frequently abandoned within a short period of time. One of the major reasons is that they do not differentiate individual PA habits and provide PA recommendations based on a unified standard, which may lead to unrealistic suggestions and thus cause frustrations. In order to motivate long-term use of activity trackers and promote PA progression in older adults, PA recommendations should adapt to the changes of an individual's PA habits. As a step towards achieving this, we introduce in this paper an innovative multiscale personalized LSTM model that can predict an individual's daily PA level with satisfied accuracy. This model is verified through a series of experimental studies.

Keywords: Physical activity level prediction · Activity tracker · Time series data analysis

1 Introduction

Obesity and related diseases are threatening the national and global health, especially the health of older adults. Recent data from the National Health and Nutrition Examination Survey (NHANES) show that 71% of adults in the US were overweight and obese between 2015–2016 [1]. Obesity prevalence is 43% among adults aged 40–59 and 41% among those 60 years or older [2]. Intentionally losing weight and *regular* physical activity (PA) can control obesity and moderate the risk of associated chronic diseases and many types of cancers [3]. It is recommended that adults engage in at least 2.5 h of moderate- or 1.25 h of vigorous-intensity aerobic activity each week [4].

Y. Zheng—This work is supported by the Texas A&M University-Corpus Christi Research Grant.

© Springer Nature Switzerland AG 2019
J. Zhou and G. Salvendy (Eds.): HCII 2019, LNCS 11593, pp. 602–614, 2019.
https://doi.org/10.1007/978-3-030-22015-0_47

The past few years have witnessed an increasing use of activity trackers to help monitor, track and hopefully motivate regular PA in older adults. However, existing activity trackers are often abandoned by older adults within a short period of time after initial adoption [5], due to issues like functional complexity, high cost, poor usability, etc [6]. Furthermore, existing activity trackers do not differentiate individual PA habits and provide PA recommendations to users based on the same standard, which may lead to unrealistic suggestions and cause frustrations. In order to motivate long-term use of activity trackers and promote PA progression in older adults, new techniques that can provide personalized PA recommendations to users and can automatically adjust the recommendations to adapt to the changes of users' PA habits are urgently needed. This can be realized by comparing PA histories with future dynamics. As a step towards achieving this, we investigate the PA level prediction problem for older adults in this paper.

Most existing studies on using wearable devices to analyze human activities focus on how to recognize different types of activities such as walking, resting, running, cycling, etc [12–15]. These studies usually use inertial sensors such as accelerometers to measure the acceleration while users are performing different activities. These acceleration data are then used to extract informative features and train a classifier that can detect and differentiate human activities. As the major challenge faced by existing wearable devices is the battery life, many studies on human activity recognition have been devoted to addressing this challenge through reducing the sensors [8,9], decreasing the sampling rate [10,11], or using alternative devices such as the kinetic energy harvesting device that converts kinetic energy from human motion to electrical energy [7].

Despite the abundant works on wearable-based human activity recognition, studies on predicting human activities using wearable devices are very limited, to the best of our knowledge. Most existing studies on human activity prediction use data collected by more advanced tools like cameras [19,20], social media [17,18], smart meter [21], etc. Among the limited studies on wearable-based human activity prediction, article [16] introduces a deep learning based model to jointly predict future activities and associated durations using data collected by smartphones. However, this approach is only suitable for predicting activity types, not activity levels.

In this paper, we aim to address the problem of predicting daily PA levels for older adults wearing low-cost activity trackers, as a step towards realizing the next-generation activity trackers that can provide adaptive and personalized PA recommendations to motivate regular PA in older adults. Developing a PA level predictor with satisfied accuracy is not easy. In addition to the challenges shared with general human activity prediction problems including the difficulty in data collection and high uncertainty in human behaviors, using low-cost wearable activity trackers introduces a number of new challenges. For instance, comparing with smartphones or cameras, low-cost activity trackers, such as the Nokia Go Activity and Sleep Tracker adopted in this study, provide less informative data, which are often limited to the variants of accelerations including step counts and walking distance [22,23]. The lack of informative data makes the development of accurate prediction models extremely difficult.

To conquer aforementioned challenges and capture the individuals' daily PA habits, we develop a multi-scale personalized LSTM model that adopts the Long Short Term Memory (LSTM) network, a state-of-the-art deep learning model with superior performance on time series data, and explores individual activity data at different temporal scales. Real PA data of older adults are collected using activity trackers. With this dataset, we then conduct extensive experimental studies to evaluate the performance of the proposed method. For comparison, various traditional time series data forecast approaches are also investigated.

In the rest of the paper, we first briefly review the fundamentals of the LSTM model in Sect. 2. We then describe the real PA dataset we acquired for this study in Sect. 3. The proposed multi-scale personalized LSTM model is introduced in Sect. 4. In Sect. 5, we conduct experimental studies to evaluate the performance of the proposed model. In Sect. 6, we conclude the paper with a brief summary.

2   Review of the LSTM Model

The LSTM model [27] has been widely used for time series data analysis, due to its promising capability in discovering hidden time-dependent information. An LSTM model is composed of a set of memory cells and a fully connected network as illustrated in Fig. 1. The memory cells address the gradient vanishing and exploding problems typical for recurrent neural networks [26].

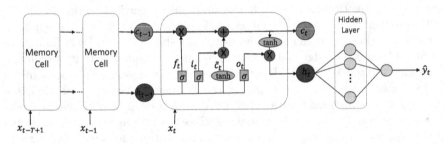

Fig. 1. Illustration of the LSTM model.

As illustrated in Fig. 1, each memory cell takes an input signal x_t, as well as the hidden state h_{t-1} and cell state c_{t-1} from the previous memory cell, and outputs the new hidden state h_t and cell state c_t. If an LSTM model consists of T memory cells, data from the previous T time steps, i.e., $\{x_{t-T+1}, x_{t-T+2}, \ldots, x_t\}$, are thus used to perform prediction. To calculate the hidden state h_t and cell state c_t, the inputs of the memory cell are passed through three gates including the forget, input, and output gates. In particular, the forget gate first decides the information to be thrown away from the cell state c_{t-1} by the following equation:

$$f_t = \sigma(W_{xf}x_t + W_{hf}h_{t-1} + b_f)$$

where f_t is the output of the forget gate. $\sigma(\cdot)$ represents the sigmoid function. $W_{xf} \in R^{T \times D}$ and $W_{hf} \in R^{T \times T}$ are weight matrices, and $b_f \in R^T$ is a bias vector. D is the dimension of the input signal.

The input gate and a candidate cell then decide the information to be stored in the cell state through

$$i_t = \sigma(W_{xi}x_t + W_{hi}h_{t-1} + b_i)$$
$$\tilde{c}_t = \tanh(W_{xc}x_t + W_{hc}h_{t-1} + b_c)$$

where i_t is the output of the input gate. $\tilde{c}_t$ is a candidate state vector. $W_{xi} \in R^{T \times D}$, $W_{hi} \in R^{T \times T}$, $W_{xc} \in R^{T \times D}$ and $W_{hc} \in R^{T \times T}$ are weight matrices, and $b_i \in R^T$ and $b_c \in R^T$ are bias vectors. $\tanh(\cdot)$ is the hyperbolic function. The new cell state c_t can then be calculated using the following equation:

$$c_t = f_t \circ c_{t-1} + i_t \circ \tilde{c}_t$$

where $\circ$ stands for element-wise multiplication.

Finally, the output gate decides the information in the cell state to be out-putted through the following equation:

$$o_t = \sigma(W_{xo}x_t + W_{ho}h_{t-1} + b_o)$$

where o_t is the output of the output gate. $W_{xo} \in R^{T \times D}$ and $W_{ho} \in R^{T \times T}$ are weight matrices, and $b_o \in R^T$ is a bias vector. The new hidden state h_t can then be obtained by

$$h_t = o_t \circ \tanh(c_t)$$

Given h_t, predictions can be made by

$$\hat{y}_t = W_y h_t + b_y \tag{1}$$

where $\hat{y}_t$ is the predicted value. W_y and b_y are weight and bias vectors, respectively.

3   Data Acquisition and Pre-processing

In this section, we briefly describe the activity data we acquired for this study and the pre-processing procedures we applied to clean the raw data.

To acquire the activity data for this study, we recruited 7 older adults aged between 50 and 70 and let them wear Nokia Go Activity and Sleep Trackers for around three months from 05/07/2018 to 07/26/2018. A data fetching application was developed that leverages the Nokia's public application programming interface to collect participants' activity data. The collected data have five fields: time, step counts, walking distance, sleeping status, and burned calories. As we are interested in PA levels in this study, the sleeping status is not considered. Furthermore, we found that the walking distance and burned calories are linearly correlated with the step counts, indicating that both the walking distance and burned calories do not provide additional information. Therefore, we end up with the time and step counts as the only data fields that are useful for this study. As the raw data is recorded when moving is detected, we pre-process the data to generate daily or hourly data through aggregation. Missing entries are filled with zeros. An example trajectory of daily step counts for one participant is shown in Fig. 2. This dataset is also used to generate the results shown in the following sections.

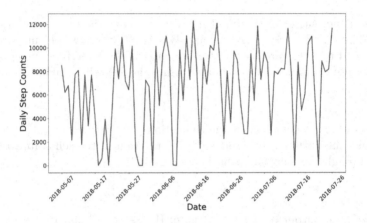

Fig. 2. An example trajectory of daily step counts.

4   Multi-scale Personalized LSTM Model

In this study, we consider the problem of predicting the daily step counts, an indicator of PA level, for an individual using the step counts data collected from the activity tracker.

As the daily dataset only contains 81 data points for each participant, which is too small to train a good prediction model, we propose to use the hourly data to predict the daily step counts. The key idea is to use the hourly data to train an LSTM model, and then let the trained LSTM model predict step counts for

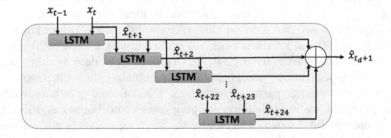

Fig. 3. Illustration of the multi-scale LSTM model with $T = 2$.

the next 24 h. The sum of the predicted step counts is the total step counts for the next day. An illustration of the proposed model with $T = 2$ is shown in Fig. 3, where x_t represents the hourly data point measured at time t (hour), $\hat{x}_t$ is the hourly data point predicted at time t (hour), and $\hat{x}_{t_d}$ denotes the daily data point predicted at time t_d (day).

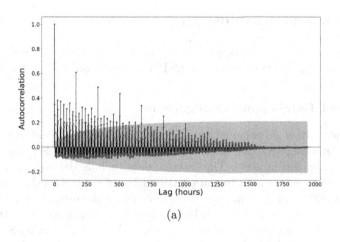

(a)

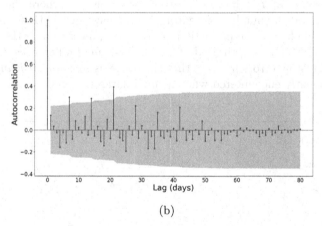

(b)

Fig. 4. Autocorrelation of (a) hourly step counts and (b) daily step counts.

Before we use the data to train the multi-scale LSTM model, we first conduct an autocorrelation analysis to understand the participant's PA patterns. As shown in Fig. 4, the PA level shows *behavior rhythms*. In particular, the hourly PA levels show high autocorrelations (see Fig. 4(a)) at lags 24, 48, 72, etc., indicating a cycle of 24 h. The strongest peaks appear at lags 24×7, 24×14, 24×21, etc., indicating a cycle of 7 days. To better illustrate the 7-day cycle, we plot in Fig. 4(b) the autocorrelation of daily PA levels, which demonstrates high autocorrelations at lags 7, 14, 21, etc., further verifying the existence of a 7-day cycle. To capture these behavior rhythms, we insert two data fields into the hourly data, one is the *hour of the day*, and the other is the *day of the week*. Therefore, each data point x_t has four fields: time, step counts, hour of the day and day of the week.

5   Experimental Evaluation

In this section, we conduct a series of experiments to evaluate the performance of the proposed multi-scale personalized LSTM model for daily PA level prediction.

5.1   Model Training and Configuration

To train the multi-scale personalized LSTM model, we use the dataset visualized in Fig. 2 from a single participant as an example. We then divide the dataset into the training and testing data. The training data include the first 51 days (63%) of activity data and are used to train the model, and the testing data include the rest 30 days (37%) of data and are used to evaluate the prediction performance of the model. To determine the optimal value of the parameter T in the LSTM models, we evaluate the prediction performance of the multi-scale LSTM model at different values of T. The results are shown in Fig. 5, where the number of hidden layers and the number of neurons in each layer are both set to 1. As we can see from the figure, the prediction performance, measured by the root mean square error (RMSE), is optimized at $T = 2$. The small differences between the training and testing errors indicate that the model is free of *overfitting*, which is an issue frequently encountered when a small dataset is used.

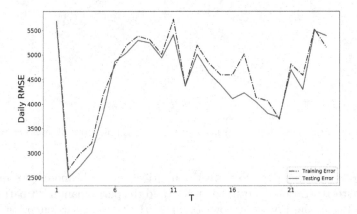

Fig. 5. Prediction performance of the multi-scale LSTM model at different values of T.

5.2   Comparison Studies

In this section, we conduct various comparison studies to evaluate the performance of the proposed model from different aspects.

Model Types. In the first experiment, we investigate the impact of different baseline models on the prediction performance. In particular, we replace the LSTM model in the proposed multi-scale framework (see Fig. 3) with different time series data forecast models including the Autoregressive Integrated Moving Average (ARIMA) [25] and the Multilayer perceptron (MLP) [24] models. We then compare the prediction performances of the resulting multi-scale ARIMA and multi-scale MLP models with the proposed multi-scale LSTM model. For both benchmark models, feature selection is performed to pick the best set of features, and model parameters are tuned to achieve the best prediction performance. In particular, a $(1, 0, 2)$-ARIMA model is implemented, which takes lag features $\{t - 1, t - 2, t - 3\}$. The MLP model takes lag features $\{t - 24, t - 48\}$, and has one hidden layer with a single neuron. The comparison results are shown in Fig. 6 with the corresponding RMSE provided in Table 1, which demonstrate the promising performance of the LSTM model.

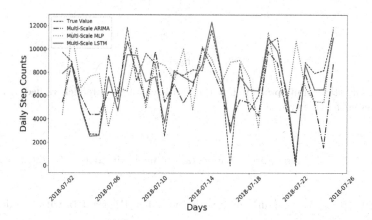

Fig. 6. Daily step counts predicted by different multi-scale prediction models.

Table 1. RMSE of different prediction models.

Multi-scale LSTM	Multi-scale ARIMA	Multi-scale MLP
2496.327	3298.723	4023.917

Feature Types. In the second experiment, we study the impact of different feature types on the prediction performance. In particular, we compare the performance of the prediction models trained using the hourly data with two fields (time, step count) and that with two additional fields, hour of the day and day of the week, inserted. The prediction performance of the multi-scale LSTM model trained using data with different feature types are shown in Fig. 7. Table 2 compares the RMSE of different prediction models. From these results, we can conclude that inserting the hour of the day and day of the week into the hourly data improves the prediction performance, as these two data fields naturally capture the participant's daily and weekly behavior rhythms.

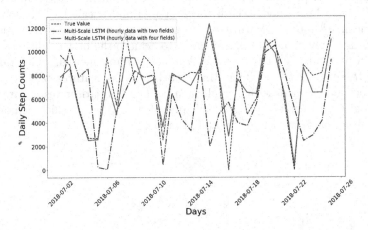

Fig. 7. Daily step counts predicted by the multi-scale LSTM model trained using data with different feature types.

Table 2. RMSE of different prediction models trained using data with different feature types.

Model type	Hourly data with four fields	Hourly data with two fields
Multi-scale LSTM	**2496.327**	3456.462
Multi-scale ARIMA	3298.723	4063.455
Multi-scale MLP	4023.917	4295.745

Temporal Scales. In the third experiment, we compare the proposed multi-scale LSTM model with the traditional single-scale LSTM, ARIMA and MLP models that are trained directly using the daily data of two fields (time, step count). In particular, a (0,0,1)-ARIMA model is implemented, whose features include lags $\{t_d - 1, t_d - 2, \ldots, t_d - 7\}$ and cycle of 7 days. Both MLP and the traditional LSTM have one hidden layer with 3 neurons. The traditional LSTM model also has a dropout layer with dropout rate of 0.4 to alleviate the overfitting issue. The features taken by the MLP and the traditional LSTM model are lags $\{t_d - 7, t_d - 11, t_d - 12, t_d - 14\}$ and $\{t_d - 1, t_d - 2, \ldots, t_d - 6\}$, respectively. The comparison results are shown in Fig. 8 and Table 3, which demonstrate the good performance of the proposed multi-scale LSTM model.

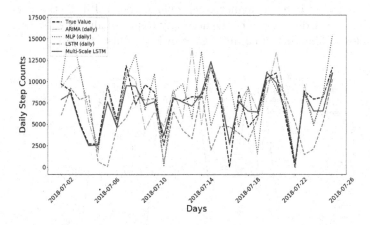

Fig. 8. Daily step counts predicted by the multi-scale LSTM model compared with traditional single-scale models trained using the daily data.

Table 3. RMSE of the multi-scale LSTM compared with traditional single-scale models trained using the daily data.

Multi-scale LSTM	ARIMA	MLP	LSTM
2496.3	2613.3	3540.0	4155. 3

We also test the performance of the traditional single-scale prediction models trained using the daily data with an additional field, day of the week, inserted. The results are shown in Table 4. As we can see, the proposed multi-scale LSTM model still achieves the best performance.

Table 4. RMSE of the multi-scale LSTM compared with traditional models trained using the daily data with an additional field inserted.

Multi-scale LSTM	ARIMA	MLP	LSTM
2496.3	2797.037	4739.270	2561.182

Model Generality. In the last experiment, we study the impact of adopting a generalized model on the prediction performance. To obtain the generalized model, we use the datasets from all 7 participants to train the multi-scale LSTM model, with T set to 12 for the best performance. We then use the same testing data described in Sect. 5.1 to evaluate the prediction performance of this generalized model. The results are shown in Fig. 9 and the corresponding RMSE is 4877.771, which is much higher than 2496.3, the RMSE of the personalized model. This study demonstrates the necessity to personalize the prediction models, considering the individual differences in PA habits.

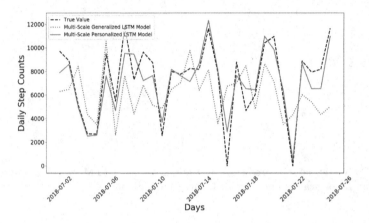

Fig. 9. Daily step counts predicted by the generalized model compared with the personalized model.

6   Conclusion

This paper explores the problem of how to accurately predict daily PA levels for individuals using data collected by low-cost activity trackers, as a step towards developing intelligent activity trackers that can suggest personalized PA goals based on individuals' PA habits. To address this problem, a systematic investigation on the characteristics of the data collected by low-cost activity trackers was first conducted. New attribute fields were inserted into the raw data to capture daily and weekly behavior rhythms. A novel multi-scale personalized LSTM model was then developed, which addresses the challenge of lack of informative data by exploring PA patterns at different temporal scales. The series of experimental studies demonstrate the good performance of the proposed model. In the future, we will explore how to set appropriate PA goals for individuals to motivate regular PA effectively.

References

1. Fryar, C.D., Carroll, M.D., Ogden, C.L.: Prevalence of overweight, obesity, and severe obesity among adults aged 20 and over: United States, 1960–1962 through 2015–2016 (2018)
2. Hales, C.M., Fryar, C.D., Carroll, M.D., Freedman, D.S., Ogden, C.L.: Trends in obesity and severe obesity prevalence in US youth and adults by sex and age, 2007–2008 to 2015–2016. JAMA **319**(16), 1723–1725 (2018)
3. Lauby-Secretan, B., et al.: Breast-cancer screening viewpoint of the IARC Working Group. N. Engl. J. Med. **372**(24), 2353–2358 (2015)
4. Office of Disease Prevention and Health Promotion: 2008 physical activity guidelines for Americans summary (2008). https://health.gov/paguidelines/2008/summary.aspx
5. Ledger, D., McCaffrey, D.: Inside wearables: how the science of human behavior change offers the secret to long-term engagement. Endeavour Partners **200**(93), 1 (2014)
6. Kim, K.I., Gollamudi, S.S., Steinhubl, S.: Digital technology to enable aging in place. Exp. Gerontol. **88**, 25–31 (2017)
7. Khalifa, S., Lan, G., Hassan, M., Seneviratne, A., Das, S.K.: Harke: human activity recognition from kinetic energy harvesting data in wearable devices. IEEE Trans. Mobile Comput. **17**(6), 1353–1368 (2018)
8. Zappi, P., et al.: Activity recognition from on-body sensors: accuracy-power trade-off by dynamic sensor selection. In: Verdone, R. (ed.) EWSN 2008. LNCS, vol. 4913, pp. 17–33. Springer, Heidelberg (2008). https://doi.org/10.1007/978-3-540-77690-1_2
9. Wang, Y., et al.: A framework of energy efficient mobile sensing for automatic user state recognition. In: 7th International Conference on Mobile Systems, Applications, and Services, pp. 179–192. ACM (2009)
10. Krause, A., et al.: Trading off prediction accuracy and power consumption for context-aware wearable computing. In: Ninth IEEE International Symposium on Wearable Computers, pp. 20–26. IEEE (2005)
11. Yan, Z., Subbaraju, V., Chakraborty, D., Misra, A., Aberer, K.: Energy-efficient continuous activity recognition on mobile phones: an activity-adaptive approach. In: 16th International Symposium on Wearable Computers (ISWC). IEEE (2012)
12. Bulling, A., Blanke, U., Schiele, B.: A tutorial on human activity recognition using body-worn inertial sensors. ACM Comput. Surv. (CSUR) **46**(3), 33 (2014)
13. Lara, O.D., Labrador, M.A.: A survey on human activity recognition using wearable sensors. IEEE Commun. Surv. Tutor. **15**(3), 1192–1209 (2013)
14. Ronao, C.A., Cho, S.B.: Human activity recognition using smartphone sensors with two-stage continuous hidden Markov models. In: 10th International Conference on Natural Computation (ICNC). IEEE (2014)
15. Guan, Y., Plötz, T.: Ensembles of deep LSTM learners for activity recognition using wearables. ACM Interact. Mobile Wearable Ubiquit. Technol. **1**(2), 11 (2017)
16. Krishna, K., Jain, D., Mehta, S.V., Choudhary, S.: An LSTM based system for prediction of human activities with durations. ACM Interact. Mobile Wearable Ubiquit. Technol. **1**(4), 147 (2018)
17. Zhu, Y., Zhong, E., Pan, S.J., Wang, X., Zhou, M., Yang, Q.: Predicting user activity level in social networks. In: 22nd ACM International Conference on Information & Knowledge Management, pp. 159–168. ACM (2013)

18. Preum, S.M., Stankovic, J.A., Qi, Y.: MAPer: a multi-scale adaptive personalized model for temporal human behavior prediction. In: 24th ACM International on Conference on Information and Knowledge Management, pp. 433–442. ACM (2015)

19. Li, K., Fu, Y.: Prediction of human activity by discovering temporal sequence patterns. IEEE Trans. Pattern Anal. Mach. Intell. **36**(8), 1644–1657 (2014)

20. Ma, S., Sigal, L., Sclaroff, S.: Learning activity progression in LSTMs for activity detection and early detection. In: IEEE Conference on Computer Vision and Pattern Recognition, pp. 1942–1950 (2016)

21. Yassine, A., Singh, S., Alamri, A.: Mining human activity patterns from smart home big data for health care applications. IEEE Access **5**, 13131–13141 (2017)

22. Lee, B.C., Ajisafe, T., Vo, T., Xie, J.: Understanding long-term adoption and usability of wearable activity trackers among active older adults. In: Human Computer Interaction (HCI) International Conference (2019, accepted)

23. Lee, B.C., Xie, J.: How do aging adults adopt and use a new technology? New approach to understand aging service technology adoption. In: Stephanidis, C. (ed.) HCI 2018. CCIS, vol. 851, pp. 161–166. Springer, Cham (2018). https://doi.org/10.1007/978-3-319-92279-9_22

24. Haykin, S.S.: Neural Networks and Learning Machines, vol. 3. Pearson, Upper Saddle River (2009)

25. George, B., Gwilym, M.J., Gregory, C.R., Greta, M.L.: Time Series Analysis: Forecasting and Control. Wiley, New York (2015)

26. Hasim, S., Andrew, S., Francoise, B.: Long short-term memory based recurrent neural network architectures for large vocabulary speech recognition, vol. 402, p. 1128 (2014)

27. Zhao, Z., et al.: LSTM network: a deep learning approach for short-term traffic forecast. IET Intell. Transp. Syst. **11**(2), 68–75 (2017)

Author Index

Printed in the United States
By Bookmasters